LETTERS FROM RUSSIA

ASTOLPHE DE CUSTINE

The 1843 Translation
Edited, Revised, and with an Introduction by
ANKA MUHLSTEIN

NEW YORK REVIEW BOOKS

New York

This is a New York Review Book
Published by The New York Review of Books
1755 Broadway, New York, NY 10019

Library of Congress Cataloging-in-Publication Data
Custine, Astolphe, marquis de, 1790–1857.
  [Russie en 1839. English]
  Letters from Russia / Astolphe de Custine ; edited and with an introduction
by Anka Muhlstein.
     p. cm.
  ISBN 0-940322-81-1 (Paperback : alk. paper)
  1. Russia—Description and travel. 2. Custine, Astolphe, marquis de,
1790–1857—Journeys—Russia. 3. National characteristics, Russian.
I. Muhlstein, Anka. II. Title.
  DK25 .C9713 2002
  947'.073—dc21   2001006477

Book design by Lizzie Scott
Printed in the United States of America on acid-free paper.
10 9 8 7 6 5 4 3 2 1

March 2002
www.nybooks.com

INTRODUCTION

ASTOLPHE DE CUSTINE arrived in St. Petersburg on July 10, 1839. He reached Moscow on the third of August. Ten days later, he headed northeast for about 150 miles. He stopped at Yaroslavl, then spent a few days in Nizhny Novgorod, and returned to Moscow and St. Petersburg. On October 1, he was back in Berlin. His entire stay in Russia lasted less than three months. Custine did not speak a word of Russian, and traveled under the protection and surveillance of a government official. Yet he produced a most explosive and unexpected account of his journey, *Russia in 1839* or, as it is also known, *Letters from Russia*, one of those rare books that refuse to die.

Banned in Russia, Custine's work was an immediate success in Europe when it appeared in 1843, and was read widely during the ten years that followed. It was rediscovered in Russia in 1910, when an abridged version was published, only to be suppressed a second time under Lenin: any reader could perceive the parallels between the Russia of Nicholas I and the Communist State. Then, in 1951, at a time when the cold war turned into bloody combat on the Korean Peninsula, another English version (again abridged) appeared with a preface by Walter Bedell Smith, who had been the United States ambassador to the Soviet Union in the late 1940s. More substantial editions were published in the United States in 1989 and in France in 1990.

In the nineteenth century, the Russian philosopher Alexander Herzen declared Custine's book the most intelligent work ever written on Russia; in the twentieth, George Kennan, himself a former chargé d'affaires to the Soviet Union, wrote that it was no doubt the best description available of the world that had given rise to Stalin. Because of its historical significance and its ongoing contemporary relevance, *Letters from Russia* has continued to be widely read and studied, and the character and the motivations of the author of this extraordinary work have also become topics of particular interest. Why, one wants to know, did Custine choose to travel to that distant and forbidding country, and why did he, an aristocrat and a dandy, a man of conservative opinions, a flattered guest of the Czar, immediately grasp the timeless cruelty of Russia's despotic regime?

As a writer, Custine's gifts included a keen eye, an avid curiosity, and a fiercely independent intellect—characteristics that explain both the motives and the success of his endeavor. Why go to Russia? The simple answer may be that Custine had a passion for travel. He discovered Italy, Germany, and Switzerland at a young age, and kept going back to those quintessential parts of Europe. He had also visited England and Scotland, and knew Spain quite well. The next step for a Romantic writer would normally have been either Jerusalem and the Middle East or America, which, thanks to Chateaubriand, had marked the new French sensibility. Russia was certainly a surprising choice but not an irrational one.

For years, Custine had published poems, novels, and plays without much success. However, in 1838 his account of a journey in Spain was well received by both the press and the public. Balzac, a much-admired friend, encouraged him to continue in that vein and suggested to him Russia or, as it was called at the time, the North:

> There are very few modern books that can be compared
> to [yours]. . . . If you do the same for every country, you
> will have a unique collection in the genre and a collec-

tion that will be of the greatest value, believe me. . . . I
will do everything in my power to persuade you to also
describe . . . the North.

But Custine hardly needed to be spurred on. Russia had
in fact been on his mind ever since Tocqueville, in 1835,
had published his *Democracy in America* to enormous ac-
claim. Tocqueville made a point of contrasting Russia and
the United States:

> There are on earth today two great peoples who, having
> started from different points, seem to be advancing to-
> wards the same end: they are the Russians and the
> Anglo-Americans. They both grew up in darkness; and
> whilst Europeans were busy elsewhere, they suddenly
> placed themselves in the forefront of nations, and the
> world learned at almost the same time of their births
> and their greatness.
>
> All other nations seem, more or less, to have reached
> the limits nature has assigned to them and within which
> they now need only to remain, but those two are still
> growing. . . . America is struggling against obstacles of
> nature; Russia against men. . . . The principal means of
> action for the one is liberty; for the other servitude.

Tocqueville believed reluctantly in the inevitable victory
of the American model; Custine, more skeptical in every
way, may well have hoped to discredit such a view through
symmetrical comparison. The two men, in any case, had
much in common. Their families had both been hounded
and ruined by the French Revolution, and they themselves
were both conservatives, troubled by the loss of their place
in society but convinced of the impossibility of going back
to pre-revolutionary principles. When Tocqueville points out
that he has an "intellectual taste" for democratic *institutions,*

but that, as an instinctive aristocrat, he despises and fears the crowd, he anticipates Custine's question whether one "ought not to impose a silence on [one's] antipathies" and accept with good grace a wise and moderate representative government. Tocqueville went to the United States to study the effects of democracy in the American republic, and Custine hoped to find in Russia "new arguments against the despot that reigns at home, against disorder baptized with the name of liberty."

Why then did he return to France with his mind entirely changed? The fact that Custine begins his book by retracing the story of his family during the Terror gives us a clue. He had been born to privilege in an aristocratic family of considerable wealth, but at the wrong time, in 1790 at the onset of the French Revolution. His paternal grandfather, who had fought on the side of the Colonies in the war of American Independence and embraced the new ideals to the point of commanding one of the French revolutionary armies, was for all that imprisoned, tried, and executed in 1792. A few weeks later, his son, Astolphe's father, was also executed. Custine's mother was arrested. The boy, entrusted to the care of a devoted servant, saw her brought back home by armed men, who pushed her around while searching for incriminating papers. They ransacked the apartment, sealing off every room except the kitchen where Astolphe and his nanny had taken refuge. For a child these must have seemed incomprehensible acts, even though the brutal scenes he had already witnessed in the streets of Paris might have prepared him for more violence.

Custine's mother miraculously escaped the guillotine and, once free, went about recovering a part of the family's fortune. But she could not erase the memories of violence and the terror that had marred her son's childhood. The Revolution had robbed Astolphe of his property and his traditional rank in society, shaken his initial confidence in his surroundings, and destroyed the world from which he sprang. But it gave him, in exchange, the assurance that he had a right to freedom. "I am certainly anything but a revolutionary, still I am revolutionized," he declared, and proved it by developing an absolute independence of spirit—independence that would prove crucial in resisting the Czar's blandishments.

But it is the legacy of fear inherited by Custine, as much as his independent spirit, that explains the insights he was able to take away from his short trip, notwithstanding his lack of Russian. Fear, Custine claimed, was the first emotion of which he had been conscious as a child; his first observations of brutality in a country under the sway of an absolute ruler awakened that memory. When Custine identifies Russia as "the empire of fear," he means it literally. He could not bear physical violence done to men or animals, and the spectacle of the streets in St. Petersburg, where men were punched and hit and hurt without awakening any reaction from passersby, exacerbated his unease and anguish:

> Under the terror which hovers over all heads, submission becomes the general rule of conduct; victims and executioners, all practice the obedience that perpetuates the evil which they inflict or to which they submit.

Custine was uninterested in statistics and industrial progress, but he was fascinated by the social consequences of violence. He may have been particularly attuned to this evil for another reason. Custine was a declared homosexual, ferociously attached to the freedom of his ways and equally conscious of the animosity his tastes could spark in others. His preternatural sensitivity to the tyrannical oppressiveness of orthodoxy and its mechanics made him quick to find means with which to outfox them. A hundred years later, another French writer, equally unconventional in his tastes,

André Gide, had a similar experience when he was invited by Stalin to make a speech at Gorky's funeral. Gide stayed a few days in Moscow, then made a short trip to the countryside, visited one or two collective farms, listened with stupefaction to the theories about art voiced by government officials, and, alone among the group of Communist sympathizers with whom he traveled, returned to write a book devoid of illusions. Men accustomed to being on the outside make clear-eyed observers.

Curiously, the enduring strength of *Letters from Russia* may in the end derive from what was perhaps Custine's greatest weakness: his tendency to trust impressions and emotions more than facts. His book is less a conventional political study than a recording of his personal response to the reality of Russia, leaving ample room for selective reporting as well as for his subjective, but very acute, judgments. Thus it is in some sense the lacunae, the omissions, in Custine's book that have kept it from becoming dated. Had Custine been interested in agrarian reforms and industrial development instead of fear, secrecy, and the arbitrary nature of the czarist system, his book would never have been perceived, when rediscovered more than a century after its initial publication, as a tantalizing beam illuminating in a new way the relation between Russia's past and its present.

Custine took four years to write his book, in which he adopted the epistolary form employed in his previous travel books on Spain and Italy. This flexible technique allowed him to vary his tone, return to a point of interest, ignore whatever bored him, and indulge in personal digressions without worrying about the strict inner logic of a conventional travelogue. The result is a bold, accessible, vivid, and persuasive account of his journey, which, to Custine's surprise and great joy, was an immediate commercial success. In part, the interest built on scandal. "Paris," Custine explained, "was full of Russians who started to screech like eagles, or rather geese—imagine the noise!! They forced everyone to read it." Foreigners living in Russia or visiting there reported that the book provoked terrible anger. The Czar was outraged, and a courtier confirmed that he had thrown down the volume of the "despicable Custine."

Within two years, three editions were sold in Germany and two in England. Further reprints appeared regularly in France until 1854, a year in which the Crimean War lent the text added topical interest. It would be the last edition of the century. Custine died three years later, in 1857.

—ANKA MUHLSTEIN

A NOTE ON THE TEXT

The present edition is based on an anonymous early translation of Custine's *La Russie en 1839*, entitled *The Empire of the Czar; or, Observations on the Social, Political, and Religious State and Prospects of Russia, Made During a Journey Through That Empire* and published by Longman, Brown, Green, and Longmans (London, 1843). It has been slightly abridged. The editor has also taken the liberty of replacing some obsolete expressions with modern equivalents.

LETTERS FROM RUSSIA

AUTHOR'S PREFACE

A TASTE for traveling has never been with me a fashion; I brought it with me into the world, and I began to gratify it in early youth. We are all vaguely tormented with a desire to know a world which appears to us a dungeon, because we have not ourselves chosen it for an abode. I should feel as if I could not depart in peace out of this narrow sphere unless I endeavored to explore my prison. The more I examine it, the more beautiful and extensive it becomes in my eyes. *To see in order to know*: such is the motto of the traveler; such is also mine: I have not adopted it; nature gave it to me.

To compare the different modes of existence in different nations, to study the manner of thinking and feeling peculiar to each, to perceive the relations which God has established between their history, their manners, and their physiognomy—in a word, to travel, is to procure for my curiosity an inexhaustible aliment, to supply my thoughts with an eternal impulse of activity: to prevent my surveying the world would be like robbing a literary man of the key of his library.

But if curiosity causes me to wander, an attachment which partakes of the nature of a domestic affection brings me back. I then take a review of my observations, and select from among the spoil the ideas which I imagine may be communicated with the greatest likelihood of being useful.

During my sojourn in Russia, as well as during all my other journeys, two thoughts, or rather sentiments, have never ceased to influence my heart,—a love of France, which renders me severe in my judgments upon foreigners, and

3

upon the French themselves, for passionate affections are never indulgent,—and a love of mankind. To find the balancing point between these two opposing objects of our affections here below, between the love of country and the love of our fellow-men, is the vocation of every elevated mind. Religion alone can solve the problem: I do not flatter myself that it has enabled me to do so; but I can and ought to say that I have never ceased bending towards attaining this means of solution, all my efforts without regard to the variations of fashion. With my religious ideas, I have passed through an unsympathizing world; and now I see, not without a pleasurable surprise, these same ideas occupying the youthful minds of the new generation.

I should like to send into Russia all Christians who are not Catholic, to show them what our religion may be brought to when taught in a *national* church, when practiced under the direction of a *national* clergy.

The spectacle of abject servility into which the sacerdotal power can fall in a land where the church is only held of the state, would make every consistent Protestant recoil. A national church or a national clergy are words which ought never to have been joined; the church is, by its very essence, superior to all national distinctions, all human associations; to abandon the church universal in order to enter into any political church, is to do worse than to err in faith,—it is to abjure the faith, it is to fall back again from heaven to earth.

And yet how many sincere, how many excellent men believed, at the birth of Protestantism, that they should be purifying their creed by adopting the new doctrines which have only served to narrow their minds! Since then, indifference, masked and extolled under the attractive name of toleration, has perpetuated error.

The circumstance which renders Russia the most singular state now to be seen in the world is that extreme barbarism, favored by the enslavement of the church, and extreme civilization, imported by an eclectic government from foreign lands, are there to be seen united. To understand how tranquillity, or at least immobility, can spring from the shock of elements so opposed, it will be necessary to follow the traveler into the heart of this singular country.

The mode which I employ of describing places and defining characters, appears to me, if not the most favorable to the author, at least the most likely to inspire confidence in the reader, whom I oblige to follow me, and whom I render the judge of the development of those ideas that may be suggested to me.

I arrived in a new country without any other prejudices than those which no man can guard against; those which a conscientious study of its history imparts. I examined objects, I observed facts and individuals, while candidly permitting daily experience to modify my opinions. Very few exclusive political notions incommoded me in this spontaneous labor, in which religion alone was my unchanging rule; and even that rule may be rejected by the reader without the recital of facts and the moral consequences that flow from them being discarded, or confounded with the reprobation that I shall meet with from those whose creeds do not agree with mine.

I may be accused of having prejudices, but I shall never be reproached with intentionally disguising the truth.

The descriptions of what I saw were made upon the spot, the stories I heard each day were committed to paper on the same evening. Thus, my conversations with the Emperor, given word for word in the ensuing chapters, cannot fail to possess a species of interest: that of exactitude. They will also serve, I hope, to render this prince, so differently viewed among us and throughout Europe, better known.

The chapters that follow were not all destined for the public. Several of the early ones were written as purely confidential letters. Fatigued with writing, but not with traveling, I resolved, this time, to observe without any methodical plan, and to keep my descriptions for my friends. The reasons that decided me to publish the whole will be seen in the course of the work.

The principal one was the feeling that my views were daily modified by the examination to which I subjected a state of society absolutely new to me. It struck me that in speaking the truth of Russia, I should be doing something bold and novel: hitherto, fear and interest have dictated exaggerated eulogies; hatred has also published calumnies: I am not afraid of making shipwreck either on the one rock or the other.

I went to Russia to seek for arguments against representative government, I return a partisan of constitutions. A mixed government is not the most favorable to action; but in their old age, nations have less need of acting: this government is the one which most aids production, and which procures for man the greatest amount of prosperity; it is, above all, the one which imparts the highest activity to mind within the sphere of practical ideas: in short, it renders the citizen independent, not by the elevation of sentiments, but by the operation of laws; assuredly these are great compensations for great disadvantages.

As I gradually grew acquainted with the tremendous and singular government, regulated, or I might say founded, by Peter I, I became aware of the importance of the mission which chance had entrusted to me.

The extreme curiosity with which my work inspired the Russians, who were evidently rendered unquiet by the reserve of my language, first led me to think that I had more power than I previously attributed to myself; I therefore became attentive and prudent, for I was not long in discovering the danger to which my sincerity might expose me. Not daring to send my letters by post, I preserved them all, and kept them concealed with extreme care; so that on my return to

France, my journey was written, and in my own hands. Nevertheless, I have hesitated to publish it for three years: this is the time which I have needed to reconcile, in the secret of my conscience, what I believed to be the conflicting claims of gratitude and of truth! The latter at last prevails, because it appears to me to be truth of a nature that will interest my country. I cannot forget that, above all else, I write for France, and I hold it my duty to reveal to her useful and important facts.

I consider myself competent and authorized to judge, even severely, if my conscience urges me, a country where I have friends, to analyze, without descending into offensive personalities, the character of public men, to quote the words of political persons, to commence with those of the highest personage in the state, to recount their actions, and to carry out to the last stage of inquiry the reflections which these examinations may suggest; provided, however, that in capriciously pursuing the course of my ideas, I do not give them to others except for just the worth that they have in my own eyes: this, it appears to me, is all that constitutes the probity of an author.

But in thus yielding to duty, I have respected, at least I hope so, all the rules of social propriety; for I maintain that there is a proper manner of expressing severe truths: this manner consists in speaking only upon conviction, whilst repelling the suggestions of vanity.

Besides, having seen much to admire in Russia, I have been able to mingle many praises in my descriptions.

The Russians will not be satisfied; when was self-love ever known to be? And yet, no one has ever been struck more than I, by the greatness and political importance of their nation. The high destinies of these people, these last comers upon the old theater of the world, engaged my mind during the whole time of my stay among them. The Russians, viewed as a body, appeared to me as being great, even in their most shocking vices; viewed as individuals, I considered them amiable. In the character of the common people I found much to interest: these flattering truths ought, I think, to compensate for others less agreeable. But, hitherto, the Russians have been treated as spoiled children by the greater number of travelers.

If the discordances that one cannot help remarking in their social state, if the spirit of their government, essentially opposed to my ideas and habits, have drawn from me reproaches, and even cries of indignation, my praises, equally voluntary, must have the greater weight.

But these Orientals, habituated as they are to breathe and dispense the most direct incense of flattery, will be sensible to nothing but blame. All disapprobation appears to them as treachery; they call every severe truth a falsehood; they will not perceive the delicate admiration that may sometimes lurk under my apparent criticisms—the regret and, on some occasions, the sympathy that accompany my most severe remarks.

If they have not converted me to their religions (they have several, and among these, political religion is not the least intolerant), if, on the contrary, they have modified my monarchical ideas in a way that is opposed to despotism and favorable to representative government, they will be offended simply because I am not of their opinion. I regret that such is the case, but I prefer regret to remorse.

If I were not resigned to their injustice, I should not print these chapters. Besides, though they may complain of me in words, they will absolve me in their consciences: this testimony will be sufficient for me. Every honest Russian will admit that if I have committed errors of detail for want of time to rectify my impressions, I have described Russia in general, as it really is. They will make allowance for the difficulties which I have had to conquer, and will give me credit for the quickness with which I have discerned the advantageous traits of their primitive character under the political mask that has disfigured it for so many ages.

The facts of which I have been witness are recorded precisely as they passed before my eyes; those which were related to me, are given as I received them; I have not endeavored to deceive the reader by substituting myself for the persons whom I consulted. If I have abstained from naming, or in any way indicating these persons, my discretion will undoubtedly be appreciated; it is one proof more of the degree of confidence which the enlightened individuals deserve, to whom I thus ventured to address myself for information respecting certain facts that it was impossible for me to observe personally. It is superfluous to add that I have only cited those to which the character and position of the men from whom I had them, gave, in my eyes, an unquestionable stamp of authority.

Aided by my scrupulous exactitude, the reader may judge for himself of the degree of authority that should be ascribed to these secondary facts, which, it may be further observed, occupy but a very small place in my narrations.

LETTER 1

ARRIVAL OF THE HEREDITARY GRAND DUKE OF RUSSIA AT EMS. — CHARACTER OF RUSSIAN COURTIERS. — THE PERSON OF THE GRAND DUKE. — HIS FATHER AND UNCLE AT THE SAME AGE. — HIS EQUIPAGES AND SUITE. — SUPERIORITY OF THE ENGLISH IN ALL EXTERNAL APPURTENANCES. — THE RHINE. — THE RIVER MORE BEAUTIFUL THAN ITS BANKS. — FIREFLIES ON THE RHINE.

I DATE FROM yesterday the commencement of my Russian Travels.* The hereditary grand duke has arrived at Ems, preceded by ten or twelve carriages, and attended by a numerous court.

What has chiefly struck me in my first view of Russian courtiers is the extraordinary submissiveness with which, as grandees, they perform their devoirs. They seem, in fact, to be only a higher order of slaves; but the moment the prince has retired, a free, unrestrained, and decided manner is reassumed, which contrasts unpleasantly with that complete abnegation of self, affected only the moment before. In a word, there appears to reign throughout the suite of the heir of the Imperial throne, a habit of servile docility from which the nobles are not more exempt than the valets. It is not merely the etiquette that regulates other courts, where official respect, the importance of the office rather than that of the person, the compulsory part, in short, that has to be played, produces ennui, and sometimes ridicule: it is something more; it is a

---

*5th June, 1839.

11

spontaneous and involuntary humility, which yet does not altogether exclude arrogance: it seems to me as though I could hear them say, "since it cannot be otherwise, we are glad to have it so." This mixture of pride and humiliation displeases me, and by no means prepossesses me in favor of the country I am about to survey.

I found myself amid the crowd of curious spectators close to the grand duke, just as he descended from his carriage; and as he stood for some time before entering the gate of the *maison des bains*, talking with a Russian lady, the Countess ———, I was able to observe him at my leisure. His age, as his appearance indicates, is twenty: his height is commanding, but he appears to me, for so young a man, rather fat. His features would be handsome were it not that their fullness destroys their expression. His round face rather resembles that of a German than a Russian; it suggests an idea of what the Emperor Alexander's must have been at the same age, without however recalling, in any degree, the physiognomy of the Kalmyk. A face of this cast will pass through many changes before assuming its definitive character. The habitual humor which it, at present, denotes, is gentleness and benevolence; but between the youthful smile of the eyes and the constant contraction of the mouth, there is, nevertheless, a discordance which does not bespeak frankness, and which, perhaps, indicates some inward suffering. The sorrows of youth—of that age in which happiness is, as it were, the right of man—are secrets the better guarded, because they are mysteries inexplicable even to those who experience them. The expression of this young prince is amiable; his carriage is graceful, imposing, and altogether princely; and his manner modest, without being timid, which must alone gain him much goodwill. The embarrassment of great people is so embarrassing to others, that their ease always wears the character of affability, to which in fact it amounts. When they believe themselves to be something more than common mortals, they become constrained, both by the direct influence of such an opinion, and by the hopeless effort of inducing others to share it. This absurd inquietude does not disturb the grand duke. His presence conveys the idea of a perfectly well-bred man; and if he ever reign, it will be by the charm inherent in graceful manners that he will cause himself to be obeyed: it will not be by terror, unless, at least, the *necessities* attached to the office of a Russian emperor should, in changing his position, change his disposition also.

Since writing the above, I have again seen the hereditary grand duke, and have examined him more nearly and leisurely. He had cast off his uniform, which appeared to fit him too closely, and gave to his person a bloated appearance. In my opinion he looks best in undress. His general bearing is certainly pleasing; his carriage is lofty, yet without military stiffness. The kind of grace by which he is distinguished, reminds one of that peculiar charm of manner which seems to belong to the Slavic race. It is not the expression of the quick passions of southern climes, neither is it the imperturbable coolness of the people of the north: it is a combination of simplicity, of southern mobility, and of Scandinavian melancholy. The Slavs are fair-complexioned Arabs; the grand duke is more than half German, but in Mecklenburg and Holstein, as in some parts of Russia, there are Germans of Slavic extraction.

The countenance of this prince, notwithstanding his youth, presents fewer attractions than his figure. His complexion has already lost its freshness*; one can observe that he is under the influence of some cause of grief; his eyelids are cast down with a sadness that betrays the cares of a riper age. His well-formed mouth is not without an expression of sweetness; his Grecian profile reminds me of antique medals,

---

*The grand duke had been ill some time before his arrival at Ems.

or of the portraits of the Empress Catherine; but notwithstanding his expression of amiableness (an expression which
almost always imparts that also of beauty), his youth, and,
yet more, his German blood, it is impossible to avoid observing in the lines of his face a power of dissimulation which
one trembles to see in so young a man. This trait is doubtless
the impress of destiny. It convinces me that the grand duke
will be called to the throne. The tones of his voice are sweet,
which is not commonly the case in his family; they say it is a
gift which he has inherited from his mother.

He shines among the young people of his suite without
our discovering what it is that preserves the distance which
may be easily observed to exist between them, unless it be
the perfect gracefulness of his person. Gracefulness always
indicates an amiable mental endowment; it depicts mind
upon the features, embodies it in the carriage and the attitudes, and pleases at the very time that it commands.
Russian travelers had spoken to me of the beauty of the
prince as quite a phenomenon. Without this exaggeration I
should have been more struck with it; besides, I could not but
recollect the romantic mien, the archangelic form, of his father and his uncle the grand duke Michael, who, when in
1815, they visited Paris, were called *"the northern lights,"*
and I felt inclined to be severe, because I had been deceived;
yet, notwithstanding this, the grand duke of Russia appears
to me as one of the finest models of a prince that I have ever
met with.

With the elegance of his equipages, the disorder of the baggage, and the carelessness of the servants, I have been much
struck. In contrasting this imperial cortege with the magnificent simplicity of English equipages, and the careful superin-
tendence that English servants bestow upon everything, one
is reminded that even to have one's carriages and harness
made in London would not be all that is requisite towards attaining that perfection in material, or external arrangements,

the possession of which constitutes the superiority of the English in so matter-of-fact an age as our own.

Yesterday I went to see the sun setting on the Rhine. It was a magnificent spectacle. It is not, however, the banks of the river, with their monotonous ruins and parched vineyards, which occupy too much of the landscape to be agreeable to the eye, that I chiefly admire in this beautiful yet overlauded country. I have seen elsewhere banks more commanding, more varied, more lovely; finer forests, a more luxuriant vegetation, and more picturesque and striking points of view: it is the river itself, especially as viewed from the shore, that appears to me the most wonderful object in the scene. This immense body of water, gliding with an ever-equal motion through the country which it beautifies and enlivens, reveals to me a power in creation that overwhelms my senses. In watching its movements I liken myself to a physician examining the pulse of a man in order to ascertain his strength. Rivers are the arteries of our globe, and before their manifestation of universal life I stand fixed in awe and admiration: I feel myself to be in the presence of my sovereign; I see eternity, I believe, and I almost grasp the infinite. This is the involuntary perception of a sublime mystery; in nature what I cannot comprehend I admire, and my ignorance takes refuge in adoration. Thus it is that science to me is less necessary than to discontented minds.

We shall literally die of heat. It is many years since the air of the valley of Ems, always oppressive, has risen to the present temperature. Last night, in returning from the banks of the Rhine, I saw in the woods a swarm of fireflies—my beloved Italian *luccioli*. I had never before observed them, except in hot climates.

I set out in two days for Berlin and St. Petersburg.

LETTER 2

FRANCE is now represented in Prussia by a minister who unites all the requisites of an enlightened modern diplomat. No mysterious airs, no affected reserve, no unnecessary concealment, betray the opinion that he might entertain of his own importance. One scarcely recollects the post he occupies, until reminded of it by the ability with which its duties are fulfilled. Appreciating with the happiest tact the wants and the tendencies of modern society, he tranquilly proceeds in advance of the future, without, however, disdaining the lessons of the past; in a word, he is one of the small remaining number of those men of former times who are now become so necessary to the present.

Originally from the same province as myself, he has related to me details connected with the history of my family, with which I was unacquainted, and from which I derived much gratification. This I admit without hesitation, for that pious admiration with which we contemplate the heroism of our fathers ought not to be identified with pride.

I knew that there existed in the archives of the French legation at Berlin, letters and diplomatic notes possessing a high interest for the world in general, and for myself in particular: they are my father's.

In 1792, when but twenty-two years old, he was selected by the ministers of Louis XVI, who had then been constitutional king for about a year, to manage a delicate and important mission to the Duke of Brunswick. The object was to induce the duke to decide in refusing the command of the army allied against France. It was hoped, and with reason, that the crisis of our revolution would prove less dangerous to the country and the king, if foreigners did not attempt violently to interfere with its progress.

My father arrived at Brunswick too late. The duke had given his word. The confidence which the character and ability of young Custine inspired in France, was, however, such, that, instead of being recalled to Paris, he was sent to the Prussian court, to make new efforts to detach King William II from that same coalition whose armies the Duke of Brunswick had promised to command.

Shortly before the arrival of my father at Berlin, M. de Ségur, the French ambassador in Prussia, had failed in this difficult negotiation. My father was sent to replace him.

Circumstances more powerful than the talents or the will of men, rendered futile the negotiations of my father with the Berlin cabinet; but notwithstanding the failure of his object, he obtained the esteem, and even the friendship, of all those with whom business brought him into contact (not excepting the king and the ministers), which indemnified him, personally, for the ill success of his political mission.

When my father was about to return to his government to give an account of his negotiations, his mother-in-law, then a French refugee at the same court at which he represented France as minister, joined her entreaties to those of his other friends at Berlin, to induce him to change his intentions, forsake the constitutional cause, and remain among the émigrés until a more favorable time for serving his country should arrive. These entreaties, though accompanied with the prediction of the evils that would await him on his return, and though the scenes of the 10th of August, the imprisonment of Louis XVI, and the frightful anarchy which reigned throughout

France, had terrified all Europe, did not influence my father, or deter him from what he considered his duty to those who had employed him, and to whom he owed an account of his mission. True to the ancient motto of his house—"*Fais ce que doys, adviegne que pourra,*"*—and, in spite of the prayers of his friends, he departed for the country where the scaffold was preparing for him.

He found public affairs there in such disorder, as to induce him to renounce politics and join the army of the Rhine, commanded by his father, General Custine. There he honorably served as volunteer in two campaigns, and when the general who had opened the road of conquest to our arms returned to Paris to die, his son accompanied him, to defend him, and to share his fate. It is the diplomatic correspondence of my father, during the period of his mission at the court of Berlin, that our present Prussian minister has kindly permitted me to peruse.

These letters are admirable models of diplomatic style. The maturity of mental power, the justice, yet determined energy of character, the extent of information, the clearness and precision of thought which they evince, are really extraordinary, when the age of the writer is considered. M. de Noailles, who was at the time French ambassador at Vienna, expressed in letters (also preserved in our archives at Berlin) sentiments the most flattering to the new diplomatist, to whom he predicted a brilliant career. Little did he imagine how short that career would be!!

The death which my father sought and met in Paris under the influence of a sense of duty, was attended with a circumstance, unknown to the public, that in my opinion invests it with a character of sublimity. The circumstance deserves to be told at length; but as my other parent will occupy a con-

---

*Do thy duty, let come what will.

spicuous part in the story, I will first relate another which will give some idea of her character.

My travels are my memoirs. I do not therefore scruple to commence those to Russia with a history that more concerns myself personally, than the topics on which I shall have to dwell hereafter.

It was while with the army, and before his recall to Paris, that General Custine was apprised of the death of the king. His expressions of indignation on this occasion were not moderated even in presence of the commissioners of the convention. These overheard him say, "I serve my country against foreign invasion, but who would fight for those who now govern us?" These words, reported to Robespierre by Thionville, decided the fate of the general.

My mother at that time lived in a retired manner in a village in Normandy. The moment she learnt the return of General Custine to Paris, this noble-minded young woman conceived it to be her duty to quit her asylum, and her child, who was then quite an infant, to repair to the assistance of her father-in-law, with whom her family had been for some years on bad terms, owing to a difference in political opinions.

It was a great trial to her to part with me, for she was a mother in the truest sense of the word; but misfortune always had the first claim upon her heart.

Could General Custine have been saved, it would have been by the devotion and courage of his daughter-in-law. Their first interview was most touching. No sooner did the veteran recognize my mother than he believed himself safe. In fact, her youth, her extreme beauty, her mingled heroism and timidity, so interested the journalists, the people, and even the judges of the revolutionary tribunal, that the men who were determined on the death of the general, felt it necessary first to silence the most eloquent of his advocates, his daughter-in-law.

The government, however, at that time, had not thrown

off all appearance of law; yet the men who hesitated to throw my mother into prison did not scruple to attempt her assassination. The *Septembriseurs*, as these hired ruffians were called, were placed for several days about the precincts of the Palais de Justice; but though my mother was warned of her danger, nothing could deter her from daily attending the trial, and seating herself at the feet of her father-in-law, where her devoted mien softened even the hearts of his murderers.

Between each sitting of the court she employed her time in privately soliciting the members of the committees and of the revolutionary tribunal. A friend of my father's, in costume *à la carmagnole*, generally accompanied her, and waited for her in the antiroom.

In one of the last sittings of the tribunal her looks had drawn tears even from the women in the gallery, commonly called "the furies of the guillotine," and the *tricoteuses* of Robespierre. This so enraged Fouquier-Tinville, the chief prosecutor, that he sent secret peremptory instructions to the assassins outside.

After the accused was re-conducted to prison, his daughter-in-law prepared to descend the steps of the palace, in order to regain, on foot and alone—for none dared openly to accompany her—the hackney coach, which waited for her in a distant street. My mother, naturally timid in a crowd, stood trembling at the head of this long flight of steps, pressed on all sides by an enraged and bloodthirsty populace. Her eyes involuntarily sought the spot where Madame de Lamballe had been murdered some time before. She felt her presence of mind departing, as from the ferocious mob the cry, "It is the daughter of the traitor, it is La Custine," mingled with horrid imprecations, reached her ears. How was she to pass through this crowd of infernal, rather than human beings? Already some, with naked swords, had placed themselves before her; others, half clothed, had caused their women to draw back—a certain sign that murder was about to be enacted. My mother felt that the first symptom of weakness she might betray would be the signal for her death: she has often related to me that she bit her hands and tongue so as to bring blood, in her endeavor to preserve a calm countenance at this juncture. At length she observed a fishwife among the foremost of the crowd. This woman, who was revolting in appearance, had an infant in her arms. Moved by the God of mothers, *the daughter of the traitor* approached this mother (a mother is something more than a woman), and said to her, "What a sweet babe you have in your arms!" "Take it," replied the parent, who understood her by one word and glance; "you can return it to me at the foot of the steps."

The electricity of maternal feeling had thrilled through these two hearts. It communicated itself also to the crowd. My mother took the child, pressed it to her bosom, and held it as an aegis in her arms.

Man, as the child of nature, resumed his superiority over man brutalized under the influence of social evils. The "civilized" barbarians were vanquished by two mothers. She, who was mine, descended, thus rescued, into the court of the Palais de Justice, unsaluted by even an abusive word. She returned the infant to her who had lent it: they parted without interchanging a syllable: the place was not favorable to thanks or explanations, and they never saw each other afterwards; but assuredly the souls of these mothers will meet in another world.

The young woman thus miraculously saved, could not save her father-in-law. He died, and to crown the glory of his life, the veteran soldier had the courage to die a Christian. A letter to his son attests this humble sacrifice, the most difficult of all, in an age of practical crimes and philosophical virtues. In proceeding to the scaffold he embraced the crucifix. This religious courage ennobled his death, as much as his military courage ennobled his life; but it gave great offense to the Brutuses of Paris.

During the trial of General Custine, my father had published a sober but manly defense of the former's political and military conduct. This defense, which had been placarded on the walls of Paris, only served to bring upon the author the hatred of Robespierre. He was imprisoned soon after the death of his father. At this period the Reign of Terror was making rapid progress: to suffer arrest was to receive sentence; the process of trial had become a mere form.

My mother had obtained permission to see her husband daily. Ascertaining that his death was determined, she put in requisition every means that might enable him to escape. By aid of large bribes and larger promises, she won over even the daughter of the jailer to second her design.

My father was not tall. He was slightly and elegantly made. It was arranged therefore that he should put on the clothes of his wife in the prison, that she should dress herself in those of the jailer's daughter, and while the latter was to reach the street by another stair, the prisoner and his wife were to pass out together by the ordinary passage, which the two women had been, purposely, in the habit of doing very frequently.

Everything was duly arranged, and a day fixed, for the execution of this plan. On that day my mother, full of hope that it was her last visit, repaired to the prison, though only on the previous evening the convention had published a decree against all who should aid or connive at the escape of a political prisoner.

This monstrous law was purposely placed before the eyes of the prisoners. My mother, on arriving at the appointed hour, found Louise, the young woman whose goodwill as well as interested services she had enlisted, in tears, on the prison stairs. Upon inquiring the cause, she learnt, to her inexpressible surprise, that it was owing to her husband having peremptorily refused to entertain any further the projected plan of escape. My mother, fearing they had been betrayed, turned, without reply, to gain her husband's apartment. Louise followed her, and apprised her, in a low voice, that he had read the law. She immediately guessed the rest. She knew his inflexible character, and his high and delicate sense of honor: despair almost deprived her of all physical power. "Come with me," she said to Louise, "you will have more influence with him than I; for it is in order to avoid exposing your life that he is about to sacrifice his own."

They both entered together, and a scene commenced which may be better imagined than described. Never but on one single occasion did my mother summon sufficient fortitude to describe it to me. Suffice to say, that nothing could shake the stoical resolution of the young prisoner: the two women on their knees, the weeping wife, the agonized mother reminding him that his child would be an orphan, the stranger urging the utmost willingness to risk her life in his service, —all was unavailing. The sentiments of honor and of duty were stronger in the soul of this man than love of life, than love for a tender and exquisitely beautiful woman, than the impulses of paternal affection. The time accorded to my mother for her visit was passed in useless remonstrances. She had, at length, to be carried out of the chamber. Louise conducted her into the street, where our friend M. Guy de Chaumont-Quitry awaited her with an anxiety that may be easily imagined.

"All is lost," said my mother; "he will not save himself."

"I was sure he would not," replied M. de Chaumont-Quitry.

This answer, worthy of the friend of such a man, appears to me almost as sublime as the conduct to which it referred.

And of all this the world has hitherto known nothing. Supernatural virtue passed unobserved in a time when the sons of France were as lavish of their heroism as they had been of their genius fifty years before.

My mother saw her husband but once more after this scene. By means of money she procured permission to bid him the last adieu, when condemned, and in the conciergerie.

This solemn interview was disturbed by so singular a circumstance, that I have felt some hesitation before concluding to recount it. It will appear like an invention of the tragicomic genius of Shakespeare, but it is strictly true. In all scenes and circumstances, reality is more strange than fiction.

My mother, Delphine de Sabran, was one of the most lovely women of those times. The devotion she displayed to her father-in-law, assures to her a glorious place in the annals of a revolution in which the heroism of the women has often atoned for the ferocity and fanaticism of the men.

She met my father for the last time, with composure, embraced him in silence, and sat with him for three hours. During this time not a word of reproach was spoken. The, perhaps, too elevated sentiment which had cost him his life was forgiven; not a regret was breathed outwardly: it was felt that the unhappy victim had need of all his powers to prepare for the sacrifice. But few words passed between the condemned man and his wife. At length my name was pronounced; this was too much—my father entreated pardon—and my mother did not name me again.

In these heroic times death became an exhibition in which the victims felt their honor staked not to betray fear before their executioners. My poor mother respected in her husband, so young, so handsome, so full of mind, and formerly so happy, the necessity he felt for preserving all his courage for the trial of the morrow. The last proof that can be given of an elevated character appeared then a primary duty, even in the eyes of a naturally timid woman: so true it is that the sublime is always within the reach of characters that are sincere! No woman could be more sincere than my mother; and no person could display more energy in trying circumstances. Midnight was drawing nigh, and fearing that her fortitude would support her no longer, she rose to retire.

Their interview had taken place in a room which served as

a hall of entrance to several apartments of the prison: it was spacious, and lighted by a single candle. Suddenly, one of the doors, hitherto unnoticed, opened. A man with a dark lantern in his hand, and grotesquely clad, issued from it. He was a prisoner proceeding to visit another in a different apartment. His costume was ludicrous in the extreme, and his visage was highly rouged. This ridiculous apparition appeared before the two young people in the moment of their darkest despair. Without thinking that the object of the rouge was—not to beautify a withered face but, probably, to prevent a man of proud spirit from appearing pale before the scaffold of the morrow—they involuntarily burst into a loud and frightful fit of laughter: a nervous electricity triumphed for one moment over the bitterest anguish of the soul. The effort they had so long made to conceal from each other their feelings, had irritated the fibers of the brain: they were thus suddenly overcome by a sense of the ridiculous, the only emotion doubtless for which they were unprepared; and in spite of their efforts, or rather in consequence of their efforts to remain calm, their laughter became inordinate, and speedily degenerated into frightful spasms. The guards, whose revolutionary experience had enlightened them on the nature of this phenomenon, had pity on my mother. The unhappy wife was carried away in convulsions: such was the last interview of this young couple, and such were the stories that nursed my infancy. My mother had commanded these subjects never to be named to me, but the common people love to recount the catastrophes they have survived. The servants scarcely spoke to me of anything but the misfortunes of my parents; and never shall I forget the consequent impression of terror which I experienced in my earliest intercourse with the world.

My first sentiment was that of a fear of life, a sentiment which must be more or less participated in by all, for all have their measure of woes to fill up. It was doubtless this sentiment which taught me to comprehend the Christian religion, before even I had been instructed in it. I felt from my infancy that my lot had been cast in a place of exile.

To return to my father:—after he had regained his composure, he occupied himself with preparing for the stern trial that impended, and towards morning wrote to his wife a letter admirable for the fortitude which it displays. It has been preserved in the memoirs of the times, together with that of my grandfather's to this same son; whose death is to be attributed, first, to a sense of duty, which would not permit him to remain a refugee at the court of Berlin; secondly, to the part he took in the defense of his parent; and, thirdly, to his refusal to save himself at the risk of the life of a young and unknown female.

If his enemies could not speak of his memory without respect, what must have been the sentiments of his friends!

M. Girard, his old tutor, preserved for him the tenderest affection. On being suddenly apprised of his fate, he was seized with an apoplectic fit, and died almost immediately.

My father had a simplicity of manners and a modesty which disarmed envy, at a time when it reigned without control, and which account for the admiration his merits inspired.

He must doubtless have thought more than once during his last night, of the predictions of his friends at Berlin; but I do not believe that he even then repented of the part he had taken. He was one of those with whom life, however bright its hopes, appears little compared with the testimony of a pure conscience. That land is not to be despaired of which produces men in whose hearts the sense of duty is stronger than the sentiments of affection.

LETTER 3

As I HAVE begun to relate the misfortunes of my family, I
will finish the story. Perhaps this episode of our revolution,
as recounted by the son of two individuals who performed
conspicuous parts in it, will not be found altogether without
interest.

My mother having lost all that could attach her to her
country, had now no duty to perform but that of saving her
life, and watching over the welfare of her child.

Her situation was, in fact, much worse than that of the
other French fugitives. Our name, tainted with Liberalism,
was as odious to the aristocrats of that period as to the
Jacobins. The prejudiced and intolerant partisans of the old
regime, could as little forgive my parents for the part they

had taken at the commencement of the revolution, as could the Terrorists for the moderation of their republican patriotism.

The Girondists, who were the Doctrinaires of this era, would have defended the cause of my father; but that party was annihilated, or had, at least, disappeared since the triumph of Robespierre.

My mother, therefore, found herself in a more isolated position than most of the Jacobin victims. Having devotedly embraced the opinions of her husband, she had been obliged to renounce the society in which her life had been passed, and she had not sought entrance into any other. The remains of those circles which had constituted the *world* of that period—the world, that is to say, of the faubourg Saint-Germain —were not propitiated by our misfortunes; and high aristocrats had well nigh come forth from their hiding places to join in the chorus of the *Marseillaise*, when they heard cried in the streets the condemnation of the *traitor* Custine.

The moderate reform party—the men whose love of France exists independently of the form of government adopted by the French—this party, which is now a nation, was not then represented in the country. My father died a martyr in the cause of that unborn nation; and my mother, when only twenty-two years old, had to undergo all the fatal consequences of her husband's virtue—a virtue too lofty to be appreciated by men who could not understand its motives. The energetic moderation of my father was ill understood by his contemporaries, and his wronged memory attached to the person of his wife, and followed her even to the tomb. Identified with a name which, in the midst of a world torn by conflicting passions, represented the principle of impartiality, she was abandoned by all parties. Others had the consolation of mourning over their wrongs in company, my mother could only weep alone!

Soon after the catastrophe which rendered her a widow,

she became aware of the necessity of leaving France. This, however, required a passport, which it was very difficult to obtain. By means of money she procured a false one, under the name of a dealer in lace about to visit Belgium. It was arranged that my nurse, Nanette, a faithful servant of our family in Lorraine, and who had brought me to Paris, should proceed with me by way of Alsace to Pyrmont in Westphalia, where we were to meet my mother, and from thence journey together to Berlin, in which city she expected to join her own mother and her brother also. To no other servant but the nurse herself was this plan confided. All preliminary arrangements having been made, Nanette departed with me for the office of the Strasburg diligence, leaving my mother, who was to set out immediately after us on her journey to Flanders, at her lodging in the Rue de Bourbon. She was employing the last minutes that were to precede her departure, in her room, assorting papers and burning such as might compromise others; for among these papers were letters from officers in the army, and from parties already suspected of being aristocrats, of a character that would have sufficed to bring to the guillotine, in four and twenty hours, herself and fifty other individuals.

Seated on a large sofa near to the fireplace, she was busy burning the most dangerous letters, and placing others, which, as having been written by her parents and dearest friends she felt unwilling to destroy, in a separate box, when suddenly she heard the door of the outer apartment open, and forewarned by one of those presentiments which had never failed to aid her in moments of danger, she said within herself, "I am betrayed; they are coming to arrest me"; whereupon, without further deliberation, for it was too late to burn the heaps of dangerous documents by which she was surrounded, she gathered them hastily together and stuffed them, with the box also, under the sofa, the hangings of which fortunately reached to the floor.

This accomplished, she arose, and received, with an air of perfect composure, the persons who instantly after entered her room. They were the members of the Committee of General Safety, with their attendants. These beings, whose external appearance was at once ridiculous and terrible, surrounded her with muskets and drawn swords.

"You are under arrest," said the president.

My mother made no answer.

"You are arrested, for intent to emigrate."

"It was my intention," she replied, on seeing her false passport already in the hands of the president; for it had been taken from her pocket by the agent of the municipality, whose first care was to search her person.

At this moment my mother observed that her servants had followed the members of the committee into the room. A single glance sufficed to show her by whom she had been denounced; the face of her *femme de chambre* betrayed the secret of a troubled conscience.

"I pity you," said my mother, addressing this person, who began to cry and to ask for pardon, pleading that she had acted through fear for herself.

"Had you watched me better," replied her mistress, "you would have found that I did not expose you to any risk."

"To which prison will you be conducted?" asked one of the members of the committee; "you are free to choose."

"I have no choice."

Before departing they examined the drawers, cabinets, and each piece of furniture in the room, and searched everywhere except beneath the sofa. The papers remained where they had been placed. My mother was conveyed to the Carmelite convent, which had been converted into a prison, and on whose walls was still to be seen the blood of the victims of the 2d September, 1792.

Meanwhile the friend who waited for her at the barrier, convinced from her non-appearance that she had been arrested, hurried to the office of the diligence to prevent Nanette from proceeding with me to Strasburg. He arrived in time, and I was taken back to our residence. My mother was no longer there; the seals had already been affixed upon the doors of her apartments; all the servants had been dismissed; not, however, before they had found time to plunder the plate and linen. The house was robbed of all its valuables, and deserted, except by the civic guard, who kept the door. The kitchen was the only room left to us. Here my poor nurse made her bed close to my cradle, and tended me for eight months with the affection of a mother; and with a devotion that could not have been exceeded had I been a great nobleman.

After the money, which had been destined for our journey, was expended, she supported me by selling, one by one, the articles of her dress. If my mother perished, her intention was to carry me to her own country, and to bring me up among the little peasants of her family. I was at that time two years old. Falling dangerously ill of a malignant fever, she found means to procure for me the attendance of three of the first medical men in Paris. Poor Nanette! she had, indeed, both a generous heart and an energetic character, though the strength of her feelings may not have been equaled by the powers of her intellect.

Her fearlessness made her often very imprudent. During the trial of my grandfather, the people in the streets would often inveigh, in the most violent language, against the *traitor Custine*. Whenever my nurse chanced to hear these imprecations she would stop in the middle of the crowd, demand who dared to say anything against General Custine, defend him against the accusations of the populace, maintaining that she, who was born his servant, knew him better than they, and conclude by heaping both on them and their revolution the most contemptuous epithets. More than once has she thus incurred danger of being killed in the streets of Paris.

On one occasion, passing with me in her arms across the Place du Carrousel, she observed the women on their knees paying their orisons before the revolutionary shrine of Marat, the martyr of atheism and inhumanity.

By a confusion of ideas, which strikingly exhibits the disorder into which minds were plunged at this epoch, the women, after finishing their prayers, rose, paying a deep reverence to their new saint, and making the sign of the cross.

Nanette was so indignant at this exhibition, that, forgetting I was in her arms, she began to load these new devotees with abuse, and from words soon came to blows. During the struggle she continued faithfully to hold me to her bosom, the fear of my suffering in the contest being her chief care. At length she fell, and the cry of "to the lantern with the aristocrat" resounded from all sides. A woman snatched me from her arms, and she was being dragged along by the hair of her head, when a man, who appeared among the most furious of the crowd, pressed near to her, and contrived to hint in her ear that she should counterfeit insanity, and that he would take care of her child. Nanette began immediately to sing and make many strange grimaces; whereupon her friendly adviser called out "she is mad."—"She is mad; she is mad; let her go," was re-echoed by other voices. Availing herself of this means of escape, she retreated, singing and dancing, towards the Pont Royal, and in the Rue du Bac received me again from the hands of her deliverer.

This lesson served to render Nanette (chiefly through fear for me) more circumspect, but her imprudence became a source of constant alarm to my mother.

The latter, in her prison, derived some consolation from the society of several distinguished female fellow-prisoners, who evinced for her the sincerest sympathy. Among others were Mademoiselle Picot, and Mesdames de Lameth, d'Aiguillon, and de Beauharnais, afterwards the Empress Josephine. This last named lady was placed in the same room with my mother, and they mutually performed for each other the offices of a *femme de chambre*.

With the exception of Madame de Beauharnais, these young and beautiful women took a pride in maintaining a high degree of courage and fortitude. The former exhibited all the thoughtlessness of the creole, and often betrayed a pusillanimity and peevish restlessness that made her companions in misfortune blush. But though she had no magnanimity of character, she was naturally graceful; and gracefulness can dispense with every other qualification. Her mien, her manner, and, above all, her way of speaking, possessed a peculiar charm.

Many curious details connected with the prison life of this period have been written. Had my mother left any memoirs, they would have revealed to the public traits and occurrences still unknown. In the ancient Carmelite convent, among other female prisoners, was an Englishwoman, very old, deaf, and almost blind. She had never been able to learn the reason of her imprisonment; to ascertain which she constantly addressed everyone with whom she had an opportunity of speaking. The executioner was the last person who replied to her inquiry.

In the same chamber with this last was the wife of a man who exhibited a puppet show. They had been arrested, they said, because their puppets were too aristocratic. The woman had a profound respect for the fallen great; and, thanks to this feeling! the prisoners of noble birth received from her a homage greater than they had ever met with in their own houses.

The plebeian voluntarily waited upon them, and was continually performing little obliging offices, actuated by the pure pleasure of the service: she never approached their persons without testifying marks of the most profound respect; and in finally bidding farewell to these illustrious companions, to proceed with her husband to the place of execution, the poor woman did not for a moment forget to use all those antiquated forms of obeisance with which she was accustomed to address them at other times.

The prisoners, both male and female, used to meet at certain hours in a kind of garden, where the men played at prisoners' bars. It was usually during these moments of recreation that the revolutionary tribunal sent to summon its victims. If the one singled out was in the midst of a game, he bade a simple adieu to his friends, *after which the party continued their play!!* This prison was a world in miniature, of which Robespierre was the god. What could so much resemble hell, as this caricature of Providence?

After having been five months in prison, my mother saw M. de Beauharnais depart for the scaffold. In passing her, he presented her with an arabesque talisman set in a ring. She always kept it, and it is now worn by me.

Time was then no longer reckoned by weeks, but by periods of ten days; the tenth was termed *décadi*, and answered to our Sunday, as they neither worked nor guillotined on that day. Its arrival, therefore, assured to the prisoners an existence of twenty-four hours; this appeared an age in prospect, and the day was always viewed as a fête in the prison.

Such was the life of my mother after the death of her husband. It continued during the last six months of the Reign of Terror. Considering her connections, her celebrity, and the circumstances of her arrest, it was wonderful that she had escaped the scaffold so long. On three different occasions she was taken from prison to her own house, where her inquisitors examined before her, and questioned her upon every insignificant paper which they could find in the drawers and secretaries; searching every corner of the apartment, and omitting only to examine the sofa, which it was the will of God should be overlooked. It may be readily imagined that my mother's heart would irrepressibly beat every time they approached this spot. She has often told me that she did not dare, in one single instance, to look towards the fatal sofa, and yet that she equally feared her eyes might have the appearance of being too consciously averted.

This was not the only token of protection which God vouchsafed her in her misfortunes. The sentiments of the men on whom her fate depended were softened by an invisible power.

Twelve members of the section superintended the searches. They invariably concluded by subjecting the prisoner to a long and scrutinizing inquiry. The first time she was thus questioned, the president of this species of revolutionary jury was a little hunchbacked shoemaker, who was as malicious as he was ugly. This man had found in a corner, a shoe, which he pretended was made of English leather. The accusation was serious. My mother at first maintained that the leather was not English, but the shoe-making president insisted on the fact.

"It is possible that it may be," my mother at length conceded; "you ought to know better than I. All that I can say is, that I have never procured anything from England."

They tried it on her foot: it fitted her. "Who is your shoe-maker?" demanded the president. She named him. He had been the fashionable shoemaker at the commencement of the revolution.

"A bad patriot," observed the jealous humpback.

"A good shoemaker!" remarked my mother.

"We would imprison him," replied the president, "but the aristocrat has concealed himself. Do you know where he is?"

My mother answered in the negative, and intimated that if she did she would not tell.

Her courageous answers, which contrasted strangely with her timid mien; the species of involuntary irony to which these scenes, alike burlesque and tragic in their character, excited her; the exquisite beauty of her person; her youth; her widow's dress; the expression of her face, at once wayward and resigned; her air, lofty in spite of herself; her perfectly easy and elegant manners; her celebrity, already national; the dignity of misfortune; the unequaled accent of her silver voice; and, finally, the instinct of the woman, that constant desire to please, which always succeeds when it is innate and consequently natural,—all contributed to win the hearts of her judges, hard and cruel as they were; in short, all felt favorably disposed towards her except the little hunchback.

My mother had a remarkable talent for drawing, especially for taking likenesses. In the intervals of her examination she amused herself by taking those of the persons who surrounded her, and in a few minutes had made an excellent sketch of the terrible picture in which she was the chief figure.

A master mason, of the name of Jérôme, one of the most ardent Jacobins of the day, was present on this occasion. He took the sketch from my mother and passed it to the others; each recognized himself, and all amused themselves at the expense of the president. The rage of the latter might have been fatal to my mother; nevertheless, it was the imprudence she on this occasion committed which saved her life.

The drawing was attached to the other documents connected with her case. Jérôme, the mason, who affected the most violent hostility to her, and who never addressed her without some horrible oath, Jérôme, ferocious though he might be, was young; and, struck with admiration of her many charms, he conceived the idea of saving her from the guillotine.

He had free access to the office of Fouquier-Tinville, the chief prosecutor, where lay the box of papers on which were inscribed the names of every prisoner in Paris. These papers were used to furnish the executions of the day, which often reached to the number of sixty or eighty, and the spectacle of which constituted the chief amusement of the people of Paris. The selection of the victims was generally made with little choice, the names that were uppermost being first taken. Jérôme was acquainted with the fatal box: during six months he did not *once fail* to enter the office every evening, and, unobserved, to place the paper on which was inscribed the name of my mother at the bottom of the box, or, at least, to assure himself that it remained there. When fresh papers were put in, they were, by a species of distributive justice, placed undermost, so that each name should come in its turn. It was the business of Jérôme constantly to search out my mother's, and restore it to the bottom place.

I am now only repeating what I have myself often heard Jérôme relate. He has told me that, at night, when everyone had retired, he has often returned to the office, under the fear that someone might at the last moment have disturbed the order of the papers—that order on which the life of my mother entirely depended. In fact on one occasion her name appeared at the top of the pile; Jérôme shuddered, and again placed it under the others.

Neither I nor the friends who listened to this fearful recital dared to ask Jérôme the names of the victims whose death he had hastened in my mother's favor. The latter knew nothing, until after her deliverance from prison, of the stratagem that had saved her life.

When the day of the 9th Thermidor arrived, the prisons were found to be almost emptied; there remained only three sheets in the box of Fouquier-Tinville, and it was not likely that many would be added; the bloody spectacles of the Place de la Révolution began to weary the public; and the project of Robespierre and his confidential counselors was to make an end of the families of the old regime, by commanding a general massacre in the interior of the prisons.

My mother, who contemplated death on the scaffold with such high resolution, has often told me that she felt her courage sink at the idea of being murdered in this manner.

During the last weeks of the Reign of Terror, the old keepers of the Carmelite prison had been replaced by the more ferocious men who were destined to aid in effecting the secret executions. They did not conceal from their victims the plan formed against them; the rules of the prison were made more severe; visitors were no longer admitted; every distant sound the prisoners caught seemed to them the signal of carnage; every night appeared to them the last.

This agony of suspense was relieved the very day that Robespierre fell.

Some who have dealt in over-refined subtleties, in reviewing the history of the Reign of Terror, pretend that Robespierre only fell because he was better than his opponents.

It is true that his accomplices did not become his enemies, until they trembled for their own lives; but in saving themselves they saved France, which would have become a den of wild beasts had Robespierre's plans been carried out. The revolution of the 9th Thermidor was, it is also true, the revolt of a banditti; but surely the fact of their captain having fallen a victim to their conspiracy, does not render him any the worthier character. If misfortune served to justify crime, what would become of the principle of conscience? Equity would perish under the influence of a false generosity—a most dangerous sentiment, for it seduces noble minds, and causes them to forget that a good man should prefer justice and truth to every other consideration.

It has been said that Robespierre was not naturally cruel. What of that? He was one in whom envy had become omnipotent. Envy, nursed and fed by the well-merited humiliations that this man had endured, under the state of society which preceded the revolution, had suggested to him the idea of a revenge so atrocious, that the meanness of his soul and the hardness of his heart scarcely suffice to persuade us that he was capable of realizing it. To write in blood, to calculate by heads, such were the processes of political arithmetic to which France submitted under the government of Robespierre. She does yet worse in the present day—she listens to those who would justify him.

To accept as an excuse for murder, that which renders it the more odious, the sangfroid and the ulterior plans of the murderer, is to contribute to one of the most crying evils of our age, the perversion of human judgment. The men of the present day, in the decisions dictated by their false sensibility, proceed with an impartiality that annihilates the principles of good and evil; to arrange matters upon earth to their own liking, they have abolished, at one blow, heaven and hell.

Such are the sophisms to which the pretended amelioration of our manners leads—an amelioration which is nothing more than a supreme moral indifference, a deeply rooted religious incredulity, and an ever-increasing avidity for sensual gratifications; but patience,—the world has ere now recovered from a yet more hopeless state.

Two days after the 9th Thermidor, the greater number of the prisons of Paris were empty. Madame de Beauharnais, through her connection with Tallien, came out in triumph; Mesdames d'Aiguillon and de Lameth were also speedily liberated. My mother was almost the only one left in the Carmelite prison. She beheld her noble companions in misfortune give place to the Terrorists, who, after the political revolution that had been effected, daily changed places with their victims. All the friends and relatives of my mother were dispersed; no one thought of her. Jérôme, proscribed, in turn, as a friend of Robespierre, was obliged to conceal himself and could not aid her.

For two months she remained thus abandoned, under a desolation of feeling, that, she has often told me, was more difficult to endure than the previous more immediate sense of peril.

The struggle of parties continued; the government was still in danger of falling again into the hands of the Jacobins. But for the courage of Boissy-d'Anglas, the murder of Feraud had become the signal for a second Reign of Terror, more terrible than the first. My mother knew all this; my illness also, though she did not know its extent, added to her griefs.

At length Nanette, having saved my life by her careful nursing, set seriously about rescuing that of her mistress. She went to the house of one Dyle, a manufacturer of china, in order to consult with about fifty workmen of our province, who were then employed by this rich individual, and who had formerly worked at a porcelain manufactory founded by my grandfather at Niderviller, at the foot of the Vosges, and subsequently confiscated with his other property.

It was to these men, among whom was Malriat her father, that Nanette applied, urging them to interest themselves in the fate of their former mistress.

They eagerly signed a petition, framed by Nanette, who both spoke and wrote the German-French of Lorraine. This document she herself carried to Legendre, formerly a butcher, and then president of the bureau to which petitions in favor of prisoners were addressed. The paper of Nanette was received and thrown aside, among a multitude of similar petitions.

One evening, three young persons, connected with Legendre, entered the bureau, rather heated with wine, and amused themselves with chasing each other over the tables, and with other similar pranks. In the midst of this sport, some of the surrounding papers were disturbed; one fell, and was picked up by a member of the party. "What have you there?" asked the others.

"No doubt a petition," replied Rossigneux, which was the name of the person addressed.

"Yes; but for what prisoner?"

They called for lights. In the interval of their appearing, the three hot-headed youths took an oath among themselves to obtain, that very evening from Legendre, the signature that would give liberty to the captive, whoever he might be, and to announce to him his freedom within the same hour.

"I swear it, though it should be the liberation of the Prince de Condé," said Rossigneux.

"No doubt," said the others, laughing; "he is no longer a prisoner."

They read the petition; it was that dictated by Nanette, and signed by the workmen of Niderviller.

"How fortunate," shouted the young men; "the lovely Custine, a second Roland! We will go and fetch her from prison in a body."

Legendre returned home at one o'clock in the morning, under the influence of wine like the others. The petition for my mother's liberty was presented by three giddy youths, signed by a drunken man, and at three o'clock in the morning, the former, empowered to open her prison gates, knocked at the door of her apartment.

She at that time slept alone; and would neither open her door, nor consent to leave the prison.

Her liberators explained to her as well as they could, the circumstances of their coming; but she resisted all their urgent entreaties; she feared to enter a hackney coach with strangers in the middle of the night; and all they could obtain from her was the permission to return at the hour of ten.

When she finally left the prison, they related to her, with many details, the circumstances to which the liberation was owing, more especially with the view of proving to her that she had nobody to thank for it; for at that time a species of traffic in liberty was carried on by certain intriguers, who would often extort largely from the liberated parties, for the most part already ruined by the revolution.

A lady of rank, and nearly related to my mother, was not ashamed to ask her for thirty thousand francs, which she pretended had been expended in bribes to procure her release. My mother replied by simply relating the story of Rossigneux, and saw her relative no more.

What a scene had she to encounter on returning to her own residence! The house bare and desolate, the seals yet on the doors, and I in the kitchen, still deaf and imbecile, in consequence of the malady that had so nearly ended in my death. My mother had remained firm before the terror of the scaffold, but she sank under this misery. The day after her return she was attacked with jaundice, which lasted five months, and left an affection of the liver, from which she suffered throughout her life.

At the end of six months, the small part of the estate of her husband that had remained unsold, was restored to her. We were then both recovered.

"On what does my lady imagine she has lived, since she left the prison?" asked Nanette, one day.

"I do not know; you must have sold the plate, the linen, or the jewels."

"There were none left to sell."

"Well then, on what?"

"On money which Jérôme forwarded to me every week, with the express command that I was not to mention it to my lady; but now that she can return it, I will tell her the real fact."

My mother had the gratification of saving the life of this man, when proscribed with the Terrorists. She concealed him, and aided his escape to America.

He returned under the consulate, with a little fortune which he had made in the United States, and which he afterwards augmented by speculations in Paris. My mother treated him as a friend, and her family loaded him with marks of grateful kindness; yet he would never form one of our society. He used to say to my mother, "I will come and see you when you are alone, you will always receive me with kindness, for I know your heart; but your friends will regard me as some strange animal; I shall not be at my ease with them. I was not born as you were; I cannot speak as you do." My mother always continued a faithful friend to him. He had the utmost confidence in her, and used often to relate to her his domestic troubles, but never spoke on politics or religion. He died while I was yet a child, about the commencement of the period of the Empire.

My poor mother passed in struggling with poverty the best years of that life which had been so miraculously preserved.

Of the enormously rich estate of my grandfather, nothing remained to us but the debts. The government took the property, but left the task of paying the creditors to those whom it had robbed of the means for so doing.

Twenty years were spent in ruinous lawsuits, with the view of recovering for me some of this estate. My mother was my guardian. Her love for me prevented her ever again marrying; besides, made a widow by the hands of the executioner, she did not feel herself free to act as do other women.

Our involved and complicated affairs were her torment. We were ever kept suspended betwixt fear and hope, and struggling meanwhile with want. At one time riches would appear within our grasp; at another, some unforeseen reverse, some chicanery of the law, deprived us of every prospect. If I have any taste for the elegancies of life, I attribute it to the privations of my early youth.

A year after her liberation, my mother obtained a passport to proceed to Switzerland. Here her mother and her brother, who did not dare to enter France, awaited her.

Their meeting, notwithstanding the renewal of griefs which it called forth, was a consolation.

This Swiss journey was one of the happiest portions of my mother's life; my grandmother was one of the most distinguished and amiable women of her time; and my uncle, the Count Elzéar de Sabran, though younger than his sister, possessed superior and precocious powers of mind.

Lavater was a friend of Madame de Sabran's, who took her daughter to Zurich purposely to present her to this oracle of the philosophy of that day. The great physiognomist, on perceiving her, turned towards Madame de Sabran, observing, "Ah, madame, what a fortunate mother you are! your daughter is transparent! Never have I seen so much sincerity; I can read through her face!"

After her return to France, she devoted herself to two objects, namely, the re-establishment of my fortune, and the direction of my education. I owe to her all that I am, and all that I have. She became also the center of a circle of distinguished persons, among whom were some of the first men of our country. M. de Chateaubriand continued her friend to the last.

For painting she had almost the talent of an artist, and never passed a day without shutting herself up in her studio for several hours. The world she loved not—it frightened, wearied, and disgusted her; she had seen it, in its depths, too early; nevertheless, she was born with, and had ever preserved, that generosity which is the virtue of more prosperous lives.

Her timidity in society was proverbial among her family; her brother used to observe that she had more fear of a salon than of the scaffold.

During the whole period of the empire, she and her friends sided with the opposition. After the death of the Duc d'Enghien, she never visited Malmaison, nor did she ever again see Madame Bonaparte.

In 1811 she made, with me, the tour of Switzerland and Italy. On this occasion she accompanied me everywhere, and, either on horseback or on foot, crossed the most dangerous passages of the Alps.

We passed the winter at Rome, in a most agreeable society. My mother was no longer young; yet the classic grace of her features made a strong impression on Canova, whose ingenuous character she much admired. One day I said to her, "With your romantic mind, I should not wonder at your marrying Canova."

"Do not dare me to do it," she replied. "If he were not Marquis d'Ischia, I might be tempted."

I had the happiness of having her life preserved to me until the 13th of July, 1826. She died of the same disease that proved fatal to Bonaparte. This malady, of which the germ had long existed, was accelerated by grief, caused by the death of my wife and only child.

It was in honor of my mother that Madame de Staël, who knew her well and loved her warmly, gave the name of Delphine to the heroine of her first romance.

At the age of fifty-six years she still retained a beauty that struck even those who had not known her in her youth, and were not, therefore, seduced by the charms of memory.

LETTER 4

THIS MORNING, at Lübeck, the landlord of the hotel, hearing that I was going to embark for Russia, entered my room with an air of compassion which made me laugh. This man is more clever and humorous than the sound of his voice, and his manner of pronouncing the French language, would at first lead one to suppose.

On hearing that I was traveling only for my pleasure, he began exhorting me, with the good-humored simplicity of a German, to give up my project.

"You are acquainted with Russia?" I said to him.

"No, sir; but I am with Russians; there are many who pass through Lübeck, and I judge of the country by the physiognomy of its people."

"What do you find, then, in the expression of their countenance that should prevent my visiting them?"

"Sir, they have two faces. I do not speak of the valets, who have only one; but of the nobles. When they arrive in Europe they have a gay, easy, contented air, like horses set free, or birds let loose from their cages: men, women, the young and the old, are all as happy as schoolboys on a holiday. The same persons, when they return, have long faces and gloomy looks; their words are few and abrupt; their countenances full of care. I conclude from this, that a country which they left with so much joy, and to which they return with so much regret, is a bad country."

"Perhaps you are right," I replied; "but your remarks, at least, prove to me that the Russians are not such dissemblers as they have been represented."

"They are so among themselves; but, they do not mistrust us honest Germans," said the landlord, retiring, and smiling knowingly.

Here is a man who is afraid of being taken for a goodnatured simpleton, thought I: he must travel himself in order to know how greatly the description, which travelers (often superficial and careless in their observations) give of different nations, tends to influence these nations' character. Each separate individual endeavors to establish a protest against the opinion generally entertained with respect to the people of his country.

Do not the women of Paris aspire to be simple and unaffected? It may be here observed, that nothing can be more opposite than the Russian and the German character.

My carriage is already in the packet boat: the Russians say it is one of the finest steamers in the world: they call it *Nicholas I*. This same vessel was burnt last year crossing from Petersburg to Travemünde: it was refitted, and has since made two voyages.

Some superstitious minds fear that misfortune will yet attach itself to the boat. I, who am no sailor, do not sympathize with this poetic fear; but I respect all kinds of inoffensive superstition, as resulting from the noble pleasures of believing and of fearing, which are the foundation of all piety, and of which, even the abuse classes man above all other beings in creation.

After a detailed account of the circumstances of the burning of the *Nicholas I.* had been made to the emperor, he cashiered the captain, who was a Russian, and who was quietly playing at cards in the cabin when the flames burst from the vessel. His friends, however, state in his excuse, or rather in his praise, that he was acquainted with the danger, and had given private orders to steer the vessel towards a sandbank on the Mecklenburg coast, his object being to avoid alarming the passengers until the moment of absolute necessity arrived. The flames burst out just as the vessel grounded; most of the passengers were saved, owing chiefly to the heroic efforts of a young and unknown Frenchman. The Russian captain has been replaced by a Dutchman; but he, it is said, does not possess authority over his crew. Foreign countries lend to Russia the men only whom they do not care to keep themselves. I shall know tomorrow what to think of the individual in question. No one can judge so well of a commander as a sailor or a passenger. The love of life, that love so passionately rational, is a guide by which we can unerringly appreciate the men upon whom our existence depends.

Our noble vessel draws too much water to get up to Petersburg; we therefore change ship at Kronstadt, whence the carriages will follow us, two days later, in a third vessel. This is tiresome, but curiosity triumphs over all: it is perhaps the chief requisite in a traveler.

I am writing at midnight, *without any lights*, on board the steamboat *Nicholas I*, in the Gulf of Finland. It is now the close of a day which has nearly the length of a month in these latitudes, beginning about the 8th of June, and ending towards the 4th of July. By degrees the nights will reappear; they are very short at first, but insensibly lengthen as they approach the autumnal equinox. They then increase with the same rapidity as do the days in spring, and soon involve in darkness the north of Russia and Sweden, and all within the vicinity of the Arctic Circle. To the countries actually within this circle, the year is divided into a day and a night, each of six months' duration. The tempered darkness of winter continues as long as the dubious and melancholy summer light.

I cannot yet cease from admiring the phenomenon of a polar night, the clear beam of which almost equals that of the day. Nothing more interests me than the various degrees in which light is distributed to the various portions of the globe. At the end of the year, all the different parts of the earth have beheld the same sun during an equal number of hours; but what a difference between the days! what a diversity also of temperature and of hues! The sun, whose rays strike vertically upon the earth, and the sun whose beams fall obliquely, do not appear the same luminary, at least if we judge by effects.

As for myself, whose existence bears a sympathetic analogy to that of plants, I acknowledge a kind of fatality in climates, and, impelled by the influence the heavens have over my mind, willingly pay respect to the theory of Montesquieu. To such a degree are my temper and faculties subject to the action of the atmosphere, that I cannot doubt of its effects upon politics. But the genius of Montesquieu has exaggerated and carried too far the consequences of this belief. Obstinacy of opinion is the rock on which genius has too often made shipwreck. Powerful minds will only see what they wish to see: the world is within themselves; they understand everything but that which is told to them.

About an hour ago I beheld the sun sinking in the ocean between the NNW and N. He has left behind a long bright track which continues to light me at this midnight hour, and enables me to write upon deck while my fellow-passengers are sleeping. As I lay down my pen to look around, I perceive already, towards the NNE the first streaks of morning light. Yesterday is not ended, yet tomorrow is begun. The sublimity of this polar scene I feel as a compensation for all the toils of the journey. In these regions of the globe the day is one continued morning, which never performs the promises of its birth. This singular twilight precedes neither day nor night; for the things which bear those names in southern countries have in reality no existence here. The magic effects of color, the religious gloom of midnight, are forgotten; nature appears no longer a painting, but a sketch; and it is difficult to preserve belief in the wonders of those blessed climates where the sun reigns in his full power.

The sun of the north is an alabaster lamp, hung breast-high, and revolving between heaven and earth. This lamp, burning for weeks and months without interruption, sheds its melancholy rays over a vault which it scarcely lightens; nothing is bright, yet all things are visible. The face of nature, everywhere equally illuminated by this pale light, resembles that of a poet rapt in vision and hoary with years. It is Ossian who remembers his loves no more, and who listens only to the voices of the tombs.

The aspect of these unvaried surfaces—of distances without objects, horizons undefined, and lines half effaced—all this confusion of form and coloring, throws me into a gentle reverie, the peaceful awakening from which is as like death as life. The soul resembles the scene, and rests suspended between day and night—between waking and sleeping. It is no lively pleasure that it feels; the raptures of passion cease, but the inquietude of violent desires ceases also. If there is not exemption from ennui, there is from sorrow: a perpetual repose possesses both the mind and the body, the image of which is reflected by this indolent light, that spreads its mortal coldness equally over day and night, over the ocean and the land, blended into one by the icy hand of winter, and the overspreading mantle of the polar snows.

The light of these flat regions near the pole accords well with the blue eyes, the inexpressive features, the fair locks, and the timidly romantic imagination of the women of the North. Those women are forever dreaming of what others are enacting; of them more especially can it be said, that life is but the vision of a shadow.

In approaching these northerly regions you seem to be

climbing the platform of a chain of glaciers; the nearer you advance, the more perfectly is the illusion realized. The globe itself seems to be the mountain you are ascending. The moment you attain the summit of this large Alp, you experience what is felt less vividly in ascending other Alps: the rocks sink, the precipices crumble away, population recedes, the earth is beneath your feet, you touch the pole. Viewed from such elevation, the earth appears diminished, but the sea rises and forms around you a vaguely defined circle; you continue as though mounting to the summit of a dome—a dome which is the world, and whose architect is God.

From thence the eye extends over frozen seas and crystal fields, in which imagination might picture the abodes of the blessed unchangeable inhabitants of an immutable heaven.

Such were the feelings I experienced in approaching the Gulf of Bothnia, whose northern limits extend to Torneo.

The coast of Finland, generally considered mountainous, appears to me but a succession of gentle, imperceptible hills; all is lost in the distance and indistinctness of the misty horizon. This untransparent atmosphere deprives objects of their lively colors; everything is dulled and dimmed beneath its heavens of mother-of-pearl. The vessels just visible in the horizon, quickly disappear again; for the glimmering of the perpetual twilight to which they here give the name of day scarcely lights up the waters; it has not power to gild the sails of a distant vessel. The canvas of a ship under full sail in northern seas, in place of shining as it does in other latitudes, is darkly figured against the gray curtain of heaven, which resembles a sheet spread out for the representation of Chinese figures. I am ashamed to confess it, but the view of nature in the north reminds me, in spite of myself, of an enormous magic lantern, whose lamp gives a bad light, and the figures on whose glasses are worn with use. I dislike comparisons which degrade the subject; but we must, at any rate, endeavor to describe our conceptions. It is easier to admire than to disparage; nevertheless, if we would describe with truth, the feeling that prompts both sentiments must be suffered to operate.

On entering these whitened deserts, a poetic terror takes possession of the soul: you pause, affrighted on the threshold of the palace of winter. As you advance amid abodes of cold illusions, of visions, brilliant, though with a silvered rather than a golden light, an indefinable species of sadness takes possession of the heart; the failing imagination ceases to create, or its feeble conceptions resemble only the undefined forms of the wanly glittering clouds that meet the eye.

When the mind reverts from the scenery to itself, it is to partake of the hitherto incomprehensible melancholy of the people of the North, and to feel, as they feel, the fascination of their monotonous poetry. This initiation into the pleasures of sadness is painful while it is pleasing; you follow with slow steps the chariot of Death, chanting hymns of lamentation, yet of hope; your sorrowing soul lends itself to the illusions around, and sympathizes with the objects that meet the sight: the air, the mist, the water, all produce a novel impression. There is, whether the impression be made through the organ of smell or of touch, something strange and unusual in the sensation: it announces to you that you are approaching the confines of the habitable world; the icy zone is before you, and the polar air pierces even to the heart. This is not agreeable, but it is novel and very strange.

LETTER 5

AMONG THE passengers on board the steamer, I observed
an elderly man, whose immensely swollen legs could hardly
support his corpulent frame. His head, well set between
his large shoulders, had a noble cast: it was a portrait of
Louis XVI.

I soon learnt that he was the Russian Prince K——, a
descendant of the conquering Varegues, and therefore one of
the most ancient of the Russian nobility.

As I observed him, supported by his secretary, and moving
with difficulty towards a seat, I could not help saying to myself, here is a sorry traveling companion; but on hearing his
name, which I well knew by reputation, I reproached myself
for this incorrigible mania of judging by appearances.

As soon as seated, the old gentleman, the expression of
whose face was shrewd, although noble and sincere, addressed me by name.

Apostrophized thus suddenly, I rose without replying. The

prince continued in that truly aristocratic tone, the perfect simplicity of which excludes all idea of ceremony:—

"You, who have seen almost all Europe, will, I am sure, be of my opinion."

"On what subject, Prince?"

"On England. I was saying to Prince ———, here," indicating with his finger, and without further presentation, the individual with whom he was talking, "that there is no noblesse among the English. They have titles and offices; but the idea which we attach to a real order of nobility, distinguished by characteristics which can neither be purchased nor conferred, is unknown to them. A monarch may create a prince; education, circumstances, genius, virtue, may make a hero; but none of these things are sufficient to constitute a nobleman."

"Prince," I replied, "a noblesse, in that sense of the word which was once understood in France, and in which you and I, I believe, understand it at present, has become a fiction, and was perhaps always one. You remind me of the observation of M. de Lauraguais, who said, on returning from an assembly of the marshals of France, 'we were twelve dukes and peers, but I was the only gentleman.' "

"He said the truth," replied the prince. "On the continent, a person of ancient family alone is considered as noble, because in countries where nobility is still something real, it is inherent in the blood, and not in fortune, favor, talent, or avocation; it is the produce of history; and, as in physics, the period for the formation of certain metals appears to have ceased, so in communities, the period for the creation of noble families has ceased also. It is this of which the English are ignorant."

"It is true," I answered, "that though still preserving much feudal pride, they have lost the spirit of feudal institutions. In England, chivalry has ceded to industry, which has readily consented to take up its abode in a baronial constitution, on condition that the ancient privileges attached to names should be placed within reach of newly founded families.

"By this social revolution, the result of a succession of political changes, hereditary rights are no longer attached to a race, but are transferred to individuals, to offices, and to estates. Formerly the warrior ennobled the land that he won; now it is the possession of the land which constitutes the noble; and what is called a noblesse in England, seems to me to be nothing more than a class that is rich enough to pay for wearing a certain dress. This monied aristocracy differs, no doubt, very greatly from the aristocracy of blood. Rank that has been bought, has an evidence of the intelligence and activity of the man; rank that has been inherited is an evidence of the favor of Providence.

"The confusion of ideas respecting the two kinds of aristocracy, that of money and that of birth, is such in England, that the descendants of a family, whose name belongs to the history of the country, if they happen to be poor and are without title, will tell you they are not noble; while my Lord —— (grandson of a tailor), forms, as member of the house of peers, a part of the high aristocracy of the land."

"I knew that we should agree," replied the prince, with a graceful gravity that is peculiar to him.

Struck with this easy manner of making acquaintance, I began to examine the countryman of the Prince K——, Prince D——, the celebrity of whose name had already attracted my attention. I beheld a man still young: his complexion wore a leaden hue; a quiet, patient expression was visible in his eye; but his forehead was full, his figure tall, and throughout his person there was a regularity which accorded with the coldness of his manners, and the harmony produced by which was not unpleasing.

Prince K——, who never tired of conversation, continued:—

"To prove to you that the English notions of nobility differ from ours, I will relate a little anecdote which will perhaps amuse you.

"In 1814 I attended the Emperor Alexander on his visit to London. At that time His Majesty honored me with much confidence, which procured for me many marks of kindness on the part of the Prince of Wales, then regent. This prince took me aside one day, and said to me, 'I should like to do something that would be agreeable to the emperor. He appears to have a great regard for the physician who accompanies him; could I confer on this person any favor that would please your master?'

" 'You could, sir,' I replied.

" 'What, then, should it be?'

" 'Nobility.'

"On the morrow the doctor was made a knight. The Emperor took pains to ascertain the nature of the distinction which thus constituted his physician a Sir, and his physician's wife a Lady; but, although his powers of comprehension were good, he died without being able to understand our explanations, or the value of the new dignity conferred upon his medical man."

"The ignorance of the Emperor Alexander," I replied, "is justified by that of many well-informed men: look at the greater number of novels in which foreigners attempt to depict English society." This discourse served as a prelude to a most agreeable conversation, which lasted several hours. The tone of society among the higher ranks in Russia is marked by an easy politeness, the secret of which is almost lost among ourselves.

Everyone, not even excluding the French secretary of Prince K——, appears modest, superior to the little cares and contrivances of vanity and self-love, and, consequently, exempt from their mistakes and mortifications. If it is this that one gains from living under a despotism, *Vive la Russie!* How can polished manners subsist in a country where nothing is respected, seeing that bon ton is only discernment in testifying respect. Let us recommence by showing respect to those who have a right to deference, and we shall then again become naturally, and, so to speak involuntarily, polite.

Notwithstanding the reserve which I threw into my answers to the Prince K——, the old diplomatist quickly discovered the tendency of my views.

"You do not belong either to your country or to your age," he exclaimed; "you are an enemy to the power of speech as a political engine."

"It is true," I replied; "any other way of ascertaining the worth of men appears to me preferable to public speaking, in a country where self-love is so easily excited as in mine. I do not believe that there could be found in France many men who would not sacrifice their most cherished opinions to the desire of having it said that they had made a good speech."

"Nevertheless," pursued the liberal Russian prince, "everything is included in the gift of language; everything that is in man, and something even beyond, reveals itself by discourse: there is divinity in speech."

"I agree with you," I replied, "and it is for that very reason that I dread to see it prostituted."

"When a genius like that of Mr. Canning's," continued the prince, "enchained the attention of the first men of England and of the world, surely political oratory was something great and glorious!"

"What good has this brilliant genius produced? and what evil would he not have caused if he had had inflammable minds for auditors? Speech employed in private, as a means of persuasion, to change the direction of ideas, to influence the action of a man, or of a small number of men, appears to me useful, either as an auxiliary or as a counterbalance to power; but I fear it in a large political assembly whose deliberations are conducted in public. It too often secures a triumph to limited views and fallacious popular notions, at the expense of lofty, far-sighted conceptions, and plans profoundly laid. To impose upon nations the domination of majorities is to subject them to mediocrity. If such is not your object, you do wrong to laud oratorical influence. The politics of large assemblies are almost always timid, sordid, and unprincipled. You oppose to this the case of England: that country is not what it is supposed to be. It is true that in its houses of parliament, questions are decided by the majority; but that majority represents the aristocracy of the land, which for a long time has not ceased, except at very brief intervals, to direct the affairs of the state. Besides, to what refuges of lies have not parliamentary forms compelled the leaders of this masked oligarchy to descend? Is it for this that you envy England?"

"Nevertheless, man must be led either by fear or by persuasion."

"True, but action is more persuasive than words. Does not the Prussian government prove this? Does not Bonaparte? Bonaparte at the commencement of his reign governed by persuasion as much as, or more than, by force, and yet his eloquence, though great, was never addressed except to individuals; to the mass he never spoke except by deeds: to discuss the laws in public is to rob them of that respect which is the secret of their power."

"You are a friend to despotism?"

"On the contrary, I dread the lawyers, and their echo the newspapers,* which are but speeches whose echo resounds for twenty-four hours. This is the despotism which threatens us in the present day."

"Come among us, and you will learn to fear some other kinds."

"It will not be you, Prince, who will succeed in imbuing me with a bad opinion of Russia."

---

*These allusions, it must be remembered, refer more especially to France under King Louis Philippe.—*Trans.*

"Do not judge of it, either by me, or by any other Russian who has traveled: our natural flexibility renders us cosmopolites the moment we leave our own land; and this disposition of mind is in itself a satire against our government!"

Here, notwithstanding his habit of speaking openly on all subjects, the prince began to distrust both himself, me, and everyone else, and took refuge in some remarks not very conspicuous for their perspicuity. He afterwards, however, availed himself of a moment when we were alone to lay before me his opinion as to the character of the men and the institutions of his country. The following, as nearly as I can recollect, forms the sum of his observations:—

"Russia, in the present age, is only four hundred years removed from the invasions of barbarian tribes, whilst fourteen centuries have elapsed since western Europe experienced the same crisis. A civilization older by one thousand years, of course places an immeasurable distance between the manners of nations.

"Many ages before the irruption of the Mongols, the Scandinavians placed over the Slavic (then altogether savages) chieftains, who reigned at Great Novgorod and at Kiev, under the name of Varangians. These foreign heroes, supported by a small retinue of armed followers, became the first princes of the Russians; and their companions in arms are the stock whence proceeds the more ancient nobility. The Varangian princes, who were a species of demigods, governed the nation while still composed of wandering tribes. It was from the emperors and patriarchs of Constantinople that they at this period derived all their notions of luxury and the arts. Such, if I may be allowed the expression, was the first-laid stratum of civilization in Russia, afterwards trampled on and destroyed by the Tartar conquerors.

"A vast body of saints, who were the legislators of a newly converted Christian people, illume, with their names, this fabulous epoch of Russian history. Princes, also, great by their savage virtues, ennoble the early period of the Slavic annals. Their names shine out from the profound darkness of the age, like stars piercing the clouds of a stormy night. The very sound of these strange names excites the imagination and challenges curiosity. Rurik, Oleg, Queen Olga, St. Vladimir, Sviatopolk, and Monomakh, are personages whose characters no more resemble those of the heroes of the West than do their appellations.

"They have nothing of the chivalrous about them; they are like the monarchs of Scripture; the nation which they rendered great remained in the vicinity of Asia; ignorant of your romance, it preserved manners that were in a great measure patriarchal.

"The Russian nation was not formed in that brilliant school of good faith, by whose instructions chivalrous Europe had so well profited, that the word *honor* was for a long period synonymous with truth, and the *word of honor* had a sanctity which is still revered, even in France, where so many things have been forgotten.

"The noble influence of the Knights of the Cross stopped, with that of Catholicism, in Poland. The Russians are warriors, but they fight under the principle of obedience, and with the object of gain; the Polish chevaliers fought for the pure love of glory; and thus, though these two people spring from the same stock, and have still many points of resemblance, the events of history have separated them so widely that it will require a greater number of ages of Russian policy to reunite them than it has required of religion and of social habitudes to part them asunder.

"Whilst Europe was slowly recovering from the efforts she had made during centuries to rescue the tomb of Christ from the unbelievers, Russia was paying tribute to the Mohammedans under Uzbek, and at the same time drawing her arts and sciences, her manners, religion, and politics, as also her principles of craft and fraud, and her aversion to the Latin cross, from the Greek Empire. If we reflect on all these civil, religious, and political influences, we shall no longer wonder at the little confidence that can be placed in the word of a Russian (it is the Russian prince who speaks), nor that the Russian character in general should bear the impress of that false Byzantine stamp which influences social life even under the empire of the czars—worthy successors of the lieutenants of Bati.

"The unmitigated despotism that reigns over us established itself at the very period when servitude ceased in the rest of Europe. From the time of the invasion of the Mongols, the Slavs, until then one of the freest people in the world, became slaves first to their conquerors, and afterwards to their own princes. Bondage was thenceforward established among them, not only as an existing state, but as a constituent principle of society. It has degraded the right of speech in Russia to such a point that it is no longer considered anything better than a snare: our government lives by lies, for truth is as terrible to the tyrant as to the slave. Thus, little as one speaks in Russia, one always speaks too much, since in that country all discourse is the expression of religious or political hypocrisy."

"Prince," I replied, after having listened attentively to this long series of deductions, "I will not believe you. It is enlightened to rise above national prejudices, and polite to deal gently with the prejudices of foreigners; but I have no more confidence in your concessions than I have in others' claims and pretensions."

"In three months you will render me greater justice; meanwhile, and as we are yet alone,"—he said this after looking round on all sides,—"I will direct your attention to a leading point, I will present you with a key which will serve to explain everything to you in the country you are about to visit.

"Think at each step you take among this Asiatic people that the chivalrous and Catholic influence has never obtained in their land; and not only have they never adopted it, they have withstood it also, with bitter animosity, during long wars with Lithuania, Poland, and the knights of the Teutonic order."

"You make me proud of my discernment. I wrote lately to one of my friends, that I conceived religious intolerance to be the secret spring of Russian policy."

"You anticipated clearly what you are going to see; you can have no adequate idea of the intense intolerance of the Russians; those whose minds are cultivated, and whom business brings into intercourse with western Europe, take the utmost pains to conceal the predominant national sentiment, which is the triumph of the Greek *orthodoxy*—with them, synonymous with the policy of Russia.

"Without keeping this in view, nothing can be explained either in our manners or our politics. You must not believe, for example, that the persecutions in Poland were the effect of the personal resentment of the emperor: they were the result of a profound and deliberate calculation. These acts of cruelty are meritorious in the eyes of true believers; it is the Holy Spirit who so enlightens the sovereign as to elevate him above all human feelings; and it is God who blesses him as the executor of his high designs. By this manner of viewing things, judges and executioners become so much the greater saints as they are greater barbarians. Your Legitimist journals little know what they are doing when they seek for allies among schismatics. We shall see a European revolution before we shall see the Emperor of Russia acting in good faith with a Catholic power; the Protestants are at least open adversaries; besides, they will more readily reunite with the Pope than the chief of the Russian autocracy; for the Protestants, having beheld all their creeds degenerate into systems, and their religious faith transformed into philosophic doubt, have nothing left but their sectarian pride to sacrifice to Rome; whereas the emperor possesses a real and positive spiritual power, which he will never voluntarily relinquish. Rome, and all that can be connected with the Romish church, has no more dangerous enemy than the autocrat of Moscow—visible head of his own church; and I am astonished that Italian penetration has not discovered the danger that threatens you from that quarter. After this veracious picture, judge of the illusion with which the Legitimists of Paris nurse their hopes."

This conversation will give an idea of all the others. Whenever the subject became unpleasant to Muscovite self-love, the Prince K—— broke off, at least until he was fully sure that no one overheard us.

The subjects of our discourse have made me reflect, and my reflections make me fear.

There is perhaps more to look forward to in this country, long depreciated by our modern thinkers, because appearing so far behind all others, than in those English colonies implanted on the American soil, and which are too highly vaunted by the philosophers whose systems have developed the real democracy, with all its abuses, which now subsists.

If the military spirit which prevails in Russia has failed to produce anything analogous to our creed of honor, or to invest its soldiers with the brilliant reputation which distinguishes ours, it should not therefore be said that the nation is less powerful. Honor is a human divinity, but in practical life duty outvalues even honor; though not so dazzling it is more sustained, and more capable of sustaining.

In my opinion the empire of the world is henceforth no longer to be committed to the turbulent, but to people of a patient spirit.* Europe, enlightened as she now is, will no longer submit, except to real strength: now the real strength

---

*I must again request the reader, who would follow me throughout this work, to wait before forming an opinion of Russia, until he shall have compared my different views made before and after my journey. The candor and good faith with which I profess to write forbid me to retrench anything that I have already written.

of nations is obedience to the power which rules them, just as discipline is the strength of armies. Henceforth, falsehood will react so as to produce most injury to those who would make it their instrument; truth will give birth to a new influence, so greatly will neglect and disuse have renewed its youth and vigor.

The curiosity which I feel to see Russia, and the admiration with which the spirit of order that must govern the administration of so vast a state inspires me, do not prevent my judging impartially of the policy of its government. The domination of Russia, when confining itself to diplomatic efforts, without proceeding to actual conquest, appears to me that which is most to be dreaded by the world. There is much misapprehension as regards the part which this state would play in Europe. In accordance with its constitutional character, it would represent the principle of order, but influenced by the character of its rulers, it seeks to propagate tyranny under pretext of remedying anarchy; as though arbitrary power could remedy any evil! It is the elements of moral principle that this nation lacks; with its military habits, and its recollections of invasions, it is still occupied with notions of wars of conquest, the most brutal of all wars; whereas the struggles of France and the other Western nations will henceforth assume the character of wars of propagandism.

The number of passengers whom I have fallen in with on board the *Nicholas I* is fortunately few. There is a young Princess D—— accompanying her husband on his return to St. Petersburg, a charming person, in appearance quite the heroine of a Scottish romance.

This amiable couple, accompanied also by the brother of the princess, have been passing several months in Silesia, subjecting themselves to the treatment of the famous cold-water remedy. It is more than a remedy, it is a sacrament: it is medical baptism.

In the fervor of their faith, the prince and princess have entertained us with the recital of wonderful results obtained by this mode of cure. The discovery is due to a peasant, who professes to be superior to all the doctors in the world, and justifies his pretensions by his works. He believes in himself; this example communicates itself to others; and many disciples of the new apostle are made whole by their faith. Crowds of strangers from every country resort to Gräfenberg, where all diseases are treated except those of the chest. The patient is subjected to showers (ice-cold water being employed), and then wrapped for five or six hours in flannel. No complaint, said the prince, could withstand the perspiration which this treatment produces.

"No complaint, and no individual either," I remarked.

"You are mistaken," replied the prince, with the zeal of a new convert; "among a multitude, there are very few who have died at Gräfenberg. Princes and princesses fix themselves near to the new savior, and after having tried his remedy, the love of water becomes quite a passion."

Here Prince D—— looked at his watch, and called a servant. The man came with a large pitcher of cold water in his hand, and poured it over his master's body between the waistcoat and the shirt. I could scarcely credit my senses.

The prince continued the conversation without noticing my astonishment.

"The father of the reigning Duke of Nassau arrived at Gräfenberg entirely deprived of the use of his limbs; the water has greatly restored him; but as he aspires to a perfect cure, it is uncertain when he leaves. No one knows on arriving at Gräfenberg how long he will remain; the duration of the treatment depends on the complaint and the temperament of the individual; besides, one cannot calculate on the influence of a passion, and this mode of using water becomes a passion with some people, who continue indefinitely to linger near the source of their supreme felicity."

"Prince, in listening to your account, I am ready to believe in these wonderful results; but when I reflect, I must still doubt their efficacy. Such apparent cures have often evil consequences; perspirations so violent decompose the blood, and often change gout into dropsy."

"I am so persuaded of the efficacy of the cold-water treatment," replied the prince, "that I am going to form near to me an establishment similar to that of Gräfenberg."

The Slavs, thought I to myself, have a mania for other things besides cold water, namely, a general passion for novelties. The thoughts of this imitative people willingly exercise themselves with the inventions of others.

Besides the personages already mentioned, there was yet another Russian princess on board our vessel. This lady, the Princess L——, was a most agreeable person in society: our evenings were passed delightfully in listening to Russian airs, which she sung with pleasing execution, and which were quite new to me. The Princess D—— took parts with her, and even sometimes accompanied the airs with a few graceful steps of some Cossack dance. These national exhibitions and impromptu concerts agreeably suspended our conversations, and made the hours pass like moments.

Our Russian ladies have admitted into their little circle a French merchant, who is one of the passengers. He is a man rather past the middle age, full of great schemes connected with steamboats and railroads, but still exhibiting all his former youthful pretensions; agreeable smiles and gracious mien blended with winning grimaces, plebeian gestures, narrow ideas, and studied language. He is, notwithstanding, a good fellow, speaking willingly, and even well, when he speaks on subjects with which he is conversant; amusing also, though self-sufficient, and sometimes rather prosy.

He is going to Russia to *electrify* certain minds in favor of some great industrial undertakings. He travels as agent for several French commercial houses who have associated, he says, to carry into effect these important objects; but his head, although full of grave commercial ideas, finds place, nevertheless, for all the songs and bon mots that have been popular in Paris for the last twenty years. Before turning merchant he had been a lancer, and he has preserved, in his air and attitudes, some amusing traces of his former profession. He never speaks of the Russians without alluding to French superiority in matters of every description; but his vanity is too palpable to become offensive, or to excite anything beyond a laugh.

When singing, he casts tender glances upon the ladies; when declaiming the *Parisienne* or the *Marseillaise* he folds his cloak around him with a theatrical air: his store of songs and sayings, although rather jovial in character, much amuses our fair strangers. In listening to him they seem to believe they are on a visit to Paris. The *mauvais ton* of this specimen of French manners by no means strikes them, because they do not comprehend its source or its scope; a language which they cannot understand cannot disgust them; besides, persons belonging to really good society are always the last to be annoyed or alarmed. The fear of being lowered in position does not oblige them to take offense at everything that is said.

The old Prince K—— and myself laugh between ourselves at the language to which they listen; they laugh on their part with the innocence of an ignorance unacquainted with the point at which good taste ceases and French vulgarity begins.

Vulgarity commences as soon as the individual thinks of avoiding it: such a thought never occurs to persons perfectly sure of their own good breeding.

When the gaiety of the ex-lancer becomes rather too exuberant, the Russian ladies moderate it by singing, in their turn, some of those national airs of which the melancholy and originality greatly charm me.

The Princess L—— has sung to us some airs of the Russian Gypsies, which, to my great surprise, bring the Spanish boleros to my mind. The Gitanos of Andalusia are of the same race as the Russian Gypsies. This population dispersed, one knows not why, throughout all Europe, has preserved, in every region, its manners, its traditions, and its national songs.

The sea voyage, so much dreaded in prospect, has proved so agreeable that I look forward to its termination with real regret. Besides, who does not feel some sense of desolation in arriving in a large city, where one has no business and no friends. My passion for travel cools when I consider that it consists entirely of departures and arrivals. But what pleasures and advantages do we not purchase by this pain! Were it only that we can by this means obtain information without laborious study, it would be well thus to *turn over*, as the leaves of a book, the different countries of the earth.

When I feel myself discouraged in the midst of my pilgrimages, I say to myself, "If I wish for the result, I must take the means," and under this thought I persevere. I do more:— scarcely am I again in my own abode, when I think of recommencing my travels. Perpetual travel would be a delightful way of passing life, especially for one who cannot conform to the ideas that govern the world in the age in which he lives. To change one's country is tantamount to changing one's century. It is a long bygone age which I now hope to study in Russia.

Never do I recollect having met in traveling, with society so agreeable and amusing as in this passage. Our life here is like life in the country in wet weather; we cannot get out, but all task themselves to amuse the others, so that the effort of each turns to the benefit of all. This however must be ascribed to the perfect sociability of some of our passengers, and more especially to the amiable authority of Prince K——. Had it not been for the part he took at the commencement of our voyage, no one would have broken the ice, and we should have continued observing one other in silence during the whole passage. Instead of such a melancholy isolation, we talk and chatter night and day. The light lasting during the whole twenty-four hours, has the effect of so deranging habits, that there are always some ready for conversation at any hour. It is now past three o'clock, and as I write, I hear my companions laughing and talking in the cabin; if I were to go down, they would ask me to recite some French verses, or to tell some story about Paris. They never tire of asking about Mademoiselle Rachel or Duprez, the two great dramatic stars of the day. They long to draw to their own country the celebrated talents which they cannot obtain permission to come and see amongst us.

When the French lancer, the mercantile *militaire*, joins in the conversation, it is generally to interrupt it. There is then sure to be laughter, singing, and Russian dances.

This gaiety, innocent as it is, has proved offensive to two Americans going to Petersburg on business. These inhabitants of the New World do not permit themselves even a smile at the foolish pleasures of the young European women. They do not perceive that liberty and carelessness are the safeguards of youthful hearts. Their puritanism rebels not only against license, but against mirth; they are Jansenists of the Protestant school; to please them, life must be made one protracted funeral. Happily, the ladies we have on board do not trouble themselves to render any reason to these pedantic merchants. Their manners are more simple than most of the women of the North, who, when they come to Paris, believe themselves obliged to distort their whole nature in order to seduce us. Our fair fellow-passengers please without seeming to think of pleasing; their French accent also appears to me better than that of most of the Polish women whom I have met in Saxony and Bohemia. In speaking our language they do not pretend to correct it, but endeavor to speak as we speak, and very nearly succeed.

Yesterday, a slight accident which happened to our engine served to exhibit some of the secret traits of character in those on board.

The recollection of the former accident that befell our boat has had the effect of making the passengers rather timid and distrustful, though the weather has remained throughout extremely fine.

Yesterday after dinner, we were seated reading, when suddenly the motion of the paddles stopped, and an unusual noise was heard to proceed from the engine. The sailors rushed forward; the captain followed, without saying a word in reply to the questions of the passengers. At length he gave the order to sound. "We are on a rock," said a female voice, the first that had dared to break our solemn silence. "The engine is going to burst," exclaimed another.

I was silent, though I began to think that my presentiments were going to be realized, and that it was not, after all, caprice which had inclined me to renounce this voyage.

The Princess L——, whose health is delicate, fell into a swoon, murmuring some broken words of grief that she should die so far from her husband. The Princess D—— pressed the arm of *hers*, and awaited the result with a calm, which one would not have expected from her slight, frail form and gentle features.

The fat and amiable Prince K—— neither changed his countenance nor his place; he would have sunk in his armchair into the sea without disturbing himself. The French ex-lancer, half merchant, half comedian, put on a bold face, and began to hum a song. This bravado displeased me, and made me blush for France, where vanity searches out of all things to extract some opportunity for display; true moral dignity exaggerates nothing, not even indifference to danger; the Americans continued their reading; I observed everybody.

At length the captain came to inform us that the nut of the screw of one of the pistons was broken, and that all would be made right again in a quarter of an hour.

At this news, the apprehensions that each party had more or less concealed betrayed themselves by a general explosion of rejoicing. Each confessed his thoughts and fears, all laughed at one another, and those who were the most candid in their confessions were the least laughed at. The evening that had commenced so ominously concluded with dance and song.

Before separating for the night, Prince K—— complimented me for my good manners in listening with apparent pleasure to his stories. One may recognize the well-bred man, he observed, by the manner he assumes in listening to another. I replied that the best way by which to seem to be listening, was to listen. This answer, repeated by the prince, was lauded beyond its merit. Nothing is lost, and every thought is done more than justice to by persons whose benevolence even is intellectual.

LETTER 6

TAKING my arm, Prince K—— begged me to assist him to his stateroom, where, offering me a seat, he said in a low voice, "As we are alone, I will recount to you a story:—it is to you alone that I relate it, because before Russians one must not talk of history.

"You know that Peter the Great, after much hesitation, destroyed the patriarchate of Moscow, in order to unite, on the same head, the crown and the tiara. The political autocracy thus openly usurped that unlimited spiritual power which it had coveted for so long—a monstrous union, unknown before among the nations of modern Europe. The chimera entertained by the popes during the Middle Ages is now actually realized in a nation of sixty millions of people, many of them Asiatics, whom nothing surprises, and who are by no means sorry to find a grand Lama in their Czar.

"The Emperor Peter sought to unite himself in marriage with Catherine, the sutler.

"To accomplish this supreme object of his heart it was necessary to begin by finding a family name for the future empress. This was obtained I believe in Lithuania, where an obscure private gentleman was first converted into a great lord *by birth,* and afterwards discovered to be the brother of the empress elect.

"Russian despotism not only pays little respect to ideas and sentiments, it will also deny facts; it will struggle against evidence, and triumph in the struggle!!! for evidence, when it is inconvenient to power, has no more voice among us than has justice."

The bold language of the prince startled me. He had been educated at Rome, and, like all who possess any piety of feeling and independence of mind in Russia, he inclined to the Catholic religion. While various reflections, suggested by his discourse, were passing in my mind, he continued his philosophical observations.

"The people, and even the great men, are resigned spectators of this war against truth; the lies of the despot, however palpable, are always flattering to the slave. The Russians, who bear so much, would bear no tyranny if the tyrant did not carefully act as though he believed them the dupes of his policy. Human dignity, immersed and sinking in the gulf of absolute government, seizes hold of the smallest branch within reach that may serve to keep it afloat. Human nature will bear much scorn and wrong; but it will not bear to be told in direct terms that it is scorned and wronged. When outraged by deeds, it takes refuge in words. Falsehood is so abasing, that to degrade the tyrant into the hypocrite is a vengeance which consoles the victim. Miserable and last illusion of misfortune, which must yet be respected, lest the serf should become still more vile, and the despot still more outrageous!

"There existed an ancient custom for two of the greatest noblemen of the empire to walk by the side of the patriarch of Moscow in solemn public processions.

"On the occasion of his marriage, the czarinian pontiff determined to choose for acolytes in the bridal procession, on one side, a famous boyar,* and on the other, the new brother-in-law that he had created; for in Russia, sovereign power can do more than create nobles, it can raise up relatives for those that are without any; with us, despotism is more powerful than nature; the emperor is not only the representative of God, he is himself the creative power; a power indeed greater than that of Deity, for it only extends its action to the future, whereas the emperor alters and amends the past: the law has no retroactive effect, the caprice of a despot has.

"The personage whom Peter wished to associate with the new brother of the empress was the highest noble in Moscow, and next to the czar, the greatest individual in the empire—his name was Prince Romodanowsky. Peter notified to him, through his first minister, that he was to attend the ceremony in order to walk by the emperor's side—an honor which he would share with the brother of the empress.

" 'Very well,' replied the prince; 'but on which side of the czar am I expected to place myself?'

" 'My dear prince,' replied the courtier, 'how can you ask such a question? Of course the brother-in-law of His Majesty will take the right.'

" 'I shall not attend, then,' responded the haughty boyar.

"This answer reported to the czar provoked a second message.

" 'You shall attend!' was the mandate of the tyrant; 'you shall either attend, or I will hang you!'

" 'Say to the czar,' replied the indomitable Muscovite, 'that I entreat him first to execute the same sentence on my only son: this child is but fifteen years old; it is possible that, after having seen me perish, fear will make him consent to walk on the left hand of his sovereign; but I can depend on myself, both before and after the execution of my

---

*The title of a Russian noble.

child, never to do that which can disgrace the blood of Romodanowsky.'

"The czar, I say it in his praise, yielded; but to revenge himself on the independent spirit of the Muscovite aristocracy, he built St. Petersburg.

"Nicholas," added Prince K——, "would not have acted thus; he would have sent the boyar and his son to the mines, and have declared by an ukase, *couched in legal terms*, that neither the father nor the son could have children; perhaps he would have decreed that the father had never been married; such things still often take place in Russia, the best proof of which is that we are forbidden to recount them."

Be this as it may, the pride of the Muscovite noble gives a perfect idea of that singular combination of which the actual state of Russian society is the result. A monstrous compound of the petty refinements of Byzantium, and the ferocity of the desert horde, a struggle between the etiquette of the Lower Empire, and the savage virtues of Asia, have produced the mighty state which Europe now beholds, and the influence of which she will probably feel hereafter, without being able to understand its operation.

We have just seen an instance of arbitrary power outbraved and humiliated by the aristocracy.

This fact, and many others, justify me in maintaining that it is an aristocracy which constitutes the greatest check on the despotism of an individual,—on an autocracy; the soul of aristocracy is pride, the spirit of democracy is envy. We will now see how easily an autocrat may be deceived.

This morning we passed Revel. The sight of that place, which has not long been Russian territory, recalled to our memories the proud name of Charles XII, and the battle of Narva. In this battle was killed a Frenchman, the Prince de Croï, who fought under the King of Sweden. His body was carried to Revel, where he could not be buried, because, during the campaign, he had contracted debts in the province, and had left nothing to pay them. According to an ancient custom of the land, his body was placed in the church of Revel until his heirs should satisfy his creditors. This corpse is still in the same church where it was laid more than one hundred years ago. The amount of the original debt has become so greatly augmented by interest, and by the daily charge made for the keeping of the corpse, that there are few fortunes which would now suffice to acquit it.

In passing through Revel about twenty years since, the Emperor Alexander visited the church, and was so shocked with the hideous spectacle presented by the corpse, that he commanded its immediate interment. On the morrow, the emperor departed, and the body of the Prince de Croï was duly carried to the cemetery. The day after, it was brought back to the church, and placed in its former position. If there is not justice in Russia, there are, it would appear, customs more powerful even than the sovereign will.

What most amused me during this too short passage was to find myself constantly obliged, in obedience to my instinctive notions of equity, to justify Russia against Prince K——'s observations. This won me the goodwill of all the Russians who heard our conversation. The sincerity of the opinions which the amiable prince pronounces on his country at least proves to me that in Russia there are some who may speak their mind.

When I remarked this to him, he replied, that he was not a Russian!! Singular assertion! However, Russian or foreigner, he says what he thinks. He has filled the most important political posts, spent two fortunes, worn out the favor of several sovereigns, and is now old and infirm, but especially protected by a member of the Imperial family, who loves wit too well to fear it. Besides, in order to escape Siberia, he pretends that he is writing memoirs, and that he has deposited the finished volumes in France. The emperor dreads publicity as much as Russia dreads the emperor.

I am much struck by the extreme susceptibility of the Russians as regards the judgment which strangers may form respecting them. The impression which their country may make on the minds of travelers occupies their thoughts incessantly. What would be said of the Germans, the English, and the French if they indulged themselves in such puerility? If the satires of Prince K—— are disagreeable to his countrymen, it is not so much because their own feelings are wounded, as on account of the influence these satires may have upon me, who am become an important person in their eyes since they have heard that I write my travels.

"Do not allow yourself to be prejudiced against Russia by this unpatriotic Russian; do not write under the influence of his statements; it is from a wish to display his French wit at our expense that he thus speaks, but in reality he has no such opinion."

This is the kind of language that is addressed to me, privately, a dozen times a day. It seems to me as though the Russians would be content to become even yet worse and more barbarous than they are, provided they were *thought* better and more civilized. I do not admire minds which hold the truth thus cheaply. Civilization is not a fashion or an artificial device, it is a power which has its result—a root which sends forth its stalk, produces its flowers, and bears its fruit.

"At least you will not call us the barbarians of the North, as your countrymen do." This is said to me every time I appear pleased by any interesting recital, national melody, or noble or poetic sentiment ascribed to a Russian. I reply to these fears by some unimportant compliment; but I think in my own mind that I could better love the barbarians of the North than the apes who are ever imitating the South.

There are remedies for primitive barbarism, there are none for the mania of appearing what one is not.

A kind of Russian savant, a grammarian, a translator of various German works, and a professor of I know not which college, has made as many advances towards me as he could during this passage. He has been traveling through Europe, and returns to Russia full of zeal, he says, to propagate there all that is valuable in the modern opinions of western Europe. The freedom of his discourse appeared to me suspicious: it was not that luxury of independence observable in Prince K——; it was a studied liberalism, calculated to draw out the views of others.

If I am not mistaken, there may be always found some savant of this kind, on the ordinary lines of route to Russia, in the hotels of Lübeck, the steamboats, and even at Le Havre, which, thanks to the navigation of the German and Baltic seas, has become the Muscovite frontier.

The individual in question extracted from me very little. He was specially desirous of learning whether I should write my travels, and obligingly offered me the lights of his experience. He left me at last, thoroughly persuaded that I traveled only to divert myself, and without any intention of publishing the relation of a tour which would be performed very rapidly. This appeared to satisfy him; but his inquietude, thus allayed, has awaked my own. If I write this journey I must expect to give umbrage to a government more artful and better served with spies than any other in the world. This is an unpleasant idea. I must conceal my letters, I must be guarded in my language; but I will affect nothing; the most consummate deception is that which wears no mask.

LETTER 7

As WE APPROACHED Kronstadt—an underwater fortress of
which the Russians are justly proud—the Gulf of Finland
suddenly assumed an animated appearance. The Imperial
fleet was in motion and surrounded us on all sides. It remains
in port, ice-locked for more than six months of the year; but
during the three months of summer the marine cadets are exercised in nautical maneuvers between St. Petersburg and the
Baltic. After passing the fleet, we again sailed on an almost
desert sea; now and then only enlivened by the distant apparition of some merchant vessel, or the yet more infrequent
smoke of a *pyroscaph,* as steamboats are learnedly called in
the nautical language of some parts of Europe.

The Baltic Sea, by the dull hues of its unfrequented waters,
proclaims the vicinity of a continent depopulated under the
rigors of the climate. The barren shores harmonize with
the cold aspect of the sky and water, and chill the heart of the
traveler.

No sooner does he arrive on this unattractive coast, than

he longs to leave it; he calls to mind, with a sigh, the remark of one of Catherine's favorites, who, when the Empress complained of the effects of the climate of Petersburg upon her health, observed, "It is not God who should be blamed, madame, because men have persisted in building the capital of a great empire in a territory destined by nature to be the patrimony of wolves and bears."

My traveling companions have been explaining to me, with much self-satisfaction, the recent progress of the Russian marine. I admire the prodigy without magnifying it as they do. It is a creation, or rather a re-creation of the present emperor's. This prince amuses himself by endeavoring to realize the favorite object of Peter I; but however powerful a man may be, he is forced, sooner or later, to acknowledge that nature is more powerful still. So long as Russia shall keep within her natural limits, the Russian navy will continue the hobby of the emperors and nothing more.

During the season of naval exercises, I am informed that the younger pupils remain performing their evolutions in the neighborhood of Kronstadt, while the more advanced extend their voyages of discovery as far as Riga, and sometimes even to Copenhagen.

As soon as I found that the sole object of all this display of naval power, which passed before my eyes, was the instruction of pupils, a secret feeling of ennui extinguished my curiosity.

All this unnecessary preparation, which is neither the result of commerce nor of war, appears to me a mere parade. Now, God knows, and the Russians know, whether there is any pleasure in a parade! The taste for reviews in Russia is carried beyond all bounds, and here, before even landing in this empire of military evolutions, I must be present at a review on the water. But I must not laugh at this. Puerility on a grand scale is a monstrous thing, impossible except under a tyranny, of which it is, perhaps, the most terrible result!

Everywhere, except under an absolute despotism, men, when they make great efforts, have in view great ends; it is only among a blindly abject people that the monarch may command immense sacrifices for the sake of trifling results.

The view of the naval power of Russia, gathered together for the amusement of the czar, at the gate of his capital, has thus caused me only a painful impression. The vessels which will be inevitably lost in a few winters, without having rendered any service, suggest to my mind images—not of the power of a great country, but of the useless toils to which the poor, unfortunate seamen are condemned. The ice is a more terrible enemy to this navy than foreign war. Every autumn, after the three months' exercise, the pupil returns to his prison, the plaything to its box, and the frost begins to wage its more serious war upon the Imperial finances. Lord Durham once remarked to the emperor himself, with a freedom of speech which wounded him in the most sensitive part, that the Russian ships of war were but the toys of the Russian sovereign.

As regards myself, this childish colossus by no means predisposes me to admire what I may expect to see in the interior of the empire. To admire Russia in approaching it by water, it is necessary to forget the approach to England by the Thames. The former is the image of death, the latter of life.

On dropping anchor before Kronstadt, we learned that one of the noble vessels we had seen maneuvering around us had just been lost on a sandbank. This shipwreck was dangerous only to the captain, who expected to be cashiered, and, perhaps, punished yet more severely. Prince K—— said to me privately, that he would have done better to have perished with his vessel. Our fellow-traveler, the Princess L——, had a son attached to the unlucky ship. She was placed in a situation of painful suspense, until news of his safety was brought to her by the governor of Kronstadt.

The Russians are incessantly repeating to me that it is requisite to spend at least two years in their country before passing a judgment upon it; so difficult is it to understand.

But though patience and prudence may be necessary virtues in those learned travelers who aspire to the glory of producing erudite volumes, I, who have been hitherto writing only for my friend and myself, have no intention of making my journal a work of labor. I have some fear of the Russian customhouse, but they assure me that my *écritoire* will be respected.

Nothing can be more melancholy than the aspect of nature in the approach to St. Petersburg. As you advance up the gulf, the flat marshes of Ingria terminate in a little wavering line drawn between the sky and the sea; this line is Russia. It presents the appearance of a wet lowland, with here and there a few birch trees thinly scattered. The landscape is void of objects and colors, has no bounds, and yet no sublimity. It has just light enough to be visible; the gray mossy earth well accords with the pale sun which illumines it, not from overhead, but from near the horizon, or almost indeed from below,—so acute is the angle which the oblique rays form with the surface of this unfavored soil. In Russia, the finest days have a bluish dimness. If the nights are marked by a clearness which surprises, the days are clothed with an obscurity which saddens.

Kronstadt, with its forest of masts, its substructures, and its ramparts of granite, finely breaks the monotonous reverie of the pilgrim, who is, like me, seeking for imagery in this dreary land. I have never seen, in the approaches to any other great city, a landscape so melancholy as the banks of the Neva. The *campagna* of Rome is a desert, but what picturesque objects, what past associations, what light, what fire, what poetry, if I might be allowed the expression, I would say, what passion animates that religious land! To reach St. Petersburg, you must pass a desert of water framed in a desert of peat earth; sea, shore, and sky, are all blended into one mirror, but so dull, so tarnished, that it reflects nothing.

The thought of the noble vessels of the Russian navy, destined to perish without having ever been in action, pursues me like a dream.

The English, in their idiom, which is so poetical when it relates to maritime objects, call a vessel of the royal navy, *a man of war*. Never will the Russians be thus able to denominate their ships of parade. These *men of court*, or wooden courtiers, are nothing more than the hospital of the Imperial service. If the sight of so useless a marine inspired me with any fear, it was not the fear of war but of tyranny. It recalled to my mind the inhumanities of Peter I, that type of all Russian monarchs, ancient and modern.

Some miserable boats, manned by fishermen as dirty as Eskimos, a few vessels employed in towing timber for the construction of the Imperial navy, and a few steamboats, mostly of foreign build, were the only objects that enlivened the scene. Such is the approach to St. Petersburg: all that could have influenced against the choice of this site, so contrary to the views of nature or to the real wants of a great people, must have passed before the mind of Peter the Great without moving him. The sea, at any cost, was the monarch's sentiment. How strange an idea in a Russian to found the capital of the empire of the Slavs in the midst of the Finns, and in the vicinity of the Swedes! Peter the Great might say that his only object was to give a port to Russia; but if he had the genius which is ascribed to him, he must have foreseen the scope of his work; and in my opinion he did foresee it. Policy, and, I fear, the revenge of Imperial self-love, wounded by the independence of the old Muscovites, have created the destinies of modern Russia.

Russia is like a vigorous person suffocating for want of external air. Peter I promised it an outlet, but without perceiving that a sea necessarily closed during eight months in the year is not like other seas. Names, however, are every-thing in Russia. The efforts of Peter, his subjects, and succes-sors, extraordinary as they are, have only served to create a city which it is difficult to inhabit; with which the Neva dis-putes the soil whenever the wind blows from the gulf, and from which the people think of flying altogether at each step that this war of elements compels them to take towards the south. For a bivouac, quays of granite are superfluous.

The Finns, among whom the Russians fixed their new capital, are of Scythian origin; they are still almost Pagans—suitable inhabitants of the soil of Petersburg. It was only in 1836 that an ukase appeared, commanding their priests to add a family name to the saint's name given to the children in baptism.

This race is almost without physiognomy. The middle of the face is flattened to a degree that renders it deformed. The men, though ugly and dirty, are said to be strong, which, how-ever, does not prevent their being small, sickly, and poor. Al-though the natives of the territory, they are seldom seen in Petersburg except upon market days. They inhabit the swamps, and slightly elevated granite hills of the environs.

Kronstadt is a very flat island in the middle of the Gulf of Finland: this aquatic fortress is raised above the sea only just sufficiently to defend the navigation to St. Petersburg. Its foundations and many of its works are under water. Its guns are disposed, according to the Russians, with great skill, and by virtue of the shower of ball that an order of the emperor's could here pour upon an enemy, the place passes for impreg-nable. I am not aware whether these guns command both the passages of the gulf; the Russians who could have informed me, would not. My experience, although of recent date, has already taught me to distrust the rodomontades and exaggera-tions in which the subjects of the czar, inspired by an excess of zeal in the service of their master, indulge. National pride appears to me to be tolerable only among a free people.

We arrived at Kronstadt around midnight, at the dawning of one of those days without real beginning or end, which I am tired of describing though not of admiring.

After casting anchor before the silent fortress, we had to wait a long time for the arrival of a host of official personages, who boarded us one after the other; commissaries of police, directors and sub-directors of the customs, and finally the comptroller himself. This important personage considered himself obliged to pay us a visit on account of the illustrious Russian passengers on board. He conversed for a long time with the returned princes and princesses. They talked in Russian, probably because the politics of the West were the subject of their discourse; but when the conversation fell on the troubles of landing and the necessity of leaving our carriages at Kronstadt, French was freely spoken.

The Travemünde packet draws too much water to ascend the Neva; the passengers, therefore, have to proceed by a smaller steamer, which is dirty and ill constructed. We are allowed to carry with us our lighter baggage, after it has been examined by the officers. When this formality is concluded, we leave for Petersburg, with the hope that our carriages, left in the charge of these people, may arrive safely on the morrow.

The Russian princes were obliged, like myself, to submit to the laws of the customhouse, but on arriving at Petersburg I had the mortification of seeing them released in three minutes, whilst I had to struggle with every species of trickery for the space of three hours.

A multitude of little superfluous precautions engender here a population of deputies and sub-officials, each of whom acquits himself with an air of importance and a rigorous precision, which seems to say, though everything is done with much silence, "Make way, I am one of the members of the grand machine of state."

Such members, acting under an influence which is not in

themselves, in a manner resembling the wheelwork of a clock, are called men in Russia! The sight of these voluntary automata inspires me with a kind of fear: there is something supernatural in an individual reduced to the state of a mere machine. If, in lands where the mechanical arts flourish, wood and metal seem endowed with human powers, under despotisms, human beings seem to become as instruments of wood. We ask ourselves, what can become of their superfluity of thought? and we feel ill at ease at the idea of the influence that must have been exerted on intelligent creatures before they could have been reduced to mere *things*. In Russia I pity the human beings, as in England I feared the machines: in the latter country, the creations of man lack nothing but the gift of speech; here, the gift of speech is a thing superfluous to the creatures of the state.

These machines, clogged with the inconvenience of a soul, are, however, marvelously polite; it is easy to see they have been trained to civility, as to the management of arms, from their cradle. But of what value are the forms of urbanity when their origin savors of compulsion? The free will of man is the consecration that can alone impart a worth or a meaning to human actions; the power of choosing a master can alone give a value to fidelity; and since, in Russia, an inferior chooses nothing, all that he says and does is worthless and unmeaning.

The numerous questions I had to meet, and the precautionary forms that it was necessary to pass through, warned me that I was entering the empire of Fear, and depressed my spirits. Fear is as catching as sadness. Thus, I was afraid and I was sad . . . out of politeness . . . to be like everybody else.

I was obliged to appear before an Areopagus of deputies who had assembled to interrogate the passengers. The members of this formidable rather than imposing tribunal were seated before a large table; some of them were turning over the leaves of the register with an attention which had a sinister appearance, for their ostensible employ was not sufficient to account for so much gravity.

Some, with pen in hand, listened to the replies of the passengers, or rather the accused, for every stranger is treated as a culprit on arriving at the Russian frontier. All the answers translated from French to German and finally to Russian were carefully written down, probably arbitrarily, and the passports minutely examined and detained, under the promise that they would be returned at Petersburg.

These formalities being satisfied, we proceeded on board the new steamboat. Hour after hour elapsed, and still there was no talk of starting. Every moment black, doleful boats proceeded from the city, and rowed towards us. Although we were moored close to the walls, the silence was profound. No voice issued from this tomb. The shadows that were gliding in their boats around were equally silent. They were clad in coarse capotes of gray wool, their faces lacked expression, their eyes possessed no fire, their complexion was of a green or yellow hue. Observing these unfortunate creatures, I wondered what man had done to God that he should condemn sixty million fellow-beings to live in Russia. I was told that they were sailors attached to the garrison, but they more resembled soldiers. Sometimes the boats passed round us in silence, sometimes six or a dozen ragged boatmen, half covered with sheepskins, the wool turned within and the filthy skin appearing without, brought us some new police agent, or tardy customhouse officer. These arrivals and departures, though they did not accelerate our matters, at least gave me leisure to reflect on the species of filthiness peculiar to the people of the North. Those of the South pass their life in the open air, half naked, or in the water; those of the North, for the most part shut up within doors, have a greasy dirtiness, which appears to me far more offensive than the neglect of a people destined to live beneath the open heaven, and born to bask in the sun.

The tedium to which these Russian formalities condemned us, gave me also an opportunity of remarking that the great lords of the country were little inclined to bear patiently the inconveniences of public regulations, when those regulations proved inconvenient to themselves.

"Russia is the land of useless formalities," they murmured to each other—but in French, that they might not be over-heard by the subaltern employees. I have retained the remark, with the justice of which my own experience has only too deeply impressed me. As far as I have been hitherto able to observe, a work that should be entitled *The Russians Judged by Themselves*, would be severe. The love of their country is with them only a mode of flattering its master; as soon as they think that master can no longer hear, they speak of everything with a frankness which is the more startling be-cause those who listen to it become responsible.

The cause of all our delay was at length revealed. The chief of chiefs, the director of the directors of the custom-house again presented himself: it was this visit we had been awaiting so long, without knowing it. At first it appeared as if the only business of the great functionary was to play the part of the man of fashion among the Russian ladies. He reminded the Princess D—— of their encounter in a house where the princess had never been; he spoke to her of court balls she had never seen: but while continuing to dispense these courtly airs, our drawing-room officer of the customs would now and then gracefully confiscate a parasol, stop a portman-teau, or recommence, with an imperturbable sangfroid, the researches already conscientiously made by his subordinates.

In Russian administration, minuteness does not exclude disorder. Much trouble is taken to attain unimportant ends, and those employed believe they can never do enough to show their zeal. The result of this emulation among clerks and commissioners is, that the having passed through one formality does not secure the stranger from another. It is like a pillage, in which the unfortunate creature, after escaping from the first troop, may yet fall into the hands of a second and a third.

The chief turnkey of the empire proceeded slowly to examine the vessel. At length this perfumed Cerberus, for he scented of musk at the distance of a league, released us from the ceremonies attending an entrée into Russia, and we were soon under weigh, to the great joy of the princes and princesses, who were going to rejoin their families. Their pleasure belied the observation of my host in Lübeck; as for me, I could not partake in it: on the contrary, I regretted leaving their delightful society to go and lose myself in a city whose vicinity was so uninviting. But the charm of that society was already broken; as we drew towards the end of our journey the ties which had united us became severed—fragile ties, formed only by the passing requirements of the voyage.

The women of the North know wonderfully well how to make us believe that they would have desired to meet with that which destiny has brought in their way. This is not falsehood, it is refined coquetry, a species of complaisance towards fate, and a supreme grace. Grace is always natural, though that does not prevent its being often used to hide a lie. The rude shocks and uncomfortably constraining influences of life disappear among graceful women and poetical men; they are the most deceptive beings in creation; distrust and doubt cannot stand before them; they create what they imagine; if they do not lie to others, they do to their own hearts; for illusion is their element, fiction their vocation, and pleasures in appearance their happiness. Beware of grace in woman, and poetry in man—weapons the more dangerous because the least dreaded!

Such were my thoughts on leaving the walls of Kronstadt: we were still all together, but we were no longer united. That circle, animated, but the previous evening, by a secret harmony which rarely exists in society, now lacked its vital principle. Few things had ever appeared to me more melancholy than this sudden change. I acknowledged it as the condition attached to the pleasures of the world, I had foreseen it, I had submitted a hundred times to the same experience; but never before did it enlighten me in so abrupt a manner. Besides, what annoyances are more painful than those of which we cannot complain? I saw each individual about to re-enter his own path; the free interchange of feeling which unites those traveling together to the same goal no longer existed among them; they were returning into real life, whilst I was left alone to wander from place to place. To be ever wandering is scarcely to live. I felt myself abandoned, and I compared the cheerlessness of my isolation to their domestic pleasures. Isolation may be voluntary, but is it on this account the more sweet? At the moment, everything appeared to me preferable to my independence, and I regretted even the cares of domestic life. I could read in the eyes of the women the thoughts of husband, children, milliners, hairdressers, the ball, and the court; and I could equally read there, that, notwithstanding the protestations of yesterday, I was no longer an object of concern to them. The people of the North have changeable hearts; their affections, like the faint rays of their sun, are always dying. Remaining fixedly attached neither to persons nor to things—willingly leaving the land of their birth—born for invasions—these people seem as though merely destined to sweep down from the pole, at the times and epochs appointed by God, in order to temper and refresh the races of the South, scorched by the fires of heaven and of their passions.

On arriving at Petersburg, *my friends*, favored by their rank, were speedily liberated from their floating prison, in which they left me, bound by the irons of the police and the customhouse, without so much as bidding me adieu. Where would have been the use of adieus? I was as dead to them. What are travelers to mothers of families? Not one cordial word, not one look, not one thought was bestowed on me. It was the white curtain of the magic lantern, after the shadows have passed. I repeat that I had expected this denouement, but I had not expected the pain which it caused me; so true it is that within ourselves exists the source of all our unforeseen emotions.

Only three days before landing, two of our fair and amiable travelers had made me promise to visit them in Petersburg, where the court is now assembled. I shall wait.

LETTER 8

APPROACH TO PETERSBURG BY THE NEVA. — INCONGRUITY
BETWEEN THE CLIMATE AND ASPECT OF THE COUNTRY AND THE
STYLE OF ARCHITECTURE. — ABSURD IMITATION OF THE
MONUMENTS OF GREECE. — THE CUSTOMHOUSE AND POLICE. —
INQUISITORIAL EXAMINATION. — DIFFICULTIES OF LANDING. —
APPEARANCE OF THE STREETS. — STATUE OF PETER THE GREAT. —
THE WINTER PALACE. — REBUILT IN ONE YEAR. — THE MEANS
EMPLOYED. — RUSSIAN DESPOTISM. — CITATION FROM HERBERSTEIN.
— KARAMSIN. — THE CHARACTER OF THE PEOPLE ACCORDS WITH
THAT OF THE GOVERNMENT.

THE STREETS of Petersburg present a strange appearance to
the eyes of a Frenchman. I will endeavor to describe them;
but I must first notice the approach to the city by the Neva. It
is much celebrated, and the Russians are justly proud of it,
though I did not find it equal to its reputation. When, at a
considerable distance, the steeples begin to appear, the effect
produced is more singular than imposing. The hazy outline of
land, which may be perceived far off between the sky and the
sea, becomes, as you advance, a little more unequal at some
points than at others; these scarcely perceptible irregularities
are found on closer approach to be the gigantic architectural
monuments of the new capital of Russia. We first begin to
recognize the Greek steeples and the gilded cupolas of convents; then some modern public buildings—the front of the
Exchange, and the white colonnades of the colleges, museums, barracks, and palaces which border the quays of granite,
become discernible. On entering the city, you pass some
sphinxes, also of granite. Their dimensions are colossal and

their appearance imposing; nevertheless these copies of the antique have no merit as works of art. A city of palaces is always magnificent, but the imitation of classic monuments shocks the taste when the climate under which these models are so inappropriately placed is considered. Soon, however, the stranger is struck with the form and multitude of turrets and metallic spires which rise in every direction: this at least is national architecture. Petersburg is flanked with numbers of large convents, surmounted by steeples; pious edifices, which serve as a rampart to the profane city. The Russian churches have preserved their primitive appearance; but it is not the Russians who invented that clumsy and capricious Byzantine style, by which they are distinguished. The Greek religion of this people, their character, education, and history, alike justify their borrowing from the Lower Empire; they may be permitted to seek for models at Constantinople, but not at Athens. Viewed from the Neva, the parapets of the quays of Petersburg are striking and magnificent; but the first step after landing discovers them to be badly and unevenly paved with flints, which are as disagreeable to the eye as dangerous to the feet, and ruinous to the wheels. The prevailing taste here is the brilliant and the striking: spires, gilded and tapering like electric conductors; porticoes, the bases of which almost disappear under the water; squares, ornamented with columns which seem lost in the immense space that surrounds them; antique statues, the character and attire of which so ill accord with the aspect of the country, the tint of the sky, the costume and manners of the inhabitants, as to suggest the idea of their being captive heroes in a hostile land; expatriated edifices, temples that might be supposed to have fallen from the summit of the Grecian mountains into the marshes of Lapland;—such were the objects that most struck me at the first sight of St. Petersburg. The magnificent temples of the pagan gods, which so admirably crown, with their horizontal lines and severely chaste contours, the promontories of the Ionian shores, and whose marbles are gilded by the sunshine amid the rocks of the Peloponnesus, here become mere heaps of plaster and mortar; the incomparable ornaments of Grecian sculpture, the wonderful minutiae of classic art, have all given place to an indescribably grotesque style of modern decoration, which substitution passes among the Finlanders as proof of a pure taste in the arts. Partially to imitate that which is perfect, is to spoil it. We should either strictly copy the model, or invent altogether. But the reproduction of the monuments of Athens, however faithfully executed, would be lost in a miry plain, continually in danger of being overflowed by water whose level is nearly that of the land. Here, nature suggests to man the very opposite of what he has imagined. Instead of imitations of pagan temples, it demands bold projecting forms and perpendicular lines, in order to pierce the mists of a polar sky, and to break the monotonous surface of the moist gray steppes which form, farther than the eye or the imagination can stretch, the territory of Petersburg. I begin to understand why the Russians urge us with so much earnestness to visit them during winter: six feet of snow conceals all this dreariness; but in summer, we see the country. Explore the territory of Petersburg and the neighboring provinces, and you will find, I am told, for hundreds of leagues, nothing but ponds and morasses, stunted firs and dark-leaved birch. To this somber vegetation the white shroud of winter is assuredly preferable. Everywhere the same plains and bushes seem to compose the same landscape; at least until the traveler approaches Finland and Sweden. There, he finds a succession of little granite rocks covered with pines, which change the appearance of the soil, though without giving much variety to the landscape. It will be easily believed that the gloom of such a country is scarcely lessened by the lines of columns which men have raised on its even and naked surface. The proper basis of Greek peristyles are mountains: there is here no harmony between the inventions of man and the gifts of nature; in short, a taste for edifices without taste has presided over the building of St. Petersburg.

But, however shocked our perceptions of the beautiful may be by the foolish imitations which spoil the appearance of the Russian capital, it is impossible to contemplate without a species of admiration an immense city which has sprung from the sea at the bidding of one man, and which has to defend itself against a periodical inundation of ice, and a perpetual inundation of water.

The Kronstadt steamboat dropped her anchor before the English quay opposite the customhouse, and not far from the famous square where the statue of Peter the Great stands mounted on its rock. One remained anchored for a long time.

I would gladly spare my reader the detail of the new persecutions, which, under the name of *simple* formalities, I had to undergo at the hand of the police, and its faithful ally the customhouse; but it is a duty to give a just idea of the difficulties which attend the stranger on the maritime frontier of Russia: the entrance by land is, I am told, more easy.

For three or four days in the year the sun of Petersburg is unbearable. I arrived on one of these days. Our persecutors commenced by impounding us (not the Russians, but myself and the other foreigners) on the deck of our vessel. We were there, for a long time, exposed without any shelter to the powerful heat of the morning sun. It was eight o'clock, and had been daylight ever since one hour after midnight. They spoke of 30 degrees of Réaumur*; which temperature, be it remembered, is much more inconvenient in the North, where the air is surcharged with vapor, than in hot climates.

At length I was summoned to appear before a new tribunal, assembled, like that of Kronstadt, in the cabin of our

---

*Nearly 100° Fahrenheit.—*Trans.*

vessel. The same questions were addressed to me with the same politeness, and my answers were recorded with the same formalities.

"What is your object in Russia?"

"To see the country."

"That is not here a motive for traveling."

(What humility in this objection!)

"I have no other."

"Whom do you expect to see in Petersburg?"

"Everyone with whom I may have an opportunity of making acquaintance."

"How long do you think of remaining in Russia?"

"I do not know."

"But about how long?"

"A few months."

"Have you a public diplomatic mission?"

"No."

"A secret one?"

"No."

"Any scientific object?"

"No."

"Are you employed by your government to examine the social and political state of this country?"

"No."

"By any commercial association?"

"No."

"You travel, then, from mere curiosity?"

"Yes."

"What was it that induced you, under this motive, to select Russia?"

"I do not know," &c. &c. &c.

"Have you letters of introduction to any people of this country?"

I had been forewarned of the inconvenience of replying too frankly to this question; I therefore spoke only of my banker.

At the termination of the session of this court of assize, I encountered several of my accomplices. These strangers had been sadly perplexed, owing to some irregularities that had been discovered in their passports. The bloodhounds of the Russian police are quick-scented, and have a very different manner of treating different individuals. An Italian merchant, who was among our passengers, was searched unmercifully, not omitting even the clothes on his person, and his pocket-book. Had such a search been made upon me, I should have been pronounced a very suspicious character. My pockets were full of letters of introduction, and though the greater number had been given me by the Russian ambassador himself, and by others equally well known, they were sealed; a circumstance which made me afraid of leaving them in my writing case. The police permitted me to pass without searching my person; but when my baggage came to be unpacked before the customhouse officers, these new enemies instituted a most minute examination of my effects, more especially my books. The latter were seized en masse, and without any attention to my protestations, but an extraordinary politeness of manner was all the while maintained. A pair of pistols and an old portable clock were also taken from me, without my being able to ascertain the reason of the confiscation. All that I could get was the promise that they would be returned.

I have now been more than twenty-four hours on shore without having been able to recover anything, and to crown my troubles, my carriage has, by mistake, been forwarded from Kronstadt to the address of a Russian prince. It will require efforts, and explanations without end, to prove this error to the customhouse agents; for the prince of my carriage is away from home.

Between nine and ten o'clock I found myself, personally, released from the fangs of the customhouse, and entered Petersburg under the kind care of a German traveler, whom I met *by chance* on the quay. If a spy, he was at least a useful one, speaking both French and Russian, and undertaking to procure me a droshky; while, in the meantime, he himself aided my valet to transport in a cart to Coulon's hotel such part of my baggage as had been given up.

Coulon is a Frenchman, who is said to keep the best hotel in Petersburg, which is not saying much. In Russia, foreigners soon lose all trace of their national character, without, at the same time, ever assimilating to that of the natives.

The obliging stranger found even a guide for me who could speak German, and who mounted behind in the droshky, in order to answer my questions. This man acquainted me with the names of the buildings we passed in proceeding to the hotel, which occupied some time, for the distances are great in Petersburg.

The too celebrated statue of Peter the Great, placed on its rock by the Empress Catherine, first attracted my attention. The equestrian figure is neither antique nor modern; it is a Roman of the time of Louis XV. To aid in supporting the horse, an enormous serpent has been placed at his feet; which is an ill-conceived idea, serving only to betray the impotence of the artist.

I stopped for one moment before the scaffolding of an edifice which, though not yet completed, is already famous in Europe, the church, namely, of St. Isaac. I also saw the façade of the new Winter Palace; another mighty result of human will applying human physical powers in a struggle with the laws of nature. The end has been attained, for in one year this palace has risen from its ashes: and it is the largest, I believe, which exists; equaling the Louvre and the Tuileries put together.

In order to complete the structure at the time appointed by the emperor, unheard-of efforts were necessary. The interior works were continued during the great frosts; six thousand workmen were continually employed; of these a considerable number died daily, but the victims were instantly replaced by other champions brought forward to perish, in their turn, in this inglorious breach. And the sole end of all these sacrifices was to gratify the whim of one man!

Among people naturally, that is to say, anciently civilized, the life of men is only exposed when common interests, the urgency of which is universally admitted, demand it. But how many generations of monarchs has not the example of Peter the Great corrupted!

During frosts when the thermometer was at 25 to 30 degrees below 0 of Réaumur, six thousand obscure martyrs—martyrs without merit, for their obedience was involuntary—were shut up in halls heated to 30 degrees of Réaumur, in order that the walls might dry more quickly. Thus, in entering and leaving this abode of death, destined to become, by virtue of their sacrifice, the abode of vanity, magnificence, and pleasure, these miserable beings would have to endure a difference of 50 to 60 degrees of temperature. The works in the mines of the Urals are less inimical to life; and yet the workmen employed at Petersburg were not malefactors. I was told that those who had to paint the interior of the most highly heated halls were obliged to place on their heads a kind of bonnet of ice, in order to preserve the use of their senses under the burning temperature. Had there been a design to disgust the world with arts, elegance, luxury, and all the pomp of courts, could a more efficacious mode have been taken? And nevertheless the sovereign was called *father* by the men immolated before his eyes in prosecuting an object of pure Imperial vanity. They were neither spies nor Russian cynics who gave me these details, the authenticity of which I guarantee.

The millions expended on Versailles supported as many families of French workmen as there were Slavic serfs destroyed by these twelve months in the Winter Palace; but, by means of that sacrifice, the mandate of the emperor has realized a prodigy; and the palace, completed to the general satisfaction, is going to be inaugurated by marriage fêtes. A prince may be popular in Russia without attaching much value to human life. Nothing colossal is produced without effort; but when a man is in himself both the nation and the government, he ought to impose on himself a law, not to press the great springs of the machine he has the power of moving, except for some object worthy of the effort. To work miracles at the cost of the life of an army of slaves may be great; but it is too great, for both God and man will finally rise to wreak vengeance on these inhuman prodigies. Men have adored the light, the Russians worship the eclipse: when will their eyes be opened?

I do not say that their political system produces nothing good; I simply say that what it does produce is dearly bought.

It is not now for the first time that foreigners have been struck with astonishment at contemplating the attachment of this people to their slavery. The following passage, which is an extract from the correspondence of the Baron Herberstein, ambassador from the Emperor Maximilian, father of Charles V, to the Czar Vasily Ivanovich, I have found in Karamzin.

Did the Russians know all that an attentive reader may gather even from that flattering historian, in whom they glory, and whom foreigners consult with extreme distrust, on account of his partiality as a courtier, they would entreat the emperor to forbid the perusal of his, and of all other historical works, and thus be left in a darkness equally favorable to the repose of the despot and the felicity of his subjects, who believe themselves happy so long as others do not stigmatize them as victims.

Herberstein, in characterizing the Russian despotism, writes as follows:—"He (the czar) speaks, and it is done; the life and fortunes of laity and clergy, nobles and burghers, all depend on his supreme will. He is unacquainted with contradiction, and all he does is deemed as equitable as though it were done by Deity; for the Russians are persuaded that their prince is the executor of the Divine decrees. Thus, *'God and the prince have willed,' 'God and the prince know,'* are common modes of speech among them. Nothing can equal their zeal for his service. One of his principal officers, a venerable gray-haired person, formerly ambassador in Spain, came to meet us on our entry into Moscow. He galloped his horse, and displayed all the activity of a young man, until the sweat fell from his brow; and when I expressed my surprise to him, '*Ah, Monsieur le Baron,*' he replied, '*we serve our sovereign in a manner altogether different from that in which you serve yours.*'

"I cannot say whether it is the character of the Russian nation which has formed such autocrats, or whether it is the autocrats themselves who have given this character to the nation."

This letter, written more than three centuries ago, describes the Russians precisely as I now see them. Like the ambassador of Maximilian, I still ask, is it the character of the Russian which has made the autocracy, or is it the autocracy which has made the Russian character? and I can no more solve the question than could the German diplomatist.

It appears to me, however, that the influence is reciprocal: the Russian government could never have been established elsewhere than in Russia; and the Russians would never have become what they are under a government differing from that which exists among them.

I will add another citation from the same author, Karamzin. He repeats the observations of the travelers who visited Muscovy in the sixteenth century. "Is it surprising," say these strangers, "that the grand prince is rich? He neither gives money to his troops nor his ambassadors; he even takes from these last all the costly things they bring back from foreign lands.* It was thus that the Prince Yaroslavsky, on his return from Spain, was obliged to place in the treasury all the chains of gold, the collars, the costly stuffs, and the silver vessels,

---

*Dickens, in his travels through the United States, informs us that the same practice is at this day observed in America.

which the emperor and the Archduke Ferdinand had given him. Nevertheless, these men do not complain. They say, 'The great prince takes away, the great prince will restore.' " It was thus the Russians spoke of the czar in the sixteenth century.

At the present day you will hear, both in Paris and in Petersburg, numbers of Russians dwelling with rapture on the prodigious effects of the word of the emperor; and, while magnifying these results, not one troubles himself with dwelling upon the means. "The word of the emperor can create," they say. Yes, it can animate stones by destroying human beings. Notwithstanding this little restrictive clause, every Russian is proud of being able to say to us, "You take three years to deliberate on the means of rebuilding a theater, whilst our emperor raises again, in one year, the largest palace in the universe." And this puerile triumph does not appear to them too dearly bought by the death of a few thousand wretched artisans, sacrificed to that sovereign impatience, that Imperial fantasy, which constitutes the national glory. Whilst I, though a Frenchman, see nothing but inhuman ostentation in this achievement, not a single protestation is raised from one end of this immense empire to the other against the orgies of absolute power.

People and government are here in unison. That a man brought up in the idolatry of self, a man revered as omnipotent by sixty millions of men (or at least of beings that resemble men), should not undertake to put an end to such a state of things, this does not surprise me; the wonder is, that among the voices that relate these things to the glory of this individual, not one separates itself from the universal chorus, to protest in favor of humanity against such autocratic miracles. It may be said of the Russians, great and small, that they are drunk with slavery.

LETTER 9

COSTUME OF THE LOWER ORDERS. — PETERSBURG IN THE MORNING.
— RESEMBLANCE OF THE CITY TO A BARRACK. — CONTRAST
BETWEEN RUSSIA AND SPAIN. — DIFFERENCE BETWEEN TYRANNY
AND DESPOTISM. — THE CHIN. — PECULIAR CHARACTER OF THE
RUSSIAN GOVERNMENT. — THE ARTS IN RUSSIA. — A RUSSIAN
HOTEL. — THE EVILS TO BE ENCOUNTERED THERE. — THE MICHAEL
PALACES. — DEATH OF PAUL I. — THE SPY BAFFLED. — THE NEVA,
ITS QUAYS AND BRIDGES. — CABIN OF PETER I. — THE CITADEL,
ITS TOMBS AND DUNGEONS. — CHURCH OF ST. ALEXANDER
NEVSKY. — RUSSIAN VETERANS. — AUSTERITY OF THE CZAR. —
RUSSIAN FAITH IN THE FUTURE, AND ITS REALIZATION. — INTERIOR
OF THE FORTRESS. — THE IMPERIAL TOMBS. — SUBTERRANEAN
PRISON. — RUSSIAN PRISONERS. — MORAL DEGRADATION OF
THE HIGHER CLASSES. — CATHOLIC CHURCH. — PRECARIOUS
TOLERATION. — TOMB OF THE LAST KING OF POLAND AND OF
MOREAU.

IT WAS ON the day before yesterday, between nine and ten
o'clock, that I obtained the liberty of entering Petersburg.

The city, whose inhabitants are not early risers, gave me,
at that hour of day, the idea of a vast solitude. Now and then I
met a few droshkies. The drivers were dressed in the costume
of the country. The singular appearance of these men, their
horses and carriages, struck me more than anything else on
my first view of the city.

The ordinary costume and general appearance of the lower
classes of Petersburg, not the porters, but the workmen,
coachmen, small tradespeople, &c. &c., is as follows:—On
the head is worn either a cap, formed somewhat in the shape
of a melon; or a narrow-brimmed hat, low crowned, and

wider at the top than the bottom. This headdress slightly resembles a woman's turban. It becomes the younger men. Both young and old wear beards. Those of the beaux are silken and carefully combed; those of the old and the careless appear dirty and matted. Their eyes have a peculiar expression, strongly resembling the deceitful glance of Asiatics—so strongly, that in casually observing them you might fancy yourself in Persia.

Their locks, worn long on each side, fall upon the cheeks and conceal the ears; but their hair is cut closely off from the nape of the neck upwards, which original mode of wearing it leaves the neck behind quite bare, for they have no cravat. The beard sometimes falls upon the breast, sometimes it is cut close round the chin. Much value is attached to this ornament, which accords with the *tout ensemble* of the costume better than with the collars, the frock coats, and the waistcoats of our young modern fops.

The Russian people have a natural perception of the picturesque; their customs, furniture, utensils, costume, and figure would all furnish subject for the painter, and the corner of every street in Petersburg might suggest material for a picture graceful in its kind.

But to complete the description of the national costume— in place of our frock and greatcoats, is substituted the caftan, a long and loose Persian robe made of gray, olive, or yet more commonly, of blue cloth. The folds of this robe, which has no collar, but is cut close to the neck, form an ample drapery, drawn together round the loins by a brightly colored silken or woolen girdle. The boots are large, and take the form of the foot. On the legs, the high leather falls down, or is doubled back over itself, in not ungraceful folds.

The movements of the men whom I met were stiff and constrained; every gesture expressed a will which was not their own. The morning is the time for errands, and not one individual appeared to be walking on his own account. I observed few good-looking women, and heard no girlish voices; everything was dull and regular as in a barrack. Military discipline reigns throughout Russia. The aspect of the country makes me regret Spain as much as though I had been born an Andalusian: it is not however the heat which I want, for that here is almost suffocating; it is joy and light.

Now appears a cavalry officer passing at full gallop to bear *an order* to some commanding officer; now a *Feldjäger*, carrying *an order* to some provincial governor, perhaps at the other extremity of the empire, whither he proceeds in a kibitka, a little Russian chariot, without springs or stuffed seat. This vehicle, driven by an old bearded coachman, rapidly conveys the courier, whose rank would prevent his using a more commodious equipage had he one at his disposal. Next are seen foot soldiers returning from exercise to their quarters, to *receive orders* from their captain. One only sees superior bureaucrats ordering inferior bureaucrats. This automaton population resembles one side of a chessboard, where a single individual causes the movements of all the pieces, but where the adversary is invisible. One neither moves nor breathes here except by an Imperial order; consequently, everything is dull, formal, and spiritless. Silence presides over and paralyzes life. Officers, coachmen, Cossacks, serfs, courtiers, all servants under the same master, blindly obey the orders which they do not understand; it is certainly the perfection of discipline; but the sight of such perfection does not gratify me; so much regularity can only be obtained by the entire absence of independence. This part of the world seems to me under the shadow of death.

Among a people thus bereft of time and of will, we see only bodies without souls, and tremble to think that for so vast a multitude of arms and legs there is only one head. Despotism is a union of impatience and of indolence; with a little more forbearance on the part of the governing power, and of activity on the part of the people, equal results might be obtained at a far cheaper cost; but what then would become of tyranny?

If I am reproached for confounding despotism with tyranny, I answer that I do so with design. They are such near relatives, that they never fail to unite in secret to the misfortune of mankind. Under a despotism, tyranny may maintain itself the longer, because it preserves the mask.

When Peter the Great established what is here called the *chin*, that is to say, when he applied the military system to the general administration of the empire, he changed his nation into a regiment of mutes, of which he declared himself and his successors the hereditary colonels.

Let the reader imagine the ambition, the rivalry, and all the other passions of war in operation during a state of peace; let his mind conceive an absence of all that constitutes social and domestic happiness; and, in place of these, let him picture to himself the universal agitation of an ever-restless though secret intrigue,—secret, because the mask is essential to success; finally, let him realize the idea of the almost complete apparent triumph of the will of one man over the will of God, and he will understand Russia. Russian government is the discipline of a military camp substituted to the order of the city; it is the state of siege turned into the normal state of society.

As the morning advances the city becomes more noisy, without however appearing more gay; one sees only carriages, little distinguished for elegance, carrying at the full speed of their two, four, or six horses, people always in haste, because their life is passed in thus *making their way*. Pleasure without any ulterior aim—pleasure for its own sake, is here a thing unknown.

Thus, almost all the great artistes who visit Russia to reap the fruit of the fame they have acquired elsewhere, never remain beyond a very brief period; if ever they prolong their stay, they wrong their talents. The air of this country is unfavorable to the finer arts. Productions that spring spontaneously elsewhere, will here only grow in the hothouse. Russian art will never be a hardy plant.

At the Hotel Coulon, I found a degenerated French innkeeper. His house is at present nearly full, on account of the marriage of the Grand Duchess Marie; indeed, he appeared almost annoyed at being obliged to receive another guest, and consequently gave himself little trouble to accommodate me. After several parleys, I was at length established on the second floor, in suffocating apartments, consisting of an entrée, a salon, and a bedchamber, the whole without curtains or window blinds, though there is a sun for twenty-two hours daily above the horizon, the oblique rays of which penetrate more fully into the houses than the sun of Africa, which falls direct upon the roofs. The air of this lodging resembles that of a limekiln choked with dust, and charged with exhalations of insects mingled with musk, forming altogether an atmosphere that is not to be endured.

Scarcely was I installed in this abode than (the fatigue of the night having got the better of my curiosity, which usually impels me to sally forth and lose myself in a large unknown city) I lay down, wrapped in a cloak, on an immense leather sofa and slept profoundly during—three minutes.

At the end of that time I woke in a fever, and on casting my eyes upon the cloak, what a sight awaited them!—a brown but living mass:—things must be called by their proper name —I was covered, I was devoured with bugs. Russia is, in this respect, not a whit inferior to Spain: but in the South we can both console and secure ourselves in the open air; here we must remain imprisoned with the enemy, and the war is consequently more bloody. I began throwing off my clothes and calling for help. What a prospect for the night! This thought made me cry out more lustily. A Russian waiter appeared. I made him understand that I wished to see his master. The master kept me waiting a long time, and when he at length did come, and was informed of the nature of my trouble, he began to laugh, and soon left the room, telling me that I should become accustomed to it, for that it was the same everywhere in Petersburg. He first advised me, however, never to seat myself on a Russian sofa, because the domestics, who always carry about with them legions of insects, sleep on these articles of furniture. To tranquilize me, he further stated, that the vermin would not follow me if I kept at a proper distance from the furniture in which they had fixed their abode.

The inns of Petersburg resemble caravansarais, where the traveler is simply housed, but not waited upon, unless by his own servants. Mine, being ignorant of the Russian language, is not only useless to me but troublesome, for I have to take care of him as well as myself!

However, his Italian quickness soon discovered in one of the dark corridors of this walled desert, called Hotel Coulon, a footman, out of place, who speaks German, and whom the keeper of the hotel recommended. I engaged him, and told him of my distress. He immediately procured for me a light iron bedstead, the mattress of which I had stuffed with the freshest straw that could be obtained, and caused the four feet to be placed in as many jars of water, in the middle of the chamber, from whence I also directed the furniture to be removed. Thus prepared for the night, I dressed, and attended by the footman, whom I had desired to forbear directing me, I issued from my magnificent hotel—a palace without, and an ornamented stable within.

The Hotel Coulon opens on a kind of square, which is tolerably lively for this city. On one side of the square stands the new Michael Palace, the stately abode of the Grand Duke Michael, brother of the emperor. It was built for the Emperor Alexander, who never inhabited it. The other sides of the square are enclosed by fine ranges of buildings with noble streets opening between. Scarcely had I passed the new

Michael Palace when I found myself before the old. It is a vast, square, and gloomy building, differing in all respects from the elegant modern edifice of the same name.

If the men are silent in Russia, the stones speak with a lamentable voice. I am not surprised that the Russians neglect their ancient architectural monuments; these are witnesses of their history, which, for the most part, they are glad to forget. When I observed the black steps, the deep canals, the massive bridges, and the deserted porticoes of this ill-omened palace, I asked its name; and the answer called to my mind the catastrophe which placed Alexander on the throne, while all the circumstances of the dark scene which terminated the reign of Paul I presented themselves to my imagination.

Nor was this all: by a sort of savage irony there had been placed opposite the principal gate of the sinister edifice, before the death, and by the order of the Emperor Paul, the equestrian statue of his brother Peter III, another victim whose memory the emperor delighted to honor in order to dishonor that of his mother. What tragedies are played in cold blood in this land, where ambition and even hate are calm in appearance! With the people of the South, their passion reconciles me, in some measure, to their cruelty; but the calculating reserve and the coldness of the men of the North, add to crime the varnish of hypocrisy. Snow is a mask. Here man appears gentle because he is impassive; but murder without hate inspires me with more horror than vindictive assassination. The more nearly I can recognize an involuntary impulse in the commission of evil, the more I feel consoled. Unfortunately, it was the calculation of interest and prudence, and not the impulses of anger, which presided over the murder of Paul. Good Russians pretend that the conspirators had only intended to place him in prison. I have seen the secret door opening into the garden, which led to the apartment of the emperor by a private staircase, up which Pahlen caused the assassins to ascend. His communication with them on the evening before, was to this effect:—"You will either have killed the emperor by five o'clock tomorrow morning, or you will be denounced by me to the emperor, at half-past five, as conspirators." The result of this eloquent and laconic harangue need not be inquired.

At five o'clock on the following morning, Alexander was an emperor, and also an imputed parricide, although he had only consented (this is true, I believe) to the confinement of his father, in order to save his mother from prison and perhaps death, to protect himself from a similar fate, and to preserve his country from the rage and caprice of an insane autocrat.

At the present day, the Russians pass the old Michael Palace without daring to look at it. In the schools and elsewhere, the death of the Emperor Paul is forbidden to be mentioned or even believed.

I am astonished that this palace of inconvenient recollections has not been pulled down. The traveler congratulates himself at the sight of a monument whose antique appearance is remarkable in a land where despotism renders everything uniform and new; where the reigning notion effaces daily the traces of the past. Its square and solid form, its deep moats, tragic associations, secret gates, and staircases favorable to crime, impart to it an imposing air, which is a rare advantage in Petersburg. At each step I take I am amazed to observe the confusion that has been everywhere made in this city between two arts so very different as those of architecture and decoration. Peter the Great and his successors seem to have taken their capital for a theater.

I was struck with the startled air of my guide, when I questioned him, in the most easy and natural manner that I could assume, on the events that had taken place in the old palace. The physiognomy of this man replied, "it is easy to see you are a newcomer." Surprise, fear, mistrust, affected innocence, pretended ignorance, the experience of an old soldier who would not easily be duped, took possession, by turns, of his countenance, and made it a book equally instructive and amusing to peruse. When your spy is at fault by reason of your apparent security, the expression of his face is truly grotesque, for he believes himself compromised by you so soon as he sees that you do not fear being compromised by him. The spy thinks only of his vocation; and if you escape his nets, he begins at once to imagine that he is going to fall into yours.

A promenade through the streets of Petersburg, under the charge of a *domestique de place*, is not without interest, and little resembles a progress through the capitals of other civilized lands. One thing is singularly connected with and dependent on another in a state governed with so close a logic as that which presides over the policy of Russia.

After leaving the old and tragical Michael Palace, I crossed a large square resembling the Champ de Mars at Paris, so spacious is it and so empty. On one side is a public garden, on the other a few houses; there is sand instead of pavement in the middle of the area, and dust in every part of it. This immense square, the form of which is vague and undefined, extends to the Neva, near which termination is a bronze statue of Suvorov.

The Neva, its bridges and quays, form the real glory of Petersburg. The scene here is so vast, that all the rest seems little in comparison. The Neva is like a vessel so full that its brim disappears under the water, which is ready to flow over on every side. Venice and Amsterdam appear to me better protected against the sea than St. Petersburg.

The vicinity of a river, large as a lake, and which flows on a level with the land through a marshy plain, lost in the mists of the atmosphere and the vapors of the sea, was assuredly of all the sites in the world the least favorable for the foundation of a capital. The water will here, sooner or later, teach a lesson to human pride. The granite itself is no security against

111

the work of winters in this humid icehouse, where the foundations of rock and the ramparts of the famous citadel built by Peter the Great, have already twice given way. They have been repaired, and will be yet again, in order to preserve this chef-d'oeuvre of human pride and human will.

I wished at once to cross the bridge, in order to examine it more closely; but my servant first conducted me in face of the fortress, to the house of Peter the Great, which is separated from it by a road and an open piece of ground.

It is a cabin, preserved, as is said, in the same state as that in which the emperor left it. In the citadel, the emperors are now buried, and the prisoners of state detained—singular manner of honoring the dead! In thinking of all the tears shed there, *under* the tombs of the sovereigns of Russia, one is reminded of the funerals of some Asian kings. A tomb bedewed with blood would, in my eyes, be less impious: tears flow for a longer period, and are perhaps accompanied with deeper pangs.

During the time that the Imperial artisan inhabited the cabin, his future capital was being built beneath his eye. It should be admitted in his praise, that, at that period, he thought much less of the palace than of the city.

One of the chambers of this illustrious cottage—that, namely, which was the workshop of the princely carpenter—is now transformed into a chapel. It is entered with as much reverence as are the most sacred churches in the empire. The Russians are ever ready to make saints of their heroes. They delight in confusing the dreadful virtues of their masters with the benevolent power of their patrons, and endeavor to view the cruelties of history through the veil of faith.

Another Russian hero, in my opinion little deserving of admiration, has been sanctified by the Greek priests; I mean Alexander Nevsky—a model of prudence, but a martyr neither to piety nor to generosity. The national church has canonized this wise rather than heroic prince—this Ulysses among the saints. An enormous convent has been built around his relics.

The tomb, enclosed within the church of St. Alexander, is in itself an edifice. It consists of an altar of massive silver, surmounted with a species of pyramid of the same metal, which rises to the vault of a vast church. The convent, the church, and the cenotaph, form one of the wonders of Russia. I contemplated them with more astonishment than admiration; for though the costliness of this pious work is immense, the rules of taste and of art have been little heeded in its construction.

In the cabin of the czar, I was shown a boat of his own building, and several other objects religiously preserved, and placed under the guard of a veteran soldier. In Russia, churches, palaces, public places, and many private houses, are entrusted to the keeping of military pensioners. These unfortunate beings would be left without means of subsistence in their old age, unless they were, on leaving the barracks, converted into porters. In such posts they retain their long military capotes, which are made of coarse wool, and are generally much worn and dirty. At each visit that you make, men, thus clad, receive you at the gates of the public buildings and at the doors of the houses. They are specters in uniform that serve to remind one of the discipline which here rules over everything. Petersburg is a camp metamorphosed into a city. The veteran who kept guard in the Imperial cottage, after having lighted several wax tapers in the chapel, led me to the sleeping apartment of Peter the Great, emperor of all the Russias. A carpenter of our days would not lodge his apprentice in such a place.

This glorious austerity illustrates the epoch and the country as much as the man. In Russia, at that period, everything was sacrificed to the future; all were employed in building the palaces of their yet unborn masters; and the original founders of the magnificent edifices, not experiencing themselves the wants of luxury, were content to be the purveyors of the future civilization, and took pride in preparing fitting abodes for the unknown potentates who were to follow them. There is certainly a greatness of mind evidenced in this care which a chieftain and his people take for the power, and even the vanity, of the generations that are yet to come. The reliance which the living have thus placed in the glory of their distant posterity has something about it which is noble and original. It is a disinterested and poetical sentiment, far loftier than the respect which men and nations are accustomed to entertain for their ancestors.

Elsewhere, great cities abound with monuments raised in memory of the past. St. Petersburg, in all its magnificence and immensity, is a trophy raised by the Russians to the greatness of the future. The hope which produces such efforts appears to me sublime. Never, since the construction of the Jewish temple, has the faith of a people in its own destinies raised up from the earth a greater wonder than St. Petersburg. And what renders more truly admirable this legacy left by one man to his ambitious country, is, that it has been ratified by history.

The prophecy of Peter the Giant, sculptured upon blocks of granite reared in the sea, has been fulfilled before the eyes of the universe. This is the first instance in which pride has appeared to me really worthy of admiration.

The history of Russia does not, however, date, as the ignorant and superficial in Europe seem to suppose, from the reign of Peter I; it is Moscow which explains St. Petersburg.

The deliverance of Muscovy, after long ages of invasion, and, afterwards, the siege and capture of Kazan by Ivan the Terrible, the determined struggles with Sweden, and many other brilliant as well as patient deeds of arms, justified the proud attitude of Peter the Great, and the humble confidence of his people. Faith in the unknown is always imposing. This man of iron had a right to put his trust in the future: charac-

LETTERS FROM RUSSIA

ters like his produce those results which others only imagine. I can see him, in all the simplicity of greatness, seated in the threshold of this cabin, planning and preparing against Europe, a city, a nation, and a history. The grandeur of Petersburg is not unmeaning. This mighty metropolis, ruling over its icy marshes, in order from thence to rule the world, is superb—more superb to the mind than to the eye! Yet it may not be forgotten, that one hundred thousand men, victims of obedience, were lost in converting the pestilential swamps into a capital!

On leaving the house of Peter the Great, I again passed before the bridge of the Neva (which leads to the Islands), and entered the celebrated fortress of Petersburg.

I have already remarked that this edifice, of which the name alone inspires fear, has twice had its ramparts and its granite foundations undermined, although it is not yet one hundred forty years old. What a struggle! The stones here seem to suffer violence like the men.

I was not permitted to see the prisons; there are dungeons under the water, and there are others under the roofs: all of which are full of human beings. I was only allowed to inspect the church, which encloses the tombs of the reigning family. My eyes were on these tombs while I was yet searching for them, so difficult was it to imagine that a square stone, of about the length and breadth of a bed, newly covered with a green cloth embroidered with the Imperial arms, could be the cemetery of the Empress Catherine I, of Peter I, Catherine II, and of so many other princes, down to the Emperor Alexander.

The Greek religion banishes sculpture from its churches, by which they lose in pomp and religious magnificence more than they gain in mystical character; while at the same time it accommodates itself to gilt work, chasings, and to pictures which do not show a very pure taste. The Greeks are the children of the Iconoclasts. In Russia they have ventured to mitigate the doctrine of their fathers; but they might have gone further than they have done.

In this funeral citadel, the dead appeared to me more free than the living. If it had been a philosophical idea which suggested the enclosing in the same tomb the prisoners of the emperor and the prisoners of death—the conspirators, and the monarchs against whom they conspired—I should respect it; but I see in it nothing more than the cynicism of absolute power—the brutal security of a despotism which feels itself safe. Strong in its superhuman power, it rises above the little humane delicacies, the observance of which is advisable in common governments. A Russian emperor is so full of what is due to himself that he cannot afford to have his justice lost sight of in that of God's. We royalist *revolutionaries* of western Europe see only in a prisoner of state at Petersburg an inno-cent victim of despotism; the Russians view him as a repro-bate. Every sound appeared to me a complaint; the stones groaned beneath my feet. Oh, how I pity the prisoners of this fortress! If the existence of the Russians confined under the earth, is to be judged of by inferences drawn from the exis-tence of the Russians who live above, there is, indeed, cause to shudder! A thrill of horror passed through me as I thought that the most steadfast fidelity, the most scrupulous probity, could secure no man from the subterranean prisons of the citadel of Petersburg, and my heart dilated, and my respira-tion came more freely, as I repassed the moats which defend this gloomy abode, and separate it from the rest of the world.

Who would not pity the Russian people? They, I speak now of the higher classes, are living under the influences of an ignorance and of prejudices which they no longer possess. The affectation of resignation is the lowest depth of abjectness into which an enslaved nation can fall: revolt or despair would be doubtless more terrible, but less ignominious. Weak-ness so degraded that it dare not indulge itself even in com-plaint, that consolation of the lower animal creation, fear calmed by its own excess—these are moral phenomena which cannot be witnessed without calling forth tears of horror.

After visiting the sepulchre of the Russian sovereigns, I proceeded to the Catholic church, the services of which are conducted by Dominican monks. I went there to demand a mass for an anniversary which none of my travels have hitherto prevented my commemorating in a Catholic church. The Dominican convent is situated in the Nevsky Prospect, the finest street in Petersburg. The church is not magnificent, but decent; the cloisters are solitary, the courts encumbered with rubbish of mason work. An air of gloom reigns throughout the community, which, notwithstanding the toleration it enjoys, appears to possess little wealth, and still less sense of security. In Russia, toleration has no guarantee, either in public opinion, or in the constitution of the state: like everything else it is a favor conceded by one man; and that man may withdraw tomorrow what he has granted today.

While waiting for the prior in the church, I saw beneath my feet a stone on which was inscribed a name that awoke in me some emotion—Poniatowski! the royal victim of folly. That too credulous lover of Catherine II is buried here without any mark of distinction; but though despoiled of the majesty of the throne, there remains for him the majesty of misfortune. The troubles of this prince, his blind fatuity punished so cruelly, and the perfidious policy of his enemies, draw the attention of all Christians, and of all travelers to his obscure tomb.

Near to the exiled king has been placed the mutilated body of Moreau. The Emperor Alexander caused it to be brought there from Dresden. The idea of placing together the remains of two men so greatly to be pitied in order to unite in the same prayer the memory of their disappointed destiny, appears to me one of the greatest conceptions of this prince, who, be it remembered, appeared great when he entered a city from whence Napoleon was flying.

Towards four o'clock in the evening I began, for the first time, to recollect that I had not come to Russia merely to inspect curious monuments of art, and to enter into the reflections, more or less philosophical, which they might suggest; and I hastened to the French ambassador's.

There I found my oversight had been great. The marriage of the Grand Duchess Marie was to take place on the day after the morrow, and I had arrived too late to be presented previously. To miss this ceremony of the court, in a land where the court is everything, would be to lose my journey.

LETTER 10

I AM JUST returned from visiting the Islands. They form an agreeable marsh; never was mud better concealed by flowers. A shallow, left dry during the summer, owing to the channels that intersect it serving as drains to the soil, planted with superb groves of birch, and covered with numerous charming villas—such is the tract called the Islands. The avenues of birch, which, together with pines, are the only trees indigenous to these icy plains, create an illusion that might lead the traveler to imagine himself in an English park. This vast garden, overspread with *"villas"* and *"cottages,"* serves instead of the country for the inhabitants of Petersburg: it is the camp of the courtiers, thickly inhabited during a brief portion of the year, and totally deserted during the remainder.

The district of the Islands is reached by various excellent carriage roads, connected with bridges thrown over the different arms of the sea.

In wandering among its shady alleys, it is not difficult to imagine one's self in the countryside, but it is a monotonous and artificial country. No undulations of the ground, always the same kind of trees,—how is it possible to produce pictorial effect from such materials! Under this zone, the plants of the hothouse, the fruit of the tropics, and even the gold and precious stones of the mines, are less rare than our commonest forest trees. With wealth, everything may be procured here that can exist under glass, and this is much towards furnishing the scenery of a fairy tale, but it is not sufficient to make a park. One of the groves of chestnut or beech which beautify our hills would be a marvel in Petersburg. Italian houses surrounded by Laponian trees, and filled with the flowers of all countries, form a contrast which is singular rather than agreeable.

The Parisians, who never forget Paris, call the tract of the Islands the Russian Champs Elysées, but it is larger, more rural, and yet more adorned and more artificial than our Parisian promenade. It is also farther distant from the fashionable quarters, and includes both town and country. At one moment, you may suppose yourself looking upon real woods, fields, and villages; in the next, the view of houses in the shape of temples, of pilasters forming the framework of hothouses, of colonnaded palaces, of theaters with antique peristyles, prove that you have not left the city.

The Russians are rightly proud of a garden raised at so much expense on the spongy soil of Petersburg. But if Nature is conquered, she remembers her defeat, and submits with a bad grace.

I should insist less on the disadvantages of this unflavored land, I should not regret so greatly, while traveling in the North, the sun of the South, if the Russians affected less to undervalue the gifts of which their country is deprived. Their perfect content extends even to the climate and the soil; naturally given to boasting, they have the folly to glory even in the physical as well as the social aspect which surrounds them. These pretensions prevent my bearing as resignedly as I ought to do, and as I had intended, with all the inconveniences of northern countries.

The delta formed between the city and one of the *embouchures* of the Neva, is now entirely covered by this species of park; it is nevertheless included within the precincts of Petersburg: the Russian cities embrace the country also. This tract would have become one of the most populous quarters of the new capital, had the plan of the founder been more exactly followed. But, little by little, Petersburg receded from the river, southward, in the hope of escaping the inundations; and the marshy isles have been reserved exclusively for the summer residences of the most distinguished courtiers. These residences are half concealed by water and snow for nine months of the year, during which time the wolves roam freely round the pavilion of the empress; but during the remaining three months, nothing can exceed the profusion of flowers which the houses exhibit. Nevertheless, under all this factitious elegance, the character of the people betrays itself; a passion for display is the ruling passion of the Russians: thus, in their drawing rooms, the flowers are not disposed in such manner as may render the interior of the apartment more agreeable, but so as to attract admiration from without; precisely the contrary of what we see in England, where, above all things, people shrink from *hanging out a sign in the streets*. The English are, of all the people on the earth, those who have best known how to substitute taste for style: their public buildings are chefs-d'oeuvre of the ridiculous; their private houses are models of elegance and good sense.

Among the Islands, all the houses and all the roads resemble each other. The shade of the birch trees is transparent, but under the sun of the North a very thick foliage is not required. Canals, lakes, meadows, groves, cottages, villas, and alleys, follow each other in constant succession. This dreamy landscape pleases without interesting, without piquing the curiosity; but it gives the idea of repose, and repose is a precious thing at the court of Russia, even though it be not valued there as it ought to be.

A distant pine forest rears at intervals its thin and spiry foliage above the roofs of some villas, built of planks and painted. These remembrances of solitude pierce through the ephemeral gaiety of the gardens, as though to witness to the rigor of winter, and the neighborhood of Finland.

The aim of civilization in the North is serious. There society is the fruit, not of human pleasures, not of interests and passions easily satisfied, but of a will, ever persisting and ever thwarted, which urges the people to incomprehensible efforts. There, if individuals unite together, it is to struggle with a rebellious nature, which unwillingly responds to the demands made upon her.

This dullness and stubbornness in the external world engender a gloom which accounts to me for the tragedies in the political world so frequent at this court. Here the drama is enacted in actual life, whilst the theater is occupied with farce. Empty amusements are those alone permitted in Russia. Under such an order of things, real life is too serious an affair to allow of a grave and thoughtful literature. Low comedy, the idyll, and the apologue well veiled, can alone flourish in presence of so terrible a reality. If in this inhospitable clime the precautions of despotism shall yet further increase the difficulties of existence, all happiness will be taken from man —repose will become impossible. Peace, felicity—these words here are as vague as is that of Paradise. Idleness without ease, inertia without quiet—such are the inevitable results of the Boreal Autocracy.

The Russians enjoy but very little of the country which

they have created at the gate of their city. The women live the same way in the summer at the Islands, as they do in the winter in Petersburg. They rise late, spend the day at their toilets, the evening in visits, and gamble through the night. To forget themselves, to lose themselves in a round of excitement, is the apparent end of their existence.

The summer of the Islands commences in the middle of June and lasts till the end of August. During these two months there is not generally (though with the exception of the present year) more than a week of hot weather. The evenings are damp, the night atmosphere clear, but cloudy above, the days gray and misty. Life would here become unbearably dull and melancholy to the individual who should allow himself to reflect. In Russia, to converse is to conspire, to think is to revolt: thought is not merely a crime, it is a misfortune also.

Man thinks only with a view of ameliorating his lot and that of his fellows, but when he can do nothing and change nothing, thought does but prey upon and envenom the mind, for lack of other employment. This is the reason why, in the Russian world of high society, people of all ages join in the dance.

As soon as the summer is over, a rain, fine as the points of needles, falls for weeks without any cessation. In two days the birch trees of the Islands may be seen stripped of their leaves, the houses of their flowers and their inhabitants, and the roads and bridges are crowded with carriages, droshkies, and carts engaged in the removal of furniture, all the different kinds of which are heaped together with a slovenliness and disorder natural to the Slavic race. It is thus that the rich man of the North, awaking from the too fleeting illusions of his summer, flies before the northeast wind, leaving the bears and wolves to re-enter into possession of their legitimate domain. Silence resumes its ancient rights over these icy swamps, and for nine months, the frivolous society of the city of wood take refuge in the city of stone. From this change of season they experience little inconvenience; for in Petersburg the snows of the winter nights reflect almost as much light as is shed by the summer's sun, and the Russian stoves give more heat than its obliquely falling rays.

That which yearly occurs in the Islands will be the fate one day of the entire city. Should this capital, without roots in history, be forgotten for even a brief space by the sovereign, should a new policy direct his attention elsewhere, the granite hid under the water would crumble away, the inundated low lands would return to their natural state, and the guests of solitude would again take possession of their lair.

These ideas occupy the mind of every foreigner who traverses the streets of Petersburg; no one believes in the duration of the marvelous city. But little meditation (and what traveler worthy of his occupation does not meditate?) enables the mind to prefigure such a war, such a change in the course of policy, as would cause this creation of Peter I to disappear like a soap bubble in the air.

In no other place have I been so impressed with the instability of human things. Often in Paris and in London have I said to myself, a time will come when this noisy abode will be more silent than Athens or Rome, Syracuse or Carthage; but to no man is it given to foresee the hour or the immediate cause of the destruction; whereas, the disappearing of St. Petersburg may be foreseen, it may take place tomorrow, in the midst of the triumphant songs of its victorious people. The decline of other capitals follows the destruction of their inhabitants, but this will perish at the moment even when the Russians will see their power extending. I believe in the duration of Petersburg, just as I believe in that of a political system, or in the constancy of man. This is what cannot be said of any other city in the world.

What a tremendous power is that which can thus cause a metropolis to spring up in the wilderness, and which, with one word, can restore to solitude all that it has taken! Here real existence seems to belong only to the sovereign: the fate, the power, the will of an entire people are all centered in one single head. The emperor is the personification of social power; beneath him reigns the equality that forms the dream of the modern Gallo-American democrats, the Fourriérists, &c. But the Russians acknowledge a cause of storm that is unknown to others, the wrath of this emperor. Republican or monarchial tyranny is preferable to autocratic equality. I fear nothing so much as a strict logic applied to politics. If France has been financially prosperous during the last ten years, it is, perhaps, because the apparent absurdity which presides over her affairs is a high practical wisdom: action, instead of speculation, now governs us.

In Russia the spirit of despotism always exerts itself with a mathematical rigor, and the result of such extreme proceeding is an extreme oppression. In beholding this effect of an inflexible policy, we feel shocked, and ask ourselves, with a kind of terror, how comes it that there is so little humanity in the actions of man? But to tremble is not to disdain; we never despise that which excites our fear.

In contemplating Petersburg, and in reflecting on the dreadful existence of the inhabitants of this camp of granite, one might be led to doubt the compassion of the Deity. There is here presented a mystery that is incomprehensible, and at the same time a greatness that is prodigious. Despotism thus organized becomes an inexhaustible subject for observation and meditation. This colossal empire, which rises before me all at once in the east of Europe—of that Europe, where society is suffering from the decay of all recognized authority—appears to me like a resurrection. I feel as though in the presence of some nation of the Old Testament, and I stop with fear, mingled with curiosity, before the feet of the antediluvian giant.

The first view of society in Russia shows that its arrangements, as contrived by the Russians themselves, are only adapted to their own social system: he must be a Russian who would live in Russia, even though outwardly everything may appear to pass as in other places. The difference lies in the foundations of things.

It was a review of the fashionable world which I took this evening at the Islands. The fashionable world, they say, is the same everywhere; nevertheless each society has a soul, and this soul will be instructed, like any other, by the fairy which is called civilization, and which is nothing more than the customs of the age.

This evening, all the city of Petersburg, that is to say, the court and its followers, were at the Islands; not for the pure pleasure of promenading on a fine day, such a pleasure would appear insipid to the Russian courtiers, but to see the *packet boat* of the empress, a spectacle of which they never tire. Here every sovereign is a god, every princess is an Armida or a Cleopatra. The train of these changeable divinities never changes: it is composed of a people ever equally faithful; the reigning prince is always in fashion with the Russian people.

Nevertheless, these submissive men, let them say and do their best, are forced and constrained in their enthusiasm. A people without liberty has instincts but not sentiments; and their instincts often manifest themselves in an officious and little-delicate manner. The emperors of Russia must be overwhelmed with submission: sometimes the incense wearies the idol. In fact, such worship admits of terrible interludes. The Russian government is an absolute monarchy moderated by assassination; and when the prince is not under the influence of lassitude, he is under that of terror. He lives, therefore, between fear and disgust. If the pride of the despot must have slaves, the feelings of the man must yearn for equals; but a czar has no equals: etiquette and jealousy maintain invidious guard around his solitary heart. He is more to be pitied than even his people, especially if he possesses any amiable qualities.

I hear much boast made of the domestic happiness of the Emperor Nicholas, but I see in it the consolations of a superior mind, rather than the proof of real happiness. Consolation is not felicity; on the contrary, the remedy proves the evil: an emperor of Russia must have a heart like other men if he has one at all. So much for the overlauded private virtues of the Emperor Nicholas.

This evening the empress, having proceeded from Peterhof by sea, landed at her pavilion on the Islands, where she will remain until the marriage of her daughter, which is to be celebrated tomorrow, in the new Winter Palace. While she remains at the Islands, the leafy shade which surrounds her pavilion serves as a shelter during the day for her regiment of chevalier guards, one of the finest in the army.

We arrived too late to see her leave her sacred vessel, but we found the crowd still under the excitement caused by the rapid transit of the Imperial star. The only tumults possible in Russia are those caused by the struggles of flatterers. This evening, the human effervescence resembled the agitation of the waves, that continue boiling in the track of some mighty vessel long after she has entered port.

At last, then, I have breathed the air of the court! though the deities who exhale it upon mortals are still unseen.

It is now one o'clock in the morning; the sun is about to rise, and I cannot yet sleep: I will, therefore, finish my night as I commenced it, by writing *without lights.*

Notwithstanding Russian pretensions to elegance, foreigners cannot find in all Petersburg one hotel that is endurable. The great lords bring with them, from the interior of the empire, a suite which is always numerous. Man is their property and their luxury. The moment the valets are left alone in the apartments of their masters, they squat themselves, in Oriental fashion, on the seats and couches, which they fill with vermin. These creatures pass into the walls and floors, and in a few days the house becomes infested past all remedy; for the impossibility of airing the houses in winter perpetuates the evil from year to year.

The new Imperial Palace, built at such cost of life and money, is already full of loathsome insects. It might be said, that the wretched workmen who were killed in order to ornament with greater celerity the habitation of their master, have avenged their own death by inoculating with their vermin those homicidal walls. If the palace is infected by these nocturnal foes, how should I be able to sleep at Coulon's? I have given up the idea; but the clearness of the night consoles me for everything.

On returning from the Islands about midnight, I again went out on foot, and occupied my mind with reviewing the scenes and conversations which had most interested me during the day; of these I will presently give the summary.

My solitary walk led me to the beautiful street called the Nevsky Prospect. I saw in the twilight, shining from afar, the little pillars of the tower of the Admiralty, surmounted with its lofty metallic spire, a Christian minaret more taper than any Gothic steeple. It is gilded all over with the gold of the ducats sent as a present to the Emperor Peter I by the States of the Netherlands.

The revolting dirtiness of my inn-chamber, and the almost fabulous magnificence of that building, present a correct picture of Petersburg. Contrasts are not wanting in a city where Europe and Asia exhibit themselves to each other in mutual spectacle. The people are handsome. The men of pure Slavic race, brought from the interior by the rich nobles, who either retain them in their service, or permit them for a certain period to carry on various trades in the city, are remarkable for their fair hair, their rosy complexions, and yet more for their perfect profiles, which equal those of Grecian statues. Their eyes have the oval Asiatic shape, with the coloring of the North; they are generally of a light blue, and unite a singular expression of gentleness, grace, and cunning. This expression, always restless, gives to the iris those changing hues which vary from the green of the serpent, and the gray of the cat, to the black of the gazelle, though the ground color still remains blue. The mouth, adorned with a golden and silky mustache, is beautifully formed, and the teeth have a brilliant whiteness that lights up the whole countenance. They are sometimes sharp and pointed, when they resemble those of the tiger, but more commonly their shape is perfectly regular. The costume of these men is always original. It consists either of the Greek tunic, with a lively colored girdle, the Persian robe, or the short Russian pelisse lined with sheepskin, the wool of which is turned outwards or inwards according to the season.

The females of the lower orders are less handsome; but few are met in the streets, and those few present few attractions: they appear degraded and stupefied. It is a singular fact, that the men take pains with their dress, and the women neglect it: this is perhaps owing to the former being attached by service to the houses of the nobles. The latter have a clumsy gait; they wear heavy boots, which deform the foot: their figures are without elegance; and their complexions, unlike those of the men, lose all freshness and clearness even while they are yet young. Their little Russian coats, short, and open before, are trimmed with fur, which is almost always hanging in rags. This costume would be pretty if it was less shabby, and if the effect was not generally spoilt by deformity or revolting dirtiness of person. The national headdress of the Russian women is handsome, but it has become rare, being now only worn, I am told, by wet nurses, and by the ladies of the court on days of ceremony. It is a species of pasteboard tower, gilt, embroidered, and much widened at the top.

The accoutrements of the horses are picturesque, and the animals themselves show speed and blood; but the equipages that I saw this evening at the Islands, not excepting those of the highest nobles, were not elegant, nor even clean. This accounts to me for the disorder and carelessness of the servants of the hereditary grand duke, and for the clumsiness and wretched varnish of that prince's carriages, which I noticed at Ems. Magnificence on a large scale, a gaudy luxury, gilded trappings, and an air of showy grandeur, are natural to the Russian nobles; but elegance, carefulness, and cleanliness, are things unknown.

I have listened this evening to several curious traits, illustrative of what we call the slavery of the Russian peasants. It is difficult for us to form a just idea of the real position of this class of men, who live in the possession of no acknowledged rights, and who yet form the nation. Deprived of everything by law, they are still not so much degraded morally as they are socially. They have good mental capacity, and sometimes even elevation of character; but, nevertheless, the principle which chiefly actuates their conduct through life is cunning. No one has a right to reproach them with this too natural consequence of their situation. Ever on their guard against their masters, who are constantly acting towards them with open and shameless bad faith, they compensate themselves by artifice for what they suffer through injustice. The relations between the peasantry and the owner of the soil, as well as their less immediate relations with the country, that is to say, with the emperor, would alone be a subject worthy of a long sojourn in the interior of Russia.

In many parts of the empire, the peasants believe themselves to belong to the soil, a condition of existence which appears to them natural, even when they have difficulty in understanding how man can be the property of man. In many other countries the peasants believe that the soil belongs to them. Such are the most happy, if they are not the most submissive of slaves. Not unfrequently, the peasants, when about to be sold send a deputation to some far-off master, of whose character for kindness reports have reached them, imploring him to buy them, their lands, their children, and their cattle; and if this lord, thus celebrated for his gentleness (I do not say his justice, for the sentiment of justice is unknown in Russia),—if this desirable lord has no money, they provide him with it, in order to be sure of belonging only to him. The benevolent lord, therefore, buys his new serfs with their own money; after which he exempts them from taxes for a certain number of years; thus indemnifying them for the price of their bodies, which they have paid to him in advance by furnishing the sum that represents the value of the domain to which they belong, and of which they have, as it were, obliged him to become the proprietor.

The greatest misfortune which can happen to these vegetating men is to see their native fields sold. They are always sold with the glebe, and the only advantage they have hitherto derived from the modern ameliorations of the law is, that they cannot now be sold without it. This provision is, however, notoriously evaded. Instead, for instance, of selling an entire estate, a few acres are often sold with one or two hundred men per acre. If the government becomes aware of such collusion it punishes the guilty parties, but it has seldom an opportunity of interfering; for between the crime and the supreme authority, that is, the emperor, are a whole multitude of people interested in concealing and perpetuating abuses. The proprietors suffer as much as the serfs from this state of things, especially those whose affairs are not in order. Estates are difficult to sell; so difficult, that a man who owes debts and is willing to pay them, is finally obliged to have recourse to the Imperial Bank, where he borrows the sum which he requires, the bank taking his property in mortgage. By this means the emperor becomes treasurer and creditor of all the Russian nobility; and the latter, thus curbed by supreme power, are placed in a situation which makes the fulfillment of their duties towards the people impossible.

On a certain day a nobleman declares his intention of selling an estate. The news of this project throws the district into alarm. The peasants send to their lord a deputation of the elders of their village, who cast themselves at his feet, imploring, with tears, that they may not be sold. "It must be," replies the lord: "I cannot conscientiously augment the tax which my peasants pay, and nevertheless I am not rich enough to keep an estate which scarcely brings me in anything."

"Is that all?" cry the deputies; "we then are wealthy enough to enable you to keep us." Whereupon, of their own free will, they raise the rent to double the amount which they have paid from time immemorial. Other peasants, with less gentleness, and greater craft of character, revolt against their masters, solely with the hope of becoming serfs of the crown. This is the highest ambition of the Russian peasant.

To emancipate suddenly such men would be to set the country on fire. The moment that the serfs, separated from the land to which they are attached, were to see it sold, let, or cultivated without them, they would rise in a mass, crying that they were despoiled of their property.

It is but a short time ago that, in a remote village which was on fire, the peasants, who complained of the tyranny of their master, availed themselves of the disorder they had perhaps caused purposely, to seize his person, impale it, and roast it in the flames of the conflagration. For such acts the emperor usually orders the transportation of the entire village to Siberia. This is called, in Petersburg, *peopling Asia.*

When I reflect upon these, and a thousand other cruelties, which, with greater or less secrecy, take place daily in the bosom of this immense empire, where the distances equally favor oppression and revolt, I am ready to conceive a hatred against the land, the government, and the entire population: an indefinable sense of uneasiness takes possession of me, and I think only of flying.

The fortune of a wealthy man is here computed by the heads of his peasants. The man who is not free is coined; he is equivalent (on an average) to ten rubles a year to his proprietor, who is called free because he is the owner of serfs. There

are districts where each peasant brings three and four times
this sum to his master. In Russia, the human money alters in
value, as, with us, the land, which doubles in price, when
markets can be opened for its produce. Here, I involuntarily
pass my time in calculating how many families it has taken
to pay for a bonnet, a shawl, or a rosebush: nothing appears to
me as it does elsewhere; everything seems tainted with
blood. The number of human beings condemned to suffer,
even unto death, in order to furnish the requisite quantity of
stuff which forms the dress of some lovely woman at court,
occupies my thoughts more than all her finery or her beauty.
Absorbed in the labor of so painful a computation, I feel myself growing unjust. The most charming face reminds me, in
spite of my efforts to banish such ideas, of those caricatures
of Bonaparte which were spread all over Europe in 1815. At a
little distance the colossal statue of the emperor appeared a
simple likeness, but, on inspecting it more nearly, each feature was found to be composed of mutilated corpses.

In all countries, the poor work for the rich, who pay them
for their labor; but these poor are not folded for life in some
enclosures like mere herds of cattle; and, though obliged to
toil at the labor which provides their children with daily
bread, they at least enjoy a semblance of liberty; now semblance, or appearance, is almost everything to a being whose
views are limited, but whose imagination is boundless. With
us, the hireling has the right of changing his employers, his
residence, and even his profession; but the Russian serf is a
chattel of his lord's; enlisted from birth to death in the service, his life represents to this proprietor a part and parcel of
the sum necessary to supply the caprices and fantasies of
fashion. Assuredly, in a state thus constituted, luxury is no
longer innocent. All communities in which a middle class of
society does not exist, ought to proscribe luxury as a scandal,
for in well-organized lands, it is the profits which that class
draws from the vanity of the superior classes which produce

general opulence. If, as is anticipated, Russia should become a land of industrial arts, the relations between the serf and the owner of the soil will be modified, and a population of independent dealers and artisans will rise up between the nobles and the peasants, but at present, the commerce of the land is scarcely born; the manufacturers, merchants, and tradesmen, are almost all Germans.

It is here only too easy to be deceived by the appearances of civilization. If you look at the court and the people who are its votaries, you may suppose yourself among a nation far advanced in social culture and political economy; but when you reflect on the relations which exist between the different classes of society, when you observe how small is the number of these classes—finally, when you examine attentively the groundwork of manners and of things—you perceive the existence of a real barbarism, scarcely disguised under a magnificence which is revolting.

I do not reproach the Russians for being what they are, what I blame in them is, their pretending to be what we are. They are still uncultivated; this state would at least allow room for hope; but I see them incessantly occupied with the desire of mimicking other nations, and this they do after the true manner of monkeys, caricaturing what they copy. They thus appear to me spoilt for the savage state, and yet wanting in the requisites of civilization; and the terrible words of Voltaire or of Diderot, now forgotten in France, recur to my mind—"The Russians have rotted before they have ripened."

At Petersburg, everything wears an air of opulence, grandeur, and magnificence; but if we should take this outward show for reality, we should find ourselves strangely deceived. Generally, the first effect of civilization is to render what may be called *material* life easy; but here everything is difficult:—a cunning apathy is the secret of existence.

If you wish to ascertain precisely what is to be seen in this great city, and if Schnitzler does not satisfy you, you will find no other guide*; no bookseller has on sale a complete directory to the curiosities of Petersburg; either the well-informed men whom you question have an interest in not answering you, or they have something else to do. The emperor, his health, his movements, the project with which he is ostensibly occupied, such are the only subjects worthy of the thoughts of a Russian who thinks at all. The catechism of the court is the only necessary knowledge. All take pleasure in rendering themselves agreeable to their master, by hiding some corner of truth from the eyes of travelers. No one has any idea of gratifying the curious; on the contrary, they love to deceive them by false data: it requires the talents of a great critic to travel to advantage in Russia. Under despotism, curiosity is synonymous with indiscretion. The empire is the emperor.

And yet this frightful extent of greatness was not sufficient for the Czar Peter. That man, not content with being the reason of his people, would also become their conscience. The sovereign who did not shrink before such a responsibility, and who, notwithstanding his long apparent or real hesitation, finally rendered himself culpable of so enormous an usurpation, has inflicted more evil on the world by this single outrage against the prerogatives of the priests, and the religious liberty of man, than he has conferred benefit on Russia by all his warlike and political talents, and his genius for the arts of industry. That emperor, type and model of the empire, and of the emperors in all ages, was a singular union of the great and the minute. With a lust for power, grasping as that of the most cruel tyrants of any age or nation, he united the ingenuity of the artisan in a degree that made him the rival of the best mechanics of his times; a sovereign scrupulously terrible, an eagle and an ant, a lion and a beaver:—this monarch, dreadful during life, now imposes himself on posterity as a

---

*Schnitzler is author of the best work on Russian statistics that has been written.

species of saint, and tyrannizes over the judgments, as he formerly tyrannized over the acts of men. To pass an impartial opinion upon him is, at the present time, a sacrilege which is not without danger, even for a stranger, in Russia. I brave this danger every day; for of all yokes, the most insupportable to me is that which imposes the necessity of admiring. In Russia, power, unlimited as it is, entertains an extreme dread of censure, or even of free speech. An oppressor is of all others the man who most fears the truth; he only escapes ridicule by the terror and mystery with which he environs himself. Hence it is that there must be no speaking of persons here: one must not allude to the *maladies* of which the Emperors Peter III and Paul I died, any more than to the clandestine amours that certain malevolent persons have ascribed to the reigning emperor. The amusements of this prince are viewed only as relaxations from the cares of greatness, and with whatever consequences they may be attended to certain families, one must profess ignorance of them under pain of being accused of the greatest of all crimes in the eyes of a people composed of slaves and diplomatists—the crime of indiscretion.

I am impatient to see the empress. She is said to be a charming, though at the same time a frivolous and haughty personage. It needs both hauteur and levity to support an existence like hers. She neither interferes with, nor informs herself respecting public affairs; knowledge is worse than useless, when there is no power to act upon it. The empress follows the example of the other subjects of the emperor: all who are born Russians, or would live in Russia, must make silence upon public affairs the motto of their life. Secret conversations would be very interesting, but who dares indulge in them? To reflect and to discern would be to render oneself suspected.

M. Repnin governed the empire and the emperor: he has been out of favor for *two years*, and for *two years* Russia has not heard his name pronounced, though that name was previously in everybody's mouth. In one day, he fell from the pinnacle of

power into the lowest depth of obscurity. No one dared to remember that he was living, nor even to believe that he ever
had lived. In Russia, on the day that a minister falls from favor,
his friends become deaf and blind. A man is, as it were, buried
the moment he appears to be disgraced. Russia does not know
today if the minister who governed her yesterday exists. Under
Louis XV the banishment of M. de Choiseul was a triumph; in
Russia, the retirement of M. Repnin is a funeral.

To whom will the people one day appeal against the mute
servility of the great? What an explosion of vengeance is not
the conduct of this cringing aristocracy preparing against the
autocratic power? What are the duties of the Russian noblesse?
To adore the emperor, and to render themselves accomplices
in the abuse of sovereign power that they themselves may
continue to oppress the people? Is such the position that Providence has ordained them to occupy in the economy of this
vast empire? They fill its posts of honor. What have they done
to merit them? In the history of Russia, no one except the
emperor has performed his part. The nobles, the clergy, and
all the other classes of society, have each failed in their own.
An oppressed people have always deserved the ills under
which they suffer. Tyranny is the work of the nation. Either
the civilized world will, before another fifty years, pass anew
under the yoke of barbarians, or Russia will undergo a revolution more terrible than that the effects of which we are still
feeling in western Europe.

I can perceive that I am feared here, which I attribute to its
being known that I write under the influence of my convic-
tions. No stranger can set foot in this country without immediately feeling that he is weighed and judged. "This is a sincere
man," they think, "therefore he must be dangerous." Under
the government of the lawyers,* a sincere man is only useless!

---

*Alluding to France under King Louis Philippe.—*Trans.*

"An indefinite hatred of despotism reigns in France," they say; "but it is exaggerated and unenlightened, therefore we will brave it. The day, however, that a traveler, who convinces because he himself believes, shall tell the real abuses which he cannot fail to discover among us, we shall be seen as we really are. France now barks at us without knowing us; when she does know us, she will bite."

The Russians, no doubt, do me too great honor by the inquietude which, notwithstanding their profound dissimulation, they cannot conceal from me. I do not know whether I shall publish what I think of their country; but I do know that they only do themselves justice in fearing the truths that I could publish.

The Russians have everything in name, and nothing in reality. They have civilization, society, literature, the drama, the arts and sciences—but they have no physicians. In case of illness, you must either prescribe for yourself, or call in a foreign practitioner. If you send for the nearest doctor, you are a dead man, for medical art in Russia is in its infancy. With the exception of the physician of the emperor, who, I am told, is, though a Russian, skillful, the only doctors who would not assassinate you are the Germans attached to the service of the princes. But the princes live in a state of perpetual motion. It is often impossible to ascertain where they may be; or, when that is known, to send twenty, forty, or sixty versts (two French leagues are equal to seven versts), after them. There are, therefore, practically speaking, no physicians in Russia. Should even the physician be sought at the known residence of his prince, and not be found there, there is no further hope. "The doctor is not here." No other answer can be obtained. In Russia, everything serves to show that reserve is the favorite virtue of the land. An opportunity for appearing discreet cannot but offer to those who know how to seize it, and what Russian would not do himself credit at so little cost? The projects and the movements of the great, and of those attached to their persons by so confidential an office as that of physician, ought not to be known, unless officially declared, to persons who are born courtiers, and with whom obedience is a passion. Here, mystery supplies the place of merit.

The most able of these doctors of the princes are far inferior to the least known among the medical men of our hospitals. The skill of the most learned practitioners will rust at court: nothing can supply the place of experience gained by the bedside of the sick. I could read the secret memoirs of a Russian court physician with great interest, but I would not follow his prescriptions. Such men would make better chroniclers than doctors. When, therefore, a stranger falls sick among this soi-disant civilized people, his best plan is to consider himself among savages, and to leave everything to nature.

On returning to my hotel this evening, I found a letter, which has very agreeably surprised me. Through the influence of our ambassador, I am to be admitted tomorrow to the imperial chapel, to witness the marriage of the grand duchess.

To appear at court before having been presented, is contrary to all the laws of etiquette, and I was far from hoping for such a favor. The Emperor has, however, granted it. Count Voronzov, Grand Master of the Ceremonies, without preinforming me, for he did not wish to amuse me with a false hope, had dispatched a courier to Peterhof, which is ten leagues from Petersburg, to solicit His Majesty in my favor. This kind consideration has not been unavailing. The emperor has given permission for me to be present at the marriage, in the chapel of the court, and I am to be presented, without ceremony, at the ball on the same evening.

LETTER 11

I AM WRITING on the 14th of July, 1839, just fifty years after
the taking of the Bastille, which event occurred on the 14th
of July, 1789. The coincidence of these dates is curious. The
marriage of the son of Eugène de Beauharnais* has taken

---

*Eugène de Beauharnais was the son of Empress Josephine and her first husband.
—Ed.

place on the same day as that which marked the commencement of our revolutions, precisely fifty years ago.

I have just returned from the palace, after having witnessed, in the Imperial Chapel, all the Greek ceremonies of the marriage of the Grand Duchess Marie with the Duke of Leuchtenberg.

I will endeavor to describe in detail, but in the first place I must speak of the emperor.

The predominant expression of his countenance is that of a restless severity, which strikes a beholder at the first glance, and, in spite of the regularity of his features, conveys by no means a pleasant impression. Physiognomists pretend, with much reason, that the hardness of the heart injures the beauty of the countenance. Nevertheless, this expression in the Emperor Nicholas appears to be the result of experience rather than the work of nature. By what long and cruel sufferings must not a man have been tortured, when his countenance excites fear, notwithstanding the voluntary confidence that noble features inspire!

A man charged with the management and direction, in its most minute details, of some immense machine, incessantly fears the derangement of one or other of its various parts. He who obeys, suffers only according to the precise measure of the evil inflicted: he who commands, suffers first as other men suffer, and afterwards, that common measure of evil is multiplied a hundredfold for him by the workings of imagination and self-love. Responsibility is the punishment of absolute power.

If he be the *primum mobile* of all minds, he becomes the center also of all griefs: the more he is dreaded, the more is he to be pitied.

He to whom is accorded unlimited rule, sees, even in the common occurrences of life, the specter of revolt. Persuaded that his rights are sacred, he recognizes no bounds to them but those of his own intelligence and will, and he is, therefore, subject to constant annoyance. An unlucky fly, buzzing in the Imperial Palace during a ceremony, mortifies the emperor; the independence of nature appears to him a bad example: everything which he cannot subject to his arbitrary laws becomes, in his eyes, as a soldier who, in the heat of battle, revolts against his officer. The emperor of Russia is a military chief, and every day with him is a day of battle.

Nevertheless, at times some gleams of softness temper the imperious looks of this monarch; and then, the expression of affability reveals all the native beauty of his classic features. In the heart of the husband and the father, humanity triumphs for a moment over the policy of the prince. When the sovereign rests from his task of imposing the yoke upon his subjects, he appears happy. This combat between the primitive dignity of the man and the affected gravity of the sovereign, appears to me worthy the attention of an observer: it occupied mine the greater part of the time I passed in the chapel.

The emperor is above the usual height by half a head; his figure is noble, although a little stiff; he has practiced from his youth the Russian custom of girding the body above the loins, to such a degree as to push up the stomach into the chest, which produces an unnatural swelling or extension about the ribs that is as injurious to health as it is ungraceful in appearance.

This voluntary deformity destroys all freedom of movement, impairs the elegance of the shape, and imparts an air of constraint to the whole person. They say that when the emperor loosens his dress, the viscera, suddenly giving way, are disturbed for a moment in their equilibrium, which produces an extraordinary prostration of amazing strength. The bowels may be displaced,—they cannot be got rid of.

The emperor has a Grecian profile, the forehead high, but receding; the nose straight, and perfectly formed; the mouth very finely cut; the face, which in shape is rather a long oval, is noble; the whole air military, and rather German than

Slavic. His carriage and his attitudes are naturally imposing. He expects always to be gazed at, and never for a moment
forgets that he is so. It may even be said that he likes this
homage of the eyes.

He passes the greater part of his existence in the open air,
at reviews, or in rapid journeys. During summer, the shade
of his military hat draws across his forehead an oblique line,
which marks the action of the sun upon the skin. It produces
a singular effect, but is not disagreeable, as the cause is at
once perceived.

In examining attentively the fine person of this individual,
on whose will hangs the fate of so many others, I have remarked, with involuntary pity, that he cannot smile at the
same time with the eyes and the mouth; a want of harmony
which denotes perpetual constraint, and which makes one
remember, with regret, that easy natural grace, so conspicuous in the less regular but more agreeable countenance of his
brother, the Emperor Alexander. The latter, always pleasing,
had yet, at times, an assumed manner. The Emperor Nicholas
is more sincere; but he has an habitual expression of severity,
which sometimes gives the idea of harshness and inflexibility. If, however, he is less fascinating, he is more firm than
his late brother; but then, it must be added, that he has also
a proportionately greater need of firmness. Graceful courtesy
insures authority by removing the desire of resistance. This
judicious economy in the exercise of power is a secret of
which the Emperor Nicholas is ignorant; he is one who desires to be obeyed where others desire to be loved.

The figure of the empress is very elegant; and, though she
is extremely thin, I find an indefinable grace about her whole
person. Her mien, far from being haughty, as I had been
informed, is expressive of an habitual resignation. On entering the chapel, she was much affected, and I thought she was
going to faint. A nervous convulsion agitated every feature of
her face, and caused her head slightly to shake. Her soft blue,

but rather sunken eyes, told of deep sufferings supported with angelic calmness. Her look, full of feeling, has the more power, from its appearing unconscious of possessing any. Faded before her time, and so weak, that it is said she cannot live long, her person gives the idea of a passing shadow, or of something that belongs no more to earth. She has never recovered from the anguish she had to undergo on the day of her accession to the throne, and conjugal duty has consumed the rest of her life.

She has given too many idols to Russia, too many children to the emperor. "Exhausting herself in Grand Dukes! What a destiny!" said a great Polish lady, who did not think herself obliged to speak reverently with her lips of what she hated in her heart.

Everyone sees the state of the empress, but no one mentions it. The emperor loves her: when confined to her chamber by illness, he attends her himself, watches by her bedside, and prepares and administers her medicine. No sooner is she better, than he destroys her health with the excitement of fêtes and journeys; but the moment that danger is again apprehended, he renounces all his projects. Of the precautions that might prevent illness he has a horror. Wife, children, servants, relations, favorites,—all in Russia must follow in the Imperial vortex, and smile on till they die. All must force themselves to conform to the wish of the sovereign, which wish alone forms the destiny of all. The nearer anyone is placed to the Imperial sun, the more is he a slave to the glory attached to his situation. The empress is dying under the weight of this slavery.

Everyone here knows this, but no one speaks of it; for it is a general rule never to utter a word which can excite much interest: neither he who speaks, nor he who listens, must allow it to be seen that the subject of conversation merits continued attention, or awakens any warm feelings. All the resources of language are exhausted in order to banish from discourse, idea and sentiment, without, however, *appearing* to repress them, which would be gauche. The excessive constraint which results from this prodigious labor,—prodigious especially through the art with which it is concealed,— embitters the life of the Russians. Such a torment serves as an expiation for the men who voluntarily deprive themselves of the two greatest gifts of God—mind and its organ, speech; in other words, thought and liberty.

The more I see of Russia, the more I approve the conduct of the emperor in forbidding his subjects to travel, and in rendering access to his own country difficult to foreigners. The political system of Russia could not survive twenty years' free communication with the west of Europe. Listen not to the fictions of the Russians: they mistake pomp for elegance, luxury for politeness, a powerful police, and a dread of government, for the fundamental principles of society. According to their notions, discipline is civilization. They forget that men in the wild can have gentle mores and soldiers can be quite cruel. Notwithstanding all their pretensions to good manners, their showy education, their precocious corruption, and their facility of comprehending and appropriating the materialism of life, the Russians are not yet civilized. They are enrolled and drilled Tartars, and nothing more.

I wish it not to be inferred that they are therefore to be despised: the more their mental rudeness is concealed under the softer forms of social intercourse, the more formidable I consider them. As regards civilization, they have been hitherto contented with exhibiting its appearance; but if ever they should find an opportunity of revenging their real inferiority upon us, we shall have to make a tremendous expiation for our advantages.

This morning, after dressing myself in haste, in order to repair to the Imperial Chapel, I entered my carriage, and followed that of the French ambassador, through the squares and streets that led to the palace, examining with curiosity all that presented itself in the way. The troops which I observed in the approaches to the palace, were less magnificent than I had been led to expect, though the horses were certainly superb. The immense square which separates the dwelling of the sovereign from the rest of the city, was crossed in various directions by lines of carriages, servants in livery, and soldiers in a variety of uniforms. That of the Cossacks is the most remarkable. Notwithstanding the concourse, the square, so vast is its extent, was not crowded.

In new states there is a void everywhere; but this is more especially the case when the government is absolute: it is the absence of liberty which creates solitude, and spreads sadness.

The equipages of the courtiers looked well without being really elegant. The carriages badly painted, and still worse varnished, are of a heavy make. They are drawn by four horses, whose traces are immoderately long. A coachman drives the wheel horses; a little postilion, clothed in the long Persian robe similar to that of the coachman, rides on a fore horse, seated upon, or rather in, a hollow saddle, raised before and behind, and stuffed like a pillow. This child, called, I believe, in German the *Vorreiter*,* and in Russian the *faleiter*, is always perched upon the right, or off-side leader; the contrary custom prevails in all other countries, where the postilion is mounted on the left, in order to have the right hand free to guide his other horse. The spirit and power of the Russian horses, which have all some blood, though all have not beauty, the dexterity of the coachmen, and the richness of their dress, greatly set off the carriages, and produce altogether an effect which, if not so elegant, is more striking and splendid than that of the equipages of the other courts of Europe.

I was occupied with a crowd of reflections which the nov-

---

*The fore rider.

elty of the objects around me suggested, when my carriage stopped under a grand peristyle, where I descended among a crowd of gilded courtiers, who were attended by vassals as barbaric in appearance as in reality. The costume of the servants is almost as brilliant as that of their masters. The Russians have a great taste for splendor, and in court ceremonies this taste is more especially displayed.

In descending from the carriage rather hastily, lest I should be separated from the persons under whose guidance I had placed myself, my foot struck with some force against the curb stone, which had caught my spur. At the moment, I paid little attention to the circumstance; but great was my distress when, immediately afterwards, I perceived that the spur had come off, and, what was still worse, that it had carried with it the heel of the boot also. Having to appear in this dilapidated state, for the first time, before a man said to be as precise as he is great and powerful, seemed to me a real misfortune. The Russians are prone to ridicule; and the idea of affording them a subject for laughter at my first presentation, was peculiarly unpleasant.

What was to be done? To return under the peristyle to search for the remnant of my boot was quite useless. To leave the French ambassador and return home, would, in itself, be the way to create a *scene*. On the other hand, to show myself as I was, would ruin me in the estimation of the emperor and his courtiers; and I have no philosophy against ridicule to which I voluntarily expose myself. The troubles that pleasure draws one into at a thousand leagues from home, appear to me unbearable. It was so easy not to go at all, that to go awkwardly were unpardonable. I might hope to conceal myself in the crowd; but, I repeat, there never is a crowd in Russia; and least of all, upon a staircase like that of the new Winter Palace, which resembles some decoration in the opera of Gustavus. This palace is, I believe, the largest and most magnificent of all existing royal or imperial residences.

I felt my natural timidity increase with the confusion which so ludicrous an accident produced, until, at length, fear itself supplied me with courage, and I began to limp as lightly as I could across the immense rooms and stately galleries, the length and strong light of which I inwardly cursed. The Russians are cool, quick-sighted quizzes, possessing, like all the ambitious, little delicacy of feeling. They are, besides, mistrustful of strangers, whose judgment they fear, because they believe we have but little good feeling towards them. This prejudice renders them censorious and secretly caustic, although outwardly they appear hospitable and polite.

I reached, at length, but not without difficulty, the further end of the Imperial Chapel. There all was forgotten, including even myself and my foolish embarrassment; indeed, in this place the crowd was more dense, and no one could see what was wanting to my equipment. The novelty of the spectacle that awaited me, restored my coolness and self-possession. I blushed for the vexation which my vanity as a disconcerted courtier had produced, and with the resumption of my part as simple traveler in the scene, recovered the composure of a philosophic observer.

One word more upon my costume. It had been the subject of grave consultation: some of the young people attached to the French legation had advised the habit of the national guard. I feared, however, that this uniform would displease the emperor, and decided upon that of a staff officer, with the epaulettes of a lieutenant-colonel, which are those of my rank.

I had been warned that the dress would appear new, and that it would become, on the part of the princes of the Imperial family, and of the emperor himself, the subject of numerous questions which might embarrass me. Hitherto, however, none have had time to occupy themselves with so small an affair.

The Greek marriage rites are long and imposing. Everything is symbolical in the Eastern church. The splendors of religion shed a luster over the solemnities of the court.

The walls and roof of the chapel, the vestments of the priests and of their attendants, all glittered with gold. There are here riches enough to astonish the least poetical imagination. The spectacle vies with the most fanciful description in the Arabian Nights; it is like the poetry of Lalla Rookh, or the Marvelous Lamp,—that Oriental poetry in which sensation prevails over sentiment and thought.

The Imperial Chapel is not of large dimensions. It was filled with the representatives of all the sovereigns of Europe, and almost of Asia; with strangers like myself, admitted in the suite of the diplomatic corps; with the wives of the ambassadors, and the great officers of the court. A balustrade separated us from the circular enclosure, within which the altar was raised. It had the form of a low square table. Places in the choir were reserved for the Imperial family: at the moment of our arrival they were vacant.

I have seen few things that could compare with the magnificence and solemnity which attended the entrance of the emperor into this chapel, blazing with gold. He appeared, advancing with the empress, and followed by the court retinue. All eyes were immediately fixed upon him and his family, among whom the betrothed pair shone conspicuously. A marriage of inclination celebrated in broidered vestments, and in a place so pompous, was a novelty which crowned the interest of the scene. This was repeated by everyone around me; for my own part I cannot give credit to the marvel, nor can I avoid seeing a politic motive in all that is said and done here. The emperor perhaps deceives himself, and believes that he is performing acts of paternal tenderness, while in the bottom of his heart he may be secretly influenced in his choice by the hope of personal advantage.

It is with ambition as with avarice; misers always calculate, not excepting even the moment when they believe they are yielding to disinterested sentiments.

Although the court was numerous, and the chapel small,

there was no confusion. I stood in the midst of the corps diplomatique, near the balustrade which separated us from the sanctuary. We were not so crowded as to be unable to distinguish the features and movements of each of the personages whom duty or curiosity had there brought together. No disorder interrupted the respectful silence that was maintained throughout the assembly. A brilliant sun illuminated the interior of the chapel, where the temperature had, I understood, risen to 30 degrees. We observed in the suite of the emperor, clothed in a long robe of gold tissue, and a pointed bonnet, likewise adorned with gold embroidery, a Tartar khan, who is half tributary, and half independent of Russia. This petty sovereign had come to pray the emperor of all the Russias to admit among *his pages* a son twelve years old, whom he had brought to Petersburg, hoping thus to secure for the child a suitable destiny. The presence of this declining power served as a contrast to that of the successful monarch, and reminded me of the triumphal pomps of Rome.

The first ladies of the Russian court, and the wives of the ambassadors of the other courts, among whom I recognized Mademoiselle Sontag, now Countess de Rossi, graced with their presence the circumference of the chapel. At the lower end, which terminated in a brilliant, painted rotunda, were ranged the whole of the Imperial family. The gilded ceiling reflecting the ardent rays of the sun, formed a species of crown around the heads of the sovereigns and their children. The attire and diamonds of the ladies shone with a magic splendor in the midst of all the treasures of Asia, which beamed upon the walls of the sanctuary, where royal magnificence seemed to challenge the majesty of the God whom it honored, without forgetting its own.

All this gorgeous display is wonderful, especially to us, if we recall the time, not distant, when the marriage of the daughter of a czar would have been scarcely heard of in Europe, and when Peter I declared, that he had a right to leave his crown to whomsoever he pleased. How great a progress for so short a period!

When we reflect on the diplomatic and other conquests of this power, which not long since was considered as of but little importance in the civilized world, we are almost led to ask ourselves if that which we see is not a dream. The emperor himself did not seem to be much accustomed to what was passing before him; for he was continually leaving his prayers, and slipping from one side to the other, in order to remedy the omissions of etiquette among his children, or the clergy. This proves that in Russia, even the court has not yet finished its education. His son-in-law was not placed quite correctly, whereupon he made him shift his position by about two feet. The grand duchess, the priests themselves, and all the great functionaries of the court seemed to be governed by his minute but supreme directions. I felt that it would have been more dignified to leave things as they were, and I could have wished that when once in the chapel, God only had been thought of, and each man had been left to acquit himself of his functions, without his master so scrupulously rectifying each little fault of religious discipline, or of court ceremonial: but in this singular country the absence of liberty is seen everywhere; it is found even at the foot of the altar. Here the spirit of Peter the Great governs the minds of all.

During the mass at a Greek marriage, there is a moment when the betrothed drink together out of the same cup. Afterwards, accompanied by the officiating priest, they pass three times round the altar, hand in hand, to signify the conjugal union, and the fidelity which should attend their walk through life. All these acts are the more imposing, as they recall to mind the customs of the primitive church.

The above ceremonies being ended, a crown was next held for a considerable time over the head of each of the newly married pair; the crown of the grand duchess, by her brother the hereditary grand duke, the position of which the emperor himself (once more leaving his prayer desk) took care to adjust, with a mixture of good nature and of minute attention that would be difficult to describe.

The crown of the Duke of Leuchtenberg was held by the Count de Pahlen, Russian ambassador at Paris, and son of the too celebrated and too zealous friend of Alexander. This recollection, banished from the conversation, and perhaps from the thoughts, of the Russians of these days, did not cease to occupy my mind the whole time that the Count de Pahlen, with the noble simplicity which is natural to him, was engaged in the performance of an act envied, doubtless, by all who aspired to court favor. That act was an invocation of the protection of Heaven, upon the head of the husband of Paul the First's grandchild! The strange coincidence most probably occurred to no one except myself. It appears that tact and propriety are here necessary only for those who possess no power. Had the recollection of the fact which occupied my mind, occurred to that of the emperor, he would have commissioned some other individual to hold the crown over the head of his son-in-law. But in a country where they neither read nor speak of public affairs, nothing has less to do with the events of today, than the history of yesterday; power consequently sometimes acts inadvertently, and commits oversights which prove that it sleeps in a security not always well advised. Russian policy is not shackled in its march either by opinions or actions; the favor of the sovereign is everything. So long as it lasts, it supplies the want of merit, of virtue, and even of innocence in the man on whom it is lavished; and, in the same manner, when it is withdrawn, it deprives him of everything.

Everyone contemplated with a species of anxious interest the immobility of the arms which sustained the two crowns. The scene lasted for a considerable time, and must have been very fatiguing for the performers. The young bride is extremely graceful; her eyes are blue, and her fair complexion has all the delicate freshness of early youth: openness and intelligence united, form the predominant expression of her face. This princess and her sister, the Grand Duchess Olga, appear to me the two most beautiful persons at the Russian court:—happy unison of the advantages of rank and the gifts of nature.

When the officiating bishop presented the married pair to their august parents, the latter embraced them with a warmth that was affecting. The moment afterwards, the empress threw herself into the arms of her husband—an effusion of tenderness which would have better suited a chamber than a chapel: but in Russia the sovereigns are at home everywhere, not excepting the house of God. The tender emotion, however, of the empress appeared altogether involuntary, and therefore did not shock the feelings. Woe to those who could find anything to ridicule in the emotions produced by true and natural feeling! Such exhibitions of sensibility are sympathetic. German kindheartedness is never lost; there must indeed be soul, when feeling is allowed to betray itself even upon the throne.

Before the benediction, two doves were, according to custom, let loose in the chapel; they quickly settled on a gilded cornice which jutted out directly over the heads of the wedded pair; and there they never ceased billing and cooing during the whole mass. Pigeons are well off in Russia: they are revered as the sacred symbol of the Holy Ghost, and it is forbidden to kill them: fortunately, the flavor of their flesh is not liked by the Russians.

The Duke of Leuchtenberg is a tall, well-made young man, but there is nothing distingué in his features. His eyes are handsome, but his mouth projects and is not well formed. His figure is good without being noble: a uniform becomes him, and supplies that want of grace that may be observed in his person. He looks more like a smart sublieutenant than a prince. Not one relation on his side had come to St. Petersburg to assist at the ceremony.

During the mass he appeared singularly impatient to be alone with his wife; and the eyes of the whole assembly were directed, by a kind of spontaneous sympathy, towards the two pigeons perched above the altar.

At one part of the Greek marriage ceremony everyone is obliged to kneel. Before prostrating himself with the others, the emperor cast around the assembly a searching, and by no means pleasing glance. It appeared as though he would assure himself that no one remained standing—a superfluous precaution: for though there were among the foreigners present both Catholics and Protestants, it never, I am certain, entered into the thoughts of one not to conform, externally, to all the ceremonies of the Greek church.

The possibility of a doubt on such a point justifies some of my previous observations, and authorizes my repeating that a restless severity has become the habitual expression of the physiognomy of the emperor.

In these times, when revolt pervades, as it were, the very air, perhaps autocracy itself begins to fear lest some insult should be offered to its power. Such an idea would clash disagreeably, and even terrifically, with the notions which it preserves of its rights. Absolute power is most to be feared when it is itself under the influence of fear. In noticing the nervous affection, the weakness, and the emaciated frame of the empress, I called to mind what this interesting woman must have suffered during the revolt at the time of her accession to the throne. Heroism repays itself; it is by fortitude, but a fortitude that exhausts life.

I have already said that everybody had fallen on their knees, and, last of all, the emperor; the lovers were united; the Imperial family and the crowd arose; the priests and choir chanted the Te Deum, and discharges of artillery, outside, announced the consecration of the marriage to the city. The effect of this exquisite music, mingled with the thunder of the cannon, the ringing of the bells, and the distant acclamations of the people, was inexpressibly grand. All musical instruments are banished from the Greek church, and the voices of human beings only there celebrate the praises of God. This rigor of the Oriental ritual is favorable to the art of singing, preserving to it all its simplicity, and producing an effect in the chants which is absolutely celestial. I could fancy I heard the heart-beating of sixty millions of subjects—a living orchestra, following, without drowning, the triumphal hymn of the priests. I was deeply moved: music can make us forget for one moment even despotism itself.

I can only compare these choruses without accompaniment, to the *Miserere* as sung during the Passion Week in the Sixtine Chapel at Rome; but the chapel of the Pope is but the shadow of what it formerly was. It is one ruin more amid the ruins of Rome. About the middle of the last century, when the Italian school shone in its brightest luster, the old Greek chants were re-arranged, without being spoilt, by composers who were brought to Petersburg from Rome. The works of these strangers are chefs d'oeuvre, which is mainly owing to all their talent and science having been applied in subservience to the works of antiquity. Their classic compositions are executed with a power worthy of the conception. The soprano, or children's parts—for no woman sings in the Imperial Chapel—are perfectly correct; the bassos have a strength, depth, and purity, that exceed anything I recollect having heard elsewhere.

To an amateur of the art, the music of the Imperial Chapel is alone worth a journey to Petersburg. The sweet, the powerful, and all the finest shades of expression, are observed with a depth of feeling and a skill which cannot be too much admired. The Russians are musical; this cannot be doubted by those who have heard the music in their churches. I listened without daring to breathe, and I longed for my learned friend Meyerbeer to explain to me the beauties which I so deeply felt, but which I was unable to comprehend. He would have understood them by the inspiration they would have communicated, for his admiration of models is expressed by his rivaling them.

During the *Te Deum*, at the moment when the two choirs

were responding to each other, the tabernacle opened, and the priests were seen, their heads adorned with sparkling tiaras of jewels, and their bodies clothed in robes of gold, over which their silver beards fell majestically; some of these beards reach as far as the waist. The assistants make as dazzling an appearance as the priests. This court is certainly magnificent, and the military costume shines also in all its splendor. I saw with delight the people bringing to God the homage of their riches and their pomp. The sacred music was listened to by a profane auditory with a silence and attention which would alone give an effect to chants less sublime than these. God was there, and his presence sanctifies even the court: the world and sense were nothing more than accessory objects—the reigning thought was heaven.

The officiating archbishop did not disgrace the majesty of the scene. If not handsome, he is venerable; his small figure is like that of a weasel, but his head is white with age. He has a careworn and sickly appearance; a priest, old and feeble, cannot be an ignoble object. At the close of the ceremony the emperor came and bent before him, respectfully kissing his hand.

The autocrat never fails to give an example of submission, when there is a hope that such an example may be of profit to himself. I was interested in the poor archbishop, who appeared dying in the midst of his glory. The majestic figure of the emperor with his noble countenance, bending before the representative of religious power—the youthful couple—the Imperial family—the spectators—in short, the whole assemblage that filled and animated the chapel, formed a subject for a picture. Before the ceremony, I thought the archbishop would have fainted. The court kept him waiting a long time, unmindful of the saying of Louis XVIII, that "Punctuality is the politeness of kings." Notwithstanding the cunning expression of his countenance, this old man inspired me with compassion. He was so feeble, and yet he sustained fatigue with so much patience, that I pitied, if I did not respect him; for whether his patience was the result of piety, or of ambition, it was cruelly tried.

The religious ceremony in the Greek chapel was followed by a second nuptial benediction by a Catholic priest, which took place in one of the halls of the palace, consecrated to this pious use for the day only. After these two marriages, the wedded pair and their family met at table. I, not having permission to witness either the Catholic marriage or the banquet, followed the greater number of the courtly crowd, and went out to breathe a less stifling air, congratulating myself on the little effect that my dilapidated boot had produced. Some persons, however, spoke to me of it laughingly, and that was all. Both in good and in evil, nothing that merely regards ourselves is as important as we fancy it.

On departing from the palace, I found my carriage again without any trouble. There is never, I repeat, a large concourse in Russia. The space is always too vast for what is done there. This is the advantage of a country where there is no nation. In a community thus ordered, a crowd would be equivalent to a revolution.

The void which is everywhere observable, causes the public structures to appear too small for the places in which they stand: they seem lost in space. The column of Alexander passes for being higher than that of the Place Vendôme, owing to the dimensions of its pedestal. The shaft consists of one single block of granite, the largest that has ever been shaped by the hand of man. This immense column, raised between the Winter Palace and the crescent which forms the other extremity of the square, when viewed from the palace, appears to the eye as nothing more than a pole, and the houses around might be taken for palisades. In the square, a hundred thousand men can perform their maneuvers, without its appearing filled or thickly peopled. It is enclosed by the Winter Palace, the façades of which are rebuilt on the model of the old palace of the Empress Elizabeth. Here is at least a relief to the eyes, after the poor and frigid imitations of the monuments of Athens and Rome. The style is that of the Regency, or Louis XIV degenerated, but the scale is very large. The opposite side of the square is terminated by a semicircle or crescent of buildings, in which are established the bureaus of various ministers of state. These edifices are mostly constructed in the ancient Grecian style. Singular taste! Temples erected to clerks! The buildings of the Admiralty are in the same square. Their small pillars and gilded turrets produce a picturesque effect. An avenue of trees ornaments the square opposite this spot, and renders it less monotonous. On the other side of the immense Russian Champ de Mars stands the church of St. Isaac, with its colossal peristyle, and its brazen dome, still half concealed by the scaffolding of the architect. Farther on, is seen the palace of the Senate, and other structures still in the form of pagan temples. Beyond, in an angle of this long square, at its extremity on the Neva, stands the statue of Peter the Great, which disappears in immensity like a pebble on the shore. These above-named edifices contain material enough to build an entire city, and yet they do not complete the sides of the great square of Petersburg: it is a vast field, not of wheat, but of pillars. The Russians may do their best to imitate all that art has produced of beautiful in other times and other lands; they forget that Nature is stronger than man. They never sufficiently consult her, and therefore she is constantly revenging herself by doing them mischief. Masterpieces have only been produced by men who have listened to, and felt the power of Nature. Nature is the conception of God; art is the relation between the conceptions of man and those of the power which has created and which perpetuates the world. The artist repeats on earth what he has heard in heaven; he is but the translator of the works of the Deity; those who would create by their own models produce only monsters.

Among the ancients, the architects reared their structures in steep and confined spots, where the picturesque character of the site added to the effect of the works of man. The Russians, who flatter themselves they are reproducing the wonders of antiquity, and who, in reality, are only caricaturing them, raise their soi-disant Grecian and Roman structures in immense plains, where they are almost lost to the eye. The architecture proper for such a land would not be the colonnade of the Parthenon, but the tower of Peking. It is for man to build mountains, when nature has not undulated the surface of the earth; but the Russians have raised their porticoes and pediments without thinking of this, and without recollecting that on a flat and naked expanse, it is difficult to distinguish edifices with so small an elevation. We still recognize the steppes of Asia in cities where they have pretended to revive the Roman Forum. Muscovy is more nearly allied to Asia than to Europe. The genius of the East hovers over its soil. The semicircle of edifices opposite the Imperial Palace, if observed sideways, at a proper distance, has the effect of an incomplete ancient amphitheater. If examined more nearly, we see only a series of decorations that have to be replastered every year, in order to repair the ravages of the winter. The ancients built with indestructible materials under a favorable sky; here, under a climate which destroys everything, they raise palaces of wood, houses of plank, and temples of plaster; and, consequently, the Russian workmen pass their lives in rebuilding during the summer, what the winter has demolished. Nothing resists the effects of this climate; even the edifices that appear the most ancient have been reconstructed but yesterday; stone lasts here no better than lime and mortar elsewhere. That enormous piece of granite which forms the shaft of the column of Alexander, is already worn by the frost. In Petersburg it is necessary to use bronze in order to support granite; yet notwithstanding these warnings, they never tire of imitating the taste of southern lands. They people the solitudes of the pole with statues and historical bas-reliefs, without considering that in their country monuments are even more evanescent than memories. Petersburg, in its present state, is but the scaffolding of a structure—when the structure is finished, the scaffolding will be removed. This chef d'oeuvre, not of architecture but of policy, is the New Byzantium, which, in the deep and secret aspirations of the Russian, is to be the future capital of Russia and of the world.

Facing the palace, an immense arcade pierces the already noticed semicircular range of buildings, and leads into the Morskoe Street. Above the enormous vault is placed a chariot with six horses in bronze, guided by I know not what kind of allegorical or historical figure. I doubt whether there could be elsewhere seen anything in such bad taste as this colossal gate opening under a house, and flanked on either side by ordinary dwellings, whose vicinity has nevertheless not prevented its being, under Russian architects, converted into a triumphal arch. I question the merit of the workmanship of the chariot, statue, and horses; but were they ever so good, they are so ill placed that I should not admire them. In objects of art, it is the harmony and keeping of the whole which invite to the examination of details; without merit in the conception, what avails a delicacy in the execution? Everything here is mean, although colossal; for in architecture it is not the dimensions of the walls which constitute excellence, but the purity of the style.

I cannot cease marveling at the passion they have conceived here for light, aerial structures. In a climate where there is sometimes a difference of eighty degrees between the temperature of winter and of summer, what have the inhabitants to do with porticoes, arcades, colonnades, and peristyles? But the Russians are accustomed to regard even nature as a slave. Obstinate imitators, they mistake their vanity for genius, and believe themselves destined to renew, on a scale yet larger than the original, all the wonders of the world. Such creations of the Russian sovereigns as I have hitherto seen, have evinced, not the love of the arts, but the love only of self.

Among other boasts, I hear it said by many Russians, that their climate also is ameliorating! Will God, then, connive at the ambition of this grasping people? Will He give them up even the sky and the breeze of the South? Shall we see Athens in Lapland, Rome at Moscow, the riches of the Thames in the Gulf of Finland, and the history of nations reduced to a question of latitude and longitude?

While my carriage, after leaving the palace, was crossing rapidly the immense square I have been describing, a violent wind raised immense clouds of dust, and I could only see, as through a veil, the equipages that were passing in all directions. The dust of summer is one of the plagues of Petersburg; it is so troublesome that I even wish for the winter snow. I had scarcely reached my hotel when a tremendous storm burst forth. Darkness at midday, thunder without rain, a wind which blew down houses, and, at the same time, a suffocating temperature, were the greeting which Heaven gave during the nuptial banquet. The superstitious viewed these signs as ominous, but soon became reassured by observing that the storm did not last long, and that the air was purer after it than before. I recount what I see, without sympathizing with it, for I have no interest here but that which actuates a curious and attentive stranger. There is between France and Russia a Chinese wall—the Slavic language and character. In spite of the notions with which Peter the Great has inspired the Russians, Siberia commences on the Vistula.

Yesterday, at seven o'clock, I returned to the palace with several other foreigners, in order to be presented to the emperor and empress.

It is easy to perceive that the former cannot for a single instant forget what he is, nor the constant attention which he excites; he studies attitude incessantly,—from whence it results that he is never natural, not even when he is sincere. He has three expressions, not one of which is that of simple benevolence. The most habitual appears to be that of

161

severity. Another, though rarer expression, suits perhaps better his fine face—it is that of solemnity; a third is that of politeness, in which are mixed some shades of gentleness and grace, that serve to temper the chill produced by the two former. But notwithstanding this grace, there is still something which injures the moral influence of the man; it is, that each expression is assumed and cast off at will, without the least trace of one remaining to modify the one next adopted. For such change we are not prepared, and it therefore appears like a mask, that can be put on or off at pleasure. Let not my meaning of the word mask be misunderstood,—I employ it according to its strict etymology. In Greek, *hypocrite* means an actor: the hypocrite was a man who masked himself to perform a play. I would only say, then, that the emperor is always engaged in acting his part.

Hypocrite or actor are ill-sounding words, especially in the mouth of one who professes to be impartial and respectful. But it appears to me that, to intelligent readers—and it is only such that I address—words are nothing in themselves; their importance depends upon the sense that is given to them. I do not say that the physiognomy of this prince lacks candor, but it lacks natural expression. Thus, the chief evil under which Russia suffers, the absence of liberty, is depicted even on the countenance of its sovereign: he has many masks, but no face. Seek for the man, and you still always find the emperor.

I believe this remark may be turned to his praise; he acts his part conscientiously. He would accuse himself of weakness were he to be for a single moment plain and simple, or were he to allow it to be seen that he lived, thought, and felt as do common mortals. Without seeming to partake of any of our affections, he is always governor, judge, general, admiral, prince,—never anything more, never anything less. He will surely grow weary of all this effort as he advances in life; yet it will place him high in the opinion of his people, and perhaps of the world, for the multitude admire the efforts which astonish them,—they pride themselves in seeing the pains that are taken to dazzle them.

Those who knew the Emperor Alexander, eulogize that prince on entirely different grounds. The qualities and the faults of the two brothers were altogether opposite; there was no resemblance, and likewise no sympathy between them. In this country, the memory of a defunct emperor is little honored, and in the present instance inclination accords with the policy that would always have the preceding reign forgotten. Peter the Great is more nearly resembled by Nicholas than by Alexander, and he is more the fashion at the present day. If the ancestors of the emperors are flattered, their immediate predecessors are invariably calumniated.

The present emperor never lays aside the air of supreme majesty, except in his family intercourse. It is there only that he recollects that the natural man has pleasures independent of the duties of state; at least, I hope that it is this disinterested sentiment which attaches him to his domestic circle. His private virtues no doubt aid him in his public capacity, by securing for him the esteem of the world; but I believe he would practice them independently of this calculation.

Among the Russians, sovereign power is respected like religion, the obligations and authority of which stand independently of the personal merit of its priests: the virtues of the prince being superfluous, are so much the more sincere.

If I lived at Petersburg I should become a courtier, not from any love of place or power, nor from any puerile vanity, but from the desire of discovering some road that might reach the heart of a man who differs from all others. Insensibility is not in him a natural vice, it is the inevitable result of a position which he has not chosen, and which he cannot quit.

To abdicate a disputed power would be sometimes a revenge, to abdicate an absolute power would be an act of cowardice.

The singular destiny of an emperor of Russia inspires me, first, with a lively emotion of curiosity, and afterwards with a feeling of pity. Who would not commiserate the state of this glorious exile? I cannot tell whether the Emperor Nicholas has received from God a heart susceptible of friendship, but I feel as though the desire of testifying a disinterested attachment to a man to whom society refuses equals, might take the place of ambition. The danger even, would give to such zeal the charm of enthusiasm. What! it will be said, attachment for a man who has nothing of humanity about him; whose severe physiognomy inspires a respect always mingled with fear, whose firm and fixed looks, in excluding familiarity, command obedience, and whose mouth, when it smiles, does not harmonize with the expression of the eyes; attachment for a man, in short, who never for a moment forgets to play his part as an absolute monarch!

And wherefore not? This want of harmony, this apparent harshness, is not a crime but a misfortune. I view in it a forced habit, not a natural character; and believing that I can see into this man, whom you calumniate as much by your fears and your precautions as your flatteries, I feel all that it must cost him to perform his duty as a sovereign, and I would not abandon so pitiable a deity of earth to the implacable envy and the hypocritical submission of his slaves. To find again the neighbor in the prince, to love him as a brother, would be a religious vocation and a work of charity that would gain the blessing of Heaven.

The more we see of the court, more especially of the court of Russia, the greater compassion must we feel for him who has to preside over it. It is a theater, on whose boards the actors pass their life in rehearsals. No one knows his part, and the day for the representation never arrives, because the manager is never satisfied with the proficiency of his corps. Actors and managers thus pass their life in preparing, correcting, and perfecting their interminable drama of society, the title of which is "The Civilization of the North." If it be so fatiguing to the audience, what must it be to the performers!

The emperor is, by extraction, more a German than a Russian. The fineness of his features, the regularity of his profile, his military figure, his bearing, naturally a little stiff, all remind one of Germany rather than of Muscovy. His teutonic temperament must have been long schooled and fettered ere he could have become, as he now is, a thorough Russian. Who knows?—he was perhaps born a plain, good-natured man! If so, what must he not have endured before he could appear only as the chieftain of the Slavs? The obligation of achieving a continual victory over himself in order to reign over others, will explain much in the character of the Emperor Nicholas.

Far from inspiring me with dislike, these things attract me. I cannot help viewing with interest one feared by the rest of the world, and who is, in reality, only so much the more to be commiserated.

To escape as much as possible from the constraint which he imposes on himself, he is as restless as a lion in a cage, or a patient in a fever; he is constantly moving on foot or on horseback; reviewing, carrying on a little war, sailing, maneuvering his fleet, giving and receiving fêtes. Leisure is that which is most dreaded at this court; whence I conclude that nowhere else is ennui so much felt. The emperor travels incessantly; he journeys over at least fifteen hundred leagues every season, and he has no notion that others have not the strength to do as he does. The empress loves him, and dreads leaving him; she therefore follows him as well as she can, and is dying of the fatigues and excitement consequent upon this life.

So complete an absence of quiet and regularity must be injurious to the education of their children. The young princes do not live sufficiently isolated to avoid the evil influences which the frivolity of a court always in motion, the absence of all interesting and connective conversation, and the impossibility of meditation, must exert upon their character. When I think of the distribution of their time, I have little hope even of the talents which they exhibit; I fear just as I would for the enduring beauty of a flower whose roots were not in their natural soil. Everything is founded on appearance in Russia; whence it is that everything inspires mistrust.

I was presented this evening, not by the French ambassador, but by the grand master of the ceremonies. Such was the order of the emperor, of which I was previously informed by our ambassador. I cannot tell whether this is the usual proceeding, but it was the manner in which I was presented to their Imperial Majesties.

All the foreigners admitted to the honor of approaching their persons were assembled together in one of the drawing rooms which they would have to cross in proceeding to open the ball. We arrived at the appointed hour, and had to wait a long time for the appearance of the illustrious personages.

There were with me two or three French, a Pole, a Genevese, and several Germans. The opposite side of the room was occupied by a row of Russian ladies, assembled there to pay their court.

The emperor received us with a refined and graceful politeness. At the first glance it was easy to recognize a man who, notwithstanding his power, is obliged and accustomed to humor the self-love of others.

In order to intimate to me that I might, without displeasing him, survey his empire, His Majesty did me the honor of saying that it was at least necessary to see Moscow and Nizhny before a just idea of the country could be formed. "Petersburg is Russian," he added, "but it is not Russia."

These few words were pronounced in a tone of voice that could not be forgotten, so strongly was it marked by authoritativeness and firmness. Everybody had spoken to me of the imposing manners, the noble features, and the commanding figure of the emperor, but no one had prepared me for the power of his voice: it is that of a man born to command. In it, there is neither effort nor study, it is a gift developed only by habitual use.

The empress, seen at close quarters, has a most winning expression of countenance, and the sound of her voice is as sweetly penetrating as that of the emperor's is naturally imperious.

She asked me if I came to Petersburg with the simple object of traveling. I replied in the affirmative. "I know that you are a curious observer," she continued.

"Yes, madame," I answered, "it is curiosity which brings me to Russia; and this time, at least, I think I shall not regret having yielded to a passion for travel."

"You really think so?" she replied, with a gracefulness of manner that was very charming.

"It appears to me that there are objects so wonderful in this country, that to believe them requires that we should see them with the eyes."

"I should wish you to see much, and to view favorably."

"This wish of Your Majesty's is an encouragement."

"If you think well of us you will say so, but it will be useless; you will not be believed: we are ill understood, and people will not understand us better."

These words, in the mouth of the empress, struck me, on account of the preoccupation of idea which they discovered. I fancied also that she meant to manifest a kind of benevolence towards me, which was expressed with a politeness and a simplicity that are rarely seen.

The empress, the moment she speaks, inspires confidence as well as respect. Through the reserve which the language and usages of court render compulsory, it is easy to see that she has a heart. This misfortune imparts to her an indescribable charm. She is more than an empress, she is a woman.

She appeared to be suffering from extreme fatigue. The thinness of her person is quite shocking. The agitation of the life she leads is consuming her, and they say that the ennui of a life more calm would be equally harmful.

The fête which followed our presentation was one of the

most magnificent that I have ever seen. The admiration and astonishment with which each reception room of this palace (rebuilt in a year) inspired the whole court, imparted a dramatic interest to the formal pomp of the usual ceremonies. Every hall and every painting was a subject of surprise to the Russians themselves, who now, for the first time, saw the marvelous abode which the word of their god had caused to spring from its ashes. What an effort of human will, I exclaimed, as I contemplated each gallery, sculpture, and painting. The style of the ornaments calls to mind the age in which the palace was originally founded, and what I saw appeared already ancient. They copy everything in Russia, not excepting even the effects of time. These wonders inspired the crowd with an admiration that was contagious, and my internal indignation at the means by which the miracle was created, began to diminish. If I could feel such an influence after only two days' abode here, what allowance should not be made for the men who are born, and who pass their life in the air of the Russian court, that is, in Russia! for it is the air of the court which is breathed from one end of the empire to the other. Even the serfs, through their relations with their lords, feel the influence of that sovereign will which alone animates the country; the courtier, who is their master, is for them the image of the Emperor, and the court is present to the Russians wherever there is a man to command and men to obey.

Elsewhere, the poor are either beggars, or unruly members of society; in Russia, they are all courtiers. The courtier is found in every rank of society, and for this reason it is that I say the court is everywhere. There is, between the sentiments of the Russian nobles and those of men of family in ancient Europe, the same difference that there is between the courtier and the aristocrat, or between emotions of vanity and of pride: true pride, which is almost as rare as virtue, is virtue. Instead of abusing courtiers, as Beaumarchais and so many others have done, these men, who, whatever may be said, are like other men, deserve pity. Poor unfortunate courtiers! they are not the monsters that our modern plays and romances, or our revolutionary journals, describe; they are merely weak creatures, corrupted and corrupting, as much as, but not more than others who are less exposed to temptation. Ennui is the curse of riches, still it is not a crime; vanity and interest are more strongly excited, and therefore more eagerly sought in a court than on any other stage of action, and these passions abridge life; but if the hearts they agitate are more tormented, they are not more perverse than those of other men. Human wisdom would accomplish much if it could succeed in showing to the multitude how much it ought to feel of pity, instead of envy, towards the possessors of a fancied good.

I saw them dancing in the very place where they had themselves nearly perished under blazing ruins, and where others had since actually died, in order that they might be amused on the day appointed by the emperor. This thought made me reflect in spite of myself, and shed (for me) a gloom over the entire fête. Elsewhere, liberty gives birth to a feeling of gladness which is favorable to illusion; here, despotism suggests meditations which make it impossible to deceive oneself.

The kind of dance that is most common at the grand fêtes of this country, does not disturb the course of ideas. The company promenade in a solemn step to the sound of music, each gentleman taking his partner by the hand. In the palace hundreds of couples thus follow in procession, proceeding from one immense hall to another, winding through the galleries, crossing the drawing rooms, and traversing the whole building in such order or direction as the caprice of the individual who leads may dictate. This is called dancing *la Polonaise*. It is amusing at first, but for those destined to dance it all their lives, balls must, I think, be a species of torture.

The polonaise at Petersburg recalled to my memory the Congress of Vienna, where I had danced it in 1814. No etiquette was observed in the European fêtes celebrated on that

occasion; everyone's place in the dance was regulated by
chance, though in the midst of all the monarchs of the earth.
My fate had placed me between the Emperor Alexander and
his consort, who was a princess of Baden. All at once the line
of the dancing couples was stopped without our perceiving
the reason, as the music continued playing. The emperor,
growing impatient, put his head over my shoulder, and addressing himself to the empress, told her, in a very rude tone,
to move on. The empress turned, and perceiving behind me
the emperor, with a lady as his partner for whom he had for
some days past betrayed a violent passion, she retorted with
an expression altogether indescribable, "Toujours poli!" The
autocrat bit his lips as he caught my eye, and the line of
dance again moved forward.

I was dazzled with the splendor of the great gallery; it
is now entirely gilded, though before the fire, it was only
painted white. That disaster has served to minister to the
taste which the emperor has for the magnificent.

What appeared to me more splendid even than the ballroom in the Winter Palace, was the gallery in which supper
was served. It is not entirely finished, and the lights in temporary paper transparencies had a fantastic appearance which
did not displease me. So unexpected an illumination in honor
of the marriage day, did not certainly correspond with the
general decorations of the magical palace, but it produced a
light clear as that of the sun, and this was enough for me.
One of the results of the progress of commercial economy is,
that we no longer see in France anything but tapers; there
seem to be yet in Russia real wax candles. The supper table
was splendid: at this fête everything was colossal, everything
was also innumerable of its kind; and I scarcely knew which
most to admire, the superb effect of the whole or the magnificence and the quantity of the objects considered separately. A
thousand persons were seated together at the table.

Among these thousand, all more or less blazing with gold

and diamonds, was the khan of the Kirgiz, whom I had seen at the chapel in the morning. I remarked also an old queen of Georgia, who had been dethroned thirty years previously. The poor woman languished unhonored, at the court of her conqueror. Her face was tanned like that of a man's used to the fatigues of the camp, and her attire was ridiculous. We are too ready to laugh at misfortune when it appears under a form that does not please us. We should wish to see a queen of Georgia rendered more beautiful by her distress; but I here saw just the contrary, and, when the eyes are displeased, the heart soon becomes unjust. It was not generous, but I confess I could not help smiling to see a royal head crowned with a kind of shako, from whence hung a very odd-looking veil. All the other ladies wore trains; but the queen of the East had on a short embroidered petticoat. There was much of the worn-out and wearied courtier in her expression, and her features were ugly. The national dress of the Russian ladies at court is antique and striking. They wear on the head a kind of tower, formed of rich stuff, and somewhat resembling in shape the crown of a man's hat, lowered in height and open at the top. This species of diadem is generally embroidered with jewels: it is very ancient, and imparts an air of nobleness and originality to handsome persons, while it singularly enhances the ugliness of plain ones. Unfortunately, these last are very numerous at the Russian court, whence people seldom retire, except to die, so attached are the aged courtiers to the posts which they there hold. In general, female beauty is rare at Petersburg; but among the higher classes, the charm of graceful manners often supplies the want of elegant forms and regular features. There are, however, a few Georgian women who unite the two advantages. These females shine amid the women of the North, like stars in the profound darkness of a southern night. The shape of the court robes, with their long sleeves and trains, gives to the whole person an Oriental aspect which, in a large assembly thus robed, has a very imposing effect.

An incident, singular enough in its character, has afforded me a specimen of the perfect politeness of the emperor.

During the ball, a master of the ceremonies had indicated to such of the foreigners as appeared for the first time at this court, the places that were reserved for them at the supper table. "When you see the ball interrupted," he said to each of us, "follow the crowd into the gallery, where you will find a large table laid out; take the side to the right, and seat yourselves in the first places you find unoccupied."

There was but one table, laid with one thousand plates, for the corps diplomatique, the foreigners, and all the attendants at court; but at the entrance of the hall, on the right-hand side, was a little round table laid for eight.

A Genevese, an intelligent and well-educated young man, had been presented the same evening in the uniform of a national guardsman, a dress which is in general anything but agreeable to the emperor; nevertheless, the young Swiss appeared perfectly at home. Whether it was owing to natural assurance, republican ease, or pure simplicity of heart, he seemed neither to think of the persons around him, nor of the effect that he might produce upon them. I envied his perfect self-confidence, which I was far from participating. Our manners, though very different, had the same success; the emperor treated us both equally well.

An experienced and intelligent person had recommended to me, in a tone half serious, half jocose, to maintain a respectful and rather timid air if I wished to please the monarch. The counsel was quite superfluous, for if I were to enter the hut of a coal miner, in order to make his acquaintance, I should experience some little degree of physical embarrassment, so naturally do I shrink from society. A man has never German blood without showing it; I possessed, therefore, naturally, the degree of timidity and reserve requisite to satisfy the jealous majesty of the czar, who would be as great as he wishes to appear, if he were less prepossessed with the notion that those who approach him are likely to fail in respect. This concern of the emperor does not, however, always operate; of which, and of the natural dignity of that prince, the following is an instance:—

The Genevese, far from partaking of my old-fashioned modesty, was perfectly at his ease. He is young, and has about him all the spirit of the age, mingled with a simplicity of his own; and I could not but admire his air of assurance each time the emperor addressed him.

The affability of the monarch was soon put by the young Swiss to a decisive proof. On passing into the banquet hall, the republican, turning towards the right, according to the instruction he had received, observed the little round table, and intrepidly seated himself before it, though there was no other person to keep him company. The moment after, the crowd of guests being placed, the emperor, followed by some officers who enjoyed his special confidence, advanced and took his seat at the same table at which was placed the worthy Swiss national guardsman. I should state that the empress was not at this table. The traveler remained in his chair with the imperturbable ease which I had already so much admired in him, and which, under the circumstances, was really miraculous.

A seat was wanting, for the emperor had not expected this ninth guest; but, with a politeness the completeness of which was equivalent to the delicacy of a kind heart, he spoke in a low voice to a servant, directing him to bring a chair and another plate, which was done without any noise or trouble.

Being placed at the extremity of the great table, close to that of the emperor's, this procedure could not escape my observation, nor, consequently, that of him who was its object. But this happily constituted young man, far from troubling himself because he perceived he had been placed contrary to the intention of the sovereign, maintained, with the most perfect sangfroid, a conversation with his two nearest neighbors, which lasted during the whole meal. I thought to myself, he has good sense; he wishes to avoid a *scene*: but, no doubt, he only waits the moment when the emperor rises, to approach him, and to offer some word of explanation. Nothing of the kind! When supper was over, the young Swiss, far from excusing himself, seemed to view the honor he had received as nothing more than was quite natural. On returning to his lodging, he would doubtless inscribe, with the most perfect simplicity, in his journal—"Supped with the emperor." However, His Majesty rather abridged the pleasure: rising, before the guests who sat at the great table, he passed round, behind our chairs, all the while desiring that we should remain seated. The hereditary grand duke accompanied his father; I observed that young prince stop behind the chair of a great English nobleman, the Marquis ———, and exchange some jest with young Lord ———, son of the same marquis. The foreigners remained seated, like everybody else, answered the prince and the emperor with their backs turned, and continued eating.

The above exhibition of English politeness shows that the emperor of Russia has greater simplicity of manners than have many of the owners of private houses.

I had scarcely expected to find at this ball a pleasure altogether foreign to the persons and objects around. I allude to the impressions which the great phenomena of nature have always produced in me. The temperature of the day had risen to 30 degrees, and notwithstanding the freshness of the evening, the atmosphere of the palace during the fête was suffocating. On rising from table, I took refuge in the embrasure of an open window. There, completely abstracted from all that passed around, I was suddenly struck with admiration at beholding one of those effects of light which we see only in the North, during the magic brightness of a polar night. It was half-past twelve o'clock, and the nights having yet scarcely begun to lengthen, the dawn of day appeared already in the direction of Archangel. The wind had fallen: numerous successive and regular belts of black and motionless clouds divided the firmament into zones, each of which was irradiated with a light so brilliant, that it appeared like a polished plate of silver; its luster was reflected on the Neva, to whose vast and unrippled surface it gave the appearance of a lake of milk or of mother-of-pearl. The greater part of Petersburg, with its quays and spires, was, under this light, revealed before my eyes; the whole formed a perfect composition of Brueghel's. The tints of the picture cannot be described by words. The domes of the church of St. Nicholas stood in the relief of lapis lazuli against a sky of silver; the illuminated portico of the Exchange, the lamps of which were partially quenched by the dawning day, still gleamed on the water of the river, and was reflected—a peristyle of gold: the rest of the city was of that blue which we see in the distances of landscapes by the old painters. This fantastic picture, painted on a ground of ultramarine, and framed by a gilded window, contrasted, in a manner that was altogether supernatural, with the light and splendor of the interior of the palace. It might have been said that the city, the sky, the sea, and the whole face of nature, had joined in contributing to the magnificence of the fête given to his daughter by the sovereign of these immense regions.

I was absorbed in the contemplation of the scene, when a sweet and penetrating female voice suddenly aroused me with the question—"What are you doing here?"

"Madame, I am indulging in admiration. I can do nothing else today."

It was the empress. She stood alone with me in the embrasure of the window, which was like a pavilion opening on the Neva.

"As for me, I am suffocating," replied Her Majesty. "It is less poetical, I admit; but you are right in admiring this picture; it is magnificent!" Continuing to contemplate it, she added—"I am certain that you and I are the only persons here who have remarked this effect of light."

"Everything that I see is new to me, madame; and I can never cease to regret that I did not come to Russia in my youth."

"The heart and the imagination are always young."

I ventured no answer; for the empress, as well as myself, had no longer any other youth but that of which she spake, and of this fact I did not wish to remind her; she would not have given me the time, nor, indeed, should I have had the boldness, to tell her how many indemnifications may be found to console us for the flight of years. On retiring, she said, with a grace which is her distinguishing attribute, "I shall recollect having suffered and admired with you": and she afterwards added, "I do not leave yet; we shall meet again this evening."

I am very intimate with a Polish family, which is that of the woman whom the empress loves best—the Baroness ———. This lady was brought up in Prussia with the daughter of the king, has followed that princess to Russia, and has never left her. She has married in Petersburg, where she has no other office but that of friend to the empress. Such constancy is honorable to both. The baroness must have been speaking well of me to the emperor and empress, and my natural timidity—a flattery so much the more refined as it is involuntary—has completed my good fortune.

On leaving the dining room to pass into the ballroom, I again approached a window. It opened into the interior court of the palace. A spectacle was there presented to me very different, but quite as unexpected as the former. The grand court of the Winter Palace is square, like that of the Louvre. During the ball, this enclosure had been gradually filling with people. The light of the dawning day had become more distinct; and in looking on the multitude, mute with admiration, motionless, fascinated, as it were, by the splendors of its master's palace, and drinking in, with a sort of timid, animal delight, the emanations of the royal festival, I experienced an impression of pleasure. At last, then, I had found a crowd in

Russia: I saw nothing below me but men: and so close was the press, that not an inch of earth could be discovered. Nevertheless, in despotic lands, the diversions of the people, when they approach those of the prince, always appear to me suspicious. The fear and flattery of the low, and the pride and hypocritical generosity of the great, are the only sentiments which I can believe to be genuine among men who live under the regime of the Russian autocracy.

In the midst of the fêtes of Petersburg, I cannot forget the journey of the Empress Catherine into the Crimea, and the façades of villages, made of planks or painted canvas, and set up, in the distance, at every quarter league of the route, in order to make the triumphant sovereign believe that the desert had become peopled under her reign. A spirit similar to that which dictated these illusions still possesses the minds of the Russians; everyone masks the evil, and obtrudes the good before the eyes of his Imperial master. There is a permanent conspiracy of smiles, plotting against the truth, in favor of the mental satisfaction of him who is reputed to will and to act for the good of all. The emperor is the only man in the empire who lives; for eating and drinking is not living.

It must be owned, however, that the people had come here voluntarily; nothing appeared to compel them to remain under the windows of the emperor: they were amusing themselves, therefore, but it was only with the pleasures of their masters, and, as Froissart says, *very sorrily*. The headdress of the women, and the Russian, that is to say the Persian, costume of the men in their long robes and brightly colored sashes, the variety of colors, and the immobility of each individual, created the illusion of an immense Turkish carpet, spread entirely over the court by the magician who presides here over every miracle:—a parterre of heads,—such was the most striking ornament of the palace of the emperor during the night of his daughter's nuptials. The monarch thought as I did, for he pointed out to the foreigners, with much complacency, the silent crowd, whose presence alone testified his participation in the happiness of its master. It was the vision of a people on their knees before the invisible gods. Their majesties are the divinities of this Elysium, where the inhabitants, trained to resignation, invent for themselves a felicity made up of privation and sacrifices.

I begin to perceive that I am here talking like the radicals in Paris. But, though a democrat in Russia, I am not the less in France an obstinate aristocrat: it is because a peasant in the environs of Paris is freer than a Russian lord, that I thus feel and write. We must travel before we can learn the extent to which the human mind is influenced by optical effects. This experience confirms the observation of Madame de Staël, who said, that in France, "One is always the Jacobin or the ultra of someone else."

I returned to my lodgings overwhelmed with the grandeur and magnificence of the emperor, and yet more astonished at seeing the disinterested admiration of his people for the good things which they do not possess, nor ever will, and which they do not dare even to regret. If I did not daily see to how many ambitious egotists liberty gives birth, I should have difficulty in believing that despotism could make so many disinterested philosophers.

LETTER 12

EXCITEMENT OF A PETERSBURG LIFE. — AFFABILITY OF THE
EMPRESS. — COMPARISON BETWEEN PARIS AND PETERSBURG. —
DEFINITION OF POLITENESS. — FÊTE AT THE MICHAEL PALACE. —
CONVERSATION WITH THE GRAND DUCHESS HELENA. — BEAUTIFUL
ILLUMINATION. — A GROVE IN A BALLROOM. — JET D'EAU. —
FUTURE PROSPECTS OF DEMOCRACY. — INTERESTING CONVERSATION
WITH THE EMPEROR. — RUSSIA EXPLAINED. — IMPROVEMENTS IN
THE KREMLIN. — AN ENGLISH NOBLEMAN AND HIS FAMILY. —
ENGLISH POLITENESS. — ANECDOTE IN NOTE. — THE GRAND
CHAMBERLAIN. — SEVERE REPRIMAND OF THE EMPEROR'S.

ONE OUGHT to be a Russian, or even the emperor himself,
to bear the fatigue of a life at Petersburg. In the evening there
are fêtes, such as are only seen in Russia; in the morning,
court ceremonies and receptions, public solemnities, or reviews upon sea or land. A vessel of one hundred twenty guns
has just been launched on the Neva before the whole court;
but, though the largest vessel that the river has ever borne, it
must not be supposed that there was any crowd at this naval
spectacle. Space is that which the Russians least want, and
through which they most suffer. The four or five hundred
thousand men who inhabit Petersburg, without peopling it,
are lost in the vast enclosure of the immense city, the heart
of which is composed of granite and brass, the body of plaster
and of mortar, and the extremities of painted wood and rotten
planks. These planks are raised in a solitary marsh like walls
around the city, which resembles a colossal statue with feet
of clay. It is like none of the other capitals of the civilized

179

world, even though, in its construction, all have been copied; but man in vain seeks for models in distant lands: the soil and the climate are his masters; they oblige him to create novelties, when he desires only to revive the antique.

I was present at the Congress of Vienna, but I do not recollect seeing anything to be compared to the richness of the jewels and dresses, the gorgeous variety of the uniforms, or the grandeur and admirable ordering of the whole spectacle, in the fête given by the emperor, on the evening of the marriage of his daughter, in this same Winter Palace—burnt down only a year ago.

Towards the end of the soirée given at court to celebrate the nuptials of the Grand Duchess Marie, the empress sent some officers to look for me, who searched for a quarter of an hour without being able to find me. I was standing apart, according to my frequent practice, still absorbed in contemplating the beauty of the heavens and admiring the night, against the same window where the empress had left me. Since supper, I had left this place only for an instant, to follow in the train of Their Majesties; but not having been observed, I returned into the gallery, where I could contemplate at leisure the romantic spectacle of the sun rising over a great city during a court ball. The officers at length discovered me in my hiding place, and hastened to lead me to the empress, who was waiting for me. She had the goodness to say before all the court, "M. de Custine, I have been inquiring for you for a long time; why did you avoid me?"

"Madame, I twice placed myself before Your Majesty, but you did not see me."

"It was your own fault, for I have been seeking for you ever since I entered the ballroom. I wish you to see everything here in detail, in order that you may carry from Russia an opinion which may rectify that of the foolish and the mischievously disposed."

"Madame, I am far from attributing to myself a power that

could effect this; but if my impressions were communicable, France would imagine Russia to be fairyland."

"You must not judge by appearances, you must look deeply into things, for you possess everything that can enable you to do this. Adieu! I only wished to say good evening;—the heat fatigues me. Do not forget to inspect my new apartments; they have been remodeled according to a plan of the emperor's. I will give orders for everything to be shown to you." On withdrawing, she left me the object of general curiosity, and of the apparent goodwill of the courtiers.

This court life is so new that it amuses me. It is like a journey in the olden times: I could imagine myself at Versailles a century ago. Politeness and magnificence are here natural. It will be seen by this how different Petersburg is from our Paris of the present day. At Paris there is luxury, riches, and even elegance; but there is neither grandeur nor courtesy. Ever since the first revolution, we have dwelt in a conquered country, where the spoilers and the spoiled consort together as well as they are able. In order to be polite, it is necessary to have something to give. Politeness is the art of doing to others the honors of the advantages we possess, whether of our minds, our riches, our rank, or our standing. To be polite, is to know how to offer and to accept with grace; but when a person has nothing certain of his own, he cannot give anything. In France at the present time, nothing is exchanged through mutual goodwill; everything is snatched by means of interest, ambition, or fear. Conversation even becomes insipid, when the secret calculations of interest cease to animate it. Mind itself is only valued, when it can be turned to personal account.

A fixed security of position in society is the basis of courtesy in all its relations, and the source also of those sallies of wit that enliven conversation.

Scarcely had we rested from the fatigues of the court ball, when we had to attend, in the Michael Palace, another fête given yesterday by the Grand Duchess Helena, sister-in-law of the emperor, wife of the Grand Duke Michael, and daughter of Prince Paul of Würtemberg, who lives at Paris. She is spoken of as one of the most distinguished personages in Europe, and her conversation is extremely interesting. I had the honor of being presented to her before the ball commenced, when she only addressed a word to me, but during the evening, she gave me several opportunities of talking with her.

The following is, as far as I recollect, the summary of what was said:—

"I hear that, in Paris and its neighborhood, you move in a very agreeable circle of society."

"It is true, madame, the conversation of persons of wit is my greatest pleasure, but I was far from venturing to suppose that your Imperial Highness would have been acquainted with this circumstance."

"We know Paris, and we are aware that there are there some few who are conversant with things as they now are, and who, at the same time, do not forget the past. These are, I doubt not, your friends. We admire, through their writings, several of the persons whom you see habitually, especially Madame Gay, and her daughter, Madame de Girardin."

"Those ladies are very clever and distinguished: I have the good fortune to be their friend."

"You possess in them friends of a superior character."

Nothing is so rare as to think ourselves obliged to feel modesty for others; it was, however, a sentiment which I, in a slight degree, experienced at this moment. It will be said that, of all modesty, this costs the least in its manifestation. However much it may be ridiculed, it is not the less true that I felt I should have wanted delicacy, had I endeavored to excite for my friends an admiration, by which my own vanity might have profited. At Paris, I should have said all that I thought; at Petersburg, I was afraid of seeming to magnify myself, under the pretense of doing justice to others. The grand duchess persisted, saying, "We take great pleasure in reading the works of Madame Gay. What do you think of them?"

"My opinion is, madame, that we may find in them a description of the society of former days written by one who understands it."

"Why does not Madame de Girardin continue to write?"

"Madame de Girardin is a poetess, madame, and in a writer of poetry, silence is the indication of labor."

"I hope that this is the cause of her silence; for, with her observing mind and poetical talent, it would be a pity that she should confine herself to the production of mere ephemeral works."

During this conversation, I made it a rule merely to listen and to reply; but I expected to hear the grand duchess pronounce other names which might flatter my patriotic pride, and put my friendly reserve to new trials.

These expectations were deceived. The grand duchess, who passes her life in a country where society is remarkable for its tact, undoubtedly knew better than myself what to speak of, and what to omit. Equally fearing the significance of my words, and of my silence, she did not utter another syllable on the subject of our contemporary literature.

There are certain names, whose sound alone would disturb the tranquillity of mind and the uniformity of thought, despotically imposed upon all who will live at the Russian court.

I must now describe some of the magic fêtes at which I am present every evening. With us the balls are disfigured by the somber attire of the men, whereas the varied and brilliant uniforms of the Russian officers give an extreme brilliancy to the reception rooms of Petersburg.

In Russia, the magnificence of the women's apparel is found to accord with the gold of the military dress; and the male dancers have not the appearance of being the clerks of attorneys, or the shopmen of their partners' apothecaries.

The whole length of the garden front of the Michael Palace is ornamented by an Italian colonnade. Yesterday, they availed themselves of a temperature of 26 degrees to illuminate the spaces betwixt each pillar of this exterior gallery with clusters of small lamps, arranged in a manner that had a very original effect. The lamps were formed of paper in the shape of tulips, lyres, vases, &c. Their appearance was both tasteful and novel.

At each fête given by the Grand Duchess Helena, it is said that she invents something altogether new. Such a reputation must be troublesome, for it is difficult to maintain. This princess, so beautiful and so quick, and so celebrated throughout Europe for the grace of her manners and the charms of her conversation, struck me as being less natural and easy than the other females of the Imperial family. Celebrity as a woman of wit and high intellectual attainment, must be a heavy burden in a royal court. She is an elegant and distinguished-looking person, but has the air of suffering from weariness and lassitude. Perhaps she would have been happier had she possessed good sense, less wit, no education, and had continued a German princess, confined to the monotonous life of a petty sovereignty.

Her obligation of doing the honors of French literature at the court of the Emperor Nicholas, makes me afraid for the Grand Duchess Helena.

The light that proceeded from the groups of lamps was reflected in a picturesque manner upon the pillars of the palace, and among the trees of the garden. The latter was full of people. In the fêtes at Petersburg, the people serve as an ornament, just as a collection of rare plants adorns a hothouse. Delightful sounds were heard in the distance, where several orchestras were executing military symphonies, and responding to each other with a harmony that was admirable. The light reflected on the trees had a charming effect. Nothing is more fantastically beautiful than the golden verdure of foliage illuminated during a fine night.

The interior of the grand gallery in which they danced was arranged with a marvelous luxury. Fifteen hundred boxes of the rarest plants, in flower, formed a grove of fragrant verdure. At one of the extremities of the hall, amid thickets of exotic shrubs, a fountain threw up a column of fresh and sparkling water: its spray, illumined by the innumerable wax lights, shone like the dust of diamonds, and refreshed the air, always kept in agitation by the movement of the dance. It might have been supposed that these strange plants, including large palms and bananas, all of whose boxes were concealed under a carpet of mossy verdure, grew in their native earth, and that the groups of northern dancers had been transported by enchantment to the forests of the tropics. It was like a dream; there was not merely luxury in the scene, there was poetry. The brilliancy of the magic gallery was multiplied a hundredfold by a greater profusion of enormous and richly gilded mirrors than I had ever elsewhere seen. The windows ranged under the colonnade were left open on account of the excessive heat of the summer night. The hall was lofty, and extended the length of half the palace. The effect of all this magnificence may be better imagined than described. It seemed like the palace of the fairies: all ideas of limits disappeared, and nothing met the eye but space, light, gold, flowers, reflection, illusion, and the giddy movement of the crowd, which crowd itself seemed multiplied to infinity. Every actor in the scene was equal to ten, so greatly did the mirrors aid the effect. I have never seen anything more beautiful than this crystal palace; but the ball was like other balls, and did not answer to the gorgeous decorations of the edifice. I was surprised that such a nation of dancers did not devise something new to perform on the boards of a theater so different from all others, where people meet to dance and to fatigue themselves, under the pretext of enjoyment. I should like to have seen the quadrilles and the ballets of other theaters. It strikes me that in the Middle Ages, the gratifications of the imagination had a greater influence in the diversions of courts than they have at present. In the Michael Palace the only dances that I saw were the polonaises, the waltz, and the degenerated country dances called quadrilles in the Franco-Russian language. Even the mazurkas at Petersburg are less lively and graceful than the real dances of Warsaw. Russian gravity cannot accommodate itself to the vivacity, the whim, and the *abandon* of the true Polish dances.

Under the perfumed groves of the ballroom, the empress rested at the conclusion of every polonaise. She found there a shelter from the heat of the illuminated garden, the air of which, during this summer night, was as stifling as that of the interior of the palace.

I found leisure during the fête to draw a comparison in my own mind between France and Russia, on a subject regarding which my observations were not in favor of the former. Democracy cannot but be uncongenial to the ordering of a grand assembly. The one which I beheld in the Michael Palace was embellished with all the care and all the tokens of homage of which a sovereign could be the object. A queen is always indispensable to elegant pleasures. But the principles of equality have so many other advantages, that we may well sacrifice to them the luxuries of pleasure. It is this which we do in France with a disinterestedness that is meritorious; my only fear is lest our great-grandchildren may have different views when the time shall have arrived to enjoy the perfections prepared for them by their too generous ancestors. Who knows if these undeceived generations will not say, when speaking of ourselves, "Seduced by a sophistical eloquence, they became vague, unmeaning fanatics, and have entailed on us absolute misery"?

To return from the contemplation of the future which

America is promising to Europe:—before the banquet the empress, seated under her canopy of exotic verdure, made me a sign to approach her; and scarcely had I obeyed, when the emperor also came to the magic fountain, where a shower of diamonds was giving us both light and a freshened atmosphere. He took me by the hand, and led me some steps from the chair of his consort, where he was pleased to converse with me for more than a quarter of an hour on subjects of interest; for this prince does not, like many other princes, speak to you merely that it may be seen he does so.

He first said a few words on the admirable arrangements of the fête; and I remarked, in reply, that, in a life so active as his, I was astonished that he could find time for everything, including even a participation in the pleasures of the crowd.

"Happily," he replied, "the machine of government is very simple in my country; for, with distances which render everything difficult, if the form of government was complicated, the head of one man would not suffice for its requirements."

I was surprised and flattered by this tone of frankness. The emperor, who understands better than any one that which is felt, though not expressed, proceeded,—replying to my thought,—"If I speak to you in this manner, it is because I know that you can understand me: we are continuing the labors of Peter the Great."

"He is not dead, sire; his genius and his will still govern Russia."

When anyone speaks in public with the emperor, a large circle of courtiers gathers at a respectful distance, from whence no one can overhear the sovereign's conversation, though all eyes continue fixed upon him.

It is not the prince who is likely to embarrass you when he does you the honor of conversing: it is his suite.

The emperor continued:—"We do not find it very easy to execute this work: submission may cause you to believe that there is uniformity among us, but I must undeceive you; there is no other country where is found such diversity of races, of manners, of religion, and of mind, as in Russia. The diversity lies at the bottom, the uniformity appears on the surface, and the unity is only apparent. You see near us twenty officers, the two first only are Russians; the three next to them are conciliated Poles; several of the others are Germans; there are even the khans of the Kirgiz, who bring me their sons to educate among my cadets. There is one of them," he said, pointing with his finger to a little Chinese monkey, in a whimsical costume of velvet all bedizened with gold.

"Two hundred thousand children are brought up and instructed at my cost with that child."

"Sire, everything is done on a large scale in this country—everything is colossal."

"Too colossal for one man."

"What man has ever stood in nearer relation to his people?"

"You speak of Peter the Great?"

"No, sire."

"I hope that you will not be content with merely seeing Petersburg. What is your plan of route in visiting my country?"

"Sire, I wish to leave immediately after the fête of Peterhof."

"To go—"

"To Moscow and Nizhny."

"Good: but you will be there too soon: you will leave Moscow before my arrival, and I should have been glad to see you there."

"This observation of Your Majesty's will cause me to change my plan."

"So much the better; we will show you the new works that we are making at the Kremlin. My object is to render the architecture of those old edifices better adapted to the uses now made of them. The palace was inconveniently small for me. You will be present also at a curious ceremony on the plain of Borodino: I am to place there the first stone of a monument which we are about to erect in commemoration of that battle."

I remained silent, and no doubt the expression of my face became serious. The emperor fixed his eyes on me, and then continued, in a tone of kindness, and with a delicacy and even sensibility of manner which touched my heart,—"The inspection of the maneuvers *at least* will interest you."

"Sire, everything interests me in Russia."

I saw the old Marquis ———, who has only one leg, dance the polonaise with the empress. Lame as he is, he can get through this dance, which is nothing more than a solemn procession. He has arrived here with his sons: they travel like real great lords; a yacht brought them from London to Petersburg, whither they have had forwarded English horses and carriages in great number. Their equipages are the most elegant, if they are not the most sumptuous, in Petersburg. These travelers are treated with marked attention. They are intimate with the Imperial family. The emperor's love of field sports, and the recollection of his journey to London when grand duke, have established between him and the Marquis ——— that kind of familiarity which, it appears to me, must be more pleasant to the princes who confer, than to the private individuals who have become the objects of such favor. Where friendship is impossible, intimacy I should think can be only constraining. One would have said, to have sometimes seen the manners of the marquis's sons towards the members of the Imperial family, that they thought on this subject as I did. If freedom of manners and speech should gain a footing at court, where will falsehood and politeness find a refuge?

In connection with the marriage fêtes given in honor of

the Grand Duchess Marie, a little incident occurred which will remind the reader of what often happened at the court of the Emperor Napoleon.

The grand chamberlain had died shortly before the marriage, and his office had been given to Count Golovkin, formerly Russian ambassador to China, to which country he could not obtain access. This nobleman, entering upon the functions of his office on the occasion of the marriage, had less experience than his predecessor. A young chamberlain, appointed by him, managed to incur the wrath of the emperor, and exposed his superior to a rather severe reprimand: it was at the ball of the Grand Duchess Helena.

The emperor was talking with the Austrian ambassador. The chamberlain received from the Grand Duchess Marie an order to carry her invitation to this ambassador to dance with her. In his zeal, the unfortunate débutant broke the circle of courtiers which I have before described as forming at a respectful distance around the emperor, and boldly approached His Majesty's person, saying to the ambassador, "Monsieur le Comte, Madame la Duchesse de Leuchtenberg requests that you will dance with her the first polonaise."

The emperor, shocked with the ignorance of the new chamberlain, addressed him, in a loud tone of voice, saying, "You have been appointed to a post, sir; learn, therefore, how to fulfill its duties; in the first place, my daughter is not the Duchess of Leuchtenberg,—she is called the Grand Duchess Marie; in the second place, you ought to know that no one interrupts me when I am talking."

The new chamberlain who received this harsh reprimand was, unfortunately, a poor Polish gentleman. The emperor, not content with what he had said, caused the grand chamberlain to be called, and recommended him to be, in future, more circumspect in his selection of deputies.

I left the ball of the Michael Palace at an early hour. I loitered on the staircase, and could have wished to remain there longer: it was a wood of orange trees in flower. Never have I seen anything more magnificent or better directed than this fête; but there is nothing so fatiguing as admiration too greatly prolonged, especially if it does not relate to the phenomena of nature, or the works of the higher arts.

I lay down my pen in order to dine with a Russian officer, the young Count ———, who took me this morning to the Cabinet of Mineralogy, the finest I believe in Europe, for the Ural mines are unequaled in the variety of their mineral wealth. Nothing can be seen here alone. A native of the country is always with you, to do the honors of the public establishments and institutions, and there are not many days in the year favorable for seeing them. In summer, they are repairing the edifices damaged by the frosts; in winter, there is nothing but receptions: everyone dances who does not freeze. It will be thought I am exaggerating when I say that Russia is scarcely better seen in Petersburg than in France. Strip the observation of its paradoxical form, and it is strictly true. Most assuredly, it is not sufficient to visit this country in order to know it. Without the aid of others, it is not possible to obtain an idea of anything, and often, this aid tyrannizes over its object, and imbues him with ideas only that are fallacious.

LETTER 13

THE LADIES OF THE COURT. — THE FINNS. — THE OPERA. —
THE EMPEROR THERE. — IMPOSING PERSON OF THAT PRINCE. —
HIS ACCESSION TO THE THRONE. — COURAGE OF THE EMPRESS.
— THE EMPEROR'S RECITAL OF THIS SCENE TO THE AUTHOR. —
ANOTHER DESCRIPTION OF THE EMPEROR. — CONTINUATION OF
HIS CONVERSATION. — HIS POLITICAL OPINIONS. — SINCERITY
OF HIS LANGUAGE. — FÊTE AT THE DUCHESS OF OLDENBURG'S. —
BAL CHAMPÊTRE. — FLOWERS IN RUSSIA. — THE FRIEND OF THE
EMPRESS. — SEVERAL CONVERSATIONS WITH THE EMPEROR. — HIS
NOBLE SENTIMENTS. — CONFIDENCE WITH WHICH HE INSPIRES
THOSE WHO APPROACH HIM. — ARISTOCRACY THE ONLY RAMPART
OF LIBERTY. — PARALLEL BETWEEN AUTOCRACIES AND DEMOCRACIES.

SEVERAL of the ladies of this court, but their number is not great, have a reputation for beauty which is deserved; others have usurped that reputation by means of coquetries, contrivances, and affectations—all copied from the English; for the Russians in high life pass their time in searching for foreign models of fashion. They are sometimes deceived in their choice, when their mistake produces a singular kind of elegance—an elegance without taste. A Russian left to himself would spend his life in dreams of unsatisfied vanity: he would view himself as a barbarian. Nothing injures more the natural disposition, and consequently the mental powers of a people, than this continual dwelling upon the social superiority of other nations. To feel humbled by the very sense of one's own assumption is an inconsistency in the actings of self-love which is not unfrequently to be seen in Russia, where the character of the parvenu may be studied under all its grades and phases.

As a general rule applicable to the different classes of the nation, beauty is less common among the women than the men; though among the latter also may be found great numbers whose faces are flat and void of all expression. The Finns have high cheekbones, small, dull, sunken eyes, and visages so flattened that it might be fancied they had all, at their birth, fallen on their noses. Their mouth is also deformed, and their whole appearance bears the impress of the slave. This portrait does not apply to the Slavs.

I have met many people marked with the smallpox, a sight rarely now seen in other parts of Europe, and which betrays the negligence of the Russian administration on an important point.

In Petersburg, the different races are so mingled, that it is impossible to form a correct idea of the real population of Russia. Germans, Swedes, Livonians, Finns (who are a species of Laplanders), Kalmyks, and other Tartar races, have so mixed their blood with that of the Slavs, that the primitive beauty of the latter has, in the capital, gradually degenerated; which leads me often to think of the observation of the emperor, "Petersburg is Russian, but it is not Russia."

I have been witnessing at the opera what is called a *gala* performance. The building was magnificently lighted: it is large, and well proportioned. Galleries and projecting boxes are unknown here: there is in Petersburg no middle class for whom to provide seats. The architect, therefore, unfettered in his plan, can construct theaters of a simple and regular design, like those of Italy, where the women who are not of the highest ranks are seated in the orchestra.

By special favor I obtained a seat in the first row of the orchestra. On gala days these chairs are reserved for the greatest nobles and the high court functionaries, and none are admitted to them except in the uniform or costume of their rank or office.

My right-hand neighbor, seeing from my dress that I was a stranger, accosted me in French, with that hospitable politeness, which in Petersburg is a characteristic of the higher, and, to a certain extent, of all classes; for here everyone is polite—the great, through the vanity of showing their good breeding, the little, through sentiments of fear.

After a few commonplace observations, I asked my obliging neighbor the name of the piece that was to be performed. "It is a translation from the French," he answered: "The Devil on Two Sticks." I puzzled my head to no purpose to make out what drama could have been translated under this title; at length it turned out that the *translation* was a pantomime founded on our ballet of the same name.

I did not much admire it, and directed my attention chiefly to the audience. At length, the court arrived. The Imperial box is an elegant salon, which occupies the back part of the theater, and which is even yet more brilliantly illuminated.

The entrance of the emperor was imposing. As he advanced to the front of his box, accompanied by the empress, and followed by their family and the attendant courtiers, the public rose simultaneously. His Majesty was dressed in a singularly splendid red uniform. That of the Cossacks looks well only on very young men: the one which the emperor wore better suited his age, and greatly set off the nobleness of his features and his stature. Before seating himself, he saluted the assembly with the peculiarly polite dignity by which he is characterized. The empress did the same, and, which appeared to me an assumption that was tantamount to a want of respect towards the public, their suite followed their example. The whole theater rendered to the sovereigns bow for bow, and, furthermore, overwhelmed them with plaudits and *hurrahs*. These demonstrations had an official character which greatly diminished their value. Wonderful, that an emperor should be applauded by a pit full of courtiers! In Russia, real flattery would be the appearance of independence. The Russians have not found out this indirect mode of pleasing; and, in truth, its use might sometimes become perilous, notwithstanding the feeling of ennui which the servility of his subjects must often produce in the prince.

The compulsory manifestations of submission with which he is everywhere received is the reason why the present emperor has only twice in his life had the satisfaction of testing his personal power upon the assembled multitude—and this was during an insurrection! The only free man in Russia is the revolted soldier.

Viewed from the point where I sat, the emperor appeared truly worthy of commanding men, so noble was his face, and so majestic his figure. My mind involuntarily recurred to the period when he mounted the throne, and the contemplation of that bright page of history led my thoughts away from the scene that was enacting before me.

What I am now about to narrate was detailed to me by the emperor himself, only a few days ago. The reason that it was not stated in the last chapter is because the papers* containing such details could not be confided either to the Russian post or to any traveler.

The day on which Nicholas ascended the throne was that in which rebellion broke out among the guards. At the first intimation of the revolt of the troops, the emperor and empress proceeded alone to their chapel, and, falling on their knees, on the steps of the altar, bound each other by mutual oath before God, to die as sovereigns, if they should be unable to triumph over the insurrection.

The emperor might well view the evil as serious, for he had been informed that the archbishop had already vainly

*Dispatched in the form of a letter to Paris.—*Trans.*

endeavored to appease the soldiers. In Russia, when religious power loses its influence, disorder is indeed formidable.

After solemnly making the sign of the cross, the emperor proceeded to confront the rebels, and to master them by his presence, and by the calm energy of his countenance. He stated this to me in terms more modest than those which I now use, and of which, unfortunately, I have not preserved the recollection, for at first I was rather taken by surprise, owing to the unexpected turn of the conversation. Of what passed after recovering from this surprise my memory is more trustworthy.

"Sire, Your Majesty drew your strength from the right source."

"I did not know what I was about to do or say—I was inspired."

"To receive such inspirations, it is necessary to merit them."

"I did nothing extraordinary: I said to the soldiers, 'Return to your ranks!' and, at the moment of passing the regiment in review, I cried, 'On your knees!' They all obeyed. What gave me power was, that the instant before I had made up my mind to perish or conquer. I am grateful for having succeeded; but I am not proud of it, for it was by no merit of my own."

Such were the noble expressions which the emperor made use of in relating to me this contemporary tragedy.

From the above relation, an idea may be formed of the interesting nature of the subjects on which he converses with the travelers whom he honors with his goodwill. It will also explain the character of the influence he exercises over ourselves, as well as over his people and his family. He is the Louis XIV of the Slavs.

Eyewitnesses have informed me that his form seemed to dilate and grow more lofty and commanding at each step that he made in advancing towards the mutineers. Taciturn, melancholy, and absorbed in trifles as he had appeared during his youth, he became a hero the moment he was a monarch. The contrary is usually the case; and princes promise more than they perform.

This prince is, on the throne, as perfectly in his proper sphere as a great actor would be on the boards. His attitude before the rebel guards was so imposing, that, while he harangued the troops, one of the conspirators, it is said, advanced four times towards him with the intention of killing him, and four times his courage failed, like the Cimbrian's before Marius.

An absurd falsehood was the instrument that the conspirators had employed to incite the army to this outbreak. They had spread a report that Nicholas had usurped the crown of his brother Constantine, who was, they said, on his way to Petersburg, to defend his rights by force of arms. The means through which they had induced the rebels to cry under the palace windows in favor of the constitution, was by persuading them that this word *constitution* was the name of the wife of Constantine. It was, therefore, an idea of duty which actuated the soldiers, who believed the emperor an usurper, and who could only be led into rebellion by a fraud. The fact is, that Constantine had refused the crown through weakness: he dreaded being poisoned. God knows, and there are perhaps some men who know also, if his abdication saved him from the peril which he thus expected to avoid.

It was, then, in support of legitimacy, that the deceived soldiers revolted against their legitimate sovereign. People remarked that, during the whole time the emperor remained among the troops, he did not once put his horse in rapid motion; but, though so calm, he was very pale. He was putting his power to the test, and the success of the proof assured him of the future obedience of his people.

Such a man cannot be judged by the standard applied to ordinary characters. His grave and authoritative voice, his magnetic and piercing look,—which is often cold and fixed rather through the habit of suppressing his passions than of dissimulating his thoughts, for he is frank,—his superb forehead, his features, which are those of an Apollo or a Jupiter, his immovable, imposing, and imperious expression, his figure, more noble than easy, more monumental than human, exercise upon all who approach his person a power which is irresistible. He becomes master of the wills of others, because it is seen that he is master of his own.

The following is what I have retained of the remainder of our conversation:—

"The insurrection thus appeased, Your Majesty must have entered the palace with feelings very different to those under which it was left; not only the throne, but the admiration of the world, and the sympathy of all lofty minds being, by this event, assured to Your Majesty."

"I did not thus view it: what I then did has been too much praised."

The emperor did not tell me that on his return, he found his wife afflicted with a nervous trembling of the head, of which she has never been entirely cured. The convulsive motion is scarcely visible; indeed, on some days, when calm and in good health, the empress is entirely free from it: but whenever she is suffering, either mentally or physically, the evil returns and augments. This noble woman must have fearfully struggled with the inquietude occasioned by her husband's daring exposure of his person to the assassin's blow. On his return, she embraced him without speaking; but the emperor, after having soothed her, felt himself grow weak, and threw himself into the arms of one of his most faithful servants, exclaiming,—"What a beginning of a reign!"

I publish these details, because it is well they should be known, in order to teach the obscure to envy less the fortune of the great.

Whatever apparent inequality legislation may have established in the different conditions of civilized men, the equity of Providence justifies itself by maintaining a secret equality, which nothing can alter or disturb. This is done by the agency of mental evils, which generally increase in the same ratio that physical evils diminish. There is less injustice in the world than the founders and legislators of nations have endeavored to produce, or than the vulgar imagine they perceive: the laws of nature are more equitable than the laws of man.

These reflections passed rapidly through my mind as I conversed with the emperor, producing in me a sentiment which he would, I believe, have been rather surprised to learn that he had inspired,—it was that of indescribable pity. I took care to conceal the emotion, and continued:—

"I can truly say, sire, that one of the chief motives of my curiosity in visiting Russia was the desire of approaching a prince who exercises such power over men."

"The Russians are good; but he must render himself worthy who would govern such a people."

"Your Majesty has better appreciated the wants and the position of this country than any of your predecessors."

"Despotism still exists in Russia: it is the essence of my government, but it accords with the genius of the nation."

"Sire, by stopping Russia on the road of imitation, you are restoring her to herself."

"I love my country, and I believe I understand it. I assure you, that when I feel heartily weary of all the miseries of the times, I endeavor to forget the rest of Europe by retiring towards the interior of Russia."

"In order to refresh yourself at your fountainhead?"

"Precisely so. No one is more from his heart a Russian than I am. I am going to say to you what I would not say to another, but I feel that you will understand me."

Here the emperor interrupted himself, and looked at me attentively. I continued to listen without replying, and he proceeded:—

"I can understand republicanism: it is a plain and straightforward form of government, or, at least, it might be so; I can understand absolute monarchy, for I am myself the head of such an order of things; but I cannot understand a representative monarchy; it is the government of lies, fraud, and corruption; and I would rather fall back even upon China than ever adopt it."

"Sire, I have always regarded representative government as a transaction inevitable in certain communities at certain epochs; but like all other transactions, it does not solve questions,—it only adjourns difficulties."

The emperor seemed to say, Go on. I continued:—

"It is a truce signed between democracy and monarchy, under the auspices of two very mean tyrants, fear and interest; and it is prolonged by that pride of intellect which takes pleasure in talking, and that popular vanity which satisfies itself on words. In short, it is the aristocracy of oratory, substituted for the aristocracy of birth; it is the government of the lawyers."

"Sir, you speak the truth," said the emperor, pressing my hand: "I have been a representative sovereign,* and the world knows what it has cost me to have been unwilling to submit to the exigences of *this infamous* government (I quote literally). To buy votes, to corrupt consciences, to seduce some in order to deceive others; all these means I disdained, as degrading those who obey as much as those who command, and I have dearly paid the penalty of my straightforwardness; but, God be praised, I have done forever with this detestable political machine. I shall never more be a constitutional king. I have too much need of saying all that I think ever to consent to reign over any people by means of stratagem and intrigue."

The name of Poland, which presented itself incessantly to our thoughts, was not once uttered in this singular conversation.

---

*In Poland.

The effect it produced on me was great. I felt myself subdued. The nobleness of sentiment which the emperor displayed, and the frankness of his language, seemed to me greatly to temper his omnipotence.

I confess I was dazzled! A man who could, notwithstanding my ideas of independence, make himself forgiven for being absolute monarch of sixty millions of fellow-beings, was, in my eyes, something beyond our common nature; but I distrusted my own admiration. I felt like the bourgeois among us, who, when surprised by the grace and address of the men of other days, are tempted by their good taste to yield to the captivating lure, but their principles resisting, they remain uncomfortably stiff, and endeavor to appear as insensible as possible. It is not in my nature to doubt a man's words at the moment they are addressed to me. A human being who speaks is, to me, the organ of God: it is only by dint of reflection and experience that I recognize the possibility of design and disguise. This may be called a foolish simplicity, which perhaps it is; but I solace myself for such mental weakness by the recollection that its source is a mental virtue: my own good faith makes me believe in the sincerity of others, even in that of an emperor of Russia.

The beauty of his face is also another instrument of persuasion; for this beauty is moral as well as physical. I attribute its effect to the truth of his sentiments, yet more than to the regularity of his features. It was at a ball at the Duchess of Oldenburg's that I had this interesting conversation with the emperor. The fête was singular, and deserves describing.

The Duchess of Oldenburg, who was a princess of Nassau, is nearly allied, through her husband, to the emperor. She wished to give a soirée on the occasion of the marriage of the grand duchess, but being unable to excel the magnificence of the former fêtes, or to vie with the splendors of the court, she conceived the idea of a *bal champêtre* at her house in the Islands.

The archduke of Austria, who arrived two days ago, to be present at the festivities of Petersburg; the ambassadors of the whole world (singular actors in a pastoral); all Russia, and finally, all the highborn foreigners, gathered together to promenade with an air of innocent simplicity, in a garden where orchestras were concealed among the distant groves.

The emperor prescribes the character of each fête: the direction for this day was, "the elegant simplicity of Horace."

The humor of all minds, including even the corps diplomatique, was throughout the evening modeled in conformity with this order. It was like reading an eclogue, not of Theocritus or Virgil, but of Fontenelle.

We danced in the open air until eleven in the evening, and then, the heavy dews having sufficiently inundated the heads and shoulders of the women, young and old, who assisted at this triumph over the climate, we re-entered the little palace which forms the usual summer residence of the Duchess of Oldenburg.

In the center of the villa* was a rotunda, quite dazzling with gold and wax lights, in which the dancers continued their amusement, while the others wandered over the rest of the house, to which this bright rotunda formed, as it were, a central sun.

There presided throughout the fête, which was smaller than the preceding ones, a species of splendid disorder that struck me more than the pomp of all the others. Without speaking of the comical constraint depicted on the countenances of certain parties who were obliged, for a time, to affect rural simplicity, it was a soirée altogether original, a species of Imperial Tivoli, where people felt themselves almost free, although in presence of an absolute master. The sovereign who enjoys himself seems no longer a despot, and this evening the emperor enjoyed himself.

---

*In Russian, "the dacha."

The excessive heats of the present summer had fortunately favored the design of the duchess. Her summerhouse is situated in the most beautiful part of the Islands, and it was in the midst of a garden radiant with flowers in pots, and upon an English lawn,—another marvel here,—that she had fixed her dancing room. This was a superb inlaid flooring, surrounded by elegant balustrades, richly embellished with flowers, and to which the sky served as ceiling. In Petersburg, the luxury of rare flowers, reared in the hothouse, supplies the place of trees. Its inhabitants—men who have left Asia to imprison themselves among the snows of the North—recollect the Oriental luxury of their earlier country, and do their best to supply the sterility of Nature, which, left to herself, produces only pine and birch trees. Art raises here an infinite variety of shrubs and plants; for as everything is artificial, it is just as easy to grow the exotic flowers of America as the violets and lilacs of France.

The empress, delicate as she is, danced, with her neck bare and her head uncovered, every polonaise at this magnificent ball in the garden of her cousin. In Russia, everybody pursues his career to the limits of his powers. The duty of an empress is to amuse herself to death.

This German princess, the victim of a frivolity which must surely press as heavily as chains upon captives, enjoys in Russia a happiness rarely enjoyed in any land, or in any rank, and unexampled in the life of an empress,—she has a friend. Of this lady, the Baroness de ——, I have already spoken. She and the empress, since the marriage of the latter, have scarcely ever been separated. The baroness, whose character is sincere, and whose heart is devoted, has not profited by her position. The man whom she has married is one of the military officers to whom the emperor is most indebted; for the Baron de —— saved his life on the day of the revolt that attended the accession to the throne, by exposing his own with a devotedness unprompted by interest. Nothing could

Astolphe de Custine

be sufficient reward for such an act of courage; it has, consequently, gone unrewarded.

As the garden became dark, a distant music answered to the orchestra of the ball, and harmoniously chased away the gloom of the night, a gloom too natural to these monotonous shades. The desert recommences on the Islands, where the pines and morasses of Finland adjoin the prettiest parks. An arm of the Neva flows slowly—for here all water appears stagnant—before the windows of the little princely house of the Duchess of Oldenburg. On this evening, the water was covered with boats full of spectators, and the road also swarmed with pedestrians. A mixed crowd of middle-class men, who are as much slaves as the peasants, and of work-people, all courtiers of courtiers, pressed among the carriages of the grandees to gaze on the livery of the master of their masters. The whole spectacle was striking and original. In Russia the names are the same as elsewhere, but the things are altogether different. I often escaped from the throng of the ball to walk beneath the trees of the park, and muse on the melancholy that insinuates itself into the entertainments of such a land. But my meditations were short, for on this day the emperor seemed as though determined to keep possession of my thoughts. Was it because he had discovered in the bottom of my heart some prejudices little favorable towards him, though the result only of what I had heard before being presented; or did he find it amusing to converse for a few moments with one who differed from those who daily came in his way; or was it that Madame de ―――― had created an influence in his mind in my favor? I could not explain to my own satisfaction the cause of receiving so much honor.

The emperor is not only accustomed to command actions, he knows how to reign over hearts: perhaps he wished to conquer mine; perhaps the ices of my shyness served to stimulate his self-love. The desire of pleasing is natural to him: to compel admiration would still be to make himself obeyed.

204

Perhaps he had a desire of trying his power on a stranger; perhaps, in short, it was the instinct of a man who had long lived deprived of the truth, and who believed he had for once met with a sincere character. I repeat, I was ignorant of his motives; but on that evening I could not stand before him, nor even place myself in a retired corner of the room where he might be, without his obliging me to approach and talk with him.

On seeing me enter the ballroom, he said, "What have you seen this morning?"

"Sire, I have been visiting the Cabinet of Natural History, and the famous Mammoth of Siberia."

"It is an object unequaled, in its kind, in the world."

"Yes, sire; there are many things in Russia that are not to be seen elsewhere."

"You flatter me."

"I respect Your Majesty too much to dare to flatter; but perhaps, sire, I do not fear you sufficiently; and I therefore ingenuously speak my thoughts, when even truth appears like compliment."

"This is a delicate compliment, monsieur: you strangers spoil us."

"Sire, Your Majesty was pleased to desire that I should be at my ease with you, and you have succeeded, as in everything else that you undertake. Your Majesty has cured me, for a time at least, of my natural timidity."

Obliged to avoid all allusion to the great political interests of the day, I wished to lead the conversation towards a subject which interested me quite as much; I added, therefore, "Each time that I am permitted to approach Your Majesty, I recognize the power which caused your enemies to fall at your feet on the day that Your Majesty ascended the throne."

"In your country, there are prejudices entertained against us, which are more difficult to triumph over than the passions of a revolted army."

"Sire, you are seen from too great a distance: if Your Majesty were better known, you would be better appreciated, and would find among us, as well as here, abundance of admirers. The commencement of Your Majesty's reign has already called forth just praises; it was also equally, or even yet more highly lauded at the time of the cholera; for in this second insurrection, Your Majesty displayed the same authority, but tempered with the most generous devotion to the cause of humanity. Energy has never failed you, sire, in times of danger."

"The moments of which you recall the recollection have been, doubtless, the best in my life; nevertheless, they have appeared to me as the most frightful."

"I can well understand that, sire; to subdue nature in ourselves and in others requires an effort—"

"An effort which is terrible," interrupted the Emperor, with an energy which startled me,—"and one that is felt long after."

"Yes; but there is the consolation of having acted heroically."

"I have not acted heroically. I only performed my part: in such circumstances none can tell what he will do or say. We run into the danger, without previously inquiring how we are to get out of it."

"It was God who inspired you, sire; and if two so dissimilar things as poetry and government may be compared, I should say that you acted in the same way that poets sing,— in listening to the voice from above."

"There was no poetry in that action."

I could perceive that my comparison had not appeared flattering, because it had not been understood in the sense of the Latin poet. At court, they are in the habit of viewing poetry as merely an exhibition of wit; and it would have been necessary to have launched into a discussion to prove that it is the purest and most brilliant light that irradiates the soul. I therefore preferred remaining silent; but the emperor, being unwilling, doubtless, to leave me under the regret of having displeased him, detained me yet further, to the great astonishment of the court, and resumed the conversation with a kindness that was very gratifying. "What is your decided plan of route?" he asked.

"Sire, after the fête at Peterhof, I propose leaving for Moscow, from whence I wish to proceed to Nizhny, to see the fair, and to return to Moscow before the arrival of Your Majesty."

"So much the better: I shall be glad for you to examine, in detail, my works at the Kremlin. My residence there was too small, I am therefore building another more suitable; and I will explain to you myself all my plans for the embellishment of this part of Moscow, which we view as the cradle of the empire. But you have no time to lose, for you have immense distances to travel over—the distances! these are the curse of Russia."

"Do not, sire, regret them: they form the canvas of pictures that are to be filled up; elsewhere the earth is too confined for the inhabitants; but it will never fail Your Majesty."

"The time fails me."

"You have the future."

"They little know me who reproach my ambition: far from seeking to extend our territory, I am desirous of drawing closer around me the entire population of Russia. It is simply over misery and barbarism that I wish to achieve conquests: to ameliorate the condition of the Russians would be more gratifying than to aggrandize myself. If you knew what an amiable people the Russians are! how gentle, and how naturally polite! You will see them at Peterhof; but it is here, on the first of January, that I would have especially desired to show them to you." Then, returning to his favorite theme, he continued: "But it is not easy to render oneself worthy of governing such a people."

"Your Majesty has already done much for Russia."

"I fear sometimes that I have not done all that might have been effected."

The emperor is the only man in the empire with whom one may talk without fear of informers; he is also the only one in whom I have as yet recognized natural sentiments and sincere language. If I lived in this country, and had a secret to conceal, I should begin by confiding it to him.

If he has, as I think, more pride than vanity, more dignity than arrogance, the general impression of the various portraits I have successively traced of him, and especially the effect his conversation produced on me, ought to be satisfactory to him: in fact, I did my best to resist the influence of his attractions. I am certainly anything but revolutionary, still I am revolutionized: such is the consequence of being born in France, and of living there. But I have a yet better reason to give in explanation of my endeavor to resist the influence of the emperor over me. Aristocrat, both from character and conviction, I feel that the aristocracy alone can withstand either the seductions or the abuses of absolute power. Without an aristocracy, there would be nothing but tyranny both in monarchies and in democracies. The sight of despotism is revolting to me in spite of myself; it offends all the ideas of liberty which spring alike from my natural feelings and my political creed. No aristocrat can submit, without repugnance, to see the leveling hand of despotism laid upon the people. This, however, happens in pure democracies as much as in absolute monarchical governments.

It appears to me, that if I were a sovereign I should like the society of those who would recognize in me the fellow-being as well as the prince, especially if, when viewed apart from my titles, and reduced to myself, I should still have a right to be called a sincere, firm, and upright man.

Let the reader seriously ask himself, if that which I have recounted of the Emperor Nicholas, since my arrival in Russia, places this prince lower in his opinion than before he had read these chapters.

Our frequent communications in public gained me numerous acquaintances, as well as renewal of acquaintances. Many persons whom I had met elsewhere cast themselves in my way, though only after they had observed that I was the object of this particular goodwill on the part of the sovereign. These men were the most exalted persons at court; but it is the custom of people of the world, and especially of placemen, to be sparing of everything except ambitious schemes. To preserve at court sentiments above the vulgar range, requires the endowment of a very lofty mind, and lofty minds are rare.

It cannot be too often repeated, that there are no great noblemen in Russia, because there are no independent characters, with the exception, at least, of those superior minds, which are too few in number to exercise any general influence on society. It is the pride inspired by high birth, far more than riches or rank acquired by industry, which renders man independent.

This country, in many respects so different from France, still resembles it in one—it is without any regulated social system. By reason of this gap in the body politic, universal equality reigns in Russia as in France, and therefore, in both countries, the minds of men are restless and unquiet: with us this is demonstrated by visible agitations and explosions; in Russia, political passions are concentrated. In France, everyone can arrive at his object, by setting out from the tribune*; in Russia by setting out at court. The lowest of men, if he can discover how to please his sovereign, may become tomorrow second only to the emperor. The favor of that god is the prize which produces as many prodigies of effort, and miraculous metamorphoses, as the desire of popularity among us. A profound flatterer in Petersburg is the same as a sublime orator

*It must be remembered that this was written during the reign of Louis Philippe. —*Trans.*

in Paris. What a talent of observation must not that have been in the Russian courtiers, which enabled them to discover that a means of pleasing the emperor was to walk in winter without a greatcoat in the streets of Petersburg. This flattery of the climate has cost the life of more than one ambitious individual. Under a despotism which is without limits, minds are as much agitated and tormented as under a republic; but with this difference, the agitation of the subjects of an autocracy is more painful on account of the silence and concealment that ambition has to impose upon itself in order to succeed. With us, sacrifices, to be profitable, have to be public; here, on the contrary, they must be secret. The unlimited monarch dislikes no one so much as a subject *publicly* devoted. All zeal that exceeds a blind and servile obedience is felt by him as both troublesome and suspicious: exceptions open the door to pretensions, pretensions assume the shape of rights, and, under a despot, a subject who fancies that he has rights is a rebel.

Before this journey, my ideas of despotism were suggested by my study of society in Austria and Prussia. I had forgotten that those states are despotic only in name, and that manners and customs there, serve to correct institutions. In Germany, the people despotically governed appeared to me the happiest upon earth; a despotism thus mitigated by the mildness of its customs caused me to think that absolutism was not, after all, so detestable a thing as our philosophers had pretended. I did not then know what absolute government was among a nation of slaves.

It is to Russia that we must go in order to see the results of this terrible combination of the mind and science of Europe with the genius of Asia—a combination which is so much the more formidable as it is likely to last; for ambition and fear—passions which elsewhere ruin men by causing them to speak too much—here engender silence. This forced silence produces a forced calm, an apparent order, more strong and more frightful than anarchy itself. I admit but few fundamental rules in politics, because, in the art of government, I believe more in the efficacy of circumstances than of principles, but my indifference does not go so far as to tolerate institutions which necessarily exclude all dignity of human character in their objects.

Perhaps an independent judiciary and a powerful aristocracy would instill a calm and an elevation into the Russian character, and render the land happy; but I do not believe the emperor dreams of such modes of ameliorating the condition of his people. However superior a man may be, he does not voluntarily renounce his own way of doing good to others.

But what right have we to reproach the emperor of Russia with his love of authority? Is not the genius of revolution as tyrannical at Paris as the genius of despotism at Petersburg?

At the same time, we owe it to ourselves to make here a restriction that will show the difference between the social state of the two countries. In France, revolutionary tyranny is an evil belonging to a state of transition; in Russia, despotic tyranny is permanent.

LETTER 14

THE POPULATION of Petersburg amounts to four hundred
and fifty thousand souls, besides the garrison. So say patriotic
Russians; but those who are well informed, and who consequently pass here for evil-disposed persons, assure me that it
does not reach to four hundred thousand, in which number
the garrison is included. Small houses of wood occupy the
quarters beyond those immense spaces called squares, that
form the center of this city of palaces.

The Russians, descended from a union of various warlike and wandering tribes, have not yet quite forgotten the life of the bivouac. Petersburg is the headquarters of an army, and not the capital of a nation. However magnificent this military city may be, it appears bare and naked in the eyes of one from the west of Europe.

"The distances are the curse of Russia," said the emperor; and it is a remark the justice of which may be verified even in the streets of Petersburg. Thus, it is not for the mere sake of display that people's carriages are drawn by four horses: here, every visit is an excursion. The Russian horses, though full of mettle and sinew, have not so much bone as ours; the badness of the pavement soon tires them; two horses could not easily draw, for any considerable time, an ordinary carriage in the streets of Petersburg. To be able to drive four is therefore an object of the first necessity to those who wish to live in the fashionable world. Among the Russians, however, all have not the right to attach four horses to their carriage. This permission is only accorded to persons of a certain rank.

After leaving the center of the city, the stranger loses himself in vaguely defined lines of road, bordered by barracks which seem as though destined for the temporary accommodation of laborers employed in some great work; they are the magazines of forage, clothes, and of other supplies for the military. The grass grows in these soi-disant and always deserted streets.

So many peristyles have been added to houses, so many porticoes adorn the barracks that here represent palaces, so great a passion for borrowed decorations has presided over the construction of this temporary capital, that I count fewer men than columns in the squares of Petersburg, always silent and melancholy, by reason of their size alone and their unchangeable regularity. The line and rule figure well the manner in which absolute sovereigns view things, and straight angles may be said to be the blocks over which despotic architecture stumbles. Living architecture, if the expression may be permitted, will not rise at command. It springs, so to speak, from itself, and is an involuntary creation of the genius and wants of a people. To make a great nation is infallibly to create an architecture. I should not be astonished if someone succeeded in proving that there are as many original styles of architecture as mother tongues. The mania for rules of symmetry is not, however, peculiar to the Russians; with us it is a legacy of the empire. Had it not been for this bad taste of the Parisian architects, we should, long since, have been presented with some sensible plan for ornamenting and finishing our monstrous Place du Carrousel; but the necessity for parallels and precedents stops everything.

The principal street in Petersburg is the Nevsky Prospect, one of the three lines which meet at the palace of the Admiralty. These three lines divide into five regular parts the southern side of the city, which, like Versailles, takes the form of a fan. It is more modern than the port, built near the Islands by Peter the Great.

The Nevsky Prospect deserves to be described in detail. It is a beautiful street, a league in length, and as broad as our boulevards. In several places, trees have been planted, as unfortunate in their position as those of Paris. Dust gnaws at them during the summer; snow buries them in the winter, and the thaw cuts and grates their bark. The Prospect serves as a promenade and rendezvous for all the idlers of the city. Of these, however, there are but few, for here people seldom move for the sake of moving; each step that is taken has an object independent of pleasure. To carry an order—to pay their court—to obey their master, whoever he may be—such are the influences which put in motion the greater part of the population of Petersburg and of the empire.

Large, uneven flint-stones form the execrable pavement of this boulevard called the Prospect; but here, as in some other principal streets, there are, deeply imbedded in the midst of the stones, blocks of fir wood in the shape of cubes, and sometimes of octagons, over which the carriages glide swiftly. Each of these pavements consists of two lines, two or three feet broad, and separated by a strip of the ordinary flint pavement, on which the shaft horse runs. Two of these roads, that is to say, four lines of wood, run the length of the Nevsky Prospect, one on the left, the other on the right of the street; they are separated from the houses by raised flags for the foot passengers. This beautiful and vast perspective extends —gradually becoming less populous, less beautiful, and more melancholy—to the undetermined limits of the habitable city; in other words, to the confines of the Asiatic barbarism by which Petersburg is always besieged; for the desert may be found at the extremity of its more superb streets.

A little below the bridge of Aniskoff is the street named Jelognaia, which leads to a desert called the Square of Alexander. I doubt whether the Emperor Nicholas has ever seen this street. The superb city created by Peter the Great, and beautified by Catherine II and other sovereigns, is lost at last in an unsightly mass of stalls and workshops, confused heaps of edifices without name, large squares without design, and in which the natural slovenliness and the inborn filthiness of the people of the land, have for one hundred years permitted every species of dirt and rubbish to accumulate. Such filth, heaped up year after year in the Russian cities, serves as a protestation against the pretension of the German sovereigns, who flatter themselves that they have thoroughly polished the Slavic nation. The primitive character of that people, however disguised it may have been by the yoke imposed upon it, at least shows itself in some of the corners of the cities; and if they have cities at all, it is not because they want them, but because their military masters compel them to emulate the west of Europe. These poor exotic birds, placed in the cage of European civilization, are victims of the mania, or rather of the ambition of the czars, conquerors of the future world, and who well know that, before subjugating us, they must imitate us.

Nothing, I am told, can give any idea of the state of the Petersburg streets during the melting of the snow. Within the fortnight which follows the breaking up of the ice on the Neva, all the bridges are carried away, and the communications between different quarters of the city are, during several days, interrupted, and often entirely broken off. The streets then become the beds of furious torrents; few political crises could cause so much damage as this annual revolt of Nature against an incomplete and impracticable civilization. Since the thaw at Petersburg has been described to me I complain no longer of the pavements, detestable though they be; for I remember they have to be renewed every year.

After midday, the Nevsky Prospect, the grand square of the palace, the quays and the bridges are enlivened by a considerable number of carriages of various kinds and curious forms: this rather relieves the habitual dullness of the most monotonous capital in Europe, a German residence built on a greater scale. The interior of the houses is equally gloomy; for notwithstanding the magnificence of certain apartments destined to receive company, and furnished in the English style, there may be seen in the background various signs of a want of cleanliness and order, which at once reminds the observer of Asia.

The articles of furniture least used in a Russian house are beds. The women servants sleep in recesses similar to those in the old-fashioned porters' lodges in France; whilst the men roll themselves up on the stairs, in the vestibule, and even, it is said, in the drawing rooms, upon the cushions which they place on the floor for the night.

This morning I paid a visit to Prince ———. He is a great nobleman, but ruined in fortune, infirm and dropsical. He suffers so greatly that he cannot get up, and yet he has no bed on which to lie,—I mean to say, nothing which would be called a bed in lands where civilization is of older date. He lives in the house of his sister who is absent. Alone in this naked palace, he passes the night on a wooden board covered with a carpet and some pillows. In all the Russian houses that I have entered, I have observed that the screen is as necessary to the bed of the Slavs as musk is to their persons:—intense dirtiness does not always exclude external elegance. Sometimes, however, they have a bed for show; an object of luxury, which is maintained through respect for European fashions, but of which no use is ever made. The residences of several Russians of taste are distinguished by a peculiar ornament—a little artificial garden in a corner of the drawing room. Three long stands of flowers are ranged round a window, so as to form a little verdant sitting room or kind of kiosk, which reminds one of those in gardens. The stands are surmounted by an ornamented balustrade, which rises to about the height of a man, and is overgrown with ivy or other climbing plants that twist around the trelliswork, and produce a cool agreeable effect in the midst of a vast apartment, blazing with gilt work and crowded with furniture. In this little verdant boudoir are placed a table and a few chairs: the lady of the house is generally seated there, and there is room for two or three others, for whom it forms a retreat, which, if not very secret, is secluded enough to please the imagination.

The effect of this household thicket is pleasing and the idea sensible, in a land where secrecy should preside over all private conversation. The usage is, I believe, imported from Asia.

I should not be surprised to see the artificial gardens of the Russian reception rooms introduced someday into the houses of Paris.* I should rejoice to see the innovation, were it only to cope with the Anglomanes, who have inflicted an injury

---

*They have been introduced into many houses in Germany; and the custom is spreading.—*Trans.*

on the good taste and the real genius of the French, which I shall never pardon.

The Slavs, grave by necessity rather than by nature, scarcely dare to laugh, except with their eyes; but words being thus repressed, these eyes, animated by silence, supply the place of eloquence, so strongly is passion depicted in their expression. That expression is almost always intelligent, and sometimes gentle, though more often anxious, even to a degree of wildness that conveys the idea of some animal of the deer kind caught in the toils.

They seem born to guide a chariot, and show good blood, like the horses which they drive. Their strange appearance and the activity of their steeds render it amusing to go about the streets of Petersburg. Thanks to its inhabitants, and in despite of its architects, this city resembles no other in Europe.

The Russian coachmen sit upright on their seats; they always drive at great speed, but with safety. The precision and quickness of their eye are admirable. Whether with two or four horses, they have always two reins to each horse, which they hold with the arms much extended. No impediment stops them in their course; men and horses, both half wild, scour the city at full speed: but nature has rendered them quick and adroit; consequently, notwithstanding the reckless daring of these coachmen, accidents are of rare occurrence in the streets of Petersburg. They have often no whip, or when they have one, it is so short that they can make no use of it. Neither do they have recourse to the voice; the reins and the bit are their only instruments. One may wander round Petersburg for hours without hearing a single shout. If the pedestrians do not get out of the way with sufficient celerity, the *faleiter*, or postilion, utters a little yelp, like the sharp cry of a marmot roused in his nest, on hearing which, everyone gives way, and the carriage rushes past without having once slackened its speed.

The carriages are in general devoid of all taste, badly varnished, and seldom cleaned. If brought from England, they do not long resist the wear and tear of the pavement of Petersburg. The harness is strong, and at the same time light and elegant: it is made of excellent leather; in short, notwithstanding the negligence of the servants, the *tout ensemble* of these equipages is original, and to a certain degree picturesque.

They only harness four horses abreast for long journeys. In Petersburg, they are placed two and two; the traces by which they are attached are long beyond all proportion. The child who guides the leaders, is, like the coachman, dressed in the Persian robe called the *armiac*. However well it may suit the man who is seated, it is not convenient on horseback; notwithstanding which the Russian postilion is bold and dexterous.

I do not know how to describe the gravity, the haughty silence, the address, and the imperturbable temerity of these little Slavic monkeys. Their pertness and dexterity are my delight every time that I go into the city; and they have, which is less often seen here than elsewhere, the appearance of being happy. It is the nature of man to experience satisfaction when what he does is done well. The Russian coachmen and postilions, being the most skillful in the world, are perhaps content with their lot, however hard it may be in some respects.

It must also be observed that those in the service of the nobles pride themselves on their personal appearance, and take pains with it; but those who ply on hire, excite, as do also their unfortunate horses, my sincere pity. They remain in the street from morning till evening, at the door of the person who lets them, or on the stands assigned by the police. The horses eat always in harness, and the men always on their seat. I pity the former more than the latter, for the Russians have a taste for servitude.

The coachmen live, however, in this manner only during the summer. In the winter, sheds are built in the midst of the most frequented squares, and near the theaters and the palaces where fêtes are most frequently given. Around this shelter large fires are lighted, where the servants warm themselves; nevertheless, in the month of January, scarcely a night passes on which there is a ball, without a man or two dying of cold in the streets.

A lady, more sincere than others to whom I addressed questions on this subject, replied, "It is possible, but I have never heard it talked about." A denial which involved a strange avowal. It is necessary to visit this city, in order to learn the extent to which the rich man will carry his contempt for the life of the poor, and the slight value which life in general has in the eyes of men condemned to live under absolutism.

In Russia, existence is painful to everybody. The emperor is scarcely less inured to fatigue than the lowest of his serfs. I have been shown his bed, the hardness of which would astonish our common laborers. Here, everyone is obliged to repeat to himself the stern truth, that the object of life is not to be found on earth, and that the means of attaining it is not pleasure. The inexorable image of duty and of submission appears at each instant, and makes it impossible to forget the hard condition of human existence—labor and sorrow!

If for a moment, in the midst of a public promenade, the appearance of a few idlers should inspire the illusive idea that there may be in Russia, as elsewhere, men who amuse themselves for the sake of amusement, men who make pleasure a business, I am soon undeceived by the sight of some *Feldjäger*, passing rapidly in his telega. The *Feldjäger* is the representative of power—he is the word of the sovereign: a living telegraph, he proceeds to bear an order to another similar automaton, who awaits him, perhaps, a thousand leagues off, and who is as ignorant as his comrade of the objects that put them both in motion. The telega, in which the man of iron travels, is of all traveling vehicles the most uncomfortable. It consists of a little cart with two leather seats, but without springs or back. No other kind of carriage could stand the roads of this savage empire. The first seat is for the coachman, who is changed at each stage; the second is reserved for the courier, who travels till he dies; and among men devoted to such a life, death arrives early.

Those whom I see rapidly crisscrossing the fine streets of this city, seem to represent the solitudes into which they are about to plunge. I follow them in imagination, and at the end of their course appear to me Siberia, Kamchatka, the Salt Desert, the Wall of China, Lapland, the Frozen Ocean, Novaya Zemlya, Persia, or the Caucasus. These historical, or almost fabulous, names produce on my imagination the effect of a dim and vapory distance in a vast landscape, and engender a species of reverie which oppresses my spirits. Nevertheless, the apparition of such blind, deaf, and dumb couriers is a poetical aliment, constantly presented to the mind of the stranger. These men, born to live and die in their telegas, impart of themselves a melancholy interest to the humblest scene of life. Nothing prosaic can subsist in the mind when in the presence of so much suffering and so much effort. It must be owned that, if despotism renders unhappy the people that it oppresses, it is conducive to the amusement of travelers, whom it fills with an astonishment ever new. Where there is liberty, everything is published and speedily forgotten, for everything is seen at a glance; but under an absolute government everything is concealed, and therefore everything is conjectured: the greater the mystery, the greater the curiosity, which is enhanced even by the necessary absence of apparent interest.

I have been describing a city without character, rather pompous than imposing, more vast than beautiful, and full of edifices without style, taste, or historic interest. But to make the picture complete, that is, faithful, I should have inserted the figures of men naturally graceful, and who, with their Oriental genius, have adapted themselves to a city built by a people which had no country, for Petersburg has been constructed by wealthy men, whose minds were formed by comparing, without deep study, the different countries of Europe. This legion of travelers, more or less refined, and rather skillful than learned, formed an artificial nation, a community of intelligent and clever characters, recruited from among all the nations of the world. They did not constitute the Russian people. These latter are roguish as the slave, who consoles himself by privately ridiculing his master; superstitious, boastful, brave, and idle as the soldier; and poetical, musical, and contemplative as the shepherd; for the habits of a nomad people prevailed for a long time among the Slavs. All this is in keeping neither with the style of the architecture nor with the plan of the streets in Petersburg: there has been evidently no connection between the architect and the inhabitant. Peter the Great built the city against the Swedes rather than for the Russians; but the natural character of its population betrays itself, notwithstanding their respect for the caprices of their master; and it is to such involuntary disobedience that Russia owes its stamp of originality. Nothing can efface the primitive character of its people; and this triumph of innate faculties over an ill-directed education, is an interesting spectacle to every traveler capable of appreciating it.

Happily for the painter and the poet, the Russians possess an essentially religious sentiment. Their churches, at least, are their own. The unchangeable form of these pious edifices is a part of their religion: superstition defends her sacred fortresses against the mania for mathematical figures in freestone oblongs, planes, and straight lines; in short, against the military, rather than classic, architecture which imparts to each of the cities of this land the air of a camp destined to remain for a few weeks during the performance of some grand maneuvers.

The genius of a nomad race is equally recognized in the various vehicles and harness, the carriages, and the droshkies. The latter is so small as quite to disappear under those who occupy it. Its singular appearance, as it passes rapidly between long straight lines of very low houses, over which are seen the steeples of a multitude of churches and other buildings, may be easily imagined.

These gilded or painted spires break the monotonous line of roofs, and rise in the air with shafts so tapered, that the eye can scarcely distinguish the point where their gilding is lost in the mists of a polar sky. They are of Asiatic origin, and appear to be of a height which, for their diameter, is truly extraordinary. It is impossible to conceive how they maintain themselves in air.

Let the reader picture to himself an immense assemblage of domes, to which are always attached the four belfries necessary to constitute a church among the modern Greeks; a multitude of cupolas covered with gold, silver, or azure; palace roofs of emerald green, or ultramarine; squares ornamented with bronze statues; an immense river bordering and serving as a mirror to the picture—let him add to it the bridge of boats thrown across the river's broadest part—the citadel, where sleep in their unornamented tombs Peter the Great and his family,* and an island covered with edifices built after the model of Grecian temples—let him embrace in one view the whole of these varied parts, and he will understand how Petersburg may be infinitely picturesque, notwithstanding the bad taste of its borrowed architecture, the marshes which surround it, the unbroken flatness of its site, and the pale dimness of its finest summer days.

Let me not be reproached for my contradictions; I have myself perceived them without wishing to avoid them, for they lie in the things which I contemplate. I could not give a true idea of objects that I describe, if I did not often seem to contradict myself. If I were less sincere, I should appear more consistent; but in physical as in moral order, truth is only an assemblage of contrasts—contrasts so glaring, that it might be said nature and society have been created, only in order to

---

*The Greek rite forbids sculpture in churches.

hold together elements which would otherwise oppose and repel each other.

How admirable is the power of the primitive endowment of nations! For more than a hundred years, the higher classes of Russians, the nobles, the learned, and the powerful of the land, have been begging ideas and copying models from all the communities of Europe; and yet this absurd fantasy of princes and courtiers has not prevented the people from remaining original.

The finely endowed Slavic race has too delicate an organization to mingle indiscriminately with the Teutonic people. The German character has, even at this day, less affinity with the Russian than has the Spanish, with its cross of Arab blood. Slowness, heaviness, coarseness, timidity, and awkwardness, have nothing in common with the genius of the Slavs. They would rather endure vengeance and tyranny. Even the German virtues are odious to the Russians; thus, in a few years the latter, notwithstanding their religious and political atrocities, have made greater progress in public opinion at Warsaw than the Prussians, notwithstanding the rare and solid qualities which distinguish the German people. I do not speak of this as desirable, I only note it as an existing fact: it is not all brothers who love, but all understand each other.

As to the analogy which I imagine I can in certain points discover between the Russians and the Spaniards, it is accounted for by the relations which may have originally existed between some of the Arab tribes, and some of the hordes which passed from Asia into Muscovy. The Moresque architecture bears an affinity to the Byzantine, which is the model of the real Muscovite. The genius of the Asiatic wanderers in Africa could not be contrary to that of other Eastern nations but recently established in Europe. History is explained by the progressive influence of races.

But for the difference in the religion and the habits of the people, I could here fancy myself on one of the most elevated and barren plains of Castile. In fact, we are enduring at present the heat of Africa; for twenty years Petersburg has not known so burning a summer.

Notwithstanding the tropical heats, I see the Russians already preparing their provision of winter fuel. Boats loaded with billets of birch wood, the only fuel used here (for the oak is a tree of luxury), obstruct the large and numerous canals which intersect the city in every direction. It is built on the model of Amsterdam: an arm of the Neva flows through the principal streets; in winter it is filled up by the ice and snow; in summer, by the innumerable boats. The wood is conveyed from the boats in narrow carts of a primitive simplicity of construction, on which it is piled to a height which makes it resemble a moving wall. The logs are held together by a chain that the driver tightens with a stick he uses as a tourniquet. He hangs on to this arrangement to keep all the parts together like a squirrel swinging on a branch. I have never once seen any of these tottering edifices fall.

Fuel is becoming scarce in Russia. Wood is as dear in Petersburg as in Paris. There are houses here which consume as much as the value of nine or ten thousand francs per winter. In beholding the inroads made upon the forests, we may ask, with inquietude, how will the next generation warm themselves?

If the jest be pardonable, I would advise, as a measure of prudence on the part of the people who enjoy a genial climate, that they should furnish the Russians wherewith to keep good fires. They might then less covet the southern sun.

The carts used for moving the filth and refuse of the city are small and inconvenient. With such machines, a man and horse can do but little work in a day. Generally speaking, the Russians show their skill rather in their manner of using inferior implements than by the pains they take to perfect those which they have. Endowed with little power of invention, they most frequently want the mechanical appliances suitable to the end they would attain. This people, who possess so much grace and so much facility of character, have no creative genius. The Russians are the Romans of the North. Both peoples have drawn their arts and sciences from strangers. The former have intelligence; but it is an imitative, and therefore ironical, intelligence; it counterfeits everything, and invents nothing. Ridicule is a prevailing trait in the character of tyrants and slaves. All oppressed people are given to slander, satire, and caricature; they revenge themselves for their inaction and degradation by sarcasm. The nature of the relation which exists between nations and their governments has yet to be elucidated. In my opinion, each nation has for a government the only one which it could have. I do not, however, pretend either to impose or expound this system. It is a labor which I leave to those who are worthier and wiser than I: my present object is the less ambitious one of describing what has most struck me in the streets and on the quays of Petersburg.

Several parts of the Neva are entirely covered with boats of hay. These rural objects are larger than many houses; they are hung with straw mattings, which give them the picturesque appearance of Oriental tents or Chinese junks. Only in Petersburg have I seen edifices of straw from which families rush out like beasts from their lair.

The trade of plasterer is important in a city where the interior of the houses is a prey to swarms of vermin, and where the appearance of the exterior is spoilt every winter. The manner in which the Russian plasterers perform their work is curious. There are only three months in the year during which they can work outside the houses; the number of workers is therefore considerable, and they are found at the corner of every street. These men, suspended at the peril of their life on little planks attached to a long hanging cord, like spiders repairing their webs torn by a storm, swing in front of the edifices which they rewhiten.

In the provinces they whitewash the towns through which

the emperor may have to pass: is this an honor rendered to the sovereign, or do they seek to deceive him as regards the wretchedness of the land? In general, the Russians carry about their persons a disagreeable odor, which is perceptible at a considerable distance. The higher classes smell of musk; the common people, of cabbage mixed with exhalations of onions and old greasy, perfumed leather. These scents never vary.

It may be supposed from this, that the thirty thousand subjects of the emperor who enter his palace on the 1st of January, to offer him their felicitations, and the six or seven thousand that we shall see tomorrow pressing into the interior of the palace of Peterhof, in honor of their empress, must leave on their passage a formidable perfume.

Among all the women of the lower orders whom I have hitherto met in the streets, not a single one has struck me as possessing beauty, and the greater number among them are ugly and dirty to a degree that is repulsive. Astonishment is excited by the recollection that they are the wives and mothers of men with features so fine and regular, profiles so perfectly Grecian, and forms so elegant and supple as those seen among even the lowest classes of the nation. There are nowhere old men so handsome, nor old women so hideous, as in Russia. I have seen few women of the middle class. One of the singularities of Petersburg is, that the number of women in proportion to that of the men is less than in other capitals. I am assured that the former do not, at the utmost, form more than a third of the total population of the city. Their scarcity causes them to be only too highly prized. They attract so eager an attention that there are few who risk themselves alone, after a certain hour, in the streets of the less populous quarters. In the capital of a country altogether military, and among a people addicted to drunkenness, this discreetness appears to me sufficiently well founded. At all times the Russian women show themselves less in public than the French: it is not necessary to go far back to find the time when they passed their lives locked up like the women of Asia. This reserve, the remembrance of which still lingers, recalls, like so many other Russian customs, the origin of the people. It contributes to the dullness of the streets and the fêtes of Petersburg. The finest sights in the city are the parades, which strengthens my former observation, that the Russian capital is but a camp somewhat more stable and pacific than a mere bivouac.

There are few cafés in Petersburg, and no authorized public balls in the interior of the city. The promenades are not much frequented, and those who are met there exhibit a gravity that conveys but little idea of enjoyment.

But if fear makes men serious, it also makes them extremely polite. I have never elsewhere seen so many men of all classes treating each other with respect. The driver of the droshky formally salutes his comrade, who never passes him without rendering reverence for reverence; the porters salute the plasterers, and so with all the others. This urbanity is, perhaps, affected; at least, I believe it overstrained: nevertheless, the mere appearance of amenity contributes to the pleasure of life. If a pretended politeness has so much about it that is valuable, what a charm must real politeness possess, the politeness, that is to say, of the heart!

A stay in Petersburg would be agreeable to any traveler of standing or character, who could believe all that he heard. The greatest difficulty would be the escaping of dinners and soirées, those real plagues of Russia, and it may be added of all societies where strangers are admitted, and, consequently, where intimacy is excluded.

I have accepted here but few private invitations. I was chiefly curious to view the solemnities of the court, but I have seen enough: one soon wearies of wonders in the contemplation of which the heart has no share.

LETTER 15

THE FÊTE of Peterhof may be viewed under two different lights, the material and the moral; thus viewed, the same spectacle produces very different impressions.

I have never seen anything more beautiful to contemplate, yet at the same time more saddening to reflect upon, than this pretended national union of courtiers and peasants, who mingle together in the same rooms without any interchange of real sympathy. In a social point of view the sight has displeased me, because it seems to me that the emperor, by this false display of popularity, abases the great without exalting the humble. All men are equal before God, and the Russians' God is the emperor. This supreme governor is so raised above earth, that he sees no difference between the serf and the lord. From the height in which his sublimity dwells, the little

229

distinctions that divide mankind escape his divine inspection, just as the irregularities which appear on the surface of the globe vanish before an inhabitant of the sun.

When the emperor opens his palace to the privileged peasants and the chosen merchants whom he admits twice a year to the honor of paying their court,* he does not say to the laborer or the tradesman, "You are a man like myself," but he says to the great lord, "You are a slave like them, and I, your God, soar equally above you all." Such is, all political fiction aside, the moral meaning of the fête; and it is this which, in my opinion, spoils it. As a spectator, I remarked that it pleased the sovereign and the serfs, much more than the professed courtiers.

To seek to become a popular idol by reducing all classes to a level, is a cruel game, an amusement of despotism, which might dazzle the men of an earlier century, but which cannot deceive any people arrived at the age of experience and reflection.

The Emperor Nicholas did not devise this imposition; and such being the case, it would be the more worthy of him to abolish it. Yet it must be owned, that nothing is abolished in Russia without peril. The people who want the guarantees of law, are protected only by those of custom. An obstinate attachment to usages, which are upheld by insurrection and poison, is one of the bases of the constitution, and the periodical death of sovereigns proves to the Russians that this *constitution* knows how to make itself respected. The adjustment of such a machine is to me a deep and painful mystery.

In point of magnificent decorations, and picturesque assemblage of the costumes of all ranks, the fête at Peterhof cannot be too highly extolled. Nothing that I had read, or that had been related to me concerning it, gave me any adequate idea of the fairy scene; the imagination was surpassed by the reality.

---

*On the 1st of January, at Petersburg, and at Peterhof on the birthday of the empress.

The reader must picture to himself a palace built upon a terrace, the height of which seems that of a mountain, in a land of plains extending farther than the eye can reach: a country so flat, that, from an elevation of sixty feet, the vision may sweep over an immense horizon. At the foot of this imposing structure lies a vast park, which terminates only with the sea, on whose bosom may be perceived a line of vessels of war, which were illuminated on the evening of the fête. This illumination was general; the fire blazed and extended, like a conflagration, from the groves and terraces of the palace to the waves of the Gulf of Finland. In the park, the lamps produced the effect of daylight. The trees were lighted up by suns of every color. It was not by thousands, nor tens of thousands, but by hundreds of thousands, that the lights in these gardens of Armida might be counted; and they could all be seen from the windows of a palace crowded with a people as profoundly respectful as if they had lived all their days at court.

Nevertheless, in this assemblage, the object of which was to efface all distinctions of rank, each class might still be separately traced. Whatever attacks despotism may have made upon the aristocracy, there are yet castes in Russia. Here is presented one more point of resemblance to the East, and not one of the least striking contradictions of social order created by the manners of the people combined with the government of the country. Thus, at this fête of the empress, this true bacchanalian revel of absolute power, I recognized the order which reigns throughout the state, amid the apparent disorder of the ball. Those whom I met were always either merchants, soldiers, laborers, or courtiers, and each class was distinguished by its costume. A dress which would not denote the rank of the man, and a man whose only worth should arise from his personal merit, would be considered as anomalies, as European inventions, imported by restless innovators and imprudent travelers. It must never be forgotten that we are here on the confines of Asia: a Russian in a frock coat, in his own country, appears to me like a foreigner.

Russia is placed upon the limits of two continents. It is not in the nature of that which is European to amalgamate perfectly with that which is Asiatic. The Muscovite community has been governed hitherto only by submitting to the violence and incoherence attendant upon the contact of two civilizations, entirely different in character. This presents to the traveler a field of interesting, if not comforting speculation.

The ball was a rout: it professed to be a masquerade, for the men wore small pieces of silk, called Venetian mantles, which floated in a ridiculous manner above their uniforms. The halls of the old palace, filled with people, resembled an ocean of heads of greasy hair, over all of which rose proudly the noble head of the emperor, whose stature, voice, and will, alike soar above his people. This prince seems worthy and capable of subjugating the minds of men, even as he surpasses their persons. A sort of mysterious influence attaches to his presence: at Peterhof, on the parade, in war, and in every moment of his life, may be seen in him the power that reigns.

This perpetual reigning, and its perpetual worship, would be a real comedy, if upon such permanent dramatic representation there did not depend the existence of sixty millions of men, who live only because the man whom you see before you, playing the part of the emperor, gives them permission to breathe, and dictates to them the mode of using that permission. It is the divine right, applied to the mechanism of social life. Such is the serious side of the representation, wherein are involved incidents of so grave a nature, that fear soon extinguishes the inclination to laughter.

There does not exist on the earth at the present time, not in Turkey, not even in China, a single man who enjoys and exercises such power as the emperor. Let the reader figure to himself all the skillfulness and experience of our modern governments, perfected as they are by centuries of practice, put into exercise in a still young and uncivilized society; the rubrics of the administrations of the West, aiding the despotism of the East; European discipline supporting the tyranny of Asia; the police employed in concealing barbarism, in order, not to destroy, but to perpetuate it; disciplined brute force and the tactics of European armies, serving to strengthen an Eastern policy;—let him conceive the idea of a half-savage people, who have been enrolled and drilled, without having been civilized, and he will be able to understand the social and moral state of the Russian nation. To profit by the progressive discoveries in the art of governing made by the European nations, in order to rule sixty millions of Orientals, has been from the time of Peter the First the problem to be studied by those who govern Russia.

The reigns of Catherine the Great and of Alexander did but prolong the systematic infancy of this nation.

Catherine had instituted schools to please the French philosophers, whose praises her vanity desired to obtain. The governor of Moscow, one of her old favorites, who was rewarded by a pompous exile in the ancient capital of the empire, wrote to her one day that no one would send their children to the schools. The empress replied pretty nearly in these words:—

"My dear prince, do not distress yourself because the Russians have no desire for knowledge: if I institute schools, it is not for ourselves, but for Europe, in whose esteem we must maintain our standing; but if our peasants should really seek to become enlightened, neither you nor I could continue in our places."

This letter has been read by a person in whose statements I have every confidence. Undoubtedly, in writing it, the empress forgot herself; and it is precisely because she was subject to such absence of mind that she was considered so amiable, and that she exercised so much power over the minds of imaginative men.

e de Custine

The Russians will, according to their usual tactics, deny the authenticity of the anecdote; but if I cannot be certain as to the strict accuracy of the words, I can affirm that they truly express the sentiments of the sovereign. In this trait may be discovered the spirit of vanity which rules and torments the Russians, and which perverts, even in its source, the power established over them.

Their unfortunate desire for the good opinion of Europe is a phantom which pursues them in the secrecy of thought, and reduces civilization to a trick of jugglery, executed more or less adroitly.

The present emperor, aided by his sound judgment and his clear apprehension, has perceived the shoal, but will he be able to avoid it? More than the strength of Peter the Great is required to remedy the evil caused by that first corrupter of the Russians.

At the present time the difficulty is of a double character; the mind of the peasant remains rude and barbarous, while his habits and his disposition cause him to submit to restraint. At the same time, the false refinement of the nobles contravenes the national character, upon which all attempts to ennoble the people can alone be built. What a complication! Who will unloose this modern gordian knot?

The mischief is so deeply rooted, that it strikes even the eye of strangers the least attentive, and that too in a country where everyone conspires to deceive the traveler.

In traveling in Russia, a light and superficial mind may feed itself on illusions; but whoever has his eyes open, and adds to some little power of observation an independent humor, will be presented with a continued and painful labor, which consists in discovering and discerning, at every point, the struggle between two nations carried on in one community. These two nations are,—Russia as she is, and Russia as they would have her to appear in the eyes of Europe.

The emperor is less secure than anyone against the snares

of illusion. The reader will remember the journey of Catherine to Cherson: she traversed deserts, but they built her lines of villages at every half league of the road by which she passed, and as she did not go behind the scenes of this theater on which the tyrant played the fool, she believed her southern provinces were well peopled, though they continued cursed with a sterility which was owing to the oppression of her government rather than to the rigor of nature. The finesse of the men charged by the emperor with the details of Russian administration, still exposes the sovereign to similar deceptions.

The diplomatic corps, and the Western people in general, have always been considered by this Byzantine government and by Russia in general, as malignant and jealous spies. There is this similarity between the Russians and the Chinese, that both one and the other always believe that strangers envy them: they judge us by their own sentiments.

The Russian hospitality also, vaunted as it is, has become an art which may be resolved into a refined species of policy. It consists in rendering its guest content at the least possible cost of sincerity. Here, politeness is only the art of reciprocally disguising the double fear that each experiences and inspires. I hear everywhere spoken the language of philosophy, and everywhere I see that oppression is the order of the day. They say to me,—"We would gladly dispense with being arbitrary, we should then be more rich and prosperous; but we have to do with an Asiatic people": at the same time, they think in their hearts, "We would gladly dispense with talking liberalism and philanthropy, we should then be more happy and more strong; but we have to do with the governments of Europe."

The Russians of all classes conspire, with an unanimity which is extraordinary, in causing duplicity to triumph among themselves. They have a dexterity in lying, a natural proneness to deceit, which is revolting. Things that I admire ate here, because I find them too dearly paid for; ....nce, calmness, elegance, respectfulness, the natural and moral relations which ought to exist between those who think and those who execute, in short, all that gives a worth and a charm to well-organized societies, all that gives a meaning and an object to political institutions, is lost and confounded here in one single sentiment—that of fear. In Russia, fear replaces, that is, paralyzes thought. This sentiment, when it reigns alone, can never produce more than the appearances of civilization; whatever shortsighted legislators may say, fear will never be the moving influence of a well-organized society; it is not order, it is the veil of chaos; where liberty is wanting, there soul and truth must be wanting also. Russia is a body without life, a colossus which subsists only by its head; and of which the members, all equally deprived of force, languish! Thence arises a profound inquietude, an inexpressible uneasiness, an uneasiness which does not, like that of the new French *révolutionnaires*, arise from a vagueness of ideas, from abuses, from the satiety of material prosperity, or the jealousies which a combination of agencies gives birth to; it is the expression of a real state of suffering, the indication of an organic malady.

I believe that in no part of the world do the men enjoy less real happiness than in Russia. We are not happy among ourselves, but we feel that happiness is in our power: among the Russians it is unattainable. Imagine republican passions (for, once again, fictitious equality reigns under a Russian emperor) boiling beneath the silence of despotism! This is a terrifying combination, especially as viewed with regard to its future influence upon the world. Russia is a cauldron of boiling water, well closed, but placed over a fire which is ever becoming more fiercely heated; I dread the explosion, and the emperor has several times experienced the same dread during the course of his laborious reign; laborious in peace as in war, for, in our days, empires, like machines, are ruined by remaining inactive. Prudence paralyzes them; anxiety in idleness devours them.

It is, then, this head without a body, this sovereign without a nation, who gives popular fêtes! It appears to me that before creating popularity, he should create a people.

In truth the country lends itself marvelously to every species of fraud: there are slaves elsewhere, but to find a nation of courtly slaves it is necessary to visit Russia. One scarcely knows at which most to wonder, the inconsistency or the hypocrisy. Catherine II is not dead; for notwithstanding the open character of her grandson, it is still by dissimulation that Russia is governed. Here, to avow the tyranny would be to make a beneficial progress.

On this point, as on many others, the foreigners who have described Russia have combined with the natives to deceive the world. Could any persons be more treacherously complaisant than the greater part of those writers who congregate here from all the corners of Europe, in order to excite a sensibility on the touching familiarity which reigns between the Russian emperor and his people? Are, then, the illusions of despotism so strong as to overpower even the simple spectator? Either this country has not hitherto been described except by men whose position or character does not permit of their being independent, or else minds the most sincere lose their ability of judgment as soon as they enter Russia.

As regards myself, I oppose this influence the aversion which I have for disguise.

I hate but one evil, and if I hate it, it is because I believe that it engenders and includes all the others: this evil is falsehood. I therefore endeavor to unmask it wherever I meet with it; it is the horror which it inspires me that gives me the desire and the courage to write these travels: I undertook them through curiosity, I relate them from a sense of duty. A passion for truth is an inspiration which supplies the place of energy, youth, and enlightened views. This sentiment influences me to such an extent as to cause me to love even the age in which we live: for though it be somewhat course, it is, at least, more sincere than that which preceded it. It distinguishes itself by the repugnance, sometimes rude and unmannerly, which it evinces for all affectations. In this repugnance I partake. A hatred for hypocrisy is the torch which serves to guide me through the labyrinth of the world: those who deceive men, whatever means they may use, seem to me as poisoners; and the more elevated and powerful they are, the more they are culpable.

Such are the sentiments which prevented my enjoying, yesterday, a spectacle which, notwithstanding, my eyes admired. It was beautiful, magnificent, singular, novel—but it appeared deceptive: this idea sufficed to deprive it of all real splendor. The passion for truth, which in the present day pervades the hearts of Frenchmen, is still unknown in Russia

After all, what is this crowd, whose respectful familiarity in presence of its sovereign has been so much extolled in Europe? Do not deceive yourselves: these are the slaves of slaves. The great lords send to the fête of the empress chosen peasants, who, it is pretended, arrive by chance. This elite of the serfs is joined by the most respectable and best-known tradespeople, for it is necessary to have a few men with beards to satisfy the old-fashioned Russians. Such is, in reality, the people whose excellent disposition has been held up as an example to other people by the sovereigns of Russia, from the time of the Empress Elizabeth. It is, I believe, from her reign that this kind of fête dates. At present, the Emperor Nicholas, notwithstanding his iron character, his admirable rectitude of intention, and the authority with which his public and private virtues invest him, could not perhaps abolish the usage. It is therefore true that, even under governments the most absolute in appearance, circumstances are stronger than men.

Nothing is so perilous for a man, however elevated his position may be, than to say to a nation, "You have been deceived, and I will be no longer accessory to your error." The vulgar cling to falsehood, even when it injures them, rather than to truth, because human pride prefers that which comes from man to that which comes from God. This is true under all governments, but doubly so under despotism.

An independence like that of the *muzhiks* of Peterhof can alarm nobody. It forms the liberty and equality which despots love. It may be boasted of without risk; but advise Russia to a gradual emancipation, and you will soon see what is said of you in the country!

I, yesterday, heard the courtiers, as they passed near me, boasting of the politeness of their serfs: "Who ever saw such a fête in France?" they said. I was strongly tempted to answer them: "In order to compare our two people, we must wait until yours exists."

I called to mind at the same time a fête which I once gave to the lower orders at Seville. It was under the despotism of Ferdinand VII, but the true politeness of those Spaniards, free de facto, if not de jure, furnished me with an object of comparison little favorable to the Russians.

Russia is a book, the table of whose contents is magnificent, but beware of going further. If you turn over the leaves, you will find no performance answering to the promise: all the chapters are headed, but all have to be filled up. How many of the Russian forests are only marshes, where you will never cut a faggot! How many distant regiments are there without men, and cities and roads which exist only in idea! The nation itself is as yet nothing more than a puff placarded upon Europe, dupe of a diplomatic fiction. I have found here no real life except that of the emperor; no constitution except that of the court.

The tradespeople who ought to form a middle class are too few in number to possess any influence in the state; besides, they are almost all foreigners. The authors amount to one or two in each generation: the artists are like the authors, their scarcity causes them to be esteemed; but though this favors their personal prospects, it is injurious to their social influence. There are no lawyers in a country where there is no justice: where, then, is to be found that middle class which constitutes the strength of other states, and without which the people are only a flock, guided by a few well-trained watchdogs? I have not mentioned another class of men who are not to be reckoned either among the great or the little. These are the sons of the priests, who almost all become subaltern employees—the commissioners and deputies who are the plagues of Russia. They form a species of obscure noblesse, very hostile to the great nobles; a noblesse whose spirit is anti-aristocratic in the true political signification of the word, and who at the same time are very burdensome to the serfs. These are the men inconvenient to the state, and fruits of the schism which permits the priest to marry who will commence the approaching revolution of Russia.

The punishment of death does not exist in this land, except for the crime of high treason; but there are certain criminals whom they nevertheless kill. The way in which they reconcile the mildness of the code with the traditional ferocity of manners, is this: when a criminal is condemned to more than a hundred strokes of the knout, the executioner, who understands the meaning of such a sentence, kills him through humanity, by striking him at the third blow on a mortal part. And yet the punishment of death is abolished! To making the law thus lie, the proclamation of the most audacious tyranny would be preferable.

Should it be thought that I judge Russia too severely, I must plead the involuntary impression that I receive each day from persons and from things, and which every friend of humanity would receive in my place, if, like me, he endeavored to look beyond the surface that would be exhibited to him.

This empire, immense as it is, is no more than a prison, of which the emperor keeps the key. Nothing can exceed the misery of the subjects unless it be that of the prince. The life of the jailer has always appeared to me so similar to that of the prisoner, that I am astonished at the mental illusion which makes the one believe himself so much less to be pitied than the other.

Man, here, knows neither the real social enjoyments of cultivated minds, nor the absolute and animal liberty of the savage, nor yet the independence of action of the half savage —the barbarian; I can see no compensation for the misery of being born under this system, except the dreams of vanity and the love of command; on these passions I stumble every time I return to the endeavor of analyzing the moral life of the inhabitants of Russia. Russia thinks and lives as a soldier! A soldier, to whatever country he may belong, is scarcely a citizen; and here less than anywhere can he be called one; he is rather a prisoner for life, condemned to look after other prisoners.

It should be observed that the word prison signifies something more here than it does elsewhere. When one thinks on all the subterranean cruelties concealed from our pity by the discipline of silence, in a land where every man serves an apprenticeship to discretion, it makes one tremble. He who would cherish a hatred for reserve should come here. Every little check in conversation, every change of expression, every inflection of voice, teaches me the danger of confidence and candor.

The very appearance of the houses brings to my mind the unhappy condition of human existence in this land.

If I cross the threshold of the palace of some great nobleman, and see there a disgusting and ill-disguised uncleanliness reigning amidst an ostentatious display of luxury; if I, so to speak, inhale vermin, even under the roof of opulence,— my mind will not stop at that which is presented merely by the senses; it wanders further, and sees all the filth and corruption which must poison the dungeons of a country where even the rich do not shrink from loathsome contact. When I suffer from the dampness of my chamber, I think of the unfortunate beings exposed to that of the underwater prison of Kronstadt, the fortress of Petersburg, and of many other political tombs of which I do not even know the name. The ghastly visages of the soldiers whom I meet in the streets remind me of the dishonesty of those employed in provisioning the army. The fraud of these traitors, paid by the emperor to feed his guards, is written in lines of lead on the livid faces of the unfortunate wretches, deprived of wholesome and even sufficient nutriment by men who care only to enrich themselves as rapidly as possible, unmindful of the disgrace they are bringing on their government, and of the maledictions of the regiments of slaves whom they kill. Finally, at each step I here take, I see rising before me the phantom of Siberia, and I think of all that is implied in the name of that political desert, that abyss of misery, that grave of living men,—a land peopled with infamous criminals and sublime heroes, a colony without which this empire would be as incomplete as a palace without cellars.

A traveler who would allow himself to be indoctrinated by the people of the country, might overrun the empire from one end to the other, and return home without having surveyed anything but a series of façades. This is what he should do in order to please his entertainers. I am aware that such is the case, but so high a price for their hospitality I cannot afford to pay.

Provided a stranger shows himself ridiculously active, rises early after having retired to rest late, never fails to attend every ball and review, in short, provided he keeps too constantly in motion to be able to think, he is well received everywhere, well thought of, and well fêted; a crowd of strangers press his hand every time that the emperor may have spoken to him, smiles are lavishly bestowed, and, on leaving, he is pronounced a distinguished traveler. He reminds me of the *Bourgeois Gentilhomme* played upon by the Mufti of Molière. The Russians have coined a French word that admirably designates their political hospitality; in speaking of foreigners whom they blind by means of fêtes—"we must *garland* them,"* they say. But let the stranger be on his guard lest he should for a moment betray any relaxation of zeal; at the least symptom of fatigue, or of penetration, he will see the Russian spirit, the most caustic of all spirits, rising up against him like an enraged serpent.

Ridicule, that empty consolation of the oppressed, is here the pleasure of the peasant, as sarcasm is the accomplishment of the noble; irony and imitation are the only natural talents which I have discovered among the Russians. The stranger once exposed to the venom of their criticism would never recover from it; he would be passed from mouth to mouth like a deserter running the gauntlet, and finally be trampled under the feet of a crowd the most hardened and ambitious in the world. The ambitious have always a pleasure in ruining others: "Destroy him as a precaution, there will at any rate be one the less; every man must be viewed as a rival because it is possible that he may become one."

I have no greater belief in the probity of the muzhik. They tell me that he would not pluck a flower in the garden of his emperor; that I do not dispute. I know that fear will produce miracles, but I know also that this model people, these peasant courtiers, do not scruple to rob their lordly rivals on a day when, too much affected by their presence at the palace, and too confident in the honorable sentiments of the serf ennobled for the hour, they cease for one moment to watch the movements of the said serf's hands.

Yesterday, at the Imperial and popular ball of the palace of Peterhof, the Sardinian ambassador had his watch very adroitly extracted, notwithstanding the chain which formed

---

*Il faut les *enguirlander*.

its guard. Several people missed also their handkerchiefs and other articles in the press. I myself lost a purse lined with a few ducats, and consoled myself for the loss in laughing at the eulogies lavished on the probity of this people by its lords. The latter well know the real value of all their fine phrases, and I am not sorry to know it also. In observing their futile finesses, I seek for the dupes of falsehoods so puerile, and I cry, with Basil, "Who is deceiving here? All the world is in the secret."

In vain do the Russians talk and pretend; every honest observer can only see in them the Greeks of the Lower Empire, formed, in accordance with the rules of modern strategy, by the Prussians of the eighteenth and the French of the nineteenth century.

The popularity of an autocrat appears to me as suspicious in Russia, as does the honesty of the men who in France preach absolute democracy in the name of liberty,—both are murderous sophisms. To destroy liberty while preaching liberality is assassination, for society lives by truth; to make tyranny patriarchal is assassination also.

I have one fixed political principle; it is that men can and ought to be governed without being deceived. If in private life falsehood is degrading, in public life it is criminal; every government that lies, is a conspirator more dangerous than the traitor whom it legally condemns to capital punishment; and—notwithstanding the example of certain great minds spoilt by an age of sophists—where truth is renounced, genius forsakes its seat, and, by a strange reversion of things, the master humbles himself before the slave; for the man who deceives is below the victim of deception. This is as applicable to politics and to literature as to religion.

The emperor has made himself the champion of monarchical power in Europe, and, it is well known, he boldly and openly maintains this position. He is not seen, as is a certain government, preaching in each different locality a different policy, according to varying and purely commercial local interests: on the contrary, he favors everywhere indiscriminately the principles which accord with his system. Is it thus that England is liberal, constitutional, and philanthropic?

The emperor reads daily, from one end to the other, one French newspaper, and only one, the *Journal des Débats*. He never looks at the others, unless some interesting article is pointed out to him.

To sustain power in order to preserve social order, is, in France, the object of the best and worthiest minds; it is also the constant aim of the *Journal des Débats*, an aim prosecuted with an intellectual superiority which explains the consideration accorded to this paper in our own country, as well as in the rest of Europe.

France is suffering under the disease common to the age, she is suffering under it more than any other land; this disease is hatred of authority; the remedy, therefore, consists in fortifying authority: such is the sentiment of the emperor at Petersburg, and of the *Journal des Débats* at Paris.

But, as they agree only in regard to the end to be obtained, they are so much the more opposed as they seem to be united. The choice of means will often cause dissension among those gathered under the same banner: they meet as allies, they separate as enemies.

The legitimacy of hereditary right appears to the emperor of Russia the only means of attaining his end; and in forcing a little the ordinary sense of the old word "legitimacy," under pretext that there exists another more sure,—that, namely, of election based upon the true interests of the country,—the *Journal des Débats* raises altar against altar, in the name of the salvation of society.

From the contest of these two legitimacies, one of which is blind as fate, the other wavering as passion, results an anger the more lively because the advocates of both systems lack decisive reasons, and use the same terms to arrive at opposite conclusions.

The site of Peterhof is the most beautiful that I have hitherto seen in Russia. A ridge of small elevation commands the
sea, which borders the extremity of the park at about a third
of a league from the palace; the latter is built on the edge of
this mount, which is almost perpendicular. Magnificent
flights of steps have been formed, by which you descend from
terrace to terrace into the park, where are found groves of
great extent and beauty, *jets d'eau*, and artificial cascades in
the taste of those at Versailles, and structures raised on certain elevated points, from whence may be seen the shores
of Finland, the arsenal of the Russian navy, the isle of
Kronstadt, and, at about nine leagues towards the right, St.
Petersburg, the white city, which at a distance looks bright
and lively, and, with its pointed-roofed palaces, its temples of
plastered columns, its forests of steeples that resemble
minarets, has the appearance towards evening of a wood of fir
trees, whose silver tops are illuminated by the ruddy glare of
some great fire.

When I think of all the obstacles which men have here
conquered in order to exist as a community, to build a city,
and to maintain in it all the magnificence necessary to the
vanity of great princes and great folks, I cannot see a lettuce
or a rose without being tempted to exclaim—"A miracle!" If
Petersburg is a Lapland in stucco, Peterhof is the palace of
Armida under glass. I can scarcely believe in the real existence of so many costly, delicate, and brilliant objects, when I
recollect that a few degrees farther north, the year is divided
into a day, a night, and two twilights, of three months each.

One may ride a league in the Imperial park of Peterhof
without passing twice under the same avenue: imagine, then,
such a park all on fire. In this icy and gloomy land the illuminations are perfect conflagrations; it might be said that the
night was to make amends for the day. The trees disappear
under a decoration of diamonds, in each alley there are as
many lamps as leaves; it is Asia, not the real modern Asia,

but the fabulous Baghdad of the Arabian Nights, or the more fabulous Babylon of Semiramis.

It is said that on the empress's birthday, six thousand carriages, thirty thousand pedestrians, and an innumerable quantity of boats leave Petersburg to proceed to, and form encampments around, Peterhof.

It is the only day on which I have seen a real crowd in Russia. A bivouac of civilians in a country altogether military, is a rarity. Not that the army was wanting at the fête, for a body of guards and the corps of cadets were both cantoned round the residence of the sovereign. All the multitude of officers, soldiers, tradesmen, serfs, lords, and masters, wandered together among the woods, where night was chased away by two hundred and fifty thousand lamps. Such was the number named to me; and though I do not know whether it was correct or not, I do know that the mass of fire shed an artificial light far exceeding in clearness that of the northern day. In Russia, the emperor casts the sun into the shade. At this period of the summer, the nights recommence and rapidly increase in length; so that, without the illumination, it would have been dark for several hours under the avenues in the park of Peterhof.

It is said, also, that in thirty-five minutes all the lamps of the illuminations in the park were lighted by eighteen hundred men. Opposite the front of the palace, and proceeding from it in a straight line towards the sea, is a canal, the surface of whose waters was so covered with the reflection of the lights upon its borders, as to produce a perspective that was magical; it might have been taken for a sheet of fire. Arioston would perhaps have had imagination brilliant enough to describe all the wonders of this illumination: to the various groups of lamps, which were disposed with much taste and fancy, were given numerous original forms; flowers as large as trees, suns, vases, bowers of vine leaves, obelisks, pillars, walls chased with arabesque work; in short, a world of fantastic imagery passed before the eye, and one gorgeous device succeeded another with inexpressible rapidity.

At the extremity of the canal, on an enormous pyramid of fire (it was, I believe, seventy feet high), stood the initials of the Empress, shining in brilliant white above all the red, blue, and green lights which surrounded it. It was like an aigrette of diamonds circled with gems of all hues. Everything was on so large a scale that the mind doubted the reality which the eye beheld. Such efforts for an annual festival appeared incredible. There was something as extraordinary in the episodes to which it gave rise, as in the fête itself. During two or three nights, all the crowd of which I have spoken encamped around the village. Many women slept in their carriages, and the female peasants in their carts. These conveyances, crowded together by hundreds, formed camps which were very amusing to survey, and which presented scenes worthy of the pencil of an artist.

The Russian has a genius for the picturesque; and the cities of a day which he raises for his festive occasions, are more amusing, and have a much more national character than the real cities built in Russia by foreigners. The painful impression I have received since living among the Russians, increases as I discover the true value of this oppressed people. The idea of what they could do if they were free, heightens the anger which I feel in seeing them as they now are.

The ambassadors with their families and suites, as well as the strangers who have been presented, are boarded and lodged at the expense of the emperor. For this object, a large and charming edifice, called the English Palace, is reserved. The building is a quarter of a league from the Imperial Palace, in a beautiful park, laid out in the English taste, and so picturesque that it appears natural. The beauty of the waters, and the undulations of the surface—undulations rarely seen in the environs of Petersburg—make it very pleasant. This year, the number of foreigners being greater than usual, there

is not room for them in the English Palace. I do not therefore sleep there, but I dine there daily with the diplomatic
corps and seven or eight hundred other individuals, at a
perfectly well-served table. This is certainly magnificent hospitality. When lodging at the village, it is necessary, after
dressing in uniform, to proceed in a carriage, in order to dine
at this table, at which presides one of the great officers of
the empire.

For the night, the director general of the theaters of the
court has placed at my disposal two actors' boxes in the theater of Peterhof, and this lodging is the envy of everyone.* It
lacks nothing except a bed; and fortunately I brought my little iron couch from Petersburg. It is an indispensable necessary for an European, traveling in Russia, who does not wish
to pass the night rolled in a rug on a bench or a staircase. We
carry our beds here as we would our cloaks in Spain. For want
of straw, which is a rare thing in a region that grows no
wheat, my mattress is filled with hay.

In any other country, so great an assemblage of people would
produce overwhelming noise and disturbance. In Russia,
everything passes with gravity, everything takes the character of a ceremony; to see so many young persons united together for their pleasure, or for that of others, not daring
either to laugh, to sing, to quarrel, to play, or to dance, one
might imagine them a troop of prisoners about to proceed to
their destination. What is wanted in all I see here is not,
assuredly, grandeur or magnificence, nor even taste and elegance: it is gaiety. Gaiety cannot be compelled; on the contrary, compulsion makes it fly, just as the line and the level
destroy the picturesque in scenery. I see only in Russia that
which is symmetrically correct, which carries with it an air
of command and regulation; but that which would give a

---

*In the village there is only a small number of dirty houses, in which the rooms are
let at the rate of from two to five hundred rubles per night.

value to this order, variety, from whence springs harmony, is here unknown.

The soldiers at their bivouac are subjected to a more severe discipline than in their barracks. Such rigor, in time of peace, in the open field, and on a day of festival, reminds me of the remark of the Grand Duke Constantine. "I do not like war," he said: "it spoils the soldiers, dirties their uniforms, and destroys discipline."

The prince did not give all his reasons for disliking war, as is proved by his conduct in Poland.

On the day of the ball and the illumination, we repaired to the Imperial Palace at seven o'clock. The courtiers, the ambassadors, the invited foreigners, and the soi-disant populace, entered the state apartments without any prescribed order. All the men, except the muzhiks, who wore their national costume, and the merchants who were robed in the caftan, carried the *tabarro,* or Venetian mantle above their uniform, which was a strictly enforced regulation, the fête being called a masked ball.

We remained a considerable time, much pressed by the crowd, waiting for the appearance of the emperor and his family. As soon as this sun of the palace began to rise, the space opened before him, and followed by his splendid cortege, he proceeded, without being even incommoded by the crowd, through the halls into which, the moment before, you might have supposed another person could not have penetrated. Wherever His Majesty passed, the waves of peasants rolled back, closing instantly behind him like waters in a vessel's track.

The noble aspect of the monarch, whose head rose above all heads, awed this agitated sea into respect. It reminded me of the Neptune of Virgil;—he could not be more an emperor than he is. He danced, during two or three successive hours, polonaises with the ladies of his family and court.

The emperor and his cortege wound, in a surprising manner, through the crowd, which, without foreseeing the direction he was about to take, always gave way in time, so as never to incommode the progress of the monarch.

He spoke to several of the men robed and bearded *à la russe*: at length, towards ten o'clock, at which hour it became dark, the illuminations, of which I have already spoken, commenced.

We had expected, during a great part of the day, that, owing to the weather, they would not have taken place. About three o'clock, while at dinner in the English Palace, a squall of wind passed over Peterhof, violently agitated the trees, and strewed the park with their branches. While coolly watching the storm, we little thought that the sisters, mothers, and friends of crowds seated at the same table with us were perishing on the water, under its terrible strength. Our thoughtless curiosity was approaching to gaiety at the very moment that a great number of small vessels, which had left Petersburg for Peterhof, were foundering in the gulf. It is now admitted that two hundred persons were drowned: others say fifteen hundred or two thousand: no one knows the truth, and the journals will not speak of the occurrence: this would be to distress the empress, and to accuse the emperor.

The disaster was kept a secret during the entire evening, nothing transpired until after the fête; and this morning the court neither appeared more nor less sad than usual. There, etiquette forbids to speak of that which occupies the thoughts of all; and even beyond the palace, little is said. The life of man in this country is such as to be deemed of trifling importance even by himself. Each one feels his existence to hang upon a thread.

Every year, accidents, similar, although less extensive, cast a gloom over the fête of Peterhof, which would change into an act of deep mourning, a solemn funeral, if others, like me, thought upon all that this magnificence costs. But here, I am the only one that reflects. Yesterday, superstitious minds were presented with more than one gloomy prognostic. The weather, which had been fine for three weeks, changed upon the birthday of the empress. The initials of that princess would not light up. The man charged with superintending this essential part of the illumination ascended to the summit of the pyramid, but the wind extinguished his lamps as quickly as he lighted them. He reascended several times; at length his foot slipped, and he fell from a height of seventy feet, and was killed on the spot.

The shocking thinness of the empress, her air of languor, the diminished luster of her eye, rendered these presages the more ominous. Her life, like a disease, may be said to be fatal: fêtes and balls every evening! There is no choice here but that of dying of amusement, or of ennui.

For the empress, as well as the zealous courtiers, the spectacle of parades and reviews commences early in the morning. These are always followed by some receptions; the empress then retires for a quarter of an hour, after which she rides out in her carriage for two hours. She next takes a bath before again going out on horseback. Returned a second time, she has some more visitors to receive: this over, she proceeds to inspect certain useful institutions superintended by herself, or by some of those honored with her intimacy. From thence she follows the emperor to the camp: there being always one somewhere near. They return to dance; and thus her days, her years, and her life are consumed.

Those who have not the courage or the strength necessary to pursue this dreadful life, are not in favor.

The empress said to me the other day, in speaking of a very distinguished but delicate woman, "She is always ill!" The tone and manner in which this was spoken convinced me that the fate of a family was decided. In a sphere where good intentions are not sufficient, an indisposition is equivalent to a disgrace.

The empress does not consider herself more excused than others from doing her share. She cannot for a moment bear that the emperor should leave her. Princes are made of iron! This high-minded woman wishes, and at moments believes, herself to be free from human infirmities; but the total privation of physical and mental repose, the want of a continuous occupation, the absence of all serious conversation, the acquired necessity of excitement, all tend to nurse a fever which is sapping life. And this dreadful mode of existence has become as indispensable as it is fatal. She cannot now either abandon it or sustain it. Consumption is feared, and, above all, the winter of Petersburg is dreaded; but nothing can induce her to pass six months away from the emperor.

While observing her interesting though emaciated figure wandering like a specter through a scene of festivity celebrated in her honor, and which she will perhaps never witness again, my heart sunk within me, and, dazzled as I may have been with human pomp and grandeur, I turned to reflect on the miseries to which our nature is exposed. Alas! the loftier the height from which we fall, the severer is the shock. The great expiate in one day, even in this world, all the privations that the poor suffer during a long life.

Yesterday, at the close of the ball, we supped; after which, almost melted, for the heat of the apartments in which the crowd was gathered was unbearable, we entered certain carriages belonging to the court, called *lignes*, and made the tour of the illuminations; beyond the influence of which the night was very dark and cool. The incredible profusion of lights spread over the enchanted forest, produced however within its shades an extraordinary heat, and we were warmed as well as dazzled.

The *lignes* are a species of carriage with double seats, on which eight persons can conveniently sit, back to back. Their shape, gilding, and the antique trappings of the horses impart to them an air of grandeur and originality.

Objects of luxury impressed with a really royal character are now rarely seen in Europe.

The number of these equipages is considerable. They form one of the magnificent displays of the fête of Peterhof. There was room in them for all invited, except the serfs and tradesmen.

A master of the ceremonies had pointed out to me the *ligne* in which I was to ride, but in the disorder of the departure no one kept his place. I could neither find my servant nor my cloak, and, at length, was obliged to mount one of the last of the *lignes*, where I seated myself by the side of a Russian lady who had not been to the ball, but who had come from Petersburg to show the illumination to her daughters. The conversation of these ladies, who appeared to know all the families of the court, was frank, in which respect it differed from that of those connected with the palace. The mother immediately commenced conversing with me: her manners had that facility and good taste about them which discovered the woman of rank. I recognized in her conversation, as I had already done elsewhere, that when the Russian women are natural, mildness and indulgence towards others is not a prominent trait in their character. She named to me all the persons we saw passing us, for in this procession the train of *lignes* often divided and filed before each other at the crossings of the alleys.

If I were not afraid of wearying the reader, I should exhaust all the formulae of admiration in repeating that I have never seen anything so extraordinary as this illuminated park traversed in solemn silence by the carriages of the court, in the midst of a crowd as dense as was that of the peasants in the rooms of the palace a few minutes before.

We rode for about an hour among enchanted groves, and made the tour of a lake situated at the extremity of the park, and called the lake of Marly. Versailles and all the magical creations of Louis XIV haunted the imagination of the princes of Europe for more than a hundred years. It was at this lake of Marly that the illuminations appeared to me the most extraordinary. At the extremity of the piece of water,—I was going to say the piece of gold, so luminous and brilliant did it appear,—stands a house which was the residence of Peter the Great, and which was illuminated like the others. The water and the trees added singularly to the effect of the lights. We passed before grottoes, whose radiant interior was seen through a cascade of water falling over the mouth of the brilliant cavern. The Imperial Palace only was not illuminated, but its white walls were rendered brilliant by the immense masses of light reflected upon them from all parts of the park.

This ride was unquestionably the most interesting feature in the fête of the empress. But I again repeat, scenes of magic splendor do not constitute scenes of gaiety. No one laughed, sung, or danced; they all spoke low; they amused themselves with precaution; it seemed as though the Russian subjects were so broken in to politeness as to be respectful even to their pleasure. In short, liberty was wanting at Peterhof, as it is everywhere else in Russia.

I reached my chamber, or rather my box, after midnight. From that time, the retreat of the spectators commenced, and while this torrent swept under my window, I sat down to write, for sleep would have been impossible in the midst of so much uproar. In this country, the horses alone have permission to make a noise. Conveyances of all forms and sizes thundered along amid a crowd of men, women, and children, on foot.

It was natural life recommencing after the constraint of a royal fête. One might have supposed them prisoners delivered from their chains. The people of the road were no longer the disciplined crowd of the park. They rushed onwards in the direction of Petersburg with a violence and a rapidity that recalled to my mind the descriptions of the retreat from Moscow. Several accidents on the road aided the illusion.

Scarcely had I time to undress and throw myself on my bed, when I found it necessary to be again on foot, to witness the review of the corps of cadets, who were to pass before the emperor.

My surprise was great to find the court already at its post; the women in their morning dresses, the men in their coats of office; everybody awaited the emperor at the place of rendezvous. The desire of proving themselves zealous, animated this embroidered crowd, who all showed so much alacrity that it seemed as if the splendor and fatigues of the night had weighed only upon me. I blushed for my indolence, and felt that I was not born to make a good Russian courtier. The chain, though gilded, did not appear to me the less heavy.

I had but just time to make my way through the crowd before the arrival of the empress, and had not yet gained my place, when the emperor started inspecting the ranks of his junior officers, while the empress, so overcome with fatigue the previous evening, waited for him in a calèche in the midst of the square. I felt for her, but the extreme exhaustion under which she had seemed to suffer during the ball had disappeared. My pity, therefore, turned upon myself, and I saw with envy the oldest people of the court lightly bearing the burden which I found so heavy. Ambition here is the condition of life: without its artificial stimulus the people would be always dull and gloomy. The emperor's own voice directed the maneuvers of the pupils. After several had been perfectly well executed, His Majesty appeared satisfied. He took the hand of one of the youngest of the cadets, led him forth from the ranks to the empress, and then, raising the child in his arms, to the height of his head, that is, above the head of everybody else, he kissed him publicly. What object had the emperor in showing himself so good-natured on this day, before the public? This they either could not or would not tell me.

I asked the people around me who was the happy father of

the model cadet, thus caressed by the sovereign: no one satisfied my curiosity. In Russia everything is turned into mystery. After this sentimental parade, the emperor and empress returned to the palace of Peterhof, where they received in the state apartments such as wished to pay their court. Afterwards, at about eleven o'clock, they appeared on one of the balconies of the palace, before which the soldiers of the Circassian guard, mounted on their superb Asiatic horses, went through some interesting exercises. The beauty of this gorgeously clad troop adds to the military luxury of a court which, notwithstanding its efforts and pretensions, is, and for a long time will remain, more Oriental than European. Towards noon, feeling my curiosity exhausted, and not possessing the all-powerful stimulus of that court ambition which here achieves so many miracles to supply my natural forces, I returned to my bed, from whence I have just risen to finish this recital.

I purpose remaining here the rest of the day, in order to let the crowd pass by; and I am also detained at Peterhof by the hope of a pleasure to which I attach some value.

Tomorrow, if I have time, I will relate the success of my machinations.

LETTER 16

I HAD EARNESTLY begged Madame —— to procure for me
admission to the English cottage of the Imperial family. It
is a small house which they have built in the midst of the
noble park of Peterhof, in the new Gothic style so much in
vogue in England. "Nothing is more difficult than to enter
the cottage," replied Madame ——, "during the time that
Their Majesties remain here, and nothing would be more easy
in their absence. However, I will try."

I therefore prolonged my stay at Peterhof, waiting, with
some impatience, but without much hope, for the answer of
Madame ——. Yesterday morning early, I received a little
note from her, thus worded, "Come to my house at a quarter
before eleven. I am permitted, as a very particular favor, to
show you the cottage at the hour when the emperor and
empress take their walk; that is at eleven o'clock precisely.
You know their punctuality."

I did not fail to keep the appointment. Madame —— resides in a very pretty mansion, built in a corner of the park.
She follows the empress everywhere, but she occupies, when

possible, some separate house, although in the immediate vicinity of the different Imperial residences. I was with her at half past ten. At a quarter before eleven, we entered a carriage-and-four, crossed the park rapidly, and in a few minutes arrived at the gate of the cottage.

It is, as I have said, quite an English residence, surrounded with flowers, shaded with trees, and built in the style of the prettiest places that may be seen near London, about Twickenham, on the borders of the Thames. We crossed a rather small vestibule raised a few steps, and had just stopped to examine a room, the furniture of which struck me as a little too recherché for the general character of the building, when a *valet de chambre* came to whisper a few words in the ear of Madame ———, who seemed surprised.

"What is the matter?" I asked, when the man had disappeared.

"The empress is returned!"

"We are betrayed!" I exclaimed: "I shall not have time to see anything."

"Perhaps not: go down into the garden by this terrace, and wait for me at the entrance of the house."

I was scarcely there two minutes before I saw the empress rapidly descending the steps of the house and coming towards me. She was alone. Her tall and slender figure possesses a singular grace; her walk is active, light, and yet noble; she has certain movements of the arms and hands, certain attitudes, a certain turn of the head, that it is impossible to forget. She was dressed in white; her face, surrounded with a white calash, appeared calm and composed; her eyes had an expression of gentleness and melancholy; a veil, gracefully thrown back, shaded her features; a transparent scarf fell over her shoulders, and completed the most elegant of morning dresses. Never had I seen her to so much advantage. Before this apparition the sinister omens of the ball disappeared: the empress seemed resuscitated, and I experienced, in beholding her, that sense of security which, after a night of trouble and agitation, returns with the dawn of day. Her Majesty must, I thought, be stronger than I, to have thus endured the fête of the day before yesterday, the review and the soiree of yesterday, and to appear today so well and beautiful.

"I have shortened my promenade," she said, "because I knew that you were here."

"I was far, madame, from expecting so much kindness."

"I said nothing of my project to Madame ———, who has been scolding me for thus coming to surprise you: she pretends that I shall disturb you in your survey. You expect then to discover all our secrets?"

"I should like, madame; one could not but gain by acquaintance with the ideas of those who know so well how to choose between splendor and elegance."

"The residence at Peterhof is unendurable to me, and it is to relieve my eyes from the glare of all that massive gold, that I have begged a cottage of the emperor. I have never been so happy as in this house; but now that one of my daughters is married, and that my sons pursue their studies elsewhere, it has become too large for us."

I smiled, without replying: I was under a charm: it seemed to me, that this woman, so different from her in whose honor was given the sumptuous fête that had just taken place, could share with me all my impressions; she has felt like me, I thought, the weariness, the emptiness, the false brilliancy of public magnificence, and she now feels that she is worthy of something better. I compared the flowers of the cottage with the chandeliers of the palace, the sun of a bright morning to the illuminations of a night of ceremony, the silence of a delicious retreat to the tumult of a palace crowd, the festival of nature to the festival of a court, the woman to the empress; and I was enchanted with the good taste and the sense which this princess had shown in fleeing the satieties of public display, to surround herself with all that constitutes the charm of private life. It was a new fairy scene, the illusion of which captivated my imagination much more strongly than the magic of splendor and power.

"I would not explain myself to Madame ———," continued the empress. "You shall see all over the cottage, and my son shall show it you. Meanwhile, I will go and visit my flowers, and will find you again before we allow you to leave."

Such was the reception I met with from this lady, who is represented as haughty, not only in Europe, where she is scarcely known, but in Russia, where they see her constantly.

At this moment, the hereditary grand duke joined his mother. He was accompanied by Madame ———, and her eldest daughter, a young person about fourteen years of age, fresh as a rose, and pretty as they were in France, in the times of Boucher. This young lady is the living model of one of the most agreeable portraits of that painter.

I was waiting for the empress to give me my *congé*, but she commenced walking backwards and forwards before the house. Her Majesty knew the interest I took in all the family of Madame ———, who is a Polish lady. Her Majesty knew also that for some years past one of the brothers of Madame ——— had lived at Paris. She turned the conversation to this young man's mode of life; and questioned me for a long time, with marked interest, regarding his sentiments, opinions, and general character. This gave me every facility for saying of him all that my attachment dictated. She listened to me very attentively. When I had ceased speaking, the grand duke, addressing his mother, continued the same subject, and said, "I met him at Ems, and liked him very well."

"And yet, it is a man thus distinguished whom they forbid to come here, because he retired into Germany after the revolution in Poland," cried Madame ———, moved by her sisterly affection, and using that freedom of expression of which the habit of living at court from her infancy has not deprived her. "But what has he done then?" said the empress, addressing me, with an accent that was inimitable for the mixture of impatience and kindness which it expressed. I was embarrassed to find an answer to a question so direct, for it involved the delicate subject of politics, and to touch upon that subject might spoil everything.

The grand duke came to my aid with an affability and a kindness which I should be very ungrateful to forget; no doubt he thought I had too much to say to dare to answer; and anticipating some evasion which might have betrayed my embarrassment, and compromise the cause I desired to plead, "My mother," he said with vivacity, "who ever asked a child of fifteen years what he had done in politics?"

This answer, full of sense and of good feeling, extricated me from the difficulty, but it put an end to the conversation. If I might dare to interpret the silence of the empress, I should say that this was her thought—"What could now be done, in Russia, with a pardoned Pole? He would always be an object of envy to the old Russians, and he would only inspire his new masters with distrust. His health and life would be lost in the trials to which he would have to be exposed in order to test his fidelity; and if, at length, they came to the conclusion that he might be trusted, they would only despise him. Besides, what could *I* do for this young man, I have so little influence!"

I do not believe I much deceive myself in saying, that such were the thoughts of the empress; such were also pretty nearly mine. We tacitly agreed in concluding that, of two evils, the least for a gentleman who had lost both his fellow-citizens and his comrades in arms, was to remain far from the land which had given him birth: the worst of all conditions would be that of a man who should live as a stranger in his own home.

On a sign from the empress, the grand duke, Madame ———, her daughter, and myself re-entered the cottage. I could have wished to have found less luxurious furniture in this house, and a greater number of objets d'art. The ground floor resembled that of all the houses of rich and elegant English people, but not one picture of a high order, not one fragment of marble, or of terra-cotta, announced that the owners of the place had a love for the arts. It is not the being able to draw more or less skillfully, but it is the taste for chefs d'oeuvre that proves a love for, and a judgment in the arts. I always regret to see the absence of this passion in those with whom it could be so easily gratified.

It may be said that statues and pictures of great value would be out of place in a cottage; but this house is the chosen and favorite resort of its possessors; and when people form for themselves an abode according to their fancy, if they have much love for the arts, that love will betray itself, at the risk even of some incongruity of style, some fault of harmony: besides, a little anomaly is allowable in an Imperial cottage. Over the distribution of the ornaments of the cottage, and the general arrangements of its interior, it could be easily discovered that family affections and habits had chiefly presided; and these are worth even yet more than an appreciation of the beautiful in the works of genius. Only one thing really displeased me in the furniture and the arrangements of this elegant retreat, and that was a too servile adherence to English fashions.

We looked over the ground floor very hastily, for fear of wearying our guide. The presence of so august a cicerone embarrassed me. I know that nothing so annoys princes as our timidity; at least, unless it be affected in order to flatter them. They love to be put at their ease, and we cannot do that without being at ease ourselves. With a grave prince, I could have hoped to save myself by conversation, but with a gay and youthful prince, I was left without resource.

A staircase, very narrow, but adorned with an English carpet, conducted us to the upper floor. We there saw the room where the Grand Duchess Marie passed a part of her childhood; it is empty: that of the Grand Duchess Olga will probably not remain long occupied. The empress might truly say that the cottage was becoming too large. These two very similar rooms are furnished with a charming simplicity.

The grand duke stopped at the top of the stairs, and said, with that perfect politeness of which (notwithstanding his extreme youth) he possesses the secret,—"I am sure that you would rather see everything here without me; and I have seen it all so often, that I would, I confess, as willingly leave you to finish your survey with Madame ———. I will therefore join my mother, and wait for you with her."

Whereupon he saluted us gracefully, and left me, charmed with the flattering ease of his manners. It is a great advantage to a prince to be really well-bred. I had not, then, this time, produced the effect that I anticipated; the constraint that I felt had not been communicated. If he had sympathized with my uneasiness, he would have remained, for timidity can do nothing but submit to its torture; it knows not how to free itself; no elevation is safe from its attacks; the victim whom it paralyzes, in whatever rank he may be placed, cannot find strength either to confront or to fly from that which produces his discomfort.

At the moment when the grand duke left us, Mademoiselle ——— was standing behind her mother. The prince, as he passed her, stopped, and in a very grave but rather humorous manner, made her a deep curtsey, without speaking a word. The young lady, perceiving that the salutation was ironical, remained in a respectful attitude, but without returning the obeisance. I admired this little expression of feeling, which appeared to me to exhibit an exquisite delicacy. I doubt whether at the Russian court, any woman of twenty-five would have distinguished herself by an act of so much courage; it was dictated only by that innocence, which to the regard due to social prerogatives knows how to join a just sentiment of its own dignity. The exhibition of tact did not pass unperceived.

"Always the same!" said the grand duke, as he turned away.

They had been children together; a difference of five years in age had not prevented them from often playing at the same games. Such familiarity is not forgotten, even at court. The silent scene which they now enacted together much amused me.

My peep into the interior of the Imperial family has interested me extremely. These princes must be viewed up close in order to be appreciated. They are made to be at the head of their country; for they are in every respect superior to their people. The Imperial family is the object the most worthy of exciting the admiration and the envy of foreigners that I have seen in Russia.

At the top of the house we found the cabinet of the emperor. It is a tolerably large and very simply ornamented library, opening on a balcony which overlooks the sea. Without leaving this watchtower, the emperor can give his orders to his fleet. For this purpose he has a spyglass, a speaking trumpet, and a little telegraph which he can work himself.

After leaving the cottage I proceeded to pay a hasty visit to Oranienbaum, the celebrated residence of Catherine II, built by Menshikov. That unfortunate man was sent to Siberia before he had completed the wonders of a palace deemed too royal for a minister.

It now belongs to the Grand Duchess Helena, sister-in-law of the present emperor. Situated two or three leagues from Peterhof, in sight of the sea, and on a continuation of the same ridge upon which is built the Imperial Palace, the castle of Oranienbaum, although constructed of wood, is an imposing edifice. Notwithstanding the imprudent luxury of the builder, and the greatness of the personages who have, after him, inhabited it, it is not remarkable for extent. Terraces, flights of steps, and balconies covered with orange trees and flowering plants, connect the house with the park, and embellish both the one and the other; but the architecture it-self is anything but magnificent. The Grand Duchess Helena has shown here the taste which presides throughout all her arrangements, and which has made Oranienbaum a charming residence, notwithstanding the dullness of the landscape, and the besetting memories of the scenes formerly enacted there.

On leaving the palace I asked permission to see the re-mains of the small but strong fortress from whence they obliged Peter III to come forth, and then carried him to Rop-scha, where he was assassinated. I was conducted to a retired hamlet, where are to be seen dry ditches, broken mounds, and heaps of stones, a modern ruin, in the production of which policy has had more to do than time. But the enforced silence, the purposely created solitude, which reign around these accursed remains, summon up before the mind precisely what is sought to be concealed: the official lie is annulled by the historic fact. History is a magical mirror, in which the people see, after the death of men who were influential in public affairs, the real, unmasked reflection of their faces. Those faces have passed away, but their images remain en-graved on this inexorable crystal. Truth cannot be buried with the dead. It rises triumphant above the fear of princes and the flattery of people, always powerless when they endeavor to stifle the cry of blood; and it finds its way through prisons, and even through the tomb, especially the tomb of the great, for obscure persons succeed better than princes in concealing the crimes which stain their memory. If I had not known that the fortress of Peter III had been demolished, I should have guessed it; but what astonishes me, in seeing the wish here exhibited to create oblivion of the past, is that anything con-nected with it should be preserved. The names ought to be destroyed as well as the walls. It was not sufficient to demol-ish the fortress, they should have also razed the palace, which is only a quarter of a league distant. Whoever visits Oranien-baum inquires, with anxiety, for the vestiges of the prison where Peter III was compelled to sign the *voluntary* abdication, which became his death warrant,—for the sacrifice once obtained, it was necessary to prevent his revoking it.

In looking over the park of Oranienbaum, which is large and beautiful, I visited several of the summerhouses which were the scenes of the empress's amorous assignations. Some of them were splendid pavilions, others exhibited bad taste. In general, their architecture lacked purity of style, though certainly pure enough for the uses to which the goddess of the place destined them.

I returned to Peterhof, and slept, for the third night, in the theater. This morning, in returning to Petersburg, I took the road by Krasnoye Selo, where a large camp is formed. Forty thousand men of the Imperial guard are, it is said, lodged there, under tents, or dispersed in the neighboring villages. Others say the number is seventy thousand. In Russia everyone imposes upon me his own estimate, to which I pay little attention, for nothing is more deceptive than these statements. They serve to show, however, the importance that is attached to leading people astray. Nations rise above such childish stratagems when they pass from infancy to a state of manhood.

I was much amused with viewing the variety of uniforms, and with comparing the expressive and savage faces of these soldiers, who are brought from every part of the empire. Long lines of white tents glistened in the sun, on a surface broken into small undulations in a manner that produced a picturesque effect.

I am constantly regretting the insufficiency of words to describe certain scenes in the North, and, above all, certain effects of light. A few strokes of the pencil would give a better idea of the original aspect of this melancholy and singular land, than whole volumes of description.

LETTER 17

ACCORDING to information that I have obtained this
morning respecting the disaster of the fête of Peterhof, its
extent has exceeded my expectations. But we shall never
ascertain the exact circumstances of the event. Every accident here is treated as an affair of state: it is God who has
failed in His duty to the emperor!

Political superstition, which is the soul of the Russian
community, exposes its chieftain to all the complaints that
impotence may bring against power, that earth may urge
against Heaven. If my dog is hurt, it is to me that he comes
for the cure of his wound; if God afflicts the Russians, they
immediately call upon their czar. This prince, who is responsible for nothing in politics, must answer for everything in
Providence: a natural consequence of man's usurpation of the

rights of God. A man who allows himself to <del>l</del>
as more than a mortal, takes upon himself all the
Heaven may send upon earth, during his reign. There resu
from this species of political fanaticism, a susceptibility and
jealous delicacy, of which no idea can be formed in other
lands. Nevertheless, the secrecy which the police believes it
necessary to maintain on the subject of misfortunes the least
dependent upon human will, fails in its object, inasmuch as
it leaves the field open to imagination. Everyone relates the
same transaction differently, according to his interest, his
fears, his ambition, or his humor; according to his situation
at court, or his position in the world. Hence it is, that truth in
Petersburg is an imaginary thing, just as it has become in
France, although from different causes. An arbitrary censorship
and an unlimited liberty may lead to the same results, and
render impossible the verification of the most simple fact.

Thus, some say that there were only thirty persons who
perished the day before yesterday, while others speak of
twelve hundred, others of two thousand, and others again of
one hundred and fifty. Imagine the uncertainty in which everything must be involved when the circumstances of an event
that took place, as it were, under our eyes, will always remain
unknown, even to ourselves. I shall never cease to marvel at
having seen a people exist, so thoughtless as to live and die
tranquilly in the twilight which the police of its masters accords it. Hitherto I had been accustomed to believe that man
could no more dispense with truth for his mind than with sun
and air for his body; but my Russian journey has undeceived
me. Truth is only needful to elevated minds or to advanced
nations: the vulgar accommodate themselves to the falsehoods
favorable to their passions and habits: here, to lie, is to protect society; to speak the truth, is to overthrow the state. The
twilight of politics is less transparent than the polar sky.

For the authenticity of one of the accidents connected with
the catastrophe of Peterhof I can vouch.

Three young Englishmen, the eldest of whom I know, had been some days in Petersburg. Their father is in England, and their mother awaits them at Karlsbad. On the day of the fête, the two youngest sailed for Peterhof without their brother, who constantly refused their solicitations to accompany them, alleging that he felt no curiosity. He saw them embark in their little vessel, and bade them adieu until the morrow. Three hours afterwards, both were corpses! They perished, together with several women and children, and two or three men, who were in the same boat: a sailor, who was a good swimmer, was alone saved. The unhappy surviving brother is plunged in a despair which would be difficult to describe. He is preparing to leave, to join his mother, and apprise her of the melancholy tidings. She had written to her sons desiring them not to omit seeing the fête of Peterhof, nor to hurry their departure, should their curiosity incline them to prolong their stay, intimating that she would wait patiently for them at Karlsbad. A little more urgency on her part would perhaps have saved their lives.

What numberless accounts, discussions, and proposals would not such a catastrophe have given rise to in any other land except this, and more especially in our own! How many newspapers would have said, and how many voices would have repeated, that the police never does its duty, that the boats were not seaworthy, the watermen greedy only of gain, and that the authorities, far from interfering, did but increase the danger by their indifference or their corruption! It would have been added that the marriage of the grand duchess had been celebrated under very gloomy auspices, like many other royal marriages; and then dates, allusions, and citations would have followed in great abundance. Nothing of the kind here. A silence more frightful than the evil itself everywhere reigns. Two lines in the gazette, without details, is all the information publicly given; and at court, in the city, in the drawing rooms of fashion, not a word is spoken. There are no coffeehouses in Petersburg where people comment upon the journals: there are, indeed, no journals upon which to comment. The petty employees are more timid than the great lords; what is not dared to be spoken of among the principals, is yet more carefully avoided by subordinates; and as to the merchants and shopkeepers, that wily caution necessary to all who would live and thrive in the land, is by them especially observed. If they speak on grave, and therefore dangerous subjects, it is only in strict and confidential privacy.

Russia has agreed to say nothing which could make the empress nervous, and thus is she left to live and die dancing! "She would be distressed, therefore hold your peace." And hereupon, children, friends, relations, all who are loved, die, and no one dares even to weep for them. People here are too unfortunate to complain.

The Russians are all courtiers. Soldiers, spies, jailers, executioners, in this land, all do more than their duty; all ply their trade as parasites. Who shall tell me to what lengths a society may not go which is not built on the foundation of human dignity?

I repeat that everything must be undone here, before Russians can constitute a people.

On the present occasion the silence of the police is not merely the result of a desire to flatter, it is also the effect of fear. The slave dreads the angry mood of his master, and employs every effort to keep him in a state of benignity and good humor. The chain, the dungeon, the knout, and Siberia, are all within reach of an irritated czar; or at the best there is the Caucasus, a Siberia mitigated to the uses of a despotism softened in accordance with the spirit of the century.

It cannot be denied that, in this instance, the first cause of the evil was the carelessness of the administration. If the authorities had prevented the boatmen of Petersburg from overloading their vessels, or from venturing on the gulf in craft too small or weak to ride the waves, no one would have perished; and yet, who knows? The Russians are generally bad seamen: wherever they are, there is danger. When Asiatics, with their long robes and long beards, are the sailors, there can be little surprise at hearing of shipwrecks.

On the day of the fête, one of the steamboats that generally run between Petersburg and Kronstadt, started for Peterhof. Although large and strong, it was in danger of foundering like the smaller vessels, and would have done so had it not been for a foreigner who was among the passengers. This man (who was an Englishman) seeing several vessels capsized around them, knowing the danger they were in, and observing, further, that the boat was badly served and badly commanded, conceived the happy idea of cutting, with his own knife, the cords which held the awning raised upon deck for the comfort and convenience of the passengers. The first thing that ought to have been done, upon the least sign of a squall, was to remove this pavilion. The Russians never dreamt of so simple a precaution, and had it not been for the foreigner's presence of mind, the boat would have infallibly capsized. It was saved, though too much damaged to continue the voyage, and its crew only too happy in being able to return to Petersburg. If the Englishman who saved it had not been an acquaintance of another Englishman, who is one of my friends, I should not have known the fact. It was confirmed to me by other informed persons, to whom I mentioned it, but they requested that I would keep it secret!

It would not do to talk about the Deluge, if that catastrophe had happened under the reign of a Russian emperor.

Among all the intelligent faculties, the only one here valued is that of tact. Imagine a whole nation bending under the yoke of this drawing-room virtue. Picture to your minds an entire people, prudent as a diplomatist who has yet his fortune to make, and you will compass the idea of the substance and worth of conversation in Russia. If the atmosphere of the court oppresses us, even when at the court, how unfriendly to life must it not be when it pursues us into the very retirement of the family circle!

Russia is a nation of mutes. Some potent magician has transformed sixty millions of human beings into automata, who must await the wand of another enchanter before they can again enjoy life. Or it reminds me of the palace of Sleeping Beauty in the Wood,—it is bright and magnificent, but it lacks one thing, which is life, or, in other words, liberty.

The emperor must suffer from such a state of things. Whoever is born to command, no doubt loves obedience; but the obedience of a man is worth more than that of a machine. A prince surrounded by complaisant flatterers must always remain in ignorance of everything which it is wished he should not know; he is, therefore, necessarily condemned to doubt every word and to distrust every individual. Such is the lot of an absolute master. In vain would he be amiable, in vain would he live as a man; the force of circumstances makes him unfeeling in spite of himself; he occupies the place of a despot, and is obliged to submit to a despot's destiny,—to adopt his sentiments, or, at least, to play his part.

The evils of dissimulation extend here further than may be imagined: the Russian police, so alert to torment people, is slow to help or enlighten them when they have recourse to its aid in doubtful situations.

The following is an example of this designed inertia. At the last carnival, a lady of my acquaintance had permitted her maid to go out on the Sunday. Night came, and she did not return. On the following morning, the lady, very uneasy, sent to obtain information from the police.

They replied that no accident had occurred in Petersburg on the preceding night, and that no doubt the *femme de chambre* had lost herself, and would soon return safe and sound.

The day passed in deceitful security. On the day following, a relation of the girl's, a young man tolerably versed in the secrets of the police, conceived the idea of going to the Hall of Surgery, to which one of his friends procured him an admission. Scarcely had he entered, when he recognized the corpse of his cousin, which the pupils were just about to start dissecting. Being a good Russian, he preserved self-command sufficient to conceal his emotion, and asked,—"Whose body is this?"

"No one knows; it is that of a girl who was found dead the night before last, in ———— Street; it is believed that she has been strangled in attempting to defend herself against men who endeavored to rape her."

"Who are the men?"

"We do not know; one can only form conjectures on the event; proofs are wanting."

"How did you obtain the body?"

"The police sold it to us secretly; so we will not talk about it."

This last is a common expression in the mouth of a Russian, or an *acclimated* foreigner.

The cousin was dead. The mistress of the victim dared not complain; and now, after a lapse of six months, I am, perhaps, the only person to whom she has related the death of her *femme de chambre*.

It will by this be seen how the subaltern agents of the Russian police perform their duties. These faithless servants gained a double advantage by selling the body of the murdered woman: they obtained a few rubles, and they also concealed the murder, which would have brought upon them severe blame, if the noise of the event had spread.

Reprimands addressed to men of this class are, I believe, accompanied with other demonstrations, of a character likely to engrave the words indelibly on the memories of the unfortunate hearers. A Russian of the lower class is as often beaten as saluted. The lifting of the rod (in Russia, the rod is a large split cane), and the lifting of the hat, are means employed in about equal measure, in the social education of this people. Beating in Russia can only be applied to certain classes, and by men of certain other classes. Here, ill-treatment is regulated like the tariff of a customhouse; it reminds us of the code of Ivan. The dignity of caste is admitted, but no one dreams of the dignity of man. The reader will recollect what I have already said of the politeness of the Russians of all ranks, and of its real value; I will now confine myself to relating one or two of the illustrative scenes that pass daily before my eyes.

I have seen, in the same street, two drivers of droshkies ceremoniously lift their hats in passing each other:—this is a common custom; if acquainted, they lift their hand to their mouth with an amicable smile, and kiss it, making at the same time a little expressive and intelligent sign with the eyes. So much for politeness.

A little farther on, I have seen a courier, a *Feldjäger*, or some other government servant, descend from his vehicle, and, running to one of these well-bred coachmen, strike him brutally and unmercifully with whip, stick, or fist, in the breast, the face, or on the head, which punishment the unlucky creature, who had not made way in sufficient haste, received without the least complaint or resistance, out of respect to the uniform and the caste of his tormentor, whose anger, however, is not always in such cases promptly disarmed by the submission of the delinquent.

I have seen one of these carriers of dispatches, the courier of some minister, or the *valet de chambre* of some aide-de-camp of the emperor's, drag from his seat a young coachman, and never cease striking him until he had covered his face with blood. The victim submitted to the torture like a real lamb, without the least resistance, and in the same manner as one would yield to some inevitable commotion of nature. The passersby were in no degree moved or excited by the cruelty; and one of the comrades of the sufferer, who was watering his horses a few steps off, obedient to a sign of the enraged *Feldjäger*, approached to hold his horse's bridle during the time that he was pleased to prolong the punishment. In what other country could a man of the lower orders be found who would assist in the infliction of an arbitrary punishment upon one of his companions?

The scene in question took place in the finest part of the city, and at the busiest hour. When the unfortunate man was released, he wiped away the blood, which streamed down his cheeks, remounted his seat, and recommenced his bows and salutations as usual. It should be recollected that this abomination was enacted in the midst of a silent crowd. A people governed in a Christian manner would protest against a social discipline which destroys all individual liberty. But here, the influence of the priest is confined to obtaining from the people and the nobles signs of the cross and genuflections.

Notwithstanding its worship of the Holy Spirit, this nation has always its god upon earth. Like Tamerlane, the emperor of Russia receives the idolatrous worship of his subjects; the Russian law has never been baptized.

I hear every day some encomium on the gentleness, politeness, and pacific humor of the people of St. Petersburg. Elsewhere, I should admire this calm; here I can only view it as the worst symptom of the evil of which I complain. The people are actuated by fear to a degree that urges them to dissimulate, and to assume the appearance of a content and tranquillity which conduces to the satisfaction of the oppressor, and the security of the oppressed. Your true tyrant likes to be surrounded with smiles. Under the terror which hovers over all heads, submission becomes the general rule of conduct; victims and executioners, all practice the obedience that perpetuates the evil which they inflict or to which they submit.

The intervention of the police between people who quarrel would expose the combatants to punishment yet more formidable than the blows they bear in silence, and they avoid therefore all noise that might call the executioner to the spot.

Of the following tumultuous scene, chance, however, rendered me a witness this morning:—

I was passing along a canal covered with boats laden with wood, which the men were carrying on shore. One of these porters got into a quarrel with his comrades, and they all started fighting, as they might have done among ourselves on a similar occasion. The aggressor, finding himself the weakest, took to flight: he climbed, with the agility of a squirrel, a large mast of the vessel, and perching himself upon a yard, set at defiance his less nimble adversaries. So far I found the scene amusing. The men, seeing themselves balked in their hope of vengeance, and forgetting that they were in Russia, manifested their fury by loud cries and savage menaces. There are found at certain distances, in all the streets of the city, policemen in uniform: two of these persons, attracted by the vociferations of the combatants, repaired to the scene of action, and commanded the chief offender to descend from his perch. This individual did not obey the summons; one of the policemen sprang on board; the refractory porter clung to the mast: the man of power reiterated his commands, and the rebel persisted in his disobedience. The former, infuriated, tried himself to climb the mast, and succeeded in seizing one of the feet of the fugitive, which, without troubling himself with any consideration as to the manner in which the unfortunate being was to descend, he pulled at with all his force. The other, hopeless of escaping the punishment that awaited him, at length yielded to his fate; he let go his hold, and fell from a height of about twelve feet upon a pile of wood, on which his body lay as motionless as a sack. The severity of the fall may be imagined. The head struck against the wood, and the sound of the concussion reached my ear, though I was about fifty paces off. I supposed the man was dead; his face was bathed in blood; nevertheless, on recovering from the first stunning effect of the fall, the unfortunate savage, thus taken in the snare, rose; his visage, wherever the blood allowed it to be seen, had a frightful paleness, and he began to bellow like an ox. His horrible cries diminished my compassion; he seemed to me as nothing more than a brute, and I could not therefore feel for him as for one of my fellows. The louder the man howled, the harder my heart grew; so true it is that the objects of our compassion must exhibit something of their proper dignity, ere we can deeply participate in their trouble. Pity is a sentiment of association, and who would mentally associate with that which he despises? They at length carried him off, although he continued to offer a desperate and protracted resistance. A small boat was brought alongside by other policemen; the prisoner was bound with cords, his hands were fastened behind his back, and he was thrown on his face into the boat. This second rude shock was followed by a shower of blows, nor did the torture end here; the sergeant who had seized the victim, no sooner saw him thus prostrate, than he jumped upon his body, and began to stamp upon him with all his force, trampling him under his feet as the grapes are trod in the winepress. I had then approached the spot, and was therefore witness of all that I relate. During this horrible torture, the frightful yells of the victim were at first redoubled, but when they began to grow fainter and fainter, I felt that I could no longer command myself, and, having no power to interfere, I hastened away.

What most disgusts me is the refined elegance which is exhibited in the same picture with such revolting barbarity. If there were less luxury and delicacy among the higher orders, the condition of the lower would inspire me with less indignation. Such occurrences, with all that they involve, would make me hate the most delightful country in the world; how much more, then, a heath of plaster—a painted marsh!

"What exaggeration!" the Russians would say. "What strong expressions, for so trifling a matter!!" I know you call it trifling, and it is for that I reproach you. Your familiarity with these horrors explains your indifference without justifying it: you make no more account of the cords with which you bind a man, than of the collar which you put on your dog.

In broad daylight, in the open street, to beat a man to death before he is tried, appears a very simple matter in the eyes of the public and of the constables of Petersburg. Merchants, lords, and soldiers, the poor and the rich, the great and small, the polite and the vulgar, the clowns and the fops, the Russians of every class, consent to let such things quietly go on in their presence, without troubling themselves about their legality. Elsewhere, the citizen is protected by the whole community against the agent of unjust power; here the public agent is protected against the just accusations of the injured individual. The serf never accuses.

The Emperor Nicholas has made a code! If the facts I have related are in accordance with the laws of that code, so much the worse for the legislator; if they are illegal, so much the worse for the administrator of the law. The emperor is, in both cases, responsible. What a misfortune to be no more than a man in accepting the office of a god, and yet to be forced to accept it! Absolute government should be confided only to angels.

I pledge myself to the accuracy of the facts that are here related. I have neither added nor retrenched one circumstance in the story, and I recount it while the slightest features of the scene continue present to my mind.*

If such details could be published at Petersburg, with the commentaries indispensable to make them noticed by minds inured to all kinds of brutality and injustice, they would not effect the good that might be expected. The Russian administration would so order matters, that the police of Petersburg

---

*It may not be useless to repeat that this chapter, like almost all the others, was preserved and concealed with care during my sojourn in Russia.

should henceforth seem to be more mild in its treatment of the people, were it only out of respect for the squeamish sentiments of foreigners; but this would be all.

The manners of a people are gradually formed by the reciprocal action of the laws upon the customs, and of the customs upon the laws; they do not change as by the stroke of a wand. Those of the Russians, in spite of the pretensions of these half savages, are, and will yet long remain cruel. It is little more than a century since they were true Tartars: it was Peter the Great who first compelled the men to admit females into their social meetings; and under all their modern elegance, several of these parvenus of civilization cannot still altogether conceal the bearskin. They simply turn it inside out.

Seeing that they can now no longer avail themselves of the age of chivalry—that age by whose spirit the nations of western Europe were so much benefited in their youth—all that can remain for the Russians is an independent and influential religion. Russia has a faith, but a political faith does not emancipate the human mind; it shuts it up in the narrow circle of its natural interests. With the Catholic faith, the Russians would soon acquire general ideas, based on a rational course of instruction, and on a liberty proportioned to their state of enlightenment. Could they but obtain this elevation, I am persuaded that they might rule the world. The evil of their system is deeply seated, and the remedies hitherto employed have only acted upon the surface—they have healed the wound over without curing it. A genuine civilization spreads from the center to the circumference, that of Russia tends from the circumference towards the center; it is a barbarism plastered over, and nothing more.

Because a savage may have the vanity of a man of the world, does it follow that his mind is cultivated? I repeat, and may, perhaps, repeat again, that the Russians care much less for being civilized than for making us believe that they are civilized. So long as this public disease of vanity shall continue to prey upon their hearts and corrupt their minds, they will have certain great lords who will be able to make a display of refinement, both among themselves and us; but they will remain barbarians at heart. Unfortunately, however, savages understand the use of firearms.

The endeavors of the Emperor Nicholas justify my views. He has thought, before I did, that the time for the display of appearances is past in Russia, and that the entire, edifice of civilization in that land has to be reconstructed.

Peter the Great would have overthrown it a second time in order to rebuild it. Nicholas is more skillful. I am filled with respect for this, man, who, with the whole energy of his mind, struggles in secret against the work of the genius of Peter the Great. While continuing to deify that mighty reformer, he is, all the while, bringing back to their proper position a nation led astray among the paths of imitation for upwards of a hundred years. The views of the present emperor manifest themselves even in the streets of Petersburg. He does not amuse himself with erecting, in haste, colonnades of stuccoed bricks; he is everywhere replacing appearance with reality; stone is everywhere superseding plaster, and buildings of a strong and massive architecture are rising above the showy monuments of a false splendor. It is by first bringing back a people to their primitive character, that they are rendered capable and worthy of true civilization, without which a nation cannot know how to work for posterity. If a people would rear a monument to their own power and greatness, they must not copy foreigners,—they must study to develop the national genius instead of thwarting it. That which in this creation most nearly approaches to Deity, is Nature. Nature calls the Russians to great things, while they, under their pretended civilization, have been occupied with trifles. The Emperor Nicholas has appreciated their capabilities better than his predecessors, and under his reign, by a general return to truth, everything is becoming great. In Petersburg stands a pillar, which is the largest piece of granite that has ever been cut by the hands of man, not excepting the Egyptian monuments. Seventy thousand soldiers, the court, the city, and the surrounding country, gathered together, without inconvenience or pressure, in the square of the Imperial Palace, to witness, in a religious silence, the miraculous erection of this monument, conceived, executed, and placed by a Frenchman, M. de Montferrand; for the French are still necessary to the Russians. The prodigious machines worked successfully, and at the moment when the column, rising from its fetters, lifted itself up as if animated with a life of its own, the army, the crowd, the emperor himself, fell on their knees to thank God for so great a miracle, and to praise him for the stupendous achievements which he permitted them to accomplish. This I call a real national fête; not a flattery that might, like the masquerade of Peterhof, have been also taken for a satire, but a grand historical picture. The great, the little, the bad, the sublime, and all other opposites, enter into the constitution of this singular country, while silence perpetuates the prodigy, and prevents the machine from breaking.

The Emperor Nicholas extends his reforms even to the language of those who surround him; he requires Russian to be spoken at court. The greater number of the women of the highest circles, especially those who have been born at Petersburg, are ignorant of their native language; but they learn a few Russian phrases, which they utter through obedience to the emperor, when he passes into the rooms of the palace where their duties may retain them. One of them acts always as a sentinel, to announce to the others, by some conventional sign, the arrival of the monarch, on whose appearance French conversation immediately ceases, and Russian phrases, destined to flatter the Imperial ear, are heard on every side. The prince observes, with self-complacency, the extent of his power as a reformer; and the fair rebels begin to laugh as soon as he has passed.

However, like every reformer, the emperor is endowed with an obstinacy which must ultimately produce success.

At the extremity of that square, vast as a mighty region, in which stands the column, is to be seen a mountain of granite,—the church of St. Isaac of Petersburg. This edifice, though less stately, less beautiful in design, and less rich in ornaments than that of St. Peter's at Rome, is quite as extraordinary. It is not finished, and one cannot therefore judge of the whole, which will be a work whose gigantic proportions will far exceed those which the spirit of the age has produced among other nations. Its materials are granite, bronze, and iron, and no other. Its color is imposing, though somber.

The marvelous temple was commenced under Alexander, and will soon be completed under the reign of Nicholas, by the same Frenchman (M. de Montferrand) who raised the column.

And such efforts for the benefit of a church crippled by the civil power! Alas! the Word of God will never be heard under this roof. The temples of the Greek church no longer serve as roofs for the pulpits of truth. In scorn of the memories of the Athanasiuses and the Chrysostoms, religion is not taught publicly to the Russians. The Greek Muscovites suppress the word of preaching, unlike the Protestants, whose religion consists of nothing but that word.

The emperor, aided by his armies of soldiers and of artists, exerts himself in vain. He will never invest the Greek church with a power which God has not given it: it may be rendered a persecuting, but it cannot be rendered an apostolical, church,— a church, that is to say, which is a *civilizer*, and a conqueror in the moral world. To discipline men is not to convert souls. This political and national church has neither moral nor spiritual life: where independence is wanting, there can be nothing else that is good. Schism, in separating the priest from his independent head, immediately throws him into the hands of his temporal prince; and thus revolt is punished by slavery. In the most bloody periods of history, the Catholic church labored to emancipate the nations: the adulterous priest sold the God of heaven to the god of the world, to enable him to tyrannize over men in the name of Christ; but that impious priest, while even killing the body, enlightened the mind: for, altogether turned from the right way as he was, he nevertheless formed part of a church which possessed life and light. The Greek priest imparts neither life nor death—he is himself a dead body.

Signs of the cross, salutations in the streets, bowing of the knees before the chapels, prostrations of old devotees upon the pavements of the churches, kissings of the hands, a wife, children, and universal contempt,—such are the fruits of the priest's abdication,—such is all that he has been able to obtain from the most superstitious people in the world. What a lesson! and what a punishment! In the midst of the triumph of his schism, the schismatic priest is struck with impotence. A priest, when he wishes to engross temporal power, perishes for the want of views sufficiently elevated to enable him to see the road that God has appointed for him;—a priest who allows himself to be dethroned by the king for the want of courage to follow that road, equally fails in his high calling.

I cannot apologize for the wandering character of my thoughts and disquisitions, for, in passing freely from object to object, from idea to idea, I describe Russia as a whole, and show the truth as it appears to me, better than if, with a more methodical style, I purposely endeavored to avoid the reproach of inconsistencies, digressions, or confusion of subjects. The state of the people, the greatness of the emperor, the aspect of the streets, the beauty of the public buildings, the degraded state of minds consequent upon the degeneration of the religious principle, all strike my eyes at the same moment, and pass, so to speak, at once under my pen; and all constitute Russia, the principles of whose life reveal themselves to my thoughts in the contemplation of objects the least significant in appearance.

Yesterday, I walked out with a Frenchman, an intelligent person, well acquainted with Petersburg, where he resides as tutor in the family of a great nobleman. He has consequently opportunities for attaining a knowledge of the truth, entirely beyond the reach of passing travelers. He considered my views of Russia too favorable. I laugh at this reproach when I think of those which the Russians will make against me, and I maintain that I am impartial, seeing that I hate only that which appears to me evil, and that I admire all which appears good, in this, as in other lands.

The Frenchman of whom I speak passes his life among Russian aristocrats.

We were walking leisurely along the beautiful promenade of the Nevsky Prospect, when suddenly a black or dark green coach passed before us. It was long, low built, and closed on all sides, and much resembled an enormous coffin raised upon wheels. Four little apertures of about six inches square, crossed with iron bars, gave air and light to this moving tomb; a child of eight, or, at the most, ten years, guided the two horses attached to the machine; and, to my surprise, a considerable number of soldiers escorted it. I had scarcely time to ask my companion the use of so singular an equipage, when my question was answered by a ghastly face, which appeared at one of the air holes, and at once informed me that the carriage served to transport prisoners to the place of their destination.

"It is the traveling cell of the Russians," said my companion; "elsewhere, no doubt, they have similar odious objects; but then they seek to hide them as much as they can from the public; here, they make as much display of them as possible. What a government!"

"Think," I replied, "of the difficulties it has to encounter!"

"Ah! you are still the dupe of their gilded words. I see the Russian authorities impose upon you whatever they please."

"I endeavor to place myself as much as possible in their situation; nothing requires more candid consideration than the position of those who govern, for it is not they who have created the existing state of things; their business is to defend it even while prudently reforming it. If the iron rod which governs this debased people were to be removed but for one moment, society would be overturned."

"They tell you that; but, trust me, they delight in this pretended necessity. Those who most complain of the severities they are obliged, as they say, to put in force, would renounce them with regret. In the bottom of their hearts they love a government without check or counterpoise; such a government works more easily than any other. No man willingly gives up anything which makes his task more easy. Could you expect a preacher to dispense with the terrors of hell, in his efforts to convert hardened sinners? Hell is the capital punishment of the theologians*; at first they make use of it with regret, as of a necessary evil, but they soon acquire a taste for dealing out damnation upon the greater part of mankind. It is the same thing with severe measures in politics; they are feared before they are tried, but after their success is witnessed, they are admired; and such, you may depend upon it, is the feeling too general in this country. I often think that they take pleasure in creating circumstances, under which it is necessary to inflict punishment, for fear they should get out of practice. Are you ignorant of what is now passing on the Volga?"

"I heard of serious troubles there, but they say that they were promptly repressed."

"No doubt: but at what price? And what should you say, were I to tell you that those frightful disorders were the result of a word of the emperor's."

"Never will you induce me to believe that he can have approved such horrors."

"Neither do I say he has. Nevertheless, a word pronounced

---

*I would beg the reader to remember that it is not I who thus speak.

by him—innocently, I believe—has caused the evil. The fact is as follows: notwithstanding the injustice of the overseers of the crown, the lot of the peasants of the emperor is still preferable to that of other serfs; and whenever the sovereign becomes proprietor of some new domain, its inhabitants are the envy of all their neighbors. The crown lately purchased a considerable estate in the district that has since revolted. Immediately, the peasants sent deputies from every part of the surrounding country to the new superintendents of the Imperial lands, to supplicate the emperor to purchase them also. The serfs chosen as ambassadors were sent on to Petersburg. The emperor received them and treated them with kindness; but, to their great regret, he did not buy them. 'I cannot,' he said to them, 'purchase all Russia, but a time will come, I hope, when each peasant of this empire will be free: if it depended only upon me, the Russians should enjoy, from this day forth, the independence which I wish for them; and to procure them which at a future period, I am laboring with all my power.' "

"Well, this answer seems to me full of reason, candor, and humanity."

"No doubt: but the emperor should have known the men to whom he addressed such words; and not have murdered his noblemen out of tenderness towards his serfs. These words, interpreted by barbarous and envious peasants, have set a whole province on fire; and thus has it become necessary to punish a people for crimes which they were instigated to commit. '*Our father* desires our deliverance,' cried the returned deputies on the borders of the Volga; 'he wishes for nothing but our happiness; he said so to us, himself: it is, then, only the nobles and their agents who are our enemies, and who oppose the good designs of *our father!* Let us avenge the emperor!' After this, the peasants believed they were performing a pious work in rising upon their masters, and thus all the nobles of a canton, and all their agents were massacred, together with their families. They spitted one,

287

and roasted him alive; they boiled another in a cauldron; they disemboweled, and killed, in various other ways, the stewards and agents of the estates; they murdered all they met, burnt whole towns, and, in short, devastated a province; not in the name of liberty, for they do not know what liberty means, but in the name of deliverance and of the emperor."

"It was perhaps some of these savages whom we saw passing in the prisoners' conveyance. How could such beings be influenced by the gentle means employed by the governments of western Europe?"

"It would be necessary gradually to change the ideas of the people; instead of which they find it more convenient to change their location. After every scene of this kind, villages and entire counties are transported. No population is sure of preserving its territory, the result of which is, that men who have become naturally attached to the soil, are deprived, in their slavery, of the only compensation which could comport with their condition. By an infernal combination, they are made moveable without being made free. A word from the monarch roots them up as though they were trees, tears them from their native soil, and sends them to perish or to languish at the world's end. The peasant, exposed to these storms of supreme power, loves not his cabin, the only thing in this world that he could love; he detests his life, and ill understands its duties; for it is necessary to impart some happiness to a man in order to make him feel his obligations; misery only instructs him in hypocrisy and revolt. If self-interest, when well understood, is not the foundation of morals, it is at least their support."

"Yet it is difficult to change the spirit of a people: it is the work neither of a day, nor of a reign."

"Is it a work at which they sincerely labor?"

"I think so, but with prudence."

"What you call prudence, I call insincerity; you do not know the emperor."

"Reproach him with being inflexible, but not with being false; in a prince, inflexibility is often a virtue."

"Do you believe the character of the emperor to be sincere? Remember his conduct at the death of Pushkin."

"I do not know the circumstances of that event."

Thus talking, we arrived at the Champ de Mars, a vast square, which appears a desert, though it occupies the middle of the city. A man may converse there with less danger of being overheard than in his chamber. My cicerone continued:—

"Pushkin was, as you are aware, the greatest of Russian poets."

"We are no judges of that."

"We are, at least, of his reputation. Whether well founded or not, his reputation was great. He was yet young, and of an irascible temper. You know he had Moorish blood on his mother's side. His wife, a very handsome woman, inspired him with more passion than confidence. His poetical temperament, and his African blood, made him easily jealous; and it was thus, exasperated by appearances and by false reports, envenomed with a perfidy which calls to mind the conception of Shakespeare, that this Russian Othello lost all reason, and sought to force the man by whom he believed himself injured, to fight with him. This person was a Frenchman, and, unfortunately, his brother-in-law; his name was M. d'Antès. A duel in Russia is a serious affair, the more so, because, instead of according, as among us, with ideas and customs in opposition to laws, it militates against all preconceived notions: this nation is more Oriental than chivalrous. Dueling is illegal here as elsewhere; but, besides this, it is less supported by public opinion than in other lands. M. d'Antès did all he could to avoid the difficulty. Urged vehemently by the unhappy husband, he refused him satisfaction, though in a manner that was dignified: but, notwithstanding, he continued his assiduities. Pushkin became almost mad. The constant presence of the man whose death he wished, appeared to him a permanent insult, and in order to rid himself of him, he acted in a way that made a duel inevitable. The two brothers-in-law fought, and M. d'Antès killed Pushkin. The man whom public opinion accused, triumphed; and the injured husband, the national poet, the innocent party, fell.

"This death excited public indignation. Pushkin, the Russian poet, par excellence, the author of the finest odes in the language, the glory of the country, the restorer of Slavic poetry, in short, the pride of the age, the hope of the future, to fall by the hand of a Frenchman! was an event that roused public passion to the highest pitch. Petersburg, Moscow, the whole empire was in excitement. The emperor, who knows the Russians better than any man in Russia, took care to join in the public affliction. He ordered a service to be performed, and I am not sure that he did not carry his pious affectation so far as to assist in person at the ceremony, in order to publish his regret by taking God to witness his admiration of the national genius removed too soon for the nation's glory.

"However this may be, the sympathy of the sovereign so flattered the Muscovite spirit as to awake a generous patriotism in the breast of a young man, endowed with considerable talent. This too credulous poet was so enraptured by the august protection accorded to the first of all arts, that he grew bold enough to believe himself inspired! In the ingenuous yearnings of his gratitude, he ventured even to write an ode— a patriotic ode, to thank the emperor for becoming the protector of literature. He concluded his remarkable production by singing the praises of the departed bard. This was all he did; I have read the verses, and I can attest the innocent intentions of the author: unless at least it might be a crime to conceal in the depths of his bosom a hope, perhaps, of becoming one day a second Pushkin,—a hope very pardonable, it seems to me, in a youthful imagination.

"Audacious youth! to aim at renown, to betray a passion for glory under a despotism! It was the same as if Prometheus had said to Jupiter,—'Take care of yourself, I am going to rob you of your thunderbolts.'

"The recompense which this young aspirant received for having thus publicly shown his confidence in his master's love for the fine arts and the belles lettres, was a SECRET order to go and pursue his poetical studies on the Caucasus, a chapel of ease to the ancient Siberia.

"After having remained there two years, he has returned, his health destroyed, his spirit broken, and his imagination radically cured of its chimeras. After this trait, will you yet put trust in the official words or the public acts of the emperor?"

"The emperor is a man; he shares human weaknesses. Something must have shocked him in the allusions of the young poet. Perhaps they were European rather than national. The emperor proceeds on a principle the very opposite to that of Catherine II, he braves Europe instead of flattering it. This is wrong, I admit; for studied opposition is in itself a species of dependence, since under it, a man is only influenced by contradiction; but it is pardonable, especially if you reflect on the evil caused to Russia by princes who were possessed all their life with the mania of imitation."

"You are incorrigible!" exclaimed the advocate of the ancient boyars. "You believe, then, in the possibility of Russian civilization? It promised well before the time of Peter the Great, but that prince destroyed the fruit in its germ. Go to Moscow, it is the center of the ancient empire; yet you will see that all minds are turned towards speculations of industry, and that the national character is as much effaced there as at St. Petersburg. The Emperor Nicholas commits today, though with different views, a fault analogous to that of Peter the Great. He does not take into account the history of an entire age, the age of the Emperor Peter: history has its fatalities,—the fatalities of faits accomplis. Woe to the prince who does not submit to these!"

291

The day was advanced; we separated, and I continued my walk, musing upon the energetic feeling of opposition which must spring up in minds accustomed to reflect under the silence of despotism. Characters which such a government does not debase, it steels and fortifies.

On my return, I sat down to read again some translations of the poems of Pushkin. They confirmed me in the opinion that a previous reading had imparted. This author has borrowed much of his coloring from the new poetical school of western Europe. Not that he has adopted the antireligious opinions of Lord Byron, the social notions of our poets, or the philosophy of those of Germany; but he has adopted their manner of describing. I therefore do not recognize him as a real Muscovite poet. The Pole, Mickiewicz, strikes me as being much more Slavic, although he, like Pushkin, has bowed to the influence of occidental literature.

The real Russian poet, did one exist, could, in the present day address only the people; he would neither be understood nor read in the salons. Where there is no language, there is no poetry; neither indeed are there any thinkers. The Emperor Nicholas has begun to require that Russian be spoken at court; they laugh at present at a novelty which is viewed as merely a caprice of their master's; the next generation will thank him for this victory of good sense over fashion.

How could the national genius develop itself in a society where people speak four languages without knowing one? Originality of thought has a nearer connection than is imagined with purity of idiom. This fact has been forgotten in Russia for a century, and in France for some years. Our children will feel the effects of the rage for English nurses which has, among us, taken possession of all fashionable mothers.

In France formerly, the first, and I believe the best French tutor, was the wet nurse. A man should study his native language throughout his whole life, but the child should not be formally taught it; he should receive it in the cradle, without study. Instead of this, our little Frenchmen of the present day lisp English, and stammer German from their birth, and are afterwards taught French as a foreign language.

Montaigne congratulated himself on having learned Latin previously to French. It is perhaps to the advantage in which the author of the *Essays* thus glories, that we owe the most pure and national style in our ancient literature; he had a right to rejoice, for Latin is the root of our language; but all purity and spontaneity of expression is lost among a people who do not respect the language of their fathers. Our children speak English, just as our footmen wear powder! I am persuaded that the want of originality in modern Slavic literature is attributable to the custom, which the Poles and Russians adopted during the eighteenth century, of introducing into their families foreign tutors and preceptors. When the Russians turn their thoughts again into their own language, they translate; and this borrowed style checks the flow of thought, at the same time that it destroys the simplicity of expression.

How is it that the Chinese have hitherto done more for the human race in literature, in philosophy, in morals, and in legislation than the Russians? It is, perhaps, because these men have not ceased to entertain a strong affection for their primitive dialect.

The confusion of languages does not injure mediocre minds; on the contrary, it aids them in their efforts. Superficial instruction, the only kind which is suited to such minds, is facilitated by a study, equally superficial, of the living languages—an easy study, or rather a mental recreation perfectly suited to indolent faculties, or to faculties devoted to material aims. But whenever, by mischance, this system is applied to the education of superior talent, it checks the work of nature, leads genius astray, and prepares for it either a future source of fruitless regrets,—or efforts which few even of the most distinguished men have the leisure or the courage, after the period of early youth is passed, to undertake. All great writers are not Rousseaus. Rousseau studied our language as a foreigner, and it would require his genius of expression and his susceptibility of imagination, joined to his tenacity of character, and also his isolation in society, in order to learn French as he learned it. Still the French of the Genevese is less at variance with that of Fénelon, than the jargon, mixed with English and German, which is now taught in Paris to the children of the highest classes. Perhaps the labored artifices that too often appear in the sentences of Rousseau would not have existed, if the great writer had been born in France at a time when (as was then the case) the children spoke French.

The study of the ancient languages, then in vogue, far from being attended with a mischievous result, afforded us the only means of attaining a profound knowledge of our own, which is derived from them. This study led us back to the pure waters of our source, and there strengthened our national genius, independently of its advantages as being the most appropriate to the development of the faculties of childhood, into whose mind, before all else, should be instilled the power of language as the instrument of thought.

Whilst Russia, slowly regenerated by the sovereign who now governs her, from the errors entailed by former monarchs, may hope to attain a language, the poets, the prose writers, the refined and soi-disant enlightened people amongst ourselves, are preparing for France a generation of scribbling imitators, of readers without independence of mind; people who understand Shakespeare and Goethe so well in the original, that they can neither appreciate the prose of Bossuet and of Chateaubriand, the winged poetry of Hugo, the classic periods of Racine, the originality and boldness of Molière and of La Fontaine, the refined wit and taste of Madame de Sévigné, nor the sentiment and the divine harmony of Lamartine!

Thus it is that they will be rendered incapable of producing anything sufficiently original to perpetuate the glory of their language, and to attract, as formerly, the men of all countries to France, there to study and to appreciate the mysteries of taste.

LETTER 18

DISTURBANCES IN RUSSIA. — PARALLEL BETWEEN FRENCH AND
RUSSIAN CRIMES AND CRUELTIES. — CHARACTERISTICS OF REVOLT
IN RUSSIA. — ORDER IN DISORDER. — DANGER OF INCULCATING
LIBERAL IDEAS AMONG IGNORANT POPULATIONS. — REASONS FOR
RUSSIAN SUPERIORITY IN DIPLOMACY. — HISTORY OF THELENEF, A
TALE OF MODERN RUSSIA.

THIS MORNING, early, I received a visit from the individual whose conversation is recounted in the last chapter. He
brought me a French manuscript, written by the young
prince, the son of his patron. It is the relation of an occurrence, only too true, that forms one of the numerous episodes
of the yet recent event with which all feeling and thoughtful
minds are still silently and secretly occupied. Is it possible
to enjoy, without any feelings of uneasiness, the luxury of
a magnificent abode, when one thinks that, at a few hundred
leagues from the palace, murder is rampant, and society
would fall to pieces, were it not for the terrific means employed to uphold it?

The young Prince ———, who has written this story,
would be ruined if it could be discovered that he was the author. It is on this account that he has confided his manuscript
to me, and entrusted me with its publication. He permits me
to insert the account of the death of Thelenef in the text of
my travels, where I shall faithfully give it, without, however,
compromising the safety of anyone. I am assured of the accuracy of the principal facts; the reader can put as much or as
little faith in them as he pleases; for my own part, I always

believe what people whom I do not know say to me. The suspicion of falsehold never enters my mind until after the proof.

The young Russian, who is the author of the fragment, wishing to justify, by the memory of the horrors of our revolution, the ferocity of his own countrymen, has cited an act of French cruelty, the massacre of M. de Belzunce at Caen. He might have increased his list: Mademoiselle de Sombreuil forced to drink a glass of blood to redeem the life of her father; the heroic death of the archbishop of Arles, and of his glorious companions in martyrdom, within the cloisters of the Carmelite convent at Paris; the massacres of Lyons; the executions, by drowning, at Nantes, surnamed by Carrier, the republican marriages; and many other atrocities which historians have not even recorded, might serve to prove that human ferocity only sleeps among nations even the most civilized. Nevertheless, there is a difference between the cold, methodical, and abiding cruelty of the Muzhiks, and the passing frenzy of the French. These latter, during the war which they carried on against God and humanity, were not in their natural state; the mood of blood had changed their character; and the extravagances of passion ruled over all their acts; for never were they less free than at the epoch when everything that was done among them was done in the name of liberty. We are, on the contrary, going to see the Russians murder each other without belying their characters; it is still a duty which they are performing.

Among this obedient people, the influence of social institutions is so great in every class—ideas and habits so rule over characters, that the fiercest excesses of vengeance still appear ruled by a certain degree of discipline. Murder is designed and executed in an orderly manner; no rage, no emotion, no words: a calm is preserved more terrible than the delirium of hate. They struggle with, overthrow, trample, and destroy each other, with the steady regularity of machines turning upon their pivots. This physical impassability in the

Astolphe de Custine

midst of scenes the most violent, this monstrous audacity in the conception and calmness in the execution, this silent passion and speechless fanaticism seem, if one might so express it, the innocence of crime. A certain order, contrary to nature, presides in this strange country over the most monstrous excesses; tyranny and revolt march in step, and perform their movements in unison.

As everything is alike, the immense extent of the territory does not prevent things being executed from one end of Russia to the other, with a punctuality, and a simultaneous correspondence, which is magical. If ever they should succeed in creating a REAL revolution among the Russian people, massacre would be performed with the regularity that marks the evolutions of a regiment. Villages would change into barracks, and organized murder would stalk forth armed from the cottages, form in line, and advance in order; in short, the Russians would prepare for pillage from Smolensk to Irkutsk, as they march to the parade in Petersburg. From so much uniformity, there results between the natural dispositions and the social habits of the people, a harmony, the effects of which might become prodigious in good as in evil.

Everything is obscure in the future prospects of the world; but, assuredly, it will see strange scenes enacted before the nations by this predestined people.

It is almost always under the influence of a blind respect for power, that the Russians disturb public order. Thus, if we are to believe what is repeated in secret, had it not been for the emperor's speech to the deputies of the peasants, the latter would not have taken up arms.

I trust that this fact, and those that I have elsewhere cited, will show the danger of inculcating liberal opinions among a population so ill prepared to receive them. As regards political liberty, the more we love it, the greater care should we take to avoid pronouncing its name before those who would only compromise a holy cause by their manner of defending

298

it. It is this which induces me to doubt of the truth of the imprudent reply attributed to the emperor. That prince knows, better than anyone, the character of his people, and I cannot believe that he could have provoked the revolt of the peasants, even unwittingly.

The horrors of the insurrection are described by the author of Thelenef, with an accuracy the more scrupulous, as the principal incident occurred in the family of the narrator.

If he has allowed himself to ennoble the character and the passion of his hero and heroine, it is because he has a poetical imagination; but while embellishing the sentiments, he has preserved the picture of national manners: in short, neither in the facts, the sentiments, nor the descriptions, does this little romance appear to me misplaced in the midst of a work, all the merit of which consists in the verisimilitude of its delineations.

I may add that the bloody scenes are yet being daily renewed in various parts of the same country where public order has been disturbed, and re-established in so terrific a manner. The Russians have no right to reproach France for her political disorders, and to draw from them consequences favorable to despotism. Let but the liberty of the press be accorded to Russia for twenty-four hours, and we should learn things that would make us recoil with horror. Silence is indispensable to oppression. Under an absolute government every indiscretion of speech is equivalent to a crime of high treason.

If there are found among the Russians, better diplomatists than among nations the most advanced in civilization, it is because our journals inform them of everything which is done or projected among ourselves, and because, instead of prudently disguising our weaknesses, we display them, with passion, every morning, whilst, on the contrary, the Byzantine policy of the Russians, working in the dark, carefully conceals from us everything that is thought, done, or feared

among them. We march exposed on all sides, they advance
under cover. The ignorance in which they leave us blinds our
view; our sincerity enlightens theirs; we suffer from all the
evils of idle talking, they have all the advantages of secrecy;
and herein lies all their skill and ability.

THE HISTORY OF THELENEF. *

The estates of Prince ——— had been for several years managed by a steward, named Thelenef. The prince, occupied with
other matters, seldom thought of his domains. Disappointed
in his ambitious views, he had traveled for a long time, in the
hope of dissipating his chagrin as a disgraced courtier. At
length, weary of seeking from the arts and from nature, consolation for his failure in politics, he returned to his own country, in order again to approach the court, and to endeavor by
dint of care and diligence to recover the favor of the sovereign.

But while fruitlessly wasting his life and fortune in playing by turns the courtier at Petersburg, and the amateur of
antiquities in southern Europe, he lost the attachment of his
peasants, exasperated by the ill-usage of Thelenef. This man
ruled as a king in the extensive estates of Vologda, where his
manner of exercising the lordly authority made him generally
execrated.

Thelenef had, however, a charming daughter, called Xenie.†
The amiability of this young person was an inborn virtue; for,
having early lost her mother, she had received no other education than that which her father could give her. He taught her
French, and she learned, as it were by heart, some of the clas-

---

*I have purposely changed the names of the persons and places, with the especial ob-
ject of disguising the true ones; and I have also taken the liberty of correcting, in the
style, a few expressions foreign to the genius of our language.

†This pretty name is that of a Russian saint.

sics of the age of Louis XIV; which had been left in the castle of Vologda by the father of the prince. The Bible, Pascal's *Pensées*, and *Telemachus* were her favorite books. When but a small number of authors are read, when those authors are well chosen, and when their works are often reperused, reading becomes very profitable. One of the causes of the frivolity of modern minds is the number of books badly read, rather than badly written, with which the world is inundated.

It would be rendering a service to the rising generation to teach them how to read, an acquirement which has become more rare since everyone has learned how to write.

Thanks to her reputation for learning, Xenie, at the age of nineteen, enjoyed a well-merited influence throughout the whole government of ———. People came to consult her from all the neighboring villages. In sickness, in disputes, in all the grievances of the poor peasants, Xenie was their guide and their support.

Her conciliating temper often brought upon her the rebukes of her father; but the knowledge of having done some good, or prevented some evil, compensated for everything. In a country where, in general, women have little influence, she exercised a power which no man in the district could dispute with her, the power of reason over brutish minds.

Even her father, violent as he was both by disposition and habit, felt the influence of her benevolent nature, and too often blushed to find himself checking the violence of his wrath through fear of giving pain to Xenie. Like a tyrannical prince, he blamed himself for his clemency, and accused himself of being too easy. He gloried in his angry passions, to which he gave the title of justice: the serfs of Prince ——— called them by another name.

The father and daughter resided in the castle of Vologda, which was situated in a widely extended plain, whose scenery, for Russia, is very pastoral.

Numerous herds and flocks, whose diminutive size and

feeble frames evince the severity of the climate, feed on the banks of the lake of Vologda, and form the only enlivening objects in the scene. Such landscapes are destitute of real beauty; nevertheless they have a tranquil, indistinct, and dreamy kind of grandeur, whose deep repose lacks neither sublimity nor poetry: it is the east without the sun.

One morning, Xenie went out with her father to assist in numbering the cattle, an operation which he himself performed every day. The herds, picturesquely grouped at different distances before the castle, animated the green banks of the lake, which were brightened by the rays of the rising sun, whilst the bell of a neighboring chapel was summoning to morning prayer some infirm, and therefore unemployed women, and several decayed old men, who enjoyed with resignation the repose of age.

The noble form of these hoary heads, the still fresh complexion of faces, whose brows were silvered with age, demonstrate the salubrity of the atmosphere, and evidence the beauty of the human race in this frozen zone. It is not to youthful countenances we must look, when we would know if beauty exists in a country.

"Look, my father," said Xenie, as she crossed the causeway which formed the isthmus that united the peninsula of the castle to the plain; "look at the flag floating over the cabin of my foster-brother."

The Russian peasants are frequently permitted to leave home, in order to exercise their industry in the neighboring towns, and sometimes even as far off as St. Petersburg. On such occasions they pay to their masters a fee, and only what they gain beyond this is their own. When one of these traveling serfs returns home to his wife, a pine, like a mast, is raised above the cabin, and a flag flutters on the top as a signal to the inhabitants of the surrounding villages, in order that when they see the joyful sign, they may sympathize with the happiness of the wife.

It was in accordance with this ancient custom that they had raised the streamer upon the pinnacle of the Pacome's cottage. The aged Elizabeth, the mother of Fedor, had been Xenie's wet nurse.

"He has returned then, this good-for-nothing foster-brother of thine," replied Thelenef.

"Oh! I am so glad he has," said Xenie.

"One knave more in the district," muttered Thelenef, "we have already enough of them"; and the face of the steward, always gloomy, assumed a yet more forbidding expression.

"It would be easy to make him good," replied Xenie; "but you will not exert your power."

"It is you who prevent me: you interfere with the duties of a master, by your soft ways and counsels of false prudence. Ah! it was not in this manner that my father and grandfather ruled the serfs of our lord's father."

"But you forget," replied Xenie, with a trembling voice, "that Fedor was from his childhood more gently brought up than other peasants; how can he be like them? His education was from the first as much cared for as mine."

"He ought to be so much the better, and he is all the worse; such are the effects of education; but it is your fault, you and your nurse would constantly bring him to the castle, and I in my kind wish to please you, forgot, and allowed him to forget, that he was not born to live with us."

"You cruelly reminded him of it afterwards," answered Xenie, with a sigh.

"Your ideas are not Russian: sooner or later, you will learn to your cost, to know how peasants must be governed." He then continued, muttering between his teeth, "What is this devil of a Fedor doing, to come back here, after my letters to the prince. The prince cannot have read them, and the steward down there is jealous of me!"

Xenie heard the self-communings of Thelenef, and anxiously watched the progress of the resentful feelings of the steward, who considered that he had been braved in his own house by an intractable serf. She hoped to appease him by these reasonable words:—

"It is now two years since you had my poor foster-brother almost beaten to death. What have you gained by your severity? Nothing; his lips did not utter one word of excuse, he would have expired under the torture, rather than have humbled himself before you: for he knew that his punishment was too severe for his fault. I confess he had disobeyed you, but he was in love with Catherine. The cause of the offense lessened its importance; this you would not take into consideration. Since that scene, and the marriage and departure which followed it, the hatred of all our peasants has become so intense, that I fear for you, my father."

"And therefore you rejoice at the return of one of my most formidable enemies," replied the exasperated Thelenef.

"Ah! I do not fear him: we have both sucked the same breast; he would die rather than make me unhappy."

"He has given good proof of this truly; he would be the first to murder me if he dared."

"You judge him too harshly. Fedor would, I am sure, defend you against them all, even though you have deeply offended him: you remember your severity too well yourself, for him to forget it. Is not this the truth, Father? He is now married, and his wife has already a little one; this domestic happiness will soften his character. The birth of children often changes the hearts of husbands."

"Silence! You will deprive me of all sense with your romantic notions. Go and read in your books about affectionate peasants and generous slaves. I know better than you do, the men I have to deal with: they are idle and vindictive like their fathers, and you will never change them."

"If you would permit me to act, and would give me your aid, we might, together, reform them; but here comes my good Elizabeth, returning from mass."

Thus speaking, Xenie ran to throw her arms around her nurse. "Now then you are happy!"

"Perhaps," replied the old woman, in a low voice.

"He is come back."

"Not for long, I fear."

"What do you mean?"

"They have all lost their senses; but, hush!"

"Well, Mother Pacome," said Thelenef, casting a sinister glance upon the old woman, "your good-for-nothing son has returned to you; his wife, I suppose, is satisfied; his return will prove to you and all, that I do not wish him ill."

"I am glad of it, sir, we need your protection; the prince is coming, and we do not know him."

"How! What!—the prince our master?" then checking himself, "doubtless," exclaimed Thelenef, much surprised, but not wishing to seem ignorant of what a peasant appeared to know, "doubtless I will protect you; but he will not be here so soon as you think: the report of his coming is current every year at this season."

"Pardon me, sir, he will be here shortly."

The steward longed to question the nurse more closely, but his dignity restrained him. Xenie saw his embarrassment, and came to his help.

"Tell me, nurse, how have you become so well acquainted with the intentions and movements of our lord the prince?"

"I learned it from Fedor. Oh, my son knows many other things besides. He is now a man—he is twenty-one years old, just a year older than you, my pretty lady. I would say, if I dare, for he is so handsome—I would say you are like each other."

"Hold thy tongue! old doter; how should my daughter resemble thy son?"

"They have sucked the same milk, and even—but, no— when you are no longer our master I will tell you what I think of them."

"When I am no longer your master!"

"Certainly. My son has seen *the father*."

"The emperor?"

"Yes; and the emperor himself has sent us word that we are going to be made free. It is his will; and if it depended only on him it would be done."

Thelenef shrugged his shoulders, and asked—"How has Fedor been able to speak to the emperor?"

"How? He was one of those who were sent by all the people of the district and of the neighboring villages, to go and ask our father"—here Mother Pacome suddenly stopped short.

"To ask what?"

The old woman, who began, a little too late, to perceive her indiscretion, took refuge in obstinate silence, notwithstanding the hasty questions of the steward. This abrupt silence had something about it that was unusual, and at the same time significative.

"Once for all, what is it that you are plotting here against us?" cried the furious Thelenef, seizing the old woman by her shoulders.

"It is easy to guess," said Xenie, advancing between her father and her nurse. "You know that the emperor bought, last year, the domain of ——, which adjoins ours. Since then our peasants dream of nothing but the happiness of belonging to the crown. They envy their neighbors, whose condition, as they believe, has become much improved, though, before, it was similar to theirs. Do not you remember that many of the old men of our district have, under various pretexts, asked your permission to travel. I was told, after their departure, that they had been chosen as deputies by the other serfs to go and entreat the emperor to purchase them, as he had done their neighbors. Various of the surrounding districts united with Vologda to present a similar request to His Majesty. They say that they offered him all the money necessary to buy the domain of the prince—both the men and the land."

"It is all true," said the old woman; "and my son, Fedor, who met them at Petersburg, went with them to speak to our father; they all came back together yesterday."

"If I did not tell you of this attempt," said Xenie, looking at her amazed father, "it was because I knew that it would end in nothing."

"You have deceived yourself, if they have seen the father."

"The *father* himself could not do what they wished; he cannot buy all Russia."

"Do you perceive their cunning!" continued Thelenef. "The knaves are rich enough to offer large presents to the emperor, and yet, with us, they are beggars. They are not ashamed to say that we spoil them of everything; whereas, if we had more sense and less mildness, we should strip them even to the very girdle with which they would strangle us."

"You will not have the time to do that, Mister Steward," said, in a very low and gentle voice, a young man who had approached unperceived, and who stood with his hat in his hand, before a bush of willows, from the midst of which he seemed to come as if by enchantment. "Ah! is it you, you villain?" cried Thelenef.

"Fedor, you say nothing to your foster-sister," interrupted Xenie, "you had so often promised not to forget me. I have kept my word better than you, for I have not omitted a single day to mention your name in my prayer there, in that chapel, before the image of St. Vladimir, which reminded me of your departure. Do you remember it? It was there that you bade me adieu, now nearly a year ago."

In concluding these words, she cast on her brother a look of tenderness and reproach, the mingled softness and severity of which made a great impression.

"I forget you!" cried the young man, lifting his eyes to heaven. Xenie was silent, awed by the religious, yet somewhat fierce expression of an eye that was generally cast down.

Xenie was one of those beauties of the North that are never

seen in other lands. Scarcely did she appear to belong to earth. The purity of her features, which reminded one of the pictures of Raphael, might have appeared cold had not a most delicate expression of sensibility softly shadowed her countenance, which, as yet, no passion had ever ruffled. Xenie had the beauty of a queen and the freshness of a village maiden. Her hair was parted in bands on a high and ivory forehead; her blue eyes, fringed with long black lashes, which cast a shadow on her fresh yet scarcely colored cheeks, were transparent as a fountain of limpid water. She needed only the silver glory to form one of the most lovely of those Byzantine Madonnas, with which it is not permitted to adorn the churches.*

Her foster-brother was one of the handsomest men of a part of the empire renowned for the tall and elegant forms, the healthful appearance, and the carelessly graceful air of its inhabitants. The serfs of this portion of the empire are, unquestionably, the men who least need pity in Russia.

The elegant costume of the peasants became him admirably. His light hair, gracefully parted, fell in silky ringlets on either side of the face, the form of which was a perfect oval. His large and powerful neck remained bare, owing to the locks being cut off close behind; whilst a band, in the form of a diadem, was fastened across the white forehead of the young laborer, keeping his hair close and smooth on the crown of his head, which shone, in the sun, like a Christ of Guido.

Fedor, humbled by an education superior to the rank he occupied in his country, and perhaps also by the instinct of his natural dignity, which contrasted with his abject condi-

---

*The use of images is always forbidden to a certain point in the Greek church, in which, the true believers admit only those of a particular conventional style, covered with various gold and silver ornaments, under which the merit of the work is entirely lost.

tion, maintained almost always the posture of a condemned man, about to receive sentence.

He had adopted this doleful attitude when nineteen years old, on the day that he underwent the punishment commanded by Thelenef, under the pretext that the young man— the foster-brother of his daughter, and hitherto his favorite, his spoiled child—had neglected to obey I know not what unimportant order. The real and serious motive for the barbarity, which was not the effect of a simple caprice, will be seen hereafter. Xenie imagined she had guessed the nature of the fault which had become so fatal to her brother. She imagined that Fedor was in love with Catherine, a young and handsome peasant girl who lived in the neighborhood; and, as soon as the unfortunate young man had been cured of his wounds, which was not until after some weeks, for the punishment had been cruelly severe, she busied herself with repairing the evil, so far as lay in her power. She thought that the only means to achieve this would be to marry him to the young girl with whom she believed him smitten. No sooner had the project been announced by Xenie, than the hatred of Thelenef appeared to diminish. The marriage was brought about and celebrated in all haste, to the great satisfaction of Xenie, who believed that Fedor would lose in the happiness of the heart, his feelings of profound grief and resentment. She deceived herself; nothing could console her brother. She alone was aware of the bitter sense of shame with which he was overwhelmed; she was his confidante, although he had confided nothing to her, for he never once complained. Indeed, the treatment of which he had been the victim was a matter of such ordinary occurrence, that no one attached any importance to it: except himself and Xenie no one thought anything about it.

He avoided, with an admirable instinct of pride, everything that could remind him of the degradation he had suffered; but he fled, involuntarily and with a shudder, whenever any of his comrades were about to be beaten; and he grew pale at the sight of a reed or a wand in a man's hand.

His sister Xenie believed she should render him again happy by procuring his marriage: he obeyed, but this compliance only served to increase his wretchedness; for the man who seeks to become virtuous by taking upon himself additional duties, does but lay open new sources of remorse.

The unhappy Fedor felt when it was too late, that, notwithstanding her friendship, Xenie had done nothing for him. Unable to bear life in the scenes that had witnessed his degradation, he abandoned his native village, his wife, and his guardian angel.

His wife felt herself humbled, but from another cause. A wife blushes for shame when her husband is not happy. Under this feeling she forebore telling him that she was enceinte. She did not wish to employ such a means for retaining near her, a husband to whose happiness she could not minister.

At length, after a year's absence, he returned. He again beheld his mother and his wife, and found also an infant in the cradle, a little angel who resembled him, but who could not cure the sorrow which preyed upon his heart. He remained motionless and silent even before his sister Xenie, whom now he only dared to call mademoiselle.

Their noble forms, which, according to the saying of the nurse, had, as well as their characters, some traits of resemblance, shone in the morning sun among the scattered groups of animals, of whom they seemed the sovereigns. One might have imagined the picture, an Adam and Eve, painted by Albrecht Dürer. Xenie was calm, though joyful; but the countenance of the young man betrayed violent emotions, ill disguised under an affected impassability.

Xenie, in spite of her unerring womanly instinct, was deceived this time by the silence of Fedor. She attributed the chagrin of her brother to painful recollections, and fancied that the sight of the scenes where he had suffered, tended to revive his grief; but she still depended on love and friendship to complete the cure of his wound.

On parting with her brother she promised often to come and see him in the cabin of her nurse.

Nevertheless, the last look of Fedor terrified the young maiden; there was something more than grief in this glance; there was the expression of a ferocious joy, blended with some unaccountable solicitude. A fear crossed her mind that he had become mad.

Madness had always inspired her with a terror which appeared to her supernatural, and as she attributed this fear to a presentiment, her superstition augmented her inquietude. When fears assume the shape of prophetic intimations, their influence becomes indomitable, a vague and fugitive presentiment takes the aspect of an impending destiny, and imagination, thus acted upon, creates what it fears, and by its influence upon intermediate events, realizes its own chimeras.

Several days passed on, during which Thelenef frequently absented himself. Xenie, entirely absorbed in the grief which was caused by the incurable melancholy of Fedor, thought only of him, and saw only her nurse.

One evening, she was sitting reading in the castle, which her father had left in the morning, saying that she was not to expect his return before the morrow: Xenie was accustomed to these journeyings; for the extent of the domains which her father superintended often obliged him to be absent for a considerable time. While thus alone, the nurse of the young girl suddenly appeared before her.

"What can you want with me so late?" asked Xenie.

"Come and take your tea with us; I have made it ready for you," replied the nurse.

"I am not accustomed to go out at such an hour."

"You must, however, today. Come, what should you fear with me?"

Xenie, used to the taciturnity of the Russian peasants, imagined that her nurse had prepared some surprise for her. She therefore rose and followed the old woman.

The village was deserted. At first Xenie believed that it only slept. The night was perfectly calm, and not dark: not a breath of wind disturbed the willows of the marsh, nor bent the long grass of the meadows; not a cloud veiled the stars of heaven. Neither the distant barking of the dog, nor the bleating of the sheep was to be heard; the cattle had ceased to low in the stall; the herdsman was no longer heard to chant his melancholy song, similar to the low trill which precedes the cadence of the nightingale; a silence more profound than the usual silence of the night, brooded over the plain, and weighed upon the heart of Xenie, who began to experience indefinable sensations of terror, though she did not dare to hazard a question. Has the angel of death passed over Vologda? Such was the silent thought of the trembling girl.

Suddenly a blaze of light appeared on the horizon.

"What is that?" cried Xenie, struck with terror.

"I cannot tell," replied the nurse, "it is perhaps the last beams of day."

"No," replied Xenie, "it is a burning village!"

"A castle," responded Elizabeth, in a hollow voice; "it is the nobles' turn now."

"What do you mean?" cried Xenie, seizing in her terror, her nurse's arm, "are the dreadful predictions of my father going to be fulfilled?"

"Let us make haste; I have to conduct you farther than our cabin."

"Where are you going to take me?"

"To a place of safety; there is no longer one for you in Vologda."

"But my father!—what has become of him? I have nothing to fear for myself; but where is my father?"

"He is saved."

"Saved! From what danger? By whom? What is it that you know? You are trying to soothe me to make me comply with your wishes!"

"I swear to you by the light of the Holy Spirit, my son has concealed him, and he has done it for your sake, at the peril of his own life; for all the traitors will perish this night."

"Fedor has saved my father! What generous conduct!"

"I am not generous, mademoiselle," said the young man, approaching to support Xenie, who seemed about to faint.

Fedor had accompanied his mother to the castle gate, which he had not ventured to enter: on the two women coming forth, he had followed them at a little distance in order to protect the flight of Xenie. The weakness that came over his sister obliged him to show himself. But she soon recovered the energy which danger arouses in strong minds.

"Fedor, explain to me all this mystery. What is going to be done?"

"The Russians are free, and they are going to avenge themselves; but make haste, and follow me," he continued, leading her on.

"Going to avenge themselves! But on whom? I have never done evil to any one!"

"'Tis true, you are an angel; yet I fear that in the first moment there will be no mercy for anybody. The madmen! they see only enemies, not alone in our former masters but in all their kindred. The hour of carnage is arrived: let us make haste. If you do not hear the tocsin, it is because they avoid sounding the bells for fear of forewarning our enemies; besides, they could not be heard far enough: it was agreed that the last glimmer of the evening sun should be the signal for the burning of the castles, and the massacre of all their inhabitants."

"Oh! you make me shudder!"

Fedor continued, still urging her forwards, "I was appointed to march with the youngest and bravest of our people on the town of ———, where we are to surprise the garrison, which consists only of a few veterans. We are the strongest, and I therefore thought they might dispense with me in the first expedition; thus I have wittingly failed in my duty, I have betrayed the sacred cause, and deserted my battalion to repair to the spot where I knew that I should find your father; he has been timely warned, and is concealed in a cabin dependent on the domains of the crown. But now I tremble lest it should be too late to save you," he continued, still hurrying her forward towards the retreat he had chosen for her. "The desire of protecting your father has lost time precious to yourself; but I thought to fulfill your wishes, and believed that you would not reproach me for the delay, when you knew the cause; besides, you are less exposed than Thelenef: we shall, I trust, yet save you."

"Yes; but you—you are lost," said the mother in a tone of anguish, which her endeavor to keep silent rendered the more impressive.

"Lost!" interrupted Xenie, "my brother lost for my sake!"

"Has he not deserted his ranks in the hour of danger?" replied the old woman, "he is guilty, and they will kill him."

"I have deserved death!"

"And I shall be the cause," cried Xenie; "no, no, you must fly—we will fly together."

"Never!"

During the precipitate retreat of the fugitives, the light of the conflagration silently spread in the horizon: not one cry, no sound of firearms, no ringing of bells, betrayed the insurrection. It was dumb massacre. The calm accord of nature, the beauty of the night smiling on so many murders, filled the soul with horror. It seemed as though Providence, in order to punish men, had removed even her frown, and was suffering them to act as they pleased.

"You will not abandon your sister?" Xenie ejaculated, trembling with terror.

"No, mademoiselle: but once assured of your safety, I will go and surrender myself."

"I will go with you," replied the young girl, pressing his arm convulsively: "I will not leave you! You think, then, that I would sacrifice anything for life!"

At this moment the fugitives saw, by the light of the stars, defiling before them, at the distance of about a hundred paces, a line of silent shadows. Fedor stopped.

"Who are they?" asked Xenie, in a low voice.

"Hush!" said Fedor, gently retreating beneath the shadow cast by some palings; then, when the last phantom had crossed the route, he continued—

"It is a detachment of our people marching in silence to surprise the castle of Count ———. We are in danger here; let us hasten."

"Whither then will you conduct me?"

"In the first place, to my mother's brother, four versts from Vologda. My old uncle is in his second childhood, he will not betray us. There you must change your dress, for that which you wear would cause you to be recognized; here is another. My mother will remain with her brother, and I hope before the close of the night to bring you to the retreat where I left Thelenef. No place is safe in our unfortunate district, but that is, at least, the safest."

"You will restore me to my father! Thank you, Fedor: but what will you yourself do then?"

"I will bid you adieu."

"Never!"

"Nay, nay, Xenie is right; you must remain with them," cried the poor mother.

"Thelenef would not suffer me," replied the young man, bitterly.

Xenie felt that it was not the moment to answer. The three fugitives pursuing their way in silence, and without accident, at length reached the door of the aged peasant.

It was fastened only with a latch. The old man slept, wrapped in a black sheepskin, and stretched on one of the rustic benches, which were ranged, like a divan, around the room. Over his head burnt a little lamp, suspended before a Greek Madonna, almost entirely concealed by the silver ornaments of her head and garments. A kettle full of hot water, a teapot, and several cups, remained on the table. A short time before the arrival of the party, the wife of Fedor had left the cottage, to seek, with her child, shelter at her father's. Fedor appeared neither surprised nor vexed at her departure; for he had not told her to wait for him, and he wished the retreat of Xenie to be unknown to the whole world.

After lighting a lamp at that of the Virgin's, he led his mother and foster-sister to a small dark closet, which formed a loft over the room before mentioned. All the houses of the Russian peasants are similar in construction.

Left alone, Fedor seated himself on the first step of the frail staircase which his sister had ascended, resting his head upon his hands, in pensive thought.

Scarcely had Xenie, whom he had urged to use all haste, opened the packet that contained her new clothes, than the young man, rising with an expression of intense anxiety, whistled softly to summon his mother.

"What is the matter?" she asked in a low voice.

"Extinguish your lamp—I hear steps; and the light will be seen through the chinks. Above all, avoid making the least noise."

The light was put out, and everything remained in silence.

A few moments passed in an agonizing suspense; at length the door opened (Xenie scarcely breathed for terror), and a man entered covered with sweat and blood. "Is it you, brother Basil?" said Fedor, advancing towards the stranger: "are you alone?"

"No; a detachment of our men wait for me before the door. No light?"

"I will get you one," replied Fedor, mounting the steps of the loft, whence he descended in an instant to rekindle the lamp, which he had taken from the hands of the trembling women, at that which glimmered before the Madonna. "Would you like some tea, brother?"

"Yes."

"Here is some."

The newcomer began to empty, by small draughts, the cup which Fedor presented. This man bore a token of command upon his breast. He was dressed as the other peasants, and armed with a naked and bloody saber; his thick and reddish beard imparted a roughness to his face that by no means tempered the glance of his eye, which resembled that of a wild animal. This glance, which cannot remain fixed on anything, is frequent among the Russians, except when they are utterly brutalized by slavery, and then the eye is vacant, and has no expression at all. His figure was not tall, his frame was thickset, his nose flat, his forehead full but low, his cheeks projecting, and red with the effect of strong liquors; his mouth, when he opened it, displayed a row of white teeth, but sharp and wide apart; it was, in fact, the mouth of a panther. His matted beard was soiled with foam, and his hands were stained with blood.

"Where did you get this saber?" said Fedor.

"I tore it from the hands of an officer, whom I killed with his own weapon. We are conquerors—the town of ——— is ours! O, we have had a glorious night! All who would not join our troop are dead—women, children, old men—all! They boiled some of the soldiers in a cauldron in the marketplace. We warmed ourselves at the same fire on which our enemies were being cooked. It was glorious!"

Fedor did not answer.

"You say nothing?"

"I think though."

"And what is it that you think?"

"I think that we are playing a desperate game. In a town without defenses, fifteen hundred inhabitants and fifty infirm veterans are easily put to the sword by two thousand peasants, falling on them suddenly; but at no very great distance there are considerable forces: we shall be crushed finally."

"Very likely! And what then is to become of the justice of God, and the will of the emperor? Coward! do you not see that the time for hesitation has passed? After what has been already done, we must conquer or die. Listen to me then, instead of turning away your head. We have spread everywhere fire and blood: do you understand me? After such a carnage, pardon is impossible. The whole town is dead. When we set to work, we do our business thoroughly. You seem to be displeased with our triumph?"

"I do not like the murder of the women."

"It is necessary to destroy an evil race, root and branch."

Fedor was silent. Basil tranquilly continued his discourse, which he only interrupted to swallow his tea. "You appear sad and melancholy, my son?"

Fedor continued silent.

"It is your foolish love for the daughter of Thelenef our mortal enemy, which has been your ruin."

"I!—a love for my foster-sister! I have a friendship for her, if you like: but—"

"Pshaw! pshaw!—a curious kind of friendship yours!"

The young man rose, and tried to place his hand on the other's mouth.

"What do you mean, boy? One would suppose you feared being overheard," continued Basil, without changing his manner.

Fedor remained motionless: the peasant continued—

"It is not I who will be your dupe; her father Thelenef was not so either, when he maltreated you."

Fedor again strove to interrupt him.

"What! you will not allow me to speak! You have not

forgotten any more than I, that he once beat you. It was to punish you, not for the trifling fault invented by himself, but for your secret love of his daughter. He wanted to drive you from the country before the evil was past remedy."

Fedor, in the most violent agitation, walked up and down the room, unable to utter any reply. He bit his hands in impotent rage, till he at length found words to say:

"You remind me of a hateful day, comrade; let us talk of something else."

"I always talk of what I please: if you do not choose to answer me, I can talk alone; but, once for all, I will not be interrupted. I am your senior, and the godfather of your newborn babe; your captain also. Do you see this sign on my breast? It is that of my rank in our army. I have therefore a right to speak before you; and if you pretend to object, I have my men bivouacking outside; with a single whistle I could bring them around me, and in a few moments the house would be in a blaze. Patience, then, and we shall understand each other better."

The young man reseated himself, affecting the most indifferent air that he could assume.

"What was I talking about?" continued Basil, grumbling between his teeth. "Oh, I was reminding you of an unpleasant recollection. Is it not true? But you have sadly forgotten it, my son, and I must bring back to your mind your own history. You will see at least that I know how to read your thoughts, and to discover whether there beats within you the heart of a traitor."

Here Basil again interrupted himself, opened a casement, and spoke in the ear of a man who presented himself at the aperture, through which were seen five other armed peasants in the background.

Fedor had seized his poniard, but he replaced it in his girdle; the life of Xenie was at stake, and the least imprudence might cause the hut to be set on fire, and all that was in it to perish! He therefore restrained himself; he wished once more to see his sister. Who can analyze all the mysteries of love? The secret of his life was being revealed to Xenie, without any contrivance or concurrence on his part. At this moment, terrible as it was, he experienced only excess of joy! What signifies the short duration of supreme felicity,—is it not eternal while it is felt? But these powerful illusions of the heart can never be known to men who are incapable of love. True love is not dependent upon time—its measure is supernatural—its movements are not to be calculated by cold human reason.

After a brief silence, the loud voice of Basil put an end to the sweet yet painful ecstasy of Fedor.

"But since you did not love your wife, why did you marry her? You acted there very foolishly."

This question again frenzied the mind of the young man.

To say that he loved his wife, was to lose all that he was about to gain. "I thought I loved her," he replied: "they told me it was necessary for me to marry. Could I know what was in my heart? I wished to please the daughter of Thelenef. I obeyed without reflection. Is it not our habit as peasants to act in this manner?"

"It is. You pretend you were ignorant of what you wished. I will tell you: you wished simply to reconcile yourself with Thelenef."

"You little know me!"

"I know you better than you know yourself. You thought our tyrants were still needful to us; and you therefore yielded, to obtain the pardon of Thelenef. In truth, we should all have done as much in your place; but what I reproach you with, is your wish to deceive me, who see through all. There was no other way of regaining the favor of the father, than by setting him at rest as to the consequences of your love for the daughter; and with this view you married, without thinking of the grief of your poor wife, whom you have condemned to eternal misery, and whom you did not scruple to abandon at the moment when she was hoping to give you a son."

"I was ignorant of that when I left her: she concealed from me her situation. Once for all, I have acted without design or premeditation. I have been ever accustomed to the guidance of my foster-sister, who has so much wisdom."

"More's the pity."

"How?"

"I say it is a pity: she will be the greater loss to the country."

"Are you capable—"

"We are capable of destroying her as we have done the others. . . . Do you suppose we shall be so foolish as not to shed the last drop of the blood of Thelenef,—the blood of our most hateful enemy?"

"But she has done you only good!"

"She is his daughter,—that is enough! We shall send the father to hell, and the daughter to paradise,—this will be the only difference."

"You will not commit so horrible a deed?"

"Who shall hinder us?"

"I!"

"Thou, Fedor! thou, traitor! thou, who art my prisoner! thou, who hast deserted the army of thy brethren in the day of combat, for—" He could not finish; for, during his last few words, Fedor, who, as the only means of safety left, had resolved to stab him, darted upon him like a tiger, and striking between the ribs, buried the poniard in his heart, stifling at the same time his scarcely commenced cry with a pelisse which he held in his hand. The last groans of the dying man did not alarm Fedor; they were too weak to be heard without. After encouraging his mother with a few words, he was about to bring her the lamp, in order to commence anew the preparations for the flight of Xenie; when, at the moment of passing by the sleeping old man, the latter started and awoke.

"Who art thou?" he said to his nephew, whom he did not recognize, and whose arm he forcibly seized. "What steam of blood!" Then, casting his eyes round the chamber, they at length fell, horror-struck, on the dead man.

Fedor had extinguished his lamp, but that of the Madonna was still burning. "Murder! murder! help!" cried the old man, in a voice of thunder. Fedor could not stop these cries, which were uttered more rapidly than they can be repeated, for the terror of the aged man was at its height, and his strength was still very great. The unfortunate Fedor knew not how to act. Heaven did not aid him.

The troops of Basil, who were lying in wait, heard the cries. Before Fedor could disengage himself from the powerful grasp of the poor senseless being, for whom he felt a respect which induced him to spare his life, though at the risk of his own, six men, furnished with cords and armed with pitchforks, stakes, and scythes, rushed into the cabin. To lay hold of Fedor, to disarm, and to bind him, was the work of a moment.

"Where are you going to take me?"

"To the castle of Vologda, to burn you there with The-lenef. You will see that your treason has not saved him."

These words were spoken by the oldest man of the troop. Fedor not replying, the man quietly continued:—"You did not think that our victory would be so complete and prompt: our army has sprung up on all sides; it is an inundation of divine justice. No one escapes us; our enemies are taken in their own snares; God is with us. We suspected you, and watched you narrowly. Thelenef was followed to the hiding place where you conducted him, and has been there seized; you shall die together; the castle is already on fire."

Fedor, without uttering a word, cast down his head, and followed his executioners. He trusted that their rapid flight from the fatal cabin might yet be the means of saving Xenie.

Six men carried before him the body of Basil, six others

escorted them with torches; the rest followed without uttering a word. The funeral cortege traversed in silence the
country, lit up with conflagrations in every direction. The
horizon appeared each moment to lessen in circumference. A
circle of fire bounded the plain. Vologda was burning; the
town of ———— was on fire, together with all the castles and
farms of the prince, and several of the surrounding villages.
The woods themselves did not escape. The carnage was universal. The conflagration illuminated the secret depths of the
forest. Solitude existed no longer. Who can conceal himself
on a plain when the forests are on fire? There can be no safe
asylum against a flood of light pouring on all sides equally.
Terror was at its height; night had fled, and yet the sun had
not risen.

The escort of Fedor was increased by the marauders who
were everywhere scouring the country. The crowd had become great by the time they reached the castle.

What a spectacle there awaited the prisoners!

The castle of Vologda, built entirely of wood, appeared like
an immense funeral pyre, the flames of which reached to the
heavens! The peasants, who had plundered this ancient mansion before setting it on fire, imagined they had burned Xenie
in the habitation of her father.

A line of boats on the water, placed closely together, completed the blockade that had been established. In the midst of
the semicircle formed by the army of the insurgents before
the castle, the unfortunate Thelenef, torn from his retreat,
and brought by force to the place destined for his execution,
stood chained to a post; while the crowd of conquerors, eager
to behold the spectacle, flocked from all parts to this place
of rendezvous.

The troop who guarded him formed a circle around their
prey, and displayed in the light of the conflagration their
loathsome banners. Great God! what colors! They were the
mangled remains of the first victims, carried upon pikes and

sabers. Heads of women with flowing hair, pieces of human bodies stuck upon pitchforks, mutilated infants, gory bones. The scene seemed peopled with hideous phantoms, which it might have been supposed had escaped from hell, to assist in the orgies of the last inhabitants of earth.

This pretended triumph of liberty was like the aspect of some great convulsion of nature. The flames and crash of the timbers of the castle resembled the eruption of a volcano. The revengeful passions of the people were like the lava, which, long boiling silently in the womb of the earth, had at length found vent, and spread in torrents on every side. Confused murmurs might be heard among the crowd, but no voice could be distinguished, unless it was that of the victim whose curses and imprecations rejoiced the hearts of the executioners. These monsters were, for the most part, men of remarkable beauty; all had a manner and bearing that was naturally noble and gentle; they seemed more like evil angels, whose faces yet retained their pristine glory, than human beings. Fedor himself much resembled his persecutors. All the Russians of pure Slavic race show by their faces that they are of the same family; even when engaged in exterminating each other it can be seen that they are brothers,—a circumstance which renders the carnage more horrible.

But then, these are no longer the children of nature; they are men perverted by a cruel and unfeeling social system. The natural man exists only in books; where he forms a theme for philosophic declamation, an ideal type, from which moralists draw their deductions just as mathematicians, in certain calculations, proceed upon given quantities. Nature, for the primitive man, as for the degenerated man, is still a state of society; and, whatever may be said, the most civilized society is the best.

The fatal circle opened for a moment, to allow of the entrance of Fedor and his execrable escort. Thelenef was so placed as not, at first, to perceive his youthful liberator. His execution was about to begin, when a murmur of terror spread among the crowd.

"A specter! a specter! It is she!" was the cry heard on all sides. The ring broke and dispersed,—the executioners fled before a phantom! Cruelty readily unites with superstition.

The flight was, however, arrested by several of the more determined ruffians, who shouted that it was Xenie herself, living, and in their power.

"Stay! stay!" cried a female voice, the agonizing accents of which went to all hearts, but above all to the heart of Fedor. "Let me pass, I will see them! They are my father and my brother! You will not forbid me to die with them?" Ere she had concluded these words, Xenie had reached the spot where Fedor stood incapable of motion, and fell insensible at his feet.

We here feel the necessity of abridging the description of this horrible scene. It was long, but we will describe it in few words. We must, however, first ask pardon for what we do relate.

Xenie, in the cabin where we left her, had forced herself to maintain silence, for fear of increasing the danger of Fedor; but, as soon as the two women were alone, she escaped, and hastened to share the fate of her father.

The execution of Thelenef commenced. Just heavens! what a death! To render it the more terrible to this unhappy being, they placed Xenie and Fedor before his eyes, seated and bound on a rude species of platform raised in haste at a short distance from him; they then cut off one by one, his feet and hands; and when at length the mutilated trunk was almost drained of blood, they stifled his death cry by stuffing into his mouth one of his own feet.

The women of the faubourg of Caen eating the heart of M. de Belzunce on the bridge of Vauxelles were models of humanity compared with the tranquil spectators of the death of Thelenef.

And this took place but a few months ago, and within a few days' journey of one of the most admired cities of Europe! After the father had ceased to suffer, one of the executioners advanced to seize the daughter; but he found her stiff and cold. During the torture of her father she had not made a single movement nor uttered a single word.

Fedor, at this sight, recovered, as though by some supernatural influence working within him, all his energy and presence of mind. By a miraculous exertion of strength he broke the cords that bound him, burst from the hands of his keepers, rushed towards his beloved sister, raised her from the earth, and pressed her for a long time to his heart; then replacing her gently and respectfully on the grass, he addressed his tormentors with that calm, composed air that appears natural to the Orientals, even in the most tragical moments of life.

"You must not touch her. God has laid his hand upon her: she is mad."

"Mad!" responded the superstitious crowd: "God is with her!"

"It is he, it is the traitor, her lover, who has told her to counterfeit madness! No, no! we must make a finish with all the enemies of God and of men," cried the most ferocious of the savages; "besides, our oath binds us: let us do our duty! *Our father* (the emperor) has willed it, and he will recompense us."

"Approach her, then, if you dare!" once more cried Fedor, in the delirium of despair; "she has suffered me to press her in my arms without resistance; you see she must be mad. But she speaks! Listen!"

They approached, and heard these words: "It was I, then, whom he loved!"

Fedor, who alone understood the meaning of this sentence, fell on his knees, and thanking God, burst into tears.

The executioners drew back from Xenie with involuntary

respect. "She is mad!" they repeated to each other, in an under tone.

Since that day she has never passed an hour without repeating the same words—"It was I, then, whom he loved!"

Many, in seeing her so calm, would question her insanity. It is supposed that the love of Fedor, thus accidentally revealed, awoke in the heart of his foster-sister, the innocent, though passionate tenderness, which the unhappy girl had, unknown either to herself or her lover, so long felt for him; and that the suddenness of the untimely discovery broke her heart.

No exhortation or advice has hitherto been able to prevent her repeating these words, which proceed from her lips mechanically, and with an incessant volubility which is frightful.

Her mind, her whole existence, has stopped, and gathered itself around the involuntary avowal of the love of Fedor, and the organs of intelligence continue their functions, as it were, by the operation of a spring, obeying that remainder of the will which bids them forever repeat the mysterious and sacred words which suffice for her mental life.

If Fedor did not perish after Thelenef, it was not to the weariness of the executioners that he owed his safety, but to that of the spectators; for the passive party tires of crime more quickly than he who is actively engaged in its perpetration. The crowd, satiated with blood, desired that the execution of the young man should be deferred until the following night. In the interval, considerable forces arrived from several sides. On the morrow, the canton in which the revolt had sprung up was surrounded, the villages were decimated, the most culpable—condemned, not to death, but to a hundred and twenty strokes of the knout—miserably perished. The remainder were banished to Siberia. Nevertheless, the populations in the neighborhood of Vologda are not yet restored to quiet and order; each day witnesses the departure of hundreds of peasants, exiled in a mass to Siberia. The lords of these deserted villages are ruined; for in estates of this kind, it is the men who constitute the wealth of the proprietor. The rich domains of the Prince ———— have become a dreary solitude. Fedor, with his mother and his wife, have been compelled to follow the inhabitants of their desolate village.

Xenie was present at the departure of the exiles, but she did not say adieu, for this new misfortune had not restored to her the light of reason.

At the moment of departing, an unexpected event cruelly aggravated the grief of Fedor and his family. His wife and mother were already in the cart, and he was about to follow them, to leave Vologda forever; but he saw only Xenie, he suffered only for his sister, an orphan, deprived of reason, or at least of memory, and whom he was going to abandon among the still warm ashes of their native hamlet. Now that she had need of the kindest aid, strangers were going to be her only protectors. The bitter feeling of despair which this thought produced, stopped his tears. A piercing cry, proceeding from the cart, recalled him to the side of his wife, whom he found fainting;—one of the soldiers was taking away his child.

"What are you going to do?" cried the distracted father.

"To place it there by the wayside that they may bury it; do you not see that it is dead?" replied the Cossack.

"I will carry it myself!"

"You shall not touch it."

At this moment, other soldiers attracted by the noise, seized Fedor, who, yielding to irresistible force, could only weep and supplicate. "He is not dead, he has fainted; let me embrace him. I promise you," he said, convulsively sobbing, "to give him up to you if his heart no longer beats. You, perhaps, have a son; have pity on me, then," said the unfortunate man, overcome with grief. The Cossack was moved; he restored to him his child. Scarcely had the father touched the icy body, than his hair stood upon his forehead,—he cast his eyes around him, they encountered the inspired look of Xenie. Neither misfortune, nor injustice, nor death, nor insanity,— nothing upon earth could destroy the sympathy of these two hearts, born to understand each other.

The young man made a sign to Xenie; the soldiers respected the poor maniac, who advanced, and received the body of the babe from the hands of its father, but without a word being uttered. The daughter of Thelenef, still without speaking, next took off her veil and gave it to Fedor; she then pressed the little corpse in her arms, and, charged with her sacred burden, remained in the same place, immovable, until she had seen her beloved brother, supported between a weeping mother and a dying wife, leave forever the village which had given him birth. She long followed with her eye the convoy of the exiled peasants: at length, when the last cart had disappeared on the road to Siberia, and she was left alone, she took away the infant, and began to play with the cold remains, bestowing upon them the most tender and endearing caresses.

"He is not dead, then!" said the lookers-on, "he will revive; she will restore him!"

Power of love! who can assign thy limits?

The mother of Fedor reproached herself without ceasing, for not having detained Xenie in the cottage of the old man; "at least she would not then have been forced to witness the punishment of her father," said the good Elizabeth.

"You would have preserved her reason, only to have increased her sufferings," replied Fedor; and again there was a dead silence.

The poor old woman had for a time been very resigned. Neither the massacres nor the fire had extorted from her a single complaint; but when it was necessary to submit with the other Vologdians to the pain of exile—to leave the cabin where her son was born, where the father of her son had died, when she was obliged to abandon her brother in helpless dotage, courage forsook her, her fortitude suddenly failed, she clung to the planks of her cottage, and at length had to be torn away, and placed by force in the telega, where we have seen her weeping for the newborn infant of her beloved son.

It will perhaps scarcely be believed that the tender cares, the vivifying breath, or perhaps the prayers of Xenie, restored at length the life of the child whom Fedor had believed to be dead. This miracle of tenderness, or of piety, causes her to be venerated as a saint by the strangers sent from the North to repeople the deserted ruins of Vologda.

Those men who believe her mad would not dare to take from her the child of her brother: no one thinks of disputing with her this precious prey, rescued thus wonderfully from the jaws of death. Such a miracle of love will console even the exiled father, whose heart will again feel a thrill of pleasure, when he knows that his son has been saved, and saved by Xenie!

A goat follows her to nourish the infant. The virgin mother may sometimes be seen, a living picture, seated in the sun among the dark ruins of the castle in which she was born, and smiling fondly on the child of her soul, the son of the hapless exile.

She cradles the little one upon her knees with a virgin grace, and his awaking brings a smile of angelic delight upon her countenance. Without knowing or hating the world, she has passed from charity to love, from love to madness, from madness to maternity. God watches over her!

Sometimes she appears struck with some sweet and sad remembrance: then her lips, the senseless echoes of the past, murmur mechanically these mysterious words—the last and only expression of her intellectual life, and of which not one of the inhabitants of Vologda can divine the meaning,—"It is I, then, whom he loved!"

Neither the Russian poet nor myself have shrunk from the

expression of *virgin mother* as applied to Xenie, and neither of us think that we have been wanting in respect for the sublime verse of the Catholic poet—"O Vergine Madre, figlio del tuo figlio,"* or profaned the profound mystery that is indicated in those few words.

---

*Dante, *Paradiso*, cant. 33. i. v.

LETTER 19

I HAD PROMISED my friends that I would not return to
France without seeing Moscow, the fabulous city—fabulous
in spite of history; for the grandeur of the events connected
with it, though they recall the most positive and clearly
defined occurrences of our age, renders its name poetical beyond all other names.

This scene of an epic poem has a sublimity which contrasts, in a whimsical manner, with the spirit of an age of
mathematicians and stockjobbers. I am therefore especially
impatient to reach Moscow, for which city I set out in two
days. My impatience will not, however, prevent my expatiating on all that may strike me before arriving there, for I mean
to complete, as far as I am able, the picture of this vast and
singular empire.

It is impossible to describe the dullness of St. Petersburg
during the absence of the emperor. At no time does the city

exhibit what may be called gaiety; but without the court, it is a desert. The reader is aware that it is constantly menaced with destruction by the sea. This morning, while roaming its solitary quays and empty streets, I said to myself, "Surely the city must be about to be inundated; the inhabitants have fled, and the water will soon recover possession of the marsh." Nothing of the kind: Petersburg is lifeless only because the emperor is at Peterhof.

The water of the Neva, driven back by the sea, rises so high, and the banks are so low, that this large inlet, with its innumerable arms, resembles a stagnant inundation, an overflowing marsh. They call the Neva a river, but it is for want of a more precise signification. At Petersburg, the Neva has already become the sea; higher up, it is a channel of a few leagues in length, which serves to convey the superfluous waters of Lake Ladoga into the Gulf of Finland.

At the period when the quays of Petersburg were built, a taste for structures of small elevation prevailed among the Russians. The adoption of this taste was very injudicious in a country where the snow, during eight months in the year, diminishes the height of the walls by six feet; and where the surface of the soil presents no variety that might, in any degree, relieve the monotony of the regular circle which forms the unchangeable line of horizon, serving as a frame for scenes level as the ocean. In my youth, I inhaled enthusiasm at the feet of the mountainous coasts of Calabria, before landscapes all of whose lines, excepting those of the sea, were vertical. Here, on the contrary, I see only one plane surface terminated by a perfectly horizontal line drawn betwixt the sky and the water. The mansions, palaces, and colleges which line the Neva, seem scarcely to rise above the soil, or rather the sea: some have only one story, the loftiest not more than three, and all appear dilapidated. The masts of the vessel overshoot the roofs of the houses. These roofs are of painted iron; they are light and elegant, but very flat, like those of Italy, whereas pointed roofs are alone proper in countries where snow abounds. In Russia, we are shocked at every step by the results of imitation without reflection.

Between the square blocks of an architecture which pretends to be Italian, run wide, straight, and empty vistas, which they call streets, and which, notwithstanding their projecting colonnades, are anything but classical. The scarcity of the women also contributes to the dullness of the city. Those who are pretty, seldom appear on foot. Wealthy persons who wish to walk, are invariably followed by a servant. The practice, is, here, one of prudence and necessity.

The emperor alone has the power to people this wearisome abode, abandoned so soon as its master has disappeared. He is the magician who puts thought and motion into the human machines,—a magician in whose presence Russia wakes, and in whose absence she sleeps. After the court has left, the superb metropolis has the appearance of a theater when the performance is over. The emperor is the light of the lamp. Since my return from Peterhof, I can scarcely recognize the city I left four days ago; but were the emperor to return this evening, everything tomorrow would recover its former interest. We should have to become Russians to understand the power of the sovereign's eye; it is a very different thing from the lover's eye spoken of by Lafontaine. Do you suppose that a young girl bestows a thought on her love affairs in the presence of the emperor? Do not deceive yourself; she is occupied with the idea of procuring some promotion for her brother. The old women, so soon as they breathe the air of the court, feel no longer their infirmities. They may have no family to provide for,—no matter, they play the courtier for the pure love of the game. They are servile without an object, just as others like play for its own sake. Thus, by an endeavor to shake off the burden of years, these wrinkled puppets lose all the dignity of age. We have no pity for busy intriguing decrepitude, because it is ridiculous. At the end of life, it is surely time to set about practicing the lesson which time is ever teaching, the grand art, namely, of giving up. Happy those who early learn to apply this lesson. To renounce, is the great proof of a powerful mind: to abdicate a position before it is lost,—this is the policy of old age.

It is, however, a policy little practiced at court, and at that of St. Petersburg less than at any other. Busy, restless old women are the plagues of the court of Russia. The sun of favor dazzles and blinds the ambitious, more especially those of the female sex; it prevents their discerning their true interest, which would be to save their pride by concealing the miseries of their hearts. On the contrary, the Russian courtiers glory in the abject meanness of their souls. The flatterer here shuffles his cards upon the table, and I am only astonished that he can win anything in a game so palpable to all the world. In the presence of the emperor the asthmatic breathes, the paralyzed becomes active, the gouty loses his pain, the lovers no longer burn, the young men no longer seek to amuse themselves, the men of mind no longer think. In lieu of all these human states, mental and physical, one combined sentiment of avarice and vanity animates life even to its latest sigh. These two passions are the breath of all courts; but here, they impart to their victims a military emulation, a disciplined rivalry, whose agitating influences extend throughout all the stages of society. To rise a step by more carefully dancing attendance,—such is the absorbing thought of this crowd, each member of which wears his badge of rank.

But then, what prostration of amazing strength, when the luminary in whose beam these flattering motes may be seen to move, is no longer above the horizon! It is like the evening dew quenching the dust.

With this continual stretch of all minds towards advancement, conversation is impossible. The eyes of the Russian courtiers are the sunflowers of the palace. They speak without interesting themselves in anything that is said, and their looks remain all the while fascinated by the sun of favor.

The absence of the emperor does not render conversation more free: he is still present to the mind. The thoughts, instead of the eyes, then become the sunflowers. In one word, the emperor is the god, the life, the passion, of this unhappy people. Imagine human existence reduced to the hope that an obeisance will procure the acknowledgment of a look! God has implanted too many passions in the human heart for the uses which are here made of it.

If I put myself in the place of the only man who has here the right to live free, I tremble for him. To have to play the part of Providence over sixty millions of souls is a dreadful office. The divinity has only the choice of two things: either to destroy his own power by showing himself a man, or to lead his votaries to the conquest of the world, in maintaining his character as a god.

It is thus, that, in Russia, the whole of life becomes nothing more than a school of ambition.

But by what road have the Russians reached this point of self-abnegation? What human means could produce such a political result? The cause of all is the *chin:* the *chin* is the galvanism, the apparent life, of souls and bodies here, —the passion which survives all other passions. I have shown its effects; it is therefore necessary that I should explain its nature.

The *chin* is a nation formed into a regiment; it is the military system applied to all classes of society, even to those which never go to war. In short, it is the division of the civil population into ranks, which correspond to ranks in the army. Since this institution has been established, a man who has never seen exercise may obtain the title of colonel.

Peter the Great—it is always to him that we must go back in order to understand the actual state of Russia—Peter the Great, troubled by certain national prejudices which had a resemblance to aristocracy, and which incommoded him in the execution of his plans, took it into his head one day to discover that the minds of his people were too independent; and, in order to remedy the evil, that great workman could devise nothing better in his profoundly deep, yet narrow penetration, than to divide the herd, that is to say, the people, into classes, entirely irrespective of name, birth, and family; so that the son of the highest noble in the empire may belong to an inferior class, whilst the son of one of the peasants may rise to the highest classes, if such be the goodwill of the emperor. Under this division of the people, every man takes his position according to the favor of the prince. Thus it is that Russia has become a regiment of sixty millions strong; and this is the *chin*,—the mightiest achievement of Peter the Great.

By its means, that prince freed himself in one day from the fetters of ages. The tyrant, when he undertook to regenerate his people, held sacred neither nature, history, character, nor life. Such sacrifices render great results easy. Peter knew better than anyone that, so long as an order of nobility exists in a community, the despotism of one man can be nothing more than a fiction. He therefore said, "To realize my government I must annihilate the remains of the feudal system; and the best way of doing this is to make caricatures of gentlemen,— to destroy the nobility by making it a creation of my own." It has consequently been, if not destroyed, at least nullified by an institution that occupies its place, though it does not replace it. There are castes in this social system, in which to enter is to acquire hereditary nobility. Peter the Great, whom I should prefer to call Peter the Strong, forestalling our modern revolutions by more than half a century, thus crushed the spirit of feudalism. Less powerful under him than it was among us, it fell beneath the half civil, half military institution which constitutes modern Russia. Peter was endowed with a clear and yet a limited understanding. In rearing his system on so great a ruin, he knew not how to profit by the exorbitant powers he had engrossed, except in mimicking, more at his ease, the civilization of Europe.

With the means of action usurped by this prince, a creative genius would have worked much greater miracles. The Russian nation, ascending after all the others upon the great stage of the world, possessed the gift of imitation in lieu of genius, and had a carpenter's apprentice for its prompter! Under a chief less fond of minutiae, less attached to details, that nation would have distinguished itself, more tardily, it is true, but more gloriously. Its power, corresponding with its own internal requirements, would have been useful to the world: it is now only astonishing.

The successors of this lawgiver in fustian have, during one hundred years, united, with the ambition of subjugating their neighbors, the weakness of copying them. In the present day, the Emperor Nicholas believes the time is arrived when Russia has no longer need of looking for models among foreigners in order to conquer and to rule the world. He is the first really Russian sovereign since Ivan IV. Peter I was a Russian in character, though not in politics; Nicholas is a German by nature, but a Russian by calculation and by necessity.

The *tchinn* consists of fourteen classes, each of which possesses its own peculiar privileges. The fourteenth is the lowest.

Placed immediately above the serfs, its sole advantage consists in its members having the title of freemen. Their freedom means that no one can strike them without rendering himself liable to prosecution. In return, every member of the class has to inscribe on his door his registered number, in order that no superior may be led to act under an ignorance that would render him liable to a penalty.

The fourteenth class is composed of persons in the lowest employ under the government, clerks of the post office, mailmen, and other subordinates charged with carrying or executing the orders of the heads of departments: it answers to the rank of petty officer in the Imperial army. The men who compose it are servants of the emperor, and serfs of no one: they possess a sense of their social dignity. But as to human dignity, it is not known in Russia.

All the other classes of the *chin* answer to as many military grades; the order that reigns throughout the entire state is analogous to the order of the army. The first class stands at the summit of the pyramid, and now consists of one single man—Marshal Paskevich, viceroy of Warsaw.

The will of the emperor is the sole means by which an individual is promoted in the *chin*; so that a man, rising step by step, to the highest rank in this artificial nation, may attain the first military dignity without having served in any army. The favor of promotion is never demanded, but always intrigued for.

There is here an immense quantity of fermenting material placed at the disposal of the head of the state. Medical men complain of their inability to communicate fever to certain patients in order to cure them of chronic maladies. The Czar Peter inoculated with the fever of ambition the whole body of his people, in order to render them more pliant, and to govern them according to his humor.

The English aristocracy is equally independent of birth; it depends upon two things, which may be acquired, office and estate. If, then, that aristocracy, moderated as it is, still imparts an enormous influence to the crown, how great must be the power of a crown whence all these things—the rank, and also the office and estate—are both de jure and de facto derived!

There results from such a social organization a fever of envy so violent, a stretch of mind towards ambition so constant, that the Russian people will become incapable of anything except the conquest of the world. I always return to this expression, because it is the only one that can explain the excessive sacrifices imposed here upon the individual by society. If the extreme of ambition can dry up the heart of a man, it may also stop the fountain of intellect, and so lead astray the judgment of a nation as to induce it to sacrifice its liberty for victory. Without this idea, avowed or disguised, and the influence of which many, perhaps, obey unconsciously, the history of Russia would seem to me an inexplicable enigma.

Here is suggested the grand question: is the idea of conquest that forms the secret aspiration of Russia, a lure, suited only to seduce for a period, more or less long, a rude and ignorant population, or is it one day to be realized?

This question besets me unceasingly, and, in spite of all my efforts, I cannot solve it. All that I can say is, that since I have been in Russia, I have formed a gloomy view of the future reserved for Europe. At the same time, my conscience obliges me to admit that my opinion is combated by wise and very experienced men. These men say that I exaggerate in my own mind the power of Russia; that every community has its prescribed destiny, and that the destiny of this community is to extend its conquests eastward, and then to become divided. Those minds that refuse to believe in the brilliant future of the Slavs, agree with me as regards the amiable and happy disposition of that people; they admit that they are endowed with an instinctive sentiment of the picturesque; they allow them a natural talent for music; and they conclude that these dispositions will enable them to cultivate the fine arts to a certain extent, but that they do not suffice to constitute the capacity for conquering and commanding which I attribute to them. They add, that "the Russians want scientific genius; that they have never shown any inventive power; that they have received from nature an indolent and superficial mind; that if they apply themselves, it is through fear rather than inclination: fear makes them apt to undertake and to draw the rough drafts of things, but it also prevents their proceeding far in any effort: genius is, in its nature, hardy as heroism; it lives on liberty; whilst fear and slavery have a reign and a sphere limited as mediocrity, of which they are the weapons. The Russians, though good soldiers, are bad seamen; in general, they are more resigned than reflective, more religious than philosophical; they have more instinct of obedience than will of their own; their thoughts lack a spring as their souls lack liberty. The task which is to them most difficult, and least natural, is seriously to occupy their minds and to fix their imaginations upon useful exercises. Ever children, they might, nevertheless, for a moment be conquerors in the realm of the sword; but they would never be so in that of thought: and a people who cannot teach anything to those they conquer, cannot long be the most powerful.

"Even physically, the French and English are more robust than the Russians; the latter are more agile than muscular, more savage than energetic, more cunning than enterprising; they possess passive courage, but they want daring and perseverance. The army, so remarkable for its discipline and its appearance on days of parade, is composed, with the exception of a few elite corps, of men well clad when they show themselves in public, but slovenly and dirty so long as they remain in their barracks. The cadaverous complexions of the soldiers betray hunger and disease: the two campaigns in Turkey have sufficiently demonstrated the weakness of the giant. Finally, a community that has not tasted liberty at its birth, and in which all the great political crises have been brought about by foreign influence, cannot, thus enervated in its germ, have a long existence in prospect."

Such, it seems to me, are the strongest reasons opposed to my fears by the political optimists. From them, it is concluded that Russia, powerful at home, and formidable when she struggles with the Asiatic people, would break herself against Europe so soon as she should throw off the mask, and make war in maintenance of her arrogant diplomacy.

I have in no degree weakened the arguments of those who thus think. They accuse me of exaggerating the danger. At any rate, my opinions are shared by other minds, quite as sober as those of my adversaries, minds which do not cease to reproach these optimists with their blindness, in exhorting them to see the evil before it become irremediable.

I stand close by the colossus, and I find it difficult to persuade myself that the only object of this creation of Providence is to diminish the barbarism of Asia. It appears to me that it is chiefly destined to chastise the corrupt civilization of Europe, by the agency of a new invasion. The eternal tyranny of the East menaces us incessantly; and we shall have to bow to it, if our extravagances and iniquities render us worthy of the punishment.

The reader must not expect from me a complete account of Russia. I neglect to speak of many celebrated things, because they make little impression upon me. I wish only to describe what strikes or interests me. Nomenclatures and catalogs disgust me with travels, and there are plenty of them without my adding to the list.

Nothing can be seen here without ceremony and preparation. Russian hospitality is so edged round with formalities as to render life unpleasant to the most favored strangers. It is a civil pretext for restraining the movements of the traveler, and for limiting the freedom of his observations. Owing to the fastidious politeness exercised in doing the honors of the land, the observer can inspect nothing without a guide: never being alone, he has the greater difficulty in forming his judgment upon his own spontaneous impressions; and this is what is desired. To enter Russia, you must, with your passport, deposit also your right of opinion on the frontier. Would you see the curiosities of a palace, they give you a chamberlain, with whom you are obliged to view everything, and, indiscriminately, to admire all that he admires. Would you survey a camp,—an officer, sometimes a general officer, accompanies you: if it be a hospital, the head surgeon escorts you; if a fortress, the governor, in person, shows it, or rather politely conceals it from you; if a school, or any other public institution, the director or the inspector must be previously apprised of your visit, and you find him, under arms, prepared to brave your examination; if an edifice, the architect himself leads you over the whole building, and explains to you all that you do not care to know, in order to avoid informing you on points which you would take interest in knowing.

All this Oriental ceremony leads people to renounce seeing many things, were it only to avoid the trouble of soliciting admissions: this is the first advantage gained! but if curiosity is hardy enough to persist in importuning official personages, it is at least so carefully watched in its perquisitions, that they end in nothing. You must communicate officially with the heads of the so-called public establishments, and you obtain no other permission than that of expressing before the legitimate authorities the admiration which politeness, prudence, and a gratitude of which the Russians are very jealous, demand. They refuse you nothing, but they accompany you everywhere: politeness becomes a pretext for maintaining a watch over you.

In this manner they tyrannize over us while pretending to do us honor. Such is the fate of privileged travelers. As to those who are not privileged, they see nothing at all. The country is so organized that, without the immediate intervention of official persons, no stranger can move about agreeably, or even safely. In all this, will be recognized the manners and the policy of the East, disguised under European urbanity. Such alliance of the East and the West, the results of which are discoverable at every step, is the grand characteristic of the Russian Empire.

A semicivilization is always marked by formalities; refined civilization dispenses with them, just as perfect good breeding banishes affectation.

The Russians are still persuaded of the efficaciousness of falsehood; and such illusion on the part of a people so well acquainted with it, amazes me. It is not that they want quick perception, but in a land where the governors do not yet understand the advantages of liberty, even for themselves, the governed naturally shrink from the immediate inconveniences of truth. One is momentarily obliged to repeat that the people here, great and small, resemble the Greeks of the Lower Empire.

I am perhaps not sufficiently grateful for the attentions which these people affect to lavish upon strangers who are at all known; but I cannot help seeing below the surface, and I feel, in spite of myself, that all their eagerness demonstrates less benevolence than it betrays inquietude.

They wish, in accordance with the judicious precept of Monomachus, that the foreigner should leave their country contented. It is not that the real country cares what is said or thought of it; it is simply that certain influential families are possessed with the puerile desire of reviving the European reputation of Russia.

If I look further, I perceive under the veil with which they seek to cloak every object, a love of mystery for its own sake. Here, reserve is the order of the day, just as imprudence is in Paris. In Russia, secrecy presides over everything; a silence that is superfluous ensures the silence that is necessary; in short, the people are Chinese disguised; they do not like to avow their aversion to foreign observation, but if they dared to brave the reproach of barbarism, as the true Chinese do, access to Petersburg would be as difficult for us as is the access to Peking.

My reasons for wearying of Russian hospitality will be now seen. Of all species of constraint the most unendurable to me is that of which I have not the right to complain. The gratitude I feel for the attentions of which I am here the object, is like that of a soldier who is made to serve by compulsion. As a traveler who specially piques himself on his independence, I feel that I am passing under the yoke; they trouble themselves unceasingly to discipline my ideas, and every evening on returning to my quarters, I have to examine my thoughts to ascertain what rank they bear, and in what uniform they are clothed.

Having carefully avoided intimacy with many great lords, I have hitherto seen nothing thoroughly except the court. My wish has been to preserve my position as an independent and impartial judge; I have feared also to incur accusations of ingratitude or want of good faith; above all, I have feared lest I should render subjects of the country responsible for my particular opinions. But, at the court, I have passed in review all the characteristics of society.

There, an affectation of French manners, without any of the tone of French conversation, first struck me. It conceals a caustic, sarcastic, Russian spirit of ridicule. If I remained here any time, I would tear away the mask from these puppets, for I am weary of seeing them copy French grimaces. At my age, a man has nothing more to learn from the spectacle of affectation; truth alone can always interest, because it imparts knowledge; truth alone is always new.

I observed from the very first, that the Russians of the lower classes, who are suspicious by nature, detest foreigners through ignorance and national prejudice; I have observed since, that the Russians of the higher classes, who are equally suspicious, fear them because they believe them hostile: "the French and the English are persuaded of their superiority over all other people"; this idea suffices to make a Russian hate foreigners, on the same principle that, in France, the provincial distrusts the Parisian. A barbarian jealousy, an envy, puerile, but impossible to disarm, influences the greater number of the Russians in their intercourse with the men of other lands.

The Russian character is in many respects the very opposite of the German. On this account it is that the Russians say they resemble the French; but the analogy is only apparent: in the inner character there is a great difference. You may, if you choose, admire, in Russia, pomp and Oriental grandeur; you may study there Greek astuteness; but you must not seek for the Gallic naïveté, the sociability and the amiableness of the French when they are natural; though I admit that you will find still less of the good faith, the sound intelligence, and the cordial feeling of the German. In Russia, you may meet with kindness, because it is to be met with wherever there are men; but good nature is never seen.

Every Russian is born an imitator; he is, consequently, a great observer.

This talent of observation, which is proper to a people in its infancy, often degenerates into a mean system of espionage. It produces questions often importunate and impolite, and which appear intolerable, coming from people always impenetrable themselves, and whose answers are seldom more than evasions. One would say that friendship itself had here some private understanding with the police. How is it possible to be at ease with people so guarded and circumspect respecting all which concerns themselves, and so inquisitive about others? If they see you assume, in your intercourse with them, manners more natural than those which they show towards you, they fancy you their dupe. Beware then of letting them see you off your guard, beware of giving them your confidence: to men who are without feeling themselves, it is an amusement to observe the emotions of others, an amusement to which I, for one, do not like to administer. To observe our manner of life is the greatest pleasure of the Russians; if we allowed them, they would amuse themselves by striving to read our hearts, and analyze our sentiments, just as people study dramatic representations at the theater.

The extreme distrust of all classes here with whom you have any business, warns you to be circumspect; the fear that you inspire discloses the danger that you run.

The other day, at Peterhof, a caterer would not permit my servant to provide me with a miserable supper in my actor's box, without being previously paid for it, although the shop of this prudent man is but two steps from the theater. What you put to your lips with one hand must be paid for with the other; if you were to give an order to a merchant without presenting him with money in advance, he would believe you were in jest, and would not undertake your business.

No one can leave Russia until he has forewarned all his creditors of his intention, that is to say, until he has announced his departure three times in the gazettes, at an interval of eight days between each publication.

This is strictly enforced, unless at least you pay the police to shorten the prescribed time, and even then, you must make the insertion once or twice. No one can obtain post-horses without a document from the authorities, certifying that he owes nothing.

So much precaution shows the bad faith that exists in the country; for as, hitherto, the Russians have had little personal intercourse with foreigners, they must have taken lessons in wariness from themselves alone.

Their experience is only such as their position with regard to each other can teach them. These men will not allow us to forget the saying of their favorite sovereign, Peter the Great, "It takes three Jews to cheat a Russian."

Among the nobles, those who do possess good manners, possess them in perfection. The proof of this may be seen daily at Paris and elsewhere; but a drawing-room Russian who has not attained true politeness, that is to say, the facile expression of a real amenity of character, has a coarseness of mind, which is rendered doubly shocking by the false elegance of his language and manners. Such ill-bred and yet well-informed, well-dressed, clever, and self-confident Russians, tread in the steps of European elegance, without knowing that refinement of habits has no value except as it announces the existence of something better in the heart of its possessor. These apprentices of fashion, who confuse the appearance with the reality, are trained bears, the sight of which inclines me to regret the wild ones: they have not yet become polished men, and they are already spoiled savages.

As there is such a place as Siberia, and as it is appropriated to the uses that are so well known, I could wish it were peopled with fastidious young officers and capricious fair ladies: "You want passports for Paris, you shall have them for Tobolsk!"

In this manner I would recommend the emperor to check the rage for traveling which is making fearful progress in Russia, among imaginative junior lieutenants and fanciful women.

If, at the same time, he were to restore the seat of his empire to Moscow, he would repair the evil caused by Peter the Great, as far as one man may atone for the errors of generations.

―――――

I have visited several churches; that of the Trinity is beautiful, but naked, as is the interior of nearly all the Greek churches that I have seen. To make up for this, the exterior of the domes is clothed with azure and strewn with brilliant gold stars. The cathedral of Kazan, built by Alexander, is vast and beautiful; but its entrance is placed in a corner of the building, out of respect to the religious law which obliges the Greek altar to be invariably turned towards the East. The street not running in such direction as to allow of the rule being obeyed except by placing the church awry, this has been done; the men of taste have had the worst of it; the faithful have carried the day, and one of the most beautiful buildings in Russia has been spoiled by superstition.

The church of Smolny is the largest and most magnificent in Petersburg. It belongs to a religious community, a kind of chapter of women and girls founded by the Empress Anna. Enormous buildings form the residence of these ladies. The noble asylum, with its cloisters, is a city of itself, but its architecture would be more appropriate for a military establishment than a religious congregation: it is neither like a convent nor a palace: it is a barrack for women.

In Russia everything is under a military system; the discipline of the army reigns even in the chapter of the ladies of Smolny.

Near to that building is seen the little palace of the Taurida, built in a few weeks by Potemkin for Catherine. The palace is elegant, but forsaken; and in this country what is forsaken is soon destroyed; even the stones will not last, except on condition of their being cared for. A winter garden occupies one side of the building. It is a magnificent hot-house, empty at the present season, and I believe neglected at all seasons. Chandeliers and other signs of elegance, old, but without the majesty which time imprints on the true antique, prove that dances and suppers have once been given there. The last ball, I believe, which the Taurida has seen, or ever will see, took place at the marriage of the Grand Duchess Helena, wife of the Grand Duke Michael.

In a corner stands a Venus de Medicis, said to be a real *antique*. This model has, as is well known, been often reproduced by the Romans.

The statue is placed upon a pedestal, on which is this inscription in Russian:—

A PRESENT FROM POPE CLEMENT XI
TO THE EMPEROR PETER I
1717–1719.

A naked Venus, sent by a pope to a schismatic prince, is certainly a singular present. The czar, who had long meditated the project of eternizing schism, by usurping the last rights of the Russian church, must have smiled at such a testimony of the goodwill of the Bishop of Rome.

I have seen also the paintings of the Hermitage, but I

cannot now describe them, as I leave tomorrow for Moscow. The Hermitage! is not this a name strangely applied to the villa of a sovereign, placed in the midst of his capital, close to the palace where he resides! A bridge thrown across a street leads from one residence to the other.

All the world knows that there are here some choice pieces, especially of the Dutch school; but I do not like paintings in Russia, any more than music in London, where the manner in which they listen to the most gifted performers, and the most sublime compositions, would disgust me with the art.

So near the pole the light is unfavorable for seeing pictures; no one can enjoy the admirable shading of the colors with eyes either weakened by snow, or dazzled by an oblique and continuous light. The hall of the Rembrandts is doubtless admirable; nevertheless, I prefer the works of that master which I have seen at Paris and elsewhere.

The Claude Lorrains, the Poussins, and some works of the Italian masters, especially of Mantegna, Giovanni Bellini, and Salvator Rosa, deserve to be mentioned.

The fault of the collection is, the great number of inferior pictures that must be forgotten in order to enjoy the masterpieces. In forming the gallery of the Hermitage, they have gathered together a profusion of names of the great masters; but this does not prevent their genuine productions from being rare. These ostentatious baptisms of very ordinary pictures weary the virtuoso, without charming him. In a collection of objects of art, the contiguity of beauty sets off the beautiful, and that of inferiority detracts from it. A judge who is wearied, is incapable of judging: ennui renders him unjust and severe.

If the Rembrandts and the Claude Lorrains of the Hermitage produce some effect, it is because they are placed in halls where there are no other pictures near them.

The collection is undoubtedly fine; but it appears lost in a city where there are so few that can enjoy it.

I leave tomorrow for Moscow.

LETTER 20

ON THE DAY of the fête at Peterhof, I had asked the minister of war what means I should take in order to obtain permission to see the fortress of Schlüsselburg.

This grave personage is the Count Chernishev. The brilliant aide-de-camp, the elegant envoy of Alexander at the court
of Napoleon, is become a sedate man, a man of importance,
and one of the most active ministers of the empire. Not a
morning passes without his transacting business with the
emperor. He replied, "I will communicate your desire to His
Majesty." This tone of prudence, mingled with an air of surprise, made me feel that the answer was very significative. My
request, simple as I had thought it, was evidently an important
one in the eyes of the minister. To think of visiting a fortress

that had become historical since the imprisonment and death of Ivan VI, which took place in the reign of the Empress Elizabeth, was enormous presumption. I perceived that I had touched a tender chord, and said no more on the subject.

Some days after, namely, on the day before yesterday, at the moment I was preparing to depart for Moscow, I received a letter from the minister of war, announcing permission to see the sluices of Schlüsselburg!

The ancient Swedish fortress, called the key of the Baltic by Peter I, is situated precisely at the source of the Neva, on an island in the lake of Ladoga, to which the river serves as a natural canal, that carries its superfluous waters into the Gulf of Finland. This canal, otherwise called the Neva, receives, however, a large accession of water, which is considered as exclusively the source of the river, and which rises up under the waves immediately beneath the walls of the fortress of Schlüsselburg, between the river and the lake. The spring is one of the most remarkable natural curiosities in Russia; and the surrounding scenery, though very flat, like all other scenery in the country, is the most interesting in the environs of Petersburg.

By means of a canal, with sluices, boats avoid the danger caused by the spring: they leave the lake before reaching the source of the Neva, and enter the river about half a league below.

This then was the interesting work which I was permitted to examine. I had requested to see a state prison; my request was met by a permission to view the floodgates.

The minister of war ended his note by informing me that the aide-de-camp, general director of the roads of the empire, had received orders to give me every facility for making the journey.

Facility! Good heavens! to what trouble had my curiosity exposed me, and what a lesson of discretion had they given me, by the exhibition of so much ceremony, qualified by so much politeness! Not to avail myself of the permission, when orders had been sent respecting me throughout the route, would have been to incur the charge of ingratitude; yet to examine the sluices with Russian minuteness, without even seeing the castle of Schlüsselburg, was to fall with my eyes open into the snare, and to lose a day; a serious loss, at this already advanced season, if I am to see all that I purpose seeing in Russia, without altogether passing the winter there.

I state facts. The reader can draw the conclusions. They have not here yet ventured to speak freely of the iniquities of the reign of Elizabeth. Anything that might lead to reflection on the nature of the legitimacy of the present power passes for an impiety. It was on this account necessary to represent my request to the emperor. He would neither grant it nor directly refuse it; he therefore modified it, and gave me permission to admire a wonder of industry which I had no intention of seeing. From the emperor, this permission was forwarded to the minister, from the minister to the director-general, from the director-general to a chief engineer, and, finally, to a petty officer commissioned to accompany me, to officiate as my guide, and to answer for my *safety* during the entire journey: a *favor* which rather reminds one of the janissary with whom they honored foreigners in Turkey. Such protection appears too much like a mark of distrust to flatter me as much as it irks me, and, while crushing in my hands the minister's letter, I think on the justice of the words of the prince whom I met on the Travemünde steamboat, and with him am ready to exclaim, that "Russia is the land of useless formalities!"

I proceeded to the aide-de-camp general director, &c. &c. &c., to claim the execution of the supreme command. The director was not at home; I must call tomorrow. Not wishing to lose another day, I persisted, and was told to return in the evening, when I was received with the usual politeness, and after a visit of a quarter of an hour, was dismissed with the necessary orders for the engineer of Schlüsselburg, but none for the governor of the castle. In accompanying me to the antechamber, he promised that a petty officer should be at my door on the morrow, at four o'clock in the morning.

I did not sleep. I became possessed with an idea that will appear quite mad; the idea that my guard might become my jailer. If this man, instead of conducting me to Schlüsselburg, eighteen leagues from Petersburg, should, when we had left the city, exhibit an order to transport me to Siberia, that I might there expiate my inconvenient curiosity, what should I say or do? The manifestations of politeness by no means reassured me: on the contrary, I had not forgotten the smiles and gracious words of Alexander, addressed to one of his ministers, who was seized by the *Feldjäger*, at the door even of the emperor's cabinet, and carried direct from the palace to Siberia.

Many other examples of sentences and executions of the same character occurred to justify my presentiments and to disturb my imagination.

The being a foreigner was not, I felt, sufficient guarantee. I called to mind the carrying off of Kotzebue, who, at the beginning of this century, was also seized by a *Feldjäger*, and transported, under circumstances similar to mine (for I already felt as if on the road), from Petersburg to Tobolsk. What had been the offense of Kotzebue? The German dramatist had made himself obnoxious because he had published his opinions, and because they were not all thought equally favorable to the order of things established in Russia. Now, who could assure me that I had not incurred the same reproach? or, which would be sufficient, the same suspicion? If I give the least umbrage here, can I hope that they will have more regard for me than they have had for others? Besides, I am watched by spies—every foreigner is. They know, therefore, that I write, and carefully conceal my papers; they are, perhaps, curious to know what these papers are about. If they seize me, my ambassador shall inquire about me. If I am judged too indesirable, they will answer that I have capsized in Lake Ladoga. These accidents happen every day. Will my ambassador try to fish me out? No. One will let him know that all efforts to recover my body have been in vain. The dignity of our nation shall be preserved and I lost forever.

Such were the fancies that possessed me the whole of the night before last; and though I visited yesterday, without any accident, the fortress of Schlüsselburg, they are not so entirely unreasonable as to make me feel quite beyond all danger for the remainder of my journey. I often say to myself, that the Russian police, prudent, enlightened, well informed, would not have recourse to any coup d'état, unless they believed it necessary, and that it would be attaching too much importance to my person and my remarks, to suppose that they could be capable of making uneasy the men who govern so great an empire. Nevertheless, these reasons for feeling secure, and many others that present themselves, are more specious than solid: experience only too clearly proves the spirit of minutia which actuates those who have too much power: everything is of importance to him who would conceal the fact that he governs by fear, and whoever depends on opinion must not despise that of any independent man who writes: a government which lives by mystery, and whose strength lies in dissimulation, is afraid of everything—everything appears to it of consequence: in short, my vanity accords with my reflection and my memory of past events, to persuade me that I here run some danger.

If I lay any stress upon these inquietudes, it is simply because they describe the country. As regards my own feelings, they dissipate as soon as it is necessary to act. The phantoms of a sleepless night do not follow me upon the road: I am more adventurous in action than in thought; it is more difficult for me to think than to act with energy. Motion imparts to me as much courage as rest inspires me with doubt.

Yesterday, at five in the morning, I set out in a calèche,

drawn by four horses harnessed abreast. Whenever they journey into the country, the Russian coachmen adopt this ancient mode of driving, in which they display much boldness
and dexterity. My *Feldjäger* placed himself before me, by the
side of the coachman, and we quickly traversed St. Petersburg, soon leaving behind us the handsome part of the city,
and next passing through that of the manufactures, among
which are magnificent glass works and immense mills for the
spinning of cotton and other factories, for the most part directed by Englishmen. This quarter of the city resembles a
colony. As a man is only appreciated here according to his
standing with the government, the presence of the *Feldjäger*
on my carriage had a great effect. Such a mark of supreme
protection made me a person of consequence in the eyes of
my own coachman, who had driven me the whole of the time
that I had been in Petersburg. He appeared suddenly to discover and to glory in the too long concealed dignity of his
master; his looks testified a respect that they had never done
before: it seemed as though he wished to indemnify me for all
the honors of which he had, mentally and in ignorance, hitherto deprived me.

The people on foot, the drivers of the carts and droshkies,
all bowed to the mystic influence of my petty officer, who,
with a simple sign of his finger, made every obstruction of
the road vanish like magic. The crowd was, as it were, annihilated before him; and I could not but think, if he had such
power to protect me, what would be his power to destroy
me, if he had received an order to that effect. The difficulty
attending an entrance into this country wearies more than
it awes me; the difficulty of flying from it would be more formidable. People say, "To enter Russia, the gates are wide; to
leave it, they become narrow."

The appearance of several villages surprised me; they display signs of wealth, and even a sort of rustic elegance, which
is very pleasing. The neat wooden houses form the line of a

single street. They are painted, and their roofs are loaded with ornaments which might be considered rather ostentatious, if a comparison were made between the exterior luxury and the internal lack of conveniences and cleanliness in these architectural toys. One regrets to see a taste for superfluities among a people not yet acquainted with necessaries; besides, on examining them more closely, the habitations are discovered to be ill built.

Always the same taste for what addresses the eye! Both peasants and lords take more pleasure in ornamenting the road, than in beautifying the interior of their dwellings. They feed here upon the admiration, or perhaps the envy, which they excite. But enjoyment, real enjoyment, where is it? The Russians themselves would be puzzled to answer the question.

Wealth in Russia is the food of vanity. The only magnificence that pleases me is that which makes no show, and I therefore find fault with everything here which they wish me to admire. A nation of decorators will never inspire me with any other feeling than that of fearing lest I should become their dupe. On entering the theater where their artificial representations are exhibited, I have but one desire; that, namely, of looking behind the curtain, a corner of which I am ever tempted to lift up. I came to see a country, I find only a theater.

I had ordered a relay of horses ten leagues from Petersburg. Four, ready harnessed, awaited me in a village, where I found a kind of Russian *venta*,* which I entered. It was the first time I had seen the peasants in their own houses.

An immense wooden shed, plank walls on three sides, plank flooring, and plank ceiling, formed the hall of entrance, and occupied the greater part of the rustic dwelling.

---

* *Venta*, a Spanish country inn.—*Trans.*

Notwithstanding the free currents of air, I found it redolent
of that odor of onions, cabbages, and old greasy leather, which
Russian villages and Russian villagers invariably exhale.

A superb stallion, tied to a post, occupied the attention of
several men, who were engaged in the difficult task of shoe-
ing him. The magnificent but untractable animal belonged, I
was told, to the stud of a neighboring lord: the eight persons
who were endeavoring to manage him, all displayed a figure,
a costume, and a countenance, that were striking. The population of the provinces adjoining the capital is not, however,
handsome: it is not even Russian, being much mixed with
the race of the Finns, who resemble the Laplanders.

They tell me that, in the interior of the empire, I shall find
perfect models of Grecian statues, several of which I have indeed already seen in Petersburg, where the nobles are often
attended by the men born on their distant estates.

A low and confined room adjoined this immense shed; it
reminded me of the cabin of some riverboat; walls, ceiling,
floor, seats, and tables, were all made of wood rudely hewn.
The smell of cabbage and pitch was extremely powerful.

In this retreat, almost deprived of air and light, for the
doors were low, and the windows extremely small, I found an
old woman busy serving tea to four or five bearded peasants,
clothed in pelisses of sheepskin, the wool of which was
turned inwards, for it has already, and for some days past, become rather cold.* These men were of short stature. Their
leather pelisses were rather tasteful in form, but they were
very ill scented: I know nothing except the perfumes of the
nobles that could be more so. On the table stood a bright copper kettle and a teapot. The tea is always of good quality, well
made, and, if it is not preferred pure, good milk is everywhere
to be obtained. This elegant beverage served up in barns, I say

---

*This is the 1st of August.

barns for politeness' sake, reminds me of the chocolate of the Spaniards. It forms one of the thousand strange contrasts with which the traveler is struck at every step he takes among these two people, equally singular, though in most of their ways as different as the climates they inhabit.

I have often said that the Russian people have a sentiment of the picturesque: among the groups of men and animals that surrounded me in this interior of a Russian farmhouse, a painter would have found subjects for several charming pictures.

The red or blue shirt of the peasants is buttoned over the collarbone, and drawn close round the loins by a sash, above which it lies in antique folds, and below, forms an open tunic that falls over the pantaloon. The long Persian robe, often left open, which, when the men do not work, partly covers this blouse, the hair worn long and parted on the forehead, but cut close behind rather higher than the nape, so as to discover all the strength of the neck—does not this form an original and graceful picture? The wild, yet, at the same time, gentle expression of the Russian peasants also possesses grace; their elegant forms, their suppleness, their broad shoulders, the sweet smile of the mouth, the mixture of tenderness and ferocity which is discernible in their wild and melancholy look, render their general appearance as different from that of our laborers as the land they cultivate differs from the rest of Europe. Everything is new here to a stranger. The natives possess a certain charm which can be felt though not expressed: it is the Oriental languor combined with the romantic reverie of a northern people; and all this is exhibited in an uncultured yet noble form, which imparts to it the merit of a primitive endowment. These people inspire much more interest than confidence. The common orders in Russia are amusing knaves: they may be easily led if they are not deceived; but as soon as they see that their masters or their masters' agents lie more than themselves, they plunge into the lowest depths of falsehood and meanness. They who would civilize a people must themselves possess worth of character—the barbarism of the serf accuses the corruptness of the noble.

Dirtiness is very conspicuous in the country, but that of the houses and the clothes strikes me more than that of the individuals. The Russians take much care of their persons. Their steam baths, it is true, appear to us disgusting; and I should for myself much prefer the contact of pure water; still, these boiling fogs cleanse and strengthen the body, though they wrinkle the skin prematurely. By virtue of their use, the peasants may be often seen with clean beards and hair, when as much cannot be said for their garments. Warm clothing costs money, and has to be worn a long time; the rooms also, in which they think only of protecting themselves from the cold, are necessarily less aired than those of southern people. Of the air that purifies, the Russians are deprived for nine months in the year, so that their dirtiness is rather the inevitable effect of their climate than of their negligence.

In some districts the workpeople wear a cap of blue cloth, bulging out in the shape of a balloon. They have several other species of headdress, all pleasing to the eye, and showing good taste as compared with the saucy affectation of negligence, visible among the lower orders in the environs of Paris.

When they work bareheaded, they remedy the inconvenience of their long hair by binding it with a kind of diadem, or fillet made of a riband, a wreath of rushes, or of some other simple material, always placed with care, and which looks well on the young people; for the men of this race have in general finely formed oval heads, so that their working headdress becomes an ornament. But what shall I say of the women? All whom I have hitherto seen have appeared to me repulsive: I had hoped in this excursion to have met some fair villagers; but here, as at Petersburg, they are broad and short in figure, and they gird their forms at the shoulders, a little above the bosom, which spreads freely under the petticoat. It is hideous! Add to this voluntary deformity, large men's boots, and a species of riding coat, or jacket of sheepskin, similar to the pelisses of their husbands, but, doubtless through a laudable economy, much less gracefully cut, and far more worn; falling indeed literally in rags—such is their toilette. Assuredly, there is no part of the world where the fair sex so completely dispenses with coquettish finery as in Russia (I speak only of the female peasants, and of the corner of the land that I have seen). Nevertheless, these women are the mothers of the soldiers of which the emperor is so proud, and of the handsome coachmen of the streets of Petersburg.

It should be observed that the greater number of the women in the government of Petersburg are of Finnish extraction. I am told that in the interior of the country I shall see very good-looking female peasants.

The road from Petersburg to Schlüsselburg is bad in many parts: there are sometimes deep beds of sand, sometimes holes of mud to be passed, over which planks have been very uselessly thrown. Still worse are the small logs of wood rudely laid across each other, on certain marshy portions of the route, which would swallow up any other foundation. This rustic, ill-joined, and movable flooring dances under the wheels; and frequent broken bones and broken carriages on Russian *grandes routes*, testify to the wisdom of reducing equipages to their most simple forms, to something about as primitive as the telega. I observed also several dilapidated bridges, one of which seemed dangerous to pass over. Human life is a small matter in Russia. With sixty millions of children, how can one have the heart of a father?

On my arrival at Schlüsselburg, where I was expected, the engineer who has the direction of the sluices, received me.

The weather was raw and gloomy. My carriage stopped before the comfortable woodhouse of the engineer, who led me himself into a parlor, where he offered me a light collation, and presented me, with a kind of conjugal pride, to a young and handsome person, his wife. She sat all alone upon a sofa, from which she did not rise on my entering. Not understanding French, she remained silent, and also motionless, I cannot tell why, unless she mistook immovability for good breeding, and starched airs for taste. Her object seemed to be to represent, before me, the statue of hospitality clothed in white muslin over a pink petticoat. I ate and warmed myself in silence: she watched me without daring to turn away her eyes, for this would be to move them, and immobility was the part she had to perform. If I had suspected there could be timidity at the bottom of this singular reception, I should have experienced sympathy, and felt only surprise; but I could hardly be deceived in such a case, for I am familiar with timidity.

My host suffered me to contemplate at leisure this curious image of rosy waxwork, dressed up in order to dazzle the stranger, though it confirmed him only in his opinion that the women of the North are seldom natural. The worthy engineer seemed flattered with the effect that his wife produced on me. He took my wonder for admiration; nevertheless, desirous of conscientiously acquitting himself of his duty, he at length said, "I regret to disturb you, but we have scarcely sufficient time to visit the works which I have received an order to show you in detail."

I had foreseen the blow, without being able to parry it. I therefore submitted with resignation, and suffered myself to be led from sluice to sluice, my mind still dwelling with useless regret upon the fortress, that tomb of the youthful Ivan, which they would not suffer me to approach. It will be seen shortly how this secret object of my journey was attained.

To enumerate all the structures of granite that I have seen this morning, the floodgates fixed in grooves worked in blocks of that stone, the flags, of the same material, employed as the pavement of a gigantic canal, would fortunately little interest the reader; it will suffice him to know that during the ten years that have elapsed since the first sluices were finished, they have required no repairs. This is an astonishing instance of stability in a climate like that of Lake Ladoga. The object of the magnificent work is to equalize the difference of the level between the canal of Ladoga and the course of the Neva near to its source. With this object, sluices have been multiplied without reference to cost, in order to render as easy and prompt as possible a navigation that the rigor of the seasons leaves open for only three or four months in the year.

Nothing has been spared to perfect the solidity and the precision of the work. The granite of Finland has been used for the bridges, the parapets, and even, I repeat it with admiration, for lining the bed of the canal; in short, all the improvements of modern science have been had recourse to, in order to complete, at Schlüsselburg, a work as perfect in its kind as the rigors of the climate will permit.

The interior navigation of Russia deserves the attention of all scientific and commercial men; it constitutes one of the principal sources of the riches of the land. By means of a series of canals, the entire extent of which is, like every other undertaking in the country, colossal, they have, since the reign of Peter the Great, succeeded in joining, so as to form a safe navigation for boats, the Caspian with the Baltic, by the Volga, Lake Ladoga, and the Neva. This enterprise, bold in conception, prodigious in execution, is now completed, and forms one of the wonders of the civilized world. Although thus magnificent to contemplate, I found it rather tedious to inspect, especially under the conduct of one of the executors of the chef d'oeuvre. The professional man invests his work with the importance which no doubt it merits; but for a mere general observer, like myself, admiration is extinguished under minute details,—details which, in the present case, I will spare the reader.

When I believed I had strictly accorded the time and the

praise that were due to the wonders I was obliged to pass in review, I returned to the original motive of my journey, and, disguising my object in order the better to attain it, I asked permission to see the source of the Neva. This wish, the apparent innocence of which could not conceal the indiscretion, was at first eluded by the engineer, who replied, "It rises up, under the water, at the outlet of Lake Ladoga, near the island on which stands the fortress."

I knew this already, but replied: "It is one of the natural curiosities of Russia. Are there no means of approaching the spring?"

"The wind is too high; we could not see the bubbling up of the waters. It is necessary that the weather be calm in order that the eye may distinguish a fountain which rises from the bottom of the waves; nevertheless I will do what I can in order to satisfy your curiosity."

At these words, the engineer ordered a very pretty boat to be manned with six rowers, who were handsomely clad. We immediately proceeded, as was said, to visit the source of the Neva, but, in reality, to approach the walls of the strong castle, or rather the enchanted prison to which I had been refused access with so artful a politeness. But the difficulties only served to excite my desire: had I had the power to give deliverance to some unhappy prisoner, my impatience could scarcely have been more lively.

The fortress of Schlüsselburg is built on a flat island, a kind of rock, very little elevated above the level of the water. This rock divides the river in two parts; it also serves, properly speaking, to separate the river from the lake, for it indicates the point where the waters mingle. We rowed round the fortress in order, as we said, to approach as nearly as possible the source of the Neva. Our rowers soon brought us immediately over the vortex. They handled their oars so well that, notwithstanding the rough weather and the smallness of our boat, we scarcely felt the heave of the waves, which, nevertheless, rolled at this spot as much as in the open sea. Being unable to distinguish the source, which was concealed by the motion of the billows, we took a turn on the lake; after which, the wind, having rather lulled, permitted our seeing, at a considerable depth, a few waves of foam. This was the spring of the Neva, above which our boat rode.

When the west wind drives back the waters of the lake, the channel which serves as its outlet remains almost dry, and then this beautiful spring is fully exposed. On such occasions, which are fortunately very rare, the inhabitants of Schlüsselburg know that Petersburg is under water. The news of such catastrophe never fails to reach them on the morrow; for the same west wind which causes the reflux of the waters of Lake Ladoga, and leaves dry the channel of the Neva near its source, drives also, when it is violent, the waters of the Gulf of Finland into the mouth of the river. The course of this stream is therefore stopped, and the water, finding its passage obstructed by the sea, makes a way by overflowing Petersburg and its environs.

When I had sufficiently admired the site of Schlüsselburg, sufficiently surveyed, with a spyglass, the position of the battery which Peter the Great raised to bombard the strong fort of the Swedes, and sufficiently praised everything which scarcely interested me, I said, in the most careless manner imaginable, "Let us go and see the interior of the fortress:"— "its situation appears extremely picturesque," I added, a little less adroitly; for in matters of finesse it is, above all, necessary to avoid overshooting the mark. The Russian cast upon me a scrutinizing look, of which I felt the full force. This diplomatic mathematician answered:—

"The fortress, sir, possesses no object of curiosity for a foreigner."

"Never mind: everything is curious in so interesting a land as yours."

"But if the governor does not expect us, we shall not be suffered to enter."

"You can ask his permission to introduce a traveler into the fortress; besides, I rather believe he does expect us."

In fact, we were admitted at the first application of the engineer; which leads me to surmise that my visit, if not announced as certain, was indicated as probable.

We were received with military ceremony, conducted under a vault, through a gate ill defended, and after crossing a court overgrown with grass, we were introduced into—the prison? Alas! no: into the apartments of the governor. He scarcely spoke a word of French, but he received me with civility, affecting to take my visit as an act of politeness of which he himself was the object, and expressing to me his acknowledgments through the engineer, accordingly. These crafty compliments were by no means satisfactory. There I was, obliged to talk to the wife of the commandant, who spoke little more French than her husband, to sip chocolate, in short, to do everything except visit the prison of Ivan—that imaginary prize, for the sake of which I had endured all the toils, the artifices, and the wearisome civilities of the day.

At length, when the reasonable time for a call had expired, I asked my companion if it was possible to see the interior of the fortress. Several words and significant glances were hereupon exchanged between the commandant and the engineer, and we all left the chamber.

I fancied myself at the crowning point of all my labors. The fortress of Schlüsselburg is not picturesque: it is a girdle of Swedish walls of small elevation, and the interior of which forms a kind of orchard, wherein are dispersed several very low buildings; including a church, a house for the commandant, a barrack, and the dungeons, masked by windows the height of which does not exceed that of the rampart. Nothing announces violence or mystery. The appearance of this quiet state prison is more terrible to the imagination than to the eye. Gratings, drawbridges, battlements, and all the somewhat theatrical apparatus of the castles of the Middle Ages,

are not here to be seen. The governor commenced by showing me the *superb ornaments of the church!* The four copes,
which were solemnly displayed before me, cost, as the governor himself took the trouble to say, thirty thousand rubles.
Tired of such sights, I simply asked for the tomb of Ivan VI.
They replied by showing me a breach made in the wall by the
cannon of the Czar Peter, when he conducted in person the
siege of the key of the Baltic.

"The tomb of Ivan," I continued, without suffering myself
to be disconcerted, "where is it?" This time they conducted
me behind the church, and, pointing to a rose brier, said, "It
is here."

I conclude that victims are allowed no tomb in Russia.

"And the chamber of Ivan," I continued with a pertinacity
which must have appeared as singular to my guides, as their
scruples, reserve, and tergiversations appeared to me.

The engineer answered in a low voice that they could
not show the chamber of Ivan, because it lay in a part of the
fortress then occupied by state prisoners.

The excuse was legitimate; I had expected it; but what
surprised me was the wrath of the commandant. Whether it
was that he understood French better than he spoke it, or that
he had only feigned ignorance of our language, he severely
reprimanded my guide, whose indiscretion, he added, would
someday ruin him. This, the latter, annoyed with the lecture
he had received, found a favorable opportunity of telling me,
stating also that the governor had warned him, in a very
significant manner, to abstain henceforward from speaking
of *public* affairs, and from introducing foreigners into state
prisons. This engineer has all the qualities necessary to constitute a good Russian; but he is young, and does not yet
understand the mysteries of his trade—it is not of his profession as an engineer that I speak.

I found it was necessary to yield; I was the weakest; and,
therefore, owning myself vanquished, I renounced the hope of

visiting the room where the unhappy heir of the throne of Russia died an imbecile, because it was found more convenient to make him an idiot than an emperor. I cannot sufficiently express my astonishment at the manner in which the Russian government is served by its agents. I remember the countenance of the minister of war, the first time that I ventured to testify a wish to visit a castle that had become historical by a crime committed in the times of the Empress Elizabeth; and I compare, with a wonder mixed with fear, the disorder of ideas that reigns among us, with the absence of all private views, of all personal opinion—the blind submission, in short, which forms the rule of conduct among all, whether heads or subordinates, who carry on the administration of affairs in Russia. The unity of action observable in this government astounds me. I admire, while I shudder, the tacit accord with which both superior and inferior employees act in making war against ideas and even events. At the time, this sentiment made me as impatient to leave the fortress of Schlüsselburg as I had been eager to enter it. I began to fear lest I should become by force one of the inmates of that abode of secret tears and unknown sorrows. In my ever-increasing sense of its oppressive influence, I longed only for the physical pleasure of walking and breathing beyond its limits. I forgot that the country into which I should return was in itself a prison; a prison whose vast size only makes it the more formidable.

A Russian fortress!—this word produces on the imagination an impression very different to that which is felt in visiting the strongholds of people really civilized, sincerely humane. The puerile precaution taken in Russia to hide what are called secrets of state, confirms me, more than would open acts of barbarity, in the idea that this government is nothing more than a hypocritical tyranny.

After having myself penetrated into a Russian state prison, and found there the impossibility of speaking of things which every stranger would naturally inquire about in such a place,

I argue with myself that such dissimulation must serve as mask to a profound inhumanity: it is not that which is commendable that people conceal with so much care.

I am assured, on good authority, that the underwater dungeons of Kronstadt contain, among other state prisoners, miserable beings who were placed there in the reign of Alexander. These unhappy creatures are reduced to a state below that of the brute, by a punishment the atrocity of which nothing can justify. Could they now come forth out of the earth, they would rise like so many avenging specters, whose appearance would make the despot himself recoil with horror, and shake the fabric of despotism to its center. Everything may be defended by plausible words, and even by good reasons: not one of the opinions that divide the political, the literary, or the religious world, lacks argument by which to maintain itself: but, let them say what they please, a system, the violence of which requires such means of support, must be radically and intensely vicious.

The victims of this odious policy are no longer men. Those unfortunate beings, denied the commonest rights, cut off from the world, forgotten by everyone, abandoned to themselves in the night of their captivity, during which imbecility becomes the fruit, and the only remaining consolation of their never-ending misery, have lost all memory, as well as all that gift of reason, that light of humanity, which no one has a right to extinguish in the breast of his fellow-being. They have even forgotten their own names, which the keepers amuse themselves by asking with a brutal derision, for which there is none to call them to account; for there reigns such confusion in the depths of these abysses of iniquity, the shades are so thick, that all traces of justice are effaced.

Even the crimes of some of the prisoners are not recollected; they are, therefore, retained forever, because it is not known to whom they should be delivered; and it is deemed less inconvenient to perpetuate the mistake than to publish it. The bad effect of so tardy a justice is feared; and thus the evil is aggravated, that its excess may not require to be justified. Infamous pusillanimity, which is called expediency, respect for *appearances*, prudence, obedience, wisdom, a sacrifice to the public good, a reason of state! Words are never wanted by oppressors; and are there not two names for everything that exists under the sun? We are unceasingly told that there is no punishment of death in Russia. To bury alive, then, is not to kill! In reflecting on so many miseries on one side, and so much injustice and hypocrisy on the other, the guilt of the prisoners is lost sight of, the judge alone seems criminal. My indignation is at its height, when I consider that this iniquitous judge is not cruel by choice. To such an extent may a bad government pervert men interested in its duration! But Russia marches in advance of her destiny. This must explain all. If we are to measure the greatness of the end by the extent of the sacrifices, we must, without doubt, prognosticate for this nation the empire of the world.

On returning from my melancholy visit, a new labor awaited me at the engineer's: a ceremonious dinner with persons of the middle classes. The engineer had gathered around him, in order to do me honor, his wife's relations and a few of the neighboring landholders. This society would have interested me as an observer, had I not at the first moment perceived that it would furnish me with no new ideas. There is no middle class in Russia; but the petty employees and the small, though ennobled, landed proprietors, represent there the middle orders of other lands. Envying the great, and themselves envied by the little, these men vainly call themselves nobles. They are exactly in the position of the French bourgeois before the Revolution: the same data produce everywhere the same results.

I could see that there reigned in this society a hostility, ill disguised, against real greatness and true elegance, to whatever land they might belong.

That starchness of manners, that acrimony of sentiment, ill concealed under an air of preciseness and propriety, recalled to my mind, only too well, the epoch in which we live, and which I had a little forgotten in Russia, where I had hitherto only seen the society of courtiers. I was now among aspiring subalterns, uneasy as to what might be thought of them; and these people are the same everywhere.

The men did not speak to me, and appeared to take little notice of me; they did not understand French, beyond perhaps being able to read it with difficulty; they therefore formed a circle in a corner of the room, and talked Russian. One or two females of the family bore all the weight of the French conversation. I was surprised to find that they were acquainted with all that portion of our literature that the Russian police suffers to penetrate into their land. The toilette of these ladies, who, with the exception of the mistress of the house, were all elderly, was wanting in taste; the dress of the men was yet more negligent; large brown topcoats, almost trailing upon the ground, had taken the place of the national costume. But what surprised me more than the careless attire, was the caustic and captious tone of the conversation. The Russian feeling, carefully disguised by the tact of the higher orders, exhibited itself here openly. This society was more candid, though less polite, than that of the court; and I clearly saw what I had only felt elsewhere, namely, that the spirit of curiosity, sarcasm, and carping criticism influences the Russians in their intercourse with strangers. They hate us as every imitator hates his model; their scrutinizing looks seek faults in us with the desire of finding them. As soon as I recognized this disposition I felt no inclination to be indulgent myself. I had thought it necessary to offer a few words of excuse for my ignorance of the Russian tongue, and I finished my speech by remarking that every traveler ought to know the language of the country he visits, as it is more natural that he should give himself the trouble of learning to speak the language of those whom he seeks, than of imposing upon them the trouble of speaking as he does.

This compliment was answered by the observation, that I must nevertheless resign myself to hearing French murdered by the Russians, unless I would travel as a mute.

"It is of this I complain," I replied; "if I knew how to murder Russian as I ought to do, I would not force you to change your habits in order to speak my language."

"Formerly, we spoke only French."

"That was wrong."

"It is not for you to reproach us."

"I invariably speak my real opinions."

"Truth, then, is still thought something of in France?"

"I cannot tell; but I know that it ought to be loved for its own intrinsic merits."

"Such love does not belong to our age."

"In Russia?"

"Nowhere; and especially in no country governed by newspapers."

I was of the same opinion as the lady, which made me desirous of changing the conversation, for I would not speak contrary to my own sentiments, nor yet acquiesce with those of a person who, when she even thought with me, expressed her views with a causticity that was capable of disgusting me with my own.

The dinner did not pass over without constraint, but it was not long, and appeared to me sufficiently good, with the exception of the soup, the originality of which passed all bounds. This soup was cold, and consisted of pieces of fish, which swam in a broth of strong, highly seasoned, and highly sweetened vinegar. With the exception of this infernal ragout, and of the sour kvass, a species of beer which is a national beverage, I ate and drank with good appetite. There was excellent claret and champagne on the table, but I saw clearly that they had put themselves out of the way on my account, which produced mutual formality and constraint. The engineer did not participate in this feeling; though a great man at his sluices, he was nothing at all in his own house, and left his mother-in-law to do its honors, with the grace of which the reader may judge.

At six in the evening my entertainers and myself parted, with a satisfaction that was reciprocal, and, it must be owned, ill-disguised. I left for the castle of ———, where I was expected. The frankness of the fair plebeians had reconciled me to the mincing affectations of certain great ladies. One may hope to triumph over affectation, but natural dispositions are invincible.

It was yet light when I reached ———, which is six or eight leagues from Schlüsselburg. I spent there the rest of the evening, walking in the twilight, in a garden, which, for Russia, is very handsome, sailing in a little boat on the Neva, and enjoying the refined and agreeable conversation of a member of the fashionable circles. What I have seen at Schlüsselburg will make me cautious how I place myself again in a position where it is necessary to face such interrogations as I submitted to in that society. Such drawing rooms resemble fields of battle. The circles of fashion, with all their vices, seem preferable to this petty world, with all its precise virtues.

I was again in Petersburg soon after midnight, having traveled during the day about thirty-six leagues, through sandy and miry roads, with two sets of hired horses.

The demands upon the animals are in proportion to those made upon the men. The Russian horses seldom last more than eight or ten years. The pavement of Petersburg is as fatal to them as it is to the carriages, and, it may be said, to the riders, whose heads nearly split as soon as they are off the few streets where the pavement is improved by two lines of wooden blocks laid down on each side of the way. It is true that the Russians have laid their detestable pavement in regularly figured compartments of large stones,—an ornament which only increases the evil, for it makes riding in the streets yet more jolting. A certain appearance of elegance or magnificence—a boastful display of wealth and grandeur, is all that the Russians care for: they have commenced the work of civilization by creating its superfluities. If such be the right way of proceeding, let us cry, *"Long live vanity, and down with common sense."*

LETTER 21

Petersburg appears to me less beautiful than Venice, but
more extraordinary. They are both colossi raised by fear.
Venice was the work of unmixed fear; the last Romans preferred flight to death, and the fruit of their fear became one
of the world's wonders. Petersburg is equally the result of terror, but of a pious terror, for Russian policy has known how
to convert obedience into a dogma. The Russian people are
accounted very religious; it may be so: but what kind of religion can that be which is forbidden to be taught? They never
preach in the Russian churches. The Gospel would proclaim
liberty to the Slavs.

This fear of things being understood which they desire
should be believed, seems to me suspicious. The more reason
and knowledge contract the sphere of faith, the stronger that
divine light, thus concentrated in its focus, becomes; the less
people believe, the more fervent is their faith. Signs of the
cross are no proofs of a right devotion; and, notwithstanding
their genuflections and other external evidences of piety, the
Russians, in their prayers, seem to me to think more of their

emperor than their God. "Awake me when you come to the subject of God," said an ambassador, about to be put to sleep in a Russian church by the Imperial liturgy.

Sometimes I feel ready to participate in the superstition of this people. Enthusiasm becomes contagious when it is, or appears to be, general; but the moment the symptoms lay hold of me, I think of Siberia, that indispensable auxiliary of Muscovite civilization, and immediately I recover my calmness and independence.

Political faith is more firm here than religious faith: the unity of the Greek church is only apparent: the sects, reduced to silence, dig their way underground; but nations will only remain mutes for a time; sooner or later, the day of discussion must arrive; religion, politics, all will speak and explain themselves at last. Wherever the right of speech shall be restored to this muzzled people, the astonished world will hear so many disputes arise, that it will believe the confusion of Babel again returned. It is by religious dissentions that a social revolution will be one day brought about in Russia.

When I approach the emperor and see his dignity and beauty, I admire the marvel. A man at his place is rarely seen anywhere, but on the throne he is a phoenix. I rejoice in living at a time when such a prodigy exists, for I take as much pleasure in showing respect as others do in offering insult.

Nevertheless, I examine, with scrupulous care, the objects of my respect, from whence it results that, when I closely consider this personage, distinguished from all others upon earth, I fancy that his head has two faces, like that of Janus, and that the words violence, exile, oppression, or their full equivalent, SIBERIA, is engraved on the face which is not presented towards me. This idea haunts me unceasingly, even when I speak to him. It is in vain that I strive only to think of what I say to him; my imagination, in spite of myself, travels from Warsaw to Tobolsk, and that single word, Warsaw, revives all my distrust.

Does the world know that, at the present hour, the roads of Asia are once again covered with exiles torn from their hearths, and proceeding on foot to their tomb, as the herds leave their pastures for the slaughterhouse? This revival of wrath is attributable to a pretended Polish conspiracy, a conspiracy of *youthful madmen*, who would have been heroes had they succeeded; and who, their attempt being desperate, only appear to me the more generously devoted. My heart bleeds for the exiles, their families, and their country. What will be the result when the oppressors of this corner of the earth, where chivalry once flourished, shall have peopled Tartary with all that was most noble and courageous amongst the sons of ancient Europe. When they have thus crowned their icy policy, let them enjoy their success. Siberia will have become the kingdom, and Poland the desert.

Ought not we to blush with shame to pronounce the name of liberalism, when we think that there exists in Europe a people who were independent, and who now know no other liberty but that of apostacy? The Russians, when they turn against the West the arms which they employ successfully against Asia, forget that the same mode of action which aids their progress against the Kalmyks, becomes an outrage of humanity when directed against a people that have been long civilized.

The scenes on the Volga continue; and their horrors are attributed to instigations of Polish emissaries; an imputation that reminds one of the justice of the wolf of La Fontaine. These cruelties and reciprocal iniquities are preludes to the convulsions of the coming result, and suffice to apprise us of its character. But in a nation governed like this, passions boil a long time before they explode; the peril may be increasing, yet the crisis is still distant, and the evil meanwhile continues: perhaps our grandchildren will not see the explosion, which, notwithstanding, we can now prognosticate as inevitable, though we cannot predict the time and the season.

We may not cease to repeat that the Russian revolution,

when it does come, will be the more terrible, because it will be proclaimed in the name of religion. The Russian policy has melted the church into the state, and confounded heaven and earth: a man who sees a god in his master, scarcely hopes for paradise, except through the favor of the emperor.

I shall never get away. Fate seems to interfere. Once more a delay; yet, this time, it is a legitimate one. I was just preparing to enter my carriage, when a friend insisted upon seeing me. He brought a letter, which he would have me read at the very moment. But what a letter, gracious God! It is from the Princess Troubetzkoy, who addresses it to a member of her family charged to show it to the emperor. I wished to copy it, in order to print it without changing a syllable, but this I was not permitted to do. "It would go the round of the whole earth," said my friend, alarmed by the effect which it produced upon me.

"The greater reason to make it known," I replied.

"Impossible. The safety of several individuals would be compromised; besides, it has only been lent me in order to show you on your word of honor, and on condition that it shall be returned in half an hour."

Unhappy land, where every stranger appears as a savior in the eyes of a herd of oppressed beings, merely because he represents truth, publicity, and liberty, among a people deprived of all these blessings.

Before alluding to the contents of this letter, it will be necessary to recount, in a few words, a lamentable history. The principal facts will be known to many, yet vaguely, like everything else that is known of a distant country, in which people only take a cold interest. Let the public read and blush—yes, blush; for whoever has not found means to protest, with his utmost power, against the policy of a country where such acts are possible, is to a certain extent an accomplice and responsible. I sent back the horses by my *Feldjäger*, under pretext of indisposition, and told him to state at the establishment of the posts that I should not leave until the morrow. Once rid of this officious spy, I sat down to write.

The Prince Troubetzkoy was condemned as a convict to hard labor, fourteen years ago. He was at that time young, and had taken a very active part in the revolt of the fourteenth December.

The first object of the conspirators on that occasion was to deceive the soldiers as regards the legitimacy of the Emperor Nicholas. They hoped by the error of the troops to produce a military revolt, and to profit by this, in order to work a political revolution, of which, whether fortunately or unfortunately for Russia, they alone at that time felt the necessity. The number of these reformers was too limited to afford any chance that the troubles excited by them could end in the result proposed. The conspiracy was defeated by the emperor's presence of mind, or rather by the intrepidity of his countenance. That prince, on the first day of his authority, drew from the energy of his bearing all the future power of his reign.

The revolution thus crushed, it was necessary to proceed to the punishment of the guilty. The Prince Troubetzkoy, one of the most deeply implicated, unable to exculpate himself, was sentenced to labor in the Ural mines for fourteen or fifteen years, and, for the remainder of his life, was exiled to Siberia, among one of those distant colonies that malefactors are destined to people.

The prince had a wife whose family was among the most distinguished in the land. This lady could not be dissuaded from following her husband to his tomb. "It is my duty," she said, "and I will fulfill it; no human power has a right to separate a wife from her husband; I will share the fate of mine."

The noble wife obtained the favor of being buried alive with her unhappy partner. I am astonished, since I have seen Russia and the spirit of its government, that, influenced by a lingering relic of shame, they have thought it right to respect this act of devotion during a period of fourteen years. That they should favor patriotic heroism is very natural, for they profit by it; but to tolerate a sublime virtue that does not accord with the views of the sovereign was an act of remissness for which they must have often reproached themselves. They feared the friends of the Troubetzkoys; an aristocracy, however enervated it may be, always preserves a shadow of its independence,—a shadow that serves to cast a cloud over despotism. Contrasts abound in this dreadful society; many men speak among themselves as freely as if they lived in France: this secret liberty consoles them for the public slavery which forms the shame and the curse of their land.

From the fear, then, of exasperating certain influential families, the government yielded to a kind of prudent compassion. The princess departed with her husband the convict, and, which is extraordinary, she reached her destination. The journey was alone a frightful trial: hundreds, thousands, of leagues in a telega, a little open cart without springs, over roads that break both carriages and human bones. The unhappy woman endured these, and many other hardships and privations, which I shall not describe for want of the precise details; for I wish to add nothing to the strict truth of this narration.

Her conduct will appear the more heroic when it is known that, until the husband's ruin, the married pair had lived somewhat coldly together. But is not a fervent devotion a substitute for love? Or rather, is it not love itself? Love flows from many sources, and of these, self-sacrifice is the most abundant.

They had never had children at Petersburg; they had five in Siberia.

This man, rendered glorious by the generosity of his wife, became a superior being in the eyes of all who approached him. Who indeed would not venerate the object of an affection so sacred?

However criminal the Prince Troubetzkoy may have been, his pardon, which the emperor will perhaps never grant, for he believes that he owes it both to his people and himself to maintain an implacable severity, has been doubtless accorded by the King of kings. The almost supernatural virtues of a wife could appease the wrath of a God, they could not disarm human justice. The reason is, that Divine Omnipotence is a reality, whilst that of the emperor of Russia is a fiction.

He would have long since pardoned the criminal had he been as great as he pretends to be; but clemency, independently of its being repugnant to his natural disposition, appears to him a weakness by which a king would degrade the kingly office: habituated as he is to measure his power by the fear which he inspires, he would regard mercy as a violation of his code of political morality.

For my own part, I judge of a man's power over others by that which I see him exercise over himself, and I cannot believe his authority safely established, until he can venture to forgive: the Emperor Nicholas ventures only to punish. Pardon might be a dangerous example to a people who are still so rude in the depths of their hearts. The prince lowers himself to the level of his savage subjects; he hardens himself with them; he does not fear to brutalize them in order to attach them: people and sovereign emulate each other in deceptions, prejudices, and inhumanity. Abominable combination of barbarism and weakness, interchange of ferocity, circulation of falsehood which warms the life of a monster!—a cadaverous body whose blood is poison. Such is despotism in its essence and its action.

The husband and wife have lived for fourteen years by the side, so to speak, of the Ural mines; for the arms of a laborer like the prince are little suited to the work of the pickax. He was there for the sake of being there, and that is all: but he was a convict, and we shall soon see to what this condition condemns a man—*and his children!*

There is no lack of good Russians in Petersburg; and I have met some, who view the life of the convicts at the mines as very bearable, and who complain of the exaggeration with which the *modern makers of fine speeches* describe the sufferings of the traitors in the Ural mountains. They own that they are not allowed to receive money, but their relations are suffered to send them provisions. Provisions! there are few that could be forwarded so great a distance, without being rendered unfit for use. But the courtiers of the executioner always find the punishment too merciful for the crime.

However great may be the luxuries of life in Siberia, the health of the Princess Troubetzkoy is injured by her sojourn at the mines. It is difficult to understand how a woman accustomed to all the delicacies of life in the highest ranks of a luxurious capital, has been able so long to tolerate the privations of every kind to which she has voluntarily submitted. She wished to live, she did live—she even gave life; she reared her offspring under a zone where the length and the rigor of winter is inimical to existence. The thermometer falls there, yearly, to a temperature that might alone suffice to destroy the human race. But this saintlike woman had other cares to think of.

At the conclusion of seven years of exile, as she saw her children growing around her, she thought it her duty to write to one of her family to beg that they would humbly supplicate the emperor to suffer them to be sent to Petersburg, or to some other civilized city, in order to receive a suitable education.

The petition was laid at the feet of the czar, and the worthy successor of the Ivans and of Peter I answered that the children of a convict—convicts themselves—would always be sufficiently learned!

After the above answer, the family—the mother and the condemned man—were silent for seven more weary years. Humanity, honor, Christian charity, outraged religion, alone pleaded in their favor; but this was done silently; not a voice was raised to appeal against such *justice*. Nevertheless, a renewal of misery has now called forth a last cry from the depths of this abyss.

The prince has completed his term of labor in the mines, and now the exiles, liberated, as they call it, are condemned to form, they and their young family, a colony in the most remote corner of the desert. The locality of their new residence, *designedly* chosen by the emperor himself, is so savage that the name of that howling wilderness is not even yet marked on the ordnance maps of Russia, the most exact and minute geographical maps that exist.

It will be easily understood that the condition of the princess (I name her only) is more wretched since she has been permitted to inhabit this solitude. It should be observed that, in the language of the oppressed, as interpreted by the oppressor, permissions are obligatory. At the mines, she could find warmth in the bosom of the earth, her family had companions in misfortune, silent consolers, admiring witnesses of her heroism. The human eye contemplated and respectfully deplored her martyrdom, a circumstance which, externally, rendered it the more sublime. Hearts beat in her presence,—in short, without even having to speak, she felt herself in society; for, let governments do their worst, pity will still spring to life wherever there are men. But what hope can there be of awakening the sympathy of bears, or of melting eternal ices, amid impenetrable woods, or marshes that have no bounds? What means can there be found of excluding the mortal cold from a hovel?—and how is subsistence for five children to be obtained a hundred leagues, perhaps more, from any human abode, unless it be that of the superintendent of the colonies?—for this is called colonizing in Siberia!

What I admire as much as the resignation of the princess, is the eloquence, the ingenious tenderness she must have possessed, to overcome the resistance of her husband, and to succeed in persuading him that she was less to be pitied in suffering with him than she would be in Petersburg, surrounded with all the comforts and elegancies of life. This triumph of devotion, recompensed by success, for her husband finally consented, I view as a miracle of delicacy, of energy, and of sensibility. To know how to sacrifice self is as noble as it is rare,—to know how to accept such a sacrifice, is sublime.

At present this father and mother, abandoned in the desert, without physical powers, stripped of every aid, lost to their fellow-men, punished in their children, whose innocence only serves to aggravate their anguish, know not how to provide food for themselves and their little ones. These young convicts by birth, these pariahs of the Imperial realm, if they have no longer a country, no longer a position in the community, have yet bodies that need food and raiment. A mother, whatever dignity, whatever elevation of soul she may possess, could she see the fruit of her body perish rather than supplicate a pardon? No; she again humbled herself, and this time it was not through Christian virtue: the lofty woman was conquered by the despairing mother. She saw her children ill, and had nothing wherewith to administer to their wants. In this extreme misery, her husband, his heart withered by his misfortune, left her to act according to her impulse, and the princess wrote a second letter from her hut of exile. The letter was addressed to her family, but meant for the emperor. This was to place herself at the feet of her enemy, to forget what she owed to herself; but who would think the less of her for so doing? God calls his elect to every species of sacrifice, even to the sacrifice of the most legitimate pride. The man who would understand life without recognizing eternity, can only have seen the things of this world on their sunny side: he must have lived on illusions, as they would have me do in Russia. The letter of the princess has reached its destination, the emperor has read it; and it was to communicate to me this letter that I was stopped at the moment of my departure. I cannot regret the delay. I have never read anything more simple and touching. Actions like the writer's can dispense with words; she uses her privilege as a heroine, and is laconic, even when imploring the life of her children. In a few lines, she states her situation, without declamation and without complaint; she concludes by imploring this single favor—the permission to live within reach of an apothecary, in order to be able to get some medicine for her children when they are ill. The environs of Tobolsk, of Irkutsk, or of Orenburg, would appear to her paradise! In the concluding words of her letter, she ceases addressing herself to the emperor, she forgets everything except her husband. With a feeling and a dignity which would merit the pardon of the worst crime, and she is innocent of any, "I am very miserable," she says; "but were it to come over again I should do as I have done."

There was in the family of this woman an individual bold enough to dare to carry her letter to the emperor, and even to support with a humble petition the request of a disgraced relative. He spoke only of that relative as a criminal, although, before any other being but the emperor of Russia, a man would have gloried in avowing his relationship with so noble a victim of conjugal duty. Well! after fourteen years of continued vengeance, continued but not glutted—(how can I moderate my indignation?—to use gentler terms in recounting such facts would be to betray a sacred cause: let the Russians object against them if they dare; I would rather fail in respect to despotism than to misfortune. They will crush me if they can; but, at least, Europe shall know that a man to whom sixty millions of men never cease saying that he is omnipotent, revenges himself!—Yes, revenge is the proper name for such a justice!)—after fourteen years, then, of vengeance, this woman, whose misery had been ennobled by so much heroism, obtained from the Emperor Nicholas no other answer than the following:—"I am astonished that anyone again dares to speak to me (twice in fifteen years!) of a family, the head of which has conspired against me!" The reader may doubt this answer,—I could yet do so myself, and nevertheless I have clear proof of its truth.

The relations of the exiles, the Troubetzkoys, a powerful family, live at Petersburg, and they attend the court! Such is the spirit, the dignity, the independence of the Russian aristocracy! In this empire of violence, fear justifies everything, —nay more, it is the only merit that is sure to receive reward.

I have no more hesitation, no more uncertainty of opinion as regards the character of the Emperor Nicholas; my judgment of that prince is at length formed. He is a man of talent and of resolution; it needs that he should be, to constitute himself the jailer of the third of the globe; but he wants magnanimity: the use that he makes of his power only too clearly proves this to me. May God pardon him! happily, I shall never see him again.

What heart would not bleed at the idea of the anguish of that unhappy mother? My God! if such be the destiny thou hast ordained upon earth for the sublimest virtue, show to it thy heaven,—open to it the gates thereof before the hour of death! Imagine what must be the feelings of this woman when she casts her eyes on her children; and when, aided by her husband, she labors to supply the education which they need! Education! it will be poison for those who have no names, but are marked and numbered like the beasts of the herd. Can the exiles deny all their recollections, all their habits, in order to hide the misfortune of their position from the innocent victims of their love? Would not the native refinement of their parents inspire these young savages with ideas that they could never realize? What danger, what momentary torment for them, and what insupportable constraint for their mother! This mental torture, added to such a load of physical sufferings, haunts me like a hideous dream from which I cannot awake. Since yesterday morning it has pursued me incessantly, whispering at every moment of the day—What is the Princess Troubetzkoy now doing?—what is she saying to her children?—with what look is she watching over them?—what prayer is she addressing to God for these beings, damned ere they were born by the providence of the Russians? This punishment inflicted upon an innocent generation disgraces an entire people!

I shall finish my journey, but without going to Borodino; without being present at the arrival of the court at the Kremlin; without speaking more of the emperor. What can I say of that prince that the reader does not now know as well as I? To form an idea of men and things in this land, it is necessary to remember that plenty of occurrences, similar to the one I have related, take place here, though they remain unknown. It required an extraordinary concurrence of circumstances to reveal to me the facts which my conscience obliges me here to record.

I am about to place in one sealed packet all the papers that I have written since my arrival in Russia, including the present chapter, and to deposit them in safe hands—things which are not easily found in Petersburg. I shall then finish the day by writing an official letter, which will leave by the post tomorrow, and in which everything will be so carefully praised and admired, that I have rational hopes it will, when seized on the frontier, assure my security during the remainder of the journey. If my friends hear no more of me, they must suppose I am sent to Siberia: that journey could alone alter my intention as regards proceeding to Moscow, which intention will be delayed in execution no longer, for my *Feldjäger* has just arrived to inform me that the post-horses will be at my door without fail tomorrow morning.

LETTER 22

I AM WRITING at Pomerania, a post town eighteen leagues
from Petersburg.

To travel post on the road from Petersburg to Moscow, is to
treat oneself for whole days to the sensation experienced in
descending the *montagnes russes* at Paris. It would be well to
bring an English carriage to Petersburg, if only for the pleasure of traveling, on really elastic springs, this famous road, the
best *chaussée* in Europe, according to the Russians, and, I believe, according to strangers also. It must be owned that it is
well kept, although hard, by reason of the nature of the materials, which, broken as they are in tolerably small pieces, form,
in encrusting over the surface, little immovable asperities,
which shake the carriages to a degree that causes something
to come out of place at every stage. As much time is thus lost
as is gained by the speed at which they drive; for we rush
along in a whirlwind of dust, with the rapidity of a hurricane
chasing the clouds before it. An English carriage is very pleasant for the few first stages; but in the long run, the necessity
of a Russian equipage, to withstand the pace of the horses, and
the hardness of the road, is discovered. The rails of the bridges

are formed of handsome iron balustrades, and the granite pillars which support them are carved with the Imperial arms. This road is broader than those of England; it is also as even, although less easy: the horses are small, but full of muscle.

My *Feldjäger* has ideas, a bearing, and a semblance, which prevent my forgetting the spirit which reigns in his country. On arriving at the second stage, one of our four horses fell on the road. Notwithstanding the advanced season, the middle of the day is still excessively hot, and the dust renders the air suffocating. It appeared to me that the horse had fallen under the influence of the heat, and that unless he were instantly bled, he would die. I therefore called the *Feldjäger*, and taking from my pocket a case containing a fleam, I offered it to him, telling him to make prompt use of it if he wished to save the life of the poor brute. He answered, with a malicious phlegm, while declining the instrument I offered, that it was of no consequence, as we were at the end of the stage. Thereupon, without aiding the unfortunate coachman to disengage the animal, he entered the stable hard by, in order to prepare another set of horses.

The Russians are far from having, like the English, a law to protect animals from the ill-treatment of men. On the contrary, it is among them as necessary to plead the cause of the men, as it is in London to plead the cause of the dogs and horses. My *Feldjäger* would not believe in the existence of such a law.

This man, who is a Livonian by birth, fortunately for me, speaks German. Under the exterior of an officious civility and obsequious language, may be discovered much obstinacy and insolence. His figure is slim; his flaxen hair gives to his features an infantile appearance which belies their really dry and harsh expression. That of his eyes, more especially, is crafty and relentless. They are gray, edged with almost white lashes; his thick eyebrows are very light, his forehead full, but low; his skin would be fair were it not tanned by the constant action of the air; his mouth is finely formed, always closed, and the lips so small that they are not seen until he speaks. His clean and neatly fitting uniform of Russian green, with a leather belt round his waist, buckled in front, gives him a certain air of elegance. He has a light step, but an extremely slow understanding.

Notwithstanding the discipline under which he has been bred, it can be perceived that he is not of Russian descent. The race, half Swedish, half Teutonic, which peoples the southern side of the Gulf of Finland, is very different from that either of the Finns or the Slavs. The real Russians are, in their primitive endowments, more to be admired than the mixed populations that defend the frontiers of their land.

This *Feldjäger* inspires me but with little confidence. Officially, he is my guide and protector; nevertheless, I see in him only a disguised spy, and feel towards him as I should towards one who might at any moment receive an order to become my jailer.

The Russian people give me the idea of being men endowed with gentle dispositions, but who believe themselves born exclusively for violence. With the easy indifference of the Orientals, they unite a taste for the arts, which is tantamount to saying that nature has given them the desire of liberty; whilst their masters have made them the machines of oppression. A man, as soon as he rises a grade above the common level, acquires the right, and, furthermore, contracts the obligation to maltreat his inferiors, to whom it is his duty to transmit the blows that he receives from those above him. Thus does the spirit of iniquity descend from stage to stage down to the foundations of this unhappy society, which subsists only by violence—a violence so great, that it forces the slave to lie to himself by thanking his tyrant; and this is what they here call public order; in other words, a gloomy tranquillity, a fearful peace, for it resembles that of the tomb. The Russians, however, are proud of this calm. So long as a man has not made up his mind to go on all fours, he must necessarily pride himself in something, were it only to preserve his right to the title of a human creature.

Some leagues from Pomerania I met a Russian of my acquaintance, who had been to visit one of his estates, and was returning to Petersburg. We stopped to talk for a short time. The Russian, after casting his eye over my carriage, began to laugh, and, pointing to its various complicated parts, said, "You see all these things, they will not keep together till you reach Moscow: foreigners who persist in using their own carriages when in our country, set out as you did, but return by the stagecoach."

"Even in going no farther than Moscow?"

"No farther even than Moscow."

"The Russians told me that it was the best road in all Europe; I took them at their word."

"There are bridges yet wanting: the road in many parts requires mending; the highway has frequently to be left in order to cross temporary bridges of rude construction, and, owing to the carelessness of our drivers, the carriages of foreigners always break in these awkward places."

"My carriage is an English one, and its quality has already been well tested by long journeys."

"They drive nowhere so fast as in Russia; the carriages, under this rapid motion, go through all the movements of a vessel in a storm, the pitching and the rolling combined. To resist such strains on a road like this, which, though even, is very hard, it is necessary, I again repeat, that the carriages should be built in the country."

"You have still the old prejudice for heavy and massive equipages; they are not, however, the strongest."

"I wish you a pleasant journey: let me hear if your carriage reaches Moscow."

Scarcely had I left this bird of ill omen when a part of the axle broke. Fortunately, we were near the end of the stage, where I am now detained. I should mention that I have yet only traveled eighteen leagues out of the one hundred eighty. . . . I shall be obliged to deny myself the pleasure of fast driving, and am learning to say in Russian, "gently," which is just the opposite of the usual motto of Russian travelers.

A Russian coachman, attired in his caftan of coarse cloth, or, if the weather be warm, as it is today, in his colored shirt or tunic, appears, at first sight, like an Oriental. In simply observing the attitude he assumes when placing himself upon his seat, we may recognize the grace of the Asiatic. In traveling post, the Russians drive from the box, dispensing with postilions, unless a very heavy carriage requires a set of six or eight horses, and even in that case, one of the men mounts the box. The coachman holds in his hands a whole bundle of cords: these are the eight reins of the team, two for each of the four horses harnessed abreast. The grace, ease, agility, and safety with which he directs this picturesque setout, the quickness of his slightest movements, the lightness of his step when he reaches the ground, his erect stature, his manner of wearing his dress, in short, his whole person reminds me of the most naturally elegant people on earth—the Gypsies of Spain. The Russians are fair-complexioned Gypsies.

The houses resemble those that I described in the excursion to Schlüsselburg, but they are not so elegant. The appearance of the villages is monotonous. A village consists always of two lines, more or less extended, of wooden cottages, regularly ranged at a certain distance backwards from the road, for, in general, the street of the village is broader than the embankment of the highway. Each cabin, constructed of pieces of roughly hewn wood, presents its gable to the street. All these habitations are of similar construction; but, notwithstanding their wearisome uniformity, an air of comfort, and even prosperity, appears to reign in the villages. They are rural without being picturesque. I breathe in them the calm of pastoral life, which is doubly agreeable after Petersburg. The country people are not gay or smiling, but they have not the miserable appearance of the soldiers and the dependents of the government. Among all the Russians, these are they who suffer least from the want of liberty. The labors of agriculture tend to reconcile man to social life, whatever it may cost; they inspire him with patience, and enable him to endure everything, provided he is allowed to give himself up to occupations which are so congenial to his nature.

The country that I have hitherto traversed is a poor, marshy forest, covered, as far as the eye can reach over a sterile plain, with miserable, stunted, and thinly scattered birch and pine; there are neither cultivated lands nor thick flourishing plantations of wood to be seen. The cattle are of a wretched breed. The climate oppresses the animals as much as despotism does the men. It might be said that nature and society vie with each other in their efforts to render life difficult. When we think of the physical obstacles that had here to be encountered in order to organize a society, we have no longer a right to be surprised at anything, unless it be that material civilization is as far advanced as we perceive it to be among a people so little favored by nature.

Can it be true that there are in the unity of ideas, and the fixedness of things, compensations for even the most revolting oppression? I think not; but were it proved to me that this system was the only one under which the Russian Empire could have been founded or maintained, I should answer by a simple question: was it essential to the destinies of the human race that the marshes of Finland should be peopled, and that the unfortunate beings brought there should erect a city marvelous to behold, but which is in reality nothing more than a mimicry of western Europe? The civilized world has only gained from the aggrandizement of the Muscovites the fear of a new invasion, and the model of a despotism without pity and without precedent, unless it be in ancient history.

The house in which I write exhibits a taste and neatness

that contrast strangely with the nakedness of the surrounding country. It is both post-house and tavern, and I find it almost clean. It might be taken for the country house of some retired, independent person. Stations of this kind, though not so well kept as that of Pomerania, are maintained, at certain distances on the road, at the expense of government. The walls and ceilings of the one I am in are painted as in Italy; the ground floor, composed of several spacious rooms, very much resembles a restaurateur in one of the French provinces. The furniture is covered with leather; large sofas are everywhere to be found, which might serve as a substitute for beds, but I have had too much experience to think of sleeping or even of sitting on them. In Russian inns, not excepting those of the best description, all wooden furniture with stuffed cushions are so many hives where vermin swarm and multiply.

I carry with me my bed, which is a masterpiece of Russian industry. If I break down again before reaching Moscow, I shall have time to make use of this piece of furniture, and shall applaud myself for my precaution.

I am now writing at Yedrova, between Great Novgorod and Valdai. There are no distances in Russia—so say the Russians, and all the travelers have agreed to repeat the saying. I had adopted the same notion, but unpleasant experience now obliges me to maintain precisely the contrary. There is nothing but distance in Russia; nothing but empty plains extending farther than the eye can reach. Two or three interesting spots are separated from each other by immense spaces. These intervals are deserts, void of all picturesque beauty: the highway destroys the poetry of the steppe; and there remains nothing but extension of space, monotony, and sterility. All is naked and poor; there is nothing to inspire awe as on a soil made illustrious by the glory of its inhabitants,—a soil like

Greece or Judea, devastated by history, and become the poetical cemetery of nations: neither is there any of the grandeur of a virgin nature; the scene is merely ugly; it is sometimes a dry plain, sometimes a marshy, and these two species of sterility alone vary the landscape. A few villages, becoming less neat in proportion as the distance from Petersburg increases, sadden the landscape instead of enlivening it. The houses are only piles of the trunks of trees, badly put together, and supporting roofs of plank, to which, in winter, an extra cover of thatch is sometimes added. These dwellings must be warm, but their appearance is as cheerless as soldiers' barracks, though dirtier. The rooms are dark, nauseating, and tainted for want of air. They have no beds; in summer the inmates sleep on benches which form a divan around the walls of the chamber, and in winter, on the stove, or on the floor around it; in other words, a Russian peasant encamps all his life. The word *reside* implies a comfortable mode of life; domestic habits are unknown to this people.

In passing through Great Novgorod I saw none of the ancient edifices of that city, which was for a long time a republic, and which became the cradle of the Russian Empire. I was fast asleep when we drove through it. If I return to Germany by Vilna and Warsaw, I shall neither have seen the Volkhov, that river which was the tomb of so many citizens,—for the turbulent republic did not spare the life of its children,—nor yet the church of St. Sophia, with which is associated the memory of the most glorious events in Russian history, before the devastation and final subjection of Novgorod by Ivan IV, that model of all modern tyrants.

I had heard much of the mountains of Valdai, which the Russians pompously entitle the Muscovite Switzerland. I am approaching this city, and, for the last thirty leagues, have observed that the surface of the soil has become uneven, though not mountainous. It is indented with numerous small ravines, where the road is so formed that we mount and descend the declivities at a gallop. It is only when changing horses that time is lost, for the Russian hostlers are slow in harnessing and putting-to.

The peasants of this canton wear a cap, broad and flat at the top, but fitting very closely round the head; it resembles a mushroom; a peacock's feather is sometimes twisted round the band, and when the men wear a hat, the same ornament is also adopted. Instead of boots, they most commonly have plats of reeds, woven by the peasants themselves, and worn as leggings fastened with packthread laces. They look better in sculpture than on the living man. Some ancient statues prove the antiquity of the attire.

The female peasants are rarely to be seen. We met ten men for one woman. Such as I have noticed wear a dress that indicates a total absence of female vanity. It consists of a species of dressing gown, very wide and loose, which fastens round the neck and reaches to the ground. A large apron of the same length, fastened across the shoulders by two short straps, completes their rustic and ungainly costume. They nearly all go barefoot; the wealthier only wear clumsy boots; Indian handkerchiefs, or other pieces of stuff, are bound closely round the head. The real national female headdress is only worn on holy days. It is the same as that of the ladies at court; a species, namely, of shako, open at the top, or rather a very lofty diadem, embroidered with precious stones when worn by the ladies, and with flowers in gold or silver thread when on the heads of the peasants. This crown has an imposing effect, and resembles no other kind of headdress, unless it be the tower of the goddess Cybele.

The peasant women are not the only Russian females who neglect their persons. I have seen ladies whose dress when traveling was of the most slovenly description. This morning, in a post-house where I stopped to breakfast, I encountered an entire family whom I had left in Petersburg, where they inhabit one of those elegant palaces which the Russians are so proud of showing to foreigners. There, these ladies were splendidly attired in the Paris fashions; but at the inn where, thanks to the new accident that had happened to my carriage, I was overtaken by them, they were altogether different persons. So whimsically were they metamorphosed that I could scarcely recognize them: the fairies had become witches. Imagine young ladies whom you had never seen except in elegant society, suddenly reappearing before you in a costume worse than that of Cinderella; dressed in nightcaps, of which it could only be said that they might have once been white, extremely dirty gowns, neck handkerchiefs that resembled ragged napkins, and old shoes in which they walked slipshod. It was enough to make a man fancy his eyes bewitched.

The fair travelers were attended by a considerable retinue. The multitude of lackeys and waiting women, muffled in old clothes more loathsome than those of their mistresses, moving about in all directions, and keeping up an infernal noise, completed the illusion that it was the scene of a meeting of witches. They screamed and scampered here and there, drank, and stuffed themselves with eatables in a manner that was sufficient to take away the appetite of the most hungry beholder; and yet these ladies could complain before me in an affected manner of the dirtiness of the post-house,—as if *they* had any right to find fault with slovenliness. I could have imagined myself amid a camp of Gypsies, except that Gypsies are without pretense or affectation. I, who pique myself on not being fastidious when traveling, find the post-houses established on this road by the government, that is, by the emperor, sufficiently comfortable. I consider that I have fared well in them: a man may even sleep at night, provided he can dispense with a bed; for this nomad people are acquainted only with the Persian carpet or the sheepskin, or a mat stretched upon a divan under a tent, whether of canvas or of wood, for in either case it is a souvenir of the bivouac. The use of a bed, as an indispensable article of furniture, has not yet been recognized by the people of Slavic race: beds are rarely seen beyond the Oder.

Sometimes, on the borders of the little lakes which are scattered over the immense marsh called Russia, a distant town is to be seen; a cluster, namely, of small houses built of gray boards, which, reflected in the water, produce a very picturesque effect. I have passed through two or three of these hives of men, but I have only particularly noticed the town of Zimagoi. It consists of a rather steep street of wooden houses, and is a league in length; at some distance, on the other side of one of the creeks of the little lake on which it stands, is seen a romantic convent, whose white towers rise conspicuously above a forest of firs, which appeared to me loftier and more thickly grown than any that I have hitherto observed in Russia. When I think of the consumption of wood in this country, both for the construction and the warming of houses, I am astonished that any forests remain in the land. All that I had hitherto seen were miserable thickets, scattered here and there, which could only serve to interfere with the culture of the soil.

I take up my pen at Torzhok. It is impossible to see far on plains, because every object is a barrier to the eye: a bush, a rail, or a building conceals leagues of land between itself and the horizon. It may also be observed that, here, no landscape engraves itself on the memory, no sites attract the eye, not one picturesque line is to be discovered. On a surface void of all objects or variety, there should at least be the hues of the southern sky; but they also are wanting in this part of Russia, where nature must be viewed as an absolute nullity.

What they call the mountains of Valdai are a series of declivities and acclivities as monotonous as the heathy plains of Novgorod.

The town of Torzhok is noted for its manufactures of leather. Here are made those beautifully wrought boots, those slippers embroidered with gold and silver thread, which are the delight of the *élégants* of Europe, especially of those who love anything that is singular, provided it comes from a distance. The travelers who pass through Torzhok pay there for its manufactured leathers a much larger price than that at which they are sold in Petersburg or Moscow. The beautiful morocco, or perfumed Russian leather, is made at Kazan: they say it is at the fair of Nizhny that it can be bought most cheaply, and that a selection may be made out of mountains of skins.

Torzhok is also celebrated for its chicken *côtelettes*. The emperor, stopping one day at a little inn of this town, was served with a hash of fattened chickens, which to his great astonishment he found excellent. Immediately, the *côtelettes* of Torzhok became celebrated throughout Russia. The following is their origin. An unfortunate Frenchman had been well received and treated here by a female innkeeper. Before leaving, he said to her, "I cannot pay you, but I will make your fortune"; whereupon he showed her how to make chicken *côtelettes*. As good luck would have it, the precious recipe was, at least so it is said, first prepared for the emperor. The innkeeper of Torzhok is dead; but her children have inherited her renown, and they maintain it.

Torzhok, when that town first breaks upon the view of the traveler, conveys the idea of a camp in the midst of an immense wheat field. Its white houses, its towers and pavilion-shaped domes, remind him of the mosques and minarets of the East. Gilded turrets, round and square steeples, some ornamented with little columns, and all painted green or blue, announce the vicinity of Moscow. The land around is well cultivated. It is a plain covered with rye, which plain, though devoid of all other objects, I greatly prefer to the sickly woods that have wearied my eyes for the last two days. The tilled earth is at any rate fertile, and the richness of a country will lead us to forgive its want of picturesque beauty; but a track that is sterile, and that yet possesses none of the majesty of the wilderness, is of all others the most tedious to travel over.

I had forgotten to mention a singular object which struck me at the commencement of the journey.

Between Petersburg and Novgorod, I remarked, for several successive stages, a second road that ran parallel to the principal highway, though at a considerable distance from it. It was furnished with bridges and everything else that could render it safe and passable, although it was much less handsome, and less smooth, than the main way. I asked the keeper of a post-house the meaning of this singularity, and was answered, through my *Feldjäger*, that the smaller road was destined for wagons, cattle, and travelers, when the emperor, or other members of the Imperial family, proceeded to Moscow. The dust and obstructions that might incommode or retard the august travelers, if the highway remained open to the public, were thus avoided. I cannot tell whether the innkeeper was amusing himself at my expense, but he spoke in a very serious manner, and seemed to consider it very natural that the sovereign should monopolize the road in a land where the sovereign is everything. The king who said, *"I am France,"* stopped to let a flock of sheep pass; and under his reign, the foot passenger, the wagoner, and the peasant who traveled the public road, repeated our old adage to the princes whom they met: "The highway belongs to everybody": what really constitutes a law is, not its letter, but the manner in which it is applied.

In France, manners and customs have in every age rectified political institutions; in Russia, their harshness increased in their application, so that, there, the consequences are worse than the principles.

LETTER 23

BOY COACHMEN. — THE ROAD. — GRACEFULNESS OF THE PEOPLE. — THE SEESAW. — BEAUTY OF THE FEMALE PEASANTS. — RUSSIAN COTTAGES. — CUSTOMS OF THE SERFS. — DEVOUT THIEVES. — WANT OF PRINCIPLE IN THE HIGHER CLASSES. — FEMALE POLITICIANS. — DOMESTIC HAPPINESS OF THE SERFS. — CASUISTICAL REFLECTIONS. — CONNECTION OF THE CHURCH AND STATE. — FUNDAMENTAL DIFFERENCE BETWEEN SECTS AND A MOTHER CHURCH. — ADVENTURES OF A FOAL. — THE AUTHOR INJURED BY THE MORAL ATMOSPHERE. — NATIONAL MORAL RESPONSIBILITY. — DEWS OF THE NORTH.

ONCE AGAIN, a delay on the road, and always from the same cause!—we break down regularly every twenty leagues. Of a truth, the Russian officer at Pomerania was a *gettatore*!

There are moments when, notwithstanding my protestations, and the reiterated word *tischné* (gently), the drivers proceed at a rate that obliges me to close my eyes in order to avoid giddiness. Among them, I have not seen one deficient in skill, and some of them possess a dexterity that is extraordinary. The Neapolitans and the Russians are the first coachmen in the world; the best among them are old men and children: the children especially surprise me. The first time that I saw my carriage and my life about to be entrusted to the care of an child of ten years old, I protested against such imprudence; but my *Feldjäger* assured me it was the custom, and as his person was exposed as much as mine, I believed him. Our four horses, whose fiery eagerness and wild appearance were by no means adapted to reassure me, set off at a gallop. The experienced child knew better than to endeavor to stop them; on the contrary, he urged them to their utmost speed, and the carriage followed as it best might. This pace, which accorded better with the temperament of the animals than the qualities of the calèche, was kept up throughout the stage, although, at the end of the first verst, the breathless horses began to tire, and the coachman to become the most impatient. Each time they relaxed their pace, he applied the whip until they resumed their former speed. The emulation which easily establishes itself between four spirited animals harnessed abreast, soon brought us to the end of the stage. These horses would rather die than give in. After observing their character, and that of their drivers, I soon perceived that the word *tischné*, which I had learned to pronounce with so much care, was utterly useless in this journey, and that I should even expose myself to accident if I persisted in checking the ordinary rate of driving. The Russians have the gift of equilibrium; men and horses would lose their balance in a slow trot. Their mode of getting over the ground would greatly divert me if my carriage were of more solid construction, but at each turn of the wheels I expect it to fall to pieces; and we break down so often that my apprehensions are only too well justified. Without my Italian valet, who officiates also as wheelwright and smith, we should already have come to a standstill. I cannot cease admiring the air of nonchalance with which the coachmen take their seats; there is a grace about it far preferable to the studied elegance of civilized drivers. In descending the hills, they rise on their feet, and drive standing, the body slightly bent, the arms stretched forward, and the eight reins drawn well up. In this attitude, which may be seen in ancient bas-reliefs, they might be taken for charioteers of the circus. When thus driving, we rush through the air amid clouds of dust, and seem scarcely to touch the earth. The English springs cause the body of the coach to sway like a vessel in a heavy gale, and there appears then to be established between the will of man and the instinct of the animals, a relation which I cannot understand. It is not by a mechanical impulse that the equipage is guided!— there seems to be an interchange of thoughts and sentiments, an animal magic, a real magnetic influence. The coachman is miraculously obeyed; he guides his four steeds abreast as if they were but one horse. Sometimes he draws them together into scarcely more space than is commonly occupied by two-wheelers; sometimes he so spreads them out that they cover the half of the highway. In point of civilization, everything is incomplete in Russia, because everything is modern. On the finest road in the world, there are still frequent interruptions; repairs going on, or temporary bridges in place of broken ones, which oblige us to turn off the road; this the driver does without for a moment slackening the pace. The road is also much obstructed by the little carts and wagons of carriers, ten of which are often guided by one man, who cannot possibly keep them all in line. Without great dexterity on the part of the Russian coachmen, it would be difficult to find a passage through such moving labyrinths. The bodies of these carriers' carts resemble large casks cut in half lengthways, and open at the top; they are each drawn by one small horse, who, without much capacity as a draft horse, is full of courage and spirit, and will pull until he falls on the road: his life is, therefore, as short as it is devoted: in Russia, a horse twelve years old is a phenomenon.

Nothing can be more original, more different to what is seen elsewhere, than the various vehicles, the men, and the horses that are met on the highways of this country. Everything that the people touch, wear, or carry, takes, unknown to themselves, a picturesque appearance: condemn a race of men, less naturally elegant, to make use of the houses, dress, and utensils of the Russians, and all these things would appear hideous; but here I find them, though foreign and unusual, striking and deserving of being painted. Oblige the Russians to wear the costume of the Paris workmen, and they would make something out of it agreeable to the eye, though never would a Russian have imagined an attire so devoid of taste. The life of this people is amusing, if not for themselves, at least for a spectator; the ingenious turn of their minds has found means to triumph over the climate, and every other obstacle that nature has opposed to social existence in a desert without poetic imagery. The contrast of the blind political submission of a people attached to the soil, with the energetic and continual struggle of that same people against the tyranny of a climate hostile to life, their conquests over nature achieved while they themselves remain under the yoke of despotism, present an inexhaustible store for both lively pictures and serious meditations. To make a journey through Russia with full advantage, it would be necessary to be accompanied by a Montesquieu and a Horace Vernet.

In none of my travels have I so much regretted my little talent for sketching. Russia is less known than India; it has been less-often described and pictorially illustrated; it is nevertheless as curious a country as any in Asia, even as relates to the arts, to poetry, and to history.

Every mind seriously occupied with the ideas which ferment in the political world, cannot but profit by examining, on the spot, a community, governed on the principles which directed the most ancient states named in the annals of the world, and yet, already imbued with the ideas that are common among the most modern and revolutionary nations. The patriarchal tyranny of the Asiatic governments, in contact with the theories of modern philanthropy, the character of the people of the East and West, incompatible by nature, yet united together by coercion in a state of society semibarbarous, but kept in order by fear, present a spectacle that can be only seen in Russia, and, assuredly, one which no man who thinks, would regret the trouble of going to contemplate.

The social, intellectual, and political state of present Russia is the result, and, so to speak, the résumé of the reigns of

Ivan IV, surnamed, by Russia herself, the Terrible; of Peter the First, called the Great, by the men who glory in aping Europe; and of Catherine II, deified by a people that dreams of the conquest of the world. Such is the formidable heritage over which the Emperor Nicholas holds sway—God knows to what purpose, and our posterity will know also!

The seesaw is the favorite amusement of the Russian peasants. This exercise develops their natural talent for adjusting the equilibrium of the body; in addition to which, it is a silent pleasure, and quiet diversions best accord with the feelings of a people rendered prudent by fear.

Silence presides over all the festivals of the Russian villagers. They drink plentifully, speak little, and shout less; they either remain silent, or sing in chorus, with a nasal voice, melancholy and prolonged notes, which form a harmonious, but by no means noisy accord. I have been surprised, however, to observe that almost all these melodies are deficient in simplicity.

On Sunday, in passing through populous villages, I observed rows of from four to eight young girls balancing themselves, by a scarcely perceptible movement of their bodies, on boards suspended by ropes, while, at a little distance beyond, an equal number of boys were fixed in the same manner, in face of the females. Their mute game lasted a long time; I have never had patience to wait its conclusion. Such gentle balancing is only a kind of interlude, which serves as a relaxation in the intervals of the animated diversion of their real swing or seesaw. This is a very lively game; it even renders the spectator nervous. Four cords hang from a lofty crossbeam, and, at about two feet from the earth, sustain a plank, on the extremities of which two persons place themselves. This plank, and the four posts which support it, are placed in such a manner that the balancing may be performed either backwards or forwards, or from side to side. The two performers, sometimes of the same, sometimes of the opposite sexes,

405

place themselves, always standing, and with legs firmly planted, on the two extremities of the plank, where they preserve their balance by taking hold of the cords. In this attitude they are impelled through the air to a frightful height, for at every swing the machine reaches the point beyond which it would turn completely over, and its occupiers be dashed to the earth from a height of thirty or forty feet, for I have seen posts at least twenty feet high. The Russians, whose frames are singularly supple, easily maintain a balance that is to us astonishing; they exhibit much grace, boldness, and agility in this exercise.

I have purposely stopped in several villages to observe the girls and young men thus amuse themselves together; and I have at last seen some female faces perfectly beautiful. Their complexion is of a delicate whiteness; their color is, so to speak, under the skin, which is transparent and exquisitely smooth. Their teeth are brilliantly white; and—rarely seen beauty!—their mouths are perfectly formed copies of the antique; their eyes, generally blue, have nevertheless the Oriental cast of expression, with also that unquiet and furtive glance natural to the Slavs, who can in general look sideways, and even behind, without turning their heads. Their whole appearance possesses a great charm; but, whether from a caprice of nature, or the effects of costume, these beauties are much less often seen united in the women than in the men. Among a hundred female peasants, we perhaps meet with but one really beautiful, whilst the great majority of the men are remarkable for the form of their heads and the gracefulness of their features. Among the old men, there are faces with rosy cheeks and silver hair and beard, of which it may be said that time has imparted of dignity more than it has taken of youth. There are heads that would be more beautiful in pictures than anything that I have seen of Rubens' or Titian's, but I have never observed an elderly female face worthy of being painted.

As a protection against the short but fervent heats of summer, a sort of veranda, a large covered open balcony, runs round some cottages, and serves as a bed for the family, who even sometimes prefer sleeping on the naked earth. Recollections of the East pursue the traveler everywhere. At all the post-houses into which I have entered at night, I have invariably found, ranged in the street before the door, numerous bundles of black sheepskins. These fleeces, which I at first took for sacks, were men, sleeping under the bright canopy of heaven. We have, this year, heats such as have not been known in the memory of man in Russia.

The sheepskins, cut out as little overcoats, serve not only for clothes, but likewise for beds, carpets, and tents to the Russian peasants. The workmen, when, during the heat of the day, they take their siesta in the fields, make a picturesque tent of these garments to protect themselves from the rays of the sun. With the ingenious address which distinguishes the Russian laborers from those of the west of Europe, they pass the sleeves of their coat over the two handles of their wheelbarrows, and then, turning this moveable roof towards the sun, they sleep tranquilly under the rustic drapery. The sheepskin coats are graceful in shape, and would be pretty if they were not generally so old and greasy. A poor peasant cannot often renew a vesture which costs so much. They wear it until it is completely worn-out.

The Russian laborer is industrious, and is ready for every difficulty in which he may be placed. He never goes out without his small hatchet, which is useful for a hundred purposes in the hands of a dexterous man in a country not yet without woods. With a Russian by your side, were you to lose yourself in a forest, you would in a very few hours have a house to pass the night in, perhaps more commodious, and assuredly more clean, than the houses of the old villages. But if the traveler possessed small articles of leather among his baggage, they would be safe nowhere. The Russians steal, with the address which they exhibit on all occasions, the straps, girths, and leather aprons of your trunks and carriages, though the same men show every sign of being extremely devout.

I have never traveled a stage without my coachman making at least twenty signs of the cross to salute as many little chapels. Ready to fulfill with the same punctilio his obligations of politeness, he salutes also with his hat every wagoner that he meets, and their number is great. These formalities accomplished, we arrive at the end of the stage, when it is invariably found that, either in putting-to or detaching the horses, the adroit, pious, polite rogue has abstracted something, perhaps a leather pouch, a strap, or a wrapper; perhaps only a nail, a screw, or a wax candle from the lamps: in short, he never leaves with altogether *clean hands*.

These men are extremely greedy of money; but they dare not complain when ill paid, which has often been the case with those who have driven us the last few days, for my *Feldjäger* retains for himself a portion of the postilion's fees, which, together with the hire of the horses for the entire journey, I paid him in advance at Petersburg. Having once observed this trick, I compensated out of my own pocket the unfortunate postilion, thus deprived of a part of the wages which, according to the ordinary custom of travelers, he had a right to expect from me; but the knavish *Feldjäger*, having perceived my generosity (for this was the name he gave to my justice), had the audacity to complain to me openly,—saying that he could no longer act for me on the journey, if I continued to thwart him in the legitimate exercise of his power.

But how can we be surprised at the want of proper principles among the common people, in a country where the great regard the most simple rules of probity as laws fit for plebeians, but which cannot extend to persons of their rank? Let it not be supposed that I exaggerate; I state what I perceive: an aristocratic pride, degenerated in its character, and at variance with the true sentiment of honor, reigns in Russia among the greater number of influential families. Recently a great lady made to me, little knowing it, an ingenious confession: it the more surprised me, because such sentiments, sufficiently common here among the men, are less so among the women, who have generally preserved better than their husbands and brothers the traditions of just and noble feelings. "It is impossible for us," she said, "to form any clear idea of a social state like that of yours in France. They tell me that, at present, the highest noble there can be put in prison for a debt of two hundred francs; this is revolting: how different from our country! There is not in all Russia a tradesman who would dare to refuse us credit for an unlimited period. With your aristocratic notions," she added, "you must surely find yourself more at home among us. There is greater similarity between the French of the old regime and us, than between any other of the European nations."

I cannot describe the effort of self-command that it required on my part to prevent myself from suddenly and loudly protesting against the affinity of which this lady boasted. Notwithstanding my obligatory prudence, I could not help saying, that a man who would now pass among ourselves for an ultra-aristocrat, might be easily classed at Petersburg with the violent liberals; and I concluded by observing, "When you assure me that, among your families, people do not think it necessary to pay their debts, I must not take you at your word."

"Many of us have enormous fortunes, but they would be ruined if they were to pay all they owed."

In order to explain to me the extent to which the fashionable world is imbued with the French genius and spirit, the same lady related to me instances of *impromptu* answers in verse, made, in a game, at the house of one of her relatives. "You see how completely French we are," she added, with a pride that made me laugh silently. "Yes, more so than we ourselves," I replied; and we changed the subject of discourse.

I can picture to myself the astonishment with which this Franco-Russian lady would enter the salons of Madame ———, in Paris, and inquire of our actual France what has become of the France of Louis XV?

Under the Empress Catherine, the conversation of the palace, and of some of the nobility, resembled that of the drawing rooms of Paris. In the present day, our discourse is more serious, or, at least, more bold than that of any of the other European people; and, in this respect, our modern Frenchmen are far from resembling the Russians, for we talk of everything, and the Russians speak of nothing.

The reign of Catherine is profoundly impressed on the memories of several Russian ladies. These fair *aspirantes* to the title of female statesmen have a talent for politics: and, as some of them add to that gift manners which altogether remind us of the eighteenth century, they are so many traveling empresses, with the reports of whose profligacy Europe resounds, but who, under this unfeminine conduct, conceal a commanding and profoundly observing mind. By virtue of the spirit of intrigue that distinguishes these Aspasias of the North, there is scarcely a capital in Europe without two or three Russian ambassadors: the one, public, accredited, recognized, and clothed with all the insignia of office; the others, secret, irresponsible, and playing, in bonnet and petticoat, the double part of independent ambassador, and spy upon the official envoy.

In all ages, women have been employed with success in political negotiations. Many of our modern revolutionists have availed themselves of female aid to conspire more skillfully, more secretly, and more safely. Spain has seen these unfortunate women become heroines in the courage with which they have submitted to the punishment entailed by their tender devotion—for love always forms a great part of the courage of a Spanish woman.

Among the Russian women, love is only the accessory.

Russia possesses a completely organized female diplomacy; and Europe is not, perhaps, sufficiently attentive to so singular a means of influence. With its concealed army of amphibious agents, its political Amazons with acute masculine minds and feminine language, the Russian court collects information, obtains reports, and even receives advice, which, if better known, would explain many mysteries, furnish a key to many inconsistencies, and reveal many petty acts, otherwise inexplicable.

The political preoccupation of mind of the greater number of Russian women renders their conversation, interesting as it might be, insipid. This is more especially the case with the most distinguished women, who are naturally the most absent when the conversation does not turn upon important subjects. There is a world between their thoughts and their discourse, from whence there results a want of accord, an absence of natural manner, in short, a duplicity, that is disagreeable in the ordinary relations of social life. Politics are, from their nature, but poor amusement; their tediousness is supported by a sense of duty, and sometimes, when statesmen speak, by flashes of mind which animate conversation; but the fraudulent politics of the amateur are the curses of conversation.

I have been assured that the moral sentiment is scarcely developed among the Russian peasants, and my daily experience confirms the accounts that I have received.

A nobleman has related to me, that a man belonging to him, who was skillful in some particular handicraft, had permission to remain in Petersburg, in order to exercise his talent there. After the expiration of two years, he was allowed to return for a few weeks to his native village, to visit his wife. He came back to Petersburg on the day appointed.

"Are you satisfied with having seen your family?" asked his master. "Perfectly so," answered the workman, with great simplicity; "my wife has presented me with two more children in my absence, and the sight of them gave me great pleasure."

These poor people have nothing of their own; neither their cottages, their wives, their children, nor even their own hearts; they have, therefore, no jealousy. Of what could they be jealous?—Of an accident? Love among them is nothing better. Such, however, is the existence of the happiest men in Russia—the serfs! I have often heard the great express envy of their lot, and perhaps not without reason.

They have no cares, they say; we take all the charge of them and their families (God knows how this charge is acquitted when the peasants become old and useless). Assured of the necessaries of life for themselves and their children, they are a hundred times less to be pitied than the free peasants are among you.

I did not reply to this panegyric on servitude; but I thought, if they have no cares, they have also no families, and therefore no affections, no pleasures, no moral sentiment, no compensation for the physical evils of life. They possess nothing; though it is individual property which makes the social man, because it alone constitutes the divisions of family.

Moral truth is the only principle that merits our devotion; to grasp it, all the efforts of the human mind tend, whatever may be their sphere of action. If, in my journeys, I take every pains to describe the world as it is, my object is to excite in the breasts of others, and in my own, regret that it is not as it should be, to arouse in human minds the sentiment of immortality, by recalling, at the sight of every injustice, every abuse inherent in the things of earth, the words of Jesus Christ, "My kingdom is not of this world."

Never have I had so frequent occasion to apply these words as since my sojourn in Russia; they occur to me at every moment. Under a despotism, all the laws are calculated to assist oppression; that is to say, the more the oppressed has reason to complain, the less has he the legal right or the temerity to do so. Surely, before God, the evil actions of a free citizen are more criminal than the evil actions of a serf. He who sees everything, takes into account the insensibility of conscience in the man debased by the spectacle of iniquity always triumphant.

It will be said that evil is evil, wherever committed; and that the man who steals at Moscow, is just as much a thief as the pickpocket in Paris. It is precisely this which I deny. On the general education that a people receives, depends in a great measure the morality of each individual; from whence it follows that a fearful and mysterious relativeness of merits and of demerits has been established by Providence between governments and subjects, and that moments arrive in the history of communities when the state is judged, condemned, and destroyed, as though it were a single individual.

The virtues, the faults, and the crimes of slaves have not the same signification as those of freemen; therefore, when I examine the character of the Russian people, I can assert as a fact which does not imply the same blame as it would with us, that in general they are deficient in spirit, delicacy, and elevation of sentiment, and that they supply the want of these qualities by patience and artifice.

"The Russian people are gentle," is often said to me. To this I answer, "I cannot give them any credit for being so: it is their habit of submission." Others say, "The Russian people are only gentle because they dare not show what is in their hearts; their fundamental sentiments are superstition and ferocity." To this I reply, "Poor creatures! they are so ill educated!"

From all that I see in this world, and especially in this country, I conclude that happiness is not the real object for which man was placed here upon earth. That object is purely religious in its character: it is moral improvement—the struggle and the victory.

The Russian people are in our days the most believing

among all the Christian nations: the chief cause of the little efficacy of their faith is easily seen. When the church abdicates its liberty, it loses its moral virtuality:—a slave, it can only give birth to slavery. It cannot be too often repeated that the only church really independent, is the Catholic church, which has alone preserved the trust of true charity. All the other churches form constituent parts of the state, which uses them as political instruments for maintaining its power. These churches are excellent auxiliaries of the government; complaisant towards the princes or magistrates who are the depositaries of the temporal power, hard upon the subjects, they call in Deity to aid the police. The immediate result is sure; it is in good order in society: but the Catholic church, quite as powerful politically, looks higher and reaches farther. The national churches make citizens; the church universal makes men. Among the sectarians, a respect for the church is confounded with a love of country; among the Catholics, the church and regenerated humanity are one and the same thing. In Russia, respect for authority continues still the only spring of the social machine. This respect is necessary, no doubt; but, in order radically to civilize the human heart, it is necessary to teach it something more than blind obedience.

The longer I stay in this country the more am I impressed with the fact that contempt for the weak is contagious. This sentiment is so natural here, that those who most severely blame it come finally to partake of it. I am myself a proof in question.

In Russia, the desire of traveling fast becomes a passion, and this passion serves as a pretext for every species of inhumanity. My courier has communicated it to me, and I often render myself, without at the time perceiving it, an accomplice in his acts of injustice. He is exceedingly angry whenever the coachman leaves his seat to readjust any portion of the harness, or when he stops on the road under any other pretext.

Yesterday evening, at the onset of a stage, a child who drove us had been several times threatened with blows by the *Feldjäger* for a fault of the kind, and I participated in the impatience and wrath of this man. Suddenly, a foal, not many days old, and well known by the boy, escaped from an enclosure bordering upon the road, and began neighing and galloping after my carriage, for he took one of the mares that drew us for his mother. The young coachman, already guilty of delay, wanted once again to stop and go to the aid of the colt, which he saw every moment in danger of being crushed under the wheels of the carriage. My courier angrily forbade him to leave his seat: the child obeyed like a good Russian, and continued to drive us at a gallop without proffering a complaint. I supported the severity of the *Feldjäger*. I thought to myself, "It is necessary to sustain authority even when it is in fault; this is the spirit of the Russian government: my *Feldjäger* is not overzealous; if I discourage him when he exhibits energy in performing his duty, he will leave everything to come and go as it pleases, and be of no use to me at all: besides, it is the custom of the country; why should I be less in haste than another? my dignity as a traveler is involved; to have time to spare would be to lose my consequence in this country: here, to be important, we must be impatient." While I was thus reasoning, night had come on. I accuse myself with having been more hard-hearted even than the Russians (for I have not, like them, the habits of early life as an excuse), thus to leave the poor colt and the unhappy child to mourn in concert; the one by neighing with all his might, the other by crying silently—a difference which gave to the brute a real advantage over the human being. I ought to have interposed my authority to cause this double punishment to cease; but no, I assisted, I contributed to the martyrdom. It was a long one, for the stage was six leagues in length. The boy, obliged to torture the animal that he wished to save, suffered with a resignation that would have touched me, had not my heart been already hardened by my abode in this country. Every time that a peasant appeared on the road, the hope of rescuing his beloved foal again revived in the bosom of the child: he made signs from afar off; he shouted when a hundred paces distant from the foot passenger, but not daring to slacken the unmerciful gallop of our horses, he never succeeded in making himself understood in time. If ever a peasant, more quick-sighted than the others, endeavored of himself to turn the foal, the speed of the carriage disconcerted him, and the young animal passed on close to the flank of one of our horses. The case was the same in the villages, and at last the despair of our youthful coachman became so great, that he no longer opened his mouth. The persevering little animal, only eight days old, according to our driver, had the spirit and muscle necessary to perform six leagues at a gallop!

When this was accomplished, our slave—it is of the boy that I speak—seeing himself at length released from the rigorous yoke of discipline, called the whole village to the rescue of the foal. The energy of this spirited little creature was so great, that, notwithstanding the fatigue of such a course, notwithstanding the stiffness of his limbs, ruined before they were formed, he was still very difficult to catch. They could only take him by driving him into a stable after the mare he had mistaken for his dam. When they had placed a halter round him, they shut him up with another mare, that gave him her milk; but he had not strength left to suck. Some said he would come round by and by, others that he was foundered and could not live. I begin to understand a little Russian, and heard this sentence pronounced by one of the elders of the village. Our little coachman completely identified himself with the young animal. Foreseeing, no doubt, the treatment that the keeper of the foals would have to suffer, he appeared in as great a consternation as if he was himself to receive the blows with which his comrade would be overwhelmed. Never have I seen the expression of despair more profoundly imprinted on the face of a child; but not one look, not one gesture of reproach against my cruel courier, escaped him. So great an empire over self, so much restraint of feeling at such an age, inspired me with fear and pity.

Meanwhile the courier, without troubling himself for a moment about the foal, or taking the least notice of the disconsolate child, proceeded gravely to make the necessary arrangements for procuring a fresh relay.

On this road, which is the finest and the most frequented in Russia, the villages where relays may be obtained are peopled with peasants purposely established there to attend to the posting. Upon the arrival of a carriage, the Imperial director sends from house to house to seek for horses and a disengaged coachman. Sometimes the distances are great enough to cause a considerable delay to the traveler. I should prefer more promptness in the changing of horses, and a little less speed in the driving. At the moment of leaving the broken-down foal and the forlorn young postilion, I felt no remorse; it came only upon reflection, and especially upon recording the circumstances in writing: shame then awoke repentance. Thus easily may those who breathe the air of despotism be corrupted. What do I say? In Russia, despotism is only upon the throne, but tyranny pervades the country.

Education and circumstances considered, it must be acknowledged that a Russian lord, the most accustomed to submit to, and to exercise arbitrary power, could not have committed, in the seclusion of his province, an act of cruelty more blamable than that of which I, yesterday evening, rendered myself guilty by my silence.

I, a Frenchman, who believe myself to possess a naturally kind disposition, who have been educated under a civilization of ancient date, who travel among a people of whose manners I am a severe observer,—lo! even I, upon the first opportunity for practicing a petty act of unnecessary cruelty,

417

yield to the temptation. The Parisian acts like a Tartar! The evil is in the atmosphere.

In France, where they respect life, even that of the brute creation, if my postilion had not thought of rescuing the colt, I should have obliged him to stop. I should myself have appealed to the peasants for aid, and should not have proceeded on my journey until I had seen the animal in safety. Here, I have aided in destroying him by an unmerciful silence. Who would be proud of his virtues, when forced to acknowledge that they depend upon circumstances more than upon self?

A great Russian lord, who, in his fits of passion, does not beat to death any of his peasants, merits praise: he is in such case humane; whilst I, a Frenchman, may be cruel for having simply suffered a foal to gallop on the road.

Even Moscow will not recompense me for the trouble I am taking to see it. Shall I give up the idea of Moscow, order the coachman to turn, and depart in all haste for Paris? To this had my reveries brought me when the day dawned. My calèche had remained open, and in my protracted doze I had not been concious of the baneful influence of the dews of the North; my clothes were saturated; my hair in a state as if dripping with perspiration; all the leather about my carriage was steeped in noxious moisture; my eyes hurt me, a veil seemed to obscure my sight; I remembered the Prince ———, who became blind in twenty-four hours after a bivouac in Poland, under the same latitude, in a moist prairie.

My servant has just entered to announce that my carriage is mended; I am therefore again about to take the road: and unless some new accident detain me, and destine me to make my entrance into Moscow in a cart, or on foot, my next chapter will be written in the holy city of the Russians, where they give me hopes of arriving in a few hours.

I must, however, first set about concealing my papers, for each chapter, even those that will appear the most inoffensive to the friends who receive them in the form of letters, would be sufficient to send me to Siberia. I take care to shut myself up when writing; and if my *Feldjäger* or one of the coachmen knock at the door, I put up my papers before opening it, and appear to be reading. I am going to slip this sheet between the crown and the lining of my hat. These precautions are, I hope, superfluous, but I think it necessary to take them; they at any rate suffice to give an idea of the Russian government.

LETTER 24

First View of Moscow. — Symbolic Architecture of Greek Churches. — Castle of Petrovsky. — Entrance of Moscow. — Aspect of the Kremlin. — Church of St. Basil. — The French at Moscow. — The Kremlin a City. — An English Hotel in Russia. — The City by Moonlight. — Population of Moscow. — Gardens under the Walls of the Kremlin. — Description of the Fortress. — Ivan III. — Napoleon and the Kremlin. — Modern Grandiloquence.

Does the reader never remember having perceived, when approaching by land some seaport town in the Bay of Biscay or the British Channel, the masts of a fleet rising behind downs, just elevated enough to conceal the town, the piers, the flat shore, and the sea itself beyond? Above the natural rampart nothing can be discovered but a forest of poles bearing sails of a dazzling white, yards, many-colored flags, and floating streamers. A fleet, apparently on land, is the apparition with which my eye has been sometimes surprised in Holland, and once in England, after having penetrated into the interior of the country, between Gravesend and the mouth of the Thames. Exactly similar is the effect that has been produced upon me by the first view of Moscow: a multitude of spires gleamed alone above the dust of the road, the undulations of the soil, and the misty line that nearly always clothes the distance, under the summer sun of these parts.

The uneven, thinly inhabited, and only half-cultivated plain resembles downs dotted with a few stunted firs. It was out of the midst of this solitude that I saw, as it were, suddenly spring up thousands of pointed steeples, star-spangled belfries, airy turrets, strangely shaped towers, palaces, and old convents, the bodies of which all remained entirely concealed.

This first view of the capital of the Slavs, rising brightly in the cold solitudes of the Christian East, produces an impression that cannot easily be forgotten.

Before the eye spreads a landscape, wild and gloomy, but grand as the ocean; and to animate the dreary void, there rises a poetical city, whose architecture is without either a designating name or a known model.

To understand the peculiarity of the picture, it is necessary to remind the reader of the orthodox plan of every Greek church. The summit of these sacred edifices is always composed of several towers, which vary in form and height, but the number of which is five at the least—a sacramental number, that is often greatly exceeded. The middle steeple is the most lofty; the four others respectfully surround this principal tower. Their form varies: the summits of some resemble pointed caps placed upon a head; the great towers of certain churches, painted and gilded externally, may be severally compared to a bishop's miter, a tiara adorned with gems, a Chinese pavilion, a minaret, and a clergyman's hat. They often consist of a simple cupola, in the shape of a bowl, and terminating in a point. All these more or less whimsical figures are crowned with large, open-worked copper crosses, gilt, and the complicated designs of which look like work of filigree. The number and disposition of the steeples have always a symbolical religious meaning: they signify the ranks in the ecclesiastical hierarchy. They image the patriarch, surrounded by his priests, his deacons, and subdeacons, lifting between heaven and earth his radiant head. A fanciful variety characterizes this more or less richly adorned roof work; but the primitive intention, the theological idea, is always scrupulously respected.

Bright chains of gilded or plated metal unite the crosses

of the inferior steeples to the principal tower; and this metallic net, spread over an entire city, produces an effect that it would be impossible to convey, even in a picture. The holy legion of steeples, without having any precise resemblance to the human form, represent a grotesque assemblage of personages gathered together on the summits of the churches and chapels,—a phalanx of phantoms hovering over the city.

The exteriors of the mystic domes of the Russian churches are worked in a most elaborate manner. They remind the stranger of a cuirass of Damascus steel; and the sight of so many scaly, enameled, spangled, striped, and checkered roofs, shining in the sun with various but always brilliant colors, strikes him with the most lively astonishment. The desert, with its dull sea-green tint, is, as it were, illuminated by this magical network of carbuncles. The play of light, in the aerial city, produces a species of phantasmagoria, in broad day, which reminds one of the reflected brilliance of lamps in the shop of a lapidary. These changing hues impart to Moscow an aspect altogether different from that of the other great European cities. The sky, when viewed from the middle of such a city, is a golden glory, similar to those seen in old paintings. Schnitzler states that, in 1730, Weber counted at Moscow 1,500 churches. Coxe, in 1778, fixes the number at 484. As for myself, I am content with endeavoring to describe the aspect of things. I admire without counting,—I must, therefore, refer the lovers of catalogs to books made up entirely of numbers.

I have, however, said enough, I hope, to impart to the reader a portion of the surprise which the first view of Moscow produced in me. To add to that surprise, he must recollect, what he will have often read, that this city is a country within itself, and that fields, lakes, and woods, enclosed within its limits, place a considerable distance between the different edifices that adorn it. The objects being so scattered, tends greatly to increase the effect. The whole plain is covered with a silver gauze. Three or four hundred churches, thus spread, present to the eye an immense semicircle, so that when approaching the city, towards sunset on a stormy evening, it would be easy to fancy you saw a rainbow of fire impending above the churches of Moscow: this is the halo of the holy city. But at about three quarters of a league from the gate, the illusion vanishes. Here the very real and heavy brick palace of Petrovsky arrests the attention. It was built by Catherine after an odd modern design: the ornaments with which it is profusely covered stand in white against the red walls. These decorations, which are formed, I think, of plaster, are in a style of extravagant Gothic. The building is as square as a die, which by no means renders its general effect more imposing. It is here that the sovereign stops, when he means to make a solemn entrance into Moscow. A summer theater, a ballroom, and a garden have been established, so as to form a kind of public café, which I shall return to see, as it is the rendezvous of the city loungers during the summer season.

After passing Petrovsky, the enchantment gradually disperses, so that by the time of entering Moscow, we feel as if waking from a brilliant dream to a very dull and prosaic reality—a vast city without any real monuments of art, that is to say, without a single object worthy of a discriminative and thoughtful approbation. Before so heavy and awkward a copy of Europe, we ask, with wonder, what has become of the Asia, whose apparition had struck us with admiration so short a time before? Moscow, viewed from without and as a whole, is a creation of sylphs, a world of chimeras; when inspected close at hand and in detail, it is a vast trading city, without regularity, dusty, ill paved, ill built, thinly peopled; in short, though it unquestionably exhibits the work of a powerful hand, it betrays also the conceptions of a head whose idea of the beautiful has failed to produce one single chef d'oeuvre. The Russian people are strong in arms, that is in numbers, but in the strength of imagination they are altogether deficient.

Without genius for architecture, without taste for sculpture, they can heap together stones, and create objects enormous in dimension; but they can produce nothing harmonious, nothing great in the perfection of its proportions. Happy privilege of art! masterpieces survive themselves, subsisting in the memory of men ages after they have been devastated by time; they share, by the inspiration which they kindle even in their latest ruin, the immortality of the minds that created them; whereas shapeless masses are forgotten while yet untouched by time. Art, when in its perfection, gives a soul to stone; it is a mystic power. This we learn in Greece, where each fragment of sculpture conduces to the general effect of each monument. In architecture, as in the other arts, it is from the superior execution of the smallest details, and from their skillfully interwoven connection with the general plan, that the sentiment of the beautiful springs. Nothing in Russia inspires this sentiment.

Nevertheless, amid the chaos of plaster, brick, and boards that is called Moscow, two points never cease to attract the eye—the church of St. Basil, and the Kremlin,—the Kremlin, of which Napoleon himself was only able to disturb a few stones! This prodigious monument, with its white irregular walls, and its battlements rising above battlements, is in itself large as a city. At the close of day when I first entered Moscow, the grotesque piles of churches and palaces embraced within the citadel rose in light against a dimly portrayed background, poor in design and cold in coloring, though we are still burning with heat, suffocating with dust, and devoured by mosquitoes. It is the long continuance of the hot season which gives the color to southern scenery; in the North, we feel the effects of the summer, but we do not see them; in vain does the air become heated for a moment, the earth remains always discolored.

I shall never forget the chilly shudder which came over me on first seeing the cradle of the modern Russian Empire: the Kremlin alone is worth the journey to Moscow.

At the gate of this fortress, but beyond its precincts—at least, according to my *Feldjäger*, for I have not yet been able to visit it—stands the church of St. Basil, Vasily Blagennoi; it is also known under the name of the Cathedral of the Protection of the Holy Virgin. In the Greek church, they are lavish of the title of cathedral; every ward, every monastery has one of its own; every city possesses several. That of Vasily is certainly the most singular, if it is not the most beautiful edifice in Russia. I have as yet only seen it at a distance. Thus viewed, it appears as an immense cluster of little turrets forming a bush, or rather giving the idea of a cantaloupe with an embroidered skin, some kind of tropical fruit all bristled over with excrescences: a crystallization of a thousand rays, the scales of a golden fish, the enameled skin of a serpent, the changeful hues of the lizard, the glossy rose and azure of the pigeon's neck, would all, as regards color, serve as comparisons: above, rise minarets of a brownish red. The effect of the whole dazzles the eye, and fascinates the imagination. Surely, the land in which such a building is called a house of prayer is not Europe; it must be India, Persia, or China!—and the men who go to worship God in this box of confectionary work, can they be Christians? Such was the exclamation that escaped me at the first view of the church of Vasily. That building must indeed possess an extraordinary style of architecture to have drawn my attention, as it did, from the Kremlin, at the moment when the mighty castle for the first time met my eyes.

Soon, however, my ideas took another turn. Where is the Frenchman who could resist an emotion of respect and of pride (for misfortune has its pride, and it is the most legitimate kind), on entering into the only city where, in our own times, took place a public event, a scene, as imposing as the most striking occurrences of ancient history?

The means that the Asiatic city took to repel its enemy was a sublime deed of despair; and thenceforward the name of Moscow became fatally united with that of the greatest captain of modern times. The sacred bird of the Greeks consumed itself in order to escape the talons of the eagle, and, like the phoenix, the mystic dove also rises again from its ashes.

God was willing to furnish the chroniclers of the age—an age the most prosaic that the world has ever seen—with one epic story. Moscow was voluntarily sacrificed, and the flames of that sacred conflagration became the signal for the revolution of Germany and the deliverance of Europe. The nations felt at last that they would have no rest until they had annihilated the indefatigable conqueror who sought peace by means of perpetual war.

Such were the recollections that absorbed my thoughts at the first view of the Kremlin. To have worthily recompensed Moscow, the emperor of Russia ought to have re-established his residence in that twice holy city.

The Kremlin is not like any other palace, it is a city in itself; a city that forms the root of Moscow, and that serves as the frontier fortress between two quarters of the world. Under the successors of Genghis Khan, Asia made her last rush upon Europe: in turning to retreat, she struck the earth with her foot, and from thence rose the Kremlin!

On first entering the city of Moscow, I forgot poetry, and even history; I thought only of what I saw, which was not very striking, for I found myself in streets similar to those in the outskirts of all great cities: I crossed a boulevard which resembled other boulevards, and then, after driving down a gentle descent, found myself amongst straight and handsome lines of houses built of stone. At last I reached the Dmitry Donskoi Street, where a handsome and comfortable chamber had been engaged for me in an excellent English hotel. I had, at Petersburg, been commended to Madame Howard, who without this introduction would not have received me into her house. I took care not to reproach her for being so scrupulous, for it is owing to this precaution that one can sleep comfortably in her establishment. The means by which she has succeeded in maintaining there a cleanliness rarely seen anywhere, and which is an absolute miracle in Russia, is the having had erected, in her courtyard, a separate building, in which the Russian servants are obliged to sleep. These men never enter the principal edifice except to wait upon their masters. In her judicious precautions, Madame Howard goes yet further. She will scarcely admit any Russian guest: consequently, neither my *Feldjäger* nor coachman knew her house, and we had some difficulty in finding it; although it is, notwithstanding its want of a sign, the best inn in Moscow and in Russia. Immediately on being installed, I sat down to write. Night is now approaching, and as there is a bright moon, I lay aside my pen in order to take a ramble over the city, which promenade I will describe on my return.

I commenced my perambulations at about ten o'clock, without guide or companion, and strolled at random from street to street, according to my usual custom. I first followed several long and wide streets, more hilly than most of those in Russia, but laid out with equal regularity. There can be no complaint of the want of straight lines in the architecture of this country, nevertheless, the line and rule have less spoilt Moscow than Petersburg. In the latter, the imbecile tyrants of modern cities found a level surface ready prepared for them; here, they had to struggle with the inequalities of the soil, and with the ancient national edifices. Thanks to these invincible obstacles presented by nature and history, the aspect of Moscow is still that of an ancient city. It is more picturesque than any other in the empire, which continues to recognize it as its capital, in spite of the almost supernatural efforts of the Czar Peter and his successors: so strong is the law of circumstances against the will of men—men even the most powerful. Despoiled of its religious honors, deprived of its patriarch, abandoned by its sovereign, and by the most courtly of its ancient boyars, without any other attractive association than that of an heroic event, too modern to be as yet duly appreciated, Moscow has been obliged to have recourse to commerce and industry. They boast of its silk manufactories. But the history and the architecture are still here to preserve its imprescriptible rights to political supremacy. The Russian government favors the pursuits of industry: being unable altogether to stem the torrent of the age, it prefers enriching the people to enfranchising them.

This evening, towards ten o'clock, the sun sank, and the moon rose. The turrets of the convents, the spires of the chapels, the towers, the battlements, the palaces, and all the irregular and frowning masses of buildings that form the Kremlin, were here and there swathed with wreaths of light as resplendent as golden fringes, while the body of the city was seen only by the remaining beams of day, which momentarily faded on the painted tiles, the copper cupolas, the gilded chains, and the metallic roofs, that make the firmament of Moscow. These edifices, the general grouping of which gives the idea of some rich tapestry, still however stood in richly colored relief against the faint blue ground of heaven. It seemed as though the sun were willing to give a parting salute to the ancient capital of Russia. This adieu appeared to me magnificent; although clouds of mosquitoes buzzed about my ears, and my eyes were filled with the dust of the streets, kept in continual motion by the thousands of vehicles moving about, at a gallop, in all directions.

The most numerous were the truly national droshkies, those tiny summer sledges, which being unable conveniently to carry more than one person at a time, are multiplied to infinity in order to meet the wants of an active population, numerous, but lost in the circuit of so immense a city. The dust of Moscow is excessively troublesome, being fine as the lightest ashes. We have still a burning temperature. The Russians are astonished at the intensity and duration of the heat of this summer.

The first thing that struck me in the streets of Moscow was the more lively, free, and careless bearing of the population as compared with that of Petersburg. An air of liberty is here breathed that is unknown to the rest of the empire. It is this which explains to me the secret aversion of the sovereigns to the old city, which they flatter, fear, and fly. The Emperor Nicholas, who is a good Russian, says he is very fond of it: but I cannot see that he resides in it more than did his predecessors, who detested it.

This evening, a few streets were partially illuminated. It is difficult to understand the taste of the Russians for illuminations, when we recollect that during the short season, when they can alone enjoy this kind of spectacle, there is scarcely any night in the latitude of Moscow, and still less in that of Petersburg.

On returning to my lodgings, I asked the cause of these moderate demonstrations of joy, and was informed that the illumination was in honor of the anniversaries of the births or baptisms of all the members of the Imperial family. There are, in Russia, so many permanent fêtes of this sort, that they pass almost unnoticed. This indifference proves to me that fear can be sometimes imprudent, that it does not always know how to flatter so well as it would wish to do. Love is the only really skillful flatterer, because its praises, even when most exaggerated, are sincere. This is a truth which conscience vainly preaches in the ear of despots.

I slowly followed the promenaders of the streets, and after having ascended and descended several declivities in the wake of a wave of idle loungers, whom I mechanically took for guides, I reached the center of the city, a shapeless square, adjoining which was a garden, with alleys of trees brilliantly lighted, and under the shade of which could be heard the sound of distant music. Several open cafés tended further to remind me of Europe; but I could not interest myself in these amusements: I was beneath the walls of the Krelim,— that colossal mountain raised for tyranny by the hands of slaves. For the modern city a public promenade has been made, a species of garden planted, in the English taste, round the walls of the ancient fortress of Moscow.

How am I to describe the walls of the Kremlin? The word *wall* gives an idea of quite too ordinary an object; it would deceive the reader: the walls of the Kremlin are a chain of mountains. This citadel, reared on the confines of Europe and Asia, is, as compared with ordinary ramparts, what the Alps are to our hills: the Kremlin is the Mont Blanc of fortresses. If the giant that is called the Russian Empire had a heart, I should say that the Kremlin was the heart of the monster; but, as it is, I would call it the head.

I wish I could give an idea of this mighty pile of stones, reared step by step into the heavens; this asylum of despotism, raised in the name of liberty: for the Kremlin was a barrier opposed to the Kalmyks by the Russians: its walls have equally aided the independence of the state and the tyranny of the sovereign. They are boldly carried over the deep sinuosities of the soil. When the declivities of the hillocks become too precipitous, the rampart is lowered by steps: these steps, rising between heaven and earth, are enormous; they are the ladders of the giants who make war against the gods.

The line of the first girdle of structures is broken by fantastic towers, so elevated, strong, and grotesque in appearance as to remind one of the peaks in Switzerland, with their many-shaped rocks, and their many-colored glaciers. The obscurity no doubt contributed to increase the size of objects, and to give them unusual forms and tints,—I say tints, for night, like engravings, has its coloring. To behold gentlemen and ladies, dressed *à la parisienne*, promenading at the feet of this fabulous palace, was to fancy myself in a dream. What would Ivan III, the restorer, or it might be said the founder of the Kremlin, have thought, could he have beheld at the foot of the sacred fortress his old Muscovites, shaved, curled, and dressed in frock coats, white pantaloons, and yellow gloves, eating ices, seated before a brightly lighted café? He would have said, as I do, it is impossible! and yet this is now seen every summer evening in Moscow.

I have, then, wandered in the public gardens planted on the glacis of the ancient citadel of the czars; I have seen the towers, wall above wall, the platforms, terrace upon terrace, and my eyes have swept over an enchanted city. It would need the eloquence of youth, which everything astonishes and surprises, to find words analogous to these prodigious things. Above a long vault through which I passed, I perceived a raised viaduct, by which carriages and foot passengers entered the holy city. The spectacle was bewildering; nothing but towers, gates, and terraces, raised one above the other, steep slopes and piled arches, all serving to form the road by which the Moscow of the present day, the vulgar Moscow, is left for the Kremlin—the Moscow of miracle and of history. These aqueducts, without water, support other stories of more fantastic edifices. I observed, raised upon one of the hanging passages, a low round tower, all bristling with battlements of spearheads. The silver brightness of this ornament contrasted singularly with the blood red of the walls. The tower seemed like a crowned giant standing before the fortress of which he was the guardian. What is there that one could not see when wandering by the light of the moon at the foot of the Kremlin? There, everything is supernatural; the mind believes in specters in spite of itself. Who could approach without a religious terror this sacred bulwark, a stone of which, disturbed by Bonaparte, rebounded even to St. Helena, and crushed the conqueror in the bosom of the ocean! Pardon, reader, I am born in the age of grandiloquence.

The newest of the new schools is endeavoring to banish it, and to simplify language upon the principle that people the most devoid of imagination are those who most carefully shun the errors of a faculty which they do not possess. I can admire a puritanical style when it is employed by superior talents, talents capable of divesting it of all monotony, but I cannot imitate it.

After having seen all that I have gazed upon this evening, it would be wise to return straight to one's own country: the excitement of the journey is exhausted.

LETTER 25

AN ATTACK of ophthalmia, which came on between
Petersburg and Moscow, gives me much pain and annoyance.
Notwithstanding this ailment, I resumed today my promenade of yesterday evening, in order to compare the Kremlin
by daylight with the fantastic Kremlin of the night. The
shade increases and distorts everything: the sun restores to
objects their forms and their proportions.

At this second view the fortress of the czars still surprised
me. The moonlight magnified, and threw out in strong relief
certain masses of the building, but it concealed others; and,
while acknowledging that I had imagined to myself too many
vaults, and galleries, hanging roads, and lofty portals, I found
quite enough of all these objects to justify my enthusiasm.
There is something of everything at the Kremlin: it is a varied
landscape in stone. The solidity of its ramparts exceeds that
of the rocks on which they stand. The multitude and the
multiformity of its parts are a marvel. This labyrinth of
palaces, museums, towers, churches, and dungeons, is terrific
as the architecture of Martin; it is as great and more irregular
than the compositions of that English painter. Mysterious
sounds rise out of the depth of its underground; such abodes
must be haunted by spirits, they cannot belong to beings like
ourselves. The sounds seem to come from the grave. The

citadel of Moscow is not merely a palace, a national sanctuary for the historical treasures of the empire; it is the bulwark of Russia, the revered asylum in which sleep the tutelary saints of the country: it is also the prison of specters.

This morning, still wandering without a guide, I penetrated even to the heart of the fortress, and found my way into the interior of some of the churches which ornament that pious city, as venerated by the Russians for its relics as for the worldly riches and the warlike trophies which it encloses. I am too excited now to describe these objects in detail, but hereafter I shall pay a methodical visit to the Treasury.

The Kremlin, on its hill, gives me the idea of a city of princes, built in the midst of a city of people. This tyrannical castle, this proud heap of stones, looks down scornfully upon the abodes of common men; and, contrary to what is the case in structures of ordinary dimensions, the nearer we approach the indestructible mass, the more our wonder increases. Like the bones of certain gigantic animals, the Kremlin proves to us the history of a world of which we might doubt until after seeing the remains. In this prodigious creation, strength takes the place of beauty, caprice of elegance: it is like the dream of a tyrant, fearful but full of power; it has something about it that disowns the age; means of defense which are adapted to a system of war that exists no longer; an architecture that has no connection with the wants of modern civilization: a heritage of the fabulous ages; a jail, a palace, a sanctuary, a bulwark against the nation's foes, a bastille against the nation, a prop of tyrants, a prison of people,—such is the Kremlin. A kind of northern Acropolis, a Pantheon of barbarism, this national sanctuary may be called the Alcazar of the Slavs.

Such, then, was the chosen abode of the old Muscovite princes; and yet these formidable walls were not sufficient shelter for the terror of Ivan IV.

The fear of a man possessing absolute power is the most

dreadful thing upon earth; and with all the imagery of this fear visible in the Kremlin, it is still impossible to approach the palace without a shudder.

Towers of every form, round, square, and with pointed roofs, belfries, dungeons, turrets, spires, sentry boxes fixed upon minarets, steeples of every height, style, and color; palaces, domes, watchtowers, walls, embattlemented and pierced with loopholes; ramparts, fortifications of every species, whimsical inventions, incomprehensible devices, kiosks by the side of cathedrals—everything announces violation and disorder, everything betrays the continual *surveillance* necessary to the security of the singular beings who were condemned to live in this supernatural world. Yet these innumerable monuments of pride, caprice, voluptuousness, glory, and piety, notwithstanding their apparent variety, express one single idea, which reigns here everywhere—war maintained by fear. The Kremlin is the work of a superhuman being, but that being is malevolent. Glory in slavery—such is the allegory figured by this satanic monument, as extraordinary in architecture as the visions of St. John are in poetry. It is a habitation which would suit some of the personages of the Apocalypse.

In vain is each turret distinguished by its peculiar character and its particular use; all have the same signification,—terror armed.

Some resemble the caps of priests, others the mouth of a dragon, others swords, their points in the air, others the forms and even the colors of various exotic fruits; some again represent a headdress of the czars, pointed, and adorned with jewels like that of the doge of Venice; others are simple crowns; and all this multitude of towers faced with glazed tiles, of metallic cupolas, of enameled, gilded, azured, and silvered domes, shine in the sun like the colossal stalactites of the salt mines in the neighborhood of Kraków. These enormous pillars, these steeples and turrets of every shape, pointed, pyramidical, and circular, but always in some manner suggesting the idea of the human form, seem to reign over the city and the land. To see them from afar, shining in the sky, one might fancy them an assembly of potentates, richly robed and decorated with the insignia of their dignity, a meeting of ancestral beings, a council of kings, each seated upon his tomb; specters hovering over the pinnacles of a palace. To inhabit a place like the Kremlin is not to reside, it is to defend one's self. Oppression creates revolt, revolt necessitates precautions, precautions increase dangers, and this long series of actions and reactions engenders a monster; that monster is despotism, which has built itself a house at Moscow. The giants of the antediluvian world, were they to return to earth to visit their degenerate successors, might still find a suitable habitation in the Kremlin.

Everything, whether purposely or not, has a symbolical sense in its architecture; but the real, the abiding, that appears after you have divested yourself of your first emotions in the contemplation of these barbaric splendors, is, after all, only a congregation of dungeons pompously surnamed palaces and cathedrals. The Russians may do their best, but they can never come out of the prison.

The very climate is an accomplice of tyranny. The cold of the country does not permit the construction of vast churches, where the faithful would be frozen at prayer: here, the soul is not lifted to heaven by the glories of religious architecture; in this zone, man can only build to his God gloomy dungeons. The somber cathedrals of the Kremlin, with their narrow vaults and thick walls, resemble caves; they are painted prisons, just as the palaces are gilded jails.

As travelers say of the recesses of the Alps, so of the wonders of this architecture—they are horribly beautiful.

Whether the Kremlin be viewed under a purely historical, or a poetical and picturesque aspect, it is the most national monument in Russia, and consequently the most interesting both for Russians and for foreigners.

This sanctuary of despotism was reconstructed in stone for Ivan III, in 1485, by two Italian architects, Marco and Pietro Antonio, who were invited to Moscow by the *Great Prince*, when he wished to again rear the ramparts, formerly wooden, of the fortress more anciently founded under Dmitry Donskoi.

But if the Kremlin was not built by Ivan IV, it was built for him. It was by a spirit of prophecy that the great king, his grandfather, constructed the palace of the tyrant. Italian architects may be found everywhere, but in no other place have they produced a work similar to that which they raised at Moscow. I may add that there have been elsewhere absolute, unjust, arbitrary, and capricious sovereigns, and yet, that the reign of none of these monsters has resembled that of Ivan IV. The same seed springing under different climates and in different soils, produces plants of the same species, but of many varieties. The earth will never see another masterpiece of despotism similar to the Kremlin, nor another nation as superstitiously patient as was the Muscovite under the monstrous reign of its greatest tyrant.

The consequences of that reign are felt even in our days. Had the reader accompanied me in this journey, he would have discovered, as I have done, in the inner depths of the Russian character, the inevitable injury produced by arbitrary power carried to its last excess; showing itself by a careless indifference to the sanctity of truth in speech, of candor in sentiment, and of justice in acts; and, when fully developed, by falsehood rampant in all its forms, fraud triumphant, and the moral sense, in fact, wholly destroyed.

I could fancy I saw a procession of vices pouring forth from all the gates of the Kremlin to inundate Russia.

Other nations have supported oppression, the Russian nation has loved it: it loves it still. Is not such fanaticism of obedience characteristic? It may not, however, be denied that this popular mania has here sometimes become the principle of sublime actions. In this inhuman land, if society has depraved the individual, it has not enervated him: he is not good, but he is also not contemptible. The same may be said of the Kremlin: it is not pleasant to behold, but it inspires awe. It is not beautiful, but it is terrible—terrible as the reign of Ivan IV.

LETTER 26

PECULIAR CHARACTER OF ARCHITECTURE IN MOSCOW. — OBSER-
VATION OF MADAME DE STAËL'S. — KITAIGOROD. — MADONNA
OF VIVELSKY. — INTERIOR OF THE TREASURY. — CROWNS AND
THRONES. — MOORISH PALACE. — NEW WORKS AT THE KREMLIN.
— DESECRATION OF THE FORTRESS. — ERROR OF THE EMPEROR
NICHOLAS. — VIEW OF MOSCOW FROM THE KREMLIN. — THE FALL
OF NAPOLEON. — REVIEW OF HIS CHARACTER.

YESTERDAY, I recommenced my travels by a methodical and minute inspection of the Kremlin, under the conduct of M. ———, to whom I had an introduction. Still the Kremlin! That building is for me all Moscow—all Russia; a world within itself! My footman went in the morning to apprise the keeper, who waited for us. I expected to find an ordinary official, instead of which we were received by a military officer, a polite and intelligent man.

The Treasury of the Kremlin is deservedly the pride of Russia. It might serve as a substitute for the chronicles of the country; it is a history in precious stones.

The golden vases, the pieces of armor, the ancient furniture, are not merely to be admired in themselves; every object is associated with some glorious or singular event worthy of commemoration. But before describing, or rather rapidly noticing, the wonders of an arsenal that has not, I believe, its second in Europe, the reader must follow me, step by step, along the way by which I was led to this sanctuary, revered by the Russians, and justly admired by strangers.

After proceeding through several straight but narrow streets, I arrived in sight of the fortress, passing under an archway, before which my footman caused the coach to stop, without deeming it necessary to consult me, so well known is the interest which attaches to the place! The vault forms the under part of a tower, singular in shape, like all the others in the old quarter of Moscow.

I have not seen Constantinople, but I believe that, next to that city, Moscow is the most striking in appearance of all the capitals in Europe. It is the inland Byzantium. Fortunately the squares of the old capital are not so immense as those of Petersburg, in which even St. Peter's of Rome would be lost. At Moscow, the sites are more confined, and therefore the edifices produce greater effect. The despotism of straight lines and symmetrical plans is opposed here both by nature and history: Moscow is everywhere picturesque. The sky, without being clear, has a silvery brightness: the models of every species of architecture are heaped together without order or plan; no structures are perfect as works of art, nevertheless the whole strikes, not with admiration, but with astonishment. The inequalities of the surface multiply the points of view. The magic glories of multitudes of cupolas sparkle in the air. Innumerable gilded steeples, in form like minarets, Oriental pavilions, and Indian domes, transport you to Delhi; dungeon-keeps and turrets bring you back to Europe in the times of the crusades; the sentinel, mounted on the top of his watchtower, reminds you of the muezzin inviting the faithful to prayer; while, to complete the confusion of ideas, the cross, which glitters in every direction, commanding the people to prostrate themselves before the Word, seems as though fallen from heaven amid an assembly of Asiatic nations, to point out to them all the narrow way of salvation. It was doubtless before this poetical picture that Madame de Staël exclaimed—*Moscow is the Rome of the North!*

The massive tower, at the foot of which my footman made

me alight, is picturesquely pierced by two arches; it separates the walls of the Kremlin, properly so called, from their continuation, which serves as a girdle to Kitaigorod, the city of the merchants, another quarter of old Moscow, founded by the mother of the czar, Ivan the Terrible, in 1534. This date appears to us recent, but it is ancient for Russia, the youngest of the European realms.

The Kitaigorod, a species of suburb to the Kremlin, is an immense bazaar, a town intersected with dark and vaulted alleys, which resemble so many subterraneous passages. These catacombs of the merchants form, however, no cemeteries, but a permanent fair. They are a labyrinth of galleries, that rather resemble the arcades of Paris, although less elegant, less light, and more solid. This mode of building is essential to the wants of commerce in such a climate: in the North, covered streets remedy, as far as it is possible, the inconveniences and severity of the open air. Sellers and buyers are there sheltered from the storm, the snow, and the frost; whereas light colonnades, open to the day, and airy porticoes have an aspect that is ridiculous. Russian architects ought to take the moles and the ants for their models.

At every step that you take in Moscow, you find some chapel, highly venerated by the people, and saluted by each passenger. These chapels, or niches, generally contain some image of the Virgin kept under glass, and honored with a lamp that burns unceasingly. Such shrines are guarded by aged soldiers. These veterans are also to be met with in the antechambers of the wealthy, and in the churches, which they keep in order. The life of an old Russian soldier, if he could not obtain an asylum among the rich, or among the priests, would be one of extreme wretchedness. A charity void of display is unknown to the government: when it wishes to perform an act of benevolence, it builds palaces for the sick, or for children; and the façades of these pious monuments attract all eyes.

In the pillar which separates the double arcade of the tower, is enshrined the Madonna of Vivelsky, an ancient image, painted in the Greek style, and highly venerated at Moscow. I observed that everybody who passed this chapel— lords, peasants, tradespeople, ladies, and military men,—all bowed and made numerous signs of the cross; many, not satisfied with so humble a homage, stopped, and well-dressed women prostrated themselves to the very earth before the miraculous Virgin, touching even the pavement with their brows; men also, above the rank of peasants, knelt, and repeated signs of the cross innumerable. These religious acts in the open streets were practiced with a careless rapidity which denoted more habit than fervor. My footman is an Italian. Nothing could be more ludicrous than the mixture of conflicting prejudices which are working in the head of this poor foreigner, who has been for a great number of years established in the ancient capital of Russia, his adopted country. His ideas of childhood, brought from Rome, disposed him to believe in the intervention of the saints and the Virgin; and, without losing himself in theological subtleties, he takes for good, in default of better, the miracles of the relics and images of the Greek church. This poor Catholic, converted into a zealous adorer of the Madonna of Vivelsky, proves to me the omnipotence of unanimity in creeds. He does not cease repeating to me, with Italian loquacity, "Signor, creda à me, questa madonna fa dei miracoli, ma dei miracoli veri, veri verissimi, non è come da noi altri; in questo paese tutti gli miracoli sono veri."

This Italian, preserving the ingenuous vivacity and the good temper of the people of his country in the empire of silence and reserve, amuses me.

I must not stay to again describe the wonderful aspect of the exterior of the Kremlin—its prodigious walls and towers, carried over hills and ravines, and rising above each other in every variety of style, shape, and design, forming altogether the most original and poetical architecture in the world. But how shall I describe my surprise when, on entering the interior of the enchanted city, I approached the building called the Treasury, and saw before me a little modern palace, with straight lines and sharp angles, ornamented in front by Corinthian pillars. This cold and puny imitation of the antique, for which I ought to have been prepared, appeared to me so ridiculous, that I stepped back some paces and asked my companion permission to delay our visit to the Treasury, under pretext of first admiring some churches. After having been so long in Russia, I ought to be surprised at no incoherence in the inventions of the Imperial architects; but on this occasion, the discordance was so glaring, that it struck me as quite a novelty.

We therefore commenced our survey by a visit to the cathedral of the Assumption. This church possesses one of those innumerable paintings of the Virgin Mary that good Christians, of all lands, attribute to St. Luke. The edifice reminds me rather of the Saxon and the Norman than of our Gothic churches. It is the work of an Italian architect of the fifteenth century. After the structure had sunk and fallen in several times, while being erected by the bad artificers and worse architects of the land, foreign aid was sought, which succeeded in making the work solid; but, in its ornaments, the taste of the country has been followed.

I am ignorant of the rule prescribed by the Greek church relative to the worship of images: but in seeing this church entirely covered with paintings in fresco, betraying bad taste, and designed in the stiff, monotonous style, called the modern Greek, because its models were brought from Byzantium, I asked myself, what then are the figures, what can be the subjects, the representation of which is forbidden in the Greek church? Apparently, they banish nothing from these buildings except good pictures.

In passing before the Virgin of St. Luke, my Italian cicerone assured me that it was genuine: he added, with the faith of a muzhik, "Signore, signore, è il paese dei miracoli!" "It is the land of miracles!" I believe him, for fear is a potent thaumaturgist. What a singular journey is this, which in a fortnight conveys you into Europe as it was four hundred years ago! Nay, with us, even in the Middle Ages, man better felt his dignity than he does at the present day in Russia. Princes as false and crafty as the heroes of the Kremlin would never have been surnamed *great* in western Europe.

The iconostasis of this cathedral is magnificently painted and gilded, from the pavement to the roof. The iconostasis is a partition, or panel, raised in Greek churches between the sanctuary, which is always concealed by doors, and the nave, where the faithful congregate. The church is nearly square, very lofty, and so small that in walking through it you feel as if in a dungeon. The building contains the tombs of numerous patriarchs; it has also very rich shrines and famous relics brought from Asia. Viewed in detail, the cathedral is anything but beautiful, yet, as a whole, there is something about it which is imposing. If we do not admire, we feel a sense of sadness; and this is something: for sadness disposes the mind to religious sentiments. But in the great structures of the Catholic church there is something more than Christian sadness; there is the song of triumph and victorious faith.

At last I summoned courage to face the Corinthian columns of the Treasury; so braving with averted eyes those dragons of bad taste, I entered the glorious arsenal, where are ranged, as in a cabinet of curiosities, the most interesting historical relics of Russia.

What a collection of armor, of vases, and of national jewels! What profusion of crowns and of thrones, all gathered into the same place! The manner in which they are arranged adds to the effect. It is impossible not to admire the good taste as well as the political wisdom which has presided over the disposition of so many insignia and trophies. The display may be a little boastful, but patriotic pride is the most legitimate of any. We forgive a passion which aids us in fulfilling our duties. There is here emblazoned a profound idea, of which the things are but symbols.

The crowns are placed on cushions raised upon pedestals, and the thrones, ranged along the wall, are reared in separate alcoves. There is wanting only in this evocation of the past, the presence of the men for whom all these things were made. Their absence is equivalent to a sermon on the vanity of human life. The Kremlin without its czars is like a theater without lights or actors.

The most venerable, if not the most imposing of the crowns, is that of Monomakh; it was brought from Byzantium to Kiev in 1116. Another crown is also said to have belonged to Monomakh, though many consider it yet more ancient than the reign of that prince. In this royal constellation of diadems, are crowns also of the kingdoms of Kazan, Astrakhan, and Georgia. The view of these satellites of royalty, maintaining a respectful distance from the star that governs all—the Imperial crown—is singularly imposing. Everything is emblematic in Russia: it is a poetical land —poetical as sorrow! What are more eloquent than the tears that fall internally and gather upon the heart? The crown of Siberia is found among the rest. It is an imaginary insignia, of Russian manufacture, deposited as though to point out a grand historical achievement, accomplished by commercial adventurers and soldiers under the reign of Ivan IV, an epoch from whence dates, not exactly the discovery, but the conquest of Siberia.

On the ground floor of the palace of the Treasury, I was shown the state-coaches of the emperors and empresses of Russia. The old coach of the last patriarch is also included in the collection. Several of its windows are of horn. It is not among the least curious of the relics in the historical repository of the Kremlin.

I was afterwards shown the little palace, which the emperor inhabits when he visits the fortress. There is nothing in it worthy of notice, unless it be the picture of the last election of a king of Poland. That extraordinary Diet which placed Poniatowski on the throne, and Poland under the yoke, has been curiously represented by a French painter, whose name I could not learn.

Other wonders awaited me elsewhere. I visited the Senate house, the Imperial palaces, and the ancient palace of the patriarch, which possess little interest beyond their names; and, finally, the little angular palace, which is a gem and a plaything. It gives the idea of a masterpiece of Moresque architecture, conspicuous by its elegance in the midst of the heavy masses which surround it. It may be compared to a carbuncle set in common freestone. The structure consists of several stories, each one less spacious than that by which it is supported; this multiplies the terraces, and gives to the edifice a pyramidal form, the effect of which is very picturesque. The topmost story is nothing more than a little pavilion. Over the whole building, squares of Delftware, polished after the manner of the Saracens, indicate the lines of architecture with much taste and precision. The interior has just been refurnished, glazed, colored, and generally restored, in a manner that shows good taste.

To describe the contrast produced by so many edifices of various styles, crowded together in one spot, which forms the center of an immense city, to convey an idea of the effect produced by the congregation of Arabesque palaces, Gothic forts, Greek temples, Indian steeples, Chinese pavilions, all confusedly mingled within a circle of Cyclopean walls, would be utterly impossible. Words cannot paint objects, except by the recollections which they recall; and the recollections of no one who has not seen the Kremlin can serve to picture it.

The basement of the little Moorish palace is almost entirely occupied by one enormous vaulted hall, the roof of which is supported by a single pillar, rising from the center. This is the hall of the throne; the emperors repair to it on leaving the church, after their coronation. Everything here revives the recollection of the magnificence of the ancient czars, and the imagination goes back to the reigns of the Ivans and Alexises. The appearance is truly Muscovite. The entirely new paintings, which cover the walls of this palace, struck me as being executed with taste; the *tout ensemble* reminds me of the pictures I have seen of the porcelain tower at Peking.

The group of these varied monuments gives to the Kremlin an aspect of theatrical decoration that is seen nowhere else in the world: but not one of the buildings in that Russian forum will bear a separate examination any better than those dispersed throughout the rest of the city. At the first view, Moscow produces a very powerful impression: to a bearer of dispatches, traveling quickly past its walls, it would, with its churches, convents, palaces, and strong castles, any one of which might be taken for the abode of unearthly beings, appear the most beautiful of cities.

Unfortunately, they are now building in the Kremlin a new palace for the emperor. Have they considered whether this sacrilegious improvement will not spoil the general aspect, unique as it is in the world, of the ancient edifices of the holy fortress? The present habitation of the sovereign is, I admit, mean in appearance; but, to remedy the inconvenience, they are entrenching upon the most venerable portions of the old national sanctuary. This is profanation. Were I the emperor, I would rather raise my new palace in the air, than disturb one stone of the old ramparts of the Kremlin.

One day at Petersburg, in speaking to me of these works, the monarch said that they would beautify Moscow. I doubt it, was the answer of my thoughts: you talk as if you could ornament history. I know that the architecture of the old fortress does not conform to any rules of art: but it is the expression of the manners, acts, and ideas of a people and of an age that the world will never see again; it is, therefore, sacred as the irrevocable past. The seal of a power superior to man is there impressed—the power of time. But in Russia authority spares nothing. The emperor, who, I believe, saw in my face an expression of regret, left me, assuring me that his new palace would be much larger and better adapted to the wants of his court than the old one. Such a reason would suffice to answer any objection in a country like this in which I travel.

In order that the court may be better lodged, they are going to include within the new palace, the little church of the Savior in the Garden. That venerable sanctuary, the most ancient, I believe, in the Kremlin and in Moscow, is then to disappear amid the fine white walls, with which they will surround it, to the great regret of all lovers of antiquity and of the picturesque.

What more provokes me is the mockery of respect with which the profanation is to be committed. They boast that the old monument will still be preserved; in other words, it will not be destroyed, but only buried alive in a palace! Such is the way in which they here conciliate the official veneration for the past with the passion for "comfort," newly imported from England. This manner of beautifying the national city of the Russians is altogether worthy of Peter the Great. Was it not sufficient that the founder of the new city should abandon the old one? No!—his successors must also demolish it, under the pretext of improvement.

There are, then, neither artists nor architects in Russia: all who preserve any sentiment of the beautiful ought to throw themselves at the feet of the emperor, and implore him to spare his Kremlin. What the enemy could not do, the emperor is accomplishing. He is destroying the holy ramparts of which the miners of Bonaparte could scarcely disturb a stone.

And I, who am come to the Kremlin to see this historical wonder thus spoiled, dare not raise one cry against the perpe-

tration of the impious work—dare not make one appeal, in
the name of history, the arts, and good taste, in favor of these
old monuments condemned to make room for the abortive
conceptions of modern architecture. I protest, but it is very
secretly, against this wrong inflicted upon a nation, upon history and good taste; and if a few of the most intelligent and
informed of the men I meet here dare to listen to me, all the
answer that they venture to give is, that "the emperor wishes
his new residence to be more *suitable* than the old one: of
what, then, do you complain?" (*Suitable* is the sacramental
word of Russian despotism.) "He has commanded that it
should be rebuilt on the very spot, even, where stood the
palace of his ancestors: he will have changed nothing."

I am, as a stranger, prudent, and answer nothing to such
reasoning: but were I a Russian, I would defend, stone by
stone, the ancient walls and enchanted towers of the fortress
of the Ivans; I would almost prefer the dungeon under the
Neva, or exile, to the shame of remaining a mute accomplice
in this Imperial vandalism. The martyr of good taste might
yet obtain an honorable place below the martyr of faith: the
arts are a religion,—a religion which, in our days, is not the
least powerful, nor the least revered.

The view obtained from the height of the terrace of the
Kremlin is magnificent, more especially at the evening hour.
I shall often return to view the setting sun from the foot
of the steeple of John the Great, the loftiest, I believe, in
Moscow.

The plantations with which for some years past the
fortress has been nearly surrounded, form an ornament characterized by much good taste. They beautify the modern
merchant city, and at the same time form a fringe for the
Alcazar of the old Russians. The trees add to the picturesque effect of the ancient ramparts. There are vast spaces in
the thickness of the walls of this castle of romance, where are
seen staircases, the boldness and height of which make one

dizzy. The eye of fancy may discern there an entire population of the dead, descending with gentle steps, wandering over the platforms, or leaning on the balustrades of the old towers; from whence they cast upon the world the cold, disdainful eye of death. The more I contemplate these irregular masses, infinite in the variety of their forms, the more I admire the biblical architecture and the poetical inhabitants.

In the midst of the promenade which surrounds the ramparts, there is an archway which I have already noticed, but which continues to astonish me each time I see it. You leave a city, the surface of which is very uneven, a city studded with towers rising to the clouds, and plunge into a dark covered way, in which you ascend a long, steep hill; on arriving at its summit, you again find yourself under the open heaven, and look down upon another part of the city, hitherto unseen, which stretches to the border of a river, half dried up by the summer heats: this river is the Moscow. When the last rays of the sun are about to withdraw, the water in its bed may be seen colored with the tint of fire. This natural mirror, embosomed amid graceful hills, is very striking. Many of the distant buildings on those hills, especially the Hospital for Foundlings, are large as a city: they consist of benevolent institutions, schools, and religious foundations. The Moscow, with its stone bridge, the convents, with their innumerable metal domes, which represent above the holy city the colossal images of priests unceasingly at prayer, the softened peal of the bells, the sound of which is peculiarly harmonious in this land, the gentle murmur and motion of a calm yet numerous crowd, continually animated, but never agitated by the silent and rapid transit of horses and carriages, the number of which is as great at Moscow as at Petersburg,—all these things will give an idea of the effect of a setting sun in this ancient capital. Every summer evening they make Moscow unlike any other city in the world: it is neither Europe nor Asia: it is Russia—and it is Russia's heart.

It was already night before I left the Kremlin. The colors of the enormous edifices of Moscow, and of the distant hills, were softly sobered; the silence of night descended upon the city. The windings of the Moscow were no longer traced in brilliant lines, the flames of western day were extinguished; but the grandeur of the spot, and all the memories which it awoke, still stirred within my heart. I fancied I saw the shade of Ivan IV—Ivan the Terrible—standing upon the loftiest tower of his deserted palace, and, aided by his sister and his friend, Elizabeth of England, endeavoring to overwhelm Napoleon in a sea of blood! These phantoms seem to glory in the fall of the giant, who, by an award of fate, was destined, in falling, to leave his two enemies more powerful than he had found them.

England and Russia have cause to return thanks to Bonaparte—nor do they refuse to do so. Such was not for France the result of the reign of Louis XIV. The hatred of Europe has survived, during the period of a century and a half, the death of the Great King, whilst the Great Captain has been deified since his fall: and even his jailers do not fear to unite their discordant voices with the concert of praise which resounds from all parts of Europe,—a historical phenomenon, which I think stands alone in the annals of the world, and which can only be explained by the spirit of opposition that now reigns among all the civilized nations. The reign, however, of that spirit is drawing to its close. We may, therefore, hope soon to read works in which Bonaparte shall be estimated by his own intrinsic merits or demerits, and without malignant allusions to the reigning* power in France or elsewhere.

I hope to see the day in which this man—as wonderful by the passions he foments after death as by the actions of his

---

*Again we must remind the reader that this was written when Louis Philippe was king of the French.—*Trans.*

life—will be fairly judged. Truth has but yet touched the pedestal of his statue, hitherto shielded against the equitable severity of history by the double influence of unparalleled successes and misfortunes.

At any rate our children will have to learn, that he had more grasp of mind than dignity of character, and that he was greater by his talent in availing himself of successes than by his constancy in struggling against reverses. Then, but not till then, will the terrible consequences of his political immorality and his Machiavellian government, be mitigated.

After leaving the terraces of the Kremlin, I returned to my rooms with a feeling of exhaustion similar to that of a man who has been just witnessing the performance of some horrible tragedy, or rather like an invalid who awakes with the nightmare in a fever.

LETTER 27

MOSCOW lies in almost the only mountainous district in the center of Russia. Not that this word is to suggest the idea of Switzerland or Italy: the soil is uneven. Nothing more to it. But the contrast presented by these hills, rising in the middle of an expanse, where both the eye and the thoughts lose themselves as on the savannas of America or the steppes of Asia, produces an effect that is very striking. Moscow is the city of panoramas. With its commanding sites and its grotesque edifices, which might serve as models for the fantastic compositions of Martin, it recalls the idea which we form, without knowing why, of Persepolis, Baghdad, Babylon, or Palmyra,—romantic capitals of fabulous lands, whose history is a poem, and whose architecture is a dream. In a word, at Moscow, we forget Europe. This was what I did not know in France, although I had read nearly all the travelers' descriptions of the city. They have, then, failed in their duty. There is one especially whom I cannot pardon for not having permitted others to enjoy his visit to Russia. No descriptions are equal to the sketches of a painter, exact, and, at the same time, picturesque, like Horace Vernet. What man was ever more gifted to perceive, and to make others perceive, the spirit that breathes in things? The truth of painting lies not so much in the form as in the expression of objects: he understood them like a poet, and transferred them like an artist; consequently, every time I feel the insufficiency of my words, I am inclined to be angry with Horace Vernet.

Here, every view is a landscape. If art has done little for Moscow, the whim of the builders and the force of circumstances have created marvels. The extraordinary forms of the edifices, and the grandeur of the masses, strongly impress the imagination. The enjoyment, it must be owned, is of an inferior order: Moscow is not the product of genius; connoisseurs will there find no monuments of art worthy of a minute examination: those monuments are rather the strange and deserted habitations of some race of giants; they are the works of the Cyclopes. In a city where no great artist has left the impress of his thoughts, we may feel astonishment, but nothing more, and astonishment is soon exhausted. However, there is nothing here, not even the disenchantment that follows the first surprise, from which I cannot draw a lesson: more particularly am I struck with the visible intimate connection between the aspect of the city and the character of the people. The Russians love all that dazzles; they are easily seduced by appearances: to excite envy, no matter at what price, constitutes their happiness. The English are gnawed by pride, the Russians are corroded with vanity.

I feel the necessity of here reminding the reader that generalities always pass for injustices. Once for all, I would state that my observations never exclude exceptions; and I avail myself of the occasion to express the respect and admiration I entertain for the merits and agreeable qualities of individuals to whom my criticisms do not apply.

Other travelers have observed before I did, that the less we know of a Russian the more amiable we find him. The

Russians have retorted upon those travelers, that they spoke in their own disparagement, and that the coolness of which they complained only proved their want of merit. "We gave you a good reception," they add, "because we are naturally hospitable; and if we afterwards changed in our manner towards you, it was because we thought more highly of you at first than you deserved." Such an answer was made a considerable time ago to a French traveler, an able writer, but whose position obliged him to be excessively reserved. I do not mean here to cite either his name or his book. The few truths which, in his prudent recitals, he allowed himself to expose, placed him in a very disagreeable position. This was the penalty for denying himself the free exercise of his intellect, in order to submit to expectations which can never be satisfied; not any more by flattering them than by doing them justice. It would cost less to brave them; and on this opinion the reader will perceive I act.

Moscow prides herself on the progress of her manufactures. The Russian silks here contend with those of both East and West. The merchant quarter, the Kitaigorod, as well as the street called the Bridge of the Marshals, where the most elegant shops are found, are reckoned among the curiosities of the city. If I mention them it is because I think that the efforts the Russians are making to free themselves from the tribute which they pay to the industry of other nations, may produce important political consequences in Europe.

The liberty that reigns in Moscow is illusive; yet it cannot be denied that, in its streets, there are men who appear to move spontaneously, who think and act under an impulse of their own. Moscow is in this respect very different from Petersburg. Among the causes of the difference, I place in the first rank the vast extent and the varied surface of the territory in the midst of which it stands. Space and inequality (I here take this word in all its acceptations) are the elements of liberty; for absolute equality is the synonym of tyranny, though it is the minority who may be placed under the yoke: liberty and equality exclude each other by the operation of reserve and combinations, more or less abstruse, which neutralize the effect of things while preserving their names.

Moscow remains almost buried in the midst of a country of which it is the capital: hence the seal of originality impressed upon its buildings, the air of liberty which distinguishes its inhabitants, and the little inclination of the czars for a residence of which the aspect is so independent. The czars, ancient tyrants mitigated by the fashion which has metamorphosed them into emperors, and even into amiable men, fly Moscow. They prefer Petersburg, with all its inconveniences, for they wish to be in continual communication with the west of Europe. Russia, as formed by Peter the Great, does not trust to herself to live and to learn. At Moscow, they could not obtain, within a week's time, the little importations of the current anecdotes and small gossip of Paris, nor the ephemeral literature of Europe. These details, contemptible as they appear to us, furnish the chief excitement of the Russian court, and consequently of Russia.

If the freezing or the melting snow did not render railroads useless in this land during six or eight months of the year, we should see the Russian government surpass all others in the construction of those roads, which are, as it were, lessening the size of earth; for that government suffers more than any other from the inconveniences of distance. But, notwithstanding acceleration of the speed of traveling, a vast extent of territory will always be the chief obstacle to the circulation of ideas: for the soil will not allow itself, like the sea, to be crossed in all directions. The water, which, at first sight, appears destined to separate the inhabitants of the world, is the medium which, in reality, unites them. Wonderful problem! Man, the prisoner of God, is yet allowed to be the king of nature.

Certainly, were Moscow a seaport, or the center of a vast

network of those metal wheel tracks, those electric conductors of human thought, destined to satisfy, in some respects,
the impatient spirit of our age, we should not see what I saw
yesterday at the English club house—military men, and fashionables of all ages, serious persons and giddy youths, making
the sign of the cross, and remaining silent for some moments
before sitting down at table—not a family table, but a table
d'hôte. Those who disclaim all religion (and there is here a
considerable number of such) viewed the others without any
surprise. It may still be seen that there are eight hundred
good leagues between Paris and Moscow.

The palace belonging to the club is large and handsome.
The entire establishment is well planned and skillfully directed; everything is about the same as in the clubs of other
places. This did not surprise me; but the pious feeling of the
Russians I sincerely admired, and said as much to the person
who had introduced me.

We were talking together, after dinner, in the garden of
the club.

"We must not be judged by appearances," replied my
companion, who is, as I am about to show, one of the most
enlightened of the Russians.

"It is precisely these appearances," I replied, "which inspire me with esteem for your nation. With us, people dread
only hypocrisy; but the sneer of cynicism is even yet more
injurious to society."

"Yes, but it is less revolting to noble minds."

"But, without further reference to general considerations,
give me an idea of the actual state of religion in your country;
tell me, how are the minds of the men who teach the Gospel
in Russia cultivated?"

Although I addressed a man of superior mind, the question
would have been an indiscreet one at Petersburg: at Moscow I
felt I might risk it, confiding in that mysterious liberty that
reigns in this city, though we can neither fully account for

nor define it; and though the confidence which it inspires may sometimes have to be dearly paid for.* The following is the summary of my Russian philosopher's reply: I use the word philosopher in its most favorable signification. After years passed in different European countries, he has returned to Russia very liberal, but very consistent. His reply then was as follows:—

"There has always been very little preaching in the schismatic churches; and among us, the political and religious authority has been opposed more than elsewhere to theological discussions. Whenever there has been a wish to commence the debate of the questions at issue between Rome and Byzantium, silence has been imposed upon both parties. The points in dispute are of so little moment that the quarrel can only be perpetuated by means of ignorance. In several public institutions for education some religious instruction has been from time to time given, but this is only tolerated, and often forbidden: it is a positive, although it may appear to you an incredible fact, that religion is not publicly taught in Russia. The result is a multitude of sects, of which the government would not endure that you should suspect the existence.

"There is one which tolerates polygamy; another goes farther, and maintains not only the principle but the practice of promiscuous intercourse between the sexes.

"Our priests are forbidden to write even historical scripture; our peasants are constantly interpreting passages from the Bible, which, taken separately, without the context, and falsely applied, frequently give rise to some new heresy, most generally Calvinistic in its character. Before the pope of the village discovers it, it has already gained a hold among the inhabitants, and often spread among the neighboring popula-

---

*The reader will hereafter see the danger of such a confidence instanced by the arbitrary detention of a French citizen.

tions. Should the priest then treat the matter publicly, the contaminated peasants are sent to Siberia, which ruins the lord of the soil, who consequently, if previously aware of the circumstance, finds more than one way of causing the pastor to preserve a silence: so that, when at last the heresy does break out and attract the eyes of the supreme authority, the number of seceders is so considerable that it is no longer possible to act against them. Violence would divulge the mischief without stifling it; persuasion would open a door for discussion—the worst of all evils in the eyes of an absolute government: they can, therefore, do nothing but have recourse to silence, under whose veil the evil is concealed, without being cured; on the contrary it gradually spreads.

"It is by religious divisions that the Russian Empire will perish; therefore to envy in us, as you do, the power of faith, is to judge us without knowing us."

Such is the opinion of the most clear-sighted and sincere men whom I have met in Russia.

A foreigner, worthy of credence and who has been long established in Moscow, has likewise informed me that he dined some years ago with a merchant of Petersburg and *his three wives*—not concubines, but legitimate wives. This merchant was a dissenter, a secret sectarian of some new church. I presume that the children borne him by his three helpmates would not be recognized as legitimate by the state; but his conscience as a Christian remained at ease.

If I had learnt this fact from a native, I might not have recounted it; for there are Russians who amuse themselves with lying, in order to perplex and lead astray too curious or too credulous travelers; a circumstance which tends to throw obstacles in the way of a pursuit, difficult everywhere, for those who would exercise it conscientiously, but doubly so here—I mean the pursuit of an observer.

The body of merchants is very powerful, very ancient, and very much esteemed in Moscow. The life of these rich dealers reminds us of the condition and manners of the Asiatic merchants, so well painted in the Arabian Nights. There are so many points of resemblance between Moscow and Baghdad, that in traveling through Russia we lose the curiosity to see Persia; we know it already.

I have just been present at a popular fête, held round the monastery of Deviche Pole. The actors are soldiers and peasants; the spectators people of the higher classes, who go there in great numbers. The tents and booths for drinking are placed close to the cemetery. The feast or fair is kept in commemoration of some Russian saint, whose relics and images are ceremoniously visited between two libations of kvass. This evening an inconceivable consumption of that national liquor has here taken place.

In general, the Russian convents have rather the appearance of a cluster of small houses, of a walled division of a city, than of a religious retreat. Being often destroyed and rebuilt, they have a modern look. In this climate nothing long resists the war of the elements. The whole country has the aspect of a colony founded but yesterday. The Kremlin alone seems destined to brave the storms, and to live as long as the empire, of which it is the emblem and the bulwark. The idea of the irrevocable is always solemn.

This evening, the tents where the holiday folks of Deviche Pole were congregated, emitted various scents, the mixture of which produced an atmosphere that was intolerable. There was perfumed Russian leather, spirituous liquors, sour beer, cabbages, the grease of the boots of Cossacks, and the musk and ambergris of numerous fashionable loiterers, who appeared determined to suffer from ennui, were it only out of aristocratic pride. I found it impossible long to breathe this mephitic air.

The greatest pleasure of the people is drunkenness; in other words, forgetfulness. Unfortunate beings! they must dream if they would be happy. As a proof of the good temper of the Russians, when the muzhiks get tipsy, these men, brutalized as they are, become softened, instead of infuriated. Unlike the drunkards of our country, who quarrel and fight, they weep and embrace each other. Curious and interesting nation! it would be delightful to make them happy. But the task is hard, if not impossible. Show me how to satisfy the vague desires of a giant, young, idle, ignorant, ambitious, and so shackled that he can scarcely stir hand or foot. Never do I pity this people without equally pitying the all-powerful man who is their master.

I soon left the taverns to walk in the square, where the promenaders raised clouds of dust. The summers of Athens are long, but the days are short, and, owing to the sea breeze, the air is scarcely hotter than it is at Moscow during the short northern heats. The unendurable summer of this year is, however, now nearly over; the nights return, and winter will soon follow. Beyond the fair, the view of the distant pine forests that surround the city with a girdle of mourning, the slowly decreasing tints of a long twilight, all tended to heighten the effect of the monotonous landscape of the North, upon the face of which poetry is written in a mystic tongue—a tongue that we do not understand.

I congratulate myself on having seen this festival, so devoid of gaiety, but, likewise, so different from those of other lands. The Cossacks were to be seen in great numbers among the promenaders and the drinkers who filled the square. They formed silent groups around singers, whose piercing voices chanted forth melancholy words set to a softly pleasing tune, although its rhythm was strongly marked. The air was the national song of the Don Cossacks. It has a kind of resemblance to some old Spanish melodies, but is more plaintive; it is soft, yet penetrating as the trill of the nightingale when

461

heard at a distance, by night, in the depths of the woods. Now and then the bystanders repeated in chorus the last words of the strophe.

There is more melancholy than passion in the songs of the northern people; but the impression which they produce is never forgotten, whereas a more lively emotion soon vanishes. Melancholy is more abiding than passion. After having listened to this air for some time, I found it less monotonous and more expressive,—such is the ordinary effect of simple music; repetition imparts to it a new power.

LETTER 28

DURING the last two days I have seen many sights;
among others, the Tartar mosque. The religion of the conquerors is now tolerated in a corner of the capital of the vanquished; and this, only on condition that the Christians have
free permission to enter the Mohammedan sanctuary.

The mosque is a small and mean edifice, and the men there allowed to worship God and the prophet, have a wretched, timid, dirty, and poverty-stricken appearance. They come to prostrate themselves in this temple every Friday, upon a filthy piece of woolen mat, which each carries with him. Their graceful Asiatic garments have become rags; their own condition is abject: they live as much apart as possible from the population which surrounds them. In seeing these beggars in appearance, creeping in the midst of actual Russia, it is difficult to realize the idea of the tyranny which their fathers exercised over the Muscovites.

The unfortunate sons of conquerors trade at Moscow in the provisions and the merchandise of Asia, and adhere as much as possible to the practice of their religion, avoiding the use of wines and strong liquors, and shutting up their women, or at least veiling them, in order to shield them from the eyes of other men; a precaution which is, however, little needed, for the Mongol race present but few attractions. High cheekbones, flat noses, small sunken black eyes, frizzled hair, a brown and oily skin, a low stature, an appearance of filth and squalor,—such were the characteristics which I remarked in the men of this degenerate race, and in the small number of women of whose features I could obtain a glimpse.

The Russians take credit for the tolerance which they accord to the faith of their ancient tyrants. I find such tolerance more ostentatious than philosophical: and, for the people to whom it is extended, it is but one humiliation more. Were I in the place of the descendants of those implacable Mongols, who were so long masters of Russia and the terror of the world, I would prefer praying to God in the secret of my heart, rather than in the shadow of a mosque accorded by the pity of my ancient tributaries.

When I wander over Moscow without aim and without guide, I never weary. Each street, each outlet, affords the view of a fresh city; a city which, studded with its embroidered, pierced, and battlemented walls, broken with towers, and supporting multitudes of turrets and watchtowers, appears as though built by genies. Then there is the Kremlin, poetical in its aspect, historical by its name, the root of an empire, the heart of a city, and which for me is all Moscow. I return there with an ever-new attraction; but it is necessary to avoid carefully examining in detail the incoherent masses of monuments with which this walled mountain is encumbered. The exquisite sense of art, the talent, that is, of finding the one only perfectly just expression of an original conception, is unknown to the Russians; nevertheless, when giants copy, their imitations always possess a kind of beauty: the works of genius are grand, the works of physical power are great: and this alone is something.

To divert my mind for a moment from the terrific Kremlin, I have paid a visit to the tower of Sukharev, built on an eminence near to one of the entrances of the city. The first story is a vast structure, containing an immense reservoir, from whence nearly all the water drunk in Moscow is distributed to the different parts of the city. The view of this walled lake, reared high in air, produces a singular impression. The architecture is heavy and gloomy; but the Byzantine arcades, the massy flights of steps, and the ornaments in the style of the Lower Empire, make the whole very imposing. This style is perpetuated in Moscow: had it been applied with discernment, it would have given birth to the only national architecture possible to the Russians: though invented in a temperate climate, it equally accords with the wants of northern people and the habits of those of the South. The interiors of Byzantine edifices are very similar to ornamented cellars; the solidity of the massive vaults, and the obscurity of the walls, offer a shelter from the cold as well as from the sun.

I have also been shown the University, the School of Cadets, the Institutions of St. Catherine and of St. Alexander, the Hospitals for Widows and for Foundlings, all vast and pompous in appearance. The Russians pride themselves in having so great a number of magnificent public establishments to show to strangers: for my part, I should be content with less of this kind of splendor; for no places are more tedious to wander over than these white and sumptuously monotonous palaces, where everything is conducted in military order, and where human life seems reduced to the action of the pendulum of a clock.

Among us, there is the fatigue of license and variety; here, we are discouraged by uniformity frozen over by pedantry, which yet we may not separate from the idea of order; whence it follows, that we hate what we ought to love. Russia, that infant nation, is nothing more than an immense college; everything is conducted there as in a military school, the only difference being, that the scholars never leave it until they die.

The new converts to civilization have not yet lost their taste, as upstarts, for everything that dazzles, everything that attracts the eye. Children and savages always love these things. The Russians are children who have the habit, but not the experience of misfortune; hence the mixture of levity and causticity which characterizes them. The enjoyments of a calm and equable life, adapted solely to satisfy the affections of intimacy, to administer to the pleasures of conversation and of mind, would never long suffice them: not that these great lords show themselves altogether insensible to refined pleasures; but, to captivate the haughty frivolity of such disguised satraps, to fix their vagrant imaginations, lively excitements are necessary. The love of play, intemperance, libertinism, and the gratifications of vanity, can scarcely fill the void in their satiated hearts: the creation of God does not furnish these unhappy victims of wealth and indolence with any means to get through their weary days. In their proud misery, they summon to their aid the spirit of destruction. All modern Europe is the prey of ennui. It is this which attests the nature of the life led by the youth of the present day: but Russia suffers from the evil worse than the other communities; for here everything is excessive. To describe the ravages of society in a population like that of Moscow would be difficult: nowhere have the mental maladies engendered in the soul by ennui—that passion of men who have no passions—appeared to me so serious or so frequent as among the higher classes in Russia: it may be said that society has here commenced by its abuses. When vice does not suffice to enable the human heart to shake off the ennui that preys upon it, that heart proceeds to crime.

The interior of a Russian coffeehouse is very curious. It consists generally of a large, low apartment, badly lighted, and usually occupying the second floor of the house. The waiters are dressed in white shirts, girded round the middle, and falling like a tunic over loose white pantaloons. Their hair is long and smooth, like that of all the lower orders of Russians; and their whole adjustment reminds one of the theophilanthropists of the French republic, or the priests of the opera when paganism was the fashion at the theater. They serve you with excellent tea, superior, indeed, to any found in other lands, with coffee and liqueurs: but this is done with a silence and solemnity very different from the noisy gaiety which reigns in the cafés of Paris. In Russia all popular pleasures are melancholy in their character: mirth is viewed as a privilege; consequently, I always find it assumed, affected, overdone, and worse than the natural sadness. Here, the man who laughs is either an actor, a drunkard, or a flatterer.

This reminds me of the times when the Russian serfs believed, in the simplicity of their abjectness, that heaven was only made for their masters: dreadful humility of misfortune! Such was the manner in which the Greek church taught Christianity to the people.

The society of Moscow is agreeable; the mixture of the patriarchal traditions of the old world with the polished manners of the modern, produces a combination that is, in a manner, original. The hospitable customs of ancient Asia and the elegant language of civilized Europe have met together at this point of the globe, to render life pleasant and easy. Moscow, fixed on the limits of two continents, marks, in the middle of the earth, a spot for rest between London and Peking.

A small number of letters of introduction suffice to put a stranger in communication with a crowd of persons, distinguished either by fortune, rank, or mind. The debut of a traveler is here easy.

I was invited a few days ago to dine at a country house. It is a pavilion situated within the limits of the city, but, to reach it, we had to traverse, for more than a league, fields that resemble steppes, to skirt solitary pools of water; and, at last, on approaching the house, we perceived, beyond the garden, a dark and deep forest of firs, which borders the exterior bounds of Moscow. Who would not have been struck with the sight of these profound shades, these majestic solitudes, in a city where all the luxuries and refinements of modern civilization are to be found? Such contrasts are characteristics; nothing similar is to be seen elsewhere.

I entered a wooden house—another singularity. In Moscow both rich and poor are sheltered by planks and boards, as in the primitive cottages. But the interior of these large cabins exhibits the luxury of the finest palaces of Europe. If I lived at Moscow, I would have a wooden house. It is the only kind of habitation the style of which is national, and, what is more important, it is the only kind that is adapted to the climate. Houses of wood are esteemed by the true Muscovites as warmer and healthier than those of stone.

We dined in the garden; and, that nothing should be wanting to the originality of the scene, I found the table laid under a tent. The conversation, although between men only, and very lively, was decent—a thing rarely known among the nations who believe themselves the first in civilization. The guests were persons who had both seen and read much; and their views appeared to me very clear and just. The Russians are apes in the manners and customs of refined life; but those who think (it is true their number is limited) become themselves again, in familiar conversation—Greeks, namely, endowed with a quickness and sagacity which is hereditary.

The dinner seemed to me short, although in reality it lasted a considerable time, and although, at the moment of sitting down at table, I saw the guests for the first time, and the master of the house for the second. This remark is worthy of notice, for great and true politeness could alone have put a stranger so quickly at his ease. Among all the recollections of my journey, that of this day will remain as one of the most agreeable.

At the moment of leaving Moscow, never to return, except merely to pass through it, I do not think it will be inappropriate for me summarily to review the character of the Russians, so far as I have been able to discern it, after a sojourn in their country, very brief, it is true, but employed without cessation in attentively observing a multitude of persons and of things, and in comparing, with scrupulous care, innumerable facts. The variety of objects which passes before the eyes of a stranger, as much favored by circumstances as I have been, and as active as I am when excited by curiosity, supplies, to a certain extent, the time and leisure which I have wanted. I naturally take pleasure in admiring: this disposition ought to procure some credit for my opinions when I do not admire.

In general, the men of this country do not appear to me inclined to generosity; they scarcely believe in that quality; they would deny it if they dared; and if they do not deny it, they despise it, because they have nothing in themselves by which to apprehend its nature. They have more finesse than delicacy, more good temper than sensibility, more pliancy than easy contentedness, more grace than tenderness, more discernment than invention, more wit than imagination, more observation than wit, more of the spirit of selfish calculation than all these qualities together. They never labor to produce results useful to others, but always to obtain some recompense for themselves. Creative genius has been denied them; the enthusiasm which produces the sublime is to them unknown; sentiments which seek only within themselves for approval and for recompense, they cannot understand. Take from them the moving influences of interest, fear, and vanity, and you will deprive them of all action. If they enter the empire of arts, they are but slaves serving in a palace; the sacred solitudes of genius are to them inaccessible; the chaste love of the beautiful cannot satisfy their desires.

It is with their actions in practical life, as with their creations in the world of thought,—where artifice triumphs, magnanimity passes for imposture.

Greatness of mind looks to itself for a recompense; but if it asks for nothing from others, it commands much, for it seeks to render men better: here, it would render them worse, because it would be considered a mask. Clemency is called a weakness among a people hardened by terror: implacable severity makes them bend the knee, pardon would cause them to lift the head; they can be subdued, but no one knows how to convince them; incapable of pride, they can yet be audacious; they revolt against gentleness, but they obey ferocity, which they take for power.

This explains to me the system of government adopted by the emperor, without, however, leading me to approve it. That prince knows how to make himself obeyed, and acts in a way to command obedience; but, in politics, I am no admirer of the compulsory system. Here, discipline is the end; elsewhere, it is the means. Is it pardonable in a prince to resist the good dictates of his heart, because he believes it dangerous to manifest sentiments superior to those of his people? In my eyes, the worst of all weaknesses is that which renders a man pitiless and unmerciful. To be ashamed of being magnanimous is to confess an unworthiness of possessing supreme power.

The people are in need of being incessantly reminded of a world better than the present world. How can they be made to believe in God, if they are not to know what is pardon? Prudence is only virtuous when it does not exclude a higher virtue. If the emperor has not in his heart more clemency than he displays in his policy, I pity Russia; if his sentiments are superior to his acts, I pity the emperor.

The Russians, when amiable, have a fascination in their manners whose spell we feel in spite of every prejudice; first, without observing it, and afterwards, without being able to throw it off. To define such an influence would be to explain the power of imagination. The charm forms an imperious, though secret attraction,—a sovereign power vested in the innate grace of the Slavs, that gift of grace which, in society, can supply the want of all other gifts, and the want of which nothing can supply.

Imagine the defunct French politeness again restored to life, and become really all that it appeared—imagine the most agreeable and unstudied complaisance—an involuntary, not an acquired, absence of egotism—an ingenuity in good taste —a pleasant carelessness of choice—an aristocratic elegance without hauteur—an easiness without impertinence—the instinct of superiority tempered by the security which accompanies rank:—but I am wrong in attempting to delineate with too finely drawn strokes; these are delicacies in the shading which must be felt. We may divine them, but we must avoid attempting to fix by words their too elusive forms. Let it suffice that all these, and many other graces, are found in the manners and conversation of the really elegant Russians, and more frequently, more completely, among those who have not traveled, but who, remaining in Russia, have nevertheless been in contact with distinguished foreigners.

These charms, these illusions, give them a sovereign power over hearts; so long as you remain in the presence of the privileged beings, you are under a spell; and the charm is double, for such is their triumph, that you imagine yourself to be to them what they are to you. Time and the world, engagements and affairs, are forgotten; the duties of society are abolished; one single interest remains—the interest of the moment; one single person survives—the person present, who is always the person liked. The desire of pleasing, carried to this excess, infallibly succeeds: it is the sublime of good taste; it is elegance the most refined, and yet as natural as an instinct. This supreme amiability is not assumed or artificial, it is a gift which needs only to be exercised; to prolong the illusion you have but to prolong your stay. The Russians are the best actors in the world: to produce an effect they need none of the accompaniments of scenery.

Every traveler has reproached them with their versatility; the reproach is but too well founded: you feel yourself forgotten in bidding them adieu. I attribute this, not only to levity of character, to inconstancy of heart, but also to the want of solid and extended information. They like you to leave them; for they fear lest they should be discovered when they allow themselves to be approached for too long a time uninterruptedly. Thence arises the fondness and the indifference which follow each other so rapidly among them. This apparent inconstancy is only a precaution of vanity, well understood and sufficiently common among people of the fashionable world in every land. It is not their faults that people conceal with the greatest care, it is their emptiness; they do not blush to be perverse, but they are humbled at being insignificant. In accordance with this principle, the Russians of the higher classes willingly exhibit everything in their minds and character likely to please at first sight, and which keeps up conversation for a few hours; but if you endeavor to go behind the decorated scene that thus dazzles you, they stop you as they would a rash intruder, who might take it into his head to go behind the screen of their bedchambers, of which the elegance is entirely confined to the outer side of the division.

They give you a reception dictated by curiosity; they after-wards repel you through prudence.

This applies to friendship as well as to love, to the society of men as well as to that of women. In giving the portrait of a Russian, we paint the nation, just as a soldier under arms con-veys the idea of all his regiment. Nowhere is the influence of unity in the government and in education so sensibly visible as here. Every mind wears a uniform. Alas! how greatly must those suffer, be they even no longer young and sensitive, who bring among this people—coldhearted and keen-witted both by nature and social education—the simplicity of other lands! I picture to myself the sensibility of the Germans, the confiding naïveté and the careless gaiety of the French, the constancy of the Spaniards, the passion of the English, the *abandon* and good nature of the true, the old Italians, all in the toils of the inherent Russian coquetry; and I pity the unfortunate foreigners who could believe for a moment they might become actors in the theater which awaits them here. In matters of the affections, the Russians are the gentlest wild beasts that are to be seen on earth; and their well-concealed claws unfortunately divest them of none of their charms. I have never felt a fascination to be compared to it, except in Polish society: a new relation, discoverable between the two families! Civil hate in vain strives to separate these people; nature reunites them in spite of themselves. If policy did not compel one to oppress the other, they would recognize and love each other. The Poles are chivalric and Catholic Rus-sians; with the further difference, that, in Poland, it is the women who form the life of society, or, in other words, who command, and that in Russia, it is the men.

These same people, so naturally amiable, so well endowed, so extremely agreeable, sometimes go astray in paths which men of the coarsest characters would avoid.

It is impossible to picture to oneself the life of many of the most distinguished young persons in Moscow. These men, who bear names, and belong to families known throughout Europe, are lost in excesses that will not bear to be described. It is inconceivable how they can resist for six months the system they adopt for life, and maintain with a constancy which would be worthy of heaven, if its object were virtuous. Their temperaments seem to be made expressly for the anticipated hell;—for it is thus that I qualify the life of a professed debauchee in Moscow.

In physical respects, the climate, and in moral respects, the government, of this land devour all that is weak in its germ: all that is not robust or stupid dies early, none survive but the debased, and natures strong in good as in evil. Russia is the land of unbridled passions or of passive characters, of rebels or of automata, of conspirators or of machines. There is here nothing intermediate between the tyrant and the slave, between the madman and the animal: the *juste milieu* is unknown; nature will not tolerate it; the excess of cold, like that of heat, pushes man to extremes.

Notwithstanding the contrasts which I here point out, all resemble each other in one respect—all have levity of character. Among these men of the moment, the projects of the evening are constantly lost in the forgetfulness of the morrow. It may be said that with them the heart is the empire of chance; nothing can stand against their propensity to embrace and to abandon. They live and die without perceiving the serious side of existence. Neither good nor evil seems in their eyes to possess any reality: they can cry, but they cannot be unhappy. Palaces, mountains, giants, sylphs, passions, solitude, brilliant crowds, supreme happiness, unbounded grief,—but it is useless to enumerate: a quarter of an hour's conversation with them suffices to bring before your eyes the whole universe. Their prompt and contemptuous glance surveys, without admiring, the monuments raised by human intelligence during centuries. They fancy they can place themselves above everything, because they despise everything. Their very praises are insults: they eulogize like people who envy; they prostrate themselves, but always unwillingly, before the objects they believe to be the idols of fashion. But at the first breath of wind, the cloud succeeds the picture, and soon the cloud vanishes in turn. Dust, smoke, and chaotic nothingness, are all that can issue from such inconsistent heads.

No plant takes root in a soil thus profoundly agitated. Everything is swept away; everything becomes leveled; all is wrapt in vapor. But from this fluid element nothing is finally expelled. Friendship or love that was imagined lost, will often again rise, evoked by a glance or a single word, and at the very moment when least thought of; though, in truth, it is only thus revived to be almost as quickly again dismissed. Under the ever-waving wand of these magicians, life is one continued phantasmagoria—one long fatiguing game, in which, however, the clumsy alone ruin themselves; for when all the world is cheating, nobody is being cheated: in a word, they are false as water, to use the poetical expression of Shakespeare, the broad strokes of whose pencil are the revelations of nature.

This explains to me why hitherto they have appeared to be doomed by Providence to a despotic government: it is in pity as much as through custom that they are tyrannized over.

If, in addressing myself to the friend to whom I send this chapter, I addressed myself to but one philosopher, here would be the place for inserting details of manners which resemble nothing that he has ever read of, even in France, where everything is written and described; but, behind him, I see the public, and this consideration stops me. My friend must therefore imagine what I do not relate; or, rather, to speak more correctly, that friend will never be able to imagine it. The excesses of despotism, which can alone give birth to the moral anarchy that here reigns around me, being only known by hearsay, their consequences would appear incredible. Where legitimate liberty is wanted, illegitimate liberty is sure to spring up; where the use is interdicted, the abuse will certainly creep in: deny the right, and you create the fraud: refuse justice, and you open the door to crime.

Under the influence of these principles, Moscow is, of all the cities in Europe, the one in which the dissolute man of the fashionable world has the widest field for his career. The government is too well informed not to know that under an absolute rule some kind of revolt must somewhere break out; but it prefers that this revolt should be in manners rather than in politics. Here lies the secret of the license of the one party and the tolerance of the other. The corruption of manners in Moscow has also other causes. One is, that the greater number of wellborn, but, by their conduct, ill-famed persons, retire when disgraced, and here establish themselves.

After the orgies which our modern literature takes pleasure in depicting, if we are to believe the authors, with a moral intention, we ought to be familiar with all the features of dissolute life. I pass over the question of the pretended utility of their aim; I can tolerate their long though useless sermons: but there is in literature something more dangerous even than the immoral; it is the ignoble. If, under the pretext of provoking salutary reforms in the lowest classes of society, the taste of the superior classes is corrupted, evil is done. To present to women the language of the pothouses, to make men of rank in love with coarse vulgarities, is to injure the manners of a nation in a way for which no legal reform can compensate. Literature is lost among us, because our most intellectual writers, forgetting all poetical sentiment, all respect for the beautiful, write for the taste of the town; and, instead of elevating their new readers to the views of delicate and noble minds, they lower themselves to the point of ministering to their coarsest appetites. They have rendered literature an ardent liquor, because, with sensibility, the faculty of tasting and feeling simple things is lost. This is a more serious evil than all the inconsistencies that have been noted in the laws and manners of the former state of society. It is another consequence of the modern materialism, which would reduce everything to the useful, and which can only discern the useful in immediate and positive results. Woe to the land where the men of genius lower themselves to play the part of commissioners of police! When an author feels himself called upon to describe vice he should at least redouble his respect for good taste; he should propose to himself the ideal truth for the type even of his most vulgar characters. But too often, under the professions of our moralist, or rather moralizing romance writers, we discover less love of virtue than cynic indifference to good taste. There is a want of poetry in their works, because there is a want of faith in their hearts. To ennoble the picture of vice, as Richardson has done in his Lovelace, is not to corrupt the mind, but to avoid soiling the imagination and lowering the tone of sentiment. Such respect for the delicacy of the reader has, if you like, a moral object; it is far more essential to civilized society than an exact knowledge of the turpitude of its bandits, and the virtues of its prostitutes. I must ask pardon for this excursion in the fields of contemporary criticism, and hasten to return to the strict and painful duties of the veracious traveler, duties that are unfortunately too often opposed to these laws of literary composition, which a respect for my language and my country has induced me to refer to.

The writings of our boldest painters of manners are but weak copies of the originals which have been daily presented to my eyes since I have been in Russia.

Bad faith injures everything, but more especially the affairs of commerce: here it has yet another sphere of action; it incommodes the libertines in the execution of their most secret contracts. The continual alterations of money, favor, in Moscow, every species of subterfuge; nothing is clear and precise in the mouth of a Russian, nothing is well defined or well guaranteed; and the purse always gains something by the slipperiness of the language. This extends even to amorous transactions: each party, knowing the duplicity of the other, requires payment in advance, whence much difficulty arises.

The female peasants are more cunning than even the women of the town. Sometimes these young and doubly corrupted savages violate the primary laws of prostitution, and escape with their booty, without paying the dishonorable debt they had contracted. The bandits of other lands observe their oaths, and maintain the good faith of comradeship in crime. The dissolute and abandoned in Russia know nothing that is sacred, not even the religion of debauchery, though it be a guarantee essential to the exercise of their profession, —so true is it that the commerce even of shame cannot be carried on without probity.

Civilization, which elsewhere elevates the mind, here perverts it. It had been better for the Russians had they remained savages:—to polish slaves is to betray society. It is needful that a man possess a basis of virtue to enable him to bear culture.

Under the influence of their government, the Russian people have become taciturn and deceitful, although naturally gentle, lively, docile, and pacific. Assuredly these are rare endowments; and yet, where there is a want of sincerity there is nothing. The Mongolian avidity of this race, and its incurable suspicion and distrust, are revealed by the least as well as the most important circumstances of life. Should you owe twenty rubles to a workman, he would return twenty times a day to ask for them, unless, at least, you were a dreaded nobleman. In Latin lands, a promise is a sacred thing—a pledge to the giver as well as the receiver. Among the Greeks, and their disciples the Russians, the word of a man is nothing better than the false key of a robber—it serves to break into the interests of others.

To make the sign of the cross in the streets before an image, and on sitting down to table, is all that the Greek religion teaches.

Intemperance is here carried to such excess, that one of the men, the most liked, and whose society is the most courted in Moscow, disappears every year for six weeks, neither more nor less. If it be asked what has become of him, the answer, "he is only gone to have a fuddling bout," satisfies everybody.

The Russians have too much levity to be vindictive; they are graceful debauchees. I take pleasure in repeating that they are supremely pleasant and agreeable; but their politeness, insinuating as it is, sometimes becomes exaggerated and fatiguing. This often makes me regret coarseness, which has at least the merit of being natural. The first law of politeness is to indulge only in praises that can be accepted; all others are insults. True politeness is nothing more than a code of flatteries well disguised. What is so flattering as cordiality? for, in order to manifest it, sympathy must first be felt.

If there are very polite persons among the Russians, some are also very impolite. The bad taste of these latter is shocking. They inquire, after the manner of savages, into things the most important, as well as into the most trifling bagatelles, without any modesty and with the utmost minuteness. They assail you with impertinent or puerile questions, and act at the same time as children and as spies. The Slavs are naturally inquisitive; and it is only good education, and the habits of the best society, that can repress their curiosity: those who have not these advantages never tire of putting you in the witness-box: they must know the objects and the results of your journey; they will ask boldly if you prefer Russia to other lands; if you think Moscow more beautiful than Paris; if the Winter Palace at Petersburg is finer than the Tuileries; if Krasnoye Selo is larger than Versailles: such interrogations are repeated unceasingly, and with each new individual to whom you are introduced you have to recommence the rehearsal of this catechism, in which national vanity hypocritically draws upon the urbanity of foreigners, and ventures its own rudeness in reliance upon the politeness of others.

I have been introduced to a person who was described to me as a singular character, worthy of observation. He is a young man of illustrious name, the Prince ———, only son of a very rich individual; this son spends twice his income, and treats his mind and body as he does his fortune. The tavern is his empire: it is there that he reigns eighteen hours out of the twenty-four; on that ignoble theater he displays, naturally and involuntarily, noble and elegant manners; his countenance is intellectual and extremely fascinating; his disposition is at once amiable and mischievous: many traits of rare liberality, and even of touching sensibility, are recounted of him.

Having had for his tutor a man of great talent, an old French abbé and émigré, he is remarkably well educated; his mind is quick and endowed with great capacity; his wit is unequaled in Moscow, but his language and conduct are such as would not be tolerated elsewhere: his charming though restless face betrays the contradiction that exists between his natural character and his course of life.

Profligacy has impressed upon his countenance the traces of a premature decay; still, these ravages of folly, not of time, have been unable to change the almost childish expression of his noble and regular features. Innate grace will last with life, and remain faithful to the man who possesses it, whatever effort he may make to throw it off. In no other land could a man be found like the young Prince ———, but there are more than one such here.

He is to be seen surrounded by a crowd of young men, his disciples and competitors, who, without equaling him either in disposition or in mind, all share with him a kind of family resemblance: it may be seen at the first glance that they are, and only can be, Russians. It is for this reason that I am about to give some details connected with their manner of life.

But already my pen falls from my hands; for it will be necessary to reveal the connection of these libertines, not with women of the town, but with the youthful sisters of religious orders,—with nuns, whose cloisters, as it will be seen, are not very securely guarded. I hesitate to relate facts which will too readily recall our revolutionary literature of 1793. I shall remind the reader of the Visitandines;—and why, he will ask, lift a corner of the veil that shrouds scenes of disorder which ought to remain carefully covered? Perhaps my passion for the truth obscures my judgment; but it seems to me that evil triumphs so long as it remains secret, whilst to publish it is to aid in destroying it; besides, I have resolved to draw a picture of this country as I see it,—not a composition, but an exact and complete copy from nature. My business is to represent things as they are, not as they ought to be. The only law that I impose on myself, under a sense of delicacy, is to forbear making any allusion to persons who desire to remain unknown. As for the man whom I select for a specimen of the most unbridled among the libertines of Moscow, he carries his contempt of opinion to the extent of desiring me to describe him as I see him. The truth of the several facts related by himself, which I cite, have been confirmed to me by others.

A story of the death of a young man, killed in the convent of ———, by the nuns themselves, he told me yesterday at a full table d'hôte, before several grave and elderly personages, employees and placemen, who listened with an extraordinary patience to this and several other tales of a similar kind, all very contrary to good manners.

I have surnamed this singular young man the Don Juan of the Old Testament, so greatly does the measure of his madness and audacity exceed the ordinary bounds of an abandoned life among modern nations. Nothing is little or moderate in Russia: if the land is not, as my Italian cicerone calls it, a land of miracles, it is truly a land of giants.

The story in question related to a young man, who, after having passed an entire month concealed within the convent of ———, began, at last, to weary of his excess of happiness to a degree that wearied the holy sisters also. He appeared dying: whereupon the nuns, wishing to be rid of him, but fearing the scandal that might ensue should they send him to die in the world, concluded that it would be better to make an end of him themselves. No sooner said than done:—the mangled remains of the wretched being were found a few days after at the bottom of a well. The affair was hushed up.

If we are to believe the same authorities, there are numerous convents in Moscow in which the rules of the cloister are little observed. One of the friends of the prince yesterday exhibited before me, to the whole legion of libertines, the rosary of a novice, which he said she had forgotten and left that very morning in his chamber. Another made a trophy of a Book of Prayers, which he stated had belonged to one of the sisters who was reputed among the most holy of the community of ———; and the audience warmly applauded.

I shall not go on. Each had his scandalous anecdote to relate, and all excited loud peals of laughter. Gaiety, ever increasing, soon became drunken riot under the influence of the wine of Ai, which overflowed in goblets, the size of which was more capable of satisfying Muscovite intemperance than our old-fashioned champagne glasses. In the midst of the general disorder, the young Prince ——— and myself alone preserved our reason,—he, because he can outdrink everybody, I, because I cannot drink at all, and had therefore abstained from attempting.

In the midst of the uproar, the Lovelace of the Kremlin rose with a solemn air, and, with the authority which his fortune, his name, his handsome face, and yet more, his superior mental capacity give him, he commanded silence, and to my great surprise obtained it. I could have fancied I was reading the poetical description of a tempest appeased by the voice of some pagan god. The young god proposed to the friends whom the gravity of his aspect had thus suddenly calmed, to indite a petition, addressed to the proper authorities, humbly remonstrating, in the name of the courtesans of Moscow, that the ancient religious institutions of nunneries so completely interfered with and rivaled their *lay community*, in the exercise of their calling, as to render that calling no longer profitable; and therefore respectfully stating that, as the expenses of these poor cyprians were not diminished in the same proportion as their gains, they ventured to hope an equitable consideration of their case would induce the authorities to see fit to deduct from a part of the revenue of the said convents, a pecuniary aid, which had become absolutely necessary, unless it was wished that the religious orders should entirely take the place of the civil recluses. The motion was put and carried with loud acclamations; ink and paper were called for; and the young madman immediately drew up, in very good French, and with magisterial dignity, a document too scandalously burlesque for me to insert here, though I have a copy. It was thrice read by the author before the meeting, with a loud emphatical voice, and was received with the most flattering marks of approbation.

Such was the scene, of which I have perhaps already recounted too much, that I witnessed yesterday in one of the best-frequented taverns of Moscow. It was the day after the agreeable dinner party in the pretty pavilion of ———. In vain is uniformity the law of the state: nature lives on variety, and knows how, at all costs, to obtain her wants.

I have spared the reader many details, and greatly moderated the expression of those which I have inflicted upon him. If I had been more exact, I should not be read. Montaigne, Rabelais, Shakespeare, and many other great describers, would chasten their style if they wrote in our age; how much more carefully, then, should they who have not the same right to independence watch over their words and allusions. The prudery of the present day, if not respectable, is at least formidable. Virtue blushes; but hypocrisy loudly exclaims.

The captain of the troop of debauchees, whose headquarters is the tavern before noticed, is endowed with so singular an elegance, his bearing is so distinguished, his person so agreeable, there is so much good taste even in his follies, so much kindly feeling painted on his countenance, so much nobleness in his manner, and even in his wildest language, that I pity more than I blame him. He rules from a high elevation the companions of his excesses; he has no appearance of being born for bad company; and it is impossible to avoid feeling a deep interest in him, although he is, in great part, responsible for the errors of his imitators. Superiority, even in evil, always exerts its influence.

He had engaged me today to accompany him on an excursion into the country, which was to occupy two days. But I have just been to find him in his usual retreat, in order to excuse myself. I pleaded the necessity of hastening my journey to Nizhny, and obtained my release. Before however leaving him to the course of folly which is dragging him onwards, I must describe the scene that was prepared for me in the court of the tavern, into which they obliged me to descend to view the decampment of this horde of libertines. The farewell was a true bacchanal.

Imagine a dozen young men already more than half drunk, loudly disputing with one another respecting their seats in three calèches, each drawn by four horses. A group of lookers-on, the tavern-keeper at their head, followed by all the servants of the house and stables, admired, envied, and ridiculed —although this last was done under the cloak of much outward reverence; meanwhile the leader of the band, standing up in his open carriage, played his part, and ruled, by voice and gesture, with unaffected gravity. There was placed at his feet a bucket, or rather a large tub, full of champagne bottles in ice. This species of portable cellar was the provision for the journey,—to refresh his throat, as he said, when the dust of the road was troublesome. One of his adjutants, whom he called the general of the corks, had already opened two or three bottles; and the young madman was dispensing huge goblets of the costly wine, the best champagne to be had in Moscow, to the bystanders, as a parting libation. Two cups, quickly emptied and incessantly replenished by his most zealous satellite, the general of the corks, were in his hands. He drank one, and offered the other to the nearest bystander. His servants were all clothed in grand livery, with the exception of the coachman, a young serf whom he had recently brought from his estates. This man was dressed in a most costly manner, far more remarkable in its apparent simplicity than the gold-lace trappings of the other servants. He had on a shirt of precious silken tissue, brought from Persia, and above it a caftan of the finest cashmere, bordered with beautiful velvet, which, opening at the breast, displayed the shirt, plaited in folds so small as to be scarcely perceptible. The dandies of Petersburg like the youngest and handsomest of their people to be thus dressed on days of ceremony. The rest of the costume corresponded with this luxury. The boots, of fine Torzhok leather, embroidered with flowers in gold and silver thread, glittered at the feet of the rustic, who seemed dazzled with his own splendor, and was so perfumed that I was almost overcome with the essences exhaled from his hair, beard, and clothes at the distance of several feet from the carriage.

After having drunk with the whole tavern, the young noble leant towards the man thus decked out, and presented him with a foaming cup, saying, "Drink." The poor, gilded muzhik was, in his inexperience, at a loss how to act. "Drink, I say," continued his master (this was translated to me); "drink, you rascal: it is not to you I give this champagne, but to your horses, who will not have strength to gallop the whole journey if the coachman is not drunk": upon which the whole assembly laughed and loudly cheered. The coachman was soon persuaded: he was already in the third bumper when his master gave the signal to start, which he did not do till he had renewed to me, with a charming politeness, his regret at having been unable to persuade me to accompany him on this party of pleasure. He appeared so distingué, that, while he spoke, I forgot the place and scene, and fancied myself at Versailles in the time of Louis XIV.

At last he departed for the château, where he is to spend three days. These gentlemen call such an excursion a summer *hunt*.

We may easily guess how they relieve themselves in the country from the ennui of town life—by continuing the same thing; by pursuing the same career; by reviving the scenes of Moscow, except, at least, that they introduce new *figurantes* upon the boards. They carry with them, in these journeys, cargoes of engravings of the most celebrated pictures of France and Italy, to furnish them with subjects for *tableaux vivants*, which they cause to be represented with certain modifications of costume.

The villages, and all that they contain, are their own; so that it may easily be supposed the privilege of the noblemen in Russia extends further than at the *opéra-comique* of Paris.

The ——— Tavern, open to all the world, is situated in one of the public squares of the city, a few steps only from a guard-house full of Cossacks, whose stiff bearing and severely gloomy air would impart to foreigners the idea of a country where no one dares to laugh even innocently.

As I have imposed upon myself the duty of communicating the ideas that I have formed of this land, I feel called upon to add to the picture already sketched, a few new specimens of the conversation of the parties already brought before the reader.

One boasted of himself and his brothers being the sons of the footmen and the coachmen of their reputed father; and he drank, and made the guests drink, to the health of all his unknown parents. Another claimed the honor of being brother (on the father's side) of all the maids of his mother.

Many of these vile boasts are no doubt made for the sake of talking: but to invent such infamies in order to glory in them, shows a corruption of mind that proves wickedness to the very core—wickedness worse even than that exhibited in the mad actions of these libertines.

According to them, the tradesmen's wives in Moscow are no better than the women of rank.

During the months that their husbands go to the fair of Nizhny, the officers of the garrison take special care not to leave the city. This is the season of easy assignations. The ladies are generally accompanied to the place of rendezvous by some *respectable* relation, to whose care their absent husbands have confided them. The goodwill and silence of these family duennas have also to be paid for. Gallantry of this kind cannot be excused as a love affair: there is no love without bashful modesty,—such is the sentence pronounced from all eternity against women who cheat themselves of happiness, and who degrade instead of purifying themselves by tenderness. The defenders of the Russians pretend that at Moscow the women have no lovers: I agree with them: some other term must be employed to designate the *friends* whose intimacy they seek in the absence of their husbands.

I repeat that I am disposed to doubt many things of this kind that are told to me; but I cannot doubt that they are related pleasantly and complacently to the first newly arrived foreigner; and the air of triumph in the narrator seems to say—We also, you see, are civilized!

The more I consider these debauchees' manner of life, the more I wonder at the social position—to use the language of the day—which they here preserve, notwithstanding conduct that in any other land would shut all doors against them. I cannot tell how such notorious offenders are treated in their own families; but I can testify that, in public, everyone pays them peculiar deference: their appearance is the signal for general hilarity; their company is the delight even of elderly men, who do not imitate them, but who certainly encourage them.

In observing the general reception which they receive, I ask myself what a person should here do to lose credit and character.

By a procedure altogether contrary to that observable among free people, whose manners become more puritanical, if not more pure, in proportion as democracy gains ground in the constitution, corruptness is here confounded with liberal institutions; and distinguished men of bad character are admired as is with us a talented opposition or minority. The young Prince ———— did not commence his career as a libertine until after finishing a three years' exile at the Caucasus, where the climate ruined his health. It was immediately after leaving school that he incurred this penalty for having broken the windowpanes of some shops in Petersburg. The government, having determined to see a political intention in this harmless riot, has, by its excessive severity, converted a hairbrained youth, while yet a child, into a profligate, lost to his country, his family, and himself. Such are the aberrations into which despotism—that most immoral of governments— can drive the minds of men.

Here all revolt appears legitimate; revolt even against reason and against God! Where order is oppressive, disorder has its martyrs. A Lovelace, a Don Juan, or yet worse if it were possible, would be viewed as a kind of liberator, merely because he had incurred legal punishments. The blame can only fall on the judge. People here avow their hatred of morals just as others would elsewhere say, "I detest arbitrary government."

I brought with me to Russia a preconceived opinion, which I possess no longer. I believed, with many others, that autocracy derived its chief strength from the equality which it caused to reign beneath it. But this equality is an illusion. I said, and heard it said, that when one man is all-powerful, the others are all equal, that is, all equally nullities; which equality, if not a happiness, is a consolation. The argument was too logical to prove practically true. There is no such thing as absolute power in the world; there are arbitrary and capricious powers; but, however outrageous they may become, they are never heavy enough to establish perfect equality among their subjects.

The Emperor Nicholas can do everything. But if he often did all that he could do, he would not retain this power very long. So long, therefore, as he forbears, the condition of the nobleman is very different from that of the muzhik or the tradesman whom he ruins. I maintain that there is at this day, in Russia, more real inequality in the conditions of men than in any other European land.

The circumstances of human societies are too complicated to be submitted to the rigor of mathematical calculation. I can see reigning under the emperor, among the castes which constitute his empire, hatreds which have their source solely in the abuses of secondary power.

In general, the men here use a very soft and specious language. They will tell you with the most benign air that the Russian serfs are the happiest peasants upon earth. Do not listen to them, they deceive you: many families of serfs in distant cantons suffer even from hunger; many perish under poverty and ill-treatment. In every class in Russia humanity suffers; and the men who are sold with the land suffer more than the others. It will be pretended that they are protected by a legal right to the necessaries of life; such right is but a mockery for those who have no means of enforcing it.

It will be further said that it is the interest of the nobles to relieve the wants of their peasants. But does every man always understand his interests? Among us, those who act foolishly lose their fortunes, and there is the end of it; but here, as the fortune of man consists in the life of a number of men, he who mismanages his property may cause whole villages to perish of famine. The government, when attracted by too glaring excesses, sometimes puts the unprincipled nobleman under guardianship; but this ever-tardy step does not restore the dead. The mass of sufferings and unknown iniquities that must be produced by such manners under such a constitution, with so great distances and so dreadful a climate, may be easily imagined. It is difficult to breathe freely in Russia when we think of all these miseries.

The nobleman has, in the government of his estates, the same difficulties to contend with, as regards the distances of places, the ignorance of facts, the influence of customs, and the intrigues of subalterns, that the emperor has in his wider sphere of action; but the nobleman has, in addition, temptations that are more difficult to resist; for being less exposed to public view, he is less controlled by public opinion and by the eye of Europe. From this firmly established order, or rather disorder of things, there result inequalities, caprices, and injustices, unknown to societies where the law alone can change the relations of society.

It is not correct, then, to say that the force of despotism lies in the equality of its victims; it lies only in the ignorance of liberty and in the fear of tyranny. The power of an absolute master is a monster ever ready to give birth to a yet greater— the tyranny of the people.

It is true that democratic anarchy never lasts; whilst the regularity produced by the abuses of autocracy are perpetuated from generation to generation.

Military discipline, applied to the government of a state, is the powerful means of oppression, which constitutes, far more than the fiction of equality, the absolute power of the Russian sovereign. But this formidable force will sometimes turn against those who employ it. Such are the evils which incessantly menace Russia,—popular anarchy carried to its most frightful excess, if the nation revolt, and the prolongation of tyranny, applied with more or less rigor according to times and circumstances, if she continue in her obedience.

Duly to appreciate the difficulties in the political position of this country, we must not forget that the more ignorant the people are, and the longer they have been patient, the more likely is their vengeance to be dreadful. A government which wields power by maintaining ignorance, is more terrible than stable: a feeling of uneasiness in the nation—a degraded brutality in the army—terror around the administration, a terror shared even by those who govern—servility in the church—hypocrisy in the nobility—ignorance and misery among the people—and Siberia for them all: such is the land as it has been made by necessity, history, nature, and a Providence ever impenetrable in its designs.

And it is with so decayed a body that this giant scarcely yet emerged out of Asia, endeavors now to influence by his weight the balance of European policy, and strives to rule in the councils of the West, without taking into account the progress that European diplomacy has made in sincerity during the last thirty years!

At Petersburg, to lie is still to perform the part of a good citizen; to speak the truth, even in apparently unimportant matters, is to conspire. You would lose the favor of the emperor, if you were to observe that he had a head cold.

But once for all, what is it that can have induced this badly armed colossus to come to fight, or at least to struggle, in the arena of ideas with which it does not sympathize—of interests which do not yet exist for it?

Simply the caprice of its masters, and the vainglory of a few traveled noblemen. Unlucky vanity of parvenus, which has enticed the government to run blindfold against difficulties that have caused modern communities to recoil backwards, and that have made them regret the era of political wars, the only wars known in former times!

This country is the martyr of an ambition which it scarcely understands; and, all wounded as it is, it strives to maintain a calm, imposing air. What a part has its head to sustain. To defend by continual artifices a glory built only upon fictions, or at least, on nothing more than hopes!

I leave tomorrow for Nizhny. Were I to prolong my stay in Moscow, I should not see this fair, which is drawing to a close. I shall not conclude the present chapter until after my return this evening from Petrovsky, where I am going to hear the Russian Gypsies.

I have been selecting a room in the hotel, which I shall continue to keep during my absence at Nizhny; having made it a hiding place for my papers: for I dare not venture on the road to Kazan with all that I have written since I left Petersburg; and I know no one here to whom I should like to confide these dangerous chapters. Exactness in the recital of facts, independence in the judgments formed, truth, in short, is more suspicious than anything else in Russia: it is truth which peoples Siberia, not, however, to the exclusion of robbery and murder, an association which frightfully aggravates the fate of political offenders.

I have returned from Petrovsky, where I saw the dancing-hall, which is beautiful; it is called, I believe, the Vauxhall. Before the opening of the ball, which appeared a dull affair, I was taken to hear the Russian Gypsies. Their wild and impassioned song has some distant resemblance to that of the Spanish gitanos. The melodies of the North are less lively, less voluptuous, than those of Andalusia, but they produce a more profoundly pensive impression. There are some which mean to be gay, but they are more melancholy than the others. The Gypsies of Moscow sing, without instruments, pieces which possess originality; but when the meaning of the words that accompany this expressive and national music is not understood, much of the effect is lost.

There is also at Moscow a French theater, where M.

Hervet, whose mother had a name in Paris, plays the parts of bouffe very naturally. I saw *Michel Perrin* given by this actor with a simplicity and a gusto which greatly pleased me. I am ignorant how far the Russians understand our theater: I do not put much faith in the pleasure which they appear to feel on seeing representations of French comedies; they have so fine a tact that they guess the fashion before it is proclaimed to them; this spares them the humiliation of owning that they follow it. The delicacy of their ear, and the varied inflections of the vowels, the multiplicity of the consonants, and the numerous hissing sounds in which they are exercised in speaking their own tongue, accustom them from infancy to master all the difficulties of pronunciation. Those, even, who only know a few words of French, pronounce them as we do. This often deceives us: we imagine that they understand our language as well as they speak it, which is a great error. The small number who have traveled, or have been born in a rank where education is necessarily carefully directed, alone understand the niceties of Parisian intellectual conversation. Our delicate strokes of wit are lost on the mass. We distrust other foreigners, because their accent of our language is disagreeable, and appears to us ridiculous; and yet, notwithstanding the labor with which they speak it, they understand us better and less superficially than the Russians, whose soft and imperceptible *cantilène* at first deceives us. As soon as they begin to talk carelessly, to relate a story, or to minutely describe a personal impression, the illusion ceases, and the deception is discovered. But they are the cleverest people in the world at concealing their deficiencies: in intimate society this diplomatic talent is wearisome.

A Russian showed me yesterday, in his cabinet, a little portable library, which struck me as a model of good taste. I approached the collection to open a volume the appearance of which had attracted me; it was an Arabic manuscript, bound in old parchment. "You are greatly to be envied; you understand Arabic?" I said to the master of the house. "No," he answered; "but I always have every kind of book around me: it sets off a room, you know."

Scarcely had this ingenuous confession escaped him than the involuntary expression of my face caused him to perceive that he had forgotten himself; whereupon, feeling very sure of my ignorance, he set about translating to me a few pretended passages of the manuscript, and did it with a volubility, a fluency, and an address, which would have deceived me, had not his previous dissimulation, and the embarrassment which he betrayed on my first perceiving it, put me on my guard. I clearly saw that he wished to obliterate the effect of his frank avowal, and to impress me with the idea, without his *actually stating it*, that in making such confession he had only been joking. The artifice, skillful as it was, failed in its object.

These are the childish stratagems of a people whose restless self-love urges them to a rivalry with the civilization of more ancient nations.

There is no kind of artifice or falsehood of which their devouring vanity is not capable, in the hope that we shall be induced to say, on returning to our several countries, "It is a great mistake to call those people the barbarians of the North." This appellation is never out of their heads; they remind strangers of it on every occasion with an ironical humility; and they do not perceive that their very susceptibility on the point furnishes their detractors with arms against them.

I have hired one of the carriages of the country to travel in to Nizhny, in order to save my own: it is a species of *tarantasse* on springs,* but scarcely more substantial than my calèche. This was the remark of a person who has just been

---

*The real *tarantasse* is the body of a calèche placed, without springs, on two shafts, which join together the axletrees of the front and hind wheels.

to aid me in expediting my departure. "You alarm me," I replied; "for I am tired of breaking down at every stage."

"For a long journey I should advise you to get another, if, at least, one could be found in Moscow at the present season: but the trip is so short that this will serve your purpose."

This short trip, including the return, and the detour that I propose making by Troitsa and Yaroslavl, is one of four hundred leagues, for one hundred and fifty of which, the roads are, I am told, detestable, abounding with logs and stumps of trees buried in the mud, deep sands full of loose stones, &c. &c. By the manner in which the Russians speak of distances, it is easy to perceive they inhabit a land large as Europe, and of which Siberia is a part.

One of the most attractive traits in their character, at least in my opinion, is their dislike to objections: they refuse to recognize either difficulties or obstacles.

The common people participate in this, it may be, a little gasconading humor, of the nobility. With his hatchet, which he never lays aside, a Russian peasant triumphs over accidents and predicaments that would altogether stop the villagers of our own provinces; and he answers, "yes," to everything that is demanded of him.

LETTER 29 *

ROADS IN THE INTERIOR. — FARMS AND COUNTRY MANSIONS.
— MONOTONY THE GREAT CHARACTERISTIC OF THE LAND. —
PASTORAL LIFE OF THE PEASANTS. — BEAUTY OF THE WOMEN
AND OLD MEN. — POLICY ATTRIBUTED TO THE POLES. — A NIGHT
AT THE CONVENT OF TROITSA. — PESTALOZZI ON PERSONAL
CLEANLINESS. — INTERIOR OF THE CONVENT. — PILGRIMS. —
TOMBS AND TREASURES. — INCONVENIENCES OF A JOURNEY IN
RUSSIA. — BAD QUALITY OF THE WATER. — WANT OF PROBITY A
NATIONAL CHARACTERISTIC.

IF WE ARE to believe the Russians, all their roads are good
during the summer season, even those that are not the great
highways. I find them all bad. A road full of inequalities,
sometimes as broad as a field, sometimes extremely narrow,
passes through beds of sand in which the horses plunge above
their knees, lose their wind, break their traces, and refuse
to draw at every twenty yards; if these sands are passed, you
soon plunge into pools of mud which conceal large stones and
enormous stumps of trees, that are very destructive to the
carriages. Such are the roads of this land, except during seasons when they become absolutely impassable, when the extreme of cold renders traveling dangerous, when storms of
snow bury the country, or when floods, produced by the thaw,
transform, for about three months in the year, the low plains
into lakes; namely, for about six weeks after the summer, and
for as many after the winter season; the rest of the year they
are marshes. The landscape remains the same. The villages

---

*Written at the convent of Troitsa, twenty leagues from Moscow, 17th of August.

still present the same double line of small wooden houses, more or less ornamented with painted carvings; their gable always faces the street, and they are flanked with a kind of enclosed court, or large shed open on one side. The country still continues the same monotonous though undulating plain, sometimes marshy, sometimes sandy; a few fields, wide pasture ranges bounded by forests of fir, now at a distance, now close upon the road, sometimes well grown, more frequently scattered and stunted: such is the aspect of all these vast regions. Here and there is to be seen a country house, or large and mansionlike farm, to which an avenue of birch trees forms the approach. These are the manor houses, or residences of the proprietors of the land; and the traveler welcomes them on the road as he would an oasis in the desert.

In some provinces the cottages are built of clay; in which case their appearance is more miserable, though still similar in general character: but from one end of the empire to the other, the greater number of the rustic dwellings are constructed of long and thick beams, carelessly hewn, but carefully caulked with moss and resin. The Crimea, a country altogether southern, is an exception; but, as compared to the whole empire, that country is but a point lost in immensity.

Monotony is the divinity of Russia; yet even this monotony has a certain charm for minds capable of enjoying solitude: the silence is profound in these unvarying scenes; and sometimes it becomes sublime on a desert plain, of which the only boundaries are our power of vision.

The distant forest, it is true, presents no variety: it is not beautiful: but who can fathom it? When we remember that its only boundary is the wall of China, we feel a kind of reverence. Nature, like music, draws a part of her potent charm from repetitions. Singular mystery!—by means of uniformity she multiplies impressions. In seeking for too much novelty and variety there is danger of finding only the insipid and the clumsy, as may be seen in the case of modern musicians devoid of genius;

but on the contrary, when the artist braves the danger of simplicity, art becomes as sublime as nature. The classic style—I use the word in its ancient acceptation—has little variety.

Pastoral life has always a peculiar charm. Its calm and regular occupations accord with the primitive character of men, and for a long time preserve the youth of races. The herdsmen, who never leave their native districts, are unquestionably the least unhappy of the Russians. Their beauty alone, which becomes more striking as I approach the government of Yaroslavl, speaks well of their mode of life.

I have met—which is a novelty to me in Russia—several extremely pretty peasant girls, with golden hair, excessively delicate and scarcely colored complexions, and eyes, which though of a light blue, are expressive, owing to their Asiatic form and their languishing glances. If these young virgins, with features similar to those of Greek Madonnas, had the *tournure* and the vivacity of movement observable in the Spanish women, they would be the most seductive creatures upon earth. Many of the females in this district are handsomely dressed. They wear over the petticoat a little habit or pelisse bordered with fur, which reaches to the knee, sits well to the shape, and imparts a grace to the whole person.

In no country have I seen so many beautiful bald heads and silver hairs as in this part of Russia. The heads of Jehovah, those chefs d'œuvre of the first pupil of Leonardo da Vinci, are not such entirely ideal conceptions as I imagined when I admired the frescoes of Luini at Lainate, Lugano, and Milan. These heads may be here recognized, living. Seated in the thresholds of their cabins, I have beheld old men, with fresh complexions, unwrinkled cheeks, blue, sparkling eyes, calm countenances, and silver beards glistening in the sun round mouths the peaceful and benevolent smile of which they heighten, who appear like so many protecting deities placed at the entrance of the villages. The traveler, as he passes, is saluted by these noble figures, majestically seated on the earth which saw them born. Truly antique statues, emblems of hospitality which a pagan would have worshiped, and which Christians must admire with an involuntary respect: for in old age beauty is no longer physical; it is the depicted triumph of the soul after victory.

We must go among the Russian peasants to find the pure image of patriarchal society; and to thank God for the happy existence he has dispensed, notwithstanding the faults of governments, to these inoffensive beings, whose birth and death are only separated by a long series of years of innocence.

May the angel, or demon of industry and of modern enlightened views, pardon me!—but I cannot help finding a great charm in ignorance, when I see its fruits in the celestial countenances of the old Russian peasants.

The modern patriarchs, laborers whose work is no longer a compulsory task, seat themselves, with dignity, towards the close of the day, in the threshold of the cottage which they themselves have, perhaps, rebuilt several times; for, under this severe climate, the house of man does not last so long as his life. Were I to carry back from my Russian journey no other recollection than that of these old men, with quiet consciences legible on their faces, leaning against doors that want no bolt, I should not regret the trouble I had taken to come and gaze upon beings so different from any other peasants in the world. The majesty of the cottage will always inspire me with profound respect.

Every fixed government, however bad it may be in some respects, has its good results; and every governed people have something wherewith to console themselves for the sacrifices they make to social life.

And yet, at the bottom of this calm which I so much admire, and which I feel so contagious, what disorder! what violence! what false security!

I had written thus much, when an individual of my acquaintance, in whose words I place confidence, having left Moscow a few hours after me, arrived at Troitsa, and, knowing that I was going to pass the night here, asked to see me while his horses were changing: he confirmed to me news that I had already heard, of eighty villages having been just burnt, in the government of Simbirsk, in consequence of the revolt of the peasants. The Russians attribute these troubles to the intrigues of the Poles. "What interest have the Poles in burning Russia?" I asked the person who related to me the fact. "None," he replied, "unless it be that they hope to draw upon themselves the wrath of the Russian government: their only fear is that they should be left in peace."

"You call to my recollection," I observed, "the band of incendiaries who, at the commencement of our first revolution, accused the aristocrats of burning their own châteaux." "You will not believe me," replied the Russian, "but I know, by close observation and by experience, that every time the Poles observe the emperor inclining towards clemency, they form new plots, send among us disguised emissaries, and even feign conspiracies when they cannot excite real ones; all of which they do solely with a view of drawing upon their country the hate of Russia, and of provoking new sentences for themselves and their countrymen: in fact, they dread nothing so much as pardon, because the gentleness of the Russian government would change the feelings of their peasants, who would soon be induced even to love the *enemy*."

"This appears to me heroical Machiavellism," I replied; "but I cannot believe in it. If it be true, why do you not pardon them in order to punish them? You would be then more adroit, as you are already more powerful, than they. But you hate them: and I am much inclined to believe that, to justify your rancor, you accuse the victims, and search, in every misfortune that happens to them, some pretext for laying your yoke more heavily upon adversaries whose ancient glory is an unpardonable crime; the more so, as it must be owned that Polish glory was not very modest."

"Not a whit more so than French glory," maliciously responded my friend, whom I had known in Paris: "but you judge unfairly of our policy, because you neither understand the Russians nor the Poles."

"This is always the burden of your countrymen's song whenever anyone ventures to tell them unpleasant truths. The Poles are easily known; they are always talking: I can trust in boasters better than in those who say nothing but what we do not care to know."

"You must, however, have a good deal of confidence in me!"

"In you, personally, I have; but when I recollect that you are a Russian, even though I have known you ten years, I reproach myself with my imprudence—I mean my candor."

"I foresee that you will give a bad account of us, on your return home."

"If I write, I perhaps may; but, as you say, I do not know the Russians, and I shall take care not to speak at random of so impenetrable a nation."

"That will be the best course for you to pursue."

"No doubt; but do not forget, that when once known to dissimulate, the most reserved men are appreciated as if already unmasked."

"You are too satirical and discriminating for barbarians such as we."

Whereupon my old friend re-entered his carriage, and went off at full gallop.

Troitsa is, after Kiev, the most famous and best-frequented place of pilgrimage in Russia. This historical monastery, situated twenty leagues from Moscow, was, I thought, of sufficient interest to allow of my losing a day, and passing a night there, in order to visit the sanctuaries revered by the Russian Christians.

To acquit myself of the task required a strong effort of reason: after such a night as the one I have passed, curiosity becomes extinguished, physical disgust overcomes every other feeling.

I had been assured at Moscow that I should find at Troitsa a very tolerable lodging. In fact, the building where strangers are accommodated, a kind of inn belonging to the convent, but situated beyond the sacred precinct, is a spacious structure, and contains chambers apparently very habitable. Nevertheless, I had scarcely retired to rest, when I found all my ordinary precautions inefficient. I had kept a candle burning as usual, and by its light I passed the night in making war with an army of vermin, black and brown, of every form, and, I believe, of every species. The death of one of them seemed to draw on me the vengeance of the whole race, who rushed upon the place where the blood had flowed, and drove me almost to desperation. "They only want wings to make this place hell," was the exclamation which escaped me in my rage. These insects are the legacy of the pilgrims who repair to Troitsa from every part of the empire; they multiply under the shelter of the shrine of St. Sergius, the founder of the famous convent. The benediction of Heaven seems to attend their increase, which proceeds in this sacred asylum at a ratio unknown elsewhere. Seeing the legions with which I had to combat, I lost all courage: my skin was burning, my blood boiled; I felt myself devoured by imperceptible enemies, and in my agony I fancied that I should prefer fighting an army of tigers to this small pest of beggars, and too often of saints; for extreme austerity sometimes marches hand in hand with filthiness—impious alliance! against which the real friends of God cannot protest sufficiently loudly.

I rose up, and found calm for a moment at the open window; but the scourge followed me—chairs, tables, ceiling, floor, walls, were teeming with life. My valet entered my room before the usual hour; he had suffered the same agonies, and even greater; for not wishing, nor being able to add to the size of our baggage, he has no bedstead, and places his *paillasse* on the floor, in preference to the sofas with all their accessories. If I dwell upon these inconveniences, it is because they form a just accompaniment to the boastings of the Russians, and serve to show the degree of civilization to which the people of this finest part of the empire have attained. On seeing poor Antonio enter the room, his eyes closed up and his face swollen, I had no need of inquiring the cause. Without uttering a word, he exhibited to me a cloak that had been blue the evening before, but was now become brown: after he had placed it on a chair, I perceived that it was moveable: at this sight, horror seized us both: air, water, fire, and all the elements were put in requisition; though in such a war victory itself is a loss. At length, purified and dressed, I made a shadow of a breakfast, and repaired to the convent, where another army of enemies awaited me: but this time, the light cavalry quartered in the folds of the Greek monks' gowns did not inspire me with the slightest fear; I had sustained the assaults of much more formidable combatants. After the battle of the night, the skirmishes of the day appeared to me a mere child's play: to speak without metaphor, the bites of bugs, and the dread of lice, had so hardened me against the attack of fleas, that I felt no more annoyance from the light clouds of these creatures that played at our feet in the churches of the convent, than I should have felt from the dust of the road. This past night has awakened all my feelings of pity for the unhappy Frenchmen who remained prisoners in Russia after the retreat from Moscow. Vermin, that inevitable product of poverty, is of all physical evils the one which inspires me with the deepest compassion. When I hear it said of a human being, he is in such wretchedness that he is dirty, my heart bleeds. Personal dirtiness is something viler even than it appears. It betrays, to the eyes of an attentive observer, a moral degradation worse than all bodily evils put together. This leprosy, for being to a certain extent voluntary, is only the more loathsome; it is a phenomenon which springs from our two natures; it embraces both the moral and the physical; it is the result of an infirmity of soul as well as of body; it is at once a vice and a malady.

I have often, in my travels, had reason to remember the sagacious observations of Pestalozzi, that great practical philosopher, the preceptor of the working classes before Fourier and the Saint-Simonians. According to his observations on the life of the lower orders, of two men who have the same habits of life, one will be dirty, the other clean. Personal cleanliness has as much to do with the health and the natural habit of body, as with the personal habits of the individual. Do we not often see among the better classes, people who take great pains with their persons, and who are yet very dirty? Among the Russians there reigns a high degree of sordid negligence: it seems to me they must have trained their vermin to survive the bath.

Notwithstanding my ill humor, I went carefully over the interior of the patriotic convent of the Trinity. It does not possess the imposing aspect of our old Gothic monasteries. The architecture is not the object that should bring people to a sacred place; yet if these famous sanctuaries were worth the trouble of being looked at, they would lose none of their sanctity, nor the pilgrims of their merits.

The convent stands on an eminence, and resembles a town surrounded with strong walls, mounted with battlements. Like the convents of Moscow, it has gilded spires and cupolas, which, shining in the evening sun, announce to the pilgrims, from afar, the end of their pious journey.

During the fine season, the surrounding roads are crowded with travelers, marching in procession. In the villages, groups of the faithful are to be seen eating and sleeping under the shade of the birch trees; and at every step, a peasant may be met walking in a species of sandal, made of the bark of the lime tree: a female often accompanies him, carrying his shoes in her hand, whilst with the other she shields herself with an umbrella from the rays of the sun, which the Muscovites dread in summer more than the inhabitants of the South. A kibitka, drawn by one horse, follows, and contains the sleeping appurtenances, and the utensils with which to prepare tea. The kibitka doubtless resembles the chariot of the ancient Sarmatians. This equipage is constructed with primitive simplicity; it consists of the half of a cask severed lengthways, and placed upon axles resembling the frame of a cannon.

The countrymen and women, who know how to sleep anywhere except in a bed, travel, stretched at their ease, in these light and picturesque vehicles: sometimes one of the pilgrims, watching over the sleepers, sits with his legs hanging over the edge of the kibitka, and lulls with national songs his dreaming comrades. In these dull and plaintive melodies, the sentiments of regret prevail over those of hope; their expression is melancholy, but never impassioned: everything is repressed, everything betrays prudence in this naturally light and cheerful people, rendered taciturn by education. If I did not view the fate of nations as written in heaven, I should say that the Slavs were born to people a more generous soil than the one on which they established themselves when they came forth from Asia, that great nursery of nations.

The first oppressor of the Russians was the climate. With every respect for Montesquieu, extreme cold appears to me more favorable to despotism than heat: the men, the freest perhaps on the face of the earth—are they not the Arabs? The rigors of nature inspire man with rudeness and cruelty.

On leaving the hostelry of the convent I crossed an open square, and entered the monastic walls. After passing under an alley of trees, I found myself among several little churches, surnamed cathedrals, with high steeples dividing them from one another; while numerous chapels, and ranges of dwellings, wherein are now lodged the disciples of St. Sergius, were scattered around without design or order.

All the names of note in Russian history have taken pleasure in enriching the convent, which overflows with gold, pearls, and diamonds. The universe has been placed under contribution to swell the pile of wealth that forms one of the miracles of the place, and which I contemplate with an astonishment more nearly approaching to stupefaction than to admiration. Czars, empresses, nobles, libertines, and true saints, have vied with one another in enriching the treasury of Troitsa. Amid so many riches, the simple dress and the wooden cup of St. Sergius shine by their very rusticity.

The tomb of the saint in the cathedral of the Trinity blazes with magnificence. The convent would have furnished a rich booty to the French; it has not been taken since the fourteenth century. It contains nine churches. The shrine is of silver gilt; it is protected by silver pillars and canopy, the gift of the Empress Anna. The image of St. Sergius is esteemed miraculous. Peter the Great carried it with him in his wars against Charles XII.

Not far from the shrine, under shelter of the virtues of the hermit, lies the body of the usurping assassin, Boris Godunov, surrounded by many of his family. The convent contains various other famous but shapeless tombs: they exhibit at once the infancy and the decrepitude of art. The house of the archimandrite and the palace of the czars present nothing of interest. The number of monks is now only one hundred; they were formerly thrice as many. Notwithstanding my persevering request, they would not show me the library. "It is forbidden" was always the answer. This modesty of the monks, who conceal the treasures of science, while they parade those of vanity, strikes me as singular. I argue from it that there is more dust on their books than on their jewels.

I am now at Dernitsky, a village between the small town of Pereslavl and Yaroslavl, the capital of the province of the same name.

It must be owned that it is a strange notion of enjoyment

which can induce a man to travel for his pleasure in a country where there are no highways, according to the application of the word in other parts of Europe,—no inns, no beds, no straw even to sleep upon,—for I am obliged to fill my mattress and that of my servant with hay,—no white bread, no wine, no drinkable water, not a landscape to gaze upon in the country,—not a work of art to study in the towns; where, in winter, the cheeks, nose, ears, and feet are in great danger of being frozen; where, in the dog days, you broil under the sun, and shiver at night. These are the amusements I am come to seek in the heart of Russia!

The water is unwholesome in nearly every part of the country. You will injure your health if you trust to the protestations of the inhabitants, or do not drink it without correcting it by effervescent powders. To be sure, you may obtain the luxury of seltzer water in the large towns; but the necessity of laying in stores of this foreign beverage, as provision for the road, is very inconvenient. The wine of the taverns, generally white and christened with the name of Sauterne, is scarce, dear, and of bad quality.

As for the scenery, there appears so little variety, that, as regards the habitations which alone enliven it, it may be said that there is but one village in all Russia. The distances are incommensurable, but the Russians diminish them by their rate of traveling: scarcely leaving their carriage until arrived at the place of their destination, they feel as though they had been in bed at home the whole length of the journey; and are astonished to find that we do not share their taste for this mode of traveling while sleeping, inherited by them from their Scythian ancestors. We must not believe, however, that their course is always equally rapid; these northern Gascons do not tell us of all their delays on the route. The coachmen drive fast when they are able, but they are often stopped by insurmountable difficulties.

Even on the road between Petersburg and Moscow, I found

that we proceeded at very unequal rates, and that at the end of the journey we had scarcely saved more time than is done in other countries. On other routes, the inconveniences are multiplied a hundredfold: the horses become scarce, the roads such as would destroy any vehicle; and the traveler asks himself, with a kind of shame, what could have been his motive for imposing upon himself so many discomforts, by coming to a country that has all the wildness, without any of the poetic grandeur of the desert. Such was the question I addressed to myself this evening, when benighted on a road, the difficulty of moving in which was greatly enhanced by a new unfinished *chaussée*, which crossed it at every fifty yards, and by tottering bridges, which had often lost the pieces of timber the most essential to their security.

My meditations at length determined me to halt, and, to the great annoyance of coachman and *Feldjäger*, I fixed on a lodging in the little house of some villagers, where I am now writing. This refuge is less disgusting than a real inn: no traveler stops in such a village; and the wood of the cabin serves as a refuge only to the insects brought from the forest. My chamber, a loft reached by a dozen steps, is nine or ten feet square, and six or seven high. The entire habitation is made of the trunks of fir trees, caulked with moss and pitch as carefully as if it were a boat. The same eternal smell of tar, cabbage, and perfumed leather, which, combined, pervades every Russian village, annoys me; but I prefer headache to mental distress, and find this bedchamber far more comfortable than the large plastered hall of the inn at Troitsa. I have fixed in it my iron bedstead: the peasants sleep, wrapped in their sheepskins, on the seats ranged round the room on the ground floor. Antonio makes his bed in the coach, which is guarded by him and the *Feldjäger*. Men are pretty safe on Russian highways, but equipages and all their appurtenances are viewed as lawful prizes by the Slavic serfs; and, without extreme vigilance, I should find my calèche in the morning, stripped of cover, braces, curtains, and apron; in short, transformed into a primitive *tarantasse*, a real telega; and not a soul in the village would have any idea what had become of the leather: or if, by means of rigid searches, it should be found at the bottom of some shed, the thief, by stating that he had found it and brought it there, would be acquitted. This is the standing defense in Russia: theft is rooted in the habits of the people, and consequently, the robber preserves an easy conscience and a serene face that would deceive the very angels. "Our Savior would have stolen," they say, "if his hands had not been pierced." This is one of their most common adages.

Nor is robbery the vice alone of the peasants: there are as many kinds of theft as there are orders in society. The governor of a province knows that he is constantly in danger of something occurring that may send him to finish his days in Siberia. If, during the time that he continues in office, he has the cleverness to steal enough to defend himself in the legal process which would precede his exile, he may get out of the difficulty; but if he continue poor and honest, he must be ruined. This is not my own remark, but that of several Russians whom I may not name, but whom I believe to be trustworthy.

The commissaries of the army rob the soldiers, and amass wealth by starving them: in short, an honest administration would be here both dangerous and ridiculous.

I hope tomorrow to reach Yaroslavl: it is a central city; and I shall stop there a day or two, in order to discover, in the interior of the country, real original Russians. I took care, with this intention, to procure several letters of introduction to that capital of one of the most interesting and important provinces of the empire.

LETTER 30

THE PREDICTION made to me at Moscow is already accomplished, although I have yet scarcely completed a quarter of my journey. I have reached Yaroslavl in a carriage, not one part of which is undamaged. It is to be mended, but I doubt whether it will carry me through.

Summer has now vanished,* not to return until the next year. A cold rain, which they here consider as proper to the season, has driven away the dog days entirely. I am so accustomed to the inconveniences of the heat, to dust, flies, and mosquitoes, that I can scarcely realize the idea of my deliverance from these scourges.

The city of Yaroslavl is an important entrepôt for the interior commerce of Russia. By it, Petersburg communicates

---

*Written 18th of August.

with Persia, the Caspian, and all Asia. The Volga, that great national and moving road, flows by the city, which is the central point of the interior navigation of the country—a navigation wisely directed, much boasted of by the subjects of the czar, and one of the principal sources of their prosperity. It is with the Volga that the immense ramifications of canals are connected, that create the wealth of Russia.

The city, like all the other provincial cities in the empire, is vast in extent, and appears empty. The streets are immensely broad, the squares very spacious, and the houses in general stand far apart. The same style of architecture reigns from one end of the country to the other. The following dialogue will show the value the Russians place on their pretended classic edifices.

A man of intelligence said to me, at Moscow, that he had seen nothing in Italy which appeared new to him.

"Do you speak seriously?" I asked.

"Quite seriously," he replied.

"It seems to me impossible," I responded, "that anyone could descend for the first time the southern side of the Alps, without the aspect of the land producing a revolution in his mind."

"In what manner?" said the Russian, with that disdainful tone and air which here too often pass for a proof of civilization.

"What!" I replied, "the novelty of those landscapes adorned by art, those hills and slopes, where palaces, convents, and villages stand surrounded with vines, mulberries, and olives, those long ranges of white pillars, which support festoons of vines, and which carry the wonders of architecture into the recesses of the steepest mountains,—all that magnificent scenery, which gives the idea of a park laid out by Lenôtre for the pleasure of princes, rather than of a land cultivated in order to yield the laborer his daily bread; all those creations of man applied to embellish the creations of

God,—is it possible that they did not appear to you as something new?"

"How," interrupted the impatient Russian,—"how can you expect us inhabitants of Petersburg and Moscow to be astonished, as you are, with Italian architecture? Do you not see models of it at every step you take in even the smallest of our towns and cities?"

This explosion of national vanity silenced me: I was at Moscow; an inclination to laugh was rising within me, but it would have been dangerous to have given way to it. The argument of my adversary was the same as though a person were to refuse to look upon the Apollo Belvedere because he had elsewhere seen plaster-of-Paris casts of it. The influence of the Mongols survives their conquests among the Russians. Was it, then, to imitate them that they drove them out? Detractors make little progress, either in the arts or in general civilization. The Russians observe with malevolence because they lack the perception of perfection: so long as they envy their models they will never equal them. Their empire is immense, but what of that: who would admire the colossus of an ape?

Such were the angry thoughts that rose in my mind, but of which I suppressed the outward expression, although I believe my disdainful opponent read them on my face, for he did not speak to me anymore, unless it was to add, with a nonchalant air, that he had seen olives in the Crimea, and mulberry trees at Kiev.

For my own part, I congratulate myself that I am only come to Russia for a short time; a long stay in this land might rob me not only of the courage, but of the desire, to say the truth, in answer to things that I hear and see. Despotism discourages and casts a spell of indifference even over minds that are the most determined to struggle against its glaring abuses.

Disdain for things that they do not know, appears to me a dominant trait in the character of the Russians. Instead of endeavoring to comprehend, they endeavor to ridicule. If they ever succeed in bringing to full light their real genius, the world will see, not without some surprise, that it is a genius for caricature. Since I have studied the Russian character, and traveled in this last of the states written in the great book of European history, I have discovered that the talent for ridicule possessed by the parvenu, may become the dowry of an entire nation.

The painted and gilded towers, almost as numerous as the houses of Yaroslavl, shine at a distance like those of Moscow, but the city is less picturesque than the old capital of the empire. It is protected on the banks of the Volga by a raised terrace, planted with trees; under it, as under a bridge, the road passes, by which merchandise is carried to and from the river. Notwithstanding its commercial importance, the city is empty, dull, and silent. From the height of the terrace is to be seen the yet more empty, dull, and silent surrounding country, with the immense river its hue a somber iron-gray, its banks falling straight upon the water, and forming, at their top, a level with the leaden-tinted plain, here and there dotted with forests of birch and pine. This soil is, however, as well cultivated as it is capable of becoming; it is boasted of by the Russians as being, with the exception of the Crimea, the richest and most smiling tract in their empire.

Byzantine edifices ought to be the models of the national architecture in Russia. Cities full of structures adapted to their location should animate the banks of the Volga. The interior arrangements of the Russian habitations are rational; their exterior, and the general plan of the towns, are not so. Yaroslavl has its columns and its triumphal arches in imitation of Petersburg, all of which are in the worst taste, and contrast, in the oddest manner, with the style of the churches and steeples. The nearer I approached this city, the more was I struck with the beauty of the population. The villages are rich and well built: I have seen a few stone houses, though too limited in number to vary the monotony of the view.

The Volga is the Loire of Russia; but instead of the gaily smiling hills of Touraine, crowned with the fairest castles of the Middle Ages, we here find only flat unvaried banks, with plains, where the small, gray, mean-looking houses, ranged in lines like tents, sadden rather than animate the landscape; such is the land that the Russians commend to our admiration.

In walking along the borders of the Volga, I had to struggle against the wind of the north, omnipotent in this country throughout the year; for three months of which it sweeps the dust before it, and for the remaining nine, the snow. This evening, in the intervals of the blast, the distant songs of the boatmen upon the river caught my ear. The nasal tones, that so much injure the effect of the national songs of the Russians, were lost in the distance, and I heard only a vague plaintive strain, of which my heart could guess the words. Upon a long float of timber, which they guided skillfully, several men were descending the course of their native Volga. On reaching Yaroslavl, they wished to land; and when I saw them moor their raft, I stopped. They passed close before me, without taking any notice of my foreign appearance; without even speaking to each other. The Russian peasants are taciturn and devoid of curiosity; I can understand why: what they know, disgusts them with all of which they are ignorant.

Melancholy, disguised by irony, is in this land the most ordinary humor of mind; in the salons especially. There, more than elsewhere, it is necessary to dissimulate sadness; hence the sneering sarcastic tone of language, and those efforts in conversation, painful both to the speaker and the listener. The common people drown their sadness in silent intoxication; the lords, in noisy drunkenness. The same vice assumes a different form in the master and the slave. The former has yet another resource against ennui—ambition, that intoxication of the mind. Among all classes, there reigns an innate elegance, a natural refinement, which is neither barbarism nor civilization; not even their affectation can deprive them of this primitive advantage.

They are, however, deficient in a much more essential quality—the faculty of loving. In ordinary affairs, the Russians want kindheartedness; in great affairs, good faith: a graceful egotism, a polite indifference, are the most conspicuous traits in their intercourse with others. This want of heart prevails among all classes, and betrays itself under various forms, according to the rank of the individuals; but the principle is the same in all. The faculty of being easily affected and tenderly attached, so rare among the Russians, is a ruling characteristic of the Germans, who call it *Gemüth*. We should call it expansive sensibility, or cordiality, if we had any need of defining a feeling which is scarcely more common among us than among the Russians. But the refined and ingenuous French *plaisanterie* is here replaced by a malignantly prying, hostile, closely observing, caustic, satirical, and envious spirit, which appears to me infinitely more objectionable than our jesting frivolity. Here, the rigor of the climate, the severity of the government, and the habit of espionage, render characters melancholy, and self-love distrustful. Somebody, or something, is always feared; and, what is worse, not without cause. This is not avowed, yet it cannot be concealed from a traveler accustomed to observe and compare different nations.

To a certain point, the want of a charitable disposition in the Russians towards strangers appears to me excusable. Before knowing us, they lavish their attentions upon us with apparent eagerness, because they are hospitable like the Orientals; but they are also easily wearied like the Europeans. In welcoming us with a forwardness which has more ostentation than cordiality, they scrutinize our slightest words, they submit our most insignificant actions to a critical examination; and as such work necessarily furnishes them with much subject for blame, they triumph internally, saying,

"These, then, are the people who think themselves so superior to us!"

This kind of study suits their quickly discerning, rather than sensitive nature. Such a disposition neither excludes a certain politeness, nor a species of grace; but it is the very opposite of true amiability. Perhaps, with care and time, one might succeed in inspiring them with some confidence; nevertheless, I doubt whether all my efforts could achieve this; for the Russians are the most unimpressible, and, at the same time, the most impenetrable people in the world.

What have they done to aid the march of human mind? They have not hitherto produced either philosophers, moralists, legislators, or literati whose names belong to history; but, truly, they have never wanted, and never will want, good diplomatists, clever politic heads; and it is the same with their inferior classes, among whom there are no inventive mechanics, but abundance of excellent workmen.

I am leading the reader into a labyrinth of contradictions, that is, I am showing the things of this world as they have appeared to me at the first and at the second view. I must leave to him the task of so reviewing and arranging my remarks as to be able to draw from them a general opinion. My ambition will be satisfied, if a comparing of, and selecting from, this crowded collection of precipitate and carelessly hazarded judgments, will allow any solid, impartial, and ripe conclusions to be drawn. I have not attempted to draw them, because I prefer traveling to composing: an author is not independent, a traveler is. I therefore record my impressions, and leave the reader to complete the book.

The above reflections on the Russian character have been suggested by several visits that I have made in Yaroslavl. I consider this central point as one of the most interesting in my journey.

I will relate tomorrow the result of my visit to the chief personage of the place, the governor, for I have just sent him my letter. I have been told, or rather given to infer, much to his disparagement, in the various houses that I have visited this morning.

I am writing in a wretched inn; there are but two good ones in Russia, and they are kept by foreigners; the English boardinghouse at St. Petersburg, and that of Madame Howard at Moscow, are those to which I refer. In the houses even of independent private people, I cannot seat myself without trembling.

I have seen several public baths, both at Petersburg and Moscow. The people bathe in different ways: some enter chambers heated to a temperature that appears to me unbearable; the penetrating vapor of these stews is absolutely suffocating. In other chambers, naked men, standing upon heated floors, are soaped and washed by others also naked. The people of taste have their own bathtubs, as in other places: but so many individuals resort to the public establishments, the warm humidity there is so favorable to insect life, the clothes laid down in them are nurseries of so many vermin, that the visitor rarely departs without carrying with him some irrefragable proof of the sordid negligence of the lower orders.

Before cleansing their own persons, those who make use of the public baths ought to insist on the cleansing out of these dens where the old Muscovites revel in their dirtiness, and hasten old age by the inordinate use of steam, and by the perspiration it provokes.

It is now ten o'clock in the evening. The governor has sent to inform me that his son and his carriage will presently call for me. I have answered, with many thanks, that having retired for the night, I cannot this evening avail myself of his kindness; but that I shall pass the whole of the morrow at Yaroslavl, and shall then make my acknowledgments in person. I am not sorry to have this opportunity of observing Russian hospitality in the provinces.

This morning, about eleven, the governor's son, who is a mere child, arrived in full uniform, to take me in a carriage-and-four, with coachman, and *faleiter* mounted on the off-side horse, an equipage precisely similar to that of the courtiers at Petersburg. This elegant apparition at the door of my inn disappointed me; I saw at once that it was not with old Muscovites, true boyars, that I had to do. I felt that I should be again among European travelers, courtiers of the Emperor Alexander, and lordly cosmopolites.

"My father knows Paris," said the young man; "he will be delighted to see a Frenchman."

"At what period was he in France?"

The young Russian was silent; my question appeared to disconcert him, although I had thought it a very simple one: at first I was unable to account for his embarrassment; after discovering its cause, I gave him credit for an exquisite delicacy,—a rare sentiment in every country and at every age.

M. ———, governor of Yaroslavl, had visited France, in the suite of the Emperor Alexander, during the campaigns of 1813 and 1814, and this was a reminiscence of which his son was unwilling to remind me. His tact recalled to my memory a very different trait. One day, in a small town of Germany, I dined with the envoy of a petty German government, who, in presenting me to his wife, said that I was a Frenchman.

"He's an enemy, then," interrupted their son, a boy of apparently thirteen or fourteen years old.

That young gentleman had not been sent to school in Russia.

On entering the spacious and brilliant reception room, where the governor, his lady, and their numerous family awaited me, I could have imagined myself in London, or rather in Petersburg; for the lady of the house was ensconced, *à la russe*, in the little bower enclosed by gilded trellis, and raised a few steps, which occupied a corner of the salon, and which is called the *altane*. The governor received me with politeness, and led me across the room, past several male and female relatives who had met there, into the verdant cabinet, where I found his wife.

Scarcely had she invited me to sit down in this sanctuary when she thus addressed me: "Monsieur de Custine, does Elzéar still write fables?"

My uncle, Count Elzéar de Sabran, had been from his boyhood celebrated in the society of Versailles for his poetical talent, and he would have been equally so in public society if his friends and relations could have persuaded him to publish his collection of fables—a species of poetical code, enlarged by time and experience; for every circumstance of his life, every public and private event, has inspired him with one of these apologues, always ingenious, and often profound, and to which an elegant and easy versification, an original and piquant turn of expression, impart a peculiar charm. The recollection of this was far from my thoughts when I entered the house of the governor of Yaroslavl, for my mind was occupied with the hope, too rarely satisfied, of finding real Russians in Russia.

I replied to the lady of the governor by a smile of astonishment, which silently said—explain to me this mystery. The explanation was soon given. "I was brought up," said the lady, "by a friend of your grandmother, Madame de Sabran; that friend has often spoken to me of her natural grace and charming wit, as well as of the mind and talents of your uncle and your mother; she has often even spoken to me of you, though she had left France before your birth. It is Madame ——— to whom I allude; she accompanied into Russia the Polignac family when they became émigrés, and since the death of the Duchess de Polignac she has never left me."

In concluding these words Madame ——— presented me to her governess, an elderly person, who spoke French better

Astolphe de Custine

than I, and whose countenance expressed penetration and gentleness.

I saw that I must once again renounce my dream of the boyars; a dream, which, notwithstanding its futility, did not leave me without awaking some regret; but I had wherewith to indemnify myself for my mistake. Madame ———, the wife of the governor, belongs to one of the great families of Lithuania; she was born Princess ———. Over and above the politeness common to nearly all people of her rank in every land, she has acquired the taste and the tone of French society, as it existed in its most flourishing epoch; and, although yet young, she reminds me, by the noble simplicity of her manners, of the elderly persons whom I knew in my childhood. Those manners are the traditions of the old court; respect for every kind of propriety, good taste in its highest perfection, for it includes even good and kindly dispositions; in short, everything that was attractive in the higher circles of Paris at the time when our social superiority was denied by none; at the time when Madame de Marsan, limiting herself to a humble pension, retired voluntarily to a small apartment in the convent of the Assumption, and for ten years devoted her immense income to paying the debts of her brother the Prince de Guémenée,—by this noble sacrifice extenuating, as far as was in her power, the disgrace and scandal of a bankrupt nobleman.

All this will teach me nothing about the country I am inspecting, I thought to myself; nevertheless it will afford me a pleasure that I should be loath to deny myself, for it is one that has now become more rare, perhaps, than is the satisfaction of the simple curiosity which brought me here.

I fancied myself in the chamber of my grandmother,* though, indeed, on a day when the Chevalier de Boufflers was

*The Countess de Sabran, afterwards Marchioness de Boufflers, who died at Paris in 1827, aged seventy-eight years.

not there, nor Madame de Coislin, nor even the lady of the house: for those brilliant models of the character of intellect which formerly adorned French conversation have gone, never to return, even in Russia; but I found myself in the chosen circle of their friends and disciples, assembled, as it were, in their absence; and I felt as though we were waiting for them, and that they would soon reappear.

I was not in the least prepared for this species of emotion: of all the surprises of my journey it has been for me the most unexpected.

The lady of the house participated in my astonishment; for she told me of the exclamation she had made the previous evening, on perceiving my name at the bottom of the note I had sent to the governor. The singularity of the rencounter, in a region where I supposed myself as little known as a Chinese, immediately gave a familiar and friendly tone to the conversation, which became general, without ceasing to be agreeable and easy. There was nothing concerted or affected in the pleasure they seemed to take in seeing me. The surprise had been reciprocal: no one had expected me at Yaroslavl; I had only decided to take that route the day before leaving Moscow.

The brother of the governor's wife, a Prince ———, writes our language perfectly well. He has published volumes of French verses, and was kind enough to present me with one of his collections.

Assuredly, he is fortunate who expresses his idea so well in a foreign language.

All the members of the ——— family vied with one another in doing me the honors of the house and of the city.

My books were lauded with indirect and ingenious praises, and were cited so as to recall to my mind a crowd of details that I had forgotten. The delicate and natural manner in which these quotations were introduced would have pleased me if they had less flattered me. The small number of books which the censorship allows to penetrate so far, remain popular a long time. I may say, not in my own personal praise, but in that of the times in which we live, that, in traveling over Europe, the only hospitality really worthy of gratitude which I have received has been that which I owe to my writings. They have created for me among strangers a small number of friends, whose kindness, ever new, has in no slight degree contributed to prolong my inborn taste for traveling and for poetry. If a position of so little importance as the one which I occupy in our literature has procured me such advantages, it is easy to conceive the influence which the talents that among us rule the thinking world, must exercise.

The wife of the governor of Yaroslavl has, at this moment, all her family united around her; several of her sisters, with their husbands and children, are lodged in her house; she admits likewise to her table the principal employees of her husband, who are inhabitants of the city; her son also is still attended by a tutor; so that at dinner there were twenty persons to sit down to table.

It is the custom of the North to precede the principal repast by a smaller refection, which is served in the drawing room a quarter of an hour before entering the dining room. This preliminary, which is destined to sharpen the appetite, is called in Russian, if my ear has not deceived me, *zakuska*. The servants bring upon trays, small plates filled with fresh caviar, such as is only eaten in this country, dried fish, cheese, salt meats, sea biscuits, and pastry; with these, bitter liqueurs, French brandy, London port, Hungarian wine, true Danzig Goldwasser, are also brought in; to which the company help themselves standing. A stranger, ignorant of the usages of the country, or an appetite easily satisfied, might very soon here make a meal, and remain afterwards a spectator only of the real dinner. The Russians eat plentifully, and keep a liberal table; but they are too fond of hashes, stuffing, little balls of mincemeat, and fish pâtés.

One of the most delicate fishes in the world is caught in the Volga, where it abounds. It is called the sterlet, and unites the flavor of the sea and freshwater fishes, without, however, resembling any that I have eaten elsewhere. This fish is large, its flesh light and fine; its head, pointed and full of cartilages, is considered delicate; the monster is seasoned very skillfully, but without many spices: the sauce that is served with it unites the flavor of wine, strong meat broth, and lemon juice. I prefer this national dish to all the other ragouts of the land, and especially to the cold and sour soup, that species of fish broth, iced, that forms the detestable treat of the Russians. They also make soups of sugared vinegar, of which I have tasted enough to prevent my ever asking for any more.

The governor's dinner was good and well served, without superfluity, and without useless recherché. The abundance and excellent quality of the watermelons astonish me: it is said that they come from the environs of Moscow, but I should rather imagine they send to the Crimea for them. It is the custom in this country to place the dessert upon the table at the commencement of the dinner, and to serve it course by course. This method has its advantages, and its inconveniences: it seems to me only perfectly proper at great dinners.

The Russian dinners are of a reasonable length; and nearly all the guests disperse upon rising from table. Some practice the Oriental habit of the siesta; others take a walk or return to their business after drinking coffee. Dinner is not here the repast which finishes the labors of the day; and when I took leave of the lady of the house, she had the kindness to engage me to return and pass the evening with her. I accepted the invitation, for I felt it would be impolite to refuse it: all that is offered to me here is done with so much good taste, that neither my fatigue nor my wish to retire and write to my friends, is sufficient to preserve my liberty: such hospitality is a pleasant tyranny; it would be indelicate not to accept it; a carriage-and-four and a house are placed at my disposal, a whole family are troubling themselves to amuse me and to show me the country; and this is done without any affected compliments, superfluous protestations, or importunate *empressement*; I do not know how to resist so much rare simplicity, grace, and elegance; I should yield were it only from a patriotic instinct, for there is in these agreeable manners a souvenir of ancient France which affects and attracts me: it seems as though I had come to the frontiers of the civilized world to reap a part of the heritage of the French spirit of the eighteenth century, a spirit that has been long lost among ourselves. The inexpressible charm of good manners, and of simple language, reminds me of a paradox of one of the most intellectual men I have ever known: "There is not," he says, "a bad action nor a bad sentiment that has not its source in a fault of manners; consequently, true politeness is virtue; it is all the virtues united." He goes yet further; he pretends there is no other vice but that of coarseness.

At nine o'clock this evening, I returned to the house of the governor. We had first music, and afterwards a lottery.

One of the brothers of the lady of the house plays the violoncello in a charming manner; he was accompanied on the piano by his wife, a very agreeable woman. This duet, as well as many national airs, sung with taste, made the evening pass rapidly.

The conversation of Madame de ———, the old friend of my grandmother and of Madame de Polignac, contributed in no slight degree to shorten it. The lady has lived in Russia for forty-seven years; she has viewed and judged the country with discernment and justice, and she states the truth without hostility, and yet without rhetorical precautions: this is new to me; her frankness strangely contrasts with the universal dissimulation practiced by the Russians. An intelligent Frenchwoman, who has passed her life among them, ought, I think, to know them better than they know themselves; for they blind themselves in order the better to impose falsehood upon others. Madame de ——— said and repeated to me, that in this country the sentiment of honor is without power, except in the heart of the women: they have made it a matter of religion to be faithful to their word, to despise falsehood, to observe delicacy in money affairs, and independence in politics; in short, according to Madame de ———, the greater number of them possess what is wanted in the great majority of the men—probity in all the circumstances of life, whether of greater or less importance. In general, the Russian women think more than the men, because they act less. Leisure, that advantage inherent in a woman's mode of life, is as advantageous to their character as to their understanding; they are better informed, less servile, and possess more energy of sentiment than the other sex. Heroism itself appears to them natural, and becomes easy. The Princess Troubetzkoy is not the only woman who has followed her husband to Siberia: many exiled men have received from their wives this sublime proof of devotion, which loses none of its value for being less rare than I imagined it: unfortunately, I do not know their names. Where will they find a historian and a poet?

Towards the close of the evening, before permitting me to leave, my hosts, with the view of paying me a compliment, expedited, by several days, a ceremony which had been looked forward to for six months in the family: it was the drawing of a lottery, the object of which was charity. All the prizes, consisting of articles made by the lady of the house, her friends and relatives, were tastefully spread upon the tables: the one which fell to me, I cannot say by chance (for my tickets had been carefully selected), was a pretty notebook with a varnished cover. I wrote in it the date, and added a few words by way of remembrance. In the times of our fathers, an impromptu in verse would have been suggested; but, in these days, when public impromptus abound ad nauseam, those of the salon are out of date. Ephemeral literature, politics, and philosophy, have dethroned the quatrain and the sonnet. I had not the ready wit to write a single couplet; but I should, in justice, add, that neither did I feel the ambition.

After bidding farewell to my amiable hosts, whom I am to meet again at the fair of Nizhny, I returned to my inn, very well satisfied with the day. The house of the peasant in which I lodged the day before yesterday, and the salon of today, in other words, Kamchatka and Versailles within a distance traversed in a few hours, present a contrast which describes Russia.

I sacrifice my nights to relate to my friends the objects that strike me during the day. My chapter is not finished, and dawn already appears.

The contrasts in this empire are abrupt; so much so, that the peasant and the lord do not seem to belong to the same land: the grandees are as cultivated as if they lived in another country; the serfs are as ignorant and savage as though they served under lords like themselves.

It is much less with the abuses of aristocracy that I reproach the Russian government, than with the absence of an authorized aristocratic power whose attributes might be clearly and constitutionally defined. Recognized political aristocracies have always struck me as being beneficent in their influence; whilst the aristocracies that have no other foundation than the chimeras, or the injustices of privileges, are pernicious, because their attributes remain undefined and ill regulated. It is true the Russian lords are masters, and too absolute masters, in their territories; whence arise those excesses that fear and hypocrisy conceal by humane phrases, softly pronounced, which deceive travelers, and, too often, the government also. But these men, though monarchs in their far-distant domains, have no power in the state; they do what they please on their own lands, defying the power of the emperor, by corrupting or intimidating his secondary agents; but the country is not governed by them; they enjoy no consideration in the general direction of affairs. It is only by becoming courtiers, by laboring for promotion in the *chin*, that they can obtain any public credit or standing. This life of the courtier excludes all elevation of sentiment, independence of spirit, and humane, patriotic views, which are essential elements of aristocratic bodies legally constituted in states organized to extend their power and to flourish long.

The government, on the other hand, equally excludes the just pride of the man who has made his fortune by his labor. It unites all the disadvantages of democracy with those of despotism, and rejects everything that is good in both systems.

Russia is governed by a class of subaltern employees, transferred direct from the public schools to the public administration. These individuals, who are very frequently the sons of men born in foreign lands, are noble so soon as they wear a cross at their buttonhole; and it is only the emperor who gives this decoration. Invested with the magical sign, they become proprietors of estates and of men; and thus, obtaining power without obtaining also that heritage of magnanimity natural in a chieftain born and habituated to command, the new lords use their authority like upstarts as they are, and render odious to the nation, and the world, the system of servitude established in Russia, at the period when ancient Europe began to destroy her feudal institutions. By virtue of their offices, these despots oppress the country with impunity, and incommode even the emperor; who perceives, with astonishment, that he is not so powerful as he imagined, though he dares not complain or even confess it to himself. This is the bureaucracy, a power, terrible everywhere, because its abuses are always made in the name of order, but more terrible in Russia than anywhere else. When we see administrative tyranny acting under Imperial despotism, we may tremble for a land where is established, without counterbalance, the system of government propagated in Europe at the time of the French Empire.

The emperors of Russia, equally mistaken in their confidence and their suspicion, viewed the nobles as rivals, and sought only to find slaves in the men they needed for ministers. Hence has sprung up the swarm of obscure agents who labor to govern the land in obedience to ideas not their own; from which it follows that they can never satisfy real wants. This class of employees, hostile in their hearts to the order of things which they direct, are recruited in a great measure from among the sons of the popes,—a body of vulgar aspirants, of upstarts without talent, for they need no merit to oblige the state to disembarrass itself of the burden which they are upon it; people who approach to all the ranks without possessing any; minds which participate alike in the popular prejudices and the aristocratic pretensions, without having the energy of the one or the wisdom of the other: to include all in one clause, the sons of the priests are revolutionists charged with maintaining the established order.

Half enlightened, liberal as the ambitious, as fond of oppressing as the slave, imbued with crude philosophical notions utterly inapplicable to the country which they call their own, though all their sentiments and semienlightened ideas come from abroad, these men are urging the nation towards a goal of which they are perhaps ignorant themselves, which the emperor has never imagined, and which is not one that true Russians or true friends of humanity will desire.

Their permanent conspiracy dates as far back as the time of Napoleon. The political Italian had foreseen the danger of the Russian power; and, wishing to weaken the enemy of revolutionized Europe, he had recourse, in the first place, to the influence of ideas. He profited by his friendly relations with the Emperor Alexander, and by the innate tendency of that prince towards liberal institutions, to send to Petersburg, under pretext of aiding in the accomplishment of the emperor's designs, a great number of political workmen,—a kind of masked army, charged with secretly preparing the way for our soldiers. These skillful intriguers were instructed to mix themselves up with the government, and especially with the system of public education, and to instill into the minds of the rising generation doctrines opposed to the political religion of the land. Thus did the great warrior—heir to the French revolution and foe to the liberties of the world— throw from afar the seeds of trouble and of discord, because the unity of despotism appeared to him a dangerous weapon in the military government which constitutes the immense power of Russia.

That empire is now reaping the fruit of the slow and profound policy of the adversary it flattered itself that it had conquered,—an adversary whose posthumous Machiavellism survives reverses unheard of in the history of human wars. To the secretly working influence of these pioneers of our armies, and to that of their children and their disciples, I attribute in a great measure the revolutionary ideas which have taken root in many families, and even in the army; and the explosion of which has produced the conspiracies that we have seen hitherto breaking themselves against the strength of the established government. Perhaps I deceive myself, but I feel persuaded that the present emperor will triumph over these ideas, by crushing, even to the last man, those who defend them.

I was far from expecting to find in Russia such vestiges of our policy, and to hear from the mouths of Russians reproaches similar to those that the Spaniards have addressed to us for thirty-five years past. If the mischievous intentions which the Russians attribute to Napoleon were real, no interest, no patriotism could justify them. We cannot save one part of the world by deceiving the other. Our religious propagandism appears to me sublime, because the Catholic church accords with every form of government and every degree of civilization, over which it reigns with all the superiority of mind over body: but political proselytism, that is to say, the narrow spirit of conquest, or to speak yet more justly, the spirit of rapine justified by that skillful sophistry called glory, is odious; for, far from drawing together the human race, this contracted ambition divides them: unity can only give birth to elevated and extended ideas; but the politics of national interference are always little; its liberality is hypocritical or tyrannical; its benefits are ever deceptive: every nation should derive from within itself the means for the improvements it requires.

To conclude: the problem proposed, not by men, but by events, by the concatenation of circumstances, to an emperor of Russia, is to favor among the nation the progress of knowledge, in order to hasten the emancipation of the serfs; and further, to aim at this object by the improving of manners, by the encouraging of humanity and of legal liberty; in short, by ameliorating hearts with the view of alleviating destinies. Such is the condition imposed upon any man who would now reign, even at Moscow: but the peculiarity of the emperor's position is, that he has to shape his course towards this object, keeping clear, on the one side, of the mute though well-organized tyranny of a revolutionary administration, and on the other, of the arrogance and the conspiracies of an aristocracy so much the more unquiet and formidable as its power is vague and undefined.

It must be owned that no sovereign has yet acquitted himself in this terrible task with so much firmness, talent, and good fortune as have been displayed by the Emperor Nicholas. He is the first of the modern Russian princes who has perceived the necessity of being a Russian in order to confer good upon the Russians. Undoubtedly history will say: This man was a great sovereign.

I have no time left for sleeping: the horses are already at my carriage, and I shall soon be on the road to Nizhny.

LETTER 31*

OUR ROAD follows the course of the Volga. Yesterday, I
crossed that river at Yarovslavl, and I have recrossed it today
at Kuniche. In many places its two banks differ in physical
aspect. On one side, stretches an immense plain level with
the water, on the other, the bank forms an almost perpendicular wall, sometimes a hundred or a hundred and fifty feet
high. This rampart or natural embankment, which extends
a considerable way backwards from the river before it again
loses itself in gradual slopes upon the plain, is clothed with
willows and birch, and is broken, from distance to distance,
by the river's tributaries. These watercourses form deep
furrows in the bank, which they have to pierce in order to
reach the mighty stream. The bank, thus broken, resembles a
mountain chain, and the furrows are real valleys, across
which the road parallel to the Volga is carried.

The Russian coachmen, although so skillful on level

---

*Written at Yurevets, a small town between Yaroslavl and Nizhny Novgorod.

ground, are, on mountainous roads, the most dangerous drivers in the world. That on which we are now traveling puts
their prudence and my sangfroid to the full proof. The continual ascending and descending would, if the declivities were
longer, be, under their mode of driving, extremely perilous.
The coachman commences the descent at a foot's pace; when
about a third of it is got over, which generally brings you to
the steepest part, man and horses begin mutually to weary of
their unaccustomed prudence; the latter get into a gallop, the
carriage rolls after with constantly increasing velocity until it
reaches the middle of a bridge of planks, frail, disjointed, uneven, and moveable: for they are placed, but not fixed, upon
their supporting beams, and under the poles which serve as
rails to the trembling structure. A bridge of this kind is found
at the bottom of each ravine. If the horses, in their wild gallop, do not bring the carriage straight on the planks, it will be
overturned. The life of the traveler depends entirely upon the
address of the driver, and upon the legs of four spirited, but
weak and tired animals. If a horse stumbles, or a strap breaks,
all is lost.

At the third repetition of this hazardous game, I desired
that the wheel should be locked, but there was no drag on my
Moscow carriage; I had been told that it was never necessary
to lock the wheel in Russia. To supply the want, it was necessary to detach one of the horses, and to use its traces. I have
ordered the same operation to be repeated, to the great astonishment of the drivers, each time that the length and steep-
ness of the declivity have seemed to threaten the safety of the
carriage, the frailness of which I have already only too often
experienced. The coachmen, astonished as they appear, do
not make the least objection to my strange fancies, nor in any
way oppose the orders that I give them through the *Feldjäger*;
but I can read their thoughts in their faces. The presence of a
government servant procures me everywhere marks of deference: such a proof of favor on the part of the authorities ren-

ders me an object of respect among the people. I would not advise any stranger, so little experienced as I am, to risk himself without such a guide on Russian roads, especially those of the interior.

When the traveler has been so fortunate as to cross safely the bottom of the ravine, the next difficulty is to climb the opposite bank. The Russian horses know no other pace but the gallop: if the road is not heavy, the hill short, and the carriage light, they bring you to the summit in a moment; but if the ascent is long, or the road, as is frequently the case, sandy, they soon come to a stop, panting and exhausted, in the middle of their task; turn stupid under the application of the whip, kick, and run back, to the imminent danger of throwing the carriage into the ditches; while at each dilemma of the kind I say to myself, in derision of the pretensions of the Russians, There are no distances in Russia!

The coachmen, however adroit they may be, want experience when they leave their native plains; they do not understand the proper manner of getting horses over mountains. At the first signs of hesitation everybody alights; the servants push at the wheels; at every few steps the horses stop to breathe, when the men rub their nostrils with vinegar, and encourage them with voice and hand. In this manner, aided by strokes of the whip, generally applied with admirable judgment, we gain the summit of these formidable ridges, which in other countries would be climbed without difficulty. The road from Yaroslavl to Nizhny is one of the most hilly in the interior of Russia; and yet I do not believe that the natural rampart or quay that crowns the banks of the Volga exceeds the height of a house of five or six stories in Paris.

There is one danger when journeying in Russia which could hardly be foreseen—the danger the traveler runs of breaking his head against the cover of his calèche. He who intends visiting the country need not smile, for the peril is actual and imminent. The logs of which the bridges and often

the roads themselves are made, render the carriages liable to
shocks so violent, that the traveler, when not warned, would
be thrown out if his equipage were open, and would break his
neck if the head were up. It is therefore advisable, in Russia,
to procure a carriage the top of which is as lofty as possible. A
bottle of seltzer water, substantial as those bottles are, has,
although well packed in hay, been broken under my seat by
the violence of the jolts.

Yesterday, I slept in a post-house, where there was a want
of every common convenience. My carriage is so uncomfortable, and the roads are so rough, that I cannot journey more
than twenty-four hours together without suffering from violent
headache, and, therefore, as I prefer a bad lodging to brain-
fever, I stop wherever we may happen to be. The greatest rarity in these out-of-the-way lodgings, and indeed in all Russia,
is clean linen. I carry my bed with me, but I cannot burden
myself with much store of sheets; and the tablecloths which
they give me at the post-houses, as substitutes, have always
been in use. Yesterday, at eleven o'clock in the evening, the
master of the post-house sent to a village more than a league
distant to search for clean sheets on my account. I should
have protested against this excess of zeal in my *Feldjäger*, but
I did not know of it until the next morning. From the window
of my kennel, by the obscured light that is called night in
Russia, I could admire at leisure the eternal Roman peristyle,
which, with its wooden, whitewashed pediment and its
plaster pillars, adorns, on the stable side, the Russian post-
houses. The constant sight of this clumsy architecture creates a nightmare that follows me from one end of the empire
to the other. The classic column has become the sign of a
public building in Russia: false magnificence here displays itself by the side of the most complete penury; but "comfort,"
and elegance well understood, and everywhere the same, are
not to be seen, either in the palaces of the wealthy, where the
halls are superb, but where the bedchamber is only a screen,

or yet in the huts of the peasants. There may, perhaps, be two or three exceptions to this rule in the whole empire. Even Spain appears to me less in want than Russia of objects of convenience and necessity.

Another precaution indispensable to a traveler in this country is a Russian lock. All the Slavic peasants are thieves, in the houses if not on the highway. When, therefore, you have got your luggage into the room of an inn full of different classes of people, it is necessary, before going out to walk, either to make your servants mount guard at the door, or to lock it. One of your people will be already engaged in keeping watch over the carriage; and there are no keys, nor even locks to the doors of apartments in Russian inns. The only expedient, therefore, is to be provided with staples, rings, and padlock. With these you may speedily place your property in safety. The country swarms with the most adroit and audacious of robbers. Their depredations are so frequent, that justice does not dare to be rigorous. Everything is here done by fits and starts, or with exceptions,—a capricious system, which too well accords with the ill-regulated minds of the people, who are as indifferent to equity in action as to truth in speech.

I, yesterday, visited the convent of Kostroma, and saw the apartments of Alexis Romanov and his mother, a retreat which Alexis left to ascend the throne, and to found the actual reigning dynasty. The convent was like all the others. A young monk, who had not been fasting, and who smelt of wine at a considerable distance, showed me the house. I prefer old monks with white beards, and popes with bald heads, to these young, well-fed recluses. The Treasury, also, resembled those I had seen elsewhere. Would the reader know in a few words, what is Russia? Russia is a country where the same persons and the same things are everywhere to be seen. This is so true, that on arriving at any place, we think always that we recognize persons whom we had left elsewhere.

At Kuniche, the ferryboat in which we recrossed the Volga had sides so low, that the smallest thing would have caused it to upset. Nothing has ever appeared to me more dull and gloomy than this little town, which I visited during a cold rain, accompanied with wind, that kept the inhabitants prisoners in their houses. Had the wind increased, we should have run much risk of being drowned in the river. I recollected that at Petersburg no one stirs a step to save those who fall into the Neva; and I thought, that should the same fate happen to me here, not an attempt would be made to save me by anyone on these banks, which are populous though they appear a desert, so gloomy and silent are the soil, the heavens, and the inhabitants. The life of man has little importance in the eyes of the Russians; and, judging by their melancholy air, I should say they are indifferent to their own lives as well as to those of others.

Existence is so fettered and restrained, that everyone seems to me secretly to cherish the desire of changing his abode, without possessing the power. The great have no passports, the poor no money, and all remain as they are, patient through despair, that is, as indifferent about death as about life. Resignation, which is everywhere else a virtue, is in Russia a vice, because it perpetuates the compulsory immobility of things.

The question here, is not one of political liberty, but of personal independence, of freedom of movement, and even of the expression of natural sentiment. The slaves dare only quarrel in a low voice; to be angry is one of the privileges of power. The greater the appearance of calm under this system, the more do I pity the people: tranquillity or the knout!—this is for them the condition of existence. The knout of the great is Siberia; and Siberia itself is only an exaggeration of Russia.

I am writing in the midst of a forest, many leagues from any habitation. We are stopped, in a deep bed of sand, by an accident that has happened to my carriage; and while my valet is, with the aid of a peasant whom Heaven has sent us, repairing the damage, I, who am humbled by the want of resources which I find within myself for such an occurrence, and who feel that I should only be in the way of the workmen if I attempted to assist them, take up my pen to prove the uselessness of mental culture, when man, deprived of all the accessories of civilization, is obliged to struggle, without any other resource but his own strength, against a wild nature, still armed with all the primitive power that it received from God.

As I have before said, handsome female peasants are scarce in Russia; but when they are handsome, their beauty is perfect. The oval or almond shape of their eyes imparts a peculiar expression; the eyelid is finely and delicately chiseled, but the blue of the pupil is often clouded, which reminds one of the ancient Sarmatians, as described by Tacitus: this hue gives to their veiled glances a gentleness and an innocence, the charm of which is irresistible. They possess all the vague and shadowy delicacy of the women of the North, united with the voluptuousness of the Oriental females. The expression of kindness in these ravishing creatures inspires a singular feeling,—a mixture of respect and confidence. He must visit the interior of Russia who would know the real gifts of the primitive man, and all that the refinements of society have lost for him. In this patriarchal land it is civilization which spoils the inhabitants. The Slav was naturally ingenuous, musical, and almost tenderhearted; the drilled Russian is false, tyrannical, imitative, and foolishly vain. It would take more than a century to establish an accord between the national manners and the new European ideas; supposing that, all the while, Russia was governed by enlightened princes,—friends of progress, as the expression now is.

, the complete separation of classes makes social
nt, immoral thing. It might be supposed that it was
from this country Rousseau took the first idea of his system;
for it is not even necessary to possess the resources of his
magic eloquence to prove that arts and sciences have done
more evil than good to the Slavs. The future will show the
world whether military and political glory can compensate
the Russian nation for the happiness of which their social organization deprives them.

The Russians are, in short, a resigned nation,—this simple
description explains everything. The man who is deprived of
liberty,—and here the definition of that word extends to natural rights and real wants,—though he may have all other advantages, is like a plant excluded from the air: in vain do you
water its roots, the languishing stem produces a few leaves,
but will never send forth flowers.

The spectacle now before my eyes proves to me the truth
of what I have always heard respecting the Russian's singular
dexterity and industry.

A Russian peasant makes it a principle to recognize no
obstacles,—I do not mean to his own desires, unhappy creature! but to the orders he receives. Aided by his inseparable
hatchet, he becomes a kind of magician, who creates in a moment all that is wanted in the desert. He repairs your carriage, or, if it is beyond repair, he makes another, a kind
of telega, skillfully availing himself of the remains of the old
one in the construction of the new. I was advised in Moscow
to travel in a *tarantasse*, and I should have done well to have
followed that advice; for with such an equipage, there is
never danger of stopping on the road. It can be repaired, and
even reconstructed, by every Russian peasant.

If you wish to camp, this universal genius will build you
a dwelling for the night, and one that will be preferable to
the taverns in the towns. After having established you as
comfortably as you can expect to be, he wraps himself in his

sheepskin and sleeps at the door of your new house, of which he defends the entrance with the fidelity of a dog; or else, he will seat himself at the foot of a tree before the abode that he has erected, and, while continuing to gaze on the sky he will relieve the solitude of your lodging by national songs, the melancholy of which awakes a response in the gentlest instincts of your heart; for an innate gift of music is still one of the prerogatives of this privileged race. The idea that it would be only just that he should share with you the cabin built by his hands, will never enter his head.

I am struck with the simplicity of the ideas and sentiments of these men. God, the King of heaven; the czar, the king of earth—this is all their theory: the orders, and even the caprices, of the master, sanctioned by the obedience of the slave; this suffices for their practice. The Russian peasant believes that he owes both body and soul to his lord.

Conforming to this social devotion, he lives without joy, but not without pride; for pride is the moral element essential to the life of all intelligent beings. It takes every kind of form, even the form of humility,—that religious modesty discovered by Christians.

A Russian does not know what it is to say *no* to his lord, who represents to him his two other greater masters, God and the emperor; and he places all his talent, all his glory, in conquering those little difficulties of existence that are magnified, and even valued, by the lower orders of other lands, as auxiliaries in their revenge against the rich, whom they consider as enemies, because they are esteemed the happy of the earth.

The Russian serfs are too completely stripped of all the blessings of life to be envious: the men who are most to be pitied are they who no longer complain. The envious among us are those whose ambitious aims have failed: France, that land of easy living and rapid fortune-making, is a nursery of envious people. I cannot feel sympathy with the regrets, full of malice, that prey on these men, whose souls are enervated by the luxuries of life; but the patience of the peasants here, inspires me with a compassion—I had almost said, with an esteem that is profound. The political self-denial of the Russians is abject and revolting; their domestic resignation is noble and touching. The vice of the nation becomes the virtue of the individual.

The plaintive sadness of the Russian songs strikes every foreigner; but this music is not only melancholy, it is also scientific and complicated: it is composed of inspired melodies, and, at the same time, of harmonious combinations exceedingly abstruse, and that are not elsewhere attained except by study and calculation. Often, in traveling through villages, I stop to listen to pieces executed by several voices with a precision and a musical instinct that I am never tired of admiring. The performers, in these rustic quintets, guess, by intuition, the laws of counterpoint, the rules of composition, the principles of harmony, the effects of the different kinds of voice, and they disdain singing in unison. They execute series of harmonies, elaborate, unexpected, and interspersed with trills and delicate ornaments, which, if not always perfectly correct, are very superior to the national melodies heard in other lands.

The song of the Russian peasants is a nasal lamentation, not very agreeable when executed by one voice; but when sung in chorus, these complaints assume a grave, religious character, and produce effects of harmony that are surprising. I had supposed the Russian music to have been brought from Byzantium, but I am assured that it is indigenous: this will explain the profound melancholy of the airs, especially of those which affect gaiety by their vivacity of movement. If the Russians do not know how to revolt against oppression, they know how to sigh and groan under it.

Were I in the place of the emperor, I should not be content with forbidding my subjects to complain; I should also forbid them to sing, which is a disguised mode of complaining. These accents of lament are avowals, and may become accusations: so true it is that the arts themselves, under despotism, are not innocent; they are indirect protestations.

Hence, no doubt, the taste of the government and the courtiers for the works, literary or artistical, of foreigners: borrowed poetry has no roots. Among a people of slaves, when patriotic sentiments produce profound emotions, they are to be dreaded: everything that is national, including even music, becomes a means of opposition.

It is so in Russia, where, from the corners of the farthest deserts, the voice of man lifts to Heaven vengeful complaints; demanding from God the portion of happiness that is refused him upon earth. Nothing more striking reveals the habitual sufferings of the people than the mournfulness of their pleasures. The Russians have consolations, but no enjoyments. I am surprised that no one before me should have warned the government of its imprudence in allowing the people an amusement which betrays their misery and their resignation. He who is powerful enough to oppress men, should, for consistency's sake, forbid them to sing.

I am now at the last stage on the road to Nizhny. We have reached it on three wheels, and dragging a prop of wood in the place of the fourth.

A great part of the road from Yaroslavl to Nizhny is a long garden avenue, traced almost always in a straight line, broader than the great avenue in our Champs Elysées at Paris, and flanked on either side by two smaller alleys, carpeted with turf and shaded by birch trees. The road is easy, for they drive nearly always upon the grass, except when crossing marshy tracts by means of elastic bridges; a kind of floating floors, more curious than safe either for the carriages or the horses. A road on which grows so much grass can be little frequented, and is therefore the more easily kept in repair. Yesterday, before we broke down, I was praising this road, which we were then traveling at full gallop, to my *Feldjäger*. "No doubt it is beautiful," replied the individual addressed, whose figure resembles that of a wasp, whose features are sharp and dry, and whose manners are at once timid and threatening, like hatred suppressed by fear: "no doubt it is beautiful—it is the great road to Siberia."

These words chilled me through. It is for my pleasure, I said to myself, that I travel this road: but what have been the thoughts and feelings of the many unfortunate beings, who have traveled it before me? These thoughts and feelings, evoked by the imagination, took possession of my mind. Siberia!—that Russian hell, is, with all its phantoms, incessantly before me. It has upon me the effect that the eye of the basilisk has upon the fascinated bird.

What a country is this! a plain without limits and without colors, with only here and there some few inequalities in the surface, a few fields of oats and rye, a few scattered birch and pine woods in the distance, villages built of gray boards along the lines of road; on rather more elevated sites, at every twenty, thirty, or fifty leagues, towns, the vast size of which swallows up the inhabitants, and immense, colorless rivers, dull as the heavens they reflect! Winter and death are felt to be hovering over these scenes, giving to every object a funereal hue: the terrified traveler, at the end of a few weeks, feels as if he were buried alive, and, stifling, struggles to burst his coffin lid, that leaden veil that separates him from the living.

Do not go to the North to amuse yourself, unless at least you seek your amusement in study; for there is much here to study.

I was then traveling upon the great road to Siberia, and while absorbed in the reflection it so naturally suggested, I saw in the distance a group of armed men, who had stopped under one of the side alleys of the road.

"What are those soldiers doing there?" I asked my courier.

"They are Cossacks," he replied, "conducting exiles to Siberia!"—

It is not then, a dream, it is not the mythology of the gazettes; I see there the real unhappy beings, the actual exiles, proceeding wearily on foot to seek the land where they must die forgotten by the world, far from all that is dear to them, alone with the God who never created them for such a fate. Perhaps I have met, or shall meet, their wives or mothers: for they are not criminals; on the contrary, they are Poles —the heroes of misfortune and devotion. Tears came into my eyes as I approached these unhappy men, near to whom I dared not even stop lest I should be suspected by my Argus. Alas! before such sufferings the sentiment of my impotent compassion humiliates me, and anger rises above commiseration in my heart. I could wish to be far away from a country where the miserable creature who acts as my courier can become formidable enough to compel me, in his presence, to dissimulate the most natural feelings of my soul. In vain do I repeat to myself that, perhaps, our convicts are still worse off than the colonists of Siberia; there is, in that distant exile, a vague poetry, which adds to the severity of the sentence all the influence of the imagination; and this inhuman alliance produces a frightful result. Besides, our convicts are solemnly convicted; but a few months' abode in Russia suffices to convince us that there are no laws there.

There were three exiles, and they were all innocent in my eyes; for under a despotism, the only criminal is the man who goes unpunished. These three convicts were escorted by six Cossacks on horseback. The head of my carriage was closed, and the nearer we approached the group, the more narrowly did the courier strive to watch the expression of my countenance. I was greatly struck with the efforts he made to persuade me that they were only simple malefactors, and that there was no political convict among them. I preserved a gloomy silence: the pains that he took to reply to my thoughts, appeared to me very significative.

Frightful sagacity of the subjects of despotism! all are spies, even as amateurs, and without compensation.

The last stages of the road to Nizhny are long and difficult, owing to the sand-beds, which get deeper and deeper,* until the carriages become almost buried in them. They conceal immense, movable blocks of wood and stone, very dangerous to the carriages and horses. This part of the road is bordered by forests, in which, at every half league, are encampments of Cossacks, designed to protect the journeying of the merchants who resort to the fair. Such a precaution reminds me of the Middle Ages.

My wheel is repaired, so that I hope to reach Nizhny before evening.

---

*A *chaussée* is being made from Moscow to Nizhny, which will be soon completed.

LETTER 32

THE SITUATION of Nizhniy is the most beautiful that I
have beheld in Russia. I see no longer a little ridge of low
banks falling upon a large river, but a real mountain, which
looks down on the confluence of the Volga and the Oka, two
equally noble rivers; for the Oka, at its mouth, appears as
large as the more celebrated stream. The lofty town of Nizhny,
built on this mountain, commands a plain, vast as the sea. A
land without bounds spreads before it, and at its foot is held
the largest fair in the world. During six weeks of the year the
commerce of the two richest quarters of the globe meet at the
confluence of the Oka and the Volga. It is a spot worthy of being painted. Hitherto, the only truly picturesque scenes that I
had admired in Russia were the streets of Moscow and the
quays of Petersburg. But those scenes were the creations of
man: here, the country is naturally beautiful. The ancient

city of Nizhny, instead, however, of seeking the rivers, and profiting by the riches they offer, hides itself behind the mountain; and there, lost in the background, seems to shrink from its glory and prosperity. This ill-advised situation has struck the Emperor Nicholas, who exclaimed the first time he saw the place—"At Nizhny, nature has done everything, but man has spoilt all." To remedy the errors of the founders of Nizhny Novgorod, a suburb, in the form of a quay, has been built under the hill, on that one of the two points of land separating the rivers, which forms the right bank of the Oka. This new town increases every year; it is becoming more populous and important than the ancient city, from which it is separated by the old Kremlin of Nizhny; for every Russian city has its Kremlin.

The fair is held on the other side of the Oka, upon a low tract, which forms a triangle between it and the Volga. The Oka is crossed by a bridge of boats, which serves as the road from the city to the fair, and which appears as long as that of the Rhine at Mainz. The two banks of the river thus connected, are very different in character: the one which is the promontory of Nizhny, rises majestically in the midst of the plain called Russia; the other, nearly on a level with the water which inundates it during a part of the year, forms a portion of this immense plain. The singular beauty of the contrast did not escape the glance of the Emperor Nicholas: that prince, with his characteristic sagacity, has also perceived that Nizhny is one of the most important points in his empire. He is very fond of this central spot, thus favored by nature, and which has become the rendezvous of the most distant populations, who here congregate from all parts, drawn together by a powerful commercial interest. His Majesty has neglected nothing that could tend to beautify, enlarge, and enrich the city. The fair of Makarev, which was held formerly on the estate of a boyar, twenty leagues below, following the course of the Volga towards Asia, was forfeited for the benefit of the crown and country; and the Emperor Alexander transferred it to Nizhny. I regret the Asiatic fair held on the domains of a Muscovite prince: it must have been more original and picturesque, though less immense and regular than the one I find here.

I have already said that every Russian city has its Kremlin, just as every Spanish city has its Alcazar. The Kremlin of Nizhny, with its many-shaped towers, its pinnacles and embattled ramparts, which circle round a mountain far loftier than the hill of the Kremlin at Moscow, is nearly half a league in circumference.

When the traveler perceives this fortress from the plain he is struck with astonishment. It is the pharos, towards whose shining turrets and white walls, rising above the stunted forest pines, he shapes his course through the sandy deserts which defend the approach to Nizhny on the side of Yaroslavl. The effect of this national architecture is always powerful: but here, the grotesque towers and Christian minarets that constitute the ornament of all the Kremlins, are heightened in effect by the striking character of the site, which in certain places opposes real precipices to the creations of the architect. In the thickness of the walls have been worked, as at Moscow, staircases, which lead, from battlement to battlement, up to the very summit of the crowning ramparts. These commanding stairs, with the towers by which they are flanked, the slopes, the vaults, the arcades which sustain them, form a picture from whichsoever point of approach they are viewed.

The fair of Nizhny, now become the most considerable in the world, is the rendezvous of the people the least alike in person, costume, language, religion, and manners. Men from Tibet, from Bukhara, from the regions bordering upon China, come to meet Persians, Finns, Greeks, English, and Parisians: it is like the merchants' doomsday. The number of strangers present at Nizhny every day during the fair, exceeds two hundred thousand. The men who compose this yearly gathering come and go daily; but the average number always continues pretty nearly the same: nevertheless, on certain days, there are at Nizhny as many as three hundred thousand. The usual consumption of bread in this pacific camp amounts to four hundred thousand pounds weight per day. Except at the season of this saturnalia of trade and industry, the city is lifeless. Nizhny scarcely numbers twenty thousand stationary inhabitants, who are lost in its vast streets and naked squares during the nine months that the fairground remains forsaken.

The fair occasions little disorder. In Russia disorder is unknown: it would be a progressive movement, for it is the child of liberty. The love of gain, and the ever-increasing need of luxuries, felt now by even barbarous nations, cause the semibarbarous populations who resort here from Persia and Bukhara to recognize the advantages of orderly demeanor and good faith: besides, it must be admitted that in general the Mohammedans are upright in money matters.

Though I have only been a few hours in the city, I have already seen the governor. I had several flattering letters of introduction to him: he appears hospitable, and, for a Russian, open and communicative. His name is illustrious in the ancient history of Russia—it is that of Burtulin. The Burtulins are a family of old boyars; a class of men that is becoming rare.

I have scarcely encountered any really dense crowd in Russia, except at Nizhny, on the bridge over the Oka, the only road which leads from the city to the fairground, and the road also by which we approach Nizhny from Yaroslavl. At the entrance of the fair, you turn to the right to cross the bridge, leaving on the left the booths, and the temporary palace of the governor, a pavilion which forms a species of administrative observatory, whither he repairs every morning, and from whence he surveys all the streets, all the rows of shops, and presides over the general arrangements of the fair. The dust, the din, the carriages, the foot passengers, the soldiers charged with maintaining order, greatly obstruct the passage of the bridge, the use and character of which it is difficult at first to understand; for the surface of the water being covered by a multitude of boats, at the first glance, you suppose the river to be dry. The boats are so crowded together at the confluence of the Volga and the Oka that the latter river may be crossed by striding from junk to junk. I use this Chinese word because a great portion of the vessels which resort to Nizhny bring to the fair the merchandise, more especially the tea, of China.

Yesterday, on arriving, I expected that our horses would have run over twenty individuals before reaching the quay of the Oka, which is New Nizhny, a suburb that will in a few years more be very extensive.

When I had gained the desired shore, I found that many other difficulties awaited me: before everything else it was necessary to obtain a lodging, and the inns were full. My *Feldjäger* knocked at the very door, and always returned with the same smile, ferocious by its very immobility, to tell me that he could not procure a single chamber. He advised me to appeal to the hospitality of the governor; but this I was unwilling to do.

At length, arrived at the extremity of the long street that forms this suburb, at the foot of the steep hill which leads to the old city, and the summit of which is crowned by the Kremlin of Nizhny, we perceived a coffeehouse, the approach to which was obstructed by a covered public market, from whence issued odors that were anything but perfumes. Here I alighted, and was politely received by the landlord, who conducted me through a series of apartments, all filled with men in pelisses, drinking tea and other liquors, until, by bringing me to the last room, he demonstrated to me that he had not one single chamber unoccupied.

"This room forms the corner of your house," I observed: "has it a private entrance?"

"Yes."

"Very good: lock the door which separates it from the other apartments, and let me have it for a bedchamber."

The air that I breathed already suffocated me. It was a mixture of the most opposite emanations: the grease of sheepskins, the musk of dressed leather, the blacking of boots, the smell of cabbage, which is the principal food of the peasants, the steam of coffee, tea, liqueurs, and brandy, all thickened the atmosphere. The whole was poison: but what could I do? it was my last resource. I hoped, also, that after being cleared of its guests, swept, and washed, the bad odors of the apartment would dissipate. I therefore insisted on the *Feldjäger* clearly explaining my proposal to the keeper of the coffeehouse.

"I shall lose by it," replied the man.

"I will pay you what you please; provided you also find somewhere a lodging for my valet and my courier."

The bargain was concluded; and here I am, quite proud of having taken by storm, in a dirty public house, a room for which I have to pay more than the price of the finest apartment in the Hôtel des Princes, at Paris. It is only in Russia, in a country where the whims of men supposed to be powerful, know no obstacle, that one is able to convert, in a moment, the public hall of a coffeehouse into a sleeping apartment.

My *Feldjäger* undertook to make the drinkers retire: they rose without offering the least objection, were crowded into the next room, and the door was fastened upon them by the species of lock I have already mentioned. A score of tables filled up the chamber: but a swarm of priests in their robes, in other words, a troop of waiters in white shirts, precipitated themselves upon the furniture, and left me with bare walls in a few moments. But what a sight then met my eyes! Under the spot where each table had stood, under every stool, multitudes of vermin were crawling, of a kind I have never before seen: they were black insects, about half an inch long, thick, soft, viscid, and tolerably nimble in their movements. This loathsome animal is known in a portion of eastern Europe, in Volhynia, the Ukraine, Russia, and a part of Poland, where it is called, I believe, *persica*, because it was brought from Asia. I cannot recollect the name given to it by the coffeehouse waiters of Nizhny. On seeing the floor of my chamber mottled over with these moving insects, crushed under the foot at every step, not by hundreds, but by thousands, and on perceiving the new kind of ill savor exhaled by this massacre, I was seized with despair, fled from my chamber to the street, and proceeded to present myself to the governor. I did not re-enter my detestable lodging until assured that it had been rendered as clean as was practicable. My bed, filled with fresh hay, was placed in the middle of the room, its four feet standing in earthen vessels full of water. Notwithstanding these precautions, I did not fail to find, on awaking from a restless unrefreshing sleep, two or three *persicas* on my pillow. They are not noxious; but I cannot express the disgust with which they inspire me. The filthiness, the apathy, which their presence in the habitations of man betrays, make me regret my journey to this part of the globe. I feel as though there were a moral degradation in being approached by these offal-bred creatures: physical antipathy triumphs over all the efforts of reason.

A merchant of Moscow, who has the most splendid and extensive silk-magazine in the fair, is coming this morning to take me over it, and to show me everything in detail.

I again find here the dust and suffocating heat of a southern clime. I was therefore well advised not to go on foot to the fair: but the concourse of strangers is at this time so great at Nizhny, that I could not get a vehicle on hire; I was therefore obliged to use the by-no-means elegant one in which I arrived from Moscow, and to attach to it two horses only, which annoyed me as much as though I had been a Russian. It is not through vanity that they drive four horses: the animals have spirit, but they want power; they soon tire when they have much weight to draw.

On entering the carriage with the merchant who was so good as to act as my cicerone, and with his brother, I told my *Feldjäger* to follow us. He, without hesitating or waiting to ask my permission, deliberately stepped into the calèche, and, with a coolness that amazed me, seated himself by the side of M. ——— 's brother, who, notwithstanding my expostulations, was determined to sit with his back to the horses. In this country, it is not unusual to see the owner of a carriage seated facing the horses, when even he is not by the side of a lady, whilst his friends place themselves opposite. This impoliteness, which would not be committed among us excepting where there was the strictest intimacy, here astonishes nobody.

Fearing lest the familiarity of the courier should shock my obliging companions, I considered it necessary to make him remove; and told him, very civilly, to mount the seat by the side of the coachman.

"I shall do nothing of the kind," answered the *Feldjäger*, with imperturbable sangfroid.

"What is the reason that you do not obey me?" I asked, in a yet calmer tone; for I know that among this half-Oriental nation, it is necessary to maintain perfect impassibility in order to preserve your authority.

We spoke in German:—"It would be a derogation," answered the Russian, in the same quiet tone.

This reminded me of the disputes about precedence among the boyars, which, under the reigns of the Ivans, were often so serious as to fill many pages of the Russian history of that epoch.

"What do you mean by a derogation?" I continued. "Is not that the place which you have occupied since we left Moscow?"

"It is true, sir, that is my place in traveling; but in taking a drive, I ought to be in the carriage. I wear a uniform."

This uniform, which I have described elsewhere, is that of an agent of the post.

"I wear uniform, sir; I possess a rank in the *chin*; I am not a private servant; I am in the employ of the emperor."

"I care very little what you are; though I never said to you that you were a servant."

"I should have the appearance of being one, were I to sit in that place when you take a ride in the city. I have been many years in the service; and, as a recompense for my good conduct, they hold out to me the prospect of nobility: I am endeavoring to obtain it, for I am ambitious."

This confusion of our old aristocratic ideas with the new vanity instilled by despots into a people diseased with envy, took me by surprise. I had before me a specimen of the worst kind of emulation—that of the *parvenant* already giving himself the airs of the *parvenu*!

After a moment's silence, I answered: "I approve your pride, if it is well founded; but being little acquainted with the usages of your country, I shall, before allowing you to enter my coach, submit your claims to the governor. My intention is to require nothing from you beyond what you owe me in accordance with the orders given you when you were sent to me: in my uncertainty as to your pretensions, I dispense with your services for today; I shall proceed without you."

I felt inclined to laugh at the tone of importance with which I spoke; but I considered this dramatic dignity necessary to my comfort during the rest of the journey. There is nothing, however ridiculous, which may not be excused by the conditions and the inevitable consequences of despotism.

This aspirant to nobility, and scrupulous observer of the etiquette of the highway, costs me, notwithstanding his pride, three hundred francs, in wages, per month. He reddened when he heard my last words, and, without making any reply, he left the carriage and re-entered the house in silence.

The ground on which the fair is held is very spacious; and I congratulated myself that I did not proceed to that city of a month on foot, for the heat continues to be great during a day in which the sun still darts his rays for fifteen hours.

The men of every land, but especially those of the extreme East, here meet together: these men are however more singular in name than in appearance. All the Asiatics resemble each other, or they may, at least, be divided into two classes: those having the faces of apes, as the Kalmyks, Mongols, Bashkirs, and Chinese; and those having the Greek profile, as the Circassians, Persians, Georgians, Indians, &c.

The fair of Nizhny is held, as I have already said, on an immense triangle of sandy and perfectly level land, which runs to a point between the Oka, at its *embouchure* into the Volga, and the broad stream of the latter river. It is, therefore, bordered on either side by one of the two rivers. The soil upon which so immense an amount of wealth is heaped, scarcely rises above the water. This merchant city consists of a vast assemblage of long and broad streets: their perfect straightness injures their picturesque effect. A dozen of buildings called Chinese pavilions rise above the shops; but their fantastic style is not sufficient to correct the dullness and monotony of the general aspect of the edifices. The whole forms an oblong bazaar, which appears solitary, so vast is it in extent. The dense crowds that obstruct the approaches disappear as soon as you penetrate the interior lines of stalls. The city of the fair is, like all the other modern Russian cities, too vast for its population, although that population, including the amphibious community scattered in boats on the river, and among the flying camps which environ the fair properly so called, amounts to two hundred thousand souls. The houses of the merchants stand upon a subterranean city, an immense vaulted sewer; in which labyrinth he would be lost who should attempt to penetrate without an experienced guide. Each street in the fair is doubled by a gallery, which follows its whole length, underground, and serves as an issue for all refuse. The sewers are constructed of stone, and are cleansed several times daily, by a multitude of pumps, which introduce the water from the neighboring rivers. They are entered by large and handsome stone staircases.

These catacombs of filth, which serve also for the prevention of everything offensive in the open streets, are placed under the charge of Cossacks, who form its police, and who politely invite any individual tempted to soil the street to descend. They are one of the most imposing works I have seen in Russia, and might suggest models to the constructors of the sewers at Paris. So much vastness and solidity reminds one of the descriptions of Rome. They were built by the Emperor Alexander, who, like his predecessors, pretended to conquer nature by establishing the fair on a soil inundated during one half of the year. He lavished millions in remedying the inconveniences of the injudicious choice made when the fair of Makarev was transported to Nizhny.

The Oka, which separates the city of the fair from the permanent city, is here more than four times the breadth of the Seine. Forty thousand men sleep every night upon its bosom, making themselves nests in boats, which form a kind of floating camp. From the surface of the aquatic city rises, at evening, the heavy murmur of voices that might be easily taken for the gurgling of the waves. All these boats have masts, and form a river-forest peopled by men from every corner of the earth: their faces and their costumes are equally strange. The sight has struck me more than any other in the immense fair. Rivers thus inhabited remind one of the descriptions of China.

Some of the peasants in this part of Russia wear white tunic shirts, ornamented with red borders: the costume is borrowed from the Tartars. At nighttime, the white linen gives them the appearance of specters moving in the dark. Yet, notwithstanding its many singular and interesting objects, the fair of Nizhny is not picturesque: it is a formal plan rather than a graceful sketch. The man devoted to political economy, or arithmetical calculations, has more business here than the poet or the painter: the subjects relate to the commercial balance and progress of the two principal quarters of the world—nothing more and nothing less. From one end of Russia to the other I perceive a minute, Dutch-taught government, hypocritically carrying on war against the primitive faculties of an ingenious, lively, poetical, Oriental people, a people born for the arts.

The merchandise of every part of the world is collected in the immense streets of the fair; but it is also lost in them. The scarcest objects are buyers. I have seen nothing yet in this country without exclaiming, "The people are too few for the space!" It is just the contrary in ancient communities, where the land is insufficient for the progress of civilization. The French and English stalls are the most elegant; while viewing them, the beholder might fancy himself at Paris or at London: but this Bond Street of the East, this Palais Royal of the steppes, does not constitute the real wealth of the market of Nizhny. To have a just idea of the importance of the fair, it is necessary to recollect its origin, and the place where it was first held. Before flourishing at Makarev it was established at Kazan. The two extremes of the ancient world, western Europe and China, met in that old capital of Russian Tartary to exchange their various products. This is now done at Nizhny. But a very incomplete idea of a market for the commodities of two continents would be formed, if the spectator did not leave the regular stalls and elegant pavilions which adorn the modern bazaar of Alexander, and survey some of the different camps by which it is flanked. The line and rule do not follow the merchants into the suburbs of the fair: these suburbs are like the farmyard of a château,—however stately and orderly the principal habitation, the disorder of nature reigns in its dependencies.

It is no easy task to traverse, even rapidly, these exterior depots, for they are themselves each as large as cities. A continual and really imposing activity pervades them,—a true merchantile chaos, which it is necessary to see in order to believe.

To commence with the city of tea: it is an Asiatic camp, which extends on the banks of the two rivers to the point of land where they meet. The tea comes from China by Kiakhta, which is in the back part of Asia. At this first depot, it is exchanged for merchandise, and from thence transported in packages, which resemble small chests in the shape of dice, about two feet square. These packages are frames, covered with skins; the buyers thrust into them a kind of probe, by withdrawing which they ascertain the quality of the article. From Kiakhta the tea travels by land to Tomsk; it is there placed in boats, and sails along several rivers, of which the Irtysh and the Tobol are the principal, till it arrives at Tyumen, from whence it is again transported by land to Perm, in Siberia, where it is reshipped on the Kama, which carries it into the Volga, and up that river it ascends to Nizhny. Russia receives yearly seventy-five to eighty thousand chests of tea, one half of which remains in Siberia, to be transported to Moscow during the winter by sledges, and the other half arrives at this fair.

The principal tea merchant in Russia is the individual who wrote for me the above itinerary. I do not answer for either the spelling or the geography of that opulent man; but a millionnaire is generally correct, for he buys the science of others.

It will be seen that this famous tea of the caravans, so delicate, as is said, because it comes overland, travels nearly all the way by water: to be sure, it is fresh water; and the mists of rivers do not produce such effects as the ocean fogs.

Forty thousand chests of tea is an amount easily named; but the reader can have no idea of the time it takes to survey them, though it be only by passing before the piles of boxes.

This year, thirty-five thousand were sold in three days. A single individual, my geographical merchant, took fourteen thousand, which cost him ten million silver rubles (paper rubles are not current here), a part payable down, the rest in one year.

It is the rate of tea which fixes the price of all the commodities of the fair: before this rate is published, the other bargains are only made conditionally.

There is another city as large, but less elegant, and less perfumed than the city of tea—that, namely, of rags. Fortunately, before bringing the tatters of all Russia to the fair, those into whose hands they have fallen, cause them to be washed. This commodity, necessary to the manufacture of paper, has become so precious, that the Russian custom-house forbids its exportation with extreme severity.

Another town which attracted my attention among the suburbs, was that of barked timber. Like the suburbs of Vienna, these secondary cities are larger than the principal. The one of which I speak serves as a magazine for the wood, brought from Siberia, destined to form the wheels of the Russian carts, and the collars of the horses—these semicircles formed of a single piece of bended wood, which are seen fixed in so picturesque a manner, at the extremities of the shafts, and which rise above the heads of all the shaft horses in the empire. The store necessary to furnish these wheels and collars to western Russia forms here mountains of wood, of which our timber-yards at Paris cannot give even an idea.

Another city, and it is, I believe, the most extensive and curious of all, serves as a depot for the iron of Siberia. I walked for a quarter of a league under galleries, in which are to be found, artistically arranged, every known species of iron bar, grating, and wrought iron; pyramids built of the utensils of husbandry and housekeeping, magazines full of vessels of cast iron; in short, a city of the metal which forms one of the principal sources of the wealth of the empire. The sight of such wealth made me shudder. How many criminals must it not have required to dig up those treasures? and if there are not criminals enough in that subterranean world which produces iron, their number is made up by the unfortunate victims of despotism. The system which regulates the miners of the Ural would be a curious subject of inquiry, if it were permitted, to foreigners. But the means of pursuing this study would be as difficult for a European from the West, as the journey to Mecca is for a Christian.

All these towns form only chapels-of-ease to the principal fair, round which, as a common center, they extend without any plan or order. Their outer, or general circumference, would equal that of the larger European capitals. A day would not afford sufficient time to pass through all the temporary suburbs. Amid such an abyss of riches it is impossible to see everything; the spectator is obliged to select.

I must abridge my descriptions. In Russia we resign ourselves to monotony; it is a condition of existence: but in France, where I shall be read, I have no right to expect the reader to submit to it with the same good grace that I do here. He has not the same obligation to be patient as he would have if he had traveled a thousand leagues to learn the practice of that virtue of the vanquished.

I forgot to notice a city of cashmere wool. In seeing this vile dusty hair, bound in enormous bales, I thought of the beautiful shoulders that it would one day cover; the splendid attires that, when transformed into shawls, it would complete.

I saw also a city of furs, and another of potash. I use this word city purposely; it alone can give an idea of the extent of the various depots which surround the fair, and which invest it with a character of grandeur that no other fair will ever possess.

Such a commercial phenomenon could only be produced in Russia. To create a fair like Nizhny requires that there should be an extreme desire for luxuries among tribes still half barbarous, living in countries separated by incommensurable distances, without prompt or easy means of communication, and where the inclemency of the seasons isolates the population during a great part of the year. The combination of these, and doubtless many other circumstances which I do not discern, could alone induce commercial people to submit to the difficulties, expenses, and personal fatigues of annually resorting, and of bringing all the riches of the soil and of industry to one single point of the country, at a fixed season. The time may be predicted, and I think it is not far distant, when the progress of material civilization in Russia will greatly diminish the importance of the fair of Nizhny, at present, as I have already said, the largest in the world.

In a suburb, separated by an arm of the Oka, is a Persian village, the shops of which are filled exclusively with Persian merchandise. Among these objects, I more particularly admired the carpets, which appeared magnificent, the raw silk, and the termolama, a species of silk-cashmere, manufactured, they say, only in Persia.

The forms and dress of the Persians do not greatly strike in this country, where the indigenous population is itself Asiatic, and preserves traces of its origin.

I also traversed a city destined solely as a receptacle for the dried and salted fish which are sent from the Caspian Sea for the Russian Lents.* The Greek devotees are great consumers of these aquatic mummies. Four months of abstinence among the Muscovites enriches the Mohammedans of Persia and Tartary. This city of fishes is situated on the borders of the river; some of the fish are piled upon earth, the remainder lay within the holds of the vessels that brought them. The dead bodies, heaped together in millions, exhale, even in the open air, a disagreeable perfume. Another divi-

---

*There are four Lents in the Greek church.—*Trans.*

sion forms the city of leather; an article of the first importance at Nizhny; as enough is brought there to supply the consumption of all the west of Russia.

Another is the city of furs. The skins of every animal may be seen there, from the sable, the blue fox, and certain bearskins,—to obtain a pelisse of which costs twelve thousand francs,—to the common foxes and wolves, which cost nothing. The keepers of the treasures make themselves tents for the night with their merchandise, savage lairs, the aspect of which is picturesque. These men, although they inhabit cold countries, live on little, clothe lightly, and sleep in the open air in fine weather. They are the true lazzaroni of the North, though less gay, witty, or buffoonish, and more dirty than those of Naples; because, to the uncleanliness of their persons is added that of their garments, which they never take off.

What I have already written will serve to give an idea of the exterior of the fair: the interior, I repeat, is much less interesting. Without, are carts and wheelbarrows moving amid a crowd where reign disorder, cries, songs, and in short, liberty: within, are regularity, silence, solitude, order, the police, and in one word, Russia! Immense files of houses, or rather stalls, separate about a dozen long and broad streets, which terminate in a Russian church and in twelve Chinese pavilions. The united length of all the streets and alleys of the fair, properly so called, and without speaking of the suburbs, is ten leagues.

The Emperor Alexander, after having selected the new ground for the fair, ordered the necessary works for its establishment, but he never saw it. He was ignorant of the immense sums that had to be added to his budget, to make this low land fitted to the use for which it was destined. By means of amazing efforts and enormous expenditure the fair is now habitable during summer, which is all that is required for commerce. But it is not the less badly situated: being rendered dusty or miry by the first ray of sun or smallest rain, and remaining unhealthy at all times; which is no small evil for the merchants, obliged to sleep above their magazines for the space of six weeks.

Notwithstanding the taste of the Russians for straight lines, many think with me that it would have been better to have placed the fair by the side of the old city, on the crest of the mountain, the summit of which might have been rendered accessible by gentle, terraced slopes. At the foot of the hill, on the borders of the Oka, the objects too heavy and bulky to be carried up, might have still remained, by the side of their vessels, while the livelier retail fair would have been held on a spacious platform at the gate of the lofty city. Imagine a hill crowded with the representatives of all the Asiatic and European nations. Such a peopled mountain would have produced a grand effect: the marsh, where the traveling population now swarms, produces very little.

The modern engineers, so skillful in all lands, would then have had whereon to exercise their talents; the poets, the painters, the admirers of noble sites and picturesque effects, the sightseers, who are become quite a nation in this century, in which the abuses of activity produce fanatics in idleness,— all these men useful through the money which they expend, would have enjoyed a magnificent promenade, far more attractive than that afforded them in a bazaar where no point of view can be gained, and where the air breathed is mephitic; while it merits consideration, that such a result would have been obtained at much less expenditure of money than it has cost the emperor to establish his aquatic fair.

The Russian peasants are the principal commercial agents in this prodigious market. Nevertheless, the law forbids the serf to ask, or the freemen to grant him, a credit of more than *five rubles*. And yet they deal with some of these people, on the strength of their word only, for from two hundred thousand to five hundred thousand francs; and the dates for pay-

ment are very distant. These slavish millionnaires, these
Aguados of the soil, do not know how to read. In Russia, men
sometimes deploy a prodigious intelligence to compensate
for their ignorance. The people are very ignorant of arithmetic. For centuries they have reckoned their accounts by
frames, containing series of movable balls. Every line has its
color; each indicates units, tens, hundreds, &c. This mode of
calculation is sure and rapid.

It must not be forgotten that the lord of these enormously
wealthy serfs could despoil them in a day of all they possess,
provided he did not injure their persons. Such acts of violence, it is true, are rare, but they are possible.

No one remembers that any merchant ever suffered by
his confidence in the peasants with whom he dealt: so true it
is, that in every society, if only it be stable, the progress of
morals corrects the faults of institutions.

I have, however, been told that, on the other hand, the
father of a Count Sheremetev, who is still living, once promised liberty to a family of peasants, in consideration of the exorbitant sum of fifty thousand rubles. He received the money,
and retained among his serfs the despoiled family.

Such is the school of good faith and probity in which
the Russian peasants are instructed, under the aristocratic
despotism which crushes them, in spite of the autocratic despotism which governs them, and which is often powerless
against its rival. Imperial pride contents itself with words,
forms, and numbers; aristocratic ambition aims at things,
and makes a profit of words. Never did a master receive more
adulation and less obedience than the deceived, soi-disant
absolute sovereign of the Russian Empire: disobedience is indeed perilous; but the country is vast, and solitude is dumb.

The governor of Nizhny, M. Burtulin, has very politely invited me to dine with him daily during my stay in the city;
tomorrow he will explain to me how conduct similar to that
of Count Sheremetev's, rare everywhere and in every age,

cannot be now repeated in Russia. I will give the summary of his conversation, if I can make anything out of it; for hitherto I have gathered little from the lips of the Russians but confused language. Is this owing to the want of logical minds, or is it done purposely, with the view of perplexing foreigners? It is, I believe, attributable to both causes. By continually endeavoring to hide truth from the eyes of others, people become at last unable to perceive it themselves, except through a veil, which daily thickens.

Nothing is cheap at the fair of Nizhny, except articles that no one cares to buy. The epoch of great differences in price in different localities, is passed: everywhere the value of things is known: the Tartars themselves, who come from the center of Asia to Nizhny to pay very dear for the objects of luxury supplied by Paris and London, bring, in exchange, commodities of which they perfectly well know the value. The merchants may still avail themselves of the situation of the buyers to refuse them articles at a just price; but they cannot deceive them. Yet they do not abate their prices; they coolly ask too much; and their probity consists in never departing from their most exaggerated demands.

From a financial point of view, the importance of the fair continues to increase yearly; but the interest which attaches to the singularity and picturesque appearance of the assemblage diminishes. In general, the fair of Nizhny would disappoint the lover of the grotesque and the amusing. Everything is dull, stiff, and regular in Russia, except, at least, in moments when the long-repressed instinct of liberty bursts forth in an explosion: then the peasants roast their lord, or the lord marries his slave; but these rare outbreaks are little talked of: the distances and the measures taken by the police prevent isolated facts from being circulated among the mass.

In my walks through the central portion of the fair, I saw the Bukharans. These people inhabit a corner of Tibet bordering upon China. They come to Nizhny to sell precious stones.

The turquoises that I bought of them are as dear, as those sold in Paris; and all stones of any value are equally high in price. The dealers in these stones pass the year in their journey, for it takes them, they say, more than eight months to go and come only. Neither their persons nor dress struck me as very remarkable. I scarcely believe in the genuineness of the Chinese at Nizhny; but the Tartars, Persians, Kirgiz, and Kalmyks suffice for curiosity.

The two last-named barbarians bring, from the solitudes of their steppes, herds of small wild horses to sell at the fair. These animals have many good qualities, both physical and moral; but their make does not recommend them. They are, nevertheless, excellent for the saddle; and their disposition causes them to be valued. Poor creatures! they have better hearts than many men: they love each other with a tenderness and a passion that prevents them from ever voluntarily separating. So long as they remain together, they forget exile and slavery, and seem to believe themselves in their own country. When one is sold, he has to be cast, and forcibly dragged with cords out of the enclosure where his brethren are confined, who, during this violence, never cease attempting to escape or rebel, and all the while neigh most piteously. Never have I seen the horses of our own country show so many proofs of sensibility. I have seldom been more affected than I was yesterday, by the sight of these unhappy creatures torn from the freedom of the desert and violently separated from those they love. I may be answered by the line of Gilbert:

Un papillon souffrant lui fait verser des larmes.

But I shall not care for being laughed at, feeling sure that if the reader had seen the carrying out of these cruel bargains, he would have shared my feeling. Crime, when recognized as such by the laws, has its judges in this world: but permitted cruelty is only punished by the pity of kindly disposed people for the victims, and, I hope also, by Divine equity. It is this tolerated barbarity which makes me regret the narrow limits of my eloquence; a Rousseau or a Sterne would know how to make the reader weep over the fate of these poor Kirgiz horses, destined to carry, in Europe, men as much slaves as themselves, but whose condition does not always deserve as great pity as that of the enslaved brute.

Towards evening the aspect of the plain became imposing. The horizon was lightly veiled in mist, which afterwards fell in dew on the dust of Nizhny, a kind of fine brown sand, the reflection of which imparted to the heavens a reddish tint. The depths of the shade were pierced by the fantastic light of a multitude of lamps in the bivouacs by which the fair was surrounded. Everything had a voice;—from the distant forest, from the bosom of the inhabited river, a murmur brought to the attentive ear the sounds of life. What an imposing gathering together of mankind! what different languages and contrasting habits! and yet what uniformity of sentiments and ideas! The object of this great meeting, of each individual it comprised, was simply to gain a little money. Elsewhere the gaiety of the people conceals their cupidity; here, commerce stands naked, and the sterile rapacity of the merchant predominates over the frivolity of the lounger; nothing is poetical; everything is mercenary. I am wrong,—the poetry of fear and of sorrow is at the bottom of everything in this country: but where is the voice that dares express it? Nevertheless, there are a few pictures to console the imagination and to refresh the eye.

On the roads which connect the different merchant encampments may be seen long files of singular vehicles, being pairs of wheels united by an axle, which, when attached to others, so as to form an equipage of four or six wheels, had served to carry the beams and poles used in the construction of some of the temporary erections of the fair. They return thus detached, drawn by one horse, guided by men who stand upright on the axle, balancing themselves with a savage grace, and managing their half-broken steeds with a dexterity I have seen nowhere but in Russia. They remind me of the charioteers of the Byzantian circus; their shirts form a Greek tunic that is truly antique. As the Russian female peasants are the only women on earth who make themselves a waist above the bosom, so are their male relatives the only men I have ever seen who wear their shirts over their pantaloons.

In wandering at night about the fair, I was struck with the brilliancy of the eating booths, the little theaters, the taverns, and the coffeehouses. But from the midst of so much light there rose no sound, save a dull suppressed murmur; and the contrast formed by the illumination of the place and the taciturnity of the people, gave the idea of magic. I could have believed the human beings had been touched by the wand of an enchanter. The men of Asia continue grave and serious, even in their diversions: and the Russians are Asiatics, drilled, but not civilized.

LETTER 33

THIS YEAR, immediately before opening the fair, the governor called around him the ablest commercial heads in
Russia, then assembled together at Nizhny, and laid before
them, in detail, the long-ago-acknowledged and deplored inconveniences of the monetary system of the empire.

The reader is aware that there are in Russia two representative signs of commodities—paper and silver money; but he,
perhaps, does not know that the latter, by a singularity that is
unique, I believe, in financial history, is constantly varying in
value, whilst the worth of the former remains fixed. Nothing
but a profound study of the political economy of the country
could explain another very extraordinary fact resulting from
this singularity, namely, that in Russia, the specie represents
the paper, although the latter was only instituted, and only
legally exists to represent the former.

Having explained this anomaly to his auditors, and expatiated on all the mischievous consequences arising therefrom, the governor added that the emperor, in his constant solicitude for his people and for the order of his empire, had at length determined to put an end to a disorder, the progress of which threatened seriously to cripple the internal commerce of the land. The only remedy recognized as efficient is the definite and irrevocable fixing of the value of the coined ruble. The edict of the emperor accomplished this revolution in one day, as far at least as words could do it; but in order to realize the reform, the governor concluded his harangue by announcing that it was His Majesty's will that the ukase should be immediately put in execution; and he added that the superior agents of the administration, and he, the governor of Nizhny, in particular, hoped that no consideration of personal interest would prevail against the duty of obeying, without delay, the supreme will of the empire's head.

The honest men consulted on this serious question, replied that the measure, though good in itself, would destroy the most secure commercial fortunes if it were applied to transactions and bargains already made, and the terms of which would have to be fulfilled during the actual fair. While continuing to laud and admire the profound wisdom of the emperor, they humbly represented to the governor that those among the merchants who had effected sales of goods at a price fixed according to the ancient rate of money, which they had done, acting in dependence upon the relations between the paper and the silver ruble being continued as they were at the last fair, would be exposed to the necessity of submitting to payments that would not be the less fraudulent because authorized by the law, since they would rob them of their just profits; and might indeed ruin them if the present edict were thus allowed a retroactive effect; the consequences of which would be a multitude of small bankruptcies, that would not fail finally to draw in the others.

The governor replied with the gentleness and calmness

which presides in Russia throughout all administrative, financial, and political discussions, that he *perfectly* entered into the views of the chief merchants interested in the business of the fair; but that after all, the mischievous results dreaded by these gentlemen only threatened a few individuals, *who would have, as a guarantee, the severity of the existing laws against bankrupts*, whereas, on the other hand, a delay would always look something like resistance; and that such example, given by the most important commercial place in the empire, would involve inconveniences far more injurious to the country than a few failures, affecting only a small number of individuals; for disobedience, approved and justified by men who had hitherto enjoyed the confidence of the government, would be an attack aimed at the dignity of the sovereign, at the administrative and financial *unity* of Russia, or, in other words, at the vital principles of the empire: he added, that, under these peremptory considerations, he did not doubt the gentlemen addressed would, by their compliance, hasten to avoid the *monstrous* reproach of sacrificing the good of the state to their personal interests.

The result of this *pacific* conference was that, on the morrow, the fair opened under the *retroactive* system of the new ukase, the solemn publication of which was made after the assent and the promises of the first merchants in the empire had been thus obtained.

This was related to me by the governor himself, with the intention of proving to me the gentleness with which the machine of despotic government works—that machine so calumniated by people governed under liberal institutions.

I took the liberty of asking my obliging and interesting preceptor in Oriental politics, what had been the result of the government measure, and of the hasty manner in which it was judged right to put it in execution.

"The result has exceeded my hopes," replied the governor,

with a satisfied air. "Not one bankrupt! . . . All the new bargains have been concluded under the new monetary system; but what will surprise you is the fact, that no debtor has availed himself, in paying his old engagements, of the power which the law gave him of defrauding his creditors."

I confess that at the first view this result appeared to me astounding; but, on reflection, I recognized the astuteness of the Russians: the law being published, it was obeyed—on paper; and that is enough for the government. It is easily satisfied, I admit; for what it principally requires, at whatever cost, is silence. The political state of Russia may be defined in one sentence: it is a country in which the government says what it pleases, because it alone has the right to speak. Thus, in the case before us, the government says—Such is the law—obey it; but, nevertheless, the mutual accord of interested parties annuls the action of this law in that iniquitous portion of it which could be applied to old debts. In a country where the governing power is patient, it would not have exposed the honest man to the danger of being deprived of his due by thieves: in justice, the law can only regulate the future. And, indeed, theory apart, such is the result here; but to obtain it, it was necessary that the sense and good management of the subjects should be opposed to the blind impetuosity of the authorities, in order to escape the evils which would otherwise have been entailed on the country by these freaks of supreme power.

There exists under all governments built on exaggerated theories, a concealed action, a de facto influence, which nearly always opposes the extravagant doctrine adopted. The Russians possess, in a high degree, the spirit of commerce, which will explain how it was that the merchants of the fair perceived that the real tradesman thrives only by acting, and by being able to act, in confidence,—every sacrifice of credit is a loss to him of cent per cent. Nor was this all; another influence checked bad faith, and made blind cupidity silent.

The temptation that might have been felt by the insolvent would be repressed purely by fear—that real sovereign of Russia. On this occasion, the evil-intentioned will have thought that if they exposed themselves to any process, or even to too notorious animadversion, the judges or the police would turn against them; and that, in such case, what is here called law would be applied with rigor. They have dreaded incarceration, the blows of the rod in the prison, or, perhaps, something worse! Under these motives, operating with double influence in the universal silence that forms the normal state of Russia, they have given this good example of commercial probity with which the governor of Nizhny took pleasure in dazzling me. If I was dazzled, it was only for an instant; for I was not long in recognizing that if the Russian merchants forbore to ruin each other, their reciprocal moderation had precisely the same source as that of the boatmen of Lake Ladoga and the coachmen and porters of Petersburg, who control their angry passions, not through motives of humanity, but under the dread of the superior authority interfering in their affairs. As I remained silent, I could see that M. Burtulin enjoyed my surprise.

"No one knows the superiority of the emperor," he continued, "unless they have seen this prince engaged in public business, especially at Nizhny, where he performs prodigies."

I answered that I greatly admired the sagacity of the emperor.

"When we visit together the works directed by His Majesty," replied the governor, "you will yet more admire him. You will see that, owing to the energy of his character and the justness of his views, the monetary revolution, which would elsewhere have required infinite precaution, works among us as if by enchantment."

The courtierlike governor had the modesty to forbear adding a word in favor of his own good management; he equally avoided giving me any occasion to allude to what evil tongues are continually repeating to me in secret, namely, that every financial measure of the kind just taken by the Russian government, gives to the superior authority means of profit, which it well knows how to use, but of which no one dares openly to complain under autocratic rule. I am ignorant of the secret maneuvers to which recourse has been had on this occasion; but to give myself an idea of them, I imagine the situation of a man who has deposited with another a considerable sum of money. If the receiver has the power to triple the value of each piece of coin of which the sum is composed, it is clear that he can return the deposit, and all the while retain two thirds of the amount deposited. I do not say that such has been the actual result of the measure ordained by the emperor, but I admit the supposition, among many others, to aid me in comprehending the insinuations, or, if you like, the calumnies of the malcontents. They, indeed, add that the profit of this so suddenly executed operation, which consists in depriving, by a decree, the paper money of a part of its ancient value, to increase in the same proportion that of the silver ruble, is designed to compensate the private treasury of the sovereign for the sums which it was necessary to draw from it, in order to rebuild, *at his own cost*, his Winter Palace, and to refuse, with a magnanimity which Europe and Russia have admired, the offers of towns and of many private individuals, great merchants, and others, emulous of contributing to the reconstruction of a national edifice which serves as a habitation for the head of the empire.

The reader may judge, by the detail which I have deemed it my duty to give of this tyrannical charlatanism, of the value here attached to words, and of the real worth of the noblest sentiments and the finest phrases. He may judge also of the constraint imposed upon generous minds and independent spirits obliged to live under a system in which peace and order are purchased by the sacrifice of truth—that most sacred of all the gifts of heaven to man. In other communities, it is the people who apply the whip, and the government which puts on the drag; here, it is the government which urges onward, and the people who hold back; for if the political machine is to keep together at all, it is essential that the spirit of conservatism should exist in some part of it. The displacement of ideas which I here note is a political phenomenon, which I have never seen except in Russia. Under an absolute despotism, it is the government which is revolutionary; for the word revolution signifies arbitrary system and violent power.

The governor has kept his promise. He has taken me to see and minutely examine the works ordered by the emperor, with a view of making Nizhny all that it is capable of being made, and of repairing the errors of its founders. A superb road rises from the banks of the Oka to the high city, the precipices are filled up, the terraces are laid out, magnificent openings are cut even in the bosom of the mountain, where enormous substructures support squares, streets, and edifices; bridges are constructed; and all these works, worthy of a great commercial city, will soon change Nizhny into one of the most beautiful in the empire. As His Majesty has taken it under his special protection, each time that any small difficulty rises as to the mode of carrying on the works commenced, or whenever the face of an old house is to be repaired, or a new one to be built, the governor is instructed to cause a special plan to be made, and to submit the question of its adoption to the emperor. What a man! exclaim the Russians. ... What a country! I should exclaim, if I dared to speak.

While on the road, M. Burtulin, whose obliging civility and hospitality I cannot sufficiently acknowledge, gave me some interesting explanations of the Russian system of administration, and of the improvement which the progress of manners is daily effecting in the condition of the peasants.

A serf may now become the proprietor even of lands, in

the name of his lord, without the latter daring to violate the *moral* guarantee by which he is bound to his wealthy slave. To despoil this man of the fruit of his labor and industry would be an abuse of power which the most tyrannical boyar dare not permit himself under the reign of the Emperor Nicholas: but who shall assure me that he dare not do so under another sovereign? Who shall assure me even, that in spite, of the return to equity which forms the glorious characteristic of the present reign, there may yet be no avaricious and needy lords, who, without openly robbing their vassals, know how skillfully, and by turns, to employ threats and kindness, in order gradually to extract from the hands of the slave a portion of the wealth which they dare not carry away at one swoop? It is difficult to believe in the duration of such relations between the master and the serf, and yet the institutions which produce this social singularity are stable.

In Russia, nothing is defined by the proper words. In theory, everything is precisely as is said; but under such a system, if carried out, life would be impossible: in practice, there are so many exceptions, that we are ready to say, the confusion caused by customs and usages so contradictory must make all government impossible.

It is necessary to discover the solution of the double problem; the point, that is, where the principle and the application, the theory and the practice, accord, to form a just idea of the state of society in Russia.

If we are to believe the excellent governor of Nizhny, nothing can be more simple: the habit of exercising the power renders the forms of command gentle and easy. Angry passions, ill-treatment, the abuses of authority, are become extremely rare, precisely because social order is based upon extremely severe laws; everyone feels that to preserve for such laws a respect without the existence of which the state would be overthrown, they should not be put in force frequently or rashly. It is requisite that the action of despotic

575

government be observed close at hand, to understand all its gentleness (it is the governor of Nizhny who now speaks): if authority preserves any force in Russia, it is to be attributed to the moderation of the men who exercise it. Constantly placed between an aristocracy which the more easily abuses its power because its prerogatives are ill defined, and a people who the more willingly misunderstand their duty because the obedience exacted from them is not ennobled by a moral feeling, the men who command can only preserve the *prestige* of sovereignty by using as rarely as possible violent means: these means would expose the measure of the government's strength; and it judges it wiser to conceal than to unveil its resources. If a noble commits any reprehensible act, he would be several times warned in secret by the governor of the province before being admonished officially. If warnings and reprimands were not sufficient, the tribunal of the nobles would threaten to place him under guardianship; and if this had no good effect, the menace would be executed.

All this superabundance of precaution does not appear to me to be very consolatory to the serf, who, if he had as many lives, might die a hundred times under the knout of his master, before the latter, thus prudently warned and duly admonished, should be obliged to give account of his injustices or his atrocities. It is true, that the day after, lord, governor, and judges might all be sent to Siberia; but this would be rather a consolation for the imagination of the poor peasants than a real protection from the arbitrary acts of subaltern authorities, who are ever disposed to abuse the power delegated to them.

The common people have very rarely recourse to the legal tribunals in their private disputes. This enlightened instinct appears to me a sure indication of want of equity in the judges. The infrequency of litigation may have two causes— the spirit of justice in the subjects, and the spirit of iniquity in the judges. In Russia, nearly every trial is stifled by an administrative decision, which very often *recommends* an arrangement onerous to both parties, who prefer the reciprocal sacrifice of a part of their claims, and even of their best-founded rights, to the danger of proceeding against the advice of a man invested with authority by the emperor. This is the reason why the Russians have grounds for boasting that there is very little litigation in their land. Fear produces everywhere the same result—peace without tranquillity.

Will not the reader have some indulgence for a traveler lost in a country where facts are not more conclusive than words? The fictions of the Russians have upon me an effect precisely the contrary to that intended: I see at the very outset the design to blind and dazzle me; I therefore stand upon my guard; and the consequence is, that instead of being the impartial spectator that I should have been but for their vain boasting, I become, in spite of myself, an unfriendly observer.

The governor was also pleased himself to show me the fair; but this time we made the tour of it rapidly, in a carriage. I admired one point of view that was worthy of forming a panorama. To enjoy the magnificent picture, we ascended the summit of one of the Chinese pavilions, which commands an entire view of the city of a month. I was there more especially struck with the immensity of the piles of wealth annually accumulated on this point of land—a focus of industry the more remarkable, because it is lost, as it were, in the midst of deserts without bounds either to the eye or the imagination.

The governor informs me that the value of the merchandise brought this year to the fair of Nizhny exceeds one hundred and fifty millions,* according to the manifestoes of the merchants themselves, who, with the mistrust natural to Orientals, always conceal a part of the value of their stock.

Although all the countries in the world send the tribute of their soil and industry to Nizhny, the principal importance

---

*The author does not state whether these are francs or rubles.—*Trans.*

of this annual market is owing to its being a depot for the provisions, the precious stones, the stuffs, and the furs of Asia. The wealth of the Tartars, the Persians, and the Bukharans, is the object which most strikes the imagination of the strangers attracted by the reputation of the fair; yet, notwithstanding its commercial importance, I, as merely a curious observer, find it below its reputation. They reply to this, that the Emperor Alexander spoiled its picturesque and amusing aspect. He rendered the streets which separate the stalls more spacious and regular; but such stiffness is dull: besides, everything is gloomy and silent in Russia; everywhere the reciprocal distrust of government and people banishes mirth. Every passion and every pleasure has to answer for its consequences to some rigid confessor, disguised as an agent of police; every Russian is a schoolboy liable to the rod; all Russia is a vast school, where discipline is enforced by severe rule, until constraint and ennui, becoming intolerable, occasion here and there an outbreak. When this takes place, it is a regular political saturnalia; but, once again, the acts of violence are isolated, and do not disturb the general quiet. That quiet is the more stable, and appears the more firmly established, because it resembles death: it is only living things that can be exterminated. In Russia, respect for despotism is confounded with the idea of eternity.

This morning early, the governor, whose obliging kindness I can never tire, took me to see the curiosities of the old city. His servants attended him, which enabled me to dispense with putting to a second proof the docility of my *Feldjäger*, whose claims the governor respects.

There is in Russia a class of persons which corresponds to the middle class among us, though without possessing the firmness of character derived from an independent position, and the experience obtained by means of liberty of thought and cultivation of mind: this is the class of subaltern employees, or secondary nobility. The ideas of these men are generally turned towards innovations, whilst their acts are the most despotic that are committed under despotism: this, indeed, is the class which, in spite of the emperor, governs the empire.

These are enemies created by the emperors themselves, in their distrust of the old nobility. An avowed aristocracy, long rooted in the land, but moderated by the progress of manners and the amelioration of customs, would have been an instrument of civilization preferable to the hypocritical obedience, the destructive influence, of a host of commissioners and deputies, the greater number of foreign origin, and all more or less imbued, in the secret of their hearts, with revolutionary notions; all as insolent in their thoughts as obsequious in their words and manners.

My courier, unwilling to perform his business because he is near attaining the prerogatives of this order of nobility, is the profoundly comic type of its nature and character. I wish I could describe his slim figure, his carefully adjusted dress, his sharp, thin, dry, pitiless, yet humble countenance— humble whilst waiting till it may have the right to become arrogant;—in short, this type of pup, in a country where conceit is not harmless as with us; for in Russia it is a sure means of rising, if only it unite itself with servility:—but this person eludes the definition of words, as an adder glides out of sight. He represents to my eyes the union of two political forces, the most opposite in appearance, although possessing much real affinity, and although detestable when combined —despotism and revolution! I cannot observe his eyes of clouded blue, bordered with nearly white lashes, his complexion, which would be delicate, but for the bronzing rays of the sun and the frequent influence of an internal and always repressed rage, his pale and thin lips, his dry yet civil words, the intonation of which utters the very opposite of the phraseology, without viewing him as a protecting spy, a spy respected even by the governor of Nizhny; and under the influence of this idea I am tempted to order post-horses, and never to stop until beyond the frontiers of Russia.

The powerful governor of Nizhny does not dare to command this ambitious courier to mount the box of my carriage; and, though the representative of supreme authority, can only advise me to be patient.

———

The thick walls of the Nizhny Kremlin wind around a hill much loftier and steeper than the hill of Moscow. The ramparts, rising in steps above each other, the terraces, arches, and battlements of this fortress, produce a striking effect: but, notwithstanding the beauty of the site, he would be deceived who should expect, in beholding it, to be seized with astonishment produced by the Kremlin of Moscow—that religious fortress in which history is written on rock. The Kremlin of Moscow is an object that has not its like, either in Russia or in the world.

We also visited a very pretty convent: the nuns are poor, but their house exhibits edifying marks of cleanliness. Afterwards, the governor took me to see his camp: the rage for maneuvers, reviews, and bivouacs is universal. The governors of the provinces, like the emperor, pass their life in playing at soldiers; and the more numerous these assemblages are, the more proudly do the governors feel their resemblance to their master. The regiments which form the camp of Nizhny are composed of the children of soldiers. It was evening when we reached their tents, reared on a plain which is a continuation of the table of the hill on which stands old Nizhny.

Six hundred men were chanting the prayers; and at a distance, in the open air, this religious and military choir produced an astonishing effect; it was like a cloud of perfume rising majestically under a pure and deep sky: prayer, ascending from that abyss of passions and sorrows, the heart of man, may be compared to the column of smoke and fire which rises through the torn crater of the volcano, until it reaches the firmament. And who knows if the pillar of the Israelites, so long lost in the desert, did not image the same thing? The voices of these poor Slavic soldiers, softened by the distance, seemed to come from on high. When the first notes struck our ears, a knoll on the plain hid the tents from our eyes. The weakened echoes of earth responded to these celestial voices; and the music was interrupted by distant discharges of musketry—a warlike orchestra, which scarcely seemed more loud than the great drums of the opera, and which appeared much more in place than they do. When the tents, whence issued the harmonious notes, were seen before us, the setting sun, glistening upon their canvas, added the magic of color to that of sounds.

The governor, who saw the pleasure that I experienced in listening to this music, allowed me to enjoy it, and enjoyed it himself for a considerable time: nothing gives greater pleasure to this truly hospitable man than to procure enjoyment for his guests. The best way of showing him your gratitude is to let him see your gratification. We finished our ride by twilight; and, returning through the low town, we stopped before a church which has not ceased to attract my eyes since I have been in Nizhny. It is a true model of Russian architecture; neither ancient Greek, nor the Greek of the Lower Empire, but a Delftware toy, in the style of the Kremlin, or of the church of Vasily Blazhenny, though with less variety in the form and color. It is so covered with flowerwork and carvings of curious form, that one cannot stop before it without thinking of a vessel of Dresden china. This little chef d'oeuvre of the whimsical is not ancient. It was raised by the munificence of the Stroganov family; great nobles descended from the merchants, at whose cost was made the conquest of Siberia under

Ivan IV. The brothers Stroganov of that period themselves raised the adventurous army which conquered a kingdom for Russia. Their soldiers were the buccaneers of terra firma.

The interior of the church of the Stroganovs does not answer to its exterior; but, such as it is, I greatly prefer it to the clumsy copies of Roman temples with which Petersburg and Moscow are encumbered.

To finish the day we attended the opera of the fair, and listened to a vaudeville in the native language. The Russian vaudevilles are still translations from the French. The people of the country appear to be very proud of this new means of civilization which they have imported. I was unable to judge of the influence of the spectacle upon the minds of the assembly, owing to the fact of the theater being empty almost to the letter. Besides the ennui and the compassion one feels in the presence of poor players, when there is no audience, I experienced on this occasion the disagreeable impression which the mixing up of singing and speaking scenes has always communicated to me in our own theaters. This barbarism, without the salt of French wit, would, but for the governor, have driven me away during the first act. As it was, I remained patient until the conclusion of the performance.

I have been passing the night in writing to dissipate my ennui; but this effort has made me ill, and I am going to bed in a fever.

LETTER 34*

A. M. JAMENT related to me, at Nizhny, that a German, a
new lord of the village, a great agriculturist and a propagator
of modes of husbandry still unused in this country, has just
been assassinated on his own domains, contiguous to those of
a M. Merline, another foreigner, through whom the fact has
come to our knowledge.

Two men presented themselves to this German lord, under the pretext of purchasing horses of him; and in the
evening, they entered his chamber and murdered him. It was,
I am assured, a blow aimed by the peasants of the foreigner in
revenge for the innovations which he sought to make in the
culture of their lands.

The people of this country have an aversion for everything

---

*Written at Vladimir, between Nizhny and Moscow, the 2d of September.

that is not Russian. I often hear it repeated, that they will someday rise from one end of the empire to the other upon the men without a beard, and destroy them all. It is by the beard that the Russians know each other. In the eyes of the peasants, a Russian with a shaved chin is a traitor, who has sold himself to foreigners, and who deserves to share their fate. But what will be the punishment inflicted by the survivors upon the authors of these Muscovite Vespers? All Russia cannot be sent to Siberia. Villages may be transported, but it would be difficult to exile provinces. It is worthy of remark, that this kind of punishment strikes the peasants without hurting them. A Russian recognizes his country wherever long winters reign: snow has always the same aspect; the winding-sheet of the earth is everywhere equally white, whether its thickness be six inches or six feet; so that, if they only allow him to reconstruct his cabin and his sledge, the Russian finds himself at home to whatever spot he may be exiled. In the deserts of the North it costs little to make a country. To the man who has never seen anything but icy plains scattered with stunted trees, every cold and desert land represents his native soil. Besides, the inhabitants of these latitudes are always inclined to quit the place of their birth.

Scenes of disorder are multiplying in the country: every day I hear of some new crime: but, by the time it is made public, it has already become ancient, which tends to weaken its impressiveness, especially as from so many isolated atrocities nothing results to disturb the general repose of the country. As I have already said, tranquillity is maintained among this people by the length and difficulties of communication, and by the secrecy of the government, which perpetuates the evil through fear of disclosing it. To these causes, I may add the blind obedience of the troops, and, above all, the complete ignorance of the country people themselves. But, singular conjunction of facts!—the latter remedy is, at the same time, the first cause of the evil: it is, therefore, difficult to see how the nation will get out of the dangerous circle in which circumstances have involved it. Hitherto, the good and the evil, the danger and the safety, have come to it from the same source.

The reader can form no conception of the manner in which a lord, when taking possession of some newly acquired domain, is received by his peasants. They exhibit a servility which would appear incredible to the people of our country: men, women, and children, all fall on their knees before their new master—all kiss the hands, and sometimes the feet, of the landholder; and, O! miserable profanation of faith!—those who are old enough to err, voluntarily confess to him their sins—he being to them the image and the envoy of God, representing both the King of Heaven and the emperor! Such fanaticism in servitude must end in casting an illusion over the mind of him who is its object, especially if he has not long attained the rank which he possesses: the change of fortune thus marked, must so dazzle him as to persuade him that he is not of the same race as those prostrate at his feet— those whom he suddenly finds himself empowered to command. It is no paradox which I put forward, when I maintain that the aristocracy of birth could alone ameliorate the condition of the serfs, and enable them to profit by emancipation through gentle and gradual transitions. Their slavery becomes unbearable under the new men of wealth. Under the old ones, it is hard enough: but these are at least born above them, and also among them, which is a consolation; besides, the habit of authority is as natural to the one party as that of slavery is to the other; and habit mitigates everything, mollifying the injustice of the strong, and lightening the yoke of the feeble. But the change of fortunes and conditions produces frightful results in a country subjected to a system of servitude: and yet, it is this very change which maintains the duration of the present order of things in Russia, because it conciliates the men who know how to benefit by it—a second example of the remedy being drawn from the source of the evil. Terrible circle, round which revolve all the populations of a vast empire! This lord, this new deity—what title has he to be adored? He is adored because he has had enough money and capacity for intrigue to be able to buy the land to which are attached all the men prostrate before him. An upstart appears to me a monster, in a country where the life of the poor depends upon the rich, and where man is the fortune of man; the onward progress of industrious enterprise, and the fixed state of serfdom, combined in the same society, produce results that are revolting: but the despot loves the upstart— he is his creature! The position of a new lord is this: yesterday his slave was his equal: today, his industry more or less honest, his flatteries more or less mean, have put it into his power to purchase a certain number of his comrades. To become the beast of burden of an equal is an intolerable evil. It is, however, a result which an impious alliance of arbitrary customs and liberal, or, to speak more justly, unstable institutions, can bring upon a people. Nowhere else does the man who makes a fortune have his feet kissed by his vanquished rivals. The most shocking incoherence has become the basis of the Russian constitution.

M. Guibal—everytime that I am authorized to cite a name, I use the permission—M. Guibal, the son of a schoolmaster, was exiled without cause, or at least without explanation, and without being able to guess his crime, into a Siberian village in the environs of Orenburg. A song, which he composed to beguile his sorrow was listened to by an inspector, who put it before the eyes of the governor; it attracted the attention of that august personage, who sent his aide-de-camp to the exile to inform himself regarding the circumstances of his situation and his conduct, and to judge if he was good for anything. The unfortunate man succeeded in interesting the aide-de-camp, who, on his return, made a very favorable report, in consequence of which he was immediately recalled. He has never known the real cause of his misfortune: perhaps it was another song.

Such are the circumstances on which depends the fate of a man in Russia!

The following story is of a different character.

A Russian, immensely rich, but who ought to have been enlightened as regards the miseries and infirmities of wealth and power—for the fortune of his family had been established for two generations—was traveling in Germany. He fell sick in a small town, and called in the chief physician of the place: at first he submitted to everything that was ordered; but not finding himself at the end of a few days any better, he grew weary of obedience, rose up angrily, and throwing off the veil of civilization in which he had deemed it advisable to muffle himself, he called the landlord, and, while rapidly marching up and down his chamber, thus addressed him: "I do not understand the manner in which I am treated: here I have taken medicine for three days without being in the least benefited: what kind of a doctor have you sent me? *he cannot know who I am!*"

Whimsical sentiments of every species abound in Russia among the higher classes, because hearts and minds are the prey of exhaustion and satiety. A lady of high rank in Petersburg has been married several times: she passes the summers in a magnificent country house, some leagues from the city, and her garden is filled with the tombs of all her husbands, whom she begins to love passionately so soon as they are dead. She raises for them mausolea and chapels, weeps over their ashes, and covers their tombs with sentimental epitaphs; in short, she renders to the dead an honor offensive to the living. The pleasure grounds of this lady have thus become a real Père-Lachaise, with quite a little gloom about them for whoever has not, like the noble widow, a love of tombs and deceased husbands.

Nothing need surprise us in the way of false sensitiveness

among a people who study elegance with the same precise minuteness that others learn the art of war or of government. The following is an example of the grave interest the Russians take in the most puerile matters whenever they affect them personally.

A descendant of ancient boyars, who was rich and elderly, lived in the country, not far from Moscow. A detachment of hussars was, with its officers, quartered in his house. It was the season of Easter, which the Russians celebrate with peculiar solemnity. All the members of a family unite with their friends and neighbors, to attend the mass, which, on this festival, is offered precisely at midnight.

The proprietor of whom I speak, being the most considerable person of the neighborhood, expected a large assembly of guests on Easter Eve, more especially as he had, that year, restored and greatly beautified his parish church.

Two or three days before the feast, he was awakened by a procession of horses and carriages passing over a pier that led to his residence. This castle is, according to the usual custom, situated close upon the edge of a small sheet of water; the church rises on the opposite side, just at the end of the pier, which serves as a road from the castle to the village.

Astonished to hear so unusual a noise in the middle of the night, the master of the house rose, and, to his great surprise, saw from the window, by the light of numerous torches, a beautiful calèche drawn by four horses and attended by outriders.

He quickly recognized this new equipage, as well as the man to whom it belonged: he was one of the hussar officers lodged in his house, an individual who had been recently enriched by an inheritance, and had just purchased a carriage and horses, which had been brought to the castle. The old lord, upon seeing him parading in his open calèche, all alone, by night, in the midst of a deserted and silent country, imagined that he had become mad: he followed with his eyes the elegant procession, and saw it advance in good order towards the church, and stop before the door; where the owner gravely descended from the carriage, aided by his people, who crowded round to support the young officer, although he, appearing quite as nimble as they, might have easily dispensed with their assistance.

Scarcely had he touched the ground, when, slowly and majestically, he re-entered his coach, took another turn on the pier, and came back again to the church, where he and his people recommenced the previous ceremony. This game was renewed until daybreak. At the last repetition, the officer gave orders to return to the castle without noise. A few minutes after, all were in their beds.

In the morning, the first question that the wondering owner of the house put to his guest, the captain of hussars, was as to the meaning of his nocturnal ride, and of the evolutions of his people around his person. "O! nothing!" replied the officer, without the least embarrassment: "my servants are novices; you will have much company at Easter; people are coming here from every quarter; I therefore merely thought it best to make a rehearsal of *my entrée* into church."

I must now give an account of my departure from Nizhny, which it will be seen was less brilliant than the nocturnal ride of the captain of hussars.

On the evening that I accompanied the governor to the empty Russian theater, I met, after leaving him, an acquaintance who took me to the café of the Gypsies, situated in the most lively part of the fair: it was nearly midnight, but this house was still full of people, noise, and light. The women struck me as being very handsome; their costume, although in appearance the same as that of other Russian females, takes a foreign character when worn by them: there is magic in their glances, and their features and attitudes are graceful, and at the same time imposing. In short, they resemble the sibyls of Michelangelo.

Their singing is about the same as that of the Gypsies at Moscow, but, if anything, I thought it yet more expressive, forcible, and varied. I am assured that they have much pride of character, that they have warm passions, yet are neither light nor mercenary, and that they often repel, with disdain, very advantageous offers.

The night was far advanced when we left the Gypsies; stormy clouds, which swept over the plain, had suddenly changed the temperature. The long, deserted streets of the fair were filled with ponds of water, through which our horses dashed without relaxing their speed; fresh squalls, bringing over black clouds, announced more rain, and drove the water, splashed aside by the horses, in our faces. "Summer is gone," said my cicerone. "I feel you are only too right," I answered; "I am as cold as if it were winter." I had no cloak: in the morning we had been suffocated with the heat; on returning to my room, I was freezing. I sat down to write for two hours, and then retired to rest in the icy fit of fever. In the morning, when I wished to get up, a vertigo seized me, and I fell again on my couch, unable to dress myself.

This annoyance was the more disagreeable, as I had intended leaving on that very day for Kazan: I wished at least to set my foot in Asia; and with this view had engaged a boat to descend the Volga, whilst my *Feldjäger* had been directed to bring my carriage empty to Kazan, to convey me back to Nizhny by land. However, my zeal had a little cooled after the governor of Nizhny had proudly displayed to me plans and drawings of Kazan. It is still the same city from one end of Russia to another: the great square, the broad streets, bordered with diminutive houses, the house of the governor, with ornamented pillars and a pediment; decorations even yet more out of place in a Tartar than in a Russian town; barracks, cathedrals in the style of temples; nothing, in short, was wanting; and I felt that the whole tiresome architectural repetition was not worth the trouble of prolonging my journey two hundred leagues in order to visit. But the frontiers of Siberia and the recollections of the siege still tempted me. It became necessary, however, to renounce the journey, and to keep quiet for four days.

The governor very politely came to see me in my humble bed. At last, on the fourth day, feeling my indisposition increase, I determined to call in a doctor. This individual said to me,—

"You have no fever, you are not yet ill, but you will be seriously so if you remain three days longer at Nizhny. I know the influence of this air upon certain temperaments; leave it; you will not have traveled ten leagues without finding yourself better, and the day after, you will be well again."

"But I can neither eat, sleep, walk, nor even move without feeling severe pains in my head: what will become of me if I am obliged to stop on the road?"

"Cause yourself to be carried into your coach: the autumn rains have commenced: I repeat, that I cannot answer for your recovery if you remain at Nizhny."

This doctor is scientific and experienced: he has passed several years at Paris, after having previously studied in Germany. His look inspired me with confidence; and the day after I received his advice I entered my carriage, in the midst of a beating rain accompanied by an icy wind. It was unpleasant enough to discourage the strongest traveler: nevertheless, at the second stage, the prediction of the doctor was fulfilled; I began to breathe more freely, though fatigue so overpowered me that I was obliged to stop and pass the night in a miserable lodging: the next day I was again in health.

During the time spent in my bed at Nizhny, my guardian spy grew tired of our prolonged stay at the fair, and of his consequent inaction. One morning he came to my *valet de chambre*, and said to him, in German, "When do we leave?"

"I cannot tell; monsieur is ill."

"*Is* he ill?"

"Do you suppose that it is to please himself that he keeps his bed in such a room as you found for him here?"

"What is the matter with him?"

"I do not know at all."

"Why is he ill?"

"Good heavens! you had better go and ask him."

This *why* appears to me worthy of being noted.

The man has never forgiven me the scene in the coach. Since that day, his manners and his countenance have changed, which proves to me that there always remains some corner for the natural disposition, and for sincerity in even the most profoundly dissimulating characters. I therefore think all the better of him for his rancor: I had believed him incapable of any primitive sentiment.

The Russians, like all newcomers in the civilized world, are excessively susceptible; they cannot understand generalities; they view everything as applied personally: nowhere is France so ill understood. The liberty of thinking and speaking is more incomprehensible than anything else to these people. Those who pretend to judge our country, say to me, that they do not really believe our king abstains from punishing the writers who daily abuse him in Paris.

"Nevertheless," I answer them, "the fact is there to convince you."

"Yes, yes, you talk of toleration," they reply, with a knowing air; "it is all very well for the multitude and for foreigners: but your government punishes secretly the too audacious journalists."

When I repeat that everything is public in France, they smile, politely abstain from further comment; but they do not believe me.

The city of Vladimir is often mentioned in history: its aspect is like all the other Russian cities—that eternal type with which the reader is only too familiar. The country, also, that I have traveled over from Nizhny resembles the rest of

Russia—a forest without trees, interrupted by towns without life—barracks, raised sometimes upon heaths, sometimes upon marshes, and the spirit of a regiment to animate them. When I tell the Russians that their woods are badly managed, and that their country will in time be without fuel, they laugh in my face. It has been calculated how many thousands of years it will require to consume the wood which covers the soil of an immense portion of the empire; and this calculation satisfies everybody. It is *written* in the estimates sent in by each provincial governor, that each province contains so many acres of forests. Upon these data the statistical department goes to work; but before performing their purely arithmetical labor of adding sums to make a total, the calculators do not think of visiting these forests upon paper. If they did, they would in most cases find only a few thickets of brushwood, amid plains of fern and rushes. But with their written satisfactory reports, the Russians trouble themselves very little about the real scarcity of the only riches proper to their soil. Their woods are immense in the bureau of the minister, and this is sufficient for them. The day may be foreseen when, as a consequence of this administrative supineness and security, the people will warm themselves by the fires made of the old dusty papers accumulated in the public offices: these riches increase daily.

My words may appear bold and even revolting; for the sensitive self-love of the Russians imposes upon foreigners duties of delicacy and propriety to which I do not submit. My sincerity will render me culpable in the eyes of the men of this country. What ingratitude! the minister gives me a *Feldjäger*; the presence of his uniform spares me all the difficulties of the journey, and therefore am I bound, in the opinion of the Russians, to approve of everything with them. That foreigner, they think, would outrage all the laws of hospitality if he permitted himself to criticize a country where so much regard has been shown towards him. Notwithstanding all this, I hold myself free to describe what I see, and to pass my opinion upon it.

To appreciate, as I ought to do, the favor accorded me by the director-general of the posts in furnishing me with a courier, it will at least be right to state the discomforts which his obliging civility has spared me. Had I set out for Nizhny with a common servant only, we should, however well he might have spoken Russian, have been delayed by the tricks and frauds of the post-masters at nearly every stage. They would at first have refused us horses, and then have showed us empty stables to convince us there were none. After an hour's parley, they would have found us a set that they would pretend belonged to some peasant, who would condescend to spare them for twice or thrice the charge established by the Imperial post-regulations. We might at first have refused; the horses would have been taken away; till at last, tired of the war, we should have concluded by humbly imploring the return of the animals, and by complying with every demand. The same scene would have been renewed at each out-of-the-way post. This is the manner in which inexperienced and un-protected foreigners here travel.

The Russians are always on their guard against truth, which they dread; but I, who belong to a community where everything is transacted openly, why should I embarrass myself with the scruples of these men, who say nothing, or merely darkly whisper unmeaning phrases, and beg their neighbors to keep them a secret? Every open and clearly defined statement causes a stir in a country where not only the expression of opinions, but also the recital of the most undoubted facts, is forbidden. A Frenchman cannot imitate this absurdity; but he ought to note it.

Russia is governed, God knows when she will be civilized.

Putting no faith in persuasion, the monarch draws every-thing to himself, under pretext that a rigorous system of cen-tralization is indispensable to the government of an empire so prodigiously extended as Russia. That system is perhaps necessary to the principle of blind obedience: but enlightened obedience is opposed to the false idea of simplification which has for more than a century influenced the successors of the Czar Peter, and their successors also. Simplification, carried to this excess, is not power, it is death. Absolute authority ceases to be real, it becomes a phantom, when it has only the images of men to exercise itself upon.

Russia will never really become a nation until the day when its prince shall voluntarily repair the evil committed by Peter I. But will there ever be found, in such a country, a sovereign courageous enough to admit that he is only a man?

It is necessary to see Russia, to appreciate all the difficulty of this political reformation, and to understand the energy of character that is necessary to work it.

———

I am now writing at a post-house between Vladimir and Moscow.

Among all the chances and accidents by which a traveler is in danger of losing his life on a Russian highway, the imagination of the reader would be at fault to single out the one by which my life has been just menaced. The danger was so great, that without the address, the strength, and the presence of mind of my Italian servant, I should not be the writer of the following account:—

It was necessary that the shah of Persia should have an object in conciliating the friendship of the emperor of Russia, and that with this view, building his expectations upon bulky presents, he should send to the czar one of the most enormous black elephants of Asia, clothed with superb hangings, which served as a caparison for the colossus, escorted by a cortege of horsemen, resembling a cloud of grasshoppers, followed by a file of camels, which appeared no larger than donkeys by the side of this elephant, the most enormous that I have ever beheld, and surmounted by a man with olive complexion and Oriental costume, carrying a parasol, and sitting cross-legged upon the back of the monster; it was further necessary, that whilst this living monument was thus forced to journey on foot towards Petersburg, where the climate will soon transfer him to the collection of the mammoths and the mastodons, I should be traveling post by the same route; and that my departure from Vladimir should so coincide with that of the Persians, that, at a certain part of the deserted road, the gallop of my Russian horses should bring me behind them, and make it necessary to pass by the side of the giant; —it required nothing less, I say, than these combined circumstances to explain the danger caused by the terror that seized my four horses, on seeing before them an animated pyramid, moving as if by magic in the midst of a crowd of strange-looking men and beasts.

Their astonishment as they approached the walking tower was at first shown by a general start aside, by extraordinary neighings and snortings, and by refusing to proceed. But the words and the whip of the coachman at length so far mastered them as to compel them to pass the fantastic object of their terror. They submitted trembling, their manes stood erect, and scarcely were they alongside of the monster when, reproaching themselves as it were for a courage, which was nothing more than fear of another object, they yielded to their panic, and the voice and reins of the driver became useless. The man was conquered at the moment when he thought himself the conqueror: scarcely had the horses felt that the elephant was behind them, when they dashed off at full speed, heedless as to where their blind frenzy might carry them. This furious course had very nearly cost us our lives: the coachman, bewildered and powerless, remained immovable on his seat, and slackened the reins; the *Feldjäger*, placed beside him, partook of his stupefaction and helplessness. Antonio

and I, seated within the calèche, which was closed on account of the weather and my ailment, remained pale and
mute: our species of *tarantasse* has no doors; it is a boat, over
the sides of which we have to step to get in and out. On a sudden, the maddened horses swerved from the road, and dashed
at an almost perpendicular bank, about ten feet high: one
of the small fore wheels was already buried in the bankside;
two of the horses had reached the top without breaking their
traces; I saw their feet on a level with our heads; one strain
more, and the coach would have followed, but certainly not
upon its wheels. I thought that it was all over with us. The
Cossacks who escorted the powerful cause of this peril, seeing our critical position, had the prudence to avoid following
us, for fear of further exciting our horses: I, without even
thinking of springing from the carriage, had commended my
soul to God, when, suddenly, Antonio disappeared. I thought
he was killed: the head and leather curtains of the calèche
partly concealed the scene from me; but at the same moment
I felt the horses stop. "We are saved!" cried Antonio. This *we*
touched me, for he himself was beyond all danger, after having succeeded in getting out of the calèche without accident.
His rare presence of mind had indicated to him the moment
favorable to springing out with the least risk: afterwards,
with that agility which strong emotions impart, but which
they cannot explain, he found himself, without knowing
how, upon the top of the bank, at the heads of the two horses
which had scaled it, and the desperate efforts of which threatened to destroy us all. The carriage was just about to over-
turn; but Antonio's activity gave time to the others to follow
his example; the coachman was in a moment at the heads of
the two other horses, while the courier propped up the coach.
At the same moment, the Cossack guard of the elephant, who
had put their horses to a gallop, arrived to our assistance;
they made me alight, and helped my people to hold the still
trembling horses. Never was an accident more nearly being

disastrous, and never was one repaired at less cost. Not a screw of the coach was disturbed, and scarcely a strap of harness broken.

In a quarter of an hour, Antonio was seated quietly by my side in the calèche; in another ten minutes he was as fast asleep as if he had not been the means of saving all our lives.

While they put the harness in order, I approached the cause of all this mischief. The groom of the elephant had prudently led him into the wood adjoining one of the side alleys of the road. The formidable beast appeared to me yet larger after the peril to which he had exposed me. His trunk, busy in the top of the birch trees, reminded me of a boa twisted among the palms. I began to make excuses for my horses, and left him, giving thanks to God for having escaped a death which at one moment appeared to me inevitable.

I am now again at Moscow. An excessive heat has not ceased to reign there for several months; I find the same temperature that I left: the summer is indeed quite extraordinary. The draft sends up into the air, above the most populous quarters of the city, a reddish dust, which, towards evening, produces effects as fantastical as the Bengal lights. This evening, at sunset, I contemplated the spectacle from the Kremlin, the survey of which I have made with as much admiration, and almost as much surprise, as I did at first.

The city of men was separated from the palace of giants, by a glory like one of Correggio's: the whole was a sublime union of the marvels of painting and poetry.

The Kremlin, as the loftiest point in the picture, received on its breast the last streaks of day, while the mists of night had already enveloped the rest of the city. The white and irregular masses of the palace reflected unequally the obliquely borne beams of a flickering twilight. This variety of shades was the effect of the different degrees of inclination of different walls, and of the projections and recesses which constitute the beauty of the barbaric architecture, whose bold caprices, if they do not charm the taste, speak impressively to the imagination. It was so astonishing, so beautiful, that I have not been able to resist once more naming the Kremlin.

But let not the reader be alarmed—this is an adieu.

The plaintive song of some workmen, echoing from vault to vault, from battlement to battlement, from precipice to precipice—precipices built by man—penetrated to my heart, which was absorbed in inexpressible melancholy. Wandering lights appeared in the depths of the royal edifice; and along the deserted galleries and empty barbicans, came the voice of man, which I was astonished to hear at that hour among these solitary palaces; as was likewise the bird of night, who, disturbed in his mysterious loves, fled from the light of the torches, and, seeking refuge among the highest steeples and towers, there spread the news of the unusual disorder.

That disorder was the consequence of the works commanded by the emperor to welcome his own approaching arrival: he fêtes himself, and illuminates his Kremlin when he comes to Moscow. Meantime, as the darkness increased, the city brightened: its illuminated streets, shops, coffeehouses, and theaters, rose out of the dark like magic. The day was also the anniversary of the emperor's coronation—another motive for illuminating. The Russians have so many joyful days to celebrate, that, were I in their place, I should never put out my lamps.

The approach of the magician has already begun to be felt. Three weeks ago Moscow was only inhabited by merchants, who proceeded about their business in droshkies: now, noble coursers, splendid equipages, gilded uniforms, great lords, and numerous valets, enliven the streets and obstruct the porticoes. "The emperor is thirty leagues off: who knows if he will not be here tomorrow, or perhaps tonight? It is said he was here yesterday, incognito: who can prove that he is not here now?" And this doubt, this hope, animates all hearts; it changes the face and language of all persons, and the aspect of everything. Moscow, the merchant city, is now as much troubled and agitated as a tradesman's wife expecting the visit of a great nobleman. Deserted palaces and gardens are reopened; flowers and torches vie with each other in brilliancy; flattering speeches begin to murmur through the crowd: I fear lest I myself should catch the influence of the illusion, if not through selfish motives, at least from a love of the marvelous.

An emperor of Russia at Moscow, is a king of Assyria in Babylon.

His presence is at this moment, they say, working miracles at Borodino. An entire city is there created—a city just sprung out of the desert, and destined to endure for a week: even gardens have been planted there round a palace; the trees, destined soon to die, have been brought from a distance at great expense, and are so placed as to represent antique shades. The Russians, though they have no past, are, like all enlightened parvenus, who well know what is thought of their sudden fortunes, more particularly fond of imitating the effects of time. In this scene of fairy work, all that speaks of duration is imitated by things the most ephemeral. Several theaters are also raised on the plain of Borodino; and the drama serves as an interlude between the warlike pantomimes.

The program of the fête is the exact repetition of the battle which we called Moscow, and which the Russians have christened Borodino. Wishing to approach as nearly as possible to the reality, they have convoked from the most distant parts of the empire, all the surviving veterans of 1812 who were in the action. The reader may imagine the astonishment and distress of these brave men, suddenly torn from their repose, and obliged to repair from the extremities of Siberia, Kamchatka, Lapland, the Caspian, or the Caucasus, to a theater which they are told was the theater of their glory —not their fortune, but their renown, a miserable recompense for a superhuman devotion. Why revive these questions and recollections? Why this bold evocation of so many mute and forgotten specters? It is the last judgment of the conscripts of 1812. If they wished to make a satire upon military life, they could not take a better course: it was thus that Holbein, in his *Dance of Death*, caricatured human life. Numbers of these men, awakened out of their sleep on the brink of their graves, have not mounted a horse for many years; and here they are obliged, in order to please a master whom they have never seen, again to play over their long-forgotten parts. They have so much dread of not satisfying the expectations of the capricious sovereign who thus troubles their old age, that they say the representation of the battle is more terrible to them than was the reality. This useless ceremony, this fanciful war, will make an end of the soldiers whom the real event spared: it is a cruel pleasure, worthy of one of the successors of the czar who caused living bears to be introduced in the masquerade that he gave on the nuptials of his buffoon: that czar was Peter the Great. All these diversions have their source in the same feeling— contempt for human life.

The emperor had permitted me—which means to say that he commanded me—to be present at Borodino. It is a favor of which I feel myself to have become unworthy. I did not at the time reflect upon the extreme difficulty of the part a Frenchman would have to perform in this historical drama: and I also had not seen the monstrous work of the Kremlin, which he would expect me to praise; above all, I was then ignorant of the history of the Princess Troubetzkoy, which I have the greater difficulty in banishing from my mind, because I may not speak of it. These reasons united have induced me to decide upon remaining in oblivion. It is an easy resolve; for the contrary would give me trouble, if I may judge by the useless efforts of a crowd of Frenchmen and foreigners of all countries, who in vain solicit permission to be present at Borodino.

All at once the police of the camp has assumed extreme severity; these new precautions are attributed to unpleasant revelations that have been recently made. The sparks of revolt are everywhere feeding under the ashes of liberty. I do not know even whether, under actual circumstances, it would be possible for me to avail myself of the invitation the emperor gave me, both at Petersburg and, afterwards when I took leave of him, at Peterhof. "I shall be very glad if you will attend the ceremony at Borodino, where we lay the first stone of a monument in honor of General Bagration." These were his last words.*

I see here persons who were invited, yet are not able to approach the camp. Permissions are refused to everybody except a few privileged Englishmen and some members of the diplomatic corps. All the rest, young and old, military men and diplomatists, foreigners and Russians, have returned to Moscow, mortified by their unavailing efforts. I have written to a person connected with the emperor's household, regretting my inability to avail myself of the favor His Majesty had accorded in permitting me to witness the maneuvers, and pleading as an excuse the state of my eyes, which are not yet cured. The dust of the camp is, I am told, unbearable to everybody; to me it might cost the loss of sight.

The Duke of Leuchtenberg must be endowed with an unusual quantum of indifference to be able coolly to witness the spectacle prepared for him. They assure me that, in the repre-

---

*I learnt afterwards, at Petersburg, that orders had been given to permit my reaching Borodino, where I was expected.

sentation of the battle, the emperor will command the corps of Prince Eugene, father of the young duke.

I should regret not seeing a spectacle so curious in its moral aspect, if I could be present as a disinterested spectator; but, without having the renown of a father to maintain, I am a son of France, and I feel it is not for me to find any pleasure in witnessing a representation of war, made at great cost, solely with the view of exalting the national pride of the Russians, on the occasion of our disasters. As to the sight itself, I can picture it very easily; I have seen plenty of straight lines in Russia. Besides, in reviews and mock fights, the eye never gets beyond a great cloud of dust.

The Russians have reason to pride themselves on the issue of the campaign of 1812; but the general who laid its plan, he who first advised the gradual retreat of the Russian army towards the center of the empire, with the view of enticing the exhausted French after it,—the man, in fact, to whose genius Russia owed her deliverance—Prince Wittgenstein, is not represented in this grand repetition; because, unfortunately for him, he is yet living, half disgraced: he resides on his estates; his name will not be pronounced at Borodino, though an eternal monument is to be raised to the glory of General Bagration, who fell on the field of battle.

Under despotic governments, dead warriors are great favorites: here, behold one decreed to be the hero of a campaign in which he bravely fell, but which he never directed.

This absence of historical probity, this abuse of the will of one man, who imposes his views upon all, who dictates to the people whatever they are to think on events of national interest, appears to me the most revolting of all the impieties of arbitrary government. Strike, torture bodies, but do not crush minds: let man judge of things according to the intimations of Providence, according to his conscience and his reason. The people must be called impious who devoutly submit to this continual violation of the respect due to all that is most holy in the sight of God and man,—the sanctity of truth.

Without waiting for the solemn entry of the emperor into Moscow, I shall leave in two days' time for Petersburg.

———————

Here end the chapters that were written by the traveler in the form of letters to his friends: the relation which follows completes his recollections; it was written at various places, commencing at Petersburg, in 1839, and afterwards continued in Germany, and more recently at Paris.

LETTER 35

RETURN FROM MOSCOW TO PETERSBURG. — HISTORY OF M.
PERNET, A FRENCH PRISONER IN RUSSIA. — HIS ARREST. —
CONDUCT OF HIS FELLOW-TRAVELER. — THE FRENCH CONSUL AT
MOSCOW. — EFFECTS OF IMAGINATION. — ADVICE OF A RUSSIAN.
— GREAT NOVGOROD. — SOUVENIRS OF IVAN IV. — ARRIVAL AT
PETERSBURG. — M. DE BARANTE. — SEQUEL OF THE HISTORY OF
M. PERNET. — INTERIOR OF A MOSCOW PRISON. — A VISIT TO
COLPINA. — THE ACADEMY OF PAINTING. — THE ARTS IN RUSSIA.
— INFLUENCE OF THE NORTH UPON THE ARTS. — MADEMOISELLE
TAGLIONI AT PETERSBURG. — SUPERIORITY OF A REPRESENTATIVE
FORM OF GOVERNMENT. — DEPARTURE FROM RUSSIA. — THE
FEELINGS OF THE AUTHOR. — A SINCERE LETTER. — REASONS FOR
NOT RETURNING THROUGH POLAND.

AT THE MOMENT I was about to leave Moscow, a singular circumstance attracted all my attention, and obliged me to delay my departure.

I had ordered post-horses at seven o'clock in the morning: to my great surprise my *valet de chambre* awoke me at four, and on my asking the cause of this unnecessary hurry, he answered that he did not like to delay informing me of a fact which he had just learnt, and which appeared to him very serious. The following is the gist of what he related.

A Frenchman, whose name is M. Louis Pernet, and who arrived a few days ago in Moscow, where he lodged at a public hotel, has been arrested in the middle of the night—this very night,—and, after being deprived of his papers, has been taken to the city prison, and there placed in a cell. Such was the account which the waiter at our inn gave to my servant, who,

605

after many questions, further learnt that M. Pernet was a young man about twenty-six years old, and in poor health; that he passed through Moscow last year, when he stayed at the house of a Russian friend, who afterwards took him into the country. This Russian was now absent, and the unfortunate prisoner had no other acquaintance in Moscow except another Frenchman, a M. R——, in whose company he had been traveling from the north of Russia. M. R—— lodged in the same hotel with the prisoner. His name struck me the moment I heard it, for it is the same as that of a man with whom I dined a few days before at the house of the governor of Nizhny. I immediately rose, and sought the waiter myself, to hear from his own lips the version of the story, and to ascertain beyond doubt the correctness of the name of M. R——, whose identity I was particularly desirous of ascertaining. The waiter told me, that having been sent on an errand by a foreigner about to leave Moscow, he was at Kopp's hotel at the moment when the police left it, and he added that M. Kopp had related to him the affair, which he recounted in words that exactly accorded with the statement of Antonio.

As soon as I was dressed, I repaired to M. R——, and found, true enough, that he was the man of Nizhny. I found him out of bed; we recognized each other in a moment; but when I told him the object of my very early morning call, he appeared embarrassed.

"It is true that I have traveled," he said, "with M. Pernet, but it was by mere chance; we met at Archangel, and from thence have proceeded in company: he has a very poor constitution, and his weak health gave me much uneasiness during the journey: I rendered him the services that humanity called for, but nothing more; I am not one of his friends; I know nothing of him."

"I know still less of him," I replied; "but we are all three Frenchmen, and we owe each other mutual aid in a country where our liberty and our life may be menaced any moment by a power which cannot be seen till it strikes."

"Perhaps M. Pernet," replied M. R——, "has got himself into this scrape by some imprudence. A stranger like himself, and without credit, what can I do? If he is innocent, the arrest will be followed by no serious consequences; if he is culpable, he will have to submit to the punishment. I can do nothing for him, I owe him nothing; and I advise you, sir, to be yourself very cautious in any steps you may take in his favor, as well as in your language respecting the affair."

"But what will decide his guilt?" I exclaimed. "It will be first of all necessary to see him, to know to what he attributes this arrest, and to ask him what can be said or done for him."

"You forget the country we are in," answered M. R——: "he is in a dungeon; how could we get access to him? the thing is impossible."

"What is also impossible," I replied, rising, "is that Frenchmen—that any men, should leave their countryman in a critical situation, without even inquiring the cause of his misfortune."

On leaving this very prudent traveling companion, I began to think the case more serious than I had at first supposed; and I considered that, to understand the true position of the prisoner, I ought to address myself to the French consul. Being obliged to wait the usual hour for seeing that personage, I ordered back my post-horses, to the great surprise and displeasure of the *Feldjäger*, as they were already at the door when I gave the countermand.

At ten o'clock, I made to the French consul the above relation of facts; and found that official protector of the French quite as prudent, and yet more cold, than M. R—— had appeared to me. Since he has lived in Moscow, this consul has become almost a Russian. I could not make out whether his answers were dictated by a fear founded on a knowledge of the usages of the country, or by a sentiment of wounded self-love, of ill-understood personal dignity.

"M. Pernet," he said, "passed six months in Moscow and its environs, without having thought fit, during all that time, to make the smallest approach towards the consul of France. M. Pernet must look, therefore, to himself alone to get out of the situation in which his heedlessness has involved him. This word," added the consul, "is perhaps not sufficiently strong." He then concluded by repeating that he neither ought, nor could, nor would, mix himself up with the affair.

In vain did I represent to him, that, in his capacity as our consul, he owed to every Frenchman, without distinction of persons, and even if they failed in the laws of etiquette, his aid and protection; that the present question was not one of ceremony, but of the liberty and perhaps the life of a fellow-countryman; and that, under such a misfortune, all resentment should be at least suspended till the danger was over. I could not extract one word, not one single expression of interest in favor of the prisoner; nor even, when I reasoned on public grounds, and spoke of the dignity of France, and the safety of all Frenchmen who traveled in Russia, could I make any impression; in short, this second attempt aided the cause no better than the first.

Nevertheless, though I had not even known M. Pernet by name, and though I had no motive to take any personal interest in him, it seemed to me, as chance had made me acquainted with his misfortune, that it was no more than my duty to give him all the aid that lay in my power. I was at this moment strongly struck with a truth which is no doubt often present to the thoughts of others, but which had only until then vaguely and fleetingly passed before my mind—the truth that imagination serves to extend the sphere of pity, and to render it more active. I went even so far as to conclude in my own mind, that a man without imagination would be absolutely devoid of feeling. All my imaginative or creative faculties were busy in presenting to me, in spite of myself, this unhappy unknown man, surrounded by the phantoms of his prison solitude: I suffered with him, I felt his feelings, I shared his fears; I saw him, forsaken by all the world, discovering that his state was hopeless: for who would ever interest themselves in a prisoner in this land, so distant and so different from ours, in a society where friends meet together for amusement and separate in adversity. What a stimulus was this thought to my commiseration! "You believe yourself to be alone in the world; you are unjust towards Providence, which sends you a friend and a brother." These were the words which I mentally addressed to the victim.

Meanwhile, the unhappy man could hope for no succor, and every hour that passed in his dreadful silence and monotony would plunge him deeper in despair: night would come with its train of specters; and then what terrors, what regrets would seize upon him! How did I pant to tell him that the zeal of a stranger should replace the loss of the faithless protectors on whom he had a right to depend! But all means of communication were impossible: the dismal hallucinations of the dungeon pursued me in the light of the sun, and notwithstanding the bright arch of heaven above my head, they shut me up, as it were, in dark, dank vaults; for in my distress, forgetting that the Russians apply the classic architecture to the construction even of prisons, I dreamt not of Roman colonnades, but of Gothic cells. Had my imagination less deeply impressed me with all these things, I should have been less active and persevering in my efforts in favor of an unknown individual. I was followed by a specter, and to rid myself of it no efforts could have been too great.

To have insisted on entering the prison would have been a step no less useless than dangerous. After long and painful doubt, I thought of another plan: I had made the acquaintance of several of the most influential people in Moscow; and though I had, two days ago, taken leave of everybody, I resolved to risk giving my confidence to the man for whom I had, among all the others, conceived the highest opinion.

Not only must I here avoid using his name, I must also take care not to allude to him in any way by which he could be identified.

When he saw me enter his room, he at once guessed the business that brought me; and without giving me time to explain myself, he told me that by a singular chance he knew M. Pernet personally, and believed him innocent, which caused his situation to appear inexplicable; but that he was sure political considerations could have alone led to such an imprisonment, because the Russian police never unmasks itself, unless compelled; that, no doubt, the existence of this foreigner had been supposed to have been altogether unknown in Moscow; but that now the blow was struck, his friends could only injure him by showing themselves; for if it were known that parties were interested in him, it would render his position far worse, as he would be removed to avoid all discovery and to stifle all complaints: he added therefore, that, for the victim's sake, extreme circumspection was necessary. "If once he departs for Siberia, God only can say when he will return," exclaimed my counselor; who afterwards endeavored to make me understand that he could not openly avow the interest he took in a suspected Frenchman; for being himself suspected of liberal principles, a word from him, intimating merely that he knew the prisoner, would suffice to exile the latter to the farther end of the world. He concluded by saying, "You are neither his relation nor his friend; you only take in him the interest that you believe you ought to take in a countryman, in a man whom you know to be in trouble; you have already acquitted yourself of the duty that this praiseworthy sentiment imposes on you; you have spoken to your consul; you had now, believe me, better abstain from any further steps; it will do no good, and you will compromise yourself for the man whose defense you gratuitously undertake. He does not know you, he expects nothing from you; continue, then, your journey, you will disappoint no hopes that he has conceived; I will keep my eye on him; I cannot appear in the affair, but I have indirect means which may be useful, and I promise to employ them to the utmost of my power. Once again, then, follow my advice, and pursue your journey."

"If I were to set out," I exclaimed, "I should not have a moment's peace; I should be pursued by a feeling that would amount to remorse, when I recollected that the unfortunate man has me only to befriend him, and that I have abandoned him without doing anything."

"Your presence here," he answered, "will not even serve to console him, as he is and must continue wholly ignorant of the interest you take in him."

"There are, then, no means of gaining access to the dungeon?"

"None," replied the individual addressed, not without some marks of impatience at my thus persisting. "Were you his brother, you could do no more for him here than you have done. Your presence at Petersburg may, on the contrary, be useful to M. Pernet. You can inform the French ambassador of all that you know about this imprisonment; for I doubt whether he will hear anything of it from your consul. A representation made to the minister by a personage in the position of your ambassador, and by a man possessing the character of M. de Barante, will do more to hasten the deliverance of your countryman than you and I, and any twenty others could do in Moscow."

"But the emperor and his ministers are at Borodino or at Moscow," I answered, unwilling to take a refusal.

"All the ministers have not followed His Majesty," he replied, still in a polite tone, but with increasing and scarcely concealed ill humor. "Besides, at the worst, their return must be awaited. You have, I repeat, no other course to take, unless you would injure the man whom you wish to serve, and expose yourself also to many unpleasant incidents, or perhaps to something worse," he added, in a significant manner.

Had the person to whom I addressed myself been a placeman, I should have already fancied I saw the Cossacks advancing to seize me, to convey me to a dungeon like that of M. Pernet.

I felt that the patience of my adviser was at an end; I had nothing, in fact, to reply to his arguments: I therefore retired, promising to leave, and gratefully thanking him for his counsel.

"As it is obvious I can do nothing here, I will leave at once," I said to myself: but the slow motions of my *Feldjäger* took up the rest of the morning, and it was past four in the afternoon before I was on the road to Petersburg.

The sulkiness of the courier, the want of horses, felt everywhere on the road on account of relays being retained for the household of the emperor and for military officers, as well as for couriers proceeding from Borodino to Petersburg, made my journey long and tedious: in my impatience, I insisted on traveling all night; but I gained nothing by this haste, being obliged, for want of horses, to pass six whole hours at Great Novgorod, within fifty leagues of Petersburg.

I was scarcely in a fitting mood to visit the cradle of the Slavic empire, and which became also the tomb of its liberty. The famous church of St. Sophia encloses the sepulchres of Vladimir Yaroslav, who died in 1051, of his mother Anna, and of an emperor of Constantinople. It resembles the other Russian churches, and perhaps is not more authentic than the ostensibly ancient cathedral at Nizhny Novgorod. I no longer believe in the dates of any old monuments that are shown me in Russia. But I still believe in the names of its rivers: the Volkhov represented to me the frightful scenes connected with the siege of this republican city, taken, retaken, and decimated by Ivan the Terrible. I could fancy I saw the Imperial hyena, presiding over carnage and pestilence, couched among the ruins of the city; and the bloody corpses of his subjects seemed to issue out of the river that was choked with their bodies, to prove to me the horrors of intestine wars. It is worthy of remark, that the correspondence of the Archbishop Pinen, and of other principal citizens of Novgorod with the Poles, was the cause which brought the evil on the city, where thirty thousand innocent persons perished in the combat, and in the executions and massacres invented and presided over by the czar. There were days on which six hundred were at once executed before his eyes; and all these horrors were enacted to punish a crime unpardonable from that epoch—the crime of clandestine communication with the Poles. This took place nearly three hundred years ago, in 1570. Great Novgorod has never recovered the stroke: she could have replaced her dead, but she could not survive the abolition of her democratic institutions: her whitewashed houses are no longer stained with blood; they appear as if they had been built only yesterday; but her streets are deserted, and three parts of her ruins are spread over the plain, beyond the narrow bounds of the actual city, which is but a shadow and a name. This is all that remains of the famous republic of the Middle Ages. Where are the fruits of the revolutions which never ceased to saturate the now almost desert soil with blood? Here, all is as silent as it was before the history. God has only too often had to teach us, that objects which men blinded with pride, viewed as a worthy end of their efforts, were really only a means of employing their superfluous powers during the effervescence of youth. Such are the principles of more than one heroic action.

For three centuries, the bell of the *veche** has ceased to summon the people of Novgorod, formerly the most glorious and the most turbulent of the Russian populations, to deliberate upon their own affairs. The will of the czar stifles

---

*Popular assembly.

in every heart all sentiments, including even regret for the memory of effaced glory. Some years ago, frightful scenes occurred between the Cossacks and the inhabitants of the country, in the military colonies established in the vicinity of the decayed city. But the insurrection was stifled, and everything has returned to its accustomed order, that is, to the silence and peace of the tomb.

I was very happy to leave this abode, formerly famous for the disorders of liberty, now desolated by what is called *good order*,—a word which is here equivalent to that of death.

Although I made all possible haste, I did not reach Petersburg until the fourth day: immediately after leaving my carriage, I repaired to M. de Barante's.

He was quite ignorant of the arrest of M. Pernet, and appeared surprised to hear of it through me, especially when he learnt that I had been nearly four days on the road. His astonishment redoubled when I related to him my unavailing endeavors to influence our consul—that official protector of the French—to take some step in favor of the prisoner.

The attention with which M. de Barante listened to me, the assurance which he gave me that he would neglect nothing to clear up this affair, the importance with which he appeared to invest the smallest facts that could interest the dignity of France and the safety of her citizens, put my conscience at ease and dissipated the phantoms of my imagination. The fate of M. Pernet was in the hands of his natural protector, whose ability and character became better warrenties for the safety of this unfortunate man than my zealous though powerless solicitations. I felt I had done all that I could for him and for the honor of my country. During the twelve or fourteen days that I remained at Petersburg, I purposely abstained from pronouncing the name of Pernet before the ambassador; and I left Russia without knowing the end of a story which had so much absorbed and interested me.

But while journeying towards France, my mind was often carried back to the dungeons of Moscow. If I had known all that was passing there, it would have been yet more painfully excited.

———

Not to leave the reader in the ignorance in which I remained for nearly six months, respecting the fate of the prisoner at Moscow, I insert here all that I have learnt since my return to France respecting the imprisonment of M. Pernet, and his deliverance.

One day, near the end of the winter of 1840, I was informed that a stranger was at my door, and wished to speak with me. I desired that he would give his name: he replied that he would give it to me only. I refused to see him; he persisted; I again refused. At last, renewing his entreaties, he sent up a line of writing without any signature, to say that I could not refuse listening to a man who owed to me his life, and who only wished to thank me.

This language appeared extraordinary. I ordered the stranger to be introduced. On entering the room he said—"Sir, it was only yesterday I learnt your address: my name is Pernet; and I come to express to you my gratitude; for I was told at Petersburg that it is to you I owe my liberty, and consequently my life."

After the first surprise which such an address caused me, I began to notice the person of M. Pernet. He is one of that numerous class of young Frenchmen who have the appearance and the temperament of the men of southern lands; his eyes and hair are black, his checks hollow, his countenance everywhere equally pale; he is short and slight in figure; and he appeared to be suffering, though rather morally than physically. He discovered that I knew some members of his family settled in Savoy, who are among the most respectable people

of that land of honest men. He told me that he was a lawyer;
and he related that he had been detained in the prison of
Moscow for three weeks, four days of which time he was
placed in the dungeon. We shall see by his recital the way in
which a prisoner is treated in this abode. My imagination had
not approached the reality.

The two first days he was left *without food!* No one came
near him; and he believed, for forty-eight hours, that they were
determined to starve him to death in his prison. The only
sound that he heard was that of the strokes of the rod, which,
from five o'clock in the morning until night, were inflicted
upon the unhappy slaves who were sent by their masters to
this place, to receive correction. Add to that frightful sound,
the sobs and screams of the victims, mingled with the menaces and imprecations of the tormentors, and you will form
some faint idea of the moral as well as physical sufferings of
our unhappy countryman during four weary days, and while
still remaining ignorant of his crime.

After having thus penetrated against his will into the profound mystery of a Russian prison, he believed, not without
reason, that he was destined to end his days there; for he said
to himself, "If there had been any intention to release me, it
is not here that I should be confined by men who fear nothing
so much as to have their secret barbarity divulged."

A slight partition alone separated his narrow cell from the
inner court, where these cruelties were perpetrated.

The rod which, since the amelioration of manners, usually
replaces the knout of Mongolic memory, is formed of a cane
split into three pieces, an instrument which fetches off the
skin at every stroke; at the fifth, the victim loses nearly all
power to cry, his weakened voice can then only utter a prolonged sobbing groan. This horrible rattle in the throat of the
tortured creatures pierced the heart of the prisoner, and pre-
saged to him a fate which he dared not look in the face.

M. Pernet understands Russian; he was therefore present,

without seeing anything, at many private tortures; among others, at those of two young girls, who worked under a fashionable milliner in Moscow. These unfortunate creatures were flogged before the eyes even of their mistress, who reproached them with having lovers, and with having so far forgotten themselves as to bring them into her house—the house of a milliner!—what an enormity! Meanwhile this virago exhorted the executioners to strike harder: one of the girls begged for mercy: they said that she was nearly killed, that she was covered with blood. No matter! She had carried her audacity so far as to say that she was less culpable than her mistress; and the latter redoubled her severity. M. Pernet assured me, observing that he thought I might doubt his assertion, that each of the unhappy girls received, at different intervals, a hundred and eighty blows. "I suffered too much in counting them," he added, "to be deceived as to the number."

A man feels the approach of insanity when present at such horrors, and yet unable to succor the victims.

Afterwards, serfs and servants were brought by stewards, or sent by their masters, with the request that they might be punished; there was nothing, in short, but scenes of atrocious vengeance and frightful despair, all hidden from the public eye.* The unhappy prisoner longed for the obscurity of night, because the darkness brought with it silence; and though his thoughts then terrified him, he preferred the evils of imagination to those of reality. This is always the case with real sufferers. It is only the dreamers who have comfortable beds and good tables, who pretend the evils we fancy exceed those that we feel.

At last, after four times twenty-four hours of a torment which would, I think, surpass all our efforts to picture, M.

---

*See, in Dickens's *American Notes*, extracts from the United States' papers, concerning the treatment of the slaves; presenting a remarkable resemblance between the excesses of despotism and the abuses of democracy.

Pernet was taken from his dungeon, still without any explanation, and transferred to another part of the prison.

From thence he wrote to M. de Barante, by General ————,
on whose good offices he thought he could reckon.

The letter did not reach its address; and when afterwards
the writer demanded an explanation of this circumstance, the
general excused himself by subterfuges, and concluded by
swearing to M. Pernet, on the Gospel, that the letter had not
been put in the hands of the minister of police, and never
would be! This was the utmost extent of devotion that the
prisoner could obtain from his *friend*: and this is the fate of
human affections when they pass under the yoke of despotism.

At the end of three weeks—which had been an eternity
to M. Pernet—he was released without any form of process,
and without even being able to learn the cause of his imprisonment.

His reiterated questions, addressed to the director of
police in Moscow, procured for him no explanations; he was
merely told that his ambassador had claimed him; and this
was accompanied with an order to leave Russia. He asked,
and obtained permission to take the route of Petersburg.

He wished to thank the French ambassador for the liberty
which he owed to him; and also to obtain some information
as to the cause of the treatment he had undergone. M. de
Barante endeavored, but in vain, to divert him from the
project of addressing M. de Benkendorff, the minister of the
Imperial police. The liberated man demanded an audience: it
was granted him. He said to the minister that, being ignorant
of the cause of the punishment that he had received, he
wished to know his crime before leaving Russia.

The statesman briefly answered, that he would do well to
carry his inquiries on the subject no further, and dismissed
him, repeating the order that he should, without delay, leave
the empire.

Such is all the information that I could obtain from M.

Pernet. This young man, like everyone else who has lived some time in Russia, has acquired a mysterious and reserved tone of language, to which foreigners are as liable as the native inhabitants. One would say that in that empire, a secret weighs upon all minds.

On my continuing my inquiries, M. Pernet further stated, that on his first journey to the country, they had given him, in his passport, the title of merchant, and on the second, that of lawyer. He added a more serious circumstance, namely, that before reaching Petersburg, while in a steamboat on the Baltic, he had freely expressed his opinion of Russian despotism, before several individuals whom he did not know.

He assured me, on leaving, that his memory could recall no other circumstance that could account for the treatment he had received at Moscow. I have never seen him since; though, by a singular chance, I met, two years after, a member of his family, who said he knew of the services I had rendered to his young relative, and thanked me for them. This family, I repeat, are respected by all who know them in the kingdom of Sardinia.

The last moments of my stay in Petersburg were employed in inspecting various establishments that I had not seen on my visit to that city.

Prince ——— showed me, among other curiosities, the immense works of Colpina, the arsenal of the Russian arsenals, which is situated some leagues from the capital. In this manufactory are prepared all the articles required for the Imperial marine. Colpina is reached by a road seven leagues in length, the last half of which is execrable. The establishment is directed by an Englishman, M. Wilson, who is honored with the rank of general (all Russia is converted into an army). He showed to us his machines, like a true Russian engineer, not permitting us to overlook a nail or a screw: under his escort we surveyed about twenty workshops, of enormous size. The extreme complaisance of the director deserved much gratitude, though I expressed but little, and that little was more than I felt; fatigue renders a man almost as ungrateful as ennui.

The day after my journey to Colpina, I visited the Academy of Painting, a superb and stately edifice, which up to the present time contains but few good works. How can they be expected in a land where the young artists wear uniform? I found all the pupils of the Academy enrolled, dressed, and commanded like marine cadets. This fact alone denotes a profound contempt for the object pretended to be patronized, or rather a great ignorance of the nature and the mysteries of art; professed indifference would be less indicative of barbarism. There is nothing free in Russia, except objects for which the government does not care; it cares only too much for the arts; but it is ignorant that they cannot dispense with liberty, and that this sympathy between the works of genius and the independence of man would alone attest the nobleness of the artist's profession.

The vicinity of the pole is unfavorable to the arts, with the exception of poetry, which can sometimes dispense with all material, except the human soul; it is then the volcano under the ice. But for the inhabitants of these dreadful climates, music, painting, the dance—all those pleasures of sensation which are partially independent of mind—lose their charms in losing their organs. What are Rembrandt, Correggio, Michelangelo, and Raphael, in a dark room? The North has doubtless it own kind of beauty, but it is still a palace without light: all the attractive train of youth, with their pastimes, their smiles, their graces, and their dances, confine themselves to those blessed regions where the rays of the sun, not content with gliding over the surface of the earth, warm and fertilize its bosom by piercing it from on high.

In Russia a double gloom pervades everything—the fear of power and the want of sun. The national dances resemble rounds led by shadows under the gleam of a twilight which never ends. Mademoiselle Taglioni herself (alas! for Mademoiselle Taglioni!) is not a perfect dancer at St. Petersburg. What a fall for La Sylphide! But when she walks in the streets —for she walks at present—she is followed by footmen in handsome cockades and gold lace; and the newspapers overwhelm her every morning with articles containing the most preposterous praises I have ever seen. This is all the Russians, notwithstanding their cleverness, can do for the arts and for artistes. What the latter want is a heaven to give them life, a public which can understand them, a society which can excite and inspire them. These are necessaries: rewards are supererogatory. It is not, however, in a country contiguous to Lapland, and governed under the system of Peter the Great, that such things are to be sought for. I must wait for the Russians' establishment in Constantinople, before I can know of what they are really capable in the fine arts and in civilization.

I left France scared by the abuses of a false liberty; I return to my country persuaded that if, logically speaking, the representative system is not the most moral form of government, it is, practically, the most wise and moderate; preserving the people on one side from democratic license, and on the other, from the most glaring abuses of despotism: I therefore ask myself if we ought not to impose a silence upon our antipathies, and submit without murmur to a necessary policy, and one which, after all, brings to nations prepared for it, more good than evil. It is true that hitherto this new and wise form of government has only been able to establish itself by usurpation. Perhaps these final usurpations have been rendered inevitable by preceding errors. This is a religious question, which time, the wisest of God's ministers upon earth, will resolve to our posterity. I am here reminded of the profound idea of one of the most enlightened and cultivated intellects in Germany, M. Varnhagen von Ense:

"I have often labored," he wrote to me one day, "to discover who were the prime movers of revolutions; and, after thirty years' meditation, I have come to the conclusion that my earliest opinion was right, and that they are caused by the men against whom they are directed."

Never shall I forget my feelings in traveling from Niemen to Tilsit: it was more especially then that I did justice to the observation of my host at Lübeck. A bird escaped from its cage could not have been more joyous. I can speak and write all that I think: I am free! were my exulting exclamations. The first real letter that I dispatched to Paris was sent from this frontier: it would cause quite a sensation in the little circle of my friends, who, until they received it, had, no doubt, been the dupes of my official correspondence. The following is the copy of that letter:

TILSIT, THURSDAY, 26TH SEPTEMBER, 1839.

You will, I hope, have as much pleasure in reading the above date as I have in writing it: here I am beyond the empire of uniformity, minutiae, and difficulties. I hear the language of freedom, and I feel as if in a vortex of pleasure, a world carried away by new ideas towards inordinate liberty. And yet I am only in Prussia: but in leaving Russia, I have again found houses the plan of which has not been dictated to a slave by an inflexible master, but which are freely built: I see a lively country freely cultivated (it is of Prussia I am speaking), and the change warms and gladdens my heart.

In short, I breathe! I can write to you without carefully guarding my words for fear of the police—a precaution almost always insufficient; for there is as much of the susceptibility of self-love as of political prudence in the espionage of the Russians. Russia is the most gloomy country, and is inhabited by the most handsome men that I have ever beheld: a country in which women are scarcely seen, cannot be gay. Here I am, escaped from it, and without the smallest accident. I have traveled two hundred and fifty leagues in four days, by roads often wretched, often magnificent; for the Russian spirit, friend as it is to uniformity, cannot attain a real state of order: the characteristics of its administration are meddlesomeness, negligence, and corruption. A sincere man in the empire of the czar would pass for a fool.

I have now a journey of two hundred leagues to perform before I reach Berlin; but I look forward to it as a mere excursion of pleasure.

Good roads throughout the distance, good inns, beds on which one may lie down, the order of houses managed by women—all seemed delightful and novel. I was particularly struck with the varied architecture of the buildings, the air of freedom in the peasants, and the gaiety of the female sex among them. Their good humor inspired me with a kind of fear: it was an independence, the consequences of which I dreaded for them, for I had myself almost lost the memory of it. I saw towns built spontaneously, before any government had imagined a plan of them. Ducal Prussia does not assuredly pass for a land of license; and yet, in passing through the streets of Tilsit, and afterwards those of Königsberg, I could have fancied myself at a Venetian carnival. My feelings brought to my memory a German of my acquaintance, who, after having been obliged, by business, to pass whole years in Russia, was at last able to leave that country forever. He was accompanied by a friend; and had scarcely set foot on deck of the English vessel, which was about to weigh anchor, when he threw himself into his companion's arms, exclaiming, "God be praised, we may now breathe freely and speak openly!"

Many people have, doubtless, felt the same sensation: but why has no traveler before recorded it? Here, without comprehending, I marvel at the *prestige* which the Russian government exercises over minds. It obtains silence, not only from its own subjects—that is nothing,—but it makes itself respected, even at a distance, by strangers escaped from its iron discipline. The traveler either praises it or is silent: this is a mystery which I cannot comprehend. If ever the publication of this journey should procure me the explanation of the marvel, I shall have additional reason to applaud myself for my sincerity.

I had intended to return from Petersburg into Germany, by way of Vilna and Warsaw; but I changed that project.

Miseries like those which Poland suffers cannot be attributed entirely to fatality: in prolonged misfortunes, we may always look to faults as well as to circumstances. To a certain point, nations, like individuals, become accomplices of the fate which pursues them; they appear accountable for the reverses which, blow after blow, they have to suffer: for, to attentive eyes, destinies are only the development of characters. On perceiving the result of the errors of a people punished with so much severity, I might not be able to abstain from reflections of which I should repent. To represent their case to the oppressors would be a task we should impose upon ourselves with a kind of joy, sustained, as we should feel, by the idea of courage and generosity which attaches to the accomplishment of a perilous, or, at least, painful duty: but to wound the heart of the victim, to overwhelm the oppressed, though even with deserved strokes, with just reproaches, is an executioner's office, to which the author who does not despise his own pen will never abase himself.

This was my reason for renouncing my proposed journey through Poland.

LETTER 36*

I LEFT EMS for Russia five months ago, and return to this elegant village after having made a tour of some thousand
leagues. My stay here during the previous spring was disagreeable to me by reason of the crowd of bathers and
drinkers: I find it delicious now that I am literally alone, with
nothing to do but to enjoy a beautiful autumn sky in the
midst of mountains the solitude of which I admire; and to review my recollections, while I at the same time seek the rest
I need after the rapid journey just completed.

With what a contrast am I presented! In Russia, I was deprived of all the scenes of nature; for I cannot give the name
of nature to solitudes without one picturesque object,—to
seas, lakes, and rivers, whose banks are on a level with the
water; to marshes without bounds, and steppes without vegetation, under a sky without light. Those plains are not, indeed, devoid of a kind of beauty; but grandeur without grace
soon fatigues. What pleasure can the traveler have in traversing immense spaces, where the surface and horizon are always destitute of feature? Such monotony aggravates the
fatigue of locomotion, by rendering it fruitless. Surprises
must always constitute a great portion of the enjoyment of

---

*Written at Ems, October, 1839.

traveling; and the hope of them must always furnish much of the stimulus that keeps alive the zeal of the traveler.

I have surveyed the Russian Empire. I hoped to see a country where should reign the calm of a power assured of its own strength: but arrived there, I found only the reign of silence maintained by fear; and I have drawn from the spectacle a lesson very different from the one which I went to seek. Russia is a world scarcely known to foreigners: the Russians who travel to escape it, pay, when at a distance, in crafty encomiums, their tribute to their country; and the greater number of travelers who have described it to us have been unwilling to discover in it anything but that which they sought to find. If people will defend their prejudices against evidence, where is the good of traveling? When thus determined to view nations as they wish to view them, there is no necessity for leaving their own country.

The following is the résumé of my journey, written since my return to Ems.

In Russia, all that strikes the eye, everything that passes around, bears the impress of a regularity that is startling; and the first thought that enters the mind of the traveler, when he contemplates this symmetrical system, is that a uniformity so complete, a regularity so contrary to the natural inclinations of men, cannot have been established, and cannot be maintained except by violence. Imagination vainly implores a little variety, like a bird uselessly beating its wings against a cage. Under such a system a man may know the first day of his life all that he will see and do until the last. This hard tyranny is called in official language, respect for unity, love of order; and it is a fruit of despotism so precious to methodical minds, that they think they cannot pay too dear for it.

In France, I had imagined myself in accord with these rigorous disciplinarians; but since I have lived under a despotism which imposes military rule upon the population of an

entire empire, I confess that I have learnt to prefer
the disorder which announces vigor to the perfect order
which destroys life.

In Russia, the government interferes with everything and
vivifies nothing. In that immense empire, the people, if not
tranquil, are mute; death hovers over all heads, and strikes
capriciously whom it pleases: man there has two coffins, the
cradle and the tomb. The Russian mothers ought to weep the
birth more than the death of their children.

I do not believe that suicide is common there: the people
suffer too much to kill themselves. Singular disposition of
man!—when terror presides over his life, he does not seek
death; he knows what it is already. *

But if the number of suicides in Russia were ever so great,
no one would know it; the knowledge of numbers is a privilege of the Russian police: I am ignorant whether they arrive
correct before the eyes of the emperor; but I do know that
no misfortune is published under his reign until he has consented to the humiliating confession of the superiority of
Providence. The pride of despotism is so great that it seeks to
rival the power of God. Monstrous jealousy! into what aberrations hast thou not plunged princes and subjects! Who will
dare to love truth, who will defend it in a country where idolatry is the principle of the constitution? A man who can do
everything is the crowned impersonification of a lie.

---

*Dickens says—speaking of the solitary prison of Philadelphia—"Suicides are rare
among the prisoners; are almost, indeed, unknown. But no argument in favor of the
system can reasonably be deduced from this circumstance, although it is very often
urged. All men who have made diseases of the mind their study, know perfectly well
that such extreme depression and despair, as to change the whole character, and beat
down all its powers of elasticity and self-resistance, may be at work within a man,
and yet stop short of self-destruction."—*American Notes for General Circulation.*

The great writer, the profound moralist, the Christian philosopher from whom I
borrow these lines, has not only the authority of talent, and of a style which engraves
his thoughts on brass, but his opinion on this particular subject is law.

It will be understood that I am not now speaking of the Emperor Nicholas, but of the emperor of Russia. We often hear mention made of customs which limit his power: I have been struck with its abuse, but have seen no remedy.

In the eyes of real statesmen, and of all practical minds, the laws are, I admit, less important than our precise logicians and political philosophers believe them; for it is the manner in which they are applied that decides the life of the people. True; but the life of the Russian people is more gloomy than that of any other of the European nations; and when I say the people, I speak not only of the peasants attached to the soil, but of the whole empire.

A government that makes profession of being vigorous, and that causes itself to be dreaded on every occasion, must inevitably render men miserable. Wherever the public machine is rigorously exact, there is despotism, whatever be the fiction, monarchical or democratical, which covers it. The best government is that which makes itself the least felt; but such lightness of the yoke is only procured by the labors of genius and superior wisdom, or by a certain relaxation of social discipline. Governments, which were beneficial in the youth of nations, when men, still half savages, honored everything that snatched them from a state of disorder, become so again in the old age of communities. At that epoch is seen the birth of mixed institutions. But these institutions, founded on a compact between experience and passion, can suit none but already wearied populations, societies the springs of which are weakened by revolutions. From this it may be concluded, that if they are not the most powerful of political systems, they are the most gentle: the people who have once obtained them cannot too carefully strive to prolong their duration, fruits as they are of a green old age. The old age of states, like that of men, is the most peaceable period of existence, when it crowns a glorious life; but the middle age of a nation is always a time of trial and violence: Russia is passing through it.

In this country, which differs from all others, nature itself has become an accomplice in the caprices of the man who has slain liberty to deify unity; it, too, is everywhere the same: two kinds of scattered and stunted trees, the birch and the pine, spread over plains always either sandy or marshy, are the only features on the face of nature throughout that immense expanse of country which constitutes northern Russia.

What refuge is there against the evils of society in a climate under which men cannot enjoy the country, such as it is, for more than three months of the year? Add to this, that during the six most inclement of the winter months, they—unless they are peasants—dare not breathe fresh air for more than two hours in the day. Such is the lot that heaven has assigned to man in these regions.

Let us see what man has done for himself: St. Petersburg is unquestionably one of the wonders of the world; Moscow is also a very picturesque city; but what can be said of the aspect of the provinces?

The excess of uniformity engendered by the abuse of unity will be seen described in my chapters. The absence of soul betrays itself in everything: each step that you take proves to you that you are among a people deprived of independence. At every twenty or thirty leagues, the same town greets your eyes.

The passion of both princes and people for classic architecture, for straight lines, buildings of low elevation, and wide streets, is a contradiction of the laws of nature and the wants of life in a cold, misty region, frequently exposed to storms of wind which case the visage in ice. Throughout my journey, I was constantly but vainly endeavoring to account for this mania among the inhabitants of a country so different from those lands whence the architecture has been borrowed: the Russians cannot probably explain it any better than I, for they are no more masters of their tastes than of their actions. The fine arts, as they call them, have been imposed on the people, olphe de Custine

just like the military exercise. The regiment, and its spirit of minuteness, is the mold of Russian society.

Lofty ramparts, high and crowded edifices, the winding streets of the cities of the Middle Ages, would have suited, better than caricatures of the antique, the climate and the customs of Muscovy; but the country the wants and genius of which are least consulted by the Russians, is the country they occupy.

When Peter the Great published from Tartary to Lapland his edicts of civilization, the creations of the Middle Ages had long been out of date in Europe; and the Russians, even those that have been called *great*, have never known how to do more than follow the fashion.

Such disposition to imitate scarcely accords with the ambition which we attribute to them; for man does not rule the things that he copies; but everything is contradictory in the character of this superficial people: besides, a want of invention is their peculiar characteristic. To invent, there must be independence; in them, mimicry may be seen pervading the very passions: if they wish to take their turn on the scene of the world, it is not to employ faculties which they possess, and the inaction of which torments them; it is simply to act over the history of illustrious communities: they have no creative power; comparison is their talent, imitation is their genius: naturally given to observation they are not themselves except when aping the creations of others. Such originality as they have, lies in the gift of counterfeit, which they possess more amply than any other people. Their only primitive faculty is an aptitude to reproduce the inventions of foreigners. They would be in history what they are in literature, able translators. The task of the Russians is to translate European civilization to the Asiatics.

The talent of imitation may become useful and even admirable in nations, provided it develops itself late; but it destroys all the other talents when it precedes them. Russia is a community of imitations: and every man who can do nothing else but copy necessarily falls into caricature.

Oscillating for the space of four centuries between Europe and Asia, Russia has not yet succeeded in distinguishing itself by its works in the field of human intellect, because its national characteristics are lost under its borrowed decorations.

Separated from the West by its adherence to the Greek schism, it returns, after many centuries, with the inconsistency of a blind self-love, to demand from nations formed by Catholicism the civilization of which a religion entirely political has deprived it. This Byzantine religion, which has issued from a palace to maintain order in a camp, does not respond to the most sublime wants of the human soul; it helps the police to deceive the nation, but that is the extent of its power.

It has, in advance, rendered the people unworthy of the culture to which they aspire.

The independence of the church is necessary to the motion of the religious sap; for the development of the noblest faculty of a people, the faculty of believing, depends on the dignity of the man charged with communicating to his fellow-men the divine revelations. The humiliation of the ministers of religion is the first punishment of heresy; and thus it is that in all schismatic countries the priest is despised by the people, in spite of, or rather because of, the protection of the prince. People who understand their liberty will never obey, from the bottom of their hearts, a dependent clergy.

The time is not far distant when it will be acknowledged that, in matters of religion, what is more essential even than obtaining the liberty of the flock, is the assuring that of the pastor.

The multitude always obey the men whom they take for guides: be they priests, doctors, poets, sages, or tyrants, the minds of the people are in their hands; religious liberty for the mass is therefore a chimera; but it is on this account the more important that the man charged with performing the office of priest for them should be free: now, there is not in the world an independent priest except the Catholic.

Slavish pastors can only guide barren minds: a Greek pope will never do more than instruct a people to prostrate themselves before violent power. Let me not be asked, then, whence it comes that the Russians have no imagination, and how it is that they only copy imperfectly.

When, in the West, the descendants of the barbarians studied the ancients with a veneration that partook of idolatry, they modified them in order to appropriate them. Who can recognize Virgil in Dante, or Homer in Tasso, or Justinian and the Roman laws in the codes of feudalism? The passionate respect then professed for the past, far from stifling genius, aroused it: but it is not thus that the Russians have availed themselves of us.

When a people counterfeit the social forms of another community, without penetrating into the spirit which animates it—when they seek lessons in civilization, not from the ancient founders of human institutions, but from strangers whose riches they envy without respecting their character—when their imitation is hostile, and yet falls into puerile precision—when they borrow from a neighbor, whom they affect to disdain, even the very modes of dress and of domestic life, they become a mere echo, a reflection; they exist no longer for themselves. Russians remind me of portraits badly painted, but very thickly varnished.

It was Peter the Great, who, with all the imprudence of an untaught genius, all the temerity of a man the more impatient because deemed omnipotent, with all the perseverance of an iron character, sought to snatch from Europe the plants of an already ripened civilization, instead of resigning himself to the slow process of sowing the seeds in his own soil. That too highly lauded man produced a merely artificial work: it may be astonishing, but the good done by his barbarous genius was transient, the evil is irreparable.

How does a power to influence the politics of Europe benefit Russia? Factitious interests! vain, foolish passions! Its real interests are to have within itself the principles of life, and to develop them: a nation which possesses nothing within itself but obedience does not live. The nation of which I speak has been posted at the window; it looks out—it listens—it feels like a man witnessing some exhibition. When will this game cease?

Russia ought not only to stop, but to begin anew: is such an effort possible? can so vast an edifice be taken to pieces and reconstructed? The too recent civilization of the empire, entirely artificial as it is, has already produced real results—results which no human power can annul: it appears to me impossible to control the future state of a people without considering the present. But the present, when it has been violently separated from the past, bodes only evil: to avert that evil from Russia, by obliging it to take into account its ancient history, which was the result only of its primitive character, will be henceforward the ungrateful task, more useful than brilliant, of the men called to govern this land.

The altogether national and highly practical genius of the Emperor Nicholas has perceived the problem: can he resolve it? I do not think so; he does not let enough be done—he trusts too much to himself and too little to others, to succeed; for in Russia, the most absolute will is not powerful enough to accomplish good.

It is not against a tyrant, but against tyranny, that the friends of man have here to struggle. There would be injustice in accusing the emperor of the miseries of the empire and the vices of the government: the powers of a man are not equal to the task imposed upon the sovereign who would suddenly seek to reign by humanity over an inhuman people.

who has been in Russia, who has seen close at
things are there conducted, can understand how
little ... an can do, who is reputed capable of doing everything; and how, more especially, his power is limited, when it
is good that he would accomplish.

The unhappy consequences of the work of Peter I have
been still further aggravated under the great, or rather the long
reign of a woman who only governed her people to amuse
herself and to astonish Europe—Europe, always Europe!—
never Russia!

Peter I and Catherine II have given to the world a great
and useful lesson, for which Russia has had to pay: they have
shown to us that despotism is never so much to be dreaded as
when it pretends to do good, for then it thinks the most revolting acts may be excused by the intention; and the evil
that is applied as a remedy has no longer any bounds. Crime
exposed to view can triumph only for a day; but false virtues
forever lead astray the minds of nations. People, dazzled by
the brilliant accessories of crime, by the greatness of certain
delinquencies justified by the event, believe at last that there
are two kinds of villainy, two classes of morals, and that necessity, or reasons of state, as they were formerly called, exculpate criminals of high lineage, provided they have so
managed that their excesses shall be in accord with the passions of the country.

Avowed, open tyranny would little terrify me after having
seen oppression disguised as love of order. The strength of
despotism lies in the mask of the despot. When the sovereign
can no longer lie, the people are free; thus I see no other evil
in this world except that of falsehood. If you dread only violent and avowed arbitrary power, go to Russia; there you will
learn to fear above all things the tyranny of hypocrisy. I cannot deny it; I bring back with me from my journey ideas
which I did not own when I undertook it. I therefore would
not have been spared, for anything in the world, the trouble

which it has cost me: if I print the relation of it, I do so precisely because it has modified my opinions upon several points. Those opinions are known to all who have read me; my change of opinion is not: it is therefore a duty to publish it.

On setting out, I did not intend writing this last journey: my method is fatiguing, because it consists in reviewing for my friends, during the night, the recollections of the day. Whilst occupied with this labor, which bears the character of confidential communications, the public appeared to my thoughts in only a dim and vapory distance—so vapory that I scarcely yet realize its presence; and this will account for the familiar tone of an intimate correspondence being preserved in my printed letters.

I liked to think that I should this time be able to travel for myself alone, which would have been a means of observing with tranquillity; but the ideas with which I found the Russians prepossessed with regard to me, from the greatest personages down to the smallest private individuals, gave me to see the measure of my importance, at least of that which I could acquire in Petersburg. "What do you think, or rather, what shall you say of us?" This was at the bottom of every conversation held with me. They drew me from my inaction: I was playing a modest part through apathy, or perhaps cowardice; for Paris renders those humble whom it does not render excessively presumptuous; but the restless self-love of the Russians restored to me my own.

I was sustained in my new resolution by a continual and visible dispersion of illusion. Assuredly, the cause of the disappointment must have been strong and active to have allowed disgust to take possession of me in the midst of the most brilliant fêtes that I have ever seen in my life, and in spite of the dazzling hospitality of the Russians. But I recognized at the first glance, that in the demonstrations of interest which they lavish upon us, there is more of the desire to appear engaging, than of true cordiality. Cordiality is unknown to the Russians: it is one of those things which they have not borrowed from their German neighbors. They occupy your every moment; they distract your thoughts; they engross your attention; they tyrannize over you by means of officious politeness; they inquire how you pass your days; they question you with an importunity known only to themselves, and by fête after fête they prevent you seeing their country. Unhappily, they have chanced to fall upon a man whom fêtes have always more tired than diverted. But when they perceive that their direct attempts upon the mind of a stranger fail, they have recourse to indirect means to discredit his statements among enlightened readers: they can lead him astray with marvelous dexterity. Thus, still to prevent him from seeing things under their true color, they will falsely depreciate when they can no longer reckon upon his benevolent credulity to permit them falsely to extol. Often have I, in the same conversation, surprised the same person changing his tactics two or three times towards me. I do not always flatter myself with having discerned the truth, but I have discerned that it was concealed from me, and it is always something to know that we are deceived; if not enlightened, we are then at least armed.

All courts are deficient in life and gaiety; but at that of Petersburg, one has not even the permission to be weary. The emperor, whose eye is on everything, takes the affectation of enjoyment as a homage, which reminds me of the observation of M. de Talleyrand upon Napoleon: "L'empereur ne plaisante pas; il veut qu'on s'amuse."

I shall wound self-love: my incorruptible honesty will draw upon me reproaches; but is it my fault if, in applying to an absolute government for new arguments against the despot that reigns at home, against disorder baptized with the name of liberty, I have been struck only with the abuses of autocracy; in other words, of tyranny-designated good order? Russian despotism is a false order, as our republicanism is a false liberty. I make war with falsehood wherever I discover it; but there is more than one kind of lie: I had forgotten those of absolute power; I now recount them in detail, because, in relating my travels I describe without reserve all that I see.

I hate pretexts: I have seen that in Russia, order serves as a pretext for oppression, as, in France, liberty does for envy. In a word, I love real liberty—all liberty that is possible in a society from whence elegance is not excluded; I am therefore neither demagogue nor despot; I am an aristocrat in the broadest acceptation of the word. The elegance that I wish to preserve in communities is not frivolous, nor yet unfeeling; it is regulated by taste; taste excludes all abuses; it is the surest preservative against them, for it dreads every kind of exaggeration. A certain elegance is essential to the arts, and the arts save the world; for it is through their agency more than any other that people attach themselves to civilization, of which they are the last and the most precious fruits. By a privilege which belongs to them alone among the various objects that can shed a halo upon a nation, their glory pleases and profits all classes of society equally.

Aristocracy, as I understand it, far from allying itself with tyranny in favor of order, as the demagogues who misunderstand it pretend, cannot exist under an arbitrary government. Its mission is to defend, on one side, the people against the despot, and, on the other, civilization against that most terrible of all tyrants, revolution. Barbarism takes more than one form: crush it in despotism and it springs to life again in anarchy; but true liberty, guarded by a true aristocracy, is neither violent nor inordinate.

Unfortunately, the partisans of a moderating aristocracy in Europe are now blinded, and lend their arms to their adversaries: in their false prudence they seek for aid among the enemies of all political and religious liberty, as though danger could only come from the side of the new revolutionaries:

they forget that arbitrary sovereigns were anciently as much usurpers as are the modern Jacobins.

Feudal aristocracy has come to an end in all except the indelible glory which will forever shine around great historical names; but in communities which wish to endure, the noblesse of the Middle Ages will be replaced, as it long has been among the English, by a hereditary magistracy: this new aristocracy, heir of the old, and composed of many different elements, for office, birth, and riches all form its basis, will not regain its credit until it supports itself upon a free religion; and I again repeat, the only free religion, the only one that does not depend on a temporal power, is that taught by the Catholic church: for as to the temporal power of the pope himself, it is now only calculated to defend his sacerdotal independence. Aristocracy is the government of independent minds, and it cannot be too often reiterated, Catholicism is the faith of free priests.

Russia still remains farther from liberty, not in words, but in things, than most of the countries upon earth. Tomorrow, in an insurrection, in the midst of massacre, by the light of a conflagration, the cry of freedom may spread to the frontiers of Siberia; a blind and cruel people may murder their masters, may revolt against obscure tyrants, and dye the waters of the Volga with blood; but they will not be any the more free: barbarism is in itself a yoke.

The best means of emancipating men is not pompously to proclaim their enfranchisement, but to render servitude impossible by developing the sentiment of humanity in the hearts of nations: that sentiment is deficient in Russia. To talk of liberalism to the Russians, of whatever class they may be, would now be a crime; to preach humanity to all classes without exception is a duty.

The Russian nation has not yet imbibed the sentiment of justice; thus, one day it was mentioned to me in praise of the Emperor Nicholas, that an obscure private individual had gained a cause against some powerful nobleman. In this instance, the encomium on the sovereign appeared to me as a satire upon the community. The too highly boasted fact proved to me positively that equity is only an exception in Russia.

Everything duly considered, I would by no means advise obscure men to act in reliance upon the success of the person thus instanced, who was favored perhaps to assure impunity to the usual course of injustice, and to furnish a specimen of equity which the dispensers of the law were in need of, to serve as a reply to reproaches of servility and corruption.

Another fact, which suggests an inference little favorable to the Russian judiciary, is that there should be so little litigation in the country. The reason is not obscure; people would more often have recourse to justice if the judges were more equitable. A similar reason accounts for there being no fighting or quarreling in the streets. A dread of chains and dungeons is the consideration which usually restrains the parties.

Notwithstanding the melancholy pictures that I draw, two inanimate objects, and one living person, are worth the trouble of the journey: the Neva of Petersburg during the nightless season, the Kremlin of Moscow by moonlight, and the emperor of Russia. These include picturesque, historical, and political Russia; beyond them everything is fatiguing and wearisome to a degree that may be judged of by the preceding chapters.

Many of my friends have written to advise me not to publish them.

As I was preparing to leave Petersburg, a Russian asked me, as all the Russians do, what I should say of his country. "I have been too well received there to talk about it,"* was my reply.

---

* "J'y ai été trop bien reçu pour en parler."

This avowal, in which I thought I had scarcely politely concealed an epigram, is brought up against me. "Treated as you have been," I am told, "you cannot possibly tell the truth; and as you cannot write except to do so, you had better remain silent." Such is the opinion of a party among those to whom I am accustomed to listen. At any rate, it is not flattering to the Russians.

My opinion is, that without wounding the delicacy, without failing in the gratitude due to individuals, nor yet in the respect due to self, there is always a proper manner of speaking with sincerity of public men and things, and I hope to have discovered this manner. It is pretended that truth only shocks, but in France, at least, no one has the right or the power to close the mouth of him who speaks it. My exclamations of indignation cannot be taken for the disguised expression of wounded vanity. If I had listened only to my self-love, it would have told me to be enchanted with everything: my heart has been enchanted with nothing.

If everything related of the Russians and their country turn into personalities, so much the worse for them: this is an inevitable evil, for things do not exist in Russia, since it is the whim of a man who makes and unmakes them; but that is not the fault of travelers.

The emperor appears to me little disposed to lay down a part of his authority. Let him suffer, then, the responsibility of omnipotence: it is the first expiation of the political lie by which a single individual declares himself absolute master of a country and all-powerful sovereign of the thoughts of a people.

Forbearance in practice does not excuse the impiety of such a doctrine. I have found among the Russians that the principles of absolute monarchy, applied with inflexible consistency, lead to results that are monstrous: and, this time, my political quietism cannot withhold me from perceiving and proclaiming that there are governments to which people ought never to submit.

The Emperor Alexander, talking confidentially with Madame de Staël about the ameliorations which he projected, said to her, "You praise my philanthropical intentions—I am obliged to you; nevertheless, in the history of Russia, I am only a lucky chance."

That prince spoke the truth: the Russians vainly boast of the prudence and management of the men who direct their affairs; arbitrary power is not the less the fundamental principle of the state; and this principle so works that the emperor makes, or suffers to be made, or allows to exist, laws (excuse the application of this sacred name to impious decrees) which, for example, permit the sovereign to declare that the legitimate children of a man legally married have no father, no name; in short, that they are numbers and not human beings. And am I to be forbidden to accuse at the bar of Europe a prince who, distinguished and superior as he is, consents to reign without abolishing such a law?

His resentment is implacable: with hatred so strong, he may yet be a great sovereign, but he cannot be a great man. The great man is merciful, the political character is vindictive: vengeance reigns, pardon converts.

I have now made my last observations upon a prince that one hesitates to judge, after knowing the country where he is condemned to reign; for men are there so dependent upon things, that it is difficult to know how high or how low to look in fixing the responsibility of actions. And the nobles of such a country pretend to resemble the French! The French kings, in barbarous times, have often cut off the heads of their great vassals; but those princes, when they destroyed their enemies and seized their goods, did not debase by an insulting decree their caste, their family, and their country: such a forgetfulness of all dignity would have rendered the people of France indignant, even in the Middle Ages. But the people of Russia suffer even worse things than these. I must correct myself—there is no people of Russia: there is an emperor, who has serfs, and there are courtiers who have serfs also; but this does not constitute a people.

The middle class, few in number as compared with others, is at present almost entirely composed of foreigners; a few peasants, enfranchised by their wealth, together with the smallest employees, begin to swell its ranks. The future fate of Russia depends upon this new class, the elements of which are so diverse that it seems scarcely possible they can combine together.

The attempt is now making to create a Russian nation; but the task is difficult for one man. Evil is quickly committed, but slowly repaired: the mortifications of despotism must often, I should think, enlighten the despot on the abuses of absolute power. But the embarrassments of the oppressor do not excuse oppression. I can pity them, because evil is always to be pitied; but they inspire me with much less compassion than the sufferings of the oppressed. In Russia, whatever be the appearance of things, violence and arbitrary rule are at the bottom of them all. Tyranny rendered calm by the influence of terror, is the only kind of happiness which this government is able to afford its people.

And when chance has made me a witness of the unspeakable evils endured under a constitution founded on such principles, is the fear of wounding this or that delicate feeling to prevent my describing what I have seen? I should be unworthy of having eyes if I ceded to such pusillanimous partiality, disguised as it has this time been under the name of respect for social propriety; as though my conscience had not the first claim to my respect. What! when I have been allowed to penetrate into a prison, where I have understood the silence of the terrified victims, must I not dare to relate their martyrdom, for fear of being accused of ingratitude, because of the complaisance of the jailers? Such reserve would be anything but a virtue. I declare then, that, after having observed well around me, after endeavoring to see what was attempted to be concealed, to understand what it was not wished I should know, to distinguish between the true and the false in all that was said to me, I do not believe I am exaggerating in affirming, that the empire of Russia is a country whose inhabitants are the most miserable upon earth, because they suffer at one and the same time the evils of barbarism and of civilization. As regards myself, I should feel that I was a traitor and a coward if, after having already boldly sketched the picture of a great part of Europe, I could hesitate to complete it, for fear either of modifying opinions of my own which I once maintained, or of shocking certain parties by a faithful picture of a country which has never been painted as it really is. On what, pray, should I ground a respect for evil things? Am I bound by any other chain than a love of truth?

In general, the Russians have struck me as being men endowed with great tact; extremely quick, but possessing very little sensibility; highly susceptible, but very unfeeling: this I believe to be their real character. As I have already said, a quick-sighted vanity, a sarcastic finesse are dominant traits in their disposition; and I repeat, that it would be pure silliness to spare the self-love of people who are themselves so little merciful: susceptibility is not delicacy. It is time that these men, who discern with so much sagacity the vices and the follies of our society, should accustom themselves to bear with our sincerity. The official silence which is maintained among them deceives them: it enervates their intellect: if they wish to be recognized by the European nations, and treated as equals, they must begin by submitting to hear themselves judged. All the nations have had to undergo this kind of process. When did the Germans refuse to receive the English, except on condition that the latter should speak well of Germany? Nations have always good reasons for being what they are, and the best of all is, that they cannot be otherwise.

This excuse could not indeed be pleaded by the Russians,

at least not by those who read. As they ape everything, they *might* be otherwise; and it is just the consciousness of this possibility which renders their government severe, even to ferocity! That government knows too well that it can be sure of nothing with characters which are mere reflections.

A more powerful motive might have checked my candor—the fear of being accused of apostasy. "He has long protested," it will be said, "against liberal declamations; here behold him ceding to the torrent, and seeking false popularity after having disdained it."

Perhaps I deceive myself; but the more I reflect, the less I believe that this reproach can reach me, or even that it will be addressed to me.

It is not only in the present day that a fear of being blamed by foreigners has occupied the minds of the Russians. That strange people unite an extremely boasting spirit with an excessive distrust of self; self-sufficiency without, uncomfortable humility within, are traits which I have observed in the greater number of Russians. Their vanity, which never rests, is, like English pride, always suffering. They also lack simplicity. Naïveté, that French word of which no other language can render the exact sense, because the thing it describes is peculiar to ourselves, naïveté, that simplicity which can become pointedly witty, that gift of disposition which can produce laughter without ever wounding the heart, that forgetfulness of rhetorical precautions which goes so far as to lend arms against itself to those with whom the individual converses, that fairness of judgment, that altogether involuntary truthfulness of expression, in one word, that Gallic simplicity, is unknown to the Russians. A race of imitators will never be naïf; calculation will, with them, always destroy sincerity.

In a country where minds are, from the cradle, fashioned in the dissimulation and finesse of Oriental policy, natural sentiment must be more rare than elsewhere; and, consequently, when it is discovered it has a peculiar charm. I have met in Russia some men who blush to feel themselves oppressed by the stern system under which they are obliged to live without daring to complain: they are only free when in the face of the enemy; they therefore go to make war in the Caucasus, that they may get rid of the yoke imposed upon them at home. The sorrows of such a life imprint prematurely on their faces a seal of melancholy, which strikingly contrasts with their military habits and the heedlessness of their age: the wrinkles of youth reveal profound griefs, and inspire deep pity. These young men have borrowed from the East their gravity, and from the North their vague, imaginative reverie: they are very unhappy and very amiable: no inhabitants of any other land resemble them.

Since the Russians possess grace, they must necessarily have some kind of natural sentiment in their character, though I have not been able to discern it. It is, perhaps, impossible for a stranger traveling through Russia as rapidly as I have done, to grasp it. No character is so difficult to define as that of this people.

Without a middle age, without ancient associations, without Catholicism, without chivalry to look back upon, without respect for their word,* always Greeks of the Lower Empire, polished, like the Chinese, by set forms, coarse, or at least indelicate, like the Kalmyks, dirty like the Laplanders, beautiful as the angels, ignorant as savages (I except the women and a few diplomatists), cunning as the Jews, intriguing as freedmen, gentle and grave in their manners as the Orientals, cruel in their sentiments as barbarians, mockers both by nature and by the feeling of their inferiority, the Russians, light-minded in appearance only, are still essentially fit for serious affairs. All have the requisite disposition for acquiring an ex-

---

*Notwithstanding all that has been already said, it may be proper here to repeat, that this applies only to the mass, who, in Russia, are led solely by fear and force.

traordinarily acute tact, but none are magnanimous enough to rise above it; and they have therefore disgusted me with that faculty, so indispensable to those who would live among them. With their continual *surveillance* of self, they seem to me the men the most to be pitied on earth. This police of the imagination is incessantly leading them to sacrifice their sentiments to those of others: it is a negative quality which excludes positive ones of a far superior character; it is the livelihood of ambitious courtiers, whose business is to obey the will and to guess the impulses of another, but who would be scouted should they ever pretend to have an impulse of their own. To give an impulse requires genius; genius is the tact of energy; tact is only the genius of weakness. The Russians are all tact. Genius acts, tact observes; and the abuse of observation leads to mistrust, that is, to inaction; genius may ally itself with a great deal of art, but never with a very refined tact, because tact—that supreme virtue of subalterns who respect the enemy, that is, the master, so long as they dare not strike—is always united with a degree of artifice. Under the influence of this talent of the seraglio, the Russians are impenetrable: it is true that we always see they are concealing something, but we cannot tell what they conceal, and this is sufficient for them. They will be truly formidable and deeply skillful men when they succeed in masking even their finesse.

Some of them have already attained to that proficiency: they are the first men of their country, both by the posts they occupy, and the superiority of their abilities. But, good heavens! what is the object of all this management? What sufficient motive shall we assign for so much stratagem? What duty, what recompense, can so long reconcile the faces of men to bear the fatigue of the mask?

Can the play of so many batteries be destined to defend only a real and legitimate power? Such a power would not need it; truth can defend herself. Is it to protect the miserable interests of vanity? Perhaps it is; yet to take so much pains to attain so contemptible a result would be unworthy of the grave men to whom I allude: I attribute to them profounder views; I think I perceive a greater object, and one which better explains their prodigies of dissimulation and longanimity.

An ambition inordinate and immense, one of those ambitions which could only possibly spring in the bosoms of the oppressed, and could only find nourishment in the miseries of a whole nation, ferments in the heart of the Russian people. That nation, essentially aggressive, greedy under the influence of privation, expiates beforehand, by a debasing submission, the design of exercising a tyranny over other nations: the glory, the riches, which it hopes for, console it for the disgrace to which it submits. To purify himself from the foul and impious sacrifice of all public and personal liberty, the slave, upon his knees, dreams of the conquest of the world.

It is not the man who is adored in the Emperor Nicholas— it is the ambitious master of a nation more ambitious than himself. The passions of the Russians are shaped in the same mold as those of the people of antiquity: among them everything reminds us of the Old Testament: their hopes, their tortures, are great, like their empire.

There, nothing has any limits,—neither griefs, nor rewards, nor sacrifices, nor hopes: the power of such a people may become enormous; but they will purchase it at the price which the nations of Asia pay for the stability of their governments —the price of happiness.

Russia sees in Europe a prey which our dissensions will sooner or later yield to her: she foments anarchy among us in the hope of profiting by a corruption which she favors because it appears favorable to her views: it is the history of Poland recommencing on a larger scale. For many years past, Paris has read revolutionary journals paid by Russia.

"Europe," they say at Petersburg, "is following the road that Poland took; she is enervating herself by a vain liberalism, whilst we continue powerful precisely because we are not free: let us be patient under the yoke; others shall someday pay for our shame."

The views that I reveal here may appear chimerical to minds engrossed with other matters; their truth will be recognized by every man initiated in the march of European affairs, and in the secrets of cabinets, during the last twenty years. They furnish a key to many a mystery; they explain also the extreme importance which thoughtful men, grave both by character and position, attach to the being viewed by strangers only on the favorable side. If the Russians were, as they pretend, the supporters of order and legitimacy, would they make use of men, and, what is worse, of means which are revolutionary?

The distance which separates Russia from the West has wonderfully aided hitherto in veiling all these things from us. If the astute Greek policy so much fears the truth, it is because it so well knows how to profit by falsehood; but what surprises me is, that it should succeed in perpetuating the reign of that influence.

Can the reader now understand the importance of an opinion, of a sarcastic word, a letter, a jest, a smile, or, with still greater reason, of a book, in the eyes of a government thus favored by the credulity of its people, and by the complaisance of all foreigners? A word of truth dropped in Russia, is a spark that may fall on a barrel of gunpowder.

What do the men who govern the empire care for the want, and the pallid visages of the soldiers of the emperor? Those living specters have the most beautiful uniforms in Europe; what signify, then, the filthy smocks in which the gilded phantoms are concealed in the interior of their barracks? Provided they are only shabby and dirty in secret, and that they shine when they show themselves, nothing is asked from them, nothing is given them. With the Russians appearance is everything, and among them, appearance deceives more than it does among others. It follows, that whoever lifts a corner of the curtain loses his reputation in Petersburg beyond the chance of retrieving it.

Social life in that city is a permanent conspiracy against the truth.

There, whoever is not a dupe, is viewed as a traitor,—there, to laugh at a gasconade, to refute a falsehood, to contradict a political boast, to find a reason for obedience, is to be guilty of an attempt against the safety of the state and the prince; it is to incur the fate of a revolutionist, a conspirator, an enemy of order, a POLE; and we all know whether this fate is a merciful one. It must be owned, the *susceptibility* which thus manifests itself is more formidable than laughable; the minute *surveillance* of such a government, in accord with the enlightened vanity of such a people, becomes fearful; it is no longer ludicrous.

People must and ought to employ all manner of precautions under a master who shows mercy to no enemy, who despises no resistance, and who considers vengeance as a duty. This man, or rather this government personified, would view pardon as apostasy, clemency as self-forgetfulness, humanity as a want of respect towards its own majesty, or, I should rather say, its divinity!

Russian civilization is still so near its source that it resembles barbarism. The Russians are nothing more than a conquering community; their strength does not lie in mind but in war, that is, in stratagem and brute force.

Poland, by its last insurrection, has retarded the explosion of the mine; it has forced the batteries to remain masked: Poland will never be pardoned for the dissimulation that she has rendered necessary, not towards herself, for she is immolated with impunity, but towards friends whom it is needful to continue making dupes, while humoring their stormy philanthropy.

If ever the Russians succeed in conquering the West, they

will not govern it from their own country, after the manner of the old Mongols; on the contrary, there will be nothing in which they will show such eager haste as to issue from their icy plains: unlike their ancient masters, the Tartars, who tyrannized over the Slavs from a distance—for the climate of Muscovy frightened even the Mongols—the Muscovites will leave their country the moment the roads of other countries are open to them.

At this moment they talk moderation; they protest against the conquest of Constantinople; they say that they fear everything that would increase an empire where the distances are already a calamity; they dread—yes! even thus far extends their prudence!—they dread hot climates! ... Let us wait a little, and we shall see what will become of all these fears.

And am I not to speak of so much falsehood, so many perils, so great an evil? ... No, no; I would rather have been deceived and speak, than have rightly discerned and remain silent. If there is temerity in recounting my observations, there would be criminality in concealing them.

The Russians will not answer me; they will say, "A journey of four months!—he cannot have fully seen things."

It is true I have not fully seen, but I have well penetrated.

Or, if they do me the honor of refuting me, they will deny facts,—facts which they are accustomed to reckon as nothing in Petersburg, where the past, like the present and the future, is at the mercy of the monarch: for, once again, the Russians have nothing of their own but obedience and imitation; the direction of their mind, their judgment and their free will belongs to their master. In Russia, history forms a part of the crown domain: it is the moral estate of the prince, as men and lands are the material; it is placed in cabinets with the other Imperial treasures, and only such of it is shown as it is wished should be seen. The emperor modifies at his pleasure the annals of the country, and daily dispenses to his people the historic truths that accord with the fiction of the moment.

Thus it was that Minin and Pozharsky—heroes forgotten for two centuries—were suddenly exhumed, and became the fashion, during the invasion of Napoleon. At that moment, the government permitted patriotic enthusiasm.

Nevertheless, this exorbitant power injures itself; Russia will not submit to it eternally. A spirit of revolt broods in the army. I say, with the emperor, the Russians have traveled too much; the nation has become greedy of information: the customhouse cannot confiscate ideas, armies cannot exterminate them, ramparts cannot arrest their progress; ideas are in the air, they pervade every region, and they are changing the world.

From all that has gone before, it follows that the future—that brilliant future dreamt of by the Russians—does not depend upon them; they have no ideas of their own; and the fate of this nation of imitators will be decided by people whose ideas are their own. If passions calm in the West, if union be established between the governments and their subjects, the greedy hope of the conquering Slavs will become a chimera.

Is it proper to repeat, that I write without animosity, that I have described things without charging persons, and that, in expatiating upon certain facts which have shocked me, I have generally accused less than I have recounted?

I left Paris with the opinion, that the intimate alliance of France and Russia could alone set to rights the affairs of Europe: but since I have seen the Russian nation, and have recognized the true spirit of its government, I have felt that it is isolated from the rest of the civilized world by a powerful political interest, supported by religious fanaticism; and I am of opinion that France should seek for allies among nations whose interests accord with her own. Alliances are not to be formed on opinions in opposition to wants. Where, in Europe, are wants which accord? I answer among the French and the Germans, and the people naturally destined to serve as satellites to those two great nations. The destinies of a progressive civilization, a civilization sincere and rational, will be decided in the heart of Europe: everything which tends to hasten the perfect agreement of French and German policy is beneficial; everything which retards that union, however specious be the motive for delay, is pernicious.

The proof that the kind of alliance to which I aspire is good, will be that a time shall come when we shall not have it in our power to choose any other.

As a foreigner, especially as a foreigner who writes, I was overwhelmed with protestations of politeness by the Russians: but their obliging civilities were limited to promises; no one gave me facilities for seeing into the depths of things. A crowd of mysteries have remained impenetrable to my intellect. A year spent in the journey would have but little aided me; the inconveniences of winter seemed to me the more formidable because the inhabitants assured me that they were of little consequence. They think nothing of paralyzed limbs and frozen faces; though I could cite more than one instance of accidents of this kind happening even to ladies in the highest circles of society; and once attacked, the individual feels the effects all his life. I had no wish uselessly to brave these evils, together with the tedious precautions that would be necessary to avoid them. Besides, in this empire of profound silence, of vast, empty space, of naked country, of solitary towns, of prudent physiognomies, whose expression, by no means sincere, made society itself appear empty, melancholy was gaining hold upon me; I fled before the spleen as much as the cold. Whoever would pass a winter at Petersburg must resign himself for six months to forget nature, in order to live imprisoned among men who have nothing in their characters that is natural.* I

---

*I have found, in the newly published letters of Lady Montague, a maxim of the Turkish courtiers, applicable to all courtiers, but more especially to the Russian; it will serve to mark the relations, of which more than one sort exist, between Turkey and Muscovy:—"Caress the favored, shun the unfortunate, and trust nobody."

admit, ingenuously, I have passed a wretched summer in Russia, because I have not been able well to understand more than a small portion of what I have seen. I hoped to arrive at solutions; I bring back only problems.

I speak without personal hatred, but also without fear or restriction; for I brave the danger even of wearying.

The country that I have just surveyed is as somber and monotonous as the Spain which I described formerly is brilliant and varied. To draw its exact picture is to renounce the hope to please. In Russia, life is as gloomy as in Andalusia it is gay; the Russians are as dull as the Spaniards are full of spirits. In Spain, the absence of political liberty is compensated by a personal independence which perhaps exists nowhere else to the same extent, and the effects of which are surprising; whilst in Russia, the one is as little known as the other. A Spaniard lives on love, a Russian lives on calculation: a Spaniard relates everything, and if he has nothing to relate, he invents; a Russian conceals everything, or if he has nothing to conceal, he is still silent, that he may *appear* discreet: Spain is infested with brigands, but they rob only on the road; the Russian roads are safe, but you will be plundered infallibly in the houses: Spain is full of the ruins and the memories of every century; Russia looks back only upon yesterday, her history is rich in nothing but promises: Spain is studded with mountains, whose forms vary at every step taken by the traveler; Russia is but a single unchanging scene, extending from one end of a vast plain to the other: the sun illumines Seville, and vivifies the whole peninsula; the mists veil the distances in Petersburg, which remain dim during even the finest summer evenings. In short, the two countries are the very opposite of each other; they differ as regards day and night, fire and ice, north and south.

He must have sojourned in that solitude without repose, that prison without leisure which is called Russia, to feel all the liberty enjoyed in the other European countries, whatever form of government they may have adopted. It cannot be too emphatically repeated: liberty is wanted in everything Russian—unless it be the commerce of Odessa. The emperor, who is endowed with prophetic tact, little loves the spirit of independence that pervades this city, the prosperity of which is due to the intelligence and integrity of a Frenchman*: it is, however, the only point in his vast dominions where men may with sincerity bless his reign.

If ever your sons should be discontented with France, try my recipe; tell them to go to Russia. It is a journey useful to every foreigner: whoever has well examined that country will be content to live anywhere else. It is always well to know that a society exists where no happiness is possible, because, by a law of his nature, man cannot be happy unless he is free.

Such a recollection renders the traveler less fastidious; and, returning to his own hearth, he can say of his country what a wit once said of himself: "When I estimate myself, I am modest; but when I compare myself, I am proud."

---

*The Duke de Richelieu, minister of Louis XVIII.

TITLES IN SERIES